The Sound of the Whistle

HARVARD EAST ASIAN MONOGRAPHS
168

Subseries on the History of
Japanese Business and Industry

Japan's rise from the destruction and bitter defeat of World War II to its present eminence in world business and industry is perhaps the most striking development in recent world history. This did not occur in a vacuum. It was linked organically to at least a century of prior growth and transformation. To illuminate this growth a new kind of scholarship on Japan is needed: historical study *in the context of a company or industry* of the interrelations among entrepreneurs, managers, engineers, workers, stockholders, bankers, and bureaucrats, and of the institutions and policies they created. Only in such a context can the contribution of particular factors be weighed and understood. It is to promote and encourage such scholarship that this subseries is established, supported by the Reischauer Institute of Japanese Studies and published by the Council on East Asian Studies at Harvard.

Albert M. Craig
Cambridge, Massachusetts

THE SOUND OF THE WHISTLE
Railroads and the State in Meiji Japan

STEVEN J. ERICSON

Published by the COUNCIL ON EAST ASIAN STUDIES, HARVARD UNIVERSITY and distributed by HARVARD UNIVERSITY PRESS, Cambridge (Massachusetts) and London   1996

Copyright © 1996 by the President and Fellows of Harvard College
Printed in the United States of America

The Council on East Asian Studies at Harvard University publishes a monograph series and, through the Fairbank Center for East Asian Research and the Reischauer Institute of Japanese Studies, administers research projects designed to further scholarly understanding of China, Japan, Korea, Vietnam, Inner Asia, and adjacent areas.

Library of Congress Cataloging-in-Publication Data

Ericson, Steven J., 1953–
The sound of the whistle : railroads and the state in Meiji Japan /
Steven J. Ericson.
p.   cm. — (Harvard East Asian monographs ; 168. Subseries on the history of Japanese business and industry)
Includes bibliographical references and index.
ISBN 0-674-82167-X
1. Railroads and state—Japan—History.   2. Railroads—Japan—History.   I. Title.   II. Series: Harvard East Asian monographs ; 168.   III. Series: Subseries on the history of Japanese business and industry.
HE3357.E75   1996
385'.0952—dc20   96-1612
                                CIP

Index by Steven J. Ericson

*To Wilbert and Irene Ericson
and in memory of Leona*

Acknowledgments

In the acknowledgments for my doctoral thesis, on which this book is largely based, I shamelessly wrote that "a long train of people has made it possible for this dissertation finally to see the light at the end of the tunnel." At the time, I mercifully restrained the impulse to push the railroad analogy further, and I will refrain from doing so now, except to add that, in the journey from thesis to book, the train has gotten a lot longer.

My greatest debt is to Professor Albert Craig of Harvard University for his unflagging support over the years. Teruko Craig once told me that her husband often sees himself in the role of midwife, helping his students give birth to their dissertations; however, he went far beyond that role in continually encouraging me to finish this book. His sage advice, particularly that I include material on the "transformative power" of Meiji railroads, significantly shaped my efforts to turn a dull dissertation into what I hope is a reasonably interesting monograph. I am also indebted to Professor William Wray of the University of British Columbia. As a junior faculty member at Harvard during my early graduate-school days, he sparked my interest in Japanese business history and introduced me to the leading business historians in Japan. He has been a valued mentor ever since. In addition, Karl Moskowitz, Donald Shively, and the late Edwin Reischauer offered helpful suggestions at the seminar-paper and dissertation stages of this project. In more recent years, colleagues at Brown University and Dartmouth College read and commented on parts of the work in progress, and for their constructive criticism, I am most grateful. I further wish to thank a fellow student of Meiji Japan, Dallas Finn, for sharing her extensive knowledge and enthusiasm.

It is a great pleasure to acknowledge the assistance I received from a number of Japanese scholars. During my period of dissertation research in Japan, Professors Nakagawa Keiichirō and Ishii Kanji kindly served as my advisers at the University of Tokyo and provided me with valuable introductions and insights. The following historians also gave generously of their time and wisdom: Professors Uda Tadashi, Oikawa Yoshinobu, Hoshino Takao, Harada Katsumasa, Tanaka Tokihiko, and Takechi Kyōzō. Professor Uda deserves special mention for inspiring me with his infectious enthusiasm for railroads and for guiding me on an unforgettable tour of what was once the main line of the Kansai Railway Company. Furthermore, I would like to thank Professors Morikawa Hidemasa and Yui Tsunehiko for their help and encouragement at critical points over the last decade.

I am indebted to librarians and archivists at the following institutions: the Harvard-Yenching Library, the Faculty of Economics Library and Meiji shinbun zasshi bunko at the University of Tokyo, the Transportation Museum in Tokyo, the National Diet Library, the Kokuritsu kōbunshokan, Hitotsubashi University, and the now-defunct Japanese National Railways (JNR). Special thanks go to Satō Toyohiko of the Transportation Museum and the staff of the JNR archives for their hospitality and generous assistance.

The University of Tokyo Press graciously gave permission to use in this book portions of my article entitled "Private Railroads in the Meiji Era: Forerunners of Modern Japanese Management?" in Tsunehiko Yui and Keiichiro Nakagawa, eds., *Japanese Management in Historical Perspective* (Tokyo: University of Tokyo Press, 1989). I am also grateful to the Transportation Museum in Tokyo for permission to include reprints of photographs in its possession as illustrations.

Principal funding for this project came from the Foreign Language and Area Studies Fellowship, the Fulbright-Hays Dissertation Fellowship, and the Reischauer Institute of Japanese Studies. Grants from the Faculty Aide Program at Harvard University enabled me to hire as a research assistant Mari Kuraishi, who played a vital role in gathering materials for Chapter One. Michael Burkhart of the Graphics Department at West Virginia University deserves recognition for his careful preparation of the maps. Especially to be commended is Lee Ann Best, of the Council on East Asian

Studies, for her excellent editorial work. I must also thank the anonymous reviewer whose extremely thoughtful comments helped improve the manuscript in significant ways. Finally, I wish to express heartfelt appreciation to my wife, Solveig, for her support and indulgence over a number of years. To all these people and institutions, I am deeply grateful. Each has contributed to whatever strengths this book may have; I alone am responsible for its weaknesses.

Contents

ACKNOWLEDGMENTS	vii
LIST OF TABLES	xiii
LIST OF FIGURES	xv
LIST OF MAPS	xvii
INTRODUCTION	3
PART ONE THE ENGINE OF CHANGE: RAILROADS AND MEIJI JAPAN	23
1 THE TRANSFORMATIVE POWER OF MEIJI RAILROADS	25

  The Expanding Network   *26*
  Railroads and the Economy   *31*
  Railroads and Society   *53*

PART TWO IN SEARCH OF A RAILROAD POLICY, 1869-1892	95
2 THE FIRST TWO DECADES	97

  The Era of State Enterprise   *97*
  The Advent of Private Railroads   *108*
  The Panic of 1890 and Its Aftermath   *122*
  Railway Companies in the Early 1890s   *132*
  Weathering the Crisis   *174*

3 The Making of the Railway Construction Law   191

The Policy Arena *191*
The Preliminaries: The Railway Bureau and the Army *197*
The Main Event: The Cabinet and the Diet *206*
The Construction Law and Its Impact *236*

Part Three Toward Nationalization   243

4 Forging a Consensus   245

The Communications Ministry *249*
The Army *261*
The Finance Ministry and the Oligarchs *277*
The Diet *291*

5 The Business Response   311

The Smaller Railway Companies *312*
The Major Railroads *322*
The Business Community at Large *346*
Buying out the Companies *351*
Capital Unbound: Investing the Compensation *359*

Conclusion   375

List of Abbreviations Used in the Notes   389

Notes   391

List of Works Cited   459

Index   493

List of Tables

1. Length of Railway Line Open, 1872–1907 — 9
2. Installment Payments on Kyushu Railway Shares, 1888–1892 — 125
3. Kyushu Railway, Sections of Line Opened, 1890–1891 — 127
4. Average Monthly Quotations for San'yō and Kyushu Railway Shares, Osaka Stock Exchange, July 1889–December 1990 — 131
5. Average Annual Quotations for Selected Railway Shares, 1888–1894 — 133
6. Private Railroad Development and Business Results, 1888–1894 — 135
7. Income Structures and Profit Rates of Selected Railway Companies, 1888–1894 — 137
8. Dividend Rates of Selected Railway Companies, 1888–1894 — 139
9. Average Monthly Quotations for San'yō and Kansai Railway Shares, 1891 — 155
10. Development and Business Results of San'yō and Kyushu Railway Companies, 1889–1894 — 177
11. Discounts on Domestic Bills by the Bank of Japan, 1890–1896 — 181
12. Discounts Outstanding on Bills with Collateral by the Bank of Japan, March 31, 1893 — 181
13. Aggregate Capital Structure of Private Railway Companies, 1888–1894 — 183
14. Corporate Bonds Outstanding, Selected Railway Companies, 1890–1894 — 185

15. Corporate Bonds Outstanding, Private Railway Companies, 1890–1904 — 187
16. Capital Structures of San'yō and Kyushu Railway Companies, 1889–1894 — 188
17. Aggregate Capital Structure of the Five Largest and the Remaining Railway Companies, 1902 — 315
18. Business Results of Private Railway Companies, 1899–1901 — 317
19. Total Number of Railway and Spinning Companies, 1897–1905 — 319
20. Top Ten Shareholders in the San'yō Railway Company, 1905 — 333
21. Construction Expenses, San'yō Railway Company, 1889–1905 — 335
22. Profit Distribution, San'yō Railway Company, 1901–1905 — 337
23. The Nationalized Railway Companies — 361
24. New Projected Capital by Industry, August 1905–February 1907 — 365

List of Figures

1. The Model Train Presented by Perry to Japanese Officials in 1854 — 5
2. A Locomotive on the Shinbashi-Yokohama Line in Early Meiji — 11
3. Shinbashi Station, circa 1879 — 19
4. Postcard Commemorating the Attainment of 5,000 Miles of Railways in 1906 — 27
5. The Locomotive *Benkei* — 35
6. A Superheater Locomotive — 37
7. "Tetsudō hitori annai" (Do-It-Yourself Railway Guide), 1872 — 67
8. Compartmentalized Passenger Carriage of Early to Mid Meiji — 75
9. Inoue Masaru — 119
10. Nakamigawa Hikojirō — 163
11. Sengoku Mitsugu — 327

List of Maps

1. Japan's Railway Network in 1900 — 29
2. The Kyushu Railway Network in 1906 — 43
3. Alternate Routes for the Chūō Line under the Railway Construction Law of 1892 — 47
4. The Railway Network between Osaka and Nagoya in 1902 — 87
5. Japan's Railway Network in 1906 — 247

The Sound of the Whistle

Kiteki issei, Shinbashi o
   haya waga kisha wa hanaretari.

With one sound of the whistle, from Shinbashi
   Swiftly departs our train.

Ōwada Takeki, *The Railway Song*, 1900

Introduction

This book is about the politics of development and the relationship between state and private enterprise in the Japanese railroad industry during its first four decades. These years stretch from the railroad's introduction into Japan as a public undertaking in the 1870s through the parallel construction of government and private railroads after 1881 to the aftermath of the railway nationalization of 1906–1907. This first chapter in the history of Japanese railroads is virtually coterminous with the Meiji period (1868–1912), the initial phase of Japan's modern era. For the Japanese of Meiji, as for their contemporaries in the West, the steam locomotive was the quintessential symbol of progress and civilization, the very epitome of modern industrial power. The railroad had an enormous impact on Meiji society, revolutionizing the overland transport of people and goods and helping engineer a sense of nationhood. Just as in the West "the nineteenth century was pre-eminently 'The Railway Age,'"[1] so too did "King Steam" rule supreme in the consciousness of Meiji Japan. The railroad not only played a vital role in the social and cultural life of the Meiji period; it was also central to political and business development, especially to the rise of industrial policy and pork-barrel politics and the evolution of state-business relations, during that era.

Sweeping the entire history of railroads in Japan from the mid-nineteenth century to the present yields a panoramic picture of dramatic change. Two sets of images illustrate strikingly different aspects of that change. In March 1854, Commodore Matthew Perry, on his return visit to pry open the closed doors of Japan, presented his Japanese hosts with examples by the crateload of the mechanical wonders of the industrial revolution in

America. Among Perry's gifts was a quarter-size model railroad complete with "Lilliputian locomotive, car, and tender" and several miles of rails (see Figure 1).[2] This was not the first model train to be seen in Japan—that honor belonged to the miniature alcohol-driven locomotive that the Russian admiral E. V. Putiatin had brought with him just half a year earlier and operated on board his flagship to the astonishment of a few Japanese officials—but the American model had a much greater impact, viewed as it was on shore by hundreds of people. Of all the gifts Perry bestowed on them, his official artist noted, "the Japanese marveled most at the railroad."[3] Behind the reception hall at Yokohama, the Americans laid down a circular track about a mile in circumference and put on demonstration runs for the assembled dignitaries. According to the official record of the Perry expedition, "crowds of Japanese gathered around, and looked on the repeated circlings of the train with unabated pleasure and surprise, unable to repress a shout of delight at each blast of the steam whistle."[4] One spectator, "not to be cheated out of a ride," even turned participant by sitting on top of the tiny carriage. The official American record portrays this "dignified mandarin" as "whirling around the circular road at the rate of 20 miles an hour, with his loose robes flying in the wind. As he clung with a desperate hold to the edge of the roof, grinning with intense interest, and his huddled-up body shook convulsively with a kind of laughing timidity, the car spun rapidly around the circle."[5] As the rider himself, an official in the shogunate's neo-Confucian academy, described the experience in his diary: "Swiftly, as though it were flying, [the train] circled repeatedly. It was most enjoyable!"[6]

Moving forward 110 years, we find that the Japanese had progressed from rapt observers of an unprecedented contrivance to global leaders in railway technology with the inauguration of the celebrated Shinkansen "bullet train" in 1964. Capable of speeds in excess of 135 miles an hour, the sleek bullet train set the international standard for rapid and efficient rail service. Westerners were now coming to Japan to acquire rather than to impart knowledge of the most advanced means of land transportation in the world. Japan remains at the cutting edge of railway technology today, as testing proceeds with the next generation of supertrains that travel by magnetic levitation at rates of up to 325 miles per hour. The trip from Tokyo to Osaka, which took some two weeks by foot or palanquin at the time of Perry's visit, can be made in two and a half hours on today's Shinkansen

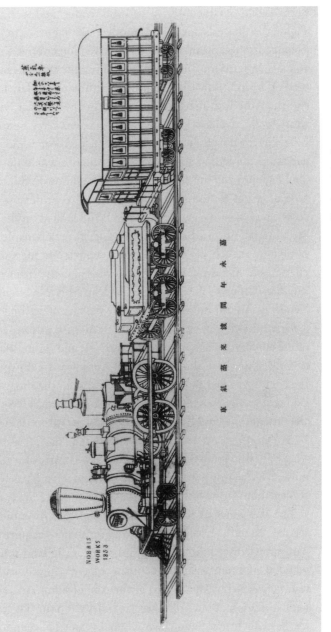

Figure 1 The model train presented by Matthew Perry to Japanese officials in March 1854. Drawing by Hibata Ōsuke. Photograph: courtesy of the Transportation Museum, Tokyo.

and, probably sometime within the next decade, will take only an hour on the "Maglev" supertrain.⁷

Another pair of images brackets a far different sequence of transformations in Japanese railway history. On October 14, 1872, the Meiji regime officially opened Japan's first railroad, the eighteen-mile line from Shinbashi (in Tokyo) to Yokohama, marking the initiation of the state railway system in Japan. The authorities planned this event as an occasion for national celebration and declared a holiday for government employees. A heavy downpour that forced a three-day postponement did nothing to dampen the festive atmosphere on the morning of the 14th. The opening ceremonies at the Shinbashi and Yokohama stations that day were held with great fanfare, highlighted by the attendance of the youthful Meiji emperor, attired in traditional court robes. At the Shinbashi depot, top government officials, also in traditional court dress, along with foreign diplomats, greeted the emperor to a trumpet flourish. They then accompanied him on the inaugural train ride to Yokohama and back, while warships in the harbor and troops on land fired 21- and 101-gun salutes.⁸ Thus, with an impressive show of central authority, did railroads begin as a public enterprise in Japan.

One hundred fifteen years later, a public ceremony of a very different sort took place in Tokyo that signalled the end of the national railway system in Japan. At midnight on April 1, 1987, the president of the Japanese National Railways, dressed in an engineer's uniform, boarded a steam locomotive specially brought back for the occasion and blew the whistle for the final run of the debt-ridden public corporation.⁹ That same morning, "JNR" gave way to "JR" or Japan Railways, a group of private companies including six regional passenger lines and a nationwide freight railway. With this denationalization of the rail network, Japan embarked upon a new age of private railway enterprise.

The first set of images represents the story of technological progress in modern Japan; the second, that of government versus private initiative in Japan's modern economic transformation. This book is concerned mainly with the latter story. It is not so much a tale of unilinear development or, as Thomas Smith once put it, of the Meiji leaders as "homing pigeons."¹⁰ Rather, it is primarily an account of trial and error, of policy changes and reversals, of consensus reached only after extended conflict and debate. The debate was over the proper role of government and the optimal balance of state and private enterprise, issues that have remained vital to this day; the consensus arrived at by the mid-1900s was for nationalization. Until then, the state-business relationship in the railway field underwent a series of shifts and turns, as Japan moved from a decade of exclusive government initiative to a quarter-century of mixed public-private development, punctuated throughout by alternating movements for nationalization and privatization.

This study seeks to explain these changes and, ultimately, the state purchase of the leading private railroads in 1906–1907. As the constantly shifting configuration of ownership indicates, the railroad industry provided a major arena for the interaction of government and private enterprise during the Meiji period. Railroad planning in that era set precedents for what has come to be known as "industrial policy," Japan's most celebrated contribution to strategies of capitalist development in the twentieth century, with Meiji bureaucrats targeting growth industries such as railroads and shipping for special promotion and eventually using the national rail system itself as an instrument of economic development.[11] Meiji railroads also helped pave the way for the pork-barrel politics that has become such a pervasive feature of Japanese government since the turn of the century, as members of the early Diet attempted to solidify electoral support through legislation for public works, above all railroad building, in their localities. Moreover, together with spinning companies, railroads are commonly regarded as having constituted a leading sector of Meiji industrialization. Yet, despite their centrality, we have hardly any full-scale works in English on the history of Japanese railroads.[12] A larger purpose of this book, therefore, is to fill this gap in our knowledge of a vital yet hitherto neglected area of the Meiji political economy.

The focus of this study is on the making and carrying out of government policy towards private railway companies with regard to two principal issues: ownership and control, and finance. The emphasis on private railroads is justified and necessitated by the fact that, after the initial decade of halting state construction, private enterprise dominated the field; by 1905, on the eve of the nationalization, the private network accounted for over two thirds of the total length of line open (see Table 1). As a result of the state purchases of 1906–1907, however, the private share of the nation's rail system plunged to 9 percent, and for the next eighty years, private action was restricted to local railroad development. The railway nationalization thus provides a natural endpoint for this study.

Regarding the issue of ownership and control, my concern is to ascertain the authorities' stand on this problem, clarifying the various perspectives that shaped government policy towards private enterprise. Key questions to be addressed here include the following: Was Meiji railroad policy basically "mercantilist" or market-conforming? Did Meiji leaders adhere consistently to the principle of government management and control, as some scholars claim, or was direct state involvement at least initially only temporary in intent? In light of the strategic and public character of railroads and especially their high capital intensity, one would expect Meiji Japan to have witnessed a greater magnitude of state intervention in this field than in most others. Yet, in relatively short order, private interests took the lead in railroad development. What does this "train" of events tell about the fundamental views of government officials? In short, railroad policy will be used as a test of the attitudes of the Meiji political leadership towards private initiative.

The second focus of this study, the financing of railroads, is inextricably related to the question of ownership and control, and in my view, access to funding was the key variable in Meiji railroad development and policy formation. By comparison, the acquisition of technology was easy. Aside from advanced techniques such as those involved in sophisticated bridge engineering and the manufacture of locomotives and rails, basic construction skills were mastered within a decade.[13] It was not as if Japan were starting from scratch; Tokugawa construction methods, including earthenwork and tunneling, were quite advanced. The Japanese could build on these, combining imported technology with traditional techniques.

In downplaying technology, however, we should not lose sight of the unprecedented nature, the sheer novelty, of railway technology. The latter was not immediately understood. Among the many woodblock prints of Meiji trains is a marvelous one from very early in the period (see Figure 2). If one looks closely, one sees that the locomotive has square wheels. This was obviously the perception of an artist rather than an engineer, but it is perhaps indicative of a more general problem in immediate comprehension. There is also the oft-told anecdote concerning the first rail passengers in Japan. In fine Japanese fashion, they would leave their sandals on the platform as they

TABLE 1 Length of Railway Line Open, 1872–1907
(unit: miles)

Year	State	Private	Total	Private as Percentage of Total
1872	18	0	18	0
1874	38	0	38	0
1876	65	0	65	0
1878	65	0	65	0
1880	98	0	98	0
1882	171	0	171	0
1884	182	81	263	30.8
1886	265	166	431	38.5
1888	506	406	912	44.5
1890	551	849	1,400	60.6
1892	551	1,320	1,871	70.6
1894	581	1,537	2,118	72.6
1896	632	1,875	2,507	74.8
1898	768	2,652	3,420	77.5
1900	950	2,905	3,855	75.4
1902	1,227	3,011	4,238	71.0
1904	1,461	3,232	4,693	68.9
1905	1,532	3,251	4,783	68.0
1906	3,116	1,692	4,808	35.2
1907	4,453	446	4,899	9.1

Source: *Tetsudō-kyoku nenpō, 1907*, Teishin-shō tetsudō-kyoku, ed. (Tetsudō-in, 1909), pp. 30–31.

boarded a train, presumably expecting to find their footwear waiting for them on the platform at their destination. Whether this story is apocryphal or not is unclear. What is apparent, however, is that such difficulties in grasping the new technology, as in mastering it, were quickly overcome.

Financing was another matter. In fact, it proved to be a much thornier issue than acquisition of technology. By way of illustration, the government raised a loan on the London market in 1870 to build the first railroads. The loan amounted to £1,000,000 and was intended to finance construction of part of the planned artery between Tokyo and Kobe, a distance of nearly four hundred miles. As it turned out, the authorities had to use over two thirds of the loan for other pressing needs, but the £300,000 actually applied to railroad construction was barely enough to lay the eighteen-mile Shinbashi-Yokohama line and part of the Osaka-Kobe section, at the outer extremities of the grand trunk railroad. State officials appear to have grossly underestimated the cost of contruction. At the time, wags ridiculed the government's program by stating that one could take apart the Chinese characters for "railroad" (*tetsudō*), or "iron way"—the character for "iron" being composed of radicals for "money" and "to lose"—and read them as "the way to lose money."[14] With its massive agenda for modernization, the government simply lacked the resources to carry out a vigorous construction program until Finance Minister Matsukata Masayoshi set the state's financial house in order in the 1880s, by the end of which decade the Tokyo-Kobe artery was finally completed as the Tokaido trunk line. The problem was only compounded by the government's decision to eschew all foreign borrowing once it had floated the railway loan and one other small industrial loan abroad. The authorities feared lest outside political intervention should follow foreign investment at a time when the nation was still weak and relatively defenseless. They therefore kept out foreign capital until the turn of the century, by which time Japan was in a much stronger position following its victory over China and its adoption of the gold standard.

Hence, a major theme of state railroad policy from early in the Meiji era was the effort to recruit domestic private capital and enterprise. That effort, however, did not succeed until the 1880s, for the huge fixed-capital requirements of railway construction posed a real obstacle to private initiative as well during the first decade of Meiji. This problem was closely intertwined with government policy on the question of ownership, inasmuch as official attitudes towards private enterprise appear to have vacillated with fluctuations in state finances and business cycles, that is, practical considerations generally outweighed ideological ones. For the private sector, the issue was as much the difficulty of mobilizing existing pools of capital for railway construction as it was the scarcity of capital per se. In this regard, one needs to look closely at government financial policy, especially private-railway subsidization and central-bank policy, and the role

Figure 2 A locomotive on the Shinbashi-Yokohama line.
Woodcut by Kuniteru II, early Meiji. Private collection.

these played in enabling private firms finally to solve the problem of raising sufficient funds.

In studying the evolution of government policy on these issues, I will try to assess the relative degree of change and continuity in Meiji railroad planning, to identify the leading actors in the decision-making process and to see how they interacted to form policy at particular points in time. A number of important events in Meiji railway history provide such reference points, and special attention will be given to two sets of events that proved to be by far the most pivotal. These were, on the one hand, the Panic of 1890 and the passage of the Railway Construction Law of 1892 and, on the other, the financial panics at the turn of the century and the railway nationalization of 1906–1907. The financial crises were catalysts for change not only in the attitudes and programs of government leaders, but also in the patterns of financing and decision making in the private railroads. Moreover, they supplied the economic context for the policy debates and legislative initiatives of the early 1890s and 1900s. In short, analysis of these panics is indispensable to understanding the politics of Meiji railroad development. The decision-making process leading to enactment of the construction and nationalization laws itself offers a microcosm of Meiji policy formation with the bureaucracy, military, Diet, and business alike entering into the equation. Railroad legislation also provided a focal point for local interests, helping to integrate them into the national scene. The evolution of Meiji railroad policy thus serves as a telling index of general political development during the period.

The existing studies of that policy, fragmentary though they are, have typically approached the subject from the standpoint of "the road to nationalization." They have usually singled out three principal actors—the railway bureaucracy, the army, and the business community—and shown how the three interacted over time, eventually coming together with the nationalization.[15] Abstracting these three groups makes for a convenient dialectic, with mutual collisions giving way to a final synthesis. Until recently, Japanese scholars, borrowing a phrase from Engels, were wont to speak of the "Bismarckian nationalization" of 1906–1907. A neat theoretical construct with a rather shallow empirical foundation, this idea basically conveys the notion that the Meiji government closely followed the Prussian pattern, buying out private lines to serve its authoritarian and imperialistic purposes, thus highlighting the strategic, statist motive behind the nationalization.[16]

More recent scholarship has been much more empirical, making use of primary, often unpublished, materials and testing these kinds of generalizations against the historical record. Yet many authors still tend to look backwards from the vantage-point of the 1906–1907 nationalization, which colors their interpretation of the development of railroad policy. This tendency probably owes much to the centennial history of the Japanese National Railways and the studies spun off from that endeavor.[17] Their assumption is that the government initially adopted a policy of public ownership and management of railroads, but, owing to financial difficulties, was compelled to permit private construction. This was only a stopgap, however, with private companies regarded merely as substituting for the state. The suggestion is that the authorities intended all along to nationalize the principal private lines and that they basically had a negative attitude towards private enterprise. I submit that this interpretation, common to many political and economic historians, is largely a distortion caused by looking at the pre-nationalization period from the viewpoint of what happened in 1906–1907.

A different perspective is offered by Japanese business historians, who are examining Meiji railroad development from the standpoint of private business. Historians in this field have taken up the study of individual railway companies as well as the general phenomena of railway management and investment.[18] In so doing, they have considered the pre-nationalization era in its own terms, pointing to a radically different view of government policy. State leaders, these scholars suggest, generally leaned towards private initiative, but early efforts at private construction failed due to the difficulty of raising capital. Hence, at the outset, the government had no choice but to pursue railroad development itself.

My own sense of the problem, which owes a debt to these business historians, is that Meiji leaders had a much more favorable attitude towards railway companies and a far greater commitment to private railway enterprise than has been commonly portrayed by Japanese writers. This attitude comes out most clearly in the implementation, as opposed to the making, of government policy. In that vein, I will look closely at the impact of state policy on the management of railway companies, particularly on the investment decisions and business strategies taken by those firms. This issue leads into the broader question of the nature and extent of government intervention in the private-railway sector and the degree of autonomy enjoyed by the companies themselves.

Western scholarship on state intervention in the Meiji economy as a whole has undergone considerable change in recent decades. Thomas Smith, in his pioneering work on government enterprise in early Meiji, voiced the initial postwar interpretation that placed great emphasis on the Meiji state as the initiator of modern economic growth in Japan.[19] This perspective mirrored the views of Alexander Gerschenkron, who argued that, in order to industrialize, late-developing countries required substitutes for individual private capital and initiative: depending on their degree of backwardness, late-comers generally turned to government-supported investment banks or to the state itself for economic leadership.[20]

Railroads offered Gerschenkron a prime example of this relationship between the timing and pattern of national development. In Britain, the first nation to industrialize, railroads followed the Industrial Revolution and therefore came to a society with an abundance of private capital. Consequently, Britain could afford to leave the railway field entirely to private enterprise unassisted by the state. In the later developers, however, railroad building either accompanied or preceded full-scale industrialization. As a result, private capital was scarce or timid, and private mechanisms for mobilizing available funds, lacking or rudimentary. This situation called for alternative means of economic development, specifically investment banks like the Crédit Mobilier and the Darmstädter in the case of France and Germany, and central governments in the case of more "backward" nations such as Russia and Japan.

Yet, in all the follower countries, the huge capital demands of railroad construction, combined with a recognition of the railroad's importance for national security and coherence, prompted at least some measure of state involvement in the creation of rail networks.[21] The United States, for example, presented a model of extensive public support for private railroads through the provision of federal land grants and state and local government funds.[22] France opted for a more direct form of government participation—an intensive partnership between the state and private interests in the construction and financing of railroads.[23] Meanwhile, Prussia until the

1870s had a genuine mixed system, with the government and private firms building separate lines, but after the enactment of a nationalization law in 1879, the Prussian state moved aggressively to buy out the private network, largely accomplishing that task by 1895.[24]

The Meiji government engaged in all these forms of state intervention, acting alternately or more often simultaneously as guarantor and creditor, partner and rival of private railway companies.[25] The regime did so partly in conscious imitation of Western precedent but more importantly in pragmatic response to fluctuating economic and financial circumstances. The scale and variety of public involvement in this field would seem to lend solid support to a Gerschenkronian view of the role of the state in Meiji industrialization.

Since the 1960s, however, Western scholars have tended to minimize that role. In what has now become the standard interpretation, the government, out of necessity, intervened directly in the economy during the 1870s, but thereafter confined its economic activity mainly to providing a favorable institutional setting for the growth of private enterprise. In short, the modern Japanese state moved quickly from a market-creating to a largely market-conforming role. Chalmers Johnson goes so far as to claim that, from the 1880s to the 1920s, "the government's overall policy toward industry and foreign trade [became] a more or less orthodox version of laissez faire,"[26] and most observers would probably concur that at least "quasi-laissez-faire" accurately describes official economic policy until the growing imposition of wartime economic controls in the 1930s. Kozo Yamamura even denies any significant contribution by the Meiji government during the 1870s, at the height of the experiment in state enterprise, pointing to private initiative as the motor of Japanese industrialization from the very start of the modern era.[27]

The experience of the railroad industry, for the most part ignored in these studies, suggests that recent scholarship in the West has overstated the case for downplaying the economic role of the Meiji government. True, private enterprise prevailed in the railway sector for much of the Meiji period. But that does not mean that the state's contribution was insignificant. Besides investing in its own rail system and offering multifaceted assistance to private railroads, the Meiji government proceeded to buy out all railway companies of a "nonlocal" character; the seventeen railroads that it took over in

1906 and 1907 accounted for roughly one quarter of the total paid-up capital of joint-stock ventures in Japan.[28] Indeed, the railway nationalization seems to stand out as the major exception to the market-conforming behavior of the Meiji regime, the one clearcut example of government displacement of private enterprise during that period. At first glance, this dramatic move towards public ownership appears to have represented a striking instance of state leadership or "bureaucratic dominance" in the economy, with the Meiji government adopting a market-displacing policy of public intervention and effectively usurping an industry from the private sector. One could counter that, at least in early Meiji, direct state involvement in this field fit the market-conforming model whereby the government supplies the requisite financial and transportation infrastructure for private industry. On the other hand, this initial activity can also be viewed as having fallen into the category of the pilot projects that the regime undertook in the 1870s in the hopes of inducing private interests to follow its lead. Granted, although the state sold off most of its model enterprises during the next decade, it retained ownership of all but one of its railroads and continued to build on them; nonetheless, the government promoted a decisive swing towards private railway enterprise from the early 1880s on. How, then, should we interpret the nationalization of late Meiji? To what degree did this action in fact mark a departure from the predominantly market-conforming pattern of state involvement in the Meiji economy? The motives of both private railway investors and government officials and the effects of the nationalization itself will be examined as important clues.

There still remains the question of what is meant by "the state." When social scientists use the term, they normally refer to the central government bureaucracy. The bureaucracy of modern Japan in particular is generally seen as a powerful, autonomous agent able to act effectively in its own or the national interest. This perspective informs Chalmers Johnson's influential model of Japan as a strong, smart state pursuing a "developmental" as opposed to "regulatory" strategy in its dealings with private business.[29] This interpretation of the state applies fairly well to Japan during the first two decades of the Meiji period: in railroad policy, government bureaucrats essentially had the field to themselves and were able to make decisions independently of private business, which had yet to organize politically or to secure formal representation in the national government.

The situation, however, changed dramatically after 1890 with the opening of the Diet and the rise in both the economic clout and political activity of business interests. The political parties, through their legislative authority in the Diet, began to have a significant input into state railroad policy, for almost all the major developments in railroad planning after 1890 involved legislative rather than strictly administrative actions. In the 1890s, as private businessmen increasingly sought to influence policy and legislation, and party politicians to court business support, a growing interpenetration of elites began to characterize Japanese government. Richard Samuels' emphasis on the constrained nature of bureaucratic power and the negotiated character of state intervention in the Japanese economy is particularly relevant to this point.[30] In any event, the notion of an autonomous, authoritative state-as-bureaucracy fails to provide as close a fit to the Japanese case from mid-Meiji on. Above all, the emergence of the political parties calls for a broader, more nuanced understanding of the Meiji state. My own conception of "the state," therefore, includes not only the oligarchs and the administrative apparatus they controlled, but also the parties and the Diet, whose appearance in the latter half of Meiji added a totally new dimension to the government-business relationship.

Within the Meiji state, then, decision making on railroads came to involve an array of participants—bureaucrats, politicians, bankers and businessmen—all jostling with one another for influence over railway policy; yet, even within the government bureaucracy, there was no unanimity on the issue. The upshot was an often-contentious process characterized by heated jurisdictional disputes between rival ministries and the growing political interventions that such conflicts invited. Chalmers Johnson offers a strikingly parallel case of industrial policy making in recent years in an article on the so-called "telecom wars" of 1983–1985.[31] In this study, Johnson presents a somewhat different view from that in his earlier work on industrial policy, one that more closely resembles the interpretation advanced here. This article examines the competition that intensified in the early 1980s between the Ministry of Posts and Telecommunications (MPT) and the Ministry of International Trade and Industry (MITI) for control over Japanese telecommunications policy. It shows how interministerial conflict, combined with the rise of policy experts or *zoku* (lit., "tribesmen") within the ruling Liberal Democratic Party, led to greater involvement by politicians in the formulation of industrial policy, hitherto an almost exclusive preserve of the bureaucracy. Johnson's study depicts much the same cluster of actors struggling to forge policy in the midst of bureaucratic turf wars as in the Meiji-railroad case.

The "telecom wars" article also provides an apt comparison with the present book in terms of the industry in question. A few decades ago, scholars drew parallels between the nineteenth-century railroad and the contemporary space program as cutting-edge industries of their day.[32] A more down-to-earth and perhaps more appropriate analogue for Meiji railroads, however, is telecommunications, one of the most important and fastest growing industries today. Telecommunications networks centering on fiber optics and digitalized equipment are in many ways heirs to the Meiji railway system, just as MPT is a direct descendant of the prewar Ministry of Communications, the agency with jurisdiction over railroads during the latter half of Meiji. As Japan gears up for the "information society" of the future, telecommunications, Johnson notes, may well "require an investment in facilities and infrastructure equal to the investment in railroads in the late nineteenth century,"[33] and the Japanese fully expect their new "information Shinkansen" to have a transformative impact comparable to that of the rail network in the first century of Japan's modern development.[34]

During the Meiji period, the railway system was part of a larger communications infrastructure that included the forerunner of today's high-tech information networks, namely, the telegraph. The latter half of the nineteenth century witnessed simultaneous revolutions in transportation and communications worldwide, and Japan was no exception. The rapid extension of the telegraph network played a key role in the creation of the Meiji transportation system, proving vital to the successful management of shipping and rail enterprises alike.[35] The first telegraph line, connecting Tokyo and Yokohama, began operation less than three years before the opening of the Shinbashi-Yokohama railway, but because telegraphs were relatively easy and cheap to build, the main lines were already in place by the mid-1880s, a full generation before the completion of the trunk-line railway system. As in the case of railroads, for both strategic and administrative reasons, the Meiji regime initially adopted a policy of state ownership and control of telegraphs; unlike for railroads, however, the government largely adhered to this policy: by 1889, only 5 percent of the telegraph

Figure 3 Shinbashi station with employees of the Inland Transport Company handling freight in the foreground, following the 1875 termination of Mitsui's monopoly. Woodcut by Hiroshige III, circa 1879. Photograph: courtesy of the Transportation Museum, Tokyo.

network was in private hands compared to over 50 percent of the railway system.[36] Yet, despite the persistence of a virtual state monopoly in the telegraph field, private interests, either directly or through local governments, had nearly as much influence on central-government plans for telegraphs as for railroads. Apart from the arteries, the telegraph system grew haphazardly, with branch lines and offices installed primarily in response to local demand, which surged in the late 1870s and early 1880s. Anticipating patterns in the expansion of the rail network, provincial notables throughout the nation came to be driven by the notion that the establishment of telegraphic service was indispensable for local economic development. Much as with the railroad, therefore, local groups began to compete against each other to have the government extend the telegraph to their localities, those areas offering to help defray the cost of construction often winning the race.[37]

For the remaining spokes of the Meiji communications network—road and water transport—Japan relied almost exclusively on private enterprise, heavily supported by the state. The resulting configuration mirrored Western practice: Britain had just joined France and other continental European countries by nationalizing its telegraph network in 1870,[38] but in most fields of transportation, private or mixed public-private systems generally prevailed in the West. To handle non-rail transport, the Meiji government during the mid-1870s nurtured three private monopolies: Mitsui for the collection and delivery of railroad freight, the Inland Transport Company (Naikoku tsuun kaisha) for general road and river conveyance, and Mitsubishi for coastal shipping; once these firms were well established, however, the state began to encourage private competition in each of these areas over the next decade (see Figure 3).[39] A similar pattern held for private railroads, with the exclusive chartering of the Nippon Railway Company, founded in 1881 with the intention of building a nationwide trunk-line network, giving way to a licensing free-for-all in the private railway boom of the late 1880s. This practice of initially protecting first-comers and subsequently fostering competitors proved on the whole effective in furthering the development of a national communications system. The expansion and integration of that system by mid-Meiji were neatly symbolized by the establishment of the Ministry of Communications in 1885. The new ministry brought together the previously scattered bureaus that had overseen the postal service, the telegraph, maritime shipping, and lighthouses; it then added to its jurisdiction telephones and electricity in 1891, railroads in 1892, and all water transport in 1893.[40] Thus did the government formally unify its supervision of practically all components of the Meiji communications network.

A growing coherence may have characterized both the network and its regulation by the state bureaucracy, but the same was not necessarily true for communications policy, which frequently became an arena of contestation among public and private interests alike. The steady development of transportation and communications infrastructure during the Meiji period resulted less from consistent central planning than from the interplay of intra-governmental negotiation and private initiative. The railway case offers a vivid illustration of these trends, helping to clarify both the nature of the policy-making process and the role of the Meiji state in the field of communications and economic development as a whole.

*Part One
The Engine of Change:
Railroads and Meiji Japan*

ONE

The Transformative Power of Meiji Railroads

"When the railway system was, for the first time, introduced into this country, . . . we virtually stepped into trains out of [palanquins]."
Inoue Masaru, former head of the Railway Bureau, in 1902[1]

In discussing government policy and state-business relations in the railway field, one can easily lose sight of the larger meaning and significance of the railroad for Meiji Japan. Simply put, railroads had the power to transform society. As the author of a recent social history of the railroad expresses it, "The modern world began with the coming of the railways. They turned the known universe upside down. They made a greater and more immediate impact than any other mechanical or industrial innovation before or since. They were the first technical invention which affected everyone in any country where they were built . . . They were the noisy, smoky, obstrusive heralds of a civilisation destined to be increasingly dominated by industrial innovations."[2] This chapter looks at the transformative impact of railroads on Meiji Japan. Its purpose is to furnish a background and context for the detailed analysis of politics and state-industry relations to follow, but it is also intended to stand alone as a case study in Meiji social and economic history. For the railroad offers a window with stunning perspectives not only on government and business but also on society at large during the Meiji period.

The Expanding Network

On July 10, 1889, some one hundred dignitaries from throughout Japan assembled in Nagoya for a gala event. The participants, all of whom had ties to the railroad industry, were there to celebrate a milestone: the nation's railway system had finally reached the 1,000-mile mark. In the eyes of the celebrants, the system had come a long way since the beginning of its construction in 1870. Japan's first railroad, the fifteen-mile stretch from Yokohama to Shinagawa, had opened in May 1872; three miles more and the line had reached Shinbashi later that year. Railroad building had proceeded fitfully for the remainder of that decade, but had started to gain momentum in the 1880s with the advent of private railroads and the laying of the government's Tokaido line, completed just nine days before the "1,000-Mile Celebration."

The festivities in Nagoya that summer day were reenacted seventeen years later, on May 11, 1906—less than two months after passage of the Railway Nationalization Law—when once again railroad officials gathered in that city to fete another milestone, this time the empire's attainment of 5,000 miles of railway line. To contemporary Japanese, this landmark appeared to symbolize the remarkably rapid change their country had undergone during the previous four decades, and it was hailed accordingly at the popular and official levels alike (see Figure 4). Compared to the industrial late-comers of continental Europe, however, Japan's record of railroad extension to that point was less than spectacular. In 1906, Germany had about 36,000 miles of track; France, nearly 25,000 miles; and even Italy, almost 11,000. Furthermore, over its first thirty-six years of railroad development, Germany's network had expanded at an average annual rate of about 320 miles and that of France, around 195; of this group, only Italy's average pace over that period—130 miles a year—was less than Japan's rate of roughly 140 miles per annum.[3] Still, in the Japanese case, the tempo of construction had quickened dramatically in the interval between the two railway celebrations, averaging more than 230 miles of track per year during that period as opposed to about 50 miles a year during the period up to mid-1889.

Given its relatively slow pace of railway construction in the early going, Japan by the middle of 1889 had achieved only the bare beginnings of a rail

Figure 4 Postcard commemorating the empire's attainment of 5,000 miles of railway line in May 1906. Depicts emblems of private railroad companies and the government railways, as well as a scene from the opening ceremony for the Shinbashi-Yokohama line in 1872. Photograph: courtesy of the Transportation Museum, Tokyo.

network. At that time, a limited number of points, mainly along the Pacific coast, was accessible by rail: more specifically, one could go by train from Sendai in the north to Himeji in the southwest; ride a few branch lines in the Kantō and Kansai areas, including one to Tsuruga on the Japan Sea; and take short rail trips on the other three main islands (see Map 1).[4]

By 1900, Japan's railway system had grown considerably, having nearly tripled in length during the previous decade. At the end of that year, a person could travel by rail almost the entire length of Honshū, from Aomori at the northern end, reached in 1891, to Asa, twenty-two miles short of Shimonoseki at the southwestern end. Also, a fair amount of track was in operation along the Japan Sea, as lines completed in 1899 linked Tsuruga with Toyama, and Naoetsu with Niigata. And the building of a cog railway to Karuizawa over the formidable Usui Pass in 1893 opened a through-route from Tokyo to Naoetsu.[5] Meanwhile, articulated regional networks were taking shape in the Kansai and Kantō; by 1900, one could ride trains from Osaka south to Wakayama or east to Nagoya by way of Yokkaichi, and from Tokyo to several points in eastern Chiba prefecture.

In addition, during the 1890s, the three biggest islands all had lines established by private railroads in connection with the mining industry. In Hokkaido, a line between the Ishikari coal fields and the port of Muroran opened in 1892, intersecting the older railroad that linked the fields with Sapporo and Otaru. Honshū saw the completion in 1895 of a branch going inland from Himeji to the gold and silver mines at Ikuno and in 1898 of an artery extending from Tokyo through the Jōban coal fields. Finally, in Kyushu, a loop through the Chikuhō coal basin was built in stages over the period 1891–1899.

Besides these mining-related railroads, in 1900, the Kyushu trunk line ran from Moji to Yatsushiro with an offshoot to Sasebo and Nagasaki, while in Hokkaido, lines connecting with the coal-mining network headed north and south from Asahikawa. Last and least, Shikoku's meager trackage inched up with the addition of two small lines in the vicinities of Takamatsu and Tokushima.[6]

By 1900, then, the rail lines open to traffic on the Japanese islands, Shikoku excepted, were beginning to constitute a respectable system. Japanese at the time celebrated this growing network by reciting the famous *Railway Song*, written by the classical scholar Ōwada Takeki and published in

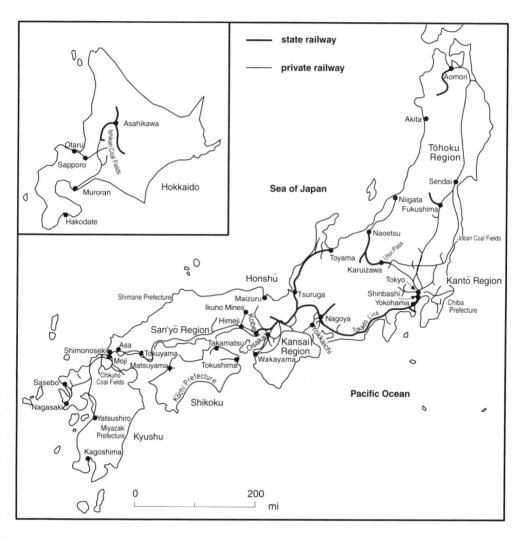

Map 1 Japan's Railway Network in 1900

five installments that year. Intended as a grammar school textbook—students were to learn their history and geography according to stops along the railroad—the *Railway Song* became highly popular among the public at large, partly owing to the imaginative promotional stunts of its Osaka publisher, who even hired a band to perform the song, set to a sprightly melody, while marching along the old Tokaido highway.[7] The first installment—the Tokaido line in sixty-six verses—opened with the famous line:

> With one sound of the whistle, from Shinbashi
> Swiftly departs our train.

Three hundred seventy-six miles and eighty-four train stops later, the song writer exclaimed:

> It's like a dream!
> Having raced past the fifty-three post stations [of the old Tokaido], we rest in a Kobe inn,
> Thanks to the fact that trains give people wings.

The other four installments of the *Railway Song* acclaimed the rail lines of the San'yō and Kyushu, Tōhoku, Japan Sea-side, and Kansai areas. Ōwada followed these with songs hailing the railroads of Hokkaido and Shikoku as well as Korea and Manchuria. His work spawned a host of imitations and even some provincial versions bursting with local pride, so that the year 1900 marked the beginning of a veritable "railway song" mania.[8] The popularity of these songs both echoed and amplified the public's growing appreciation of railroads as an integral part of Meiji life.

By the time of the nationalization and the "5,000-Mile Celebration," the rail network had expanded sufficiently to warrant new editions of the *Railway Song*. In Kyushu, construction northward from Kagoshima left only a small gap, closed in 1909, in the trans-island trunk line. In Honshū, the San'yō line reached Shimonoseki in 1901, while the Hokkaido network had extended to Hakodate by 1904. As a result, it was then possible to travel by rail, with ferry links between the main islands, from northern Hokkaido to west-central Kyushu. Considerable development of interior and connecting lines had also taken place on the big island. A line running from Osaka to Maizuru on the Japan Sea was completed in 1904. An inland railway from Tokyo to Nagoya, the Chūō line, was over three quarters finished in 1906; its 2.9-mile tunnel at Sasago was the longest of the tunnels built in the Meiji period. By 1905, a line branching off from the Tōhoku artery at Fukushima and swinging through Akita on the Japan Sea had been opened all the way to Aomori.[9]

With the establishment of through-service to Kagoshima in 1909, Ōwada came out with entirely new versions of the first two numbers of his *Railway Song*, incorporating the changes that had occurred in the main-line network west of Kobe. Whereas the earlier editions had Kagoshima-bound passengers catching the ferry for Moji at Tokuyama and ending their railroad journey at Yatsushiro, the new "train songs" celebrated the extensions to Shimonoseki and Kagoshima, concluding with the paean:

> How quickly we reach Kagoshima city!
> Thanks to the train, we arrive
> Only three days after leaving Tokyo![10]

Thus, by the latter half of the 1900s, Japan had acquired the basic skeleton of a national railway system and begun the process of fleshing it out. In 1906, the principal arteries were largely in place on the three biggest islands, and only three prefectures—Shimane, Kōchi, and Miyazaki—all on the periphery in western Japan, were as yet without any railroads.[11] On the other hand, gaps still remained in the trunk-line network, especially in the interior and along the Sea of Japan. Moreover, the vast majority of branch and connecting lines had yet to be constructed, with the system as a whole comprising less than one third of its eventual mileage. The fact that the railway network had barely begun to fill out in the Meiji period had, in turn, important implications for the role of railroads in the Meiji economy.

Railroads and the Economy

Qualifying the Linkages: Rails, Locomotives, and Markets. In recent years, economic historians, reacting to the conventional view of the railroad as a vital agent of industrialization, have tended to play down the impact of railroads on the economies of various Western countries.[12] In reassessing that impact, scholars have generally divided the economic effects of railroads into two categories: first, backward linkages or feedbacks, that is, demand for industrial products and other inputs; and second, forward linkages, namely, reduction in transport costs and the resultant widening of markets. On both counts, revisionists have argued, the data demonstrate that traditional accounts inflated the railroad's contribution to economic growth in the West.

On the face of it, using these categories, one could make an even stronger case for the relative unimportance of railroads to the economy of Meiji Japan. To begin with, the feedbacks from railroad development were severely circumscribed during the Meiji period by Japan's almost total reliance on imported rails and locomotives until after the turn of the century. In the case of rails, British makes dominated the Japanese market until the mid-1880s when they started to face competition from German and Belgian products; then, in the 1890s, Carnegie and other U.S. steel makers entered the market in force, so that by the end of the Meiji period, cheaper and superior imports from the later Western industrializers had almost totally displaced their British counterparts.[13] Meanwhile, it was not until 1901 that the state-owned Yawata Iron and Steelworks produced the first Japanese-made rails; by the following year, it was meeting just over 40 percent of domestic demand, thanks to a monopoly on orders from the state railways. Private iron-and-steel companies founded during the next decade added slightly to the total home output. Yet, well into the 1920s, Japan continued to import rails from the United States and Germany on a large scale.[14]

As for locomotives, Japanese trains were pulled exclusively by foreign engines until 1893 when the government railroads' Kobe workshop produced the first locomotive made in Japan. The British supervisor of the project was, fittingly enough, the grandson and namesake of Richard Francis Trevithick, who in 1804 had constructed the world's first locomotive steam engine.[15] In the ensuing years, several private establishments also started manufacturing engines, but as late as 1912, domestic products accounted for less than 7 percent of the locomotives on the national railways.[16] By that time, British imports, which had begun to lose ground to faster and cheaper American makes in the 1890s, had yielded first place to them, with German engines running a distant third.

German imports had initially prevailed in Kyushu and Shikoku. On the latter island, the Iyo Railway Company, established in 1887, had purchased two Krauss tank engines for its tiny 2'6"-gauge line, forerunner of the local light railways that proliferated after 1910. In 1895, when the novelist Natsume Sōseki came to teach in Matsuyama, the Iyo Railway was operating about six miles of track in the vicinity of that city; the hero of his popular novel *Botchan* (Little Master), upon boarding one of the railroad's German-made carriages, which seated twelve to sixteen passengers, described the car as being "so small it looked just like a match box."[17] One of the two Krauss engines, appropriately nicknamed "Botchan," is preserved, together with an original "match-box" carriage, in a Matsuyama park.[18]

The Kyushu Railway Company, the major carrier on the southern island, bought its first set of locomotives from Germany as well. These engines, like almost all others imported into Meiji Japan, were designed for the more typical narrow gauge of 3'6", which the government authorities had adopted in 1870 on the advice of their British engineer-in-chief and nearly every private railroad was to follow thereafter.[19] In 1887, the promoters of the Kyushu Railway hired as their technical adviser a portly German engineer named Hermann Rumschöttel. Their choice of German expertise came at a time when state railroad officials had, on the main island, begun supplementing British rails with German imports "for diplomatic reasons,"[20] presumably with the ongoing drive to revise the unequal treaties with the various Western powers in mind, but also when Germany was fast establishing itself as a world leader in railroad technology. Once the Kyushu Railway obtained its license in 1888, Rumschöttel proceeded to order everything from rails to bridge girders from German firms, including a fleet of tank engines from Krauss and Hohenzollern.[21] The German ascendance in Kyushu, however, did not outlast Rumschöttel's departure in 1892, for on the eve of the Kyushu Railway's nationalization in 1907, German products accounted for less than one fifth of the company's 244 locomotives, fully three quarters of which were American-made.[22]

While the British originally monopolized locomotive orders on the main island and the Germans did the same in Kyushu, the Americans were initially the exclusive suppliers in Hokkaido. The Meiji regime had from the outset entrusted the overall development of the northern island to experts from the United States. As a result, the first two locomotives to operate in Hokkaido were unmistakably American (see Figure 5). These pioneer engines arrived in 1880 complete with bells, diamond stacks, and cowcatchers, presenting a sharp contrast to contemporary locomotives in Honshū with their "proper British buffers"[23] and cyclindrical smokestacks. Dubbed *Yoshitsune* and *Benkei* after the heroic medieval warrior and his legendary retainer, these two engines have both survived in museums.[24]

The big island with its comparatively developed rail network was naturally the most coveted market among foreign locomotive makers. British hegemony there began to crumble in the mid-1890s when the San'yō Railway purchased powerful new American engines, a far cry from the earlier cowcatcher classics. This American breakthrough marked the beginning of fierce competition among U.S., British, and German manufacturers in Honshū. American firms increasingly won the choice orders, as in 1906 when they outbid British companies for "special express" locomotives for the Tokaido line. Symbolic of the U.S. ascendance by the end of Meiji was the fact that at the head of the funeral train bearing the body of the Meiji Emperor in September 1912 was a shiny new engine from the American Locomotive Company.[25]

That locomotive was part of the last significant batch of engines that Japan bought from foreign manufacturers. In July 1911, the final phase of treaty revision went into effect, as Japan recovered full tariff autonomy. In order to encourage domestic production of locomotives, the government immediately raised customs duties on imported engines. In anticipation of this hike, the national railways in early 1911 rushed to place orders abroad for a new generation of main-line locomotives. These engines, most of them featuring the latest superheating technology, were far larger and faster than any locomotive previously seen in Japan. The Japanese distributed the orders among the top three manufacturing nations roughly in proportion to their current reputation in the field, with the American Locomotive Company winning contracts for thirty-six engines, two German firms for twelve each, and the North British Company for twelve. At the time, Britain, unlike the United States and Germany, had not yet developed the capability to produce superheaters; apparently, diplomatic considerations once again impinged on Japan's acquisition of railroad equipment overseas, as the Japanese authorities bowed to pressure from Britain and, despite the dated technology of British manufacturers, ordered a portion of the locomotives from their Western ally. Upon receiving their orders, the foreign makers raced to complete them so as to beat the impending tariff increase. The German companies, for instance, finished their complement of mas-

Figure 5 The locomotive *Benkei*, imported from the United States in 1880 for use on the Hokkaido state railways. Photograph: courtesy of the Transportation Museum, Tokyo.

sive superheaters within the remarkably short time of two and a half months. The knocked-down engines were then loaded onto freighters for the three-month voyage to East Asia, just making it under the wire as their carriers steamed into the territorial waters of the Japanese colony of Taiwan at the very end of June.[26]

In addition to these six dozen locomotives, the Japanese in 1911–1912 purchased sixty-four engines designed for steep inclines from the United States and Germany. After the arrival of these imports, however, Japan, with rare exceptions, ceased buying standard locomotives from abroad. Domestic manufacturers, led by the Train Manufacturing Company (Kisha seizō kaisha) and Kawasaki Shipbuilding, started producing engines on a large scale after 1911, having acquired the necessary expertise by assembling imported locomotives and making dead copies of them in the process (see Figure 6). Following the railway nationalization and especially the achievement of tariff autonomy, these firms also began receiving official support in the form of exclusive orders and technical help from the national railways and protection from foreign competitors in the home market. Thus, as the Meiji period came to a close, Japan finally became self-sufficient in locomotive production.[27]

The rise in domestic manufacturing of rails and locomotives after the turn of the century naturally had a significant effect on the activities of trading companies that had been handling imports of railroad equipment. Mitsui Bussan, the largest Japanese trading firm, had entered this field in the mid-1890s, serving as agent initially for British producers and then increasingly for U.S. manufacturers such as Carnegie Steel, American Locomotive, and General Electric.[28] At the end of Meiji, Bussan was supplying nearly half of all the equipment ordered from abroad by the national railways. Yet, by that time, such orders had begun to decline as the government railway administration adopted a policy of giving preference to Japanese manufacturers. In the case of locomotives, the Railway Department announced this policy in 1909 and then declared in 1912 that, from the following year, it would purchase only domestic products. Accordingly, Bussan's delivery of twenty-four foreign-made engines in 1912 was to be its final such delivery to the national railways, and from then on, the company had to place much greater weight on importing raw materials and parts for domestic locomotive producers.[29] State railway policy contributed not only

Figure 6 A superheater locomotive, Type 8850, produced in 1913 by Kawasaki Shipbuilding Company copying engines imported from Germany in 1911. Photograph: courtesy of the Transportation Museum, Tokyo.

to a restructuring of Bussan's import business, but also to an expansion of its export operations. Following the nationalization, the government railways sought to increase export-related traffic by offering substantial rebates on such key commodities as silk cocoons; partly reflecting these discounts, the value of the raw silk distributed by Mitsui Bussan more than doubled in 1907. For the rest of the Meiji period, this product rivaled coal and cotton goods for the top position among export items handled by the firm.[30]

In any case, until very late in the period, railroads contributed little to the emergence of the iron-and-steel and engineering industries that were critical to sustaining an industrial revolution. Three forms of state intervention proved decisive in making it possible for the railroad to begin to have a considerable impact on those sectors after the turn of the century. First of all, the government initiated the Japanese steel industry by using part of the indemnity it extracted from China after the Sino-Japanese War of 1894–1895 to establish its integrated iron-and-steel mill at Yawata. That plant and the private mills for which it paved the way were to meet a growing proportion of the domestic demand for rails and steel for railroad equipment. Second, the nationalization of the major private railroads in 1906–1907, by placing some 90 percent of the total network in government hands, created a huge guaranteed market for domestic steel and engineering works. To foster home manufacture of rolling stock, for instance, the expanded national railway administration increasingly funneled orders to a cartel of private Japanese makers, even directing its own works to cease production of locomotives in 1909.[31] Following the rush order for foreign locomotives in 1911, the state railway policy of preferential buying from home manufacturers, a policy shared by other government agencies at the time, naturally became all the more pronounced, driven as it was by a new program of increased tariff protection. The state thus extended a third helping hand with Japan's complete recovery of tariff control in mid-1911. From then on, the authorities were able to shelter fledgling domestic producers by slapping heavy duties on imports.[32] All these initiatives, however, came late in the Meiji period, more than a full generation after the start of railroad construction in Japan. In this regard, Japan's early experience in railway development differed markedly from that of France and Germany, where, within the first decade or so of railroad building, "rapid and decisive moves toward import substitution," reinforced by protective tariffs, gave a significant boost to home metallurgical and engineering industries.[33]

Railroads had a limited impact on the Meiji economy not only in terms of feedbacks but also of forward linkages. Through the Meiji era, the rail network played a comparatively minor, albeit a steadily growing, role in overall market extension and integration, for the country's insular geography and the already well-developed state of coastal shipping meant that waterborne transport would continue to be the principal mode of domestic freight carriage until the end of the period.[34]

In the case of rice, for example, it was probably not until the latter half of the Taishō era that trains pulled ahead of riverboats and coastal steamers in the movement of this key commodity.[35] Delaying the shift from water to rail transport in Meiji was a lack of facilities, particularly of through-traffic arrangements and even of freight cars. For instance, the Nippon Railway Company, which serviced the rice basket in northeastern Japan, faced constant complaints about the shortage of freight cars it made available to that region for hauling rice.[36] The bottleneck of inadequate facilities was not overcome until after the railway nationalization. Another obstacle was that feeder lines were as yet underdeveloped in the Meiji era. It was really only in the Taishō period, with the rapid extension of the branch-line network, that trains came to link most of the rice-growing areas directly with the leading consumer centers and finally to overtake boats in the conveyance of rice.

Related to the inadequacy of freight service prior to the nationalization was that, unlike contemporary Western railroads, those of Meiji Japan were geared mainly to passenger traffic. Passengers consistently brought in more revenue than did goods, a pattern that, with the exception of a few years during World War I, has persisted to this day.[37] Nevertheless, as the railway system expanded, the transport of freight increased at a faster rate than did that of passengers. Between 1890 and 1906, the tonnage of goods moved shot up by a factor of sixteen, while the number of passengers carried rose less than sixfold. During the same time, income from freight grew steadily in importance, its share of total rail receipts rising from 26 to 43 percent.[38] Yet, even in late Meiji, railroads probably captured only a small proportion of Japan's aggregate freight traffic. As late as 1908, for example, less than 3 percent of the tonnage of goods transported between Tokyo and Yokohama was carried by rail.[39] For many coastwise rail lines, competition from waterborne transport remained intense until the latter part of the Meiji period, when rail fares began to fall relative to wholesale prices.[40] Even in overland transport, simpler innovations like the building of local dirt roads and the replacement of porters and pack horses by rickshaws and horsecarts probably made a greater immediate contribution to economic progress than did the more celebrated construction of railroads.[41]

NARROWING THE FIELD: INDUSTRY- AND AREA-SPECIFIC EFFECTS. In aggregate terms, railroads may not have pulled the Meiji economy toward accelerated growth, but they did have a substantial economic impact on certain industries and localities. One such industry was coal mining. By weight, coal was far and away the most important item carried by rail during the Meiji period. In 1907, for instance, it accounted for 44 percent of the total tonnage of rail freight, with wood products and grain coming in a distant second and third at 11 and 10 percent, respectively.[42] By that time, trains, which had the advantage over boats in terms of speed, reliability, and stable fares, had come to move about 70 percent of all the coal mined in Japan.[43] By improving the distribution of coal, railroads helped make it into a major export item, the third biggest after silk and tea, with coal exports accounting for about 6 percent of Japan's total exports and 40 percent of its total coal production in the mid-Meiji years.[44]

Although trains came to handle the bulk of Japan's coal output, they did not necessarily displace ships in doing so. In the Meiji period, railroad transport of coal, as of rice, was mainly short haul in nature, serving to connect inland producing or consuming centers with nearby ports. As a result, coastal shipping remained decisive in the overall movement of coal, with rail and marine transport in this case interacting in a complementary rather than competitive fashion.[45] As the railway network expanded and ramified, trains gradually supplanted ships in conveying surplus rice from northern and western Honshū to the principal deficit areas centering on Tokyo and Osaka.[46] The carriage of coal, however, did not undergo a similar shift. Because the major producing and consuming districts were on different islands, coastal shipping continued long after the Meiji era to be the pivot of the domestic transportation system for coal.[47] Where displacement did occur was in the area of short-distance movement, as the opening of railroads dealt a crippling blow to the conveyance of coal by riverboat. Yet even this change took time to unfold, with river transport of coal holding its own through much of the Meiji era. Until late in the period, then, it was not so much a case of trains replacing boats as of railroads stimulating the rapid growth of the coal-mining industry and largely capturing the resulting increase in freight.

This pattern is clearly borne out by the example of the Chikuhō coal fields of northern Kyushu (see Map 2). Before the coming of the railroad, coal mined in the Chikuhō fields had moved by river, in particular on the Onga, to points north for transshipment to the Kansai area and elsewhere. After the opening by private railway companies of direct rail links to the ports of Wakamatsu and Moji in 1891, railroads quickly came to dominate this traffic. The amount of coal carried to the ports by riverboat stagnated for the remainder of the Meiji period, but with the total output of Chikuhō coal leaping from just under one million tons in 1891 to nearly six-and-a-half million in 1906, the railroads' share of the port-bound traffic likewise jumped during that period from 3 percent to 84 percent.[48] Thanks to the extension of the railway system, the Chikuhō during those years solidified its position as the country's top coal-mining region, raising its proportion of total Japanese coal production from less than a third to over one half.[49]

Railroads had an even more dramatic impact on the Jōban coal fields north of Mito along the Pacific Ocean. Before the Nippon Railway Company extended its Jōban line to those fields in 1897, coal-mining concerns there had been small-scale, locally oriented affairs. For example, the Iwaki Coal-Mining Company, founded in 1883, had failed to heed the colliers' adage "before you buy a mine, buy a road" and, despite the installation of modern equipment in 1884, had seen its growth stunted by inadequate transportation. Production finally began to increase in 1887 when the firm built two light railways connecting its mine with the nearly harbor of Onahama. It was not until the Jōban line reached the area a decade later, however, that the operation really started to take off. The mine's output, which had edged up to about 30,000 tons by 1895, more than tripled in the ensuing four years, and by 1907, it had exceeded 300,000 tons. With the Jōban line providing a direct rail link to Tokyo, the average cost of transporting a ton of coal there from the Jōban fields fell by over a quarter.⁵⁰ The reduction in freightage and the resultant drop in price of Jōban coal triggered a surge in demand for the commodity and a sharp increase in the region's aggregate coal production, which soared from 81,174 tons in 1896 to over 1,100,000 tons in 1906. During those years, Jōban's share of all coal mined in Japan rose from 1.6 to 8.7 percent, making the Jōban fields the fourth biggest producer of Japanese coal after the Chikuhō, Miike, and Hokkaido fields.⁵¹

Meiji railroads also had an important feedback effect on the coal-mining industry since they were users as well as transporters of coal. In 1907–1909, for example, the railroads consumed 9 percent of Japan's total coal output, rendering them the fourth largest market for coal after exports, factories, and steamships.⁵² In terms of both forward and backward linkages, therefore, railroad development played a significant, if not crucial, role in the growth of the Japanese coal-mining industry.

Along with industries like coal-mining, specific localities derived great economic benefit from Meiji railroads. Prominent among these were places situated in the interior of the country. Tokugawa Japan, with its relatively limited systems of overland and riverine transport and thus heavy dependence on coastal shipping for the long-haul movement of freight, had resembled an animal whose circulatory system rests on the outside of its skin.⁵³ To a large degree, then, railroad building provided much of Japan with an effective internal circulatory system for the first time.

Railroad construction exerted this impact especially on mountainous, landlocked prefectures such as Nagano, Yamanashi, and Gunma, which were also centers of the Japanese silk industry.⁵⁴ Railroads made a signal contribution to the economic development of these areas and, in particular, to the growth of their primary industry, sericulture. Indeed, with speed of delivery so critical to the silk industry owing to the perishability of cocoons and the instability of market prices for both cocoons and raw silk, the poor accessibility of major silk-producing localities meant that railroads proved "all but decisive"⁵⁵ to the rapid expansion of that industry. Moreover, the extension of rail service into such areas, by furnishing a vital link between local filatures and increasingly distant suppliers and markets, facilitated the mechanization of silk manufacturing in the latter half of Meiji. After the late 1880s, modern machine-reeling technology spread quickly in

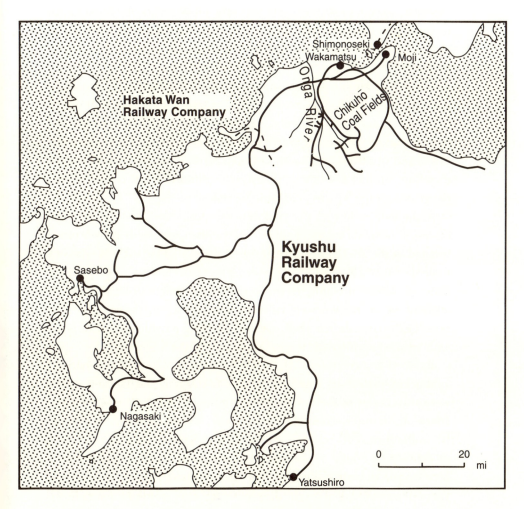

Map 2 The Kyushu Railway Network in 1906

Japan, especially in the above three prefectures, yielding a marked improvement in quality as well as productivity over traditional hand-reeling methods.[56] Railroads also began to reach those prefectures in the middle to late Meiji years. Modernization in manufacturing and in transport then combined to produce an explosion in local raw silk output from the late 1880s on. In this respect, the importance of railroad development actually transcended its local or regional impact inasmuch as raw silk was Japan's leading export item and foreign-exchange earner until well after the Meiji era.[57]

The Meiji government realized this economic function of railroads from the start. In 1870, for example, the Public Works Ministry assigned two of its officials to investigate the relative merits of building the planned Tokyo-Kyoto artery by way of the interior Nakasendō route or the coastal Tokaido. In their report, these men recommended construction via the Nakasendō, explaining that, "since there are many places [along that route] where transportation is inconvenient, if branch roads are added here and there, it will open the way to the conveyance of products and the civilization of mountainous districts (*yamaguni kaika*)."[58] The government subsequently opted for the Nakasendō route mainly on the strategic grounds that a coastal line would be vulnerable to foreign attack, but as the aforementioned report of 1870 indicates, state planners recognized from the outset that railroad building, in addition to advancing national goals, could also serve as a powerful instrument of regional economic development.

Yet it was not until the very end of the Meiji period that the government completed a trunk line through the central silk-producing regions between Tokyo and Kyoto. The state Railway Bureau started building a Nakasendō line in the mid-1880s, but after laying track at both ends of the proposed artery, concluded that the rugged terrain in between made construction of the railroad too difficult and costly. At the bureau's request, therefore, the government in 1886 reversed its earlier decision, abandoning the Nakasendō route in favor of the Tokaido.[59] Only after passage of the Railway Construction Law in 1892 did the state commence work on an alternate central railroad, the Chūō line, which opened in stages from 1901 to 1911. So, for many sericultural communities, especially in Nagano and Yamanashi, the full benefits of interior railroad building did not arrive until late in the Meiji era.

Nevertheless, inland construction of both state and private railways that preceded the laying of the Chūō line did make a difference to a number of localities with extensive involvement in the silk industry. One of the first sericultural areas to profit from such construction was the region centering on Maebashi in Gunma prefecture. In 1884, the Nippon Railway Company extended its Ueno-Takasaki line to Maebashi and the following year built most of the present-day Yamanote loop in Tokyo, connecting the Takasaki line with the state railway from Shinagawa to Yokohama (see Map 3). The company thereby established a direct rail link between the silk-producing communities of Gunma and the port of Yokohama. An 1890 report on agricultural conditions in Gunma described the impact of this railway connection on the shipment of locally manufactured raw silk as follows:

> ... the environs of Maebashi are the number-one producer of raw silk in the prefecture. Before the opening of the railroad, conveying [raw silk from this area] to Yokohama involved sending it by pack horse to the bank [of the Tone River], ... and from there by boat down the river to Yokohama via Tokyo; this took three to four days and cost ¥2.8 per horse load. But since the building of the railroad in 1884, transportation has become convenient, and it takes only one day to reach [Yokohama], while the freight charge has fallen to about ¥0.5 per load.[60]

The Takasaki and Yamanote lines thus facilitated the export of raw silk from the Maebashi area by affording distributors enormous savings in domestic carrying time and expense. The lines quickly drew the silk traffic away from the Tone River and helped boost Gunma's raw silk production, which rose nearly threefold from 1885 to 1895.[61]

Between those years, Gunma actually lost its position as Japan's top silk-producing prefecture to Nagano, whose output of raw silk jumped almost sevenfold during that time.[62] Nagano also benefited from the Nippon Railway's Takasaki line, particularly after the government began extending it into the prefecture as the first section of the abortive Nakasendō railroad, filling in the gap at the Usui Pass in 1893. This line had a marked impact on the Suwa district, a major silk-reeling center in Nagano. In the decade after 1885, raw-silk production in Suwa rose by a factor of almost nine, and by the 1890s, the district had come to account for about 30 percent of total production in the prefecture and 6 to 7 percent in all of Japan.[63] With the opening of the railway through-route in 1893, the shipment of raw silk from Suwa to Yokohama switched entirely from the Kōshū highway to the much cheaper and quicker rail line. Yet, to reach the railroad, the goods still had to travel some thirty miles by road over the steep Wada Pass. For both incoming cocoons and outgoing silk, the situation had improved considerably since the bridging of the Usui Pass; prior to that feat, transporting cocoons by road from the end of the Takasaki line extension to the Suwa region had taken about seven days at a loss of around 40 percent of the cocoons.[64] After 1893, the carrying time from the railroad was reduced to perhaps two or three days, but the silk reelers of Suwa were understandably anxious to cut that time as well by obtaining a direct rail connection to the Tokyo area.

A golden opportunity to achieve that goal came with passage of the Railway Construction Law in 1892. Among the lines designated for priority building by the state under this act was an interior road, the so-called Chūō line, to run through Yamanashi and Nagano prefectures. The law provided for alternative routes at various points along the projected line, but stipulated that the railroad pass through Kōfu and Suwa, the silk-reeling centers of Yamanashi and Nagano. Stirred by enactment of this law, silk manufacturers from those prefectures banded together and in late 1892 petitioned the government for speedy planning and construction of the proposed central artery. Since sericulture was "a principal source of profit to the nation," they argued, servicing their industry ought to be "the most important criterion in selecting railway lines"; from that standpoint, they urged that the Chūō line be built along "the spinal cord of the Japanese silk industry" from Nagoya to Suwa and thence via the Kōshū highway to Hachiōji, thus linking their localities directly with Yokohama.[65]

This route was essentially the course chosen by the government, which started laying the line from Hachiōji in 1896. The work proceeded at an agonizingly slow pace, however, with the builders having to perform difficult engineering feats, the most challenging being the construction of a nearly three-mile-long tunnel under the Sasago Pass. As a result, the first major section of track, the fifty-three miles from Hachiōji to Kōfu, took over seven years to build. Then, as the line approached Nagano prefecture, the Russo-Japanese War broke out, causing a temporary suspension of all state railroad construction. Alarmed by this turn of events, silk reelers in Suwa organized to lobby the central authorities for rapid completion of the Chūō line. The Suwa sericulturalists emphasized in their petitions the im-

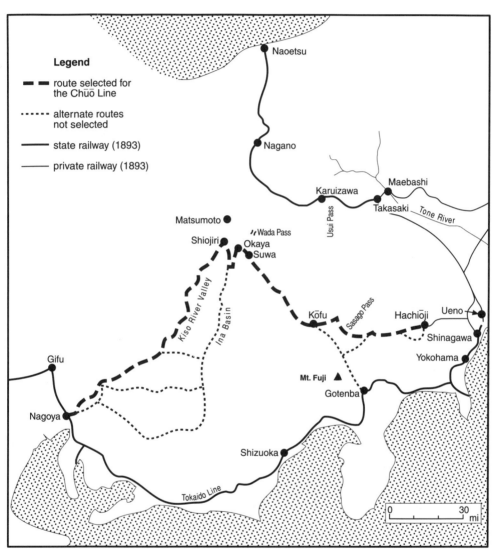

Map 3 Alternate Routes for the Chūō Line Under the Railway Construction Law of 1892

portance of the railroad for promoting silk exports and thereby raising war funds. To press their point, they went on to collect almost half a million yen in local donations and offered to lend this money to the government so that it could resume construction work.[66] Their actions carried the day, as the authorities decided in mid-1904 to make an exception in this case and accept the offer of a loan to continue extending the Chūō line. In November 1905, the railroad finally reached Okaya, in the heart of the Suwa region, more than thirteen years after the start of the silk reelers' campaign for an interior railway line.

Rail transport thus came relatively late to the great silk-producing districts of central Japan, but, however delayed, its arrival had an enormous impact on the silk industry in Yamanashi and Nagano. The opening of the Chūō line provided Kōfu and Suwa with an express route to the foreign silk market via Yokohama, while the westward extension of the railroad in the years after 1905 enabled filatures in both areas to continue expanding their access to supplies. Suwa, for example, began drawing cocoons not only from throughout the Kantō region, but also from Gifu prefecture to the west.[67] Moreover, the savings in time and expense of cocoon delivery were substantial. Cocoons that had required up to ten days to reach Nagano from the Kantō before the coming of the railroad took no more than three days thereafter.[68] Freight charges fell, too, often dramatically: with the completion of the seventeen-mile section between Okaya and Shiojiri in 1906, the cost of carrying cocoons from Shiojiri to Suwa plunged to a tenth of the previous charge.[69] The railroad also helped meet the industry's growing demand for fuel by making possible large-scale deliveries of coal, especially from the rapidly developing Jōban fields. Several months after the opening of the Chūō line to Kōfu in 1903, a reporter noted that filatures in the Kōfu area had all switched from charcoal to coal; the price of charcoal had been on the rise, but thanks to the railroad, silk reelers were now able to import coal at a much cheaper price, so the cost of producing silk had dropped significantly.[70] The same was true of the Suwa region. There, the cost reductions and other advantages afforded by the railroad contributed to a marked expansion of the local reeling industry. From 1895 to 1904, the number of filatures in Suwa had remained largely unchanged and raw-silk output had increased by only a third, but in the eight years after the Chūō line reached the area, the number of filatures doubled and production rose nearly threefold.⁷¹

As the examples of Suwa and Kōfu illustrate, Meiji railroads had a positive economic effect on the interior communities they traversed; by the same token, the economies of inland areas that failed to attract rail lines tended to experience relative stagnation or decline. Such was the case with the Ina basin, a sizable producer of rice and raw silk, located southwest of Suwa. The Ina region engaged in a fierce competition with the parallel Kiso River valley over the routing of the Chūō line beyond Suwa, both districts mounting aggressive lobbying campaigns as Diet deliberations on railroad-building legislation began in 1891. The intensity of their rivalry is captured in the "fight song" composed by supporters of the Kiso cause:

> Slaughter all those Ina swine! *Don, don.*
> So they're not going to let us lay a railroad along the Kiso, are they?
> *Don, don.*⁷²

Members of an Ina railway mission dispatched to Tokyo in 1892 showed they were no less aware of the high stakes involved in the line-selection game when they wired home the following telegram upon inclusion of the Ina basin as an "alternate route" for the Chūō line in the newly enacted Railway Construction Law: "Ten last night, bill passed. Long live the railroad (*tetsudō banzai*)!"⁷³ When the government finally opted for the Kiso-valley route in 1894, the disappointment of the Ina representatives in Tokyo was palpable; this time, their telegram to the officials back home read: "Ina line defeated. Regrets endless."⁷⁴

In the end, the economic argument for building the Chūō line through the more developed Ina basin lost out to other claims. For one thing, the military pushed for the more direct Kiso route, as did the Imperial Household Ministry, which happened to own valuable forest land in the Kiso region.⁷⁵ The decisive factor, though, was probably the opinion of the state railroad authorities. The choice between alternate routes, in this case as in most others, ultimately hinged on engineering concerns, in particular the Railway Bureau's insistence on keeping the gradient of the line to no more than 1/40.⁷⁶ After surveying the Ina and Kiso valleys in 1892, the bureau determined that the Ina route would require unacceptably steep grades whereas a line through the Kiso valley would be quicker and easier to build. The railroad authorities did not ignore the potential economic benefits of the latter route—after all, they noted, the Kiso was an area with prospects for future development[77]—but economic reasons were clearly secondary in their minds to technical considerations.

In any event, the failure to obtain a railroad dealt a sharp blow to the Ina region. As a sop, the Railway Bureau agreed to have the line from Suwa to Shiojiri loop down to the northern end of the Ina valley instead of running straight through a tunnel under the Shiojiri Pass. The urgings of a Dietman from Ina who was also a member of the Railway Council, the state organ that decided on the routing of lines under the Construction Law, appear to have played a part in this move. Railway officials needed little convincing, however, as the circuitous route fit in with their engineering priorities, enabling them to avoid a difficult tunnel excavation and save ¥260,000 to boot.[78] This dividend was small consolation to the silk manufacturers and other residents of the Ina basin. Lacking a railroad and hence the advantages of transport enjoyed by its counterpart in Suwa, the Ina silk industry fell into a long-term decline.

Ina residents might have responded to the defeat of their bid for a state railway by building a private line with their own funds; after all, the late 1890s witnessed a surge in private railroad development at the local level. At the time, they were undoubtedly dissuaded from doing so by the huge capital requirements of railway construction, a burden compounded in their case by the difficult terrain they would have to deal with.[79] They may also have been deterred by the experience of the Kōshin Railway Company. The Kōshin was a Nagano-based private railroad that had only recently collapsed in the wake of the financial panic of 1890. Landlords and merchants of Matsumoto city, joined by investors from Yamanashi prefecture and the Tokyo area, had founded the railroad in the late 1880s, at the height of the first private railway boom. The company had proposed to build a line from Matsumoto to Gotenba, a course that roughly corresponded to what the 1892 Construction Law was to list as an alternate route for the eastern end of the Chūō line. To supervise the project, the Kōshin had hired a recent graduate of the Engineering College of Tokyo Imperial University by the name of Saburi Kazutsugu. Saburi had ended up acting as more than just chief engineer. In his capacity as cheerleader and publicist, he had expressed what he believed to be the proper goal of this and other private railroads in an 1891 pamplet on "The Railway Problems in Japan, Present and Future." Echoing the state railroad officials of early Meiji, he had argued in this treatise that "it is of urgent importance to lay out lines through the central mountainous districts," for such lines would "serve to open the hitherto undeveloped resources of the interior, and to carry modern civilization into the most backward localities of the Empire."[80] The Kōshin Railway in particular was to have linked up the central silk-producing regions of Nagano with the Tokaido and Naoetsu trunk lines. Unfortunately for Saburi and his colleagues, the company had been hard hit by the Panic of 1890 and, before even starting construction work, had been forced to dissolve in 1891.[81] In the short run, at least, the fate of this railroad, combined with the renewed commitment to inland railroad building by the government after 1892, may well have put a damper on any subsequent plans for private rail development in the interior.

The motives, respectively, of private shareholders in *successful* railway companies and of government railway decision makers had led by mid-Meiji to a kind of division of labor in railroad construction between the private sector and the state; their individual agendas also insured that, insofar as Meiji railroads had linkages with the economy, they would be particularly bound up with the development of exports. The private railroads that succeeded in the Meiji period almost invariably depended on extensive equity participation by big-city capitalists and the nascent zaibatsu. Such investors were chiefly interested in obtaining high dividends or in furthering their main business concerns. Consequently, the private railroads they financed tended to follow profitable routes along the coast or in urban areas, or to service major coal fields. With state railway subsidies restricted as a matter of policy to trunk-line firms, it was left to the government to lay the bulk of the nonremunerative interior lines that nonetheless had considerable potential for generating external economies. The state was prompted to build such lines in part by the strategic demands of army officials, in part by the pork-barrel requirements of elected Diet members. Another, equally vital impulse for state authorities, however, was the national economic imperative of promoting exports, especially of silk.[82] To the extent that the zaibatsu and other coal-mine owners invested in railroads to advance their mining operations and the government did so to foster the manufacture of silk and other foreign-exchange earners, the Meiji railway system became closely tied to the leading export industries of that era. In fact, government officials were inclined to view the railway network, apropos of its economic function, primarily as a domestic adjunct to overseas shipping.[83]

These observations point to a qualified assessment of the role of railroads in the Meiji economy. At the microeconomic level, the Meiji rail network had a significant impact on particular localities and industries, especially export-oriented ones. In fact, railroads proved critical to the rapid development of such inland areas as the coal fields of Chikuhō and the silk-producing districts of Nagano. In the absence of rail transport, the coal mines and filatures of these regions would doubtless have continued to undergo moderate expansion simply through the diffusion of modern machinery and improvements in existing river and overland connections; however, rail lines clearly helped make the difference between measured and explosive growth such as occurred in both the Chikuhō and Suwa basins after the opening of railway through-routes to the ports. Moreover, the effects of railroads on individual sectors like coal mining and sericulture added up to a qualitatively important influence, one out of proportion to the aggregate data on freight movement and the like.

At the macroeconomic level, the Meiji railway system was certainly instrumental in forwarding economic growth, but it was not indispensable. In the larger scheme of things, railroad development made less of an impact on the Meiji economy than, say, the spread of traditional best practice in agriculture, the rise of a modern shipping industry, or the introduction of modern financial and business organizations, although railway companies themselves played a part in bringing about the latter set of innovations. During the Meiji period, railroads contributed to the beginnings of industrialization mainly by facilitating the production and distribution of key export items like coal, raw silk, and cotton yarn.[84] In doing so, they furthered the integration of mining, textile manufacturing, and shipping—all leading sectors of the Meiji economy—and enabled the government and private business to accumulate much of the funds needed to finance the next phase of economic development, which centered on heavy and chemical industries. The growing interdependence of these various sectors indicates that, however subsidiary the railway industry may have been, it still performed a significant integrative function in the Meiji economy.

Nevertheless, the full economic effect of railroad development did not set in until the very close of the Meiji era, some two generations after the beginning of railway construction in Japan. In this respect, the Japanese experience diverged from that of European followers like Germany. Admittedly, the German states initially relied on imported rails and rolling stock, primarily from Britain. Furthermore, in Germany, since railroad building started before industrialization really got under way, the early railroads all depended chiefly on passenger traffic for revenue; the pioneer German railroad, opened between Nürnberg and Fürth in 1835, hauled its first freight—"appropriately two barrels of beer!"—six months after commencing operation.[85] Yet, compared to Japan, Germany moved rapidly in the direction of import substitution and goods transport, thanks to tariff protection and relatively swift extension of its rail network. In Japan, the railroads began to exert substantial feedbacks on engineering and heavy industry only after the turn of the century with the establishment of virtual state monopolies in the steel-making and railway fields and the recovery of tariff independence. Even the railroads' provision of forward linkages remained limited until the government unified and filled out the system in the decades following the 1906–1907 nationalization. In macroeconomic terms, then, the significance of Meiji railroads lay not so much in their immediate impact as in the promise they held for the future, a promise that was not to be fully realized until after the Meiji era.

Railroads and Society

The Train as Symbol. More profound, although less precisely measurable, than the effect of railroads on the Meiji economy was their influence on the society and culture of the period. This was true especially in the realm of images and metaphors. In Japan as in the West, the railroad became a potent and pervasive emblem of civilization and progress.[86] The locomotive in particular was "a perfect symbol," as Leo Marx has pointed out in his discussion of American railroads, for its meaning did not have to be "attached to it by a poet" but was "inherent in its physical attributes": its power, speed, noise, and smoke.[87] As such, it appeared as the very embodiment of the new age— "the industrial revolution incarnate," in the words of one economic historian.[88] For Japanese as much as for Westerners embarking on industrialization, the notion of progress did not have to be "spelled out": the railroads made the idea "palpable" and "visible to all"[89]— at least all who came in direct contact with them, which in the case of Meiji Japan, as both the network and its use expanded, came to include a substantial part of the population.

The rest could experience the railroads vicariously through song and print of every description, for during the Meiji period, probably no other innovation approached the railroad in capturing the imagination of writers and artists alike.[90] From the beginning, accounts of railway projects, railway openings, and railway travel figured prominently in newspapers and magazines. In early Meiji journals, it was the novelty of train speed that drew the most coverage. Shortly before the Shinbashi-Yokohama line opened in 1872, for example, a reporter marveled that people would soon be able to cover the eighteen miles traversed by the railroad in only fifty-four minutes, exclaiming that this was something that previously would have been "impossible to do without wings."[91] A rash of books describing the changes sweeping early Meiji society also introduced the railroad to the reading public. A prototype of this genre entitled *A Record of Tokyo's New Prosperity* (*Tōkyō shin hanjō ki*) sold over ten thousand copies after it came out in 1874. The author included a graphic account of the train ride between Shinbashi and Yokohama, concluding in a flight of exaltation with the usual avian metaphor: "truly this is a wonderful means of putting wings on people!"[92] Later that year, in one of the many imitations of this work, another writer offered an earthier comparison; the train went from Shinbashi to Yokohama, this commentator explained, "faster than it takes a hemorrhoid sufferer to empty his bowels."[93] In the latter half of the Meiji period, there emerged a new body of literature reflecting the growing popularity of railway travel. In the mid-1890s, a succession of writers began publishing accounts of personal journeys and explorations by rail, and by the last decade of Meiji, novelists from Tokutomi Roka to Natsume Sōseki were frequently setting their narratives in railway stations or train cars.[94]

Railroads reached a wide audience in the Meiji era not only through prose but also through song and art. In the 1870s, scores of popular ditties voiced the universal astonishment at the speed and power of the locomotive. After the opening of the Shinbashi-Yokohama line, children counted the bounces of the ball with a song that contained the verse "The locomotive runs as fast as a shooting arrow; the trip to Yokohama takes only an instant."[95] They learned their syllabary by playing an 1875 version of *iroha karuta*, the traditional card game but with a modern twist, the poem for the syllable *ha* reading, "Prosperity (*hanjō*) is the matchless locomotive; passengers throng the station."[96] Meanwhile, artists, both famous and obscure, were inundating the public with lively woodblock prints of the early trains. These prints, although not always accurate in their depictions of the new technology, did as much as anything to promote the railroad in early Meiji as the leading symbol of "civilization and enlightenment." Towards the end of the period, probably the greatest influence on popular images of trains was the celebrated *Railway Song*. Taking the musical ride on the Tokaido, schoolchildren, no less their elders, hymned the advantages of the railroad and the joys of rail travel. By the time the song came out in revised form in 1909, the train had whistled its way into the hearts and minds of almost all Japanese and, for much of the populace, had become a welcome "fact of daily life."[97]

The positive image of the railroad as both symbol and convenience of civilization was clearly the most widely held. As in the West, however, this image had its dark side, representing the costs that invariably seem to accompany modernization. Charles Dickens epitomized the early Victorian version of this ambivalence. On the one hand, Dickens hailed the speedy locomotive for "realising the Arabian Nights in these prose days"[98] and for bringing prosperity in its train; on the other, he condemned it as a "monster" or "mad dragon" that threatened life and the older ways of living.[99] Writers in North America expressed similarly conflicting views of the railroad during the nineteenth century. In the dominant perception, the steam engine was the "triumphant machine," conquering the vast expanses of the continent and forging a nation out of the wilderness, but this image had its sinister counterpart, which sometimes joined ambiguously with the positive view and at other times stood unmistakably alone. In the latter case, the train appeared as a "menacing machine"—a demonic, serpentine monster symbolizing the despoilment of nature and rural life and the alienation of the individual that attended industrial "progress."[100]

An Englishman who toured Japan in 1898 reflected this subordinate negative image of the railroad in the West when, in a curious mixture of insight and obtuseness, he remarked of the Japanese:

> What should that placid little people know of the rattle and rush of an express train, typical as it is of the nerve-wasting haste with which we Westerners live our lives? Those shining metals are as the veritable trail of the serpent; they follow inevitably in the wake of civilisation, and give rise to crowded and smoky manufacturing towns, while spreading abroad an unrestful desire for travel, with all its concomitant worries and brainwear. Moreover, the destruction of all peaceful village life comes in their train.... I cannot resist saying that when Japan finally exchanges her peaceful simplicity, her admiration for, and artistic appreciation of, Nature's beauties, and her contented national life, for the storm, stress, and hurry of that feverish existence known to the West, she will have given up the substance for the shadow. Happily for her, that day is not yet within measurable distance...[101]

In fact, "that day" was fast approaching, if not already dawning in the burgeoning urban centers of Japan, as suggested in the morbidly fascinating short story "Terror" written by Tanizaki Jun'ichirō in 1913. The tale concerns a man afflicted with "railroad phobia"; this ailment causes him to "suffer the agony of pure terror" whenever he rides the train, which, "with its utter indifference and its tremendous energy, hurtles down the track at full speed. 'What's the life of one human being?' it seems to ask."[102]

Even before the appearance of Tanazaki's story, the dark imagery of the railroad had found pellucid expression in the work of the late-Meiji novelist Natsume Sōseki. For Sōseki, one of the greatest of Japan's modern writers, the train was the quintessential emblem of modernity with all its devastating effects on the individual, and nowhere did he make this more evident than in his 1906 novel *The Three-Cornered World*. In it, Sōseki used the railroad to drive home his favorite themes of alienation and dehumanization. Believing "there is nothing more typical of twentieth-century civilization ... [in its] contempt for individuality than the train," the narrator muses at the end of the novel:

> Whenever I see the violent way in which a train runs along, indiscriminately regarding all human beings as so much freight, I look at the individuals cooped up in the carriages, and at the iron monster itself ... and I think, 'Look out, look out, or you'll find yourselves in trouble.' The

railway train which blunders ahead blindly into the pitch darkness is one example of the very obvious dangers which abound in modern civilization.[103]

In the final scene, the railroad also symbolizes the shattering of rural tranquility, as the conscripted country boy climbs onto a horrific "serpent born of civilization," which has come "belching black smoke from its mouth, . . . slithering its way over the silver rails," to take him away to a distant world of modern warfare and carnage.[104]

Novelists like Sōseki were not alone in decrying the corrosive influence of the railroad on the "soul" of Japan. From a quite different perspective, agrarian moralists had by the late Meiji period become equally alarmed at the train's impact on rural life. For them, the railroad had emerged as "the Japanese version of the serpent in Eden,"[105] corrupting village youth by exposing them to the enticements of the city and, in so doing, endangering the rural repository of traditional values. A popular rendition of this fiendish metaphor also turned up in folklore. The traditional folk belief in bewitchment by foxes or badgers had assumed a modern cast by the end of Meiji, with people in certain localities claiming that the spirits of these animals took the form of ghost trains to retaliate for the depredation of their homes and lives by railroad employees. Such beliefs long outlasted the Meiji era; as John Embree noted in the mid-1930s, villagers in one area still imagined that an avenging fox train, made up of "a row of many lights," could frequently be seen gliding along the railroad tracks.[106] These tales seemed to verbalize the negative side of provincial ambivalence toward the railroad for being not only a facilitator of progress, but also a disrupter of land and community and "a destroyer of pure and simple local customs."[107]

Demonic and destructive images of the train were clearly in evidence during the Meiji period, but after the shock of first encounter had worn off, these perceptions were largely confined to the world of disaffected novelists, agrarian ideologues, and rural storytellers. For the vast majority of the population, the darker images paled before the bright symbol of the railroad as the engine of civilization and enlightenment.

EARLY REACTIONS TO THE RAILROAD. By the end of Meiji, the positive image as well as the reality of trains had gained widespread acceptance; at the outset, however, many Japanese were less than receptive to the "sound of the whistle." Indeed, railway development initially met with considerable resistance, especially within the government itself. Most vehement in their opposition were military officials and like-minded civilian bureaucrats who demanded that armaments expansion take precedence over "such a nonessential" venture as railroad building.[108] Underlying their arguments was a strong current of xenophobia spilling over from the late Tokugawa period. One War Ministry official made this explicit in June 1870 when he called for immediate suspension of the construction work already under way on the Shinbashi-Yokohama line, charging that to make railroads instead of weapons would serve "only to increase facilities for foreigners at the expense of our national polity."[109] Failing to secure a work stoppage, the War Ministry raised as many obstacles as it could, repeatedly objecting to the use of its land as right of way and forcing the railway authorities to lay one stretch of the line on land reclaimed from the sea.[110] Opposition rooted in antiforeignism came from members of the former ruling class who were outside the new regime as well. In an angry petition to the authorities in May 1870, one of them blasted the government's railway program as "a strategem for rending the imperial land and giving it to foreign barbarians."[111] His voice joined the chorus of samurai outrage at the introduction of "an abominable alien machine" into "the land of the gods."[112] As Councilor Kido Takayoshi confessed in his diary in August 1871, "since last year, public debate on the issue of the steam railroad has been extremely heated, and because of this, on several occasions, I have wanted to give up this undertaking."[113]

Anti-railroad sentiment among the samurai had actually peaked in mid-1870 after the news broke that government leaders were in the process of borrowing the money for railroad construction from England. By the time trial runs began on completed sections of the Shinbashi-Yokohama line in the summer of 1871, much of this hostility appears to have dissipated. For a number of public officials, witnessing the wonders of rail travel firsthand dispelled any lingering doubts. Ōkubo Toshimichi, one of the most powerful men in the regime and originally an opponent of railroad building, rhapsodized after his first train ride in September 1871: "Truly seeing is believing! It was thoroughly enjoyable! Without this convenience, we will never be able to establish the nation."[114] Later that fall, Ōkubo and the forty-eight other members of the Iwakura Mission, who left Japan for two years on a goodwill-cum-observation tour of the United States and Europe, kicked off their journey by taking the train from Shinagawa to the port of Yokohama. This ride on the latest in modern land transport was a fitting symbolic sendoff for a mission that would prove a genuine eye-opener to the West for much of Japan's new leadership.

The railroad evoked open resistance not only within the former ruling class but also among the general public, some of which lasted into the mid-Meiji period. The initial reaction of many a commoner resembled the xenophobic outbursts of the more conservative samurai. Much as in the case of the telegraph, "about which the wildest rumors spread, associating it with the black magic of the Christians and human sacrifice,"[115] the railroad encountered a good measure of animosity stemming from popular ignorance and superstition. One writer captured the mood in *A Dialogue on Civilization* (*Kaika mondō*), published in 1874, which presented an imaginary discussion between Kyūhei ("Old-fashioned"-*hei*) and Kaijirō ("Enlightened"-*jirō*). Rumors are afloat, reports Kyūhei, that, in order to build railroads, "people must be buried alive . . . according to the Christian method"; moreover, Westerners are planning to use the telegraph and the railroad "to break the Japanese spirit and seize Japan." Kaijirō replies by refuting these ideas, assuring Kyūhei "there is nothing Christian or miraculous about railroads" and explaining to him in detail their construction and operation.[116] Hostility born of ignorance was most pronounced in the rural hinterland where people resisted the coming of the railroad for a variety of superstitious reasons. In some places, villagers opposed the railroad for fear that it would cause an influx of strangers or an outflow of wealth; in at least one locality in Nagano prefecture, residents objected to railroad construction in the mid-1880s in the belief that the sound of the train whistle, so enchanting in a far different sense to the Japanese of late Meiji, would shorten people's life expectancy.[117] No doubt for a number of Japanese, the noisy, sooty, smelly locomotive could do nothing but arouse revulsion as a frightful manifestation of dreaded pollution.

The bulk of the popular opposition to railroads, and the most persistent, sprang from more rational considerations, however. Especially as knowledge of the railway spread, people resisted less out of fear of a mysterious and alien "fire-wheeled vehicle" than out of concern over the direct impact of the railroad on their daily lives. This was particularly true of those whose livelihood was threatened by the train. Farmers protested the obstruction of drainage channels from paddy fields and, much more critically, the expropriation of their ancestral lands. Even after receiving compensation for their land, angry farmers at the beginning of the period were known to vent their displeasure by digging up the railway ties at construction sites.[118] Incidents of rural sabotage were still occurring in 1890 when during a period of just three weeks local officials in Nagano prefecture reported twenty-two cases of vandalism along the Shin'etsu line, ranging from the placement of rocks and gravestones on the tracks to the destruction of train signals and storage sheds. The prefectural authorities issued a stern warning to the public not to commit such "wicked" acts; the governor had to repeat the admonition in 1891–1892 when the incidents continued.[119]

In the more urban areas, the threat of railroad "pollution" assumed concrete form in the very real danger of fire posed by the train. As early as January 1873, sparks from a locomotive set fire to several houses along the Shinbashi-Yokohama line. As one irate victim fumed in a petition to the governor of Tokyo: "Western machines are devils!" Government leaders, anxious to avoid negative publicity so soon after the opening of the first railroad, tried to hush up the incident by handsomely compensating the victimized households.[120] Yet news of the fire spread anyway, prompting residents of Osaka to oppose construction of the line from Kobe through their city. Bowing to this resistance, the authorities decided in 1874 to build the initial terminus of the railroad on the outskirts of Osaka rather than at a more central location.[121]

Other urban dwellers objected to railroad development because it endangered their occupations. Residents of the old post-station towns who had traditionally provided services to travelers along the major roadways were among the most vocal opponents of railroads. Such towns lived in mortal dread that they would simply fall by the wayside as the train carried its passengers right on through. In many cases, the response of the townspeople, far from jumping on the band wagon, was to fight bitterly the routing of rail lines through their towns, which ironically served only to assure their long-term decline. Along the Tokaido, for example, several post-station towns successfully resisted the railroad in the late 1880s, forcing the authorities to build the line around those towns. In one of the localities, inn keepers and transport workers fearful of losing business to the railroad were joined by a brothel owner who reasoned that, "if such a convenient means of transportation as the train comes into being, the prostitutes will run away."[122] Around the same time, the private Kōbu Railway also ran into opposition from former post-station towns on the outskirts of Tokyo. Thanks to the resistance of Chōfu and Fuchū residents—much to their regret later on—the company ended up laying its railroad in a straight line from Nakano to Tachikawa rather than along the circuitous but more developed Kōshū highway.[123] Among the inhabitants of such towns, trains presented the most immediate challenge to pack-horse drivers, rickshawmen, and others engaged in competing forms of transport. The Sanuki Railway Company, which built a line from the port of Marugame to the shrine of Konpira on Shikoku in 1888–1889, met with fierce opposition from such workers. Once construction began on the railroad, local horse drivers and rickshaw pullers mobbed the company president's house and threatened to burn it down. The president took no chances while at the construction site, constantly keeping a bodyguard at his side and a dagger in his belt. In this case, the conflict had a happy resolution, for no sooner was the railroad completed than the company hired all the protesting transport workers as station employees.[124]

The degree of opposition to railroad building in Meiji Japan should not be exaggerated, however.[125] True, the fear that the steam locomotive at first inspired in almost everyone turned to outright resistance for a number of Japanese, but for the majority, the initial response soon gave way to acceptance and then to active solicitation of the railroad, as suggested by how quickly the positive image of railways gained ascendance. Those who witnessed the official opening of the Shinbashi-Yokohama line in October 1872 typified the reactions of awe and amazement with which most Japanese first greeted the railroad. On the morning of the opening ceremony, people crowded along the railway line, some of them having camped out the night before with box lunches in hand, and awaited the passage of the inaugural train bearing the emperor and other dignitaries. Among the spectators was eleven-year-old Kiyohara Tama, the future wife of the Italian sculptor Vincenzo Ragusa, who came to Japan in 1876 to teach in the government's technical fine arts school. Tama recalled that, when the locomotive finally came by, thundering and billowing smoke, she felt as though it were "a monster . . . leaping at me." Most of those around her "covered their ears with both hands, shut their eyes, and faced downward as if waiting for a frightful thing to pass."[126]

The mood at the terminals, where the actual ceremonies took place, was far more festive, even boisterously jubilant. As a Western correspondent observed of the proceedings at Yokohama, "the day was so bright, the scene so wondrously gay, and the great mass of people in the seats and on the ground, looked so joyous and happy."[127] Once the ceremony was over and the emperor had withdrawn from the special pavilion set up for the occasion, continued the reporter, "the people made a rush upon it, and in a few minutes, the chair on which his Majesty had sat was broken up into little bits, and the carpet on which he had trodden was torn into shreds—all who were able to secure a scrap of either the one or the other deeming themselves extremely fortunate."[128] At the Shimbashi end, the lined-up spectators welcomed the returning train with shouts of *banzai*. Among the assembled, those who were witnessing a train for the first time were "loud in their exclamations of surprise."[129] One man reported that he had come expecting "to see some ordinary carriage such as foreigners had introduced, drawn along at a great speed on a smooth iron road. But when he saw the real thing, it appeared to him like the moving of a small town, for the carriages were as big as many a Japanese house."[130] Instead of being intimidated by the locomotive, many of the spectators appeared rather solicitous for its welfare. One of them expressed concern that, having to pull such a load, the engine would "surely break a bone," while another, thinking that the "perspiring" locomotive "must be very hot indeed," scrambled up the embankment and began throwing water on it, much to the disapproval of a nearby official.[131]

DAWNING OF THE "RAILWAY AGE." These varied responses to the first railway line are indicative of just how rapidly the train switched in the popular perception from an alien "fire dragon" to a familiar and increasingly valued "convenience of civilization" (*bunmei no riki*). As the state and the initial private rail company, the Nippon, proceeded with planning and construction of the first trunk lines in the early 1880s, the railroad started to impinge on the lives of ever larger numbers of communities. In the process, a majority of the local elites affected, if not the populace at large, came to realize that the railroad was not just an exciting and useful innovation but a powerful catalyst of local and regional economic development. The upshot was that, by the mid-1880s, most localities, far from resisting or even passively accepting the new mode of transport, had begun to solicit and to embrace it with fervor.

An early indication of this heightened local consciousness appeared in October 1882 when two residents of Saitama prefecture offered to donate their own land as right of way for the Nippon Railway's projected line from Ueno to Maebashi. As prefectural officials noted in reporting this offer to the state railroad authorities, who were building the line on behalf of the Nippon, the prospective donors "cannot help being deeply impressed that you are carrying out such a great enterprise as railroad construction, which not only benefits the general public but serves as a basis for increasing production and enriching the nation." The officials went on to assure the central authorities of their determination that the offer "stems entirely from true feelings of patriotism."[132] For landlords and other provincial notables like these two public-spirited men, such "patriotism" had a decidedly local thrust to it, not to mention a good measure of self-interest, with a view to the "external economies" that the railroad was sure to bring their localities and businesses.

There was also a growing element of competition, as local communities and whole prefectures began vying to have railway lines pass through their lands. When the government initially chose an interior route for the Tokyo-Kyoto artery in 1883, residents of the Ina basin in Nagano prefecture, nearly a decade before their ill-fated movement to influence the course of the Chūō line, mounted a campaign to persuade the authorities to build the railroad through their valley. In May 1884, area representatives promised to contribute 50,000 laborers if the line were so built. Officials of Matsumoto city, however, topped their offer by pledging 50,000 laborers *and* ¥30,000 should the railroad take a more northerly course via their town. In the event, both offers proved in vain, as the government switched to the coastal Tokaido route in 1886.[133]

This change coincided with the outbreak of Japan's first private railway boom, which lasted until 1889. Stimulated by the economic upturn following the Matsukata deflation of the first half of the decade as well as by the high dividends and indirect benefits that the Nippon Railway had been affording since 1884, wealthy individuals all over Japan started inundating the authorities with proposals for private railroads. If the call for a national constitution and parliament had dominated the local agenda in the late 1870s and early 1880s, the demand for railroad development took its place after 1886. A newspaper reported, just over a week before the government's decision to opt for the Tokaido route, that the people of several localities without railroad connections had become alarmed over the loss of commerical business to areas linked by rail and had begun plans to establish such connections themselves; the paper concluded, "Thus, throughout the country, the people have been aroused to the practical importance of railways by considerations directly affecting their own welfare and prosperity, and we believe that before long the public zeal for the construction of railways will become even more intense than was the eagerness in 1883 for the opening of a National Assembly, when petition after petition was submitted to the Government."[134] Later that year, another journal commented on the frenzy caused by the initial stock offer of the Ryōmō Railway Company, proclaiming that the era was "turning, as it were, into a railway age."[135] Local men of means were ready and eager to invest in private railroads that would serve their localities, but better yet if the state was prepared to build them. Indeed, once the regime announced the switch to the Tokaido route, although some towns along the projected line resisted it, many more campaigned aggressively to have the railroad traverse their communities. In August 1886, for instance, several people in Shizuoka prefecture petitioned the authorities to build the line through their locality, sweetening their request with an offer to donate the necessary land from their own holdings,[136] and residents of numerous other communities along the way followed suit.

By the late 1880s the nationwide enthusiasm for railroad development had reached a feverish pitch. As a Tokyo newspaper observed of the situation in mid-1888, "Since people [have become] persuaded . . . that the country's material progress depends, in a great measure, on the extension of railways, there has . . . developed something very like a mania for this species of enterprise, and the appetite having been whetted by issues of public securities, few localities could now be named where projects of railway construction have not been formed. It may be said, in short, that Japan has entered her railway age."[137] By then, local elites had come to view the railroad not only as a means of local economic betterment but also as a kind of status symbol.[138] The Railway Bureau, in offering a typology of "railway promoters of the present day" in its annual report for 1888, listed such elites as forming one of three classes of promoters, the other two consisting of speculative investors and those intending to make railroads their career. The bureau described these provincial notables as "wealthy local people who are popularly called 'enthusiasts for railways' (*tetsudō nesshinka*)." These individuals, it explained, "are wont to say: 'In our locality there is not yet a line of railway; this makes us ashamed before the people of other districts.'" Such being the rationale behind their railway projects, "their imagination is engrossed with the hopes of the vast indirect benefits that may be conferred on their districts by railway construction."[139] The train would deliver concrete returns in the form of wider markets and easier travel, but equally important were the intangible dividends that localities would reap by being put on the railroad map.

The popular zeal for railroad building, already marked in the late 1880s, intensified dramatically during the second private railway boom following the Sino-Japanese War of 1894–1895. Whereas the authorities had gotten almost forty formal applications for railway charters over the entire course of the first railway boom, in 1896 alone they received a staggering total of over four hundred fifty applications.[140] With the extension of government lines picking up steam under the Construction Law of 1892, petitions for state rail connections also kept pouring in from the provinces. By the mid-1890s, even the opposition to railroads of former post-station towns was a thing of the past. A newspaper reported in late 1895, as the second railroad boom was getting under way, that a movement was being organized among the inhabitants of post stations bypassed by the Tokaido line "to have the course of the railway altered so that it shall touch at these villages, and that there shall be a depôt at each of them." The leaders of the campaign were threatening that, if the railway bureaucrats rejected their demands, they would lobby members of the Diet to vote down the construction bills about to be submitted by the cabinet. "Men are going from one village to another along the Tokaido haranguing in this fashion," the paper noted, "and of course their speeches meet with the approval of the villagers."[141] Nothing came of this movement, but a different outcome awaited petitioners along the route ultimately chosen for the Chūō line, the main focus of local agitation for state railway building in the 1890s. When that line finally reached Kōfu in 1903, the opening ceremony was met with a burst of excitement and jubilation matching, if not surpassing, that which had greeted the inauguration of the Shinbashi-Yokohama line in 1872. According to a contemporary account, news of the opening "reverberated throughout the prefecture like a thunderbolt, and twenty thousand people stormed [Kōfu station] to see the steam locomotive."[142] By that time, there could be no doubt that the "railway age" had arrived in Japan and that the train had become an almost universally welcomed and sought-after convenience.

RIDING THE RAILS. As the railway grew and gained acceptance during the Meiji period, more and more people traveled by rail, and as they did, the railroad came to exert a variety of influences on the life and outlook of the Japanese. Among other things, it altered people's consciousness of time and distance, changed their attitude towards travel and recreation, and affected their patterns of work and residence. Such changes did not, however, begin to reach the populace at large immediately, since fares were initially set at high levels, in line with prevailing rates for competing modes of transport, with the effect of discouraging all but the well-to-do from riding trains regularly. When the Shinbashi-Yokohama line opened, the charge for a third-class ticket was 37.5 sen (100 sen equaled ¥1), slightly more than the steamship fare between Tokyo and Yokohama, while a second-class ticket cost 75 sen, about 13 sen over the comparable rickshaw fare; first-class passengers paid ¥1 and 12.5 sen. This was at a time when one shō (1.8 liters) of rice, enough to feed a man for roughly half a week, fetched around 4 sen. Small wonder the general public in early Meiji should have seen rail travel as an exorbitant luxury and have thought, in the words of a popular ditty, "I'd like to leave my dresser at the pawnshop and ride the steam locomotive!"[143]

Yet, for those with means, there was no question the train was the way to go. The railroad simply outclassed its competitors in speed, frequency, and comfort. Whereas walking from Tokyo to Yokohama took eight to ten hours on average and the steamship barely allowed for a round trip in a day, the first trains covered the distance each way in less than an hour. Moreover, they did so nine times a day, leaving both terminals on the hour from eight to eleven a.m. and from two to six p.m. (see Figure 7). With the railway, a day trip presented no problem whatsoever; indeed, it was possible, if one were so inclined, to make several round trips in a day. This point was brought home to the newspaper-reading public in mid-1873 when a jour-

Figure 7 "Tetsudō hitori annai" (Do-It-Yourself Railway Guide), with a timetable and fares for Yokohama station, from a series on the Shinbashi-Yokohama line. Woodcut by Yoshitora, 1872. Photograph: courtesy of the Transportation Museum, Tokyo.

nalist broke the incredible story of a woman whose baby napped the whole time she made the thirty-mile round trip from Yokohama to Shinagawa on an errand; the journey "barely took two hours, and the infant had yet to wake up!"[144] The rickshaw came the closest to the train in overall convenience, but as late as 1886 the *Japan Weekly Mail* ridiculed a proposal by rickshaw pullers to compete against the Shinbashi-Yokohama railroad by lowering their fees and running faster so as to negotiate the nineteen-mile trip in one hour and forty minutes; how could the rickshawmen imagine, the paper wondered, "that a number of their country-men and country-women will sacrifice forty-five minutes and endure a deal of jolting and discomfort for the sake of saving six *sen*."[145] The upshot was that, in spite of the relatively high fares, many people took the train right from the start, with the occupancy of passenger cars even then averaging about 80 percent.[146]

The number of railway passengers grew steadily during the Meiji period. In the first year alone, nearly half a million passengers—mostly bureaucrats, businessmen, and foreigners—rode the Shinbashi line. As more lines were added and fares were reduced, more people, especially ordinary people, took the train. The most dramatic increase occurred between 1890 and 1900 when Japan's total population rose from about forty million to forty-five million, but the number of rail passengers leaped from twenty-three million to one hundred fourteen million.[147] Indicative of the growing popularity and sophistication of railway travel around this time was the appearance in 1889 of the first train schedule in book form and in 1894 of the first guidebook for railway travel.[148]

The government's Tokaido line, opened in 1889, accounted for well over a third of all the train riders in its first year of operation. For such long distances—the Tokaido extended 376 miles from Shinbashi to Kobe—the impact of the railroad on travel was revolutionary. In the Tokugawa period, going the length of the Tokaido by foot or palanquin had taken twelve to fourteen days. Beginning in 1881, the horse-drawn omnibus cut this time in half, while the steamship could make the trip in only a few days. But the train outdid them all, covering the distance in just twenty hours. Traveling from the Tokyo area to the Kansai by rickshaw or other means of overland transport cost anywhere from ¥9 to ¥11. By contrast, third-class passengers on the Tokaido line paid less than ¥4, besides saving on hotel fees along the way.[149] In March 1889, a newspaper had heralded the impending completion of the Tokaido railway by trumpeting, "How convenient! From Shinbashi to Kobe within a day!"—and for only a few yen, no less—adding hyperbolically that a "person of taste" would soon be able to "view the cherry blossoms along the Sumida River [in Tokyo] in the morning and take a walk in Arashiyama [on the outskirts of Kyoto] in the evening."[150] With trains offering such possibilities, "it was inevitable," declares one scholar, "that the railroad would alter the popular attitude toward travel."[151]

Part of this alteration involved a drastic change in people's conception of time and distance. Riding the train, with its unprecedented speed, led to a compression of space for the early passengers that left them incredulous and disoriented. In the West, the phrase most commonly used to describe this dizzying effect of railway travel was "the annihilation of space and time," taken from one of Pope's more obscure poems.[152] As a rider on one of the first American railroads put it in 1830, "we flew in the wings of the wind at the varied speed of fifteen to twenty-five miles an hour, annihilating 'time and space.'"[153] At the outset, many Westerners believed that, if a person traveled much faster than that, he "might actually burst and be scattered across the railway lines."[154] Moving at the breath-taking rate of about twenty miles an hour, the average speed of Japanese trains throughout the Meiji period, was more than enough to instill in the first rail passengers in Europe both "the notion of instant death to all upon the least accident happening" (1829) and the perception that "space is killed by the railways" (1843).[155] The favorite contemporary metaphor for this early Western experience of railroad travel was the train "as a projectile . . . being shot through the landscape"[156]—a fitting characterization of the sudden loss of continuity suffered by the initial railway travelers, deprived as they were of the natural rhythms and perspectives of the horse-drawn carriage.

All these perceptions had their counterparts in Meiji Japan. For Japan's first railway passengers, whose only means of overland travel had been by foot or, in the case of the elite, by palanquin or horse, the sense of discontinuity was even greater than in the West. Reportedly, when one of the first trains to leave Shinbashi arrived at Yokohama station, the passengers initially refused to get off, even after a station employee announced that this was the last stop and asked that they kindly disembark. Apparently, the travelers, knowing full well that it took an entire day to walk from Tokyo to

Yokohama, could not believe they had already reached their destination; to their mind, no matter how fast the train went, there was no way that it could cover the distance in less than an hour.[157] That the speed of the new means of transport was disorienting even to the point of nausea is suggested by the fact that, within a year of the Shinbashi line's opening, the manufacturer of a seasickness pill had begun advertising his product as an antidote to trainsickness and was enjoying brisk sales of the remedy at Shinbashi and Yokohama stations.[158] From the beginning, the Japanese used familiar metaphors to express the giddying impact of the railroad on their traditional space-time consciousness. Besides the ubiquitous avian comparisons, the train was likened to a projectile in Meiji Japan as well, specifically to an arrow in flight: as the lyrics of early Meiji songs had it, the steam locomotive was "as fast as a shooting arrow" or, better yet, "*faster* than an arrow."[159] And in 1898, a Japanese writer echoed the imagery employed by Western commentators since the advent of the railroad when he observed that "the train has shrunk the world."[160]

The railroad altered popular conceptions of time in still other ways. In particular, trains, "with their emphasis on timetables and precision,"[161] strengthened their riders' appreciation of the economic value of time while also promoting the habit of punctuality among them. In 1886, on the eve of the explosion in popular railway travel, the *Japan Weekly Mail* criticized the reluctance of producers to avail themselves of rail transport, attributing it to "the conservatism of the Japanese farmer, who has not learned to set a pecuniary value on his time . . ."[162] Thomas Smith, however, has shown to the contrary that even "late Tokugawa peasants had a lively, morally rooted sense of the preciousness of time,"[163] that their awareness of time was by no means so casual that they had to be taught its value. Whatever the pre-Meiji appreciation of time, there is no question that the railroad, by offering unheard-of opportunities for saving and managing time, deepened that appreciation substantially, for the train not only went fast, it also ran—or at least tried to run—"on time." Emblematic of this heightened sense of the value of time was a story recounted by the poet Handa Ryōhei. When the Sasago tunnel was completed on the Chūō line in 1903, wrote Handa, "the travel time of three hours by foot over the pass shrank to ten minutes by train"; after the opening of the line, then, some enterprising beggars in the area paid six *sen* to ride between the stations at either end of the tunnel, figuring that, with the time and energy they saved, they would be able to make the rounds of that many more houses on the other side of the pass and thereby more than make up the train fare.[164]

Another aspect of the change in time sense furthered by the spread of railroads was a growing emphasis on punctuality and attendant awareness of clock time. As the authors of a recent history of the railway station have noted, "the common characteristic of the trains was that they did not wait and this single fact bred the habit of punctuality in their users."[165] Railroads, with their inflexible schedules, demanded that customers arrive at the station on time lest they miss their train. This was one facet of time consciousness that did have to be learned, and along with the school, factory, and public office, the railroad was a leading teacher of time discipline during the Meiji period.

As far as travel time was concerned, precision had not really been an issue in the Tokugawa era. River ferries, for instance, had had no fixed timetables: when enough customers arrived, the ferry would take them across the river; until then, everyone simply waited. As a result, travelers in the pre-railway age had had to allow plenty of time for delays.[166] This relaxed attitude toward travel time carried over into the Meiji era. Would-be passengers on the early railroads were often nonchalant about catching their trains. Some would leisurely spend an entire day just getting to the station while others who missed their train would return the next day with box lunch in hand to wait for its departure.[167]

The railway authorities realized the need to impress on their clientele the importance of punctuality as well as to inform it accurately of the time, and their efforts in this direction did much to promote an appreciation of clock time among the public. When the Shinbashi-Yokohama line opened in October 1872, the Railway Bureau posted a notice that prospective passengers should arrive at the station no later than ten minutes before the departure time of their train and that the gates to the platform would be closed three minutes before departure.[168] Trains may have conveniently left on the hour at the terminals, but at the intermediate stations they came and went at various fractions of the hour. All of this introduced a radically new conception of time, one much more finely calibrated and "minute" than anything the Japanese had previously held. Before the advent of the railroad, the smallest unit of time by which people had ordered their lives had generally been half an hour (*kohandoki*). All of a sudden, then, the requirements of the train world reduced this minimum unit to a minute, a dramatic change indeed for the users of the railroad.[169]

By demanding precision, railroads also furthered the use of clocks and watches among the general public to the point where, in 1898, a writer could report the following complaint by the elderly owner of a station-front restaurant: "If it weren't for that damn train, I wouldn't need this clock!"[170] At the outset of the Meiji period, however, hardly any Japanese possessed timepieces, nor was there anything comparable to the town clock of the West. About the only indication people got of the exact time was the ringing of temple bells at six in the morning and six in the evening, while those within earshot of the inner citadel of the old Edo castle also had the benefit of the noon gun report after October 1871.[171] For the train-riding public, to be notified of the time every six hours at an optimum was hopelessly inadequate. The railway authorities thought they had come up with a practical solution to this problem. In a petition to the Council of State in early 1872, they proposed that the large temple bell at Zōjō-ji, which housed the mausoleum of successive Tokugawa shogun, be moved to a hilltop near Shinbashi station where the bell would be rung on the hour twenty-four hours a day.[172] The State Council, perhaps wishing to underscore its ascendancy over the defeated Tokugawa, accepted this proposal and, through the prefectural authorities, instructed the temple to comply. Startled by this order, temple officials immediately raised a protest. The bell was a gift from the shogunate, they exclaimed, and it weighed over fifteen tons: to transport such a massive object would require the demolition of temple buildings that stood in the way. The latter objection apparently carried the day, as the government rescinded its order to the temple.[173] Thus, the Railway Bureau's early plan to inform the populace of the passage of the hours failed to materialize, and the railroads ended up having to count mainly on the dissemination of clocks and watches, which they themselves encouraged, for a sense of time discipline to become ingrained in their customers.

As Smith notes, however, "it was a slow process."[174] Ironically, even as the railroads tried to inculcate punctuality among their users, they tended to be less than models of precision themselves through most of the Meiji period. An employee of the Nippon Railway Company recalled, for example, that, when he was an assistant at one of the railroad's local stops in the mid-1890s,

> ... things were easy-going, and occasionally on fair-weather days in early spring, while waiting for the next train ... , the staff would leave one member at the station as a caretaker (*rusuban*), and the stationmaster and everyone else would head for the nearby hills to view the cherry blossoms. No one at that time had anything like a pocket watch. So when it came time for the train to arrive, the caretaker would hoist a signal flag attached to a long pole, which was clearly visible from the hills. Seeing the flag, the staff would break off their flower-viewing and return to the station, each member taking up his post.[175]

As late as 1903, newspapers were still grumbling about "the lax and perfunctory methods" of the Nippon Railway.[176] When the *Japan Weekly Mail* complained in 1901 of "the long delays and the unpunctuality"[177] of Japanese railroads, it was referring not only to private firms like the Nippon but also to the state railways. In 1898, a British visitor remarked on the basis of his experience with the government's Tokaido line that "all notion of speed, haste, or flurry are [sic] utterly foreign to [the Japanese] nature" and that the Japanese railway terminal presents "an air of rest and quiet, which is in singular contrast to the bustle and noise of an European railway station."[178] This leisurely air was even more pronounced on state lines that were off the beaten track; in Shimazaki Tōson's 1906 novel *The Broken Commandment*, the Tokyo-bound train for which the protagonist waits at a provincial stop on the government's Shin'etsu line is "twenty minutes late."[179] Much as in the case of Japanese factory workers in the early twentieth century, then, time discipline among railwaymen in late Meiji "was unquestionably lax by present standards ... ."[180] The railroads had to make their employees, no less than their passengers, acutely aware of clock time before such laxness could be overcome. In the event, the precision for which Japanese trains have become world-famous was not to be attained until after the nationalization when the newly unified railway regime could begin to raise levels of efficiency and punctuality across the board.

During the Meiji era, railroads altered popular conceptions not only of time and distance but also of travel and recreation. This, too, was a gradual process, which depended largely on changes in the attitudes and practices of the railroads themselves as they started to introduce travel discounts and, in general, to emphasize customer service in the latter half of the period. Still, even in the early years of train operation in Japan, hundreds of thousands of people traveled by rail, and a good part of this traffic may well have represented not so much a newfound wanderlust as a continuation of Tokugawa patterns of recreational travel. During the latter half of the Tokugawa period, pedestrians had crowded the system of major roadways administered by the shogunate. In spite of the public checkpoints and other controls designed to restrict the movement of people, many had found it relatively easy to circumvent these barriers, and in any case, officials at the checkpoints had become "increasingly reluctant from the eighteenth century to enforce the letter of the law in regulating the passage of travelers,"[181] especially those who had left their domains for the purpose of visiting shrines or temples. The Japanese of the Tokugawa era were undoubtedly more religious than their modern counterparts, but for many of them, the sacred pilgrimage had merely served as a pretext for travel and in fact had amounted to a form of recreation. This habit of tourism-by-pilgrimage unmistakably carried over into the railway age. Several private rail companies such as the Sanuki and Narita were founded in mid-Meiji with the express goal of transporting worshipers to famous religious sites, and it is not difficult to imagine that a sizable proportion of the passengers on earlier state and private lines had had similar objectives in taking the train.

The popularization of more explicitly secular forms of recreational travel by rail, however, did not occur until late in the Meiji period. Indeed, through much of the era, it almost seemed as though the railroads, with their generally shoddy facilities and imperious attitudes, were doing their level best to discourage passengers. Most of the Meiji railroads were notoriously laggard in providing amenities for travelers, even though passenger income accounted for over two thirds of their total revenue as late as the mid-1890s. The early trains were a far cry from the well-appointed Shinkansen of today. Well into the Meiji era, the railroads mainly employed British-style "matchbox" carriages divided into compartments furnished with wooden benches (see Figure 8).[182] Once inside, passengers were literally confined to their compartments, for there was no way to pass through the car, and shortly before departure, a railroad employee would lock all

Figure 8 Third-class passenger carriage divided into five compartments. Manufactured by the state railways' Kobe workshop beginning in 1876, this type of car was a standard model through mid-Meiji. Photograph: courtesy of the Transportation Museum, Tokyo.

the doors from the outside "in the approved paternal government style," as an American tourist put it in 1891.[183] To top it off, the third-class carriages were "absolutely destitute of upholstery"[184] as well as heat. And none of the early cars had lavatories, which made for a mad scramble for platform facilities at train stops and forced the government, ever eager to present a civilized front to the West, to impose stiff fines of up to ¥10 for passengers caught urinating from the windows en route and a prorated ¥5 for those caught breaking wind therefrom.[185]

Riders began to find on-board relief only in 1889 when the state lines, which thereafter would follow the lead of the more progressive private railroads in service improvements, had the distinction of introducing the first passenger cars equipped with toilets. What prompted this innovation was a tragic accident that occurred on the Tokaido line that year. On April 27th, a prominent official in the Imperial Household Ministry by the name of Hida Hamagorō got off his train during a brief stop at Fujieda station to use the facilities there. When Hida emerged from the station restroom, his train was already pulling away from the platform. Hida frantically tried to reboard the moving train, but slipped and fell to his death "between the first- and second-class cars."[186] To a people increasingly familiar with the inconveniences of rail travel, this accident was perhaps less shocking than the "notable death" with which railroads had begun in England when the president of the Board of Trade had been run down and killed on the inaugural run of the Liverpool and Manchester Railway in 1830, an incident that had "rocked [British] society at a moment of supreme self-congratulation."[187] But Hida's demise was certainly treated as a major scandal by the contemporary Japanese press, which described him as "the victim of the lack of toilets on trains"[188] and pressed the authorities to remedy the situation. The state railways took heed; within a month of the accident, newspapers were already reporting the unveiling of third-class carriages installed with central toilets accessible to the compartments on either side. The *Jiji shinpō* explained that these cars would ease restroom traffic at station stops for first- and second-class passengers but cautioned third-class riders "to refrain from using [the on-board lavatories] while at stations and to do their business when farthest away from human habitation."[189]

Still, it was some time before such facilities became widespread. In 1903, for example, a writer in a leading economic journal complained about the lack of on-board toilets on the Chūō line, adding that station restrooms were always "one or two blocks away from the stopping point of the train so that, even with a five-minute stop, women and children cannot help but experience great difficulty in going to the bathroom."[190] The problem persisted even after the nationalization, as the novelist Shiga Naoya suggested in a short story published in 1908: while riding in a toiletless carriage on the main line of the former Nippon Railway, the narrator endures the worried pleas of a mother to her distressed boy—"Can't you hold it just a little longer?"—only to overhear the conductor inform them that the next stop will be too brief for them to use the station restroom.[191]

Meiji trains also had poor interior lighting at night. As evening approached, railroad employees would clamber on to the tops of the carriages at a station stop and suspend oil lamps through holes in the roof. The feeble light thus generated was barely enough for one to make out the figures of fellow passengers. The resulting ambiance, as a mystery writer put it in 1901, was like "the inside of the catacombs in the ancient city of Rome."[192] The railroads began to install electric lighting in the late 1890s, but this innovation, too, was slow to disseminate; for instance, while traveling on the Tokaido line after the Russo-Japanese War, the title character of Natsume Sōseki's 1908 novel *Sanshirō* observes at one train stop: "The sun was down.... Station workers were tramping along the roof of the train, inserting lighted oil lamps into holders from above."[193] In short, the following complaint by a Westerner in 1898 was not entirely off the mark a decade later: "The miserable oil lamps of ancient days still defy the traveler to read by their light, and the carriages present an unaltered aspect of conservative comfortlessness."[194]

Not surprisingly, the railroads were late in developing a sense of service toward the traveling public. On the national railways, it was only after the San'yō Railway Company had begun pioneering consumer services in the late 1890s and the Kansai Railway had engaged the parallel state line in a fierce rate war in 1902 that the authorities "descended from their eminence of official magnificence and consented to address their customers in polite phraseology."[195] In the early days, by contrast, state railroad employees had sold tickets "as though they were doing the passenger a great favor," but for their part, passengers had "often stood up for their rights, some even going so far as to haggle over the fare."[196] Upon actually boarding the train, however, customers had tended to bow submissively to the overbearing station workers, and, should they encounter the prestigious stationmaster with his glittering uniform and lofty social status—one of the true "role models" of the Meiji era, they had bent over almost to the point of prostration.[197]

In the latter half of Meiji, the press began to voice the growing discontent of passengers over their shabby treatment on the state railways. In the aftermath of Hida's death, several journals called on the railway authorities to "treat passengers as customers" by taking such measures as instructing employees to be considerate of riders and having passenger trains stop at the larger stations for fifteen minutes to facilitate visits to the foodstand and restroom.[198] Such importunities seem to have had little effect: almost a decade later, for instance, the Nagano prefectural assembly was still accusing station workers on the government's Shin'etsu line of being "arrogant towards passengers."[199] The same haughty ethos pervaded the Nippon Railway, whose staff "smelled like bureaucrats."[200] As late as 1903, a newspaper assailed "the *de-haut-en-bas* temper in which the Company's business is conducted. . . . In the parlance of the railway officials, its clients in the northern regions are known generically as *dobiyakusho* (rustics) [sic], the petty officials of the Company regarding themselves as people quite above such an agricultural herd."[201]

In fairness to Meiji railroads, it should be noted that they lagged just slightly behind their Western counterparts in introducing passenger amenities. In the United States, "sleeping cars did not come into general use until after the Civil War,"[202] and trains on one of the industry leaders, the Pennsylvania Railroad, began to feature sanitary facilities only in 1878, diners in 1882, steam heating in 1885, and electric lighting in 1902.[203] On the British railroads, these amenities had all made their appearance by the early 1890s, but they did not become widespread until a decade later. And in class-conscious Great Britain, where cheaper fares had originally ridden in open freight cars, railway company attitudes towards customer service resembled those on the more conservative of the Japanese railroads. In 1892, the Great Western put into service the first British train with a corridor running its entire length; this gave third-class passengers access to lavatories, "a startling innovation on the Great Western, which never forgot that they were the 'lower orders.'" When this firm added dining cars in 1896, it restricted their use to first-class passengers, "a rule that was only gradually relaxed from 1900 onwards."[204]

Thus, even in late Meiji, Japanese railroads may not actually have been far behind those in the West in terms of customer service, but from the middle of the period on, the perception that they *were* behind became more and more prevalent. As early as 1889, for example, an article in the *Tōkyō keizai zasshi* contrasted the "inconvenience and discomfort" of Japanese railroads with "the joys of travel" on American trains, whose special advantages could be summed up by "'the three W's:' warm, water, and water-closet."[205] And in two areas related to service—speed and the condition of lines and rolling stock—late Meiji railroads, as Japanese plainly recognized at the time, were decisively laggard by contemporary Western standards.

In early Meiji, the speeds attained by Japanese trains had been roughly comparable to those in the West. Around 1860, for example, American railroads had averaged ten to fifteen miles an hour, and speeds of more than thirty miles an hour had been "virtually unknown."[206] By the middle of the Meiji era, though, Japanese trains had clearly fallen behind their Western counterparts in this regard. Traveling at speeds of up to twenty miles an hour may have seemed revolutionary at the start of the period; by the late 1880s, however, the novelty of such speeds had begun to wear off. The article in the above-mentioned economic journal, for instance, pointed out that, whereas trains in Japan occasionally surpassed twenty miles per hour, those in the West could go almost three times as fast, so "the difference in quality is obvious."[207] The gap had hardly narrowed by the turn of the century. As another journal complained in December 1898, the railroads "have never advanced one step since the time of their construction, with the exception of the San'yō road. . . . The trains creep along at the same slow pace as of old."[208] A 1903 study of the three principal trunk lines on the main island showed the average speed of trains on the Tokaido to be twenty-five miles an hour compared to only twenty for those on the Nippon Railway and nearly thirty for those on the San'yō.[209] In fact, beginning in 1898, trains on the level portion between Shinbashi and Yokohama did achieve a maximum speed of forty miles an hour, and with the introduction of express service late in the Meiji period, the travel time on the Tokaido line was gradually whittled down. Yet, as late as 1904, a British railroad executive reported that "trains are scheduled to run at about eighteen miles an hour, and seldom exceed twenty-five . . ."[210] Moreover, when limited express service was finally inaugurated on the Tokaido with the importation of the latest superheating engines in 1912, the new trains still averaged only thirty miles an hour compared to fifty-five for the fastest trains in Germany.[211]

Granted, financial and technical factors, specifically, the relative shortage of investment capital in Meiji Japan and the choice of the narrow gauge, placed constraints on the speed of Japanese trains, but the fact that the San'yō Railway was at least partly able to overcome these limitations suggests that, on other Japanese railroads, managerial shortcomings were to blame as well.[212] Deficiencies of finance and management also caused Meiji railroads to fall behind their Western contemporaries in another key area, namely, investment in plant and equipment. Most railroads in Meiji Japan sought to minimize capital expenditures by avoiding tunneling and double-tracking as well as by neglecting or delaying needed repairs and improvements. As the aforementioned British executive observed in 1904, "Japan must be congratulated on the cheap construction of her railway system, but it is impossible to have a thoroughly efficient system without paying for it. . . . Nothing strikes one more forcibly in Japan than the impermanence of things."[213] In this regard, Meiji railroads resembled their U.S. counterparts of a generation or two earlier. On antebellum American lines, durability was also "sacrificed for lower capital costs,"[214] with the result that roadbeds and rails "were almost toylike. Most lines were poorly built, sometimes not with rails at all but iron straps that could pop up, pierce the car floor, and impale the passengers."[215] Such conditions were a far cry from the highly capitalized and solidly constructed railroads of both Europe and late-nineteenth-century America.

In Japan, on the other hand, excessive economizing on fixed investments continued throughout the pre-nationalization era, reaching a peak during the recession triggered by the financial panic of 1890. In 1893, for instance, an army officer criticized "the over-economical methods of construction adopted by private companies, whose lines follow winding routes and ascend steep gradients simply because the engineers were required to cut everything as low as possible." The officer cited as examples a branch of the Nippon Railway Company "where gradients as steep as 1 in 40 exist" and a section of the Kyushu Railway "where the sinuosity of the road is quite remarkable. It would have been possible to make the former comparatively level and the latter much less tortuous had not paramount importance been given to the question of outlay."[216]

The Kyushu Railway reversed its "cheap construction" policy once the nascent Mitsubishi zaibatsu gained control of the firm in the late 1890s and pushed for upgrading the railroad so as better to serve Mitsubishi's coal-mining interests in Kyushu, but to the bitter end, the Nippon Railway did little to renovate its shoddy lines and equipment. The Nippon, like most Meiji railroad concerns, was pressured by its stockholders to pay profits out almost entirely as dividends rather than to plow them back into the enterprise. To meet such investor demands, the company simply had to ignore or postpone essential improvements. In 1900, the Nippon's president admitted that private railroads, including his own, were poorly equipped as compared to those of the state, then added lamely that, "since the funding needed to [upgrade facilities] is lacking, circumstances do not permit it."[217]

The failure to carry out necessary renovations meant that the Nippon and most other Meiji railway companies remained well behind Western railroads in the solidity and repair of their plant and equipment. In 1902, the former railway commissioner of India, Sir William Bisset, visited Japan on behalf of British capitalists to investigate the suitability of Japanese railroads as collateral for loans to Japan. Bisset concluded that, although the country's railroads on the whole were "at least equal to the railways of India,"[218] the San'yō and the state's Tokaido line were in fact the only Japanese railroads "worthy of the name."[219] Yet even government lines, particularly the less traveled routes, were not immune to undercapitalization or obsolescence. In 1897, for instance, members of the Nagano prefectural assembly petitioned the central authorities to make badly needed improvements on the Shin'etsu line, punctuating their request with a long list of grievances about "incomplete" facilities, "cramped" stations, and "squalid" passenger cars.[220] The novelist Shimazaki Tōson seconded the complaints about the rolling stock on the Shin'etsu when he wrote in *The Broken Commandment* in the mid-1900s, "Up here in Shinshu even the trains, unlike those of the Tokaido line, were old and crudely built, resembling the mountain cottages among which they ran. The higher they climbed, the more violent the lurching from side to side and rattling of windows, till the passengers could no longer hear one another talk."[221] Evidently, however, even the Tokaido did not offer a much smoother ride, for in 1909, a British resident of Yokohama sued the Railway Department for ¥3,000 in damages, claiming to have suffered a nervous breakdown while traveling to Kobe on account of the "violent shaking" of the train.[222] Also that year, the government apparently had yet to begin in earnest the pressing task of renovating the railroads after the recent nationalization: in May, the *Japan Weekly Mail* was prompted to complain in particular about the lack of progress in upgrading the rolling stock; "it is scarcely too much to say," the paper declaimed, "that more mediaeval cars are not to be found anywhere."[223]

Yet, despite the inconveniences, people rode the trains in ever-increasing numbers during the Meiji era, while songwriters and poets continued to sing the praises of rail travel. The growing use and the continued acclaim both seemed to reflect the fact that, for all its discomforts, the train was still much faster and far more convenient than any alternative.

In addition, however, the surge in ridership from mid-Meiji on coincided with the start of some positive developments in railroad policy that pointed the way to a more service-oriented future. Although the Nippon Railway was among the most conservative of Japanese railroads, it did take the lead in offering special discounts and other attractions to passengers. As early as 1886, the company began selling round-trip first-class tickets valid for one week; as the *Tōkyō nichinichi* newspaper suggested to its local readers on February 20th of that year, these tickets "*will be most handy for mailing to acquaintances and thereby encouraging them to come to Tokyo* [underlined in the original]."[224] The Nippon also appears to have been the first railroad to make available reduced rates both to groups and to commuters. As the National Industrial Exhibition of 1890 was getting under way, the *Tōkyō nichinichi* reported that the railroad "is giving a discount to graduating students who wish to round out their education by visiting the Ueno Exhibition in Tokyo. The offer applies to schools in all districts through which the company's lines pass. For groups of fifty persons or more, including supervisors, the discount is 30 percent of the regular fare. For individuals, it is 20 percent."[225] Such promotions undoubtedly did a great deal to establish among schools the custom of sending students on graduation trips and set a precedent for the extension of fare reductions to non-student groups as well. Furthermore, in 1891, after the Nippon Railway had completed part of what is now the Yamanote line encircling Tokyo, it began offering commuter passes at discounts of 20 to 25 percent for general riders and 40 to 50 percent for students.[226] Finally, in July 1892, the company started running special excursion trains to the sightseeing mecca of Nikkō, a service that "was subsequently continued on weekends every summer."[227] Spreading from the Nippon to other railroads, these marketing practices all contributed to the rapid increase in rail use during the latter half of Meiji.

The Nippon, for all its conservatism, thus led the way in introducing certain forms of customer service, but in terms of amenities and attitudes toward passengers, the most progressive railroad was the San'yō Railway Company, followed by the Kansai. Underlying the forward-looking behavior of these two firms was the fact that they probably faced greater competition for customers than did any other railroad concern during the Meiji period. For the San'yō, the competition came from steamship companies whose vessels plied the Inland Sea routes adjacent to the course of the railroad; for the Kansai, it was initially a multitude of local private railroads, most of which the company eventually bought out, and later the parallel state line between Osaka and Nagoya. Such rivalry put pressure on both firms to cut rates and improve facilities and thereby acted as a powerful stimulus for innovation. The San'yō had the added impetus of having an ownership dominated by Mitsubishi, which supported the ascendance in the railroad of enterprising career managers committed to positive expansion of the enterprise.

Under the direction of such managers, the San'yō Railway achieved high standards of both construction and service. With the exception of a brief period during the recession following the 1890 Panic, the company invested heavily in plant and equipment and, from the mid-1890s on, led the industry in introducing a variety of customer services and amenities. The innovations came in rapid succession. In 1895, the San'yō began operating express trains pulled by the latest American locomotives; the trains all featured American-style bogie cars with corridors running their length. The company installed "red caps" at principal stations in 1896 and porters on through-trains in 1898. In the latter year, the railroad initiated an express package-delivery service, and in 1899, it adopted electric lighting for all classes of passenger carriages. The firm also pioneered the use of dining cars in 1899 and sleeping cars in 1900 and opened Japan's first station hotel, at

Shimonoseki, in 1902. The following year, it inaugurated the country's first limited express train.[228]

The spirit underlying these improvements was epitomized by the company's chief of transportation. Sent overseas in 1899 to observe Western railroads, this official was particularly struck by the politeness of ticket agents on one British line who invariably said "thank you" when handing tickets or change to customers. After returning to Japan, he immediately set about enforcing this practice among San'yō agents in the hopes that their "attitude of doing passengers the favor of selling them tickets will thereby unconsciously change to a sense of receiving the favor of having them buy tickets."[229] These and other innovations made the San'yō far and away the country's most modern and progressive railroad; as a Western observer noted in 1898, "its cars [are] incomparably the best appointed in Japan, as its service is the best organized."[230]

The San'yō managed to keep abreast of the latest advances in Western railroads by taking such measures as despatching middle-level managers on inspection tours of the West and distributing among its staff an in-house translation of a recently published British handbook on railway operation and management.[231] Yet even in the industry-leading San'yō Railway, decisions were not always made on the basis of superior knowledge or information. Around 1900, when the company was deliberating on the design for Japan's first sleeping car, a split occurred between those in favor of four-wheeled bogies and those advocating six-wheeled ones. No one was able to offer an expert opinion one way or the other. The impasse reportedly was broken only when the head of the Transportation Department exclaimed: "I don't know anything from a technical standpoint, but even a palanquin would ride more smoothly if six coolies carried it rather than four! Likewise, a six-wheeled bogie is bound to be better than a four-wheeled one."[232] This argument carried the day, and the San'yō ended up with the vastly superior sleeper with six-wheeled bogies.

The San'yō was actually not the first Japanese railroad to introduce "open" as opposed to strictly compartmentalized carriages. In fact, each of the initial set of cars imported for the government's Shinbashi line had modified compartments with a central aisle and entrances at either end of the carriage.[233] It was probably in such a car that an activist in the Popular Rights Movement found a novel use for the railroads in early 1881. The

Tōkyō nichinichi reported on January 21st of that year that, when a train had recently arrived at a station on the government's Kyoto-Osaka line, a station employee had gone to investigate "uproarious sounds of cheering and applause" coming from one of the passenger cars; what he had discovered was an "imposing" orator, standing in the middle of the carriage, successfully circumventing the repressive public-assembly ordinance by delivering a rousing political speech to his fellow passengers.[234] Although Japan's first passenger cars were of the "open" variety, the state began putting into service compartmentalized carriages in 1874. These quickly supplanted their open counterparts to become the dominant form of passenger car through the middle of the Meiji era. In adopting this type of car, the Japanese were simply following British practice, whose influence, as in the choice of rails and locomotives, also prevailed in the design of carriages until the 1890s. As late as 1901, a writer of a mystery novel entitled *The Notorious Train Robber* (*Kisha no taizoku*) premised his entire story on the commission of crimes in passenger compartments—the perfect setting for avoiding witnesses to foul play—on two separate trains leaving Shinbashi for points west. On one train, the "notorious" title character slips into a first-class compartment occupied by the daughter of an upper-house Diet member and her maid; after drugging them, he rapes the young mistress and steals her diamond engagement ring. On the other train, a woman encounters a Kyushu mine owner and former Dietman in a second-class compartment and, while feigning romantic interest in the man, steals money and valuables from him. This was clearly a transitional period for carriage construction, as the next two train scenes in the novel both take place in open cars. In one scene, the maid of the victimized woman, while making a round trip on the Tokaido in the hopes of spotting the robber, happens to meet the mine owner in an open second-class car, while in the other scene, the two criminals likewise chance to encounter each other in an open second-class carriage and, after matching wits, get off the train together to become lovers and eventually meet a violent death.[235] After the San'yō Railway introduced the latest American-style open cars in the mid-1890s, these gradually became the industry norm, displacing the British-style compartmentalized carriages of old. The new open bogie cars were a far cry, however, from the simple four-wheeled "open" carriages imported at the beginning of the Meiji period.

The Kansai Railway Company was a close second to the San'yō in terms of pioneering customer services. In 1897, the Kansai initiated the practice of color-coding passenger carriages to indicate their class: it did so by painting each of its cars with a stripe whose color matched that of the corresponding grade of ticket—white for first class, blue for second, red for third. Thus, for customers, the proper class of carriage was rendered conveniently, if not painfully, clear. Also in 1897, the Kansai led the way in installing electric lighting in passenger cars before switching to gas lighting the following year.[236]

The Kansai Railway made its greatest contribution to customer services in 1902–1904 when it waged a furious rate war with the parallel state line and, in doing so, forced the government railways to adopt a more "user-friendly" policy toward their clientele.[237] The Kansai had set the stage for this conflict in 1900 by establishing a direct route between Osaka and Nagoya, one that was considerably shorter than the more circuitous route taken by the state railways (see Map 4). The opening salvo came in early August 1902. At that time the Kansai slashed its roundtrip fares, prompting the national railways to retaliate in kind. Then, in an effort to capitalize on the Bon festival that month, the company cut its fares in half and ran extra trains for those desiring to "enjoy the evening cool." It even provided passengers with onboard musical entertainment, presented them with garish fans and other souvenirs, and invited them to a restaurant and beer hall it had set up in Nara Park.

The state railways responded to their competitor's lavish customer service in a somewhat more restrained manner. Their countermeasure was to distribute among the public written invitations with timetables and discount schedules appended. In these notices, the government railways boasted that along their route, "there are many places rich in scenery. In particular, since it is said that the sweeping view of Lake Biwa is enough to dispel the sweltering heat, travelers taking this route do not in the least feel tired, and it is therefore a most convenient way to travel between these two great cities that are the center of our nation's commerce and industry."[238]

In September, the two sides tentatively put an end to the rate war by agreeing to adopt the same fare schedules, to secure the other's consent before offering discounts, and to avoid "unusual methods" of attracting business. Either party could, however, dissolve the agreement by giving thirty days' notice to that effect. In accordance with these terms, the Kansai Rail-

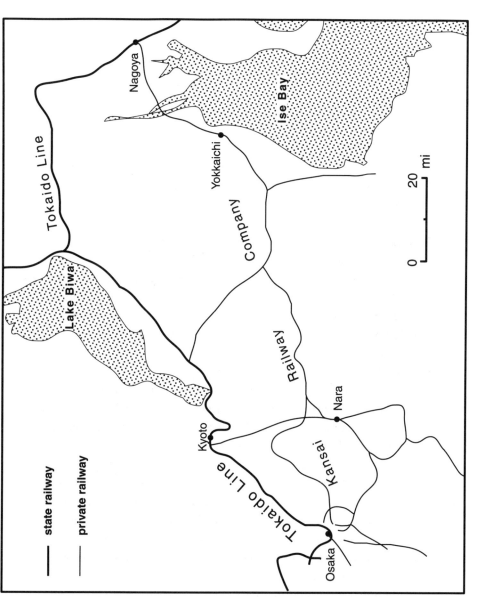

Map 4 The Railway Network Between Osaka and Nagoya in 1902

way applied for a rate reduction in October 1903 and, when the state authorities denied this request, went ahead and lowered its rates anyway after giving the required notice. The upshot was renewed competition for passenger and freight business alike. A prize especially sought by both railways for publicity reasons was the patronage of touring sumo wrestlers. Around this time, wrestlers from Tokyo and the Kansai area held a joint exhibition tournament in Nagoya. As the sumo men prepared to move their show to Osaka, the Kansai and state railways jostled for the privilege of transporting them. In choosing between the two carriers, the wrestlers divided along regional lines. The Tokyo troupe decided to take the government line reportedly for fear that otherwise the state railways might refuse to give them passage home from Nagoya. Meanwhile, the Kansai wrestlers displayed their regional pride by opting for the Kansai line. The Kansai Railway put festive decorations on the outside of the cars carrying the wrestlers as well as a brass band on board and ran its "sumo train" so as to reach Osaka twenty minutes before the Tokyo troupe arrived. Fresh from this publicity stunt, in January 1904, the Kansai unveiled yet another innovation in customer service when it began offering passengers free box lunches. By that time, the company's discount had reached the point where there was hardly any difference between roundtrip and one-way fares, with the predictable result that enterprising customers sought to recoup their fare by purchasing roundtrip tickets and selling the return portion upon arriving at their destination.

The local business community, although presumably benefiting from the bargain rates, was concerned about the negative effects of the rate war such as the inconveniences to freight transport resulting from the instability of charges and the over-concentration of rolling stock in the Kansai area. In late January 1904, the Nagoya Chamber of Commerce cited these and other related problems in appealing to the communications minister to bring an end to the competition once and for all. Finally, in April, with the governor of Osaka and two Diet members serving as mediators, the Kansai and state railways agreed once again to institute the same fares. This time the agreement held, for with the outbreak of the Russo-Japanese War in February, the government was not about to let such rivalry interfere with orderly military transport.

Although the intense competition for clients ended, the rate war with the Kansai proved a turning point for the state railways, setting them on a course leading away from their old bureaucratic arrogance towards a new customer-first attitude. Magnifying this impact of the rate war was the fact that it coincided with the emergence of young progressive bureaucrats within the national railways, men who were bent on changing their organization's policy in a service-oriented direction. Chief among these officials was Kinoshita Yoshio.[239] An engineering graduate of Tokyo Imperial University, Kinoshita at the age of twenty-eight had become head of passenger operations in the Railway Bureau in April 1902. When the rate war broke out four months later, he took full advantage of the conflict to promote a fundamental shift in state-railway policy towards users along the lines of what he had seen on an observation tour of the West in 1900–1901. The effects of his campaign were almost immediately apparent, extending beyond the section of line in direct competition with the Kansai Railway. No sooner had the rivalry begun than the government's Tokaido line announced a fare reduction of 20 percent for passengers intending to climb Mount Fuji. In making this announcement, the state railway authorities drew praise from the Japanese press for addressing their clientele in "polite phraseology" for the first time. The authorities still had much to learn in the way of marketing, for as the *Japan Weekly Mail* observed at the time, "they have not yet risen to the idea of advertising. They still deem it sufficient to post a notice in an obscure corner of a railway station on the off-chance that some one may see it."[240] Nonetheless, the language of this announcement, however circumscribed its publicity, represented a significant departure from previous practice. Another breakthrough came in February 1903 when the Railway Bureau decided to give "greater facilities . . . to the traveling public" such as making books of tickets available in smaller blocks "so as to bring them within reach of a wider circle of travelers" and reducing the minimum time limit on commuter passes from three months to one. The result of these changes, the *Jiji shinpō* predicted, "will be to extend the privilege of cheaper and easier travel to the lower orders, whereas it has hitherto been limited to first- and second-class travelers."[241] In November 1903, the state railways took yet another step to improve their public image by hiring female ticket agents. The four teenagers who began selling tickets at Shinbashi station that month were the first of many women to work in the ticket offices of major national railway terminals. Their initial appearance caused a sensation, and with the press of curious onlookers threatening to obstruct services, the authorities had to "strictly forbid peering into the ticket windows."[242]

Such service innovations did much to popularize railway travel after the turn of the century. Particularly marked was the rise in recreational travel, which theretofore had been largely confined to the upper classes. By the late 1890s, wealthy residents of Tokyo were increasingly going off for the weekend during the summer, taking the train to pleasure resorts south of the city. As a newspaper commented on this growing traffic in August 1898, "Railroads are gradually being built all over the country, and many places that were once quiet and lonely have overnight become prosperous and lively. Since the opening of the Tokaido Line, there has been an increasing stream of visitors from Tokyo to Kamakura, Enoshima, and the Seven Springs of Hakone. . . . Maybe times aren't so bad after all."[243] Times were not, however, particularly rosy for ordinary city folk, few of whom could afford a weekend getaway. In a report on July 22, 1901, the *Tōkyō nichinichi* made clear that the weekend travelers who were swarming to the recreational areas south of Tokyo were for the most part well-to-do individuals: "With the heat getting more unbearable by the day, there is a growing stream of travelers to summer resorts. Traffic is particularly heavy between Saturday and Monday mornings. There is an especially large number of second- and first-class train passengers on these days, and one notices many ladies with their children. . . . Since Westerners are also numerous, the first- and second-class cars on the Tokaido Line, as well as the Yokosuka Line, seem especially crowded."[244] Those travelers continuing to the hot-spring resort of Atami transferred at Odawara to a rather primitive man-powered railroad, built in 1895. Two to three workers pushed each carriage, taking four hours to cover the sixteen miles to Atami. Even this tiny railroad had its proper three classes of travel: when the cars came to a hill, second- and third-class passengers were let off, and the third-class fares had to help push. Nothing better illustrates the way in which the railroads with their service hierarchy tended to reinforce the stratified class system of Meiji Japan. Despite the inconveniences of the man-powered railroad, the charges even for third-class passengers were high, so that local people rode only on special occasions such as during festivals, and most of the customers were tourists of considerable means.[245]

It was not until the 1900s that recreational travel came within easy reach of ordinary people, as the government and private railroads increasingly ran special excursion trains and extended discounts to third-class passengers. On July 15, 1905, for instance, the Sōbu Railway Company, following the lead of the Nippon Railway and its highly successful Nikkō line, took advantage of the Bon festival to operate its first excursion train from Tokyo to the seaside resort of Chōshi; as a newspaper reported on the departure scene in Tokyo, "Tradespeople of every description flocked into [the station], and the platform was mobbed. Among the passengers, many wore straw bonnets, leggings, and straw sandals. There was a good number of madams and prostitutes who had come to peddle their charms, and the old ladies, too, had turned out in force. There were couples holding on to each other and young and old helping each other along. Altogether there must have been more than four hundred people. . . . The railway company is delighted with the success of the venture and will probably run a second excursion train in the near future."[246] Making rail travel even more accessible to the "lower orders" in the latter half of the 1900s was the growing availability of special group rates. During those years, railroads began one after another to promote group excursions at substantially discounted rates. In September 1909, for example, the national railways announced to the owners of factories employing fifty or more workers: "We have decided to make an unprecedented reduction of from 40 percent to 60 percent of the regular fare for laborers traveling in groups."[247] The result of such promotions was that in the latter years of Meiji, as one Japanese scholar puts it, "many people . . . who otherwise would have had little chance to travel went on group excursion to shrines, temples, and famous scenic spots with their neighbors or fellow workers."[248] Thus, the railroads, while reflecting and institutionalizing social divisions with their gradation of services, came to have a certain leveling effect as well by enabling more and more people to ride the train. And as the railroads steadily expanded their customer services in late Meiji, it is no wonder that popular attitudes toward travel and recreation should have changed markedly by the end of the period.

By facilitating the movement of people, the railway system also helped to transform the relationship between work place and residence in Japan. In the major urban areas, in particular, the ramification of the network combined with the increasing availability of season tickets had made it possible by the 1900s for growing numbers of Japanese to commute from home to relatively distant office or factory. When the state railways announced cheaper rates and easier terms for commuter passes in February 1903, Japanese newspapers, according to the *Japan Weekly Mail*, observed "that the tendency of the time is for well-to-do folks to move out of the crowded streets and establish their residence in the suburbs of cities, which wholesome movement will be greatly facilitated by the proposed reductions."[249] In Tokyo, such provisions for commuters contributed to the quickening "drift of the population to the towns and villages west of the Yamanote hills . . . through the mid- and late-Meiji era."[250] Yet, at the end of the period, this demographic shift was still only in its early stages and was confined almost entirely to the wealthy and new middle classes. It was not until the late Taishō era, with the proliferation of electric commuter railroads, that the rise of suburban bedtowns and the separation of home from work became distinct features of Japanese society.[251] The pattern, however, had been set in late Meiji when electric railways in the Kansai area pioneered the acquisition and development by private rail companies of suburban residential land along their tracks. This management innovation, then, pointed the way to the commuter culture that became increasingly characteristic of twentieth-century Japan.

FORGING A NATION. Along with changing patterns of work and residence, railroads in the Meiji era helped further the mobility of labor as well as the process of urbanization by linking the agrarian labor reservoir with urban industrial areas and by blurring the distinction between city and environs. From a wider perspective, the train served to break down regional differences and to drive forward a sense of nationhood. From the start, railway promoters in America and continental Europe had underscored the promise that the iron road held of binding a nation together; as an Italian statesman had put it around the time of his country's unification in 1861, "Railways will serve to sew up the Italian boot."[252] Citing Western precedent, Japanese leaders in early Meiji placed equal stress on the potential contribution of railroads to national unity. Their hopes were not to be disappointed. By the end of Meiji, the railroad had emerged as a powerful agent of social integration, helping to create both a national market and a national identity.

As iron rails connected more and more localities with the metropolis, Tokyo increasingly set the tempo for the country's economic and social life. Prefectures in the interior or along the Japan Sea that prior to the railroad had traded mainly with areas west of Tokyo tended to reorient their commercial relationships dramatically upon the opening of rail lines and to become closely tied to the Tokyo market.[253] The spread of the railway network outward from Tokyo also enabled the fashions and tastes of the capital to circulate ever more widely along the rails. In Nagano city, for instance, before the coming of the railroad in 1888, the local dress was influenced by Niigata fashions, with women in particular wearing *chanchanko* or sleeveless jackets instead of the more stylish *haori*; but after the railroad arrived, Nagano residents underwent a complete change in appearance, as male and female clothing both switched to the Tokyo style.[254] With the expansion of the rail system, goods also disseminated more rapidly from the capital, accelerating the standardization of styles and tastes. In 1889, for example, a businessman from Kōriyama observed that a popular toy he had seen in Tokyo around March of that year had come to be in vogue in the Kōriyama area from the middle of April. "That a fashionable item should spread this quickly to the provinces," he asserted, "is really nothing but a result of the opening of the Tōhoku line. In my opinion, before the completion of the railroad, it would have taken more than half a year for such an item to reach these parts."[255] In fact, goods that in pre-railroad days had required weeks or months to arrive from Tokyo could now often be shipped out by train in the evening and displayed in provincial shop windows the next morning.[256] Thanks to such speed of delivery, in November 1903, a traveler on the recently opened Chūō line could report having dined in Kōfu on the same kind of bonito sashimi as served in Tokyo.[257]

The railroads promoted national integration in a political as well as social and economic sense. As we will see, state railroad legislation became a particular focus of local political activity, serving to tie the localities into the national political scene. In addition, the railroad supplied common images to the very language of politics; exemplifying this influence was an 1889 pamphlet listing as one of the desired qualifications for candidates for the Diet that, "like railroad engineers," they possess specialized knowledge suitable to their professional calling as "engineers of the political locomotive of a civilized nation."[258] For the Meiji leaders, there was no question that railroads were vital to political unification and the building of a modern state. This conviction was fittingly symbolized by the calligraphy engraved at either end of the monumental Sasago tunnel, which served to link mountainous Yamanashi prefecture with the Tokyo area in 1903. Providing the celebratory inscriptions over the tunnel entrances, like bookends to a magnum opus, were the two great statesmen of the Meiji era, Itō Hirobumi and Yamagata Aritomo. "To benefit through the earth," read Itō's handwriting at the eastern end of the tunnel, to which Yamagata's at the western end, equally steeped in the gospel of material progress, replied: "To build in Heaven's stead."[259]

Part Two
In Search of a Railroad Policy, 1869–1892

TWO

The First Two Decades

"In general, applicants [for private railroad construction] have contracted the railway disease, which has been epidemic of late, and are behaving as though they were afflicted by an outbreak of fever and were speaking deliriously."
    Memorial from Railway Bureau Chief Inoue Masaru to
    Prime Minister Itō Hirobumi, March 15, 1887[1]

THE ERA OF STATE ENTERPRISE

Meiji leaders, like their counterparts in the West, came to see railway construction as virtually synonymous with nation building. This equation gave the state a strong basis for action and helped propel the railroad to a central place in the political landscape of Meiji Japan. At the outset of the period, however, there was no such unanimity among government officials; in fact, there was heated debate over the very necessity of railroad development. The issue was settled in short order, as the more progressive members of the new regime carried the day, and the Council of State decided in late 1869 to introduce railroads into Japan.[2] Far more difficult to resolve were the interrelated problems of ownership, control, and finance. A partial answer to these questions did not emerge until passage of the Railway Construction Law in 1892. Until then, policy on all these matters remained fluid and ambiguous, characterized by a great deal of experimentation and vacillation.

From the start, Meiji leaders grappled with the problem of government versus private enterprise, and, with the decision to introduce railway technology, they tentatively adopted a program of state construction and management. Several factors combined to dictate this policy choice. First of all, railroad building entailed an immense outlay of capital, and private investors, faced with a totally unfamiliar enterprise, were unlikely to sink funds on the scale required. In addition, the private sector lacked the technical and managerial skills needed for large-scale business ventures. These conditions called for state initiative not only in railroad development, but in a wide range of industrial activities in early Meiji.[3]

In the case of railroads, other factors reinforced these general circumstances necessitating a market-creating role for the government. One was the public character of the railroad. As early as 1872, state officials were pointing out the shortcomings of private rail companies in the West and were grouping railroads with telegraphs as public utilities.[4] Yet more important for the initial decision in favor of state enterprise were political considerations. In its first two years, the Meiji government faced a number of requests for railroad concessions from American and British nationals. As long as the Japanese themselves failed to embark on railway construction, Meiji leaders felt it would be difficult to refuse such foreign demands. Thus, fear of losing control over railroad development to foreigners provided the immediate stimulus for government action in this field.[5]

Besides having this preemptive reason, state authorities also realized that a railway system would promote administrative centralization, a pressing concern for the fledgling government. This latter point was stressed particularly by Ōkuma Shigenobu and Itō Hirobumi, then the leading advocates of railroad development within the regime. These two received strong backing from British Minister Sir Harry Parkes, who on the eve of the fateful council decision in 1869 met with Japanese leaders and recommended public ownership of railroads as a powerful lever for enhancing the government's authority.[6]

By opting for state enterprise, the government did not rule out private investment in railroads. Paradoxically, the huge capital demands that contributed to making state action a necessity drove the government, in turn, to seek the cooperation of private investors. Since Meiji leaders were determined to promote railroads under a policy of Japanese control, foreign loans had to be avoided as much as possible. Furthermore, competing claims on public finances meant that relatively little investment could be expected out of state revenues. Enlistment of private capital was, therefore, imperative if the government were to build essential railroads expeditiously.

The Council of State officially recognized this need when it accepted Maejima Hisoka's "Railway Estimates" in April 1870. An assistant bureau chief in the Finance and Civil Affairs ministries, Maejima had produced this memorandum after Ōkuma, then vice-minister of finance and civil affairs, had asked him to make projections as to the cost of construction and the operating revenue and expenditure for each of the rail lines slated for construction. At its meeting in late 1869, the council had resolved to build an artery from Tokyo to Kobe with branch lines to Yokohama and Tsuruga. Despite this decision, resistance to railroad development remained strong both within the government and without. Such opposition imperiled the official railway program at a time when the very survival of the regime still hung in the balance. Ōkuma and Itō must have feared for their *own* lives, branded as they were by reactionaries within the government as "corrupt officials" who had sold out the nation by contracting a railway loan abroad.[7] Critics were especially alarmed at the huge capital requirements of railway construction; in the eyes of many, the government was planning to squander on what was at best a nonessential enterprise money that ought to be allocated for such urgent priorities as armaments expansion.

Naturally such views were expressed most forcefully by military authorities. For example, Saigō Takamori, upon joining the government as supreme military commander in late 1870, deplored the frittering away of limited national resources on construction projects and urged the regime to "cancel altogether major works like railroad building and strive to consolidate the foundations [of the nation] and strengthen military affairs."[8] In short, the tightness of government finances dictated that military buildup take precedence over such premature endeavors as railway construction. Ironically, it was not until the railroads had proved their worth as instruments of military transport in 1877, when the Meiji regime quashed the Saigō-led Satsuma Rebellion and thereby firmly established its authority, that military leaders finally came around to recognize the necessity of railroad development.[9]

In the first years of the Meiji era, however, the vehement opposition of military men and other reactionary bureaucrats put the advocates of railroad building in a most difficult position. As Ōkuma disclosed to Maejima in 1870, lacking detailed knowledge of railroads, he could only argue at the pivotal council meeting of the previous year that railroad development would benefit the nation.[10] This explanation had no persuasive power with the diehards, concerned as they were about the expense of railway construction and operation. Hence, it was absolutely vital for someone to come up with statistical data on these matters if railway proponents were to have any hope of overcoming the objections of dissenting officials. Maejima seemed the right man for the task.

Born in 1835 in present-day Niigata prefecture, Maejima had studied gunnery and naval engineering in Edo during the 1850s and then continued his "Dutch studies" in Nagasaki, where he also mastered and taught English, during the early 1860s. In 1866 he was adopted into the family of a Bakufu retainer. Back in Edo, he taught mathematics for the next year and a half at the Kaiseijo, the Bakufu's school for Western studies.[11] Maejima thus possessed at least the minimum of qualifications needed to make the required estimates, which was more than most officials in the early Meiji regime could boast. Thanks to his Dutch studies, he had some technical knowledge of railroads, albeit of a strictly book-learning variety; moreover, he was "extremely good at figures."[12] Nevertheless, in drawing up his railway budget, Maejima had absolutely nothing in the way of practical guidelines; as he himself admitted, "for me to present these estimates without yet knowing a thing about this enterprise was a reckless and brazen act."[13] Maejima's calculations, therefore, were more in the nature of conjectures than of estimates, and in fact "Railway Surmises" is a closer, if less flattering, translation of the title of his memorandum ("Tetsudō okusoku"). In that sense, it is doubtful whether his calculations had much effect on the opponents of railroad development.[14]

The most telling rejoinder to the financial misgivings of state railway opponents came in the section of Maejima's report that followed those in which he presented his "conjectures." In this part of his memorandum, Maejima proposed a concrete method for raising the necessary construction capital for the Tokyo-Kobe line. The formula he recommended called for concentration of private funds through the issue of shares, that is, through the establishment of a joint-stock company. As Maejima put it, the government, "after selecting popular individuals of sincerity and moral character from among the country's rich merchants and farmers, should have them become promoters and form a railway company." The latter then was to float shares with a par value equivalent to the total estimated construction cost. The government was to guarantee a return of 12 percent on the paid-up capital until the shares were fully paid in, after which time profits were to be distributed among the shareholders.[15] Shibusawa Eiichi undoubtedly had a hand in the drafting of this section, for as head of both of the Finance Ministry bureaus in which Maejima was serving, Shibusawa was "striving to raise public opinion in favor of promoting railway construction . . . by refuting [the opposition]"[16] as well as working to introduce the corporate form of business enterprise into Japan.

Thus Maejima, with the active support of his immediate superior, advocated railroad building through private investment; however, there was no intention for the time being of turning construction or management over to the private sector. In fact, the so-called "railway company" proposed by Maejima was primarily a means for the government to raise construction capital by having the company sell shares to the public.[17] In that sense, one could argue, Maejima's report conformed to the basic policy of government control of railroads.

In several crucial respects, however, Maejima's reasoning deviated from the original policy of the Council of State. To be sure, Maejima insisted on government construction and operation. Nevertheless, he strongly implied that this was only meant to be a temporary measure stemming from the inability of private interests to manage railroads forthwith. As he asserted in his memorandum, the government "should become a strict instructor, imparting clear methods to the people and teaching them how to combine their resources, and should commence with the most convenient and profitable project [namely, construction of the Shinbashi-Yokohama line]." Beginning with railroads, Maejima continued, "shipping, commerce, and manufacturing should all be developed in accordance with this method."[18] In short, the government, by becoming a "strict instructor," should guide the private sector until the latter was fully prepared to operate such ventures on its own.

Maejima's proposal thus aimed at placing railroads in the mainstream of the incipient industrial promotion policy whereby the state sought to encourage private industry through model enterprises. Hence, as one writer sees it, the "Railway Estimates" contained "the germ of the argument for private railroads."[19] Maejima's proposal clearly represented a departure from the public ownership decision of 1869. Yet, in spite of this fact, it was unanimously accepted by the Council of State, suggesting that the initial policy was not as sweeping or unshakable as some have made it out to be.

Maejima's plan for introducing private capital seemed to bear fruit in 1871 with the establishment of the Kansai Railway Company.[20] In April 1871, the Kyoto prefectural office summoned representatives of the Mitsui, Ono, and Shimada merchant houses and urged them to contribute construction capital for the Kyoto-Osaka section of the grand artery. After considerable hesitation, the merchants finally agreed and in August formed a joint-stock company later known as the Kansai Railway. The company's preliminary articles of incorporation, approved by the Council of State in September, closely mirrored Maejima's proposal. The articles stipulated that the sole function of the enterprise was to raise construction capital. This capital was to be turned over to the government, which would pay the firm an annual dividend of 10 percent on its investment. Meanwhile, the government would undertake all construction and management. On the other hand, the preliminary articles also provided that, after twenty years, the company could assume operation of the railroad. By approving these articles, the authorities seemed to recognize the possibility of private railway management, in direct contradiction to the original Council of State decision.[21] Nevertheless, the regime's attitude towards the company was still uncertain. As one source puts it, "concerning the relationship between the government and the investors, the state had no fixed policy."[22]

This government indecision was resolved by the Yamao memorial, one of the most central documents on railroad policy during the 1870s. Submitted to the Council of State by Public Works Minister Yamao Yōzō in September 1872, the memorial proposed specific guidelines for enlistment of private capital. Yamao began by referring to developments in Europe. "Regarding such works as railroads and telegraphs, in European countries," he observed, "shortcomings have become apparent in private enterprise, and a trend towards nationalization has arisen." Even in Britain, that paragon of free enterprise, "telegraphs, hitherto owned by companies, have been purchased by the state at a huge price."[23] Heeding the experience of Europe, therefore, Japan should avoid the trouble of buying out private concerns by having the government take charge of these activities from the start.

At the root of Yamao's argument was his belief in the public nature of railroads and telegraphs. As in the case of telegraphs, the government had the responsibility to build and operate railroads itself. However, in view of its strained finances, the state, Yamao suggested, should borrow the necessary construction funds from the Kansai Railway Company at 7-percent interest and, in exchange for certain profit guarantees, should stipulate that, after twenty years, the railroad would come entirely under government ownership.[24]

The Council of State approved this plan in October 1872, and in May of the following year, a new agreement was concluded between the Kansai Railway and the government. Under the revised charter, the earlier condition on future ownership was completely reversed so that, after twenty years, the state could return the company's investment at will, and the firm would then have "no connection at all with the above railroad."[25]

Despite generous government support, the Kansai Railway soon ran into a series of difficulties. The Kansai region was mired in a business slump at the time, and the company was unable to raise even half the required construction capital. Moreover, since the promoters had been half-coerced into forming the concern in the first place, their enthusiasm quickly died. As a result, the government decided in 1874 to let the company dissolve and to build the Kyoto-Osaka line with its own money.[26] Yet, with other endeavors, including development of a modern shipping industry, having prior claim on the state's limited resources, the consequence for railroad construction, as one British employee of the government railways put it, was "a period of extreme dullness, ending in complete standstill" by the late 1870s.[27]

Adoption of the Yamao formula meant that, by and large, the authorities had upheld the principle of state ownership; efforts to enlist private enterprise had not gone beyond the level of soliciting construction capital. The Yamao memorial clearly reflected the attitude of the Public Works Ministry, particularly the Railway Bureau, which perceived railroads fundamentally as a public enterprise and insisted on strict government control. By contrast, Maejima had expressed in his "Railway Estimates" the views of a Finance Ministry bureaucrat, concerned with sound finances and leaning towards private enterprise. These two positions epitomized the budding conflict between the Finance and Public Works ministries over railroad policy, a conflict that would continue to hamper the formulation of policy in the coming decades.

Compounding this problem during the early years was the fact that the Public Works Ministry had to share railway policy making with the finance bureaucracy. After the Yamao memorial was approved, the Finance Ministry requested that financial arrangements for private companies be placed under its jurisdiction. Asserting that "it would be inappropriate to entrust capital raising, interest payment, and profit distribution to the Public Works Ministry," Finance Minister Inoue Kaoru urged that these matters "be entrusted to this ministry and construction work alone to the Public Works Ministry."[28] This proposal was adopted by the government in January 1873, and it was not until 1876 that the Public Works Ministry regained complete control over railway affairs.[29] Consequently, the economizing concerns of the finance bureaucracy, magnified by the expenses incurred in 1874 in quashing a samurai rebellion in Saga and dispatching a military expedition to Taiwan, would impinge heavily on railroad policy. This fact would reappear in sharp relief during the second major attempt to establish a private railway company, this time based not on the capital of merchants, but on the wealth of the former ruling class.

In seeking the participation of private interests in capital-intensive railroad development, the early Meiji regime could basically turn to just two sources of private funding. One of these was merchant capital, of which the first efforts to mobilize were seen in the Kansai Railway Company. The other concentration of private wealth consisted of the annual stipends paid by the government to the former daimyo and samurai. Inherited from the shogunate, these transfer payments totaled about twenty million yen a year in the early seventies.[30]

The movement to establish railway companies based on the investment of feudal pensions represented the second important stream in the history of private railway schemes during the 1870s. This movement originated with a Yokohama merchant named Takashima Kaemon, who beginning in 1871 repeatedly urged construction of a Tokyo-Aomori line to be financed by the nobility. Owner of the construction firm that contracted the reclamation work for the Shinbashi-Yokohama railroad, the enterprising Takashima recommended that the government build the northern artery with funds borrowed from the former daimyo, paying them 7-percent interest until the completion of the line and distributing profits to them thereafter.[31] The Council of State, however, turned down Takashima's proposal in mid-1872 on the grounds that it conflicted with the principle of government ownership of trunk lines.[32]

Takashima's proposal was soon echoed by the former daimyo themselves. In 1871, Minister of the Right Iwakura Tomomi impressed on Hachisuka Mochiaki, the former daimyo of Awa, the urgency of building railroads and the necessity for that purpose of forming a partnership among the nobility. Responding to Iwakura's plea, Hachisuka petitioned the government in October 1872 recommending the establishment of a nobles' company to finance construction of the Tokyo-Aomori and Tokyo-Niigata lines. In November, Iwakura backed up this plan by advising the Council of State: "the government should speedily grant [Hachisuka] permission and provide him with adequate support."[33]

Encouraged by these developments, a group of ten former daimyo applied in March 1873 for permission to organize a railroad firm based on Hachisuka's proposal. Takashima Kaemon also joined this movement, and the government found it impossible to ignore the importunities of the company promoters. In September 1874, the Council of State finally instructed the group to submit detailed plans to the Public Works Ministry. Thereupon, the promoters set up the Tokyo Railway Association and, on Takashima's advice, decided to capitalize the company at ¥2,500,000 and to start with construction of the Tokyo-Aomori line.[34]

The question of whether or not to approve the nobles' plan produced a split within the regime. Under the Yamao formula, construction and management were to remain in government hands with private companies acting merely as subsidiary financial organs. The exact character of the Tokyo Railway Association, however, was still unclear, and the Public Works Ministry, which insisted on state ownership, apparently feared losing control over a vital trunk line to private investors. On the other hand, the Finance Ministry had intruded heavily into railway policy making since 1873. A number of finance officials, led by Inoue Kaoru, favored approval of the nobles' association, arguing for revision of the Yamao formula to permit private construction of railroads. Yet even the Finance Ministry was divided, as Ōkuma Shigenobu asserted that "major works such as railway construction . . . should be managed by the state"[35] and financed through the issue of public bonds. As a result of these disagreements, the government was unable to reach any decision on the nobles' application.

In an effort to break this deadlock, Inoue Kaoru urged the association to abandon its plans for railroad building and to apply instead for purchase of the existing state line between Shinbashi and Yokohama. The nobles accepted Inoue's advice and in June 1875 altered their petition, requesting permission to acquire the government line. After heated debate, the Council of State finally approved this request. Under an agreement reached in August 1876, the government was to sell the Shinbashi-Yokohama railway for ¥3,000,000 and to guarantee a return of 6 percent on the paid-up capital.[36]

Why did the government consent to this plan, apparently in violation of the original state ownership policy? To begin with, the proposal had the firm backing of several government leaders, especially Inoue and Iwakura. The latter two proved to be persuasive advocates of the sale. Iwakura, an unflagging promoter of private railway development under the leadership of the nobility, pointed out two major advantages to the plan. On the one hand, he argued, the sale would enable the government to acquire part of the nobles' stipends for railway construction; at the same time, it would allow the former daimyo to secure a means of livelihood for the period after the commutation of their stipends.[37] Predictably, Inoue stressed the benefits to state finance. By selling the line, he maintained, the government would be able to offset its "lack of funds with which to continue the work of railway construction."[38]

Nevertheless, the sale proposal was by no means unanimously accepted by the Council of State. In fact, there was sharp discord over the terms of the sale agreement drafted in 1876. To be sure, the contract conformed to the Yamao formula insofar as it subordinated the company to the principle of government construction. On the other hand, the agreement contained a crucial provision on management that would have spelled the total collapse of the Yamao policy of government control by stipulating that, after the sale, the railroad "will become the exclusive property of the association, and [the latter] will permanently manage the enterprise."[39]

One source claims that the decision to sell the Shinbashi-Yokohama railroad "did not conflict with previous policy because it was not a trunk line."[40] However, the nobles had in mind far more than just private ownership of feeder lines, for in support of the sale agreement they had argued: "The state must sell its existing (already profitable) lines, build new ones with the proceeds, and sell these latter when they are in good running order."[41] By sanctioning the sale, therefore, the government was plainly deviating from its original policy. As Nakanishi Ken'ichi puts it, the sale agreement marked "the first step in the retreat of the state ownership principle."[42]

Yet, in the end, the sale was never consummated, and government ownership was maintained in practice, if not in principle, throughout the seventies. The nobles' association did manage to pay the first two installments on the sale price. But, in July 1877, the compulsory commutation of stipends went into effect, proving an immediate obstacle to further payments. As a result of the commutation, the nobles' annual income fell by about 40 percent.[43] Moreover, the price of commuted pension bonds declined sharply, with the result that banks refused to accept them as collateral for loans. Weakened and dispirited, the nobles' association finally requested cancellation of the sale in December 1877. The government approved this request, and the company disbanded in March 1878.[44]

After the collapse of the Tokyo Railway Association, the movement to establish private railroads under the former ruling class branched off in two main directions. The first centered around the Tōzan Company, founded in May 1878 by a group of former samurai. This company aimed at building a railroad between Tokyo and Takasaki based on the investment of commuted stipends. Unable to secure government approval of this plan, the promoters followed the example of the nobles' association and requested the sale of the Shinbashi-Yokohama railroad, but the Council of State refused to grant this request as well.[45]

Undoubtedly, this refusal reflected a more cautious attitude on the part of the regime in light of its experience with the Tokyo Railway Association. As for the earlier Takasaki railroad proposal, Nakanishi suggests that it was turned down because it "conflicted with the government's policy of the state ownership of trunk lines."[46] Probably more to the point, the government at the time was planning to build the Tokyo-Takasaki line itself, and state railway construction, largely stalled since 1874, picked up at the very end of the decade following the successful flotation of the first domestic industrial loan, of which ¥5,700,000 was appropriated for railroads.[47]

The second offshoot of the Tokyo Railway Association centered around Iwakura and the 15th National Bank.[48] After the nobles' association dissolved, its former leaders joined Iwakura in an effort to revive the original plan of constructing a Tokyo-Aomori line. This time, however, they sought to concentrate commuted pension bonds in the 15th National Bank, founded by Iwakura and other nobles in 1877, and to use this "peers' bank" as a springboard for setting up a sound private railway enterprise. In 1881, after the government had cancelled its plans for building the Takasaki line, promoters of the Tōzan Company merged with Iwakura's group, and their combined efforts culminated in the establishment of the Nippon Railway Company, the first successful private railroad in Japan.[49]

The Advent of Private Railroads

In November 1880, the Council of State withdrew the permission it had earlier granted the Railway Bureau to start building the Tokyo-Takasaki line.[50] This move, which served as a direct catalyst for the formation of the Nippon Railway Company, attended a pivotal shift in government policy. In early November, the Council of State embarked on a vigorous program of financial retrenchment, compelled to action by the serious depreciation in paper currency following the Satsuma Rebellion. As part of this program, all government departments were ordered "insofar as possible [to] postpone new enterprises . . . , thereby effecting a reduction of expenditures."[51] Once again, the requirements of public finance dominated railroad planning, and the retrenchment policy rendered the Council of State doubly receptive to plans for private railway enterprise.

One of the government leaders responsible for this renewed interest in private railroads was Matsukata Masayoshi, the principal architect of the new financial policy. Matsukata was a forceful advocate of private initiative. As finance minister during most of the 1880s, he spearheaded the transition away from direct state involvement in industry to the encouragement of private companies through subsidies and other forms of public assistance. Railroads were no exception, as Matsukata pressed for state subvention of private firms in place of government enterprise.

Matsukata had received confirmation of his ideas while visiting France as Japan's delegate to the Paris International Exhibition in 1878. In an interview with the head of the exhibition, Matsukata had asked the French official for his opinion as to whether trunk railroads should be built by the government or by private interests. The Frenchman had replied that private railway construction was "ideal" whereas railroad building by the state carried the danger of poor workmanship or of needless expenditure. He had then seconded Matsukata's emphasis on the need to "establish a railway constitution and to set up guidelines for government assistance [to private railroads]."[52] One can infer from this exchange that Matsukata had been duly impressed by the French system of public-private cooperation in the railway field. Under that system, French authorities had promoted mostly private development of the nation's rail network by offering generous concessions, including subsidies and interest guarantees, to private concerns.[53]

It is not surprising, therefore, that, when a group of private railway promoters sought his cooperation in 1880, Matsukata should have extended firm support. In November 1880, immediately after the government announced the cancellation of its Takasaki railroad plans, four of the Tōzan Company promoters called on Matsukata, then home minister, to discuss the possibility of private construction of the line. During this meeting, Matsukata observed that, without backing from the state, private railway enterprise would be difficult. Accordingly, he suggested, "the government should guarantee the interest [on investment], and if profits fail to meet a certain amount, it should make up the difference."[54]

Heartened by Matsukata's encouragement, the Tōzan Company promoters approached Iwakura in January 1881, armed with draft petitions for the establishment of a railway company and for the granting of a government profit guarantee. Iwakura responded with enthusiasm, agreeing wholeheartedly to back their plans. His participation opened the way for the merger of the two movements stemming from the Tokyo Railway Association. In February, representatives of the Tōzan Company and the peers' bank gathered at Iwakura's residence and decided jointly to promote a railway company. Iwakura then offered the group a concrete plan for railroad building. His proposal was ambitious: beginning with the Tokyo-Aomori railroad, it called for the construction of four trunk lines stretching over the entire country. Appropriate to this scale of construction, Iwakura suggested that the firm be named the Nippon Railway Company. The promoters accepted these proposals and in May 1881 submitted a founding application to the government. Approval came swiftly with a temporary license in August and a "Special Charter" in November. The following month, the first stockholders' meeting was held, and the Nippon Railway, capitalized at ¥20,000,000, was officially launched.[55]

In the composition of its investors, the Nippon Railway Company departed significantly from its predecessors. Admittedly, the railroad, like the Tōzan Company and the peers' group, tried to enlist funds from the nobility and relied heavily on investment by the 15th National Bank.[56] In contrast to its forerunners, however, the Nippon Railway aimed at raising capital not just from the former ruling class, but from the general public as well. At Iwakura's urging, the promoters had decided to seek funds from all classes "without distinguishing between the nobility and the people."[57] In his February proposal, Iwakura had estimated the company's capital requirements at ¥19,000,000, ¥2,000,000 of which would be borne by the promoters and the rest "widely solicited."[58] Iwakura thus sought to broaden the investment base of the company, hoping thereby to avoid the difficulties in raising capital that had frustrated previous attempts at establishing private railroads.

Under Iwakura's leadership, the Nippon Railway Company adopted a threefold approach to "soliciting capital widely." First, the company relied on the direct mediation of Iwakura and other top government officials in enlisting funds from the nobility. Secondly, Iwakura had the promoters obtain the cooperation of prefectural authorities in raising capital from local elites along the projected route of the Tokyo-Aomori line. And finally, Iwakura appealed to the general public by persuading journalists to publicize the company's plans.[59]

Despite these elaborate steps, the promoters realized from the start that mobilizing the necessary capital would be no simple task.[60] Seen against the backdrop of previous failure and the sheer novelty of the railway enterprise, the strategy of seeking capital from all classes was no guarantee by itself of securing the necessary funding. Government leaders were also aware of this fact, and, in line with the new financial policy, many of them were prepared to extend enough state aid to make investment in the railroad an attractive proposition.

Matsukata had been the first to express this tendency when, in his November 1880 meeting with the Tōzan Company promoters, he had voiced support for a government profit guarantee. If the railroad were to receive such a guarantee, he had asserted, "the floating of share capital should not be a difficult matter."[61] Iwakura vigorously followed up on Matsukata's suggestion, urging the Nippon Railway promoters to apply for liberal terms of assistance. Furthermore, Iwakura played a crucial mediating role within the government, negotiating with councilors Ōkuma, Itō, and Terajima Munenori on behalf of the company.[62]

These efforts bore fruit in a most generous program of state aid. Under the "Special Charter" issued by the government in November 1881, all the forms of assistance requested by the firm were granted. The state promised to pay an annual interest of 8 percent on subscribed capital while each section of the railroad was under construction and, after the completion of each section, to guarantee a net return of 8 percent per annum for ten years on the Tokyo-Sendai line and for fifteen years on the Sendai-Aomori line. The government also agreed to lend state land free of charge, to waive taxes on company-owned land, and to direct the Railway Bureau to build the branch line between Tokyo and Maebashi.[63] In the end, however, the bureau also laid the entire trunk line to Aomori, taking charge of maintenance and operation as well. As the aforementioned British employee of the state railways aptly concluded, "The position of the Japan Railway Company was indeed a very happy one. It received from the Government the right to construct and own railways in certain populous districts; it received also a guarantee of 8 per cent. upon all its subscribed capital; and finally, the whole trouble and responsibility of surveying and constructing the lines was assumed by the Railway Bureau, the company stepping in and undertaking the management when everything was completed."[64]

Did this lavish government support effect a clean break with previous policy? The aggressive promotion of a private trunk-line company appears to have signified the final negation of the state-ownership principle. The Yamao formula of state management and private capital also seems to have been repudiated with the entrusting of managerial functions to the firm.[65]

On the other hand, both the Yamao policy and the original principle of state ownership had been wavering throughout the 1870s, and to a large extent, the Nippon Railway Company simply marked the culmination of earlier efforts, frequently backed by the government, to establish private railroads.

There is another sense, however, in which state support of the Nippon Railway did not represent a major departure from past policy. A strong case can be made that, from the outset, the government regarded the "Special Charter" as an exception, that the assistance program was aimed at introducing private capital for railway construction by the state, and that ultimately the railroad did not conflict with the principle of public ownership. The government itself had intended to build the Tokyo-Aomori line since the early seventies, but with the retrenchment order of 1880, all plans for further construction had to be dropped for the time being. Yet, for a variety of strategic and economic reasons, the government still regarded as a high priority the building of this vital trunk line. At this juncture, therefore, the proposal of the Nippon Railway promoters was particularly welcome, and one could argue that, in generously supporting the firm, the Council of State was merely seeking to enlist private investors to take up the slack while the government restored its finances.

Still, the Nippon Railway Company remained totally dependent on the state for both construction and operation of its lines. In fact, it was not until 1892 that the firm became fully independent of the state railways.[66] As a result, the Nippon appeared throughout the 1880s to be little more than a semi-private concern; its complete subordination to the Railway Bureau even prompted one contemporary observer to remark that the railroad was "a company only in name and was really a government office."[67] In short, during its first decade at least, the Nippon Railway bore a striking resemblance to the Yamao formula under which railroad companies were to serve as supplementary financial organs for state railway construction.

Not only did the "Special Charter" provide for numerous forms of public assistance, but it also imposed several important obligations on the firm. The Nippon Railway was to begin construction within six months and to complete all sections within seven years. Moreover, the authorities reserved the right of state ownership, however tenuously, by stipulating that the charter would expire in ninety-nine years and that the state could purchase the railroad after a period of fifty years. According to one writer, these provisions meant that "the government could bring pressure to bear for a speedy completion of construction and could await a favorable moment for nationalization."[68] In addition, the authorities set strict terms of financial disclosure as a condition for granting subsidies to the Nippon. The charter empowered the government to appoint inspectors to "audit all the company's accounts" for the duration of the profit guarantee.[69] It also required the firm to submit monthly business reports,[70] whereas most of the private railroads to follow were obliged to make reports only twice a year.

Given the degree of state intervention in the nascent Nippon Railway, official support of that company appears to have been less a policy reversal than a temporary measure, designed to offset the government's lack of construction funds. Nevertheless, the establishment of the firm set a precedent for private ownership of trunk lines, clearly in contradiction to past policy, and paved the way for the parallel development of private and state railroads from the 1880s on.

The financial retrenchment order of 1880, by forcing suspension of state railway plans, had provided the mainspring for government support of the Nippon Railway Company. In addition to postponement of new undertakings, that directive had also called for the sale of existing state enterprises. Among the ventures initially slated for transfer to the private sector were railroads.[71] A dramatic plan for putting this into effect soon appeared within the government. In December 1881, Councilor Itō Hirobumi submitted a "Proposal for the Issue of Railway Stock" in which he recommended divestiture of government rail lines through the sale of "railway shares." Itō aimed at having these shares concentrated in a private company that would be set up to manage the railroads. The proceeds from the sale would be used partly to "supplement funds for redeeming paper notes" under the program of currency reform that Matsukata as the new finance minister was beginning to implement, and partly to "improve means of transportation on sea and land," thereby relieving state finances.[72]

Itō's proposal, had it been adopted, would have occasioned a major departure from previous policy. The transfer of government lines into private hands would clearly have upset the principle of state ownership and represented a far more drastic step than the granting of assistance to the Nippon Railway. Yet, insofar as the need for financial reform underlay Itō's plan, its aims were not unlike those of the Nippon's "Special Charter." Moreover, the fact that Itō lumped railroads together with other forms of transportation as "public works that naturally fall under the responsibility of the government"[73] suggests that, under his plan, financial policy was simply to take precedence over state railway operations for the time being.

In any case, Itō's proposal failed to win State Council approval. Public Works Minister Yamagata Aritomo charged that the proposed sale price—the total construction cost, less the value of railroad bonds redeemed—was far too low, since it did not take into account such factors as inflation. Not surprisingly, finance authorities, for once, agreed with their public works counterparts, adding that the sale itself was inopportune.[74] And well they might have so argued, since the state railways were returning almost 9 percent on fixed investment in the years 1880–1881.[75] At a time when the Meiji regime was desperately trying to stabilize its finances, government officials were simply in no hurry to unload the moneymakers among state enterprises. Finance bureaucrats may have resisted expansion of the state railway system, but they doubtless had no misgivings about hanging on to the profitable lines already completed. Thus, when Chief Councilor Sanjō Sanetomi called off further discussion of Itō's proposal in July 1882, railroads were in effect removed from the list of government industries scheduled for disposal. Immediately after the announcement of Itō's plan the previous December, the president of the Nippon Railway had asked that his company be allowed to purchase the state lines. The authorities, however, denied this request in August 1882.[76] Even after 1884, when other state enterprises were turned over to the private sector in rapid succession, the government made no move to sell off the railroads it had built on the main island. Admittedly, on the northern island, the state did transfer its Temiya-Horonai line to the newly established Hokkaido Colliery and Railway in 1889, but inasmuch as that line and the coal-mining operation it serviced were sold as a package, it was clearly an exception.[77] Thus, it would seem that the authorities by and large adhered to the principle of state ownership of railroads.

Although public ownership was maintained in the case of existing state railways, this principle was not necessarily observed in the construction of new lines. In fact, during the enterprise boom of the late 1880s, the government granted licenses to a host of private rail firms, suggesting a basic shift towards private enterprise. Moreover, the Nippon Railway Company provided a precedent for an extensive program of assistance to private railroads and prepared the way for the adoption of a policy under which, "even if it is a trunk line, depending on the circumstances, [the government] will permit private construction."[78]

The private company boom of 1886–1889 supplied the immediate backdrop for this apparent reversal of policy. A number of factors converged to trigger the enterprise boom. First, the fall in prices produced by the Matsukata deflation of the early eighties had encouraged savings, and once the deflation had run its course, these savings "rushed out seeking profitable areas of investment."[79] The other wing of the Matsukata financial reform, the establishment of a sound convertible currency system centering on the Bank of Japan, had led to a significant drop in interest rates, and together, low interest rates and stable prices encouraged long-term investments. Secondly, along with these favorable investment conditions, the price of stocks rose, increasing the chances for speculative gains. Moreover, in 1886, the rate of interest on public bonds, which hitherto had dominated the securities market, was fixed at 5 percent, making them less attractive as objects of speculation. Consequently, after 1886, stocks overwhelmingly replaced public bonds as the primary target of investment.[80] A third factor underlying the enterprise boom was the marked expansion in exports after 1885, stimulated by the global decline in the price of silver.[81]

The enterprise mania that grew out of these conditions first infected railroads, "then spread to the spinning industry, next hit the mining industry, and finally became universal."[82] The main reason railroads spearheaded the company boom was the dramatic success of the Nippon Railway. In 1884, that concern made public its first business results, revealing a profit of over 10 percent on invested capital. This announcement dispelled any doubts about the profitability of the railway enterprise and prompted a lively demand for shares. As one writer puts it, "From this time on railroad projects sprang up like mushrooms."[83]

Between 1885 and 1892, fifty applications were made for the establishment of private rail companies. The majority of these were of a purely speculative character so that, by the end of 1892, only fourteen firms, including the Nippon Railway, had actually been set up.[84] Nevertheless, private railway construction, propelled by the investment mania, made remarkable progress. In 1889, the total length of the private lines surpassed that of the government railways, and by 1892, the former had reached 1,320 miles compared to 551 for the state network.[85]

The government's attitude towards the private railway boom was expressed in a wide-ranging program of state support. The authorities offered railroad companies generous assistance, patterned after that accorded the Nippon Railway, by lending state property free of charge, granting tax exemptions, and expropriating private land on behalf of the companies. Further, in the case of trunk-line firms such as the San'yō and Kyushu, the state extended interest subsidies and profit guarantees. All told, ten of the fourteen companies founded by 1892 received some form of state aid.[86]

Government recognition of railroad concerns was made official with the enactment of the Private Railway Regulations of 1887. These prescribed for the first time definite standards according to which private railroads were to be licensed. Proposed by the Railway Bureau,[87] the regulations were actually meant to control more than to assist railway companies. Nevertheless, they did provide for some forms of public support, chief among these being official help in acquiring the necessary land. As such, the Private Railway Regulations echoed Matsukata's earlier views concerning the need for a "railway constitution" to provide guidelines for government support.

Indeed, it was Matsukata who was the leading proponent of state aid to private railways during the 1880s. In March 1887, when promoters of the Kyushu and San'yō railway companies applied for state assistance, Matsukata submitted to the cabinet a major policy statement in which he developed a strong argument for public support. Construction of the proposed trunk lines by the government, he contended, would require another huge issue of public bonds, the liquidation of which would take several decades. By contrast, if private companies were to build the lines, the state could subsidize them at a cost several times less than the interest on the necessary public bonds. Moreover, it made little sense for the government to exhaust its resources on railroad construction when "the public has been aroused and is planning enterprises." Matsukata thus concluded: "By far the best policy is to permit construction of the railroads west of Kobe by private companies and to grant them appropriate subsidies."[88]

The cabinet accepted Matsukata's proposal and approved the establishment of the San'yō and Kyushu railway companies in 1888. At that time, the government also granted the Kyushu Railway an interest subsidy of 4 percent, but at the company's request, it changed the subvention the following year to a lump-sum payment of ¥2,000 per mile of completed track. The San'yō began receiving a subsidy on the same terms in 1890. The Hokkaido Colliery and Railway came in for even better treatment with an interest subsidy as well as a profit guarantee of 5 percent.[89] The principle of the state ownership of trunk lines, which could still be regarded as having been preserved in the case of the Nippon Railway, seemed at this point to have finally collapsed.

Matsukata's views were not shared by all government leaders, however. In particular, his subsidization plan met with stiff opposition from Inoue Masaru, head of the Railway Bureau, who insisted vehemently on the principle of state ownership (see Figure 9). Inoue had been in charge of the Railway Bureau since its inauguration in 1871. During the seventies, this department had exerted little impact on railroad policy, remaining for the most part a subordinate engineering body. In fact, it was not until the early eighties that the bureau had any real input into policy making.[90] By then, the railway bureaucracy had built a strong base from which to wield its influence.

A principal component of that base was the managerial independence that the Railway Bureau enjoyed within the Public Works Ministry.[91] More central, however, was the bureau's virtual monopoly of railroad technology. By the end of the seventies, government engineers had, for the most part, managed to free themselves of foreign technical assistance; with few private engineers versed in railway technology, they were soon called upon to assist private railroads. The Nippon Railway Company, in particular, was totally dependent on the Railway Bureau in technical matters. A number of other firms also entrusted construction work to the bureau or hired members of its staff as chief engineers.[92] The effect of this heavy reliance by private railroads on the technical expertise of the Railway Bureau was to enhance the latter's voice in policy matters as well.

No doubt the most important reason for the Railway Bureau's influence was the firm leadership provided by Inoue Masaru. Described by one of his foreign employees as "a man of strong will and self-confidence,"[93] Inoue was an outspoken advocate of unified state control over the railroad network. After the breakthrough to private enterprise, the Railway Bureau chief seemed to grasp every opportunity to resist private development of railroads as well as demand swift nationalization of private lines. Inoue trumpeted these views fairly consistently through the 1880s, and it is around him that one could make the strongest case for a coherent state-ownership policy. His adamant stand on government initiative clashed loudly with Matsukata's program for the promotion of private railroads. The confrontation between the Railway Bureau chief and the finance minister represented a continuation of the classic conflict between the Public Works Ministry, imbued with a sense of the public character of railroads, and the Finance Ministry, determined to relieve the government of a heavy financial burden by encouraging private railway enterprise.

Unlike many proponents of state railways within the regime, Inoue had become a convert to national ownership not while touring the European continent with its efficient state networks, but while studying in the temple of private enterprise, Great Britain. Born into a samurai family of the Chōshū domain in 1843, he had his first exposure to Western learning in Nagasaki. There, at the age of sixteen, Inoue studied military science under the Dutch instructors at the shogunate's naval training school. Then, in 1863, he defied the shogunate's prohibition of unauthorized foreign travel by voyaging to England with a group of fellow Chōshū samurai. These were ambitious young men destined for leadership, including as they did Itō Hirobumi, Inoue Kaoru, and Yamao Yōzō. After arriving in London, Masaru eventually devoted himself to mastering railroad and mining technology as his contribution to "meeting the needs of [his] nation."[94] He apparently received an unfavorable impression of England's unregulated private system, for he returned to Japan in 1868 convinced of the total inadequacy of private railroads. The establishment of the Nippon Railway Company, therefore, profoundly disturbed Inoue, who rightly saw it as the first step in the "piecemeal denial" of his cherished principle of government ownership.[95] Accordingly, he insisted at the time that, "because the Nippon Railway Company has been founded for special reasons, . . . it should be regarded for the moment as an exception."[96]

Lest there be any doubt about his position, in March 1883, Inoue submitted to the public works minister an "Argument against Private Railroads," marking the first significant thrust into the policy-making field by the Railway Bureau.[97] Drawing on his knowledge of the West, Inoue as-

Figure 9 Inoue Masaru (1843–1910), head of the state Railway Bureau from 1871 to 1893. Photograph: courtesy of the Transportation Museum, Tokyo.

serted in this document that railroads were by nature a responsibility of the state, and "not only is it an axiom that they should not be entrusted to private companies, but the harmful effects of [doing so] would be extremely great."[98] Among these "harmful effects," Inoue cited the following: (1) because private firms are profit-driven, railroad companies would refuse to build unremunerative lines even if they were necessary from the standpoint of national policy; (2) reluctant to expand their capital, private railroads would refrain from making necessary improvements; (3) they would tend towards hypercompetition by duplicating each other's lines; (4) the local orientation of small railroads would hamper nationwide railway planning; (5) private lines with local monopolies might harass the residents of the areas they service by refusing them transportation; and (6) in a national emergency, they might try to gain excessive profits by raising rates. Such abuses had been appearing among private railroads in Europe and America since the 1840s, and Inoue therefore concluded that, "judging from the experience of Western countries . . . , the government itself should undertake railway enterprises."[99]

The Railway Bureau chief continued his criticism of private rail companies, this time based on Japan's own experience during the intervening years, in a memorial that he presented to Prime Minister Itō Hirobumi in March 1887. In this document, Inoue firmly opposed Matsukata's proposal for granting subsidies to the Kyushu and San'yō railways. Inoue admitted that, "in cases where the government has a private firm construct a line that the government itself should build," the granting of assistance was permissible. However, private railroads lacked the experience and technical knowledge needed to carry out construction work. Consequently, they would probably have to hire foreign technicians, resulting in unreasonably high costs. In addition to this, Inoue pointed out that many company promoters, swept along by the speculative craze, had become deluded by the expectation of huge profits and were making careless plans. Besides, he argued, government engineers would soon be finished with the Tokyo-Kobe artery,[100] and the state itself could undertake construction of the lines west of Kobe. In short, Inoue declared that he could not agree "to entrusting [railroad development] to companies that have yet to come up with construction plans," let alone to granting them subsidies.[101]

In these several petitions, the head of the state railways appeared to voice a consistent theme in favor of government control. Yet even Inoue, the stubborn champion of state initiative, was forced to alter his approach in the light of continued government support of private railroads. In 1883, for example, Inoue shifted from his original opposition to private companies to endorsement of the Yamao formula of state construction using private funds. In response to an application for the founding of the Kyushu Railway Company made in July 1883, Inoue submitted a memorandum urging state leaders to establish the principle that the government should "manage the capital, the lines, and the business affairs . . . as well as distribute the profits" of private railroads.[102]

When this tack failed, Inoue attempted a third course, that of strengthening the government's supervisory powers and giving them the force of law. Once the authorities granted a provisional license to the Kyushu Railway in 1886, the head of the Railway Bureau was forced to concede: "Now that private construction has been approved, it is necessary to enact regulations that will serve as standards for the control and supervision of the same."[103] Inoue thus proceeded to draft the Private Railway Regulations of 1887. As noted earlier, these provided not only for state assistance to railroad companies, but also for strict government supervision. To begin with, the regulations obliged railroad firms to start construction work within three months of receiving their licenses, the better to limit the possibility of speculation. They also authorized the government to oversee the building and operation of private lines and to order the companies to make necessary connections between their systems. Furthermore, the regulations reserved for the state the right to requisition private railroads in time of emergency as well as to purchase them after twenty-five years had elapsed from the date of their licensing.[104] Thus, in spite of Inoue's shifts and compromises, the minimum of his policy was observed.

In contrast to these changes in policy, Inoue showed no signs of wavering in the face of demands made by the army in 1887. These demands, which centered on inland construction of arteries, adoption of the standard gauge for track, and double-tracking of lines, signaled the intrusion of the military into the railway policy-making equation. To be sure, the army had recognized the importance of railway transport as early as the time of the Satsuma Rebellion, but until 1887, its activities in this field had been confined mainly to investigating the strategic role of railroads in

Europe. In particular, after the army began to take the German military system as a model in the late 1870s, it displayed a keen interest in the part played by rail transport during the Franco-Prussian War.[105] By 1887, the Army General Staff had formulated a comprehensive railway policy, which it was determined to realize through the demands it placed on Inoue.

The Railway Bureau chief responded by flatly denying the army's demands. Inoue contended that, since the changes desired by the General Staff would require an enormous outlay of resources, they could not possibly be accepted. He could, however, agree to one condition, namely, the participation of an army representative in railroad policy deliberations, provided the delegate was a competent person, well versed in railway matters. Inoue's firm stand revealed his determination to preserve the independence of the railway bureaucracy. The upshot of his intransigence was a total deadlock, a situation the army tried to overcome by appealing to public opinion, publishing in the following year a book on the strategic importance of railroads.[106] Though the views of the army and the Railway Bureau appeared to be diametrically opposed at this time, Inoue would soon take advantage of the military's demands to push his own proposal for a comprehensive railway policy.

During the 1880s, two new contestants, the Railway Bureau and the army, had thrust themselves into the railroad policy-making field. The Panic of 1890 and the ensuing recession triggered a further broadening of the policy arena, as business groups and local assemblies began to inundate the new Diet with demands for relief measures, including the nationalization of private lines. Inoue would seize the occasion to advance a coherent policy of railroad development under state control and would see this policy at least partly realized with the enactment of the Railway Construction Law of 1892.

THE PANIC OF 1890 AND ITS AFTERMATH

The Panic of 1890, Japan's first modern financial crisis, provided the immediate economic context for the making of the Railway Construction Law.[107] By disrupting the capital-raising mechanism of the boom years, the panic and the recession it brought on presented railway companies with their first real test. How did the private railroads, their financial backers, and their customers respond to the crisis? Were the rail firms actually in such dire straits in the early 1890s as to cause private business to welcome and even demand their nationalization?

The Panic of 1890 was basically a reaction to the excessive promotion and speculation accompanying the enterprise boom of the late 1880s. Ever since the beginning of the Meiji period, investment in joint-stock companies, both speculative and sound, had hinged on an installment system of stock payment, supported by the stock-collateral lending of commercial banks. Prior to the implementation of the Commercial Code in 1893, there were no legal regulations concerning the proportion of the par value of corporate shares that subscribers had to pay up at the time of a company's establishment, and fairly lenient requirements thereafter.[108] As a result, until the practice was legally abolished in 1948, almost all joint-stock enterprises, including railroad concerns, used an installment system for the payment of subscribed stock whereby shareholders would initially pay up only a portion of the par value of their shares, gradually paying up the rest as the business developed. This method enabled a company to collect payments commensurate with its immediate need for funds, thereby avoiding idle capital and reducing the weight of dividend payouts, and it also lightened the burden on stockholders of paying up high-denomination shares. Moreover, commercial banks underpinned the whole system by actively lending funds to stockholders on the security of the paid-up portion of their shares.[109]

The Kyushu Railway Company offers a clear example of how the installment-payment method worked in the case of private railroads. The installment schedule and actual record of payment for most of the Kyushu's first stock issue, as well as the railroad's initial construction program, are shown in Tables 2–3. As this firm's experience illustrates, railway companies laid their lines section by section, scheduling stock payments roughly in such a way as to have each installment cover the construction cost of the section about to be built. In the case of the Kyushu Railway, collection of the installment payments that financed the company's first six sections of line went relatively smoothly, especially after the firm started posting a favorable dividend rate and its shares began to be traded on the Tokyo and Osaka stock exchanges in 1889. But two years later, at the height of the post-panic recession, stockholders forced the firm to postpone work on the seventh and eighth sections of line and to collect only minimal sums for the corresponding installments.[110]

The installment-payment system and stock-collateral lending by banks greatly facilitated the founding and expansion of joint-stock companies, particularly under favorable business conditions such as prevailed after the Matsukata financial reform of the early 1880s. In so doing, these practices played a crucial role not only in giving rise to the enterprise boom of the late 1880s, but also in bringing about its collapse. In the absence of legal provisions governing the ratio of subscribed capital that a newly established firm had to raise forthwith, the installment method of stock payment allowed companies to be set up with only a fraction of their stock actually paid up. The result was a proliferation of joint-stock ventures, many of them unstable or purely speculative. Furthermore, payment by installment and borrowing on shares made it possible for investors to oversubscribe to newly issued stock in terms of their personal resources.[111] Such overextended holding was masked so long as the boom continued, but any significant decline in stock prices had the potential for disrupting the supply of share capital to corporations by causing banks to balk at making further loans on shares and stockholders to default on their payments.

As calls on share capital multiplied during the course of the boom, a growing proportion of available funds became tied up in the financing of joint-stock companies, much of it in the form of fixed investment that would remain unproductive for some time to come. Private rail firms, as proponents of their nationalization would argue in 1891, represented the leading "culprits" in this regard, for railroads had on the average the largest capital requirement and one of the longest gestation periods among joint-stock enterprises.[112] In fact, railroad concerns accounted for nearly a third of the increase in authorized capital, and probably for an even greater share of the rise in paid-up capital, for joint-stock companies as a whole between 1887 and 1889.[113]

During 1889, the pressure exerted on the money market by the paying up of corporate shares rose sharply, as the installment payments for companies founded during the enterprise boom fell due in growing numbers that year. By the end of 1889, for instance, residents of Osaka and its environs had paid up nearly twelve million yen in corporate stock, of which

TABLE 2 Installment Payments on Kyushu Railway Shares
(Total Par Value: ¥7,500,000), 1888–1892

Installment	Payment Deadline	Payment Due Per Share	Total Payment Due	Amt. Paid up by Deadline	Percentage Paid up	Date Paid up in Full
1	Nov. 30, 1888	¥5	¥750,000	¥285,000	38.0	July 4, 1889
2	Mar. 31, 1889	5	750,000	87,320	11.6	July 4, 1889
3	Aug. 31, 1889	10	1,500,000	1,168,730	77.9	June 24, 1890
4	May 31, 1890	5	750,000	570,275	76.0	Sep. 30, 1891
5	Oct. 31, 1890	5	750,000	555,895	74.1	Sep. 30, 1891
6	Mar. 5, 1891	5	750,000	522,285	69.6	Sep. 30, 1892
7	Aug. 5, 1891	2	300,000	106,812	35.6	Sep. 30, 1892
8	Nov. 30, 1891	1	150,000	121,624	81.1	Sep. 30, 1892
	Total Paid up:		¥5,700,000			

Source: "Kyūshū tetsudō kaisha chōsa hōkokusho," February 1900, in *Shibusawa Eiichi denki shiryō*, vol. 9, Shibusawa seien kinen zaidan ryūmonsha, ed. (Shibusawa Eiichi denki shiryō kankōkai, 1956), p. 277.

railway shares accounted for about four and a half million yen; roughly half of the latter, as well as over one million yen in spinning-company stock held by residents of that region, was paid up during 1889 alone. Bank loans undoubtedly financed most of the payments made on these shares that year, for partial evidence suggests that more than half of the eight and a half million yen in loans advanced by Osaka banks in 1889 had corporate stock as collateral, the majority of the latter being railway shares.[114]

This heightened demand for share capital, combined with the issuance of eleven million yen in government bonds and an increase in the price of rice owing to the poor harvest of 1889, produced a tightening of the money market. As a consequence, interest rates climbed, triggering a decline in stock prices. That, in turn, prompted banks to stop lending on the security of shares or to insist on more collateral. As early as July 4, 1889, the *Chōya* newspaper reported a sudden increase in stock payments and a suspension of stock-collateral lending by banks "fearful lest a panic should break out among the public." These trends intensified at the very close of the year, setting off the dreaded crisis with a panic on the Tokyo stock exchange in early January 1890. Stock prices plummeted. By increasingly refusing to make loans on shares, banks simply added to the financial stringency and the rise in interest rates, which further depressed stock prices.[115] Caught in this vicious circle, many joint-stock companies were thrust into a serious financial crisis. A number of the speculative ventures went bankrupt or dissolved, and even solid enterprises faced difficulties in raising capital. The panic itself lasted until March 1890, after which time the money market began to ease, but the ensuing recession let up only in 1893.

Thus, the major cause of the Panic of 1890 was the speculative mania of the late 1880s, which generated a flood of unsound firms and put heavy pressure on the money market. Inasmuch as the panic represented the collapse of the mania, it did not deal that severe a blow to established companies. In fact, contemporary business leaders, especially those in Tokyo, tended to discount the gravity of the crisis. In March 1890, for instance, Shibusawa Eiichi asserted that, "since the current tight money market was not caused by a lack of national power, but occurred just as national power was increasing, it is nothing to be deeply concerned about. If one were speaking of a human being, it would be as though a fever broke out not because the person became weak from an illness, but because he exercised

TABLE 3 Kyushu Railway, Sections of Line Opened, 1890–1891

Section	Date Opened	Length (miles)	Estimated Construction Cost
Hakata-Kurume	Mar. 1, 1890	23	¥924,954
Hakata-Ongagawa	Nov. 15, 1890	27	1,105,940
Ongagawa-Moji	Apr. 1, 1891	20	829,950
Kurume-Takase	Apr. 1, 1891	34	1,078,970
Takase-Kumamoto	Jul. 1, 1891	17	546,163
Tosu-Saga	Aug. 20, 1891	15	476,163
		Total:	¥4,962,140

Sources: *Nihon kokuyū tetsudō hyaku nen shi*, vol. 2 (Nihon kokuyū tetsudō, 1970), pp. 589, 601; *Tetsudō-kyoku nenpō, 1907*, appendix, pp. 3–4.

too much."[116] Yet, in view of the standard emphasis on the speculative nature of private railway enterprise during the boom, one would expect railroad companies to have been hard-hit by the panic. A close examination of the data, however, reveals a more complicated picture.

Scholars who stress the speculative character of railroad investment during the enterprise boom are apt to cite the critical observations of Railway Bureau Chief Inoue Masaru, who, as an outspoken advocate of state railway development, obviously had his own ax to grind. In March 1887, for example, Inoue depicted private promoters as wild-eyed speculators who had "contracted the railway disease, which has been epidemic of late," and two years later he was still harping on "the want of substantiality in the plans of railway projectors" and the prevalence of "capitalists whose sole object is to gain money by speculating in the sale and purchase of shares."[117] Certainly, speculative investors abounded during the boom, as the currency of the term *railway mania* in contemporary newspapers and journals attests, and undoubtedly they furthered a number of questionable schemes. Indeed, twenty of the thirty-seven promoters' groups that applied for licenses to establish railway companies during the years 1886–1889 failed, fourteen because their applications were rejected by the government and the rest because they were forced to disband at various stages prior to commencing construction.[118]

The important fact, however, is that nearly half these groups did succeed in establishing railroad firms and that the majority of the latter already had lines open to traffic by 1890. Moreover, most of these railroads, despite relying on direct and largely public stock subscriptions, managed to sell all their shares on schedule during the boom.[119] They did so by capitalizing on the very outburst of stock speculation that was giving rise to so many bubble companies during that time. As M. C. Reed observes of early Victorian railroads in a passage equally applicable to their mid-Meiji counterparts, speculation played an important part in "widening and deepening the sources from which railways were able to draw their capital. . . . The very possibility of speculative gains . . . attracted investors who in a more quiescent market would not have been prepared to accept the risks involved."[120] That such investors were enlisted in large numbers is suggested by the fact that, by the end of 1889, 62 percent of the operating rail companies' total authorized capital stock of ¥45,390,000 had been paid up.[121] As a whole, therefore, railroad firms during the enterprise boom were far from the fragile schemes that some observers have made them out to be.

By the time the panic struck, private railroads had made solid progress in the construction of lines. Twelve companies, all but three of them still in the process of extending their lines, had track open by March 1890 for a total length of 586 miles compared to 551 for the state railways.[122] The fact that these private firms were already operating lines indicates that they were by no means speculative ventures. Nevertheless, many had just recently been set up and were still in the early stages of construction. Having yet to show much in the way of profits, these companies were still struggling to win the confidence of lenders and investors. Thus, the panic found them in a much more precarious position than the older and more established firms.

Insofar as the speculative mania had markedly promoted private railroad investment during the enterprise boom, the reaction to that mania had at least some impact on all the railroad concerns. In particular, the decline in stock prices and the tight money situation made it extremely difficult for many of the companies' shareholders to meet payments on the outstanding portion of their subscribed stock. The plight of railroad stockholders is vividly described in a petition urging the nationalization of private railroads that brokers on the Tokyo stock exchange submitted to the Diet in late 1891:

Although their stock prices have fallen, railway companies have been steadily moving ahead with their construction work and have been urgently calling for stock payments. Even if the shareholders wish to comply with their demands, however, they are not free to do so because of the tight money market. As the enterprise mania has subsided, stock prices have dropped daily, and even if shareholders wish to sell on the stock market and sever their relationship with the companies, they can by no means make use of the exchange when a company has given notification and payment is unfinished, the market having strict regulations to that effect. Therefore, shareholders have increasingly rushed to liquidate their holdings by incurring debts and paying up their shares; stocks have flooded the market, and prices have dropped even further, with the result that selling at a loss has become more and more frequent. Circulating capital has poured into railway shares . . . With the money market tightening all the more, almost everyone shows signs of panic.[123]

The statistical data show that the current prices of most railway shares did indeed fall, some precipitously. In February 1890, the average monthly price of San'yō Railway shares on the Osaka exchange dropped below the paid-up value of the shares, remaining there throughout the recession (see Table 4). Similarly, in March 1890, the average monthly price of Kyushu Railway shares on the Osaka exchange fell below their paid-up value, equaling or surpassing that value in only one of the remaining months that year. In December 1890, these two kinds of shares hit their lowest point for the year, San'yō shares dropping 23 percent below their paid-up value and Kyushu shares, 18 percent. Data on the average annual prices of railway shares give a rough indication of the same trend. Of the eleven kinds of railway shares listed on the Tokyo or Osaka stock exchanges or both in 1890, the prices of eight either fell or remained below their paid-up values that year (see Table 5). Five of those eight did not recover their paid-up values until after 1892. Naturally, banks were reluctant to extend loans on the security of such depressed shares. The upshot was that a number of the more recently established railroads were forced to suspend construction work owing to the inability of stockholders to pay up.

Several scholars have downplayed the difficulties railway companies as a whole faced in raising construction capital at this time. Nakanishi, for example, argues that the panic had little impact on the expansion of private railroads: "Overall one can see no marked decline in the pace with which capital was paid in or lines were extended."[124] The data, however, suggest otherwise. In 1889, the total paid-up capital of railroad firms in operation had risen 86 percent over that of the previous year. The figure then dropped sharply during the panic and recession, falling below the 10-percent mark during the years 1892–1893 (see Table 6, Column 3). The comparable figures for length of line open show basically the same trend, albeit with a slight lag. Allowing for building time, one can see from the data in Table 6, Column 2, that little new construction was undertaken during the recession.

The panic also had a noticeable effect on the profit and dividend rates of several of the operating companies. The aggregate figures reveal a definite drop in the profit rate at the time of the panic, followed by a gradual recovery during the recession years. The overall dividend rate, however, remained fairly stable through this period, with government subsidies playing a critical role in maintaining that rate, particularly in 1890 when they accounted for 44 percent of all rail company dividends (see Table 6, Columns 5, 7, and 9).

The impact exerted by the panic on railway dividends as well as profits can be characterized more precisely through analysis of the rates of individual companies. The extent to which the crisis affected a given railroad depended not only on the level of development of that enterprise, but also on its primary source of revenue. Railroads such as the Hokkaido Colliery that derived their income mainly from the conveyance of goods, especially coal, sustained a sharp drop in profit rates, as the coal-mining industry was hard-hit by the recession (see Table 7). Also experiencing a decline or at least stagnation in their rates of profit were trunk-line firms in the early stages of construction, specifically the Kansai, San'yō, and Kyushu railways.[125] The returns of small interurban railroad concerns, however, fell little, if at all, since the demand for passenger transport, on which companies of this kind heavily relied, was much less influenced by business fluctuations than the demand for freight transport. Indeed, railroads like the Kōbu and Osaka enjoyed a steady increase in their rates of profit in spite of the panic and recession. These trends are also reflected in the companies' dividend rates, with the interurban railroads generally raising their rates throughout the period and most of the trunk-line firms either cutting theirs or keeping them at a low level (see Table 8).

The financial crisis placed in a far more serious predicament unsubsi-

TABLE 4 Average Monthly Quotations for San'yō and Kyushu Railway Shares, Osaka Stock Exchange, July 1889–December 1890

Year/Month	San'yō Railway	Kyushu Railway
1889/Jul.	¥42.19 (40)	¥24.79 (20)
Aug.	19.65 (20)	22.80 (20)
Sep.	20.00 (20)	24.40 (20)
Oct.	20.03 (20)	24.10 (20)
Nov.	21.25 (20)	26.15 (20)
Dec.	20.75 (20)	24.40 (20)
1890/Jan.	20.20 (20)	21.70 (20)
Feb.	18.10 (20)	20.05 (20)
Mar.	17.25 (20)	24.70 (25)
Apr.	16.08 (20)	23.70 (25)
May	17.40 (20)	25.20 (25)
Jun.	15.80 (20)	23.85 (25)
Jul.	17.95 (20)	24.00 (25)
Aug.	17.23 (20)	22.75 (25)
Sep.	16.70 (20)	26.65 (30)
Oct.	15.55 (20)	26.05 (30)
Nov.	15.60 (20)	24.60 (30)
Dec.	15.43 (20)	24.55 (30)

Source: Takizawa Naoshichi, Kōhon Nihon kin'yū shi ron (Yūhikaku, 1912), pp. 248–250.

Note: Figures in parentheses represent paid-up values.

dized concerns that had yet to begin operation and hence were unable as yet to offer investors any returns whatsoever to induce them to pay up their shares. The Sangū and Sōbu railways of the Kansai and Kantō areas, respectively, both came to a standstill during the early 1890s due to their inability to collect stock payments. Licensed in December 1889, the Sōbu Railway, despite having "completed arrangements to start construction,"[126] was forced to postpone work in 1890 when a number of stockholders defaulted on their payments. The normal practice in such instances was for the company to confiscate and put up for resale the shares of delinquent stockholders, but apparently the firm was too recently established for this step to be taken. On December 25, 1890, the Chōya newspaper reported that "the company is planning not to adopt such an extreme measure, but to supplement [its capital] by specially inviting new stock subscriptions through a broker." This course of action notwithstanding, the firm was unable to begin construction work until 1893.

Companies with lines open to traffic were not immune to such difficulties. This was particularly true of the Kyushu and San'yō railways, which, as recently founded trunk-line firms, had massive capital requirements and heavy construction loads, but nonetheless received relatively little assistance from the government. The crisis dealt these concerns a severe blow in the form of delays in both stock payments and construction work.

Significantly, however, the enterprise boom immediately following the post-panic recession would once again center on railroad firms, reflecting the fact that during the early 1890s, as one journal subsequently noted, "even if they did not reach their anticipated goals, relatively few companies had the misfortune of failing badly and then dissolving."[127] In fact, only one railroad that had obtained a full license—the prerequisite for issuing shares in the company's name and for starting construction work—namely, the Kōshin Railway, folded on account of the financial problems it experienced during the crisis.[128] Yet, apart from the Mito Railway, which merged with the Nippon in 1892, no railway enterprise with open track disbanded during the early 1890s. Cotton-spinning firms actually did not fare much worse in this regard—just two of them went bankrupt during the crisis—but they were clearly hit much harder than railway companies in terms of difficulties raising capital and sustaining profit and dividend rates.[129]

RAILWAY COMPANIES IN THE EARLY 1890S

Sound enterprises to begin with, operating railroads were, for the most part, never in grave peril during the crisis and, with passenger-oriented profit structures, government subsidies, and the like,[130] managed to come through it in comparatively good shape. Still, many railroad firms reacted to the panic and its aftermath as though the latter did constitute a life-threatening situation. To understand fully the behavior of private railroads at this time, one needs to examine the impact not only of the financial crisis itself, but also of the various groups that influenced railway-company decisions.

TABLE 5 Average Annual Quotations for Selected Railway Shares, 1888–1894 (unit: yen)

	Tokyo Stock Exchange				
Year	Nippon 1st Issue	Chikuhō Industrial	Ryōmō	Kōbu	Sanuki
1888	90.0 (50)	–	80.9 (100)	87.6 (75)	78.0 (65)
1889	–	25.9 (10)	47.8 (50)	107.5 (85)	69.9 (65)
1890	88.3 (50)	21.0 (25)	45.5 (50)	54.5 (45)	28.0 (50)
1891	–	–	42.5 (50)	–	30.2 (50)
1892	–	–	52.6 (50)	71.4 (45)	37.8 (50)
1893	102.5 (50)	55.7 (50)	81.2 (50)	108.1 (45)	47.9 (50)
1894	94.8 (50)	74.8 (50)	70.6 (50)	106.0 (45)	52.6 (50)

	Osaka Stock Exchange					
Year	San'yō 1st Issue	San'yō 2nd Issue	Kyushu	Hokkaido Colliery	Kansai	Osaka
1888	24.4 (25)	–	–	–	31.1 (25)	29.3 (32)
1889	20.3 (20)	5.3 (5)	24.6 (20)	–	45.3 (35)	41.0 (40)
1890	17.2 (20)	7.2 (10)	24.0 (25)	15.4 (15)	29.9 (38)	42.5 (50)
1891	22.9 (27)	19.3 (23)	28.8 (35)	52.2 (45)	33.2 (47)	44.3 (50)
1892	23.4 (27)	–	34.3 (38)	56.2 (50)	37.9 (47)	58.2 (50)
1893	31.8 (27)	–	41.2 (38)	77.5 (50)	57.6 (47)	85.3 (50)
1894	30.5 (27)	–	40.1 (38)	–	54.4 (47)	72.2 (50)

Sources: *Tōkyō kabushiki torihikijo gojū nen shi* (Tōkyō kabushiki torihikijo, 1928), Table 5; *Ō-kabu gojū nen shi* (Ōsaka kabushiki torihikijo, 1928), statistical appendix.

Note: Figures in parentheses represent paid-up values.

MAJOR RAILROAD STOCKHOLDERS. For any given railroad firm, the group most influential in decision making consisted of the company's top shareholders. During the Meiji period, private railroads on average raised about 80 percent of their financing through stock issues.[131] This high ratio of equity capital gave shareholders a sure basis for affecting, if not determining, the business strategies of railway enterprises.

The leading category of railway-company owners in the early 1890s comprised banks and their representatives. One is struck by the extent to which lists of major stockholders at this time are studded with bank executives. For example, in the October 1890 list for the Ryōmō Railway, which was founded in 1886, bank officers formed the largest class of investors whose occupations could be determined, accounting for at least fourteen of the eighty holders of 100 or more shares. These fourteen bankers possessed 25 percent of the railroad's total stock issue.[132]

Admittedly, many railway investors who were engaged in banking were concurrently involved in other fields of activity such as stockbroking or manufacturing. Such was the case, for example, with Tanaka Ichibei, Imamura Seinosuke, Matsumoto Jūtarō, and Hara Rokurō, who together held over 5 percent of the San'yō's 260,000 shares in September 1891.[133] One can assume, however, that, in many instances, sizable portions of the shares held by bank officials represented nominal holdings on behalf of the banks with which they were associated. This was particularly true of national banks, which evaded the prohibition against their ownership of corporate stock by investing in companies in the form of stock-collateral loans to their own directors and employees. In October 1890, for instance, the 4th National Bank of Niigata owned stock in the Ryōmō Railway in the name of one of its directors, Nishiwaki Kunisaburō. Nishiwaki's nominal and personal holdings in the company, amounting to 4,678 shares, made him the railroad's largest shareholder with over 15 percent of its entire stock.[134] Institutional investors, especially banks and life insurance companies, generally begin to surface on railway stockholders' lists only in the latter half of the 1890s; national banks do so after their conversion to ordinary bank status, at which time they were able to make public their holdings of railroad stock.[135] Until then, many private banks and insurance companies as well as national banks appear to have owned railway stock under their officers' names. In 1891, for instance, the Mitsui Bank held 1,012 shares of San'yō Railway stock under the name of its Kobe branch manager, and the Meiji Life Insurance Company, 1,000 shares under the name of its president.[136]

The most clearly documented case of bank investment in railroad stock is that of the 15th National Bank's involvement in the Nippon Railway Company.[137] Hugh Patrick and Kozo Yamamura have rightfully pointed out the uniqueness of this so-called "peers' bank," established as an investment organ for the nobility by Iwakura Tomomi and showered with special privileges by the government, and Yamamura claims that one should

TABLE 6 Private Railroad Development and Business Results, 1888–1894

Year	No. of Firms	Length of Line Open (miles)		Paid-up Capital (¥1,000)		Profit (¥1,000)	Profit as Percentage of Capital (%)	Dividend (¥1,000)	Dividend as Percentage of Capital (%)	State Subsidy (¥1,000)	Subsidy as Percentage of Dividend (%)
	(1)	(2)		(3)		(4)	(5)	(6)	(7)	(8)	(9)
1888	6	406		14,997		1,127	7.5	1,342	8.9	311	23.2
1889	12	525	(29.3)	27,943	(86.3)	1,427	5.1	1,927	6.9	648	33.6
1890	12	849	(61.7)	38,493	(37.8)	1,630	4.2	2,612	6.8	1,147	43.9
1891	13	1,166	(37.3)	43,441	(12.9)	2,122	4.9	3,099	7.1	1,017	32.8
1892	13	1,320	(13.2)	46,737	(7.6)	2,659	5.7	2,782	6.0	955	34.3
1893	15	1,368	(3.6)	48,870	(4.6)	3,470	7.1	3,725	7.6	887	23.8
1894	20	1,537	(12.4)	59,177	(21.1)	4,648	7.9	4,564	7.7	779	17.1

Sources: Tetsudō-kyoku nenpō, 1907, appendix, pp. 22–46 passim, p. 102; Nihon teikoku tōkei nenkan, vol. 13 (Naikaku shokikan-shitsu tōkei-ka, 1894), p. 703; and vol. 14 (1895), p. 712.

Note: Figures in parentheses represent percentage increase over previous year.

therefore exclude this institution from discussion of the role of banks in industrial financing during the Meiji period.[138] Yet, as Hoshino Takao has shown, the 15th National, like the Nippon Railway with which it was so closely tied, gradually lost the favored status it had enjoyed at its founding. In particular, following the revocation of its most important privileges with the revision of the National Bank Act in 1883, that bank came to operate by and large under the same constraints as the other national banks. Moreover, although the peers' bank was apparently exempted from the ban on corporate stockholding by national banks, it nevertheless complied with this regulation and, like other national banks, invested in railway shares under the names of its directors and employees.[139] Regardless of the bank's degree of uniqueness, however, one simply cannot omit from consideration of bank financing, at least of railway companies, an institution that, through its investment in the Nippon Railway alone, accounted for a minimum of 9 percent and more likely for 15 percent of the total paid-up capital of private railroads in the early 1890s.[140]

According to Hoshino, at the time of the establishment of the Nippon Railway in 1881, the 15th National Bank accepted 26,000 shares in the company with a par value of ¥1,300,000, or 22 percent of the railroad's first stock issue, making it the Nippon's largest stockholder.[141] Because of the prohibition against corporate stockholding by national banks, however, the 15th National concealed its investment in the Nippon Railway by having its shares held under the names of former daimyo and samurai who were directors and employees of the bank. It then advanced stock-collateral loans to these individuals in order to finance installment payments on its shares. In 1881, the Nippon Railway required stockholders to make an initial payment of ¥1 per share. The nominal holders of the shares owned by the 15th National thus had to pay in ¥26,000, which was precisely the amount of stock-collateral loans made by the bank in 1881. The same correlation held at the end of the following year, when the sum of installment payments on Nippon Railway stock that the bank's nominal holders had to have met—¥260,000—equaled the total amount of funds lent by the bank on the collateral of corporate shares. Thereafter, the 15th National began to make loans on shares other than those it possessed in the Nippon Railway, so that by the end of 1892, the minimum amount that the bank had to have paid in on its share of Nippon Railway stock, assuming that it had contin-

TABLE 7 Income Structures and Profit Rates of Selected Railway Companies, 1888–1894 (unit: ¥1,000)

Year	*Hokkaido Colliery (Licensed Nov. 1889)*			*San'yō (Licensed Jan. 1888)*			*Kansai (Licensed Mar. 1888)*			*Osaka (Licensed Mar. 1888)*			*Kōbu (Licensed Mar. 1888)*		
	Passenger Income	*Freight Income*	*Profit Rate*	*Passenger Income*	*Freight Income*	*Profit Rate*	*Passenger Income*	*Freight Income*	*Profit Rate*	*Passenger Income*	*Freight Income*	*Profit Rate*	*Passenger Income*	*Freight Income*	*Profit Rate*
			(%)			(%)			(%)			(%)			(%)
1888	–	–	–	–	–	2.1	–	–	–	–	–	–	–	–	–
1889	–	–	–	136	14	2.9	10	0	0.1	46	4	2.4	55	12	5.8
1890	71	219	6.1	154	26	1.9	47	11	0.4	76	9	3.3	70	20	6.5
1891	106	276	4.7	281	48	2.9	120	40	2.9	141	34	5.9	70	21	7.3
1892	120	304	2.6	349	87	4.0	150	28	1.8	173	39	7.0	75	31	9.4
1893	123	336	5.1	415	112	5.0	146	46	4.2	212	48	8.3	83	39	10.9
1894	148	412	4.4	712	301	8.4	187	65	3.8	231	62	8.0	100	46	12.2

Source: Tetsudō-kyoku nenpō, 1907, appendix, pp. 22–104 passim.

ued to pay up its initial subscription and had accepted all three of its capital-increase allotments since then, had declined to about one fourth of its outstanding stock-collateral loans.[142]

However, in May 1897, when the 15th National became an ordinary bank and made public its ownership of Nippon Railway stock, it held some 260,000 shares in the railroad—about a third of all the shares of Nippon stock—with a combined paid-up value of around ten million yen.[143] That is over one and a half times the minimum investment the bank had to have made by the middle of 1897 under the aforementioned assumptions. This fact indicates that the 15th National had increased its equity participation in the Nippon Railway by purchasing additional shares beyond its capital-increase allotments. It further suggests that, in 1892, the proportion of the bank's outstanding stock-collateral loans that actually represented investment in Nippon Railway shares owned by the bank was in fact closer to one half than to one quarter. The 15th National thus maintained its position as Japan's leading railway shareholder, despite the proliferation of private rail companies during the Meiji era (the bank was to acquire an interest—a relatively minor one—in only one other railroad concern[144]).

A second group of railway stockholders, significant in terms not of their numbers but of the level of their investment, comprised the future zaibatsu builders, particularly Mitsubishi and Mitsui. Mitsubishi was the second largest shareholder in private railroads throughout the period until the nationalization of 1906–1907. By the early 1890s, it had considerably narrowed the gap between its holdings of railroad stock and those of the 15th National Bank. In 1891, whereas the 15th National held at least 79,000 shares in the Nippon Railway, Mitsubishi had 28,371 shares in the San'yō,[145] more than 11,000 in the Nippon,[146] and substantial interests in several other railway companies. (All these shares had par values of ¥50.) Mitsubishi plainly capitalized on the panic and recession to snatch up railroad stocks at depressed prices. Between 1889 and 1892, for instance, Iwasaki Hisaya raised his share of the San'yō Railway's total stock from 5.4 to 11.2 percent. In Kyushu, he purchased a large block of shares in the Chikuhō Industrial Railway in March 1891 to become its top shareholder and, from July 1891 to April 1893, more than tripled his holdings in the Kyushu Railway, solidifying his position at the head of its stockholders' list with a 6.9-percent stake in the firm. The financial crisis enabled Mitsubishi to optimize the

TABLE 8 Dividend Rates of Selected Railway Companies, 1888–1894
(unit: %)

Year/Semester		Nippon	San'yō	Kyushu	Hokkaido Col.	Kansai	Osaka	Kōbu	Hankai
1888	1st	12.0	–	–	–	–	–	–	–
	2nd	12.0	4.08	6.0	–	–	–	–	10.0
1889	1st	11.0	3.28	6.0	–	–	2.5	6.3	–
	2nd	11.0	3.0	6.0	–	2.1	2.5	6.0	12.0
1890	1st	11.0	6.0	6.0	10.0	0.9	2.4	7.0	–
	2nd	10.0	6.0	6.0	10.0	0	3.6	5.0	11.0
1891	1st	9.0	4.1	6.0	10.0	1.7	5.0	7.0	–
	2nd	10.0	2.76	4.25	8.0	3.8	5.0	6.2	12.0
1892	1st	10.0	3.33	4.0	7.5	3.6	6.6	8.0	–
	2nd	10.0	4.0	4.0	7.2	4.3	6.6	8.3	13.0
1893	1st	10.0	4.5	4.74	7.5	0	8.0	10.0	–
	2nd	10.0	4.5	5.53	8.0	4.0	8.0	10.0	15.0
1894	1st	10.0	5.5	7.0	12.0	6.8	8.5	12.0	–
	2nd	10.0	7.0	7.5	12.0	4.7	9.6	10.0	17.0

Sources: Teikoku tetsudō yōkan, 3rd ed. (Tetsudō jihō-kyoku, 1906), pp. 65–367 passim; Ōsaka tetsudō ryaku reki (Osaka: Kakehi Teizō, 1901), appendix, Table 4; Hankai tetsudō keireki shi (Matsumoto Jūtarō, 1899), appendix, Table 5.

conversion of its principal stockholding assets from shipping-company, specifically N.Y.K., stocks to those of private railroad concerns.[147]

Mitsui embarked on large-scale investment in railroads somewhat later than Mitsubishi, although, by 1893, it had surpassed the Imperial Household to become the third largest stockholder in railway companies, a position it held until the 1906–1907 nationalization.[148] Mitsui did enter the recession with roughly a 1-percent interest—3,000–4,000 shares—in the Nippon Railway and a 3-percent interest in the Ryōmō.[149] But as for the two companies that would eventually be the primary targets of its railway investment activities, Mitsui under the names of its representatives fails to appear on an 1894 list of leading stockholders in the Hokkaido Colliery and Railway and barely does so on the 1891 list for the San'yō Railway.[150] On the other hand, Mitsui in the early 1890s may have had as many as 8,125 shares in the Kyushu Railway, a number second only to that of Mitsubishi, and by 1893, it had also become the second largest stockholder in the San'yō Railway with 17,399 shares compared to the 32,220 held by Iwasaki Hisaya.[151]

Another major class of railway stockholders consisted of former daimyo and aristocrats, including nominal investors representing the Imperial Household Ministry. With a 10-percent interest in the Hokkaido Colliery and Railway, approximately a 2-percent interest in the Nippon, and minor holdings in one or two smaller companies, the Imperial Household was the third largest shareholder in private railroads during at least the first two years of the recession.[152] Railroad financing by members of the nobility likewise centered in the heavily subsidized Nippon and Hokkaido Colliery. In the Nippon Railway, besides the huge sums of money based on daimyo commutation bonds that were channeled through the 15th National Bank, nobles sank in personal funds around nine hundred thousand yen, equivalent to about 16 percent of the company's total stock issue, at the time of its establishment. Members of this class also invested fairly extensively in smaller unsubsidized railroads like the Kōbu and Sōbu of the Kantō region. Ex-daimyo often did so in cases where such firms built and operated lines within their former domains.[153]

A fourth category of major railway stockholders encompassed industrial capitalists, exclusive of bank and emergent zaibatsu executives. These investors hailed chiefly from the Tokyo and Osaka areas, although local industrialists, such as the Kyushu coal-mine operators who helped to finance the Chikuhō Industrial Railway, figured prominently in certain companies. Of the big-city capitalists, Fujita Denzaburō, who was involved in shipping as well as in various industrial enterprises in Osaka, had motives for investing in private railroads that were more in tune with those of local businessmen than of his metropolitan colleagues. Like the Kyushu mining entrepreneurs, who poured money into railroads mainly to secure improved transport and enlarged markets for their coal, Fujita was principally interested in the indirect benefits resulting from his railway investment, specifically, in the railroad-building contracts that would accrue to his construction firm.[154] More typical of the big-city industrial capitalists was Amenomiya Keijirō. A diversified entrepreneur in the Tokyo area, Amenomiya took a strong interest in railway finance mainly out of a desire to reap direct returns in the form of stock dividends. By the early 1890s, with substantial holdings in the highly profitable Hokkaido Colliery and Kōbu railroads, he was well on the way to earning his eventual sobriquet of "private railway king."[155]

A final group of principal railway owners consisted of capitalists who financed their purchases of railroad stock using income drawn primarily from the more traditional activities of land ownership, trade, and moneylending. Perhaps the biggest railway stockholder among the pure landlord capitalists was Moroto Seiroku of Mie Prefecture, who invested heavily in Kyushu railroads.[156] Among traders, the leading railway shareholder at this time—and eventually one of the top investors among all groups—was Tanaka Shinshichi, a Yokohama cotton-yarn merchant.[157] A related field of activity widely engaged in by railway investors, although one might quibble with its inclusion under the rubric "traditional," was the stock- and commodity-exchange business. The prominence of this subgroup of shareholders, many of whom were stockbrokers, bespeaks the speculative character of a good portion of railway investment.

Major railway stockholders engaged in the brokerage business naturally tended to come from Tokyo and Osaka, cities with relatively developed markets in commodities and securities, as did those involved in trade and, to a much less extent, in land ownership. Yet the landlord-merchant category represents another group, in addition to that of industrial capitalists, in which one would expect to find fairly extensive participation by local investors eager to reduce transport costs and to expand markets for locally produced rice, raw silk, and so on. Indeed, descriptions of the sources of railway-share capital during the Meiji period commonly list capitalists residing along the projected routes of rail lines as forming one of the principal classes of railroad investors, especially in the case of smaller companies serving local markets. Sugiyama Kazuo, for example, states that "most local railroads were established and planned by local notables (*meibōka*) such as landlords and merchants."[158] Certainly, such investors played an important role in the promotion not only of local companies such as the Ryōmō and Chikuhō Industrial, but also of trunk-line firms such as the San'yō and Kyushu. Moreover, local landlords and merchants did on occasion become major stockholders of railroads that ran through their communities. For instance, Onishi Shin'yuemon, a large landlord and sake brewer of Hyōgo prefecture, helped to promote as well as finance the San'yō Railway, in which he was the tenth largest stockholder with almost a 1-percent interest in September 1891.[159] In the Ryōmō Railway, which traversed the textile manufacturing districts of Gunma and Tochigi prefectures north of Tokyo, local merchants connected with the textile industry were represented by at least eight of the company's top eighty stockholders in October 1890. Together, these eight traders held nearly 6 percent of the railroad's total stock.[160] Meanwhile, "local" merchants were naturally heavily involved in the financing of the Osaka and Kōbu railways, since parts of these companies' lines lay within the city limits of Osaka and Tokyo, respectively.

Yet, looking more closely at the geographical distribution of investors and expanding the field of vision to encompass small and medium shareholders, one obtains a very different picture of local investment. In the Kōbu Railway, for example, in March 1891, textile manufacturers, raw-silk dealers, and other investors from the Santama region, at the western end of the line opposite Tokyo, accounted for less than one quarter of the total number of stockholders and barely 8 percent of all the shares.[161] In the case of the Ryōmō Railway, a prefectural breakdown of the stockholders in 1890 reveals that Tokyo prefecture held first place with almost half the total, followed by Tochigi and Gunma, the prefectures in which the line was situated, together with over one quarter. In terms of percentage of total stock accounted for, Tokyo again topped the list with some 39 percent; Tochigi and Gunma, however, came a distant fourth and fifth, respectively, with only 18 percent of the total combined.[162]

These examples point out the need to qualify the notion of the importance of local investment in smaller railroads, at least for the early 1890s. Takechi Kyōzō presents data indicating that, by the mid-1890s, local financing of such railroads had increased substantially, especially with the proliferation of local lines during the second railway boom. Even in the established Ryōmō Railway, nineteen of the top forty-five stockholders hailed from Tochigi and Gunma in 1896 whereas only ten had done so in 1890.[163] Sugiyama suggests that this trend continued into the mid-1900s, by which time there was "extensive participation [in railway finance] by local men of wealth, particularly landlords and capitalists residing along railroad lines."[164] However, practically all of the evidence for the panic and recession years as well as for the preceding boom period attests to the limited scale of local investment, even though most railroads established during this heyday of trunk-railroad incorporation were actually local in character.[165] In the late 1880s and early 1890s, whether because of the shortage or timidity of local capital, railway stockholders living along the line in which they invested rarely held enough shares as a group to give them majority ownership in the operating company.

Even in cases where local capitalists did take the lead at this time in the promotion and initial financing of railroad firms, the companies concerned tended to draw increasingly on sources of capital outside the areas served by their lines. For example, the local coal-mine owners who founded the Chikuhō Industrial Railway in July 1889 faced serious financial problems with the outbreak of the 1890 Panic. According to an employee of the railroad, "since the majority of stockholders were all having difficulty meeting the expenses of their main business—coal mining—they could not possibly afford to pay up their shares in the railroad, which was from the beginning [only] a side business"; consequently, the company "could not avoid changes among its stockholders."[166] At the end of September 1889, residents of the Chikuhō region accounted for 48 percent of the total number of stockholders in the railroad. By the end of March 1890, this figure had dropped to 37 percent, at which time most of the investors holding 200 or more shares in the company were nobles and other capitalists from Tokyo.[167]

The pattern of limited local, and large-scale metropolitan, investment was particularly marked in the case of trunk-line concerns. In the San'yō Railway, the second largest rail company at this time in terms of paid-up capital, residents of Osaka prefecture accounted for 35 percent of all the shares in September 1891; those of Tokyo prefecture, for 31 percent; and those of the four prefectures through which the railroad would eventually run, for only 21 percent combined.[168] As with most other railroad firms, the San'yō's heavy reliance on capital from distant urban centers, especially Osaka and Tokyo, was to have serious implications for its business strategy during the panic and recession.

This overview of the occupational and geographical distribution of railway stockholders during the early 1890s points to the conclusion that private railroads had attracted investors who were by and large cautious and risk-avoiding. To be sure, as a result of the mania preceding the panic, railway investment included a significant risk-taking component in the form of short-term, speculative finance, as suggested by the prominence of stockbrokers on railway shareholders' lists. Risk-taking in a far different sense from such passive, impersonal investment was that of local capitalists and many nonlocal merchants and industrialists, including the emergent zaibatsu. Presumably, these investors were more concerned with the external economies of railroad building than with the direct return on their investment.

The vast majority of railway-share capital, however, represented an investment attitude that fell in between these two extremes. Like the speculators, investors of this persuasion—bankers, nobles, and most other big-city capitalists—had their eye primarily on profits, though in the form of steady dividends rather than capital gains; yet generally, they also had a long-term commitment to the interests of particular companies and, as we shall see, frequently took part in their management. On the other hand, to the extent that such capitalists were from distant urban centers and were unlikely to share in the indirect benefits of railroad development, their vested interest in the companies they helped to finance, except for the few who made railroads their career, was rather qualified and their sense of ownership, closer to that of speculative investors than of local capitalists.

Railway companies drew bankers and nobles, in particular, by offering safe and remunerative investment opportunities. One reason railroads had such attraction, aside from government subsidization in the case of the large, trunk-line firms, was that most of them centered their operations on passenger transport, and therefore business cycles exerted relatively little impact on their revenues and dividends.[169] As indicated earlier, this was especially true of interurban lines such as the Kōbu and Hankai railways, whose dividends were stabilized at a comparatively high level because of the constant or rising demand for passenger transport in the more densely populated parts of the country (see Table 8). In the case of the Kyushu, San'yō, and Kansai railways, however, the passenger orientation of their business was of little advantage to them at the time of the panic when they were still far from completing their lines and received only moderate or no subsidies from the government. For these companies, the expectation that, once the lines were finished, shareholders would enjoy stable but high dividends, though based increasingly on freight income, seems to have been the operative factor in drawing cautious yet profit-seeking investors. Such capitalists had good reason, therefore, to push for completion of railroad construction work; nevertheless, when faced with a choice, as Sugiyama puts it, "they naturally sought security rather than positive growth in the enterprise."[170]

The tendency towards risk avoidance and profit maximization on the part of railway investors had several consequences for railway company policy during the panic and recession. First, railroad firms were increasingly pressed by shareholders to economize. Such retrenchment involved cutting back not only on operating expenditures so as to increase net income, but also on capital investment so as to reduce immediate demand for stock payments. One form of the latter economy was curtailment of construction costs. Albert Fishlow, writing of antebellum American railroads, offers a positive appraisal of such economizing. In the United States, according to Fishlow, cheap construction methods constituted one of several procedures that served to maximize the rate of return on railway investment and hence to make railroad projects more attractive to private investors. Fishlow states that "engineering considerations always ranked second to early completion, as the small extent of tunneling and double tracking, among other characteristics, bears witness"; these and other building practices enabled railroad firms not only to foreshorten the gestation period, but also "to economize on the absolute quantities of capital needed. Durability was sacrificed for lower capital costs . . ."[171] In sum, these methods helped to reduce the huge capital requirements of railroad construction, thereby easing railway companies' access to needed funds. Much of what Fishlow says here of American private railroads applies equally to their Japanese counterparts during the Meiji period. In Meiji railroads as well, the use of high gradients, single-tracking, and the like represented efforts to lessen the difficulty of raising construction capital by minimizing expenditure on plant. Such practices, which began before the 1890 Panic, were, to a large degree, simply ways in which railroad firms coped as best they could with an underdeveloped capital market.

Nevertheless, during the crisis years of the early 1890s, economy measures of this sort appear at times to have been carried to such an extreme that they ultimately proved detrimental to the companies concerned. Such was the case, for instance, with the Kyushu Railway. A committee appointed to investigate the company's business affairs in 1899 reported that, from its founding in 1888 until the Sino-Japanese War of 1894–1895, the Kyushu Railway had been compelled by stockholders "to make its policy the curtailment of construction expenses to the fullest extent possible."[172] As another observer put it, "the Kyushu Railway was dominated from the beginning by the vulgar view that it should economize on construction expenditures"; such economizing reached a peak during the recession, when the company left various facilities in an "excessively makeshift" state and employed extremely steep gradients in building its line.[173] The 1899 committee remarked that Hermann Rumschöttel, the German engineer employed as an adviser by the railroad, "knew from the start that the [company's construction] plans were inadequate and predicted that the firm would some day regret it"; under pressure from its shareholders, however, the railroad was in the end forced to proceed "as if it were carrying out temporary construction work."[174] And, just as Rumschöttel had anticipated, the company in later years had to spend enormous sums of money to offset the shortcomings of its original plans.

Meanwhile, the San'yō Railway witnessed another form of stockholder-induced retrenchment of capital expenditure, namely, a lowering of fixed investment in rolling stock. In anticipation of future demand, President Nakamigawa Hikojirō had imported large quantities of passenger and freight cars from Britain, especially during 1890–1891, when the number of cars rose from 270 to 684. Nakamigawa's policy was to spare no expense in order to obtain rolling stock of the highest quality. Accordingly, all the cars he purchased featured state-of-the-art vacuum brakes, making the San'yō the first private railroad to use such equipment.[175] Once Nakamigawa resigned in October 1891, however, the company "was dominated by the Osaka school of economization."[176] Osaka capitalists, who together held a majority interest in the railroad and had long been clamoring for retrenchment, prevailed on the firm to sell off much of the rolling stock that Nakamigawa had imported. Thus, in 1892, the company sold to the state Railway Bureau and the Nippon Railway about a third of its freight and passenger cars on the grounds that the previous management "had made unnecessary purchases."[177] As with the Kyushu Railway and its cheap construction policy, though, the San'yō would eventually pay for its decision to economize on rolling stock: during the post-Sino-Japanese War boom, the company faced a shortage of cars and had to buy back for over twice the sale price those it had unloaded only a few years earlier.[178]

A second result of the cautious investment behavior of railway shareholders was that, once the recession set in, they were quick to demand suspension of installment payments and construction work alike. In early 1891, for instance, over a hundred stockholders in the Kyushu Railway petitioned the company to postpone scheduled construction work once the line had reached Kumamoto and Saga and, for the time being, to suspend the collection of stock payments.[179] The firm's officers agreed to accept these demands in view of the financial crisis. Finance Minister Matsukata Masayoshi, in reporting his approval of the company's application for an extension of the construction deadlines for the seventh and eighth sections of line beyond Kumamoto and Saga, quoted Kyushu Railway President Takahashi Shinkichi as explaining, "One after another, the majority of principal stockholders from Tokyo, Osaka, and so on have requested suspension of the construction work because of the tight money market and the difficulty of paying up shares. Since the circumstances are unavoidable, the board of directors has voted to postpone [the deadlines] . . ."[180] As for stock payments, the company decided to call in ¥2 per share, instead of the usual ¥5, for the seventh installment, due August 5, 1891, and ¥1 per share for the eighth installment, due November 30, 1891, and to put off subsequent collections.[181] Despite the lenient terms of payment, these installments, together with the preceding one, were not fully paid in until September 30, 1892.

In the meantime, in late 1891, stockholders pressured the Kyushu Railway to apply for a second extension of the deadlines for the seventh and eighth sections of line. In his new application to the government, President Takahashi again suggested that big-city capitalists represented the driving force behind the railroad's decision for postponement: "Since finance is still not smooth and the value of the stock continues to decline, the principal stockholders from Tokyo, Osaka, and so on have one after another requested suspension of the construction work, citing the difficulty of paying up their shares, and, because raising construction funds for both of these sections would only give rise to various complaints, there is no prospect of proceeding smoothly . . ."[182] Approved by the government in April 1892, the new extension pushed the deadline for both sections back a full year from the initial one-year extension date, to December 1894. In fact, the two sections were not completed until 1895–1896, as the company recovered only slowly from the recession.[183]

Another consequence of the conservative character of railway investors, and perhaps the clearest expression of stockholder domination of railroad firms, was the tendency for profits to be paid out almost completely as dividends. In the Kyushu Railway, for instance, dividends accounted for all the profits and subsidies for 1889 and apparently for 1890 as well. In the following year, ¥3,000, or 1 percent of the profits and subsidies, was applied to directors' bonuses, ¥45 to retained earnings, and the rest to dividends. The year 1892 was the first in which the company put profits into reserves, although the amount allocated for that purpose—¥3,400—represented only 1.5 percent of the railroad's net income.[184] Beginning in 1893, the company raised the reserve rate to a more substantial 4 to 5 percent of annual profits.[185] Nonetheless, the overwhelming majority of those profits continued, as before, to be paid out as dividends.

Other railroads experienced a similar pattern of profit distribution; for example, the Osaka and Kansai, both founded in 1888, did not begin to put profits into reserves until 1891 and 1893, respectively, and other firms generally allotted only nominal amounts for that purpose in the early 1890s. The major exception was the Nippon Railway, which routinely allocated for reserves around 5 percent of its profits and subsidies during the recession. The Nippon, of course, was a well-established company with a healthy cash flow, thanks in part to generous government subvention, and it could well afford to build up its reserves. By contrast, younger firms could spare little, if any, of their profits other than for dividends, faced as they were with the need to attract investors and encourage them to meet installment deadlines during the critical early stages of construction.[186] Moreover, as Patrick points out, the railroads had to satisfy the demands of stockholders for "dividend payouts at least sufficient to cover the interest charges on the [bank] loans" that many of them used to pay up their shares; few companies at this time had rates of return that exceeded the loan interest rate, "so profits tended to be paid out fully."[187]

The railroads were also constrained in their dividend policy by the conservative attitudes or, as Patrick puts it, "the relatively short-run time horizons of many investors, . . . who preferred to receive profits as income rather than plow them back as retained earnings."[188] Such attitudes were slow to change. Whereas in 1890 the combined reserves of private railroads amounted to 1.3 percent of their total paid-up capital, in 1900, after a decade of growth in profit rates, the figure had risen to only 2 percent.[189] Nearsighted profit distribution thus characterized Meiji railway companies well beyond the early years of comparatively low profitability. This fact strongly suggests that, during the early 1890s, stockholder conservatism was no less important than business performance in determining the dividend policies of private railroads.

Finally, the risk-avoiding proclivity of railway shareholders and particularly their weak sense of ownership in the railroad firms in which they invested meant that, as the recession unfolded, many of them were apparently prepared to go to the extreme of dissolving the corporation through merger or nationalization. The level of stockholder demand for either form of corporate disbandment, however, bears important qualification. During the early 1890s, there were two instances of attempted amalgamation between established railway companies. Each involved the Nippon Railway and one of two Nippon "affiliates," the Mito and Ryōmō. The latter two firms had from the start entrusted the building and operation of their lines entirely to the Nippon and by extension to the state railways, and in August 1887, the government had approved a joint request by the three firms that the Mito and Ryōmō "be regarded as branch lines of the Nippon

Railway Company and that all their construction work and the like be carried out by the Railway Bureau, as in the case of the Nippon . . ."[190] These arrangements naturally predisposed the companies to merge with each other, a tendency reinforced by the fact that President Naraharu Shigeru of the Nippon served concurrently as president of the other two railroads in 1890–1891.[191] The only other railway company in a comparable situation was the Kōbu, which operated another "branch line" of the Nippon and whose relationship to the latter was similar to that of the Ryōmō and Mito. In the case of the Kōbu Railway, however, a relatively high dividend rate (6 percent in 1890 compared to 4.68 percent for the Ryōmō and 4.6 for the Mito)[192] militated against the rise of pro-merger sentiment. In fact, by vote of the stockholders, that company took over operation of its line from the Nippon Railway in late 1891, by which year its dividend rate had risen to 6.6 percent.[193]

By contrast, investor dissatisfaction over the poor business results of the Mito Railway was enough to produce the only successful merger attempt among railway companies during the recession. In early 1891, the view prevailed among Mito stockholders that they had more to gain by combining their firm with the Nippon Railway than by maintaining it as a separate entity. As the preponderance of nonlocal men among the directors of the Mito suggests, the reason why this view gained ascendancy within the firm was that cautious, nonlocal capitalists predominated among its stockholders.[194] The latter voted at their general meeting on April 29, 1891, to convey all the company's assets to the Nippon Railway. In return, in February 1892, they received from the Nippon ¥810,000 in corporate bonds bearing 6-percent interest, equivalent to a modest but secure return of 5.4 percent on their investment in the railroad.[195]

The experience of the Ryōmō stood in between those of its fellow Nippon affiliates and presents a vivid illustration of the dominant tendencies among railway stockholders. Like the Mito Railway, the Ryōmō witnessed a strong merger movement, but in this case the movement failed, and the company followed the Kōbu lead in opting for independent management. In May 1892, three months before the appointed expiration of the contract whereby the railroad entrusted operation of its line to the Nippon, the Ryōmō called a special stockholders' meeting to decide whether the firm should manage the line on its own or sell out to the Nippon. At the meeting, according to the *Tōkyō keizai zasshi*, local and Tokyo capitalists clashed sharply over the issue, with "the local stockholders mainly advocating independence and the Tokyo stockholders primarily advocating sale." As no agreement could be reached at the time, it was finally decided to set up a committee to resolve the matter. Significantly, three of the five men elected to the committee were local capitalists involved in the textile trade. Given the composition of the committee, it comes as no surprise that its members "decided in the end to [have the railroad] become independent in accordance with the majority opinion of the stockholders."[196] At the committee's request, the Ryōmō's newly elected president then consulted with his opposite number in the Nippon Railway in order to determine whether the latter would be willing to renew its contract to operate the Ryōmō line. In the course of this discussion, the president of the Nippon made it clear that his firm would not be able to do so, the Nippon having just taken over operation of its own lines from the Railway Bureau in April 1892, but that it would give the Ryōmō every facility in order to ease its transition to self-management. Having received this assurance of cooperation from the Nippon Railway, the Ryōmō stockholders at a special general meeting in July "voted unanimously to [have their firm] become independent as of October 1st,"[197] and in September, the Ryōmō and Nippon so notified the Railway Bureau.[198]

On the face of it, it would appear that the local stockholders in the Ryōmō Railway had scored a stunning victory over their numerically superior Tokyo counterparts: they had somehow managed to stave off the merger bid of the rapacious big-city capitalists (at least for the time being—the company eventually did sell out to the Nippon Railway in 1896, at the start of a wave of mergers largely accompanying the panics of 1897–1898 and 1900–1901).[199] One might conclude from this case that, when a proposed action threatened the independent existence of a railway line, local investors were at times able to muster sufficient strength to prevent that action from being taken; in short, there were limits to what nonlocal capitalists could do.

In fact, however, the experience of the Ryōmō Railway was much more complicated than the above interpretation would imply. The leader of the pro-merger faction was indeed a Tokyo capitalist, Imamura Seinosuke, who was also acting president of the company until the latter part of May

1892. Imamura campaigned aggressively on behalf of selling out to the Nippon, appealing directly to the conservative instincts of the shareholders. By withdrawing from the railroad, he argued, investors "would not have to worry about future difficulties," and, since the Nippon Railway "has from the beginning regarded the Ryōmō as its own branch line, it is sure to agree readily to [its acquisition], . . . and it will not be hard at all to sell out for a high price."[200]

On the other hand, proponents of independent management also seem to have been led by a Tokyo investor, the famous journalist Taguchi Ukichi. The first president of the Ryōmō, Taguchi had envisioned the company at its founding as an "industrial railway," likening it to the Liverpool and Manchester in England, and he had close ties to at least one of the local promoters of the firm.[201] Hence, to that extent, one can perhaps view Taguchi as a spokesman for local interests. Yet, local merchants and industrialists were by no means the only stockholders with a vested interest in the railroad transcending their immediate investment, as suggested by the appearance of metropolitan dry-goods dealers and the like on the major stockholders' list for 1890.[202]

Taguchi and his supporters, however, centered their argument not on the wider regional benefits of railway investment and control, but on the terms and timing of the proposed merger. Prior to the May meeting of the shareholders, Imamura had negotiated an unofficial agreement with President Ono Yoshimasa of the Nippon Railway whereby the latter would buy out the Ryōmō's stock at ¥48.5 a share, or about ¥13 above the market price.[203] Opponents of the plan countered that, in the event of a merger, the stockholders should at least get back what they had invested, namely, ¥50 a share, and that, "even if we do eventually merge with the Nippon Railway Company, now is not the time for that."[204]

The key to the failure of the merger bid, then, was not so much local initiative as profit-seeking on the part of the Ryōmō Railway's principal owners. Imamura indicated as much when he lamented that his proposal was defeated in the end because "all the major stockholders tended to regard the sale as premature and opposed it."[205] Underlying this opposition was the improved business performance of the railroad. The merger movement took place at the tail end of the recession, and by then, the company was showing definite signs of recovery from the crisis. Moreover, contrary to the expectations of its promoters, the Ryōmō, like its fellow "branch lines," derived the majority of its income—over two thirds of it—from passenger transport, the development of freight traffic having fallen far short of the founders' projections.[206] This income structure meant, on the one hand, that the external benefits accruing to local investors, especially those involved in textile manufacturing or trade, were rather limited; on the other hand, as was noted earlier, it meant that the railroad was spared the full impact of the economic recession. Indeed, the firm's dividend rate rose steadily during the crisis years, reaching a relatively healthy 7 percent in 1892.[207] This trend alone may explain why, in the final analysis, a majority of the stockholders, local and nonlocal alike, voted for independence from the Nippon Railway.

In entrusting line construction and operation initially to the Nippon, the Ryōmō, Mito, and Kōbu railways were in fact doing so to the government, inasmuch as the Railway Bureau built and largely ran the Nippon lines until April 1892. In other words, these companies' arrangement with the Nippon Railway represented an indirect form of dependence on the state, which, as Sugiyama points out, was a hallmark of the conservative investment behavior of railway capitalists.[208] During the panic and recession, this proclivity manifested itself in a far more conspicuous manner, as railway investors clamored for a variety of government relief measures, including the ultimate such measure—nationalization. Railway stockholders, however, were by no means the only ones demanding state purchase of private railroads at this time; to the contrary, the nationalization movement that broke out in late 1891 seems to have encompassed all the interested parties—local elites, government bureaucrats, as well as railway owners and managers. Moreover, the nature and extent of stockholder involvement in the movement both need to be qualified.

The nationalization campaign centered on a massive petition drive and lobbying effort directed at members of the second Diet as they began deliberations on the government's proposed legislation for state railway construction and private railroad purchase in December 1891. As we will see, in proposing the gist of this legislative program to the cabinet in July, Inoue Masaru sought to take advantage of the decline in railroad-stock prices in order to realize his pet project of nationalization. Yet, by getting the cabinet to place nationalization on the legislative agenda, Inoue unwittingly contributed to the amelioration of the very condition on which he had hoped to capitalize. During the second and third quarters of 1891, railroad stocks recorded steady gains on both the Tokyo and Osaka exchanges; the third-quarter increases appear to have been based in part on rumors that the government was planning to nationalize the railway companies (see Table 9).[209] Then, at the end of the third quarter, railroad-stock prices leaped in the wake of reports that, on September 14th, the cabinet had indeed decided to buy out the firms. On the other hand, those same prices reacted sharply to the news that the opposition parties controlling the lower house of the Diet had agreed on November 8th to join forces to defeat the cabinet's railway legislation as part of their all-out offensive against the ruling oligarchy. But the stocks again rallied when the administration finally presented its program to the Diet in mid-December.[210]

It is against this background of price movements and political maneuvering that one needs to evaluate the participation of railroad stockholders in the nationalization campaign. Not surprisingly, most railway investors who took part in the movement were engaged in banking or stockbroking, professions whose fortunes were closely tied to those of railway companies.[211] Among the organizations that petitioned for passage of the nationalization bill in late 1891, for example, were the Tokyo and Osaka bankers' associations and a group of brokers on the Tokyo stock exchange, all of which numbered railway investors among their members.[212] Similar petitions came from a variety of other bodies, ranging from the Sendai Chamber of Commerce and the Hiroshima City Assembly to a group of Tokyo merchants and the Tokyo City Firefighters' Union.[213] Almost all these associations contained railway shareholders as well, and one can safely assume, as Harada Katsumasa does, that many of the members of the petitioning chambers of commerce and city assemblies, in particular, were railway investors.[214]

Unfortunately, the memorials submitted to the Diet by the latter organizations were signed solely by their presiding officers, so it is difficult to ascertain the extent to which railway stockholders within their rank and file actually endorsed the government purchase of private railroads. Nonetheless, one can compare the hundreds of signatories of the nationalization petitions presented by the other associations, which included, for instance, groups of residents of Okayama and Yamaguchi prefectures, with the 272

TABLE 9 Average Monthly Quotations for San'yō and Kansai Railway Shares, 1891
(unit: yen)

	San'yō Railway				Kansai Railway	
	Osaka Stock Exchange		Tokyo Stock Exchange		Osaka Stock Exchange	
Month						
Jan.	19.25	(23)	19.00		32.50	(45)
Feb.	17.50	(23)	17.40		28.00	(45)
Mar.	16.60	(23)	16.60		–	
Apr.	18.35	(25)	18.30		23.35	(45)
May	19.45	(25)	19.25		24.25	(45)
Jun.	21.50	(25)	21.65		30.08	(45)
Jul.	22.45	(25)	22.50		34.55	(45)
Aug.	23.60	(27)	23.70		35.33	(45)
Sep.	24.18	(27)	24.10		38.15	(45)
Oct.	23.15	(27)	23.20		35.30	(45)
Nov.	21.50	(27)	21.50		33.75	(45)
Dec.	22.08	(27)	21.55		35.10	(45)

Source: Takizawa, pp. 288–290.

Note: Figures in parentheses represent paid-up values.

holders of 200 or more shares in the San'yō Railway in September 1891.[215] Correlating these two contemporaneous sets of names reveals the somewhat startling fact that, as far as can be determined, only 13 of the 272 top shareholders in the San'yō Railway signed petitions calling for state purchase of railway companies in late 1891; 10 of the 13 affixed their names to a bankers' or stockbrokers' memorial. This fact suggests either that railway-stockholder involvement in the campaign was not as extensive as commonly maintained or that such involvement was limited, for the most part, to relatively small investors, such as the 1,590 shareholders in the San'yō Railway, amounting to 85 percent of the total, who were excluded from the list of owners of 200 or more shares in the company.[216]

The former inference receives some confirmation from an article published in the *Miyako shinbun* in late 1891. The author, who was clearly an advocate of nationalization, complained that, although journalists, businessmen, and politicians had joined the nationalization movement, "railway-company stockholders, the ones most concerned, appear not to have taken the lead themselves; rather they have been vacillating over [the issue], . . . and bankers and the like have taken charge in lieu of railway stockholders . . ."[217] The writer noted that recently Governor Kawada Koichirō of the Bank of Japan had persuaded members of the Tokyo Bankers' Association to submit a petition to the Tokyo Chamber of Commerce urging the latter to endorse the nationalization bill. According to another source, on November 25, 1891, Kawada had summoned Shibusawa Eiichi, Nakamigawa Hikojirō, Yasuda Zenjirō, and other members of the bankers' association and, declaring his support of the government's purchase of private railroads or at least of their amalgamation, had expressed dismay over the fact that business organizations in Tokyo had failed to make information on the issue available to Dietmen.[218] The bankers had responded by drafting their petition and presenting it to the Chamber of Commerce on November 30th; the chamber had then adopted this document as the basis of its memorial, which was submitted to the Diet on December 22nd.[219]

The bankers' memorial contained arguments common to virtually all of the nationalization petitions, and one can therefore regard it as fairly representative of the petition drive as a whole. Like most of the other petitioning bodies, the Tokyo Bankers' Association placed blame for the current financial crisis squarely on the private railway companies and their voracious appetite for capital, which had caused funds "that ought to be employed for commercial purposes to be converted into fixed capital . . ." As a result, "commercial and industrial enterprises of all sorts have gradually become lacking in sources of finance and unable to avoid losing vitality and experiencing decline . . ." The solution, then, was for the government to buy out the railroad firms, thereby enabling the private sector to "increase the supply of funds available for business by recovering capital tied up [in railroad investment]."[220]

The author of the *Miyako shinbun* article asserted that this petition "was the bankers' own idea and was not made at the urging of railroad stockholders."[221] True, the memorial did not originate with railway investors as such, but, in making this claim, the writer ignored the fact that many of the members of the bankers' association were themselves substantial, if not major, owners of railroad stock. Such was the case, for example, with Nakamigawa Hikojirō, who held 803 shares in the San'yō Railway in September 1891, and Yasuda Zenjirō, who had 400 shares in the Ryōmō in October 1890.²²² Furthermore, Kawada, the apparent catalyst behind the bankers' petition drive, was a former Mitsubishi executive who may well have been acting on behalf of Japan's second largest railroad stockholder.

Having established that at least some railway investors joined the nationalization movement, one must still explain why they did so at such a late date, when most companies appeared to be on the road to recovery from the panic. Bankers in particular had initially reacted to the crisis by demanding the much less dramatic measure of expanded lending by the Bank of Japan; only after the disclosure of the cabinet's decision to push for nationalization and the opposition parties' determination to oppose it did they come out in support of the state purchase of private railroads, and then only with prodding from the head of the central bank. The motives of these and other major railway stockholders for advocating nationalization are difficult to fathom without reference to the previously mentioned pattern of railroad-stock price movements. One might contend, of course, that the conservative investment outlook of most railroad owners would naturally have led them to back nationalization in earnest as a way of extricating themselves from an industry hard-hit by the recession, but, as noted above, the market already seemed to have turned the corner by the time railway investors declared themselves in favor of a railroad purchase bill. The emergent zaibatsu and other like-minded shareholders, while concerned with protecting their investments, were equally, if not more, interested in expanding the enterprise with a view to the wider benefits to be gained. Both of these ends would have been served by government purchase and extension of struggling private lines. Yet, there was another dimension, and in this case an overriding one, to the concerns of such investors, namely, a desire to influence the management of particular railroads through stock ownership. Mitsubishi and Mitsui, in particular, were acutely aware of the strategic importance of railroad control for the running of other businesses, especially coal-mining operations. Accordingly, these capitalists, though eager to obtain relief from the economic crisis, were fundamentally committed to private ownership and management of railroads.²²³

These considerations cast doubt on the seriousness of the nationalization demands of major railway stockholders, as represented by the petitions of the Tokyo and Osaka bankers' associations. Nakanishi asserts that the real objective of these petitioners was "to restrain the Diet, so that stock prices, which had begun to recover in anticipation of the government's presentation to the Diet of a bill for the purchase of private railroads, would not fall again owing to Diet opposition."[224] Indeed, considerable evidence can be marshaled in support of this claim. It was plainly concern over the sudden drop in stock prices triggered by reports of the opposition parties' resolution to derail the cabinet's nationalization plans that prompted Kawada to summon Shibusawa and his fellow Tokyo financiers on November 25th. As Kawada declared to the assembled bankers, "This year, the argument for railway nationalization has come to be expressed frequently among the public, and it has had its advocates within the government as well. As a result, this has had an effect on the economy, railway shares have gradually been restored in value, and business is very much on the verge of recovering its vitality. Nevertheless, if, at present, another major decline in stock prices were suddenly to occur, into what dreadful state would that throw our economy?"[225] In the event that the administration submitted a nationalization bill to the Diet, Kawada warned, should the Diet members "flatly reject this [bill], it may cause serious fluctuations within the business world." It would be extremely deplorable, he continued, if the Dietmen simply ignored the measure for lack of understanding of the current economic situation or voted it down for partisan political reasons; "however, if they were to reject it having rationally and factually analyzed its pros and cons on the basis of a full understanding of the present state of our business world, then, of course, there would be nothing to argue about . . ."[226]

Kawada's comments suggest that Tokyo business leaders, including major railway stockholders, were under no illusion as to the chance of passage by the Diet of the cabinet's nationalization bill in light of the vehement opposition of the parties controlling the lower house. Rather, the businessmen's primary concern was none other than to prevent violent fluctuations in railroad-stock prices, thereby assuring the continued recovery of private railroad enterprise.

Tokyo investors were not the only ones whose support of railway nationalization was less than wholehearted. In Osaka, which sustained a much greater blow from the panic than did Tokyo, businessmen seemed equally ambivalent about the state purchase of private railroads. This attitude is clearly revealed in the report of an investigative committee appointed by the Osaka Chamber of Commerce, whose members included some of the aforementioned Osaka bankers as well as other railway shareholders. In its report, on which the chamber based its petition to the Diet, the committee recommended that the government buy out all the private railroads by exchanging 5-percent public bonds, which "compared to stocks are extremely creditworthy and readily negotiable," for the paid-up portion of the companies' shares. On the other hand, it also insisted on the following condition: "[Each] purchase requires the consent of the company, and the government may not violate [that company's] vested interests by decree."227 The committee's explanation for this proviso read as follows:

> Under Article 35 of the Private Railway Regulations, the government does not have the right to purchase a private railroad until a full twenty-five years have elapsed from the date of its licensing (or, in the case of a company for which a [different] term of operation is stipulated, until that term has expired). Hence, the government naturally needs the consent of a company to purchase it [prior to that time] and clearly cannot violate [that company's] vested interests arbitrarily. If so, then in the present case, although many companies will surely agree to their nationalization, if they do not consent, there is no alternative for the government but to wait until the expiration of their licenses. No matter how necessary nationalization is, since the government has already legally granted [railway companies] special rights, it cannot violate these arbitrarily.228

This stipulation severely qualified the committee's endorsement of blanket nationalization, tantamount as it was to exempting from state purchase railroads that were relatively profitable or otherwise of value to their owners. Again, it suggests that businessmen in Osaka and Tokyo alike viewed the nationalization movement merely as an expedient for reviving the financial market through the stabilization of railroad-stock prices, and not as a way of realizing the principle of national ownership espoused by Railway Bureau Chief Inoue.

At any rate, the lower house, as expected, rejected the government's Railway Purchase Bill by a wide margin on December 24th. Nevertheless, although stock prices in the immediate aftermath "fluctuated sharply," the dreaded financial cataclysm did not occur, and "at the end of December, following the dissolution of the Diet, the [Tokyo] market showed signs of recovery."[229] Railway capitalists would again join with other businessmen in calling for nationalization during the panics of 1897–1898 and 1900–1901. At that time, stockholder participation would center much more heavily on stockbrokers and other speculative owners, clearly reflecting the passive, impersonal behavior of such investors.

RAILWAY MANAGERS. The extent to which the risk-avoiding and profit-seeking proclivities of stockholders affected railway-company decision making during the early 1890s was a function not only of the strength of those attitudes, but also of the degree of overlap between management and ownership. Most top managers of private railroads at that time appear to have been drawn from the aforementioned groups of principal stockholders and hence shared their cautious views on business strategy.[230] In fact, almost every one of the individuals cited above in illustration of those groups served as a senior executive of one or more railway companies during the early 1890s. This overlap helps to explain why, with one or two notable exceptions, there was surprisingly little tension between managers and owner-capitalists over corporate policy during the crisis and, more specifically, why shareholders were able to influence that policy to the point of dominating it, as revealed in corporate decisions on capital expenditures, dividend payouts, and the like.

Admittedly, to be eligible for a directorship in a joint-stock company during the Meiji period, one generally had to be a shareholder with a specified minimum interest in the enterprise. Railroad firms were no exception. The articles of incorporation of the San'yō Railway, for example, stipulated that its directors be elected from among holders of 100 or more shares in the company; the cutoff was raised to 200 shares in 1889.[231] This revision meant that the company's directors were ipso facto included on its 1891 list of "major stockholders," broadly defined. Although this roll covered less than 15 percent of the railroad's total number of shareholders, there was still a vast difference in holdings even within this list between a director like Fujita Denzaburō with 300 shares or a 0.1-percent interest in the firm and one like Ōtsuka Osamu, the third largest stockholder with 4,935 shares or a 1.9-percent interest in the company.[232] Indeed, President Nakamigawa, who held sixty-fourth place on the list with 803 shares, is described by the recent compilers of his biographical materials as "just a minor stockholder," on which point, among others, "he was an exceptional and remarkable figure as a manager of the Meiji era."[233] In addition, his successor, Matsumoto Jūtarō, the San'yō's eighteenth largest shareholder in April 1892 with 1,400 shares, is represented by Sugiyama as a top manager whose "character as an owner-type president was extremely weak."[234]

Whether these men had uncommonly small holdings for railway executives at the time is debatable. Four of the nine directors of the San'yō Railway in September 1891, for instance, possessed fewer shares than did Nakamigawa, while in October 1890, President Narahara of the Ryōmō Railway was only the fifty-fifth largest stockholder in that company with all of 100 shares.[235] Nonetheless, judging from available data, one can probably assume that over a third of the presidents and directors of private railroads during the early 1890s numbered among the top ten shareholders in their firms; over half of them, among the top thirty.[236] This distribution would mean that Matsumoto was fairly typical of railway-company officers in terms of his stockholder rank in the San'yō, but one might question from the standpoint of the absolute, if not of the relative, magnitude of his share the claim that his interest in that company was in fact weak.

Nakamigawa, for his part, may not have been unusual among railway managers in the size of his holdings either; however, he definitely was unique both in the progressiveness of his policies and in the amount of friction his pursuit of those policies generated between management and ownership in the San'yō Railway (see Figure 10). As noted earlier, Osaka led all prefectures in terms of the number of shares it accounted for in the San'yō in 1891, with Hyōgo prefecture occupying third place after Tokyo. Five Osaka investors and two from Hyōgo counted among the railroad's top ten shareholders that year.[237] The Kansai capitalists had originally intended that a local government official, Murano Sanjin, become president of the company. In addition, they had initially planned to lay the line only from Kobe to Himeji, a section equivalent to one tenth of the railroad's eventual mileage, and one that "would be easy to build and certain to bring profits."[238] The government, however, set as its condition for licensing the railroad the extension of the proposed line to Shimonoseki. In order to meet this requirement, the promoters solicited a major investment from Mitsubishi, which, in turn, made its participation contingent on the appointment of its candidate for the presidency, Nakamigawa.[239]

Duly elected president of the railroad in April 1888, Nakamigawa introduced management techniques that were highly innovative for the times; in Tsunehiko Yui's view, "his activities as manager were idiosyncratic and epoch-making."[240] In particular, he pursued a positive investment strategy. Besides purchasing sufficient land for double-tracking and importing the most up-to-date rolling stock from England, Nakamigawa insisted on building the line to exacting engineering standards. Specifically, he required that curves be no more than fifteen degrees and gradients, 1/100 or less, the latter stipulation for which he earned the epithet "One Hundredth (*wan handoretsu*)" from his beleaguered engineers.[241]

Nakamigawa adhered to these policies even at the height of the recession, despite pressure from many of the stockholders to retrench on construction expenditures. The financial crisis served only to sharpen the differences between Nakamigawa and these investors, as the tight money market, combined with the railroad's initially poor business results, made shareholders all the more unwilling, if not unable, to support the president's expansionary program. Criticism of those programs mounted especially among the major Osaka investors, who were openly dissatisfied with the low dividend rate as well as the princely salaries enjoyed by Nakamigawa and his staff. In October 1890, these owners managed to secure the appointment of one of their numbers, Ōtsuka Osamu, to the board of directors. No sooner had he joined the board than Ōtsuka, according to one observer, "voiced opposition to President Nakamigawa on everything."[242] In the end, he and his fellow "Osaka-style economizers," in the words of another contemporary, "conspired with the [other] stockholders to set up an investigative committee and intervened in the internal affairs of the company . . ." As this commentator put it, the "mediocre men" on this committee "concluded that the pay of the staff was too high and decided that, with the exception of the engineers, the salaries of office workers earning ¥50 or more a month should be curtailed."[243]

Nakamigawa himself proved to be the prime target of this retrenchment drive. While he was away on company business in 1891, the directors held a special meeting, attended by Vice-President Murano Sanjin, and moved to cut the president's monthly salary from ¥400 to ¥250.[244] As Yui notes somewhat understatedly, "this was obviously tantamount to an expression of nonconfidence in Nakamigawa."[245] Finding it increasingly

Figure 10 Nakamigawa Hikojirō (1854–1901), first president of the San'yō Railway Company, 1888–1891. Photograph: courtesy of the Transportation Museum, Tokyo.

difficult to carry out his programs in the face of stockholder interference and personal attacks, Nakamigawa finally resigned from the presidency of the railroad in October 1891 to become full-time director of the Mitsui Bank. Following his departure, the Osaka investors gained control over the San'yō board, increasing their representation from two to four of the nine directorships.[246] Murano took charge of the management until the appointment of a new president in April 1892. Reversing Nakamigawa's course, he "adopted an extremely conservative policy," one more in keeping with the cautious views of the major stockholders, under which he "raised passenger fares, abolished the biennial bonuses for employees, and reduced the staff in the head office."[247]

Nakamigawa was clearly ahead of his times in his aggressive championship of strategies for business expansion, for both the nature of his programs and the intensity of stockholder resistance to them were unparalleled at the time. Yet two factors suggest that one should not attribute the progressive features of San'yō management solely to Nakamigawa's genius and foresight, as an uncritical reading of his biographical materials might lead one to do. For one thing, Nakamigawa was probably not alone in his advocacy of expensive construction methods. At least on that score, he no doubt received strong backing from one of the founders and directors of the railroad, Fujita Denzaburō. For, although a colleague of the Osaka "economizers," Fujita, as the chief building contractor for the line, stood to gain immensely from large construction outlays. Second, the San'yō faced far greater competition from alternative forms of transport than any other railroad. Specifically, the firm was at the outset "constantly overwhelmed by steamship companies" whose routes paralleled the course of the railroad along the Inland Sea.[248] In order to vie with these shipping firms, the San'yō was compelled from the first to offer rates that were substantially below those set by the government; many of the other aspects of Nakamigawa's program, such as the use of cars equipped with vacuum brakes, can be seen as attempts to provide superior service and thereby to draw traffic away from the company's formidable rivals at sea. Long after Nakamigawa's resignation, competition from shipping remained a powerful impetus for innovation in the San'yō, as the railroad continued to be the industry leader in customer service.

Yet, despite the rather unusual set of circumstances affecting the management of the San'yō Railway, the fact remains that it was Nakamigawa who first established the kinds of policies necessitated by those circumstances. Moreover, the adoption of those types of policies in the short run at least was by no means a foregone conclusion, as evidenced by the sudden turnabout in strategy immediately following his departure from the railroad.

At any rate, Nakamigawa's programs contrasted sharply with those of an owner-executive like Imamura Seinosuke, who in terms of his attitudes was much more representative of top railroad managers in the early 1890s. We have already mentioned Imamura's role in the abortive merger bid between the Ryōmō and Nippon railways. As a director of the Kyushu Railway, he played a key part as well in that company's adoption of a retrenchment program in 1891. According to the railroad's first president, Takahashi Shinkichi, Imamura from the outset urged him "to try to curtail expenditures and to raise the dividend..."[249] Once the panic struck, his biographer notes, Imamura stepped up his pressure and, "as a temporary expedient, advised President Takahashi to reduce the company's operations, to take a very conservative policy, and to endeavor to maintain the status quo..."[250] His biographer further claims that Imamura was also behind the stockholders' petition demanding a second postponement of the railroad's scheduled construction work in late 1891. As this source puts it, the director privately persuaded his acquaintances among the owners to come out with the petition, suggesting that management's decision to suspend construction work was by no means forced upon it by recalcitrant shareholders.[251] On the other hand, Imamura himself was a leading investor in the company. In this capacity, he would have had a strong personal motive for desiring an increase in dividends as well as a delay in the collection of stock payments, his own disavowal of self-interest notwithstanding.[252]

Imamura exemplified senior railway executives in mid-Meiji not only in the kinds of policies he supported and in his dual status as director and principal stockholder, but also in his primary occupation. As a banker with experience in the stock-exchange business, he fits into the mainstream of top managers, who, as we have noted, came largely from the predominant classes of major railway investors. By contrast, Nakamigawa, together with President Taguchi Ukichi of the Ryōmō, was an exceptional figure in this regard as well, having as he did a background in journalistic management.

A more significant category of senior railway officers not included among the dominant investor groups consisted of former public servants, specifically, government bureaucrats and state railway engineers. Among the top executives with experience in state administration were Narahara Shigeru, president of the various companies in the Nippon Railway network, who had served as a prefectural governor and a secretary in several government ministries, and Takahashi Shinkichi, who resigned his post as head of the Commerce Bureau in the Ministry of Agriculture and Commerce to become the first president of the Kyushu Railway.[253]

The prominence of such managers at this time reflected the necessity, especially marked in the case of trunk-line firms, of obtaining state assistance and cooperation in the early stages of the enterprise and thus the desirability of securing a chief executive with connections in the central bureaucracy. Another factor impelling railway companies to recruit government bureaucrats was the shortage of qualified administrators in the private sector. From the authorities' standpoint, the placement of government officials in the companies as top managers was a means of exercising influence and ensuring accountability during the period of state subvention. In fact, the government itself appointed several of the ex-bureaucrat executives in the private railroads. Takahashi, for example, owed his position to a request by the promoters of the Kyushu Railway that the authorities select the company's president.[254] In the case of the Hokkaido Colliery and Railway, which at the outset was almost as closely tied to government policy as the Nippon, the state reserved for itself the power to appoint and dismiss for the duration of the government subsidy not only the president, but the vice-president and directors as well.[255] Under this authority, the government named as the first president Hori Motoi, who had worked as a department head in the Hokkaido government office.[256]

State railway engineers, with their virtual monopoly of railroad technology in the early years, were active from the beginning in private rail companies as technical advisers or chief engineers. While some were on loan from the state railways, others formally resigned from their official posts to enter private employment. It was generally not until later in the 1890s, however, that former government engineers like Minami Kiyoshi and Sengoku Mitsugu moved into managerial positions, as a new generation of engineers emerged to take their place as technical functionaries in the companies.[257]

Two government engineers who did make the transition to private railway manager in the early 1890s were Hirai Seijirō and Mōri Jūsuke. Originally an employee of the state railways in Hokkaido, Hirai had left government service in 1888 to supervise the construction successively of the Osaka, Sanuki, and Hokkaido Colliery railways; in January 1892, he was appointed a director of the Hokkaido Colliery.[258] Mōri, on the other hand, had overseen the construction of a section of the Nippon Railway while in the employ of the Railway Bureau in the early 1880s. He resigned from the bureau in 1885 to become chief engineer of the Nippon and was promoted to vice-president in April 1892.[259] A unique variant on the engineer-to-manager pattern is provided by Shiraishi Naoji, an engineering professor at Tokyo Imperial University from 1887 to 1890. During his tenure at the university, Shiraishi served as chief engineer of the nascent Kansai Railway, then left his faculty position to become the third president of the company in October 1890.[260]

The presence of ex-government officials in the top management of private railroads helped to ensure that, on certain issues, company policy was more in tune with that of the state than would otherwise have been the case. This policy alignment was particularly apparent during the nationalization movement of late 1891, when former public servants presided over the five largest railroads and at least two of the smaller ones as well.[261] No doubt because of the influence of these executives, the railway companies seemed to be much more supportive of the government's nationalization program than the firms' stockholders. According to the biographies of three men connected with the management of the San'yō, the private railroads joined forces to press for enactment of the Railway Purchase Bill by the Diet.[262] And, indeed, a petition backing the state's proposed railway legislation was submitted to the Diet by the top managers of five railroad firms, including Murano Sanjin of the San'yō, Takahashi Shinkichi of the Kyushu, and Shiraishi Naoji of the Kansai.[263]

In contrast to these former state officials, railway managers with nongovernmental backgrounds tended to reflect the largely ambivalent attitudes of the major stockholders towards the issue of nationalization. For example, Ban Naonosuke, who had been a journalist prior to becoming superintendent of the Ryōmō Railway under his mentor Taguchi Ukichi,[264] asserted in September 1891:

> Although I advocate the nationalization of private railroads as a temporary expedient, I am adamantly opposed to a permanent state railway system. Now that the government has decided to purchase the private railroads, I hope that it will nationalize all of them for a period of time ... and, once the various railway systems have been put in order, will again return them all to the private sector.[265]

Ban was a full-time salaried manager responsible to the part-time senior executives for the actual operation of the Ryōmō, and as such, he probably had a greater commitment to the continued existence of his enterprise, and a less sanguine view of nationalization, than did most railway presidents and directors at this time.[266]

Dominating the top-level decision making of railroad firms in the early 1890s, then, were the major stockholders who filled most of the directorships and some of the presidencies, together with the former state officials appointed to many of the chief executive posts, though possessing only minor interests in their companies. A corollary to the overlap between principal owners and top managers was the limited involvement of local investors in railway management. To be sure, local entrepreneurs typically participated in the promotion and early administration of railway companies. In fact, in the case of the Nippon Railway, a provision was written into the articles of incorporation expressly calling for local representation on the firm's initial board of directors.[267] The Tokyo investors who dominated the company, however, were required to observe this concession to interests along the route of the railroad only until the first section of line, that between Tokyo and Maebashi, had been completed.

In smaller railroads serving narrower markets, one might expect to find a fairly strong local presence on the companies' boards, and indeed, this was often the case, at least in the beginning. Yet, as was true with the Nippon Railway, local participation in the management of such firms was largely tied to their need to obtain cooperation from the localities in raising construction funds and purchasing rights of way. Once majority ownership had passed into the hands of nonlocal investors, as capital demand exceeded local supply, or the companies had finished their construction work, the tendency was for local influence over management to diminish markedly in railroads where it had originally been significant. In the Chikuhō Industrial Railway, for example, the sharp decline in the local share of the company's ownership from 1889 to 1890 was followed in April 1891 by a management shake-up that left an auditor as the sole remaining officer from the Chikuhō region.[268] Meanwhile, the Ryōmō Railway Company, commonly regarded as the quintessential local railroad, initially had two local men, one of whom was the vice-president, on its six-member board of directors. From 1889, when the company's line was completed, until 1890, however, there was no local representative on the Ryōmō's board and, thereafter, only one.[269] With local shareholders having such a weak say in the operation even of railroads with a local character, it is no wonder that the communities served generally had little input into railway management decisions during the panic and recession.

The inability of local interests to influence corporate policy directly was clearly evident in the case of the Kyushu Railway. That company's decision in 1891 to suspend construction work provoked area residents to flood the firm with petitions demanding a reversal of the decision.[270] Despite the local uproar, the railroad went ahead with the postponement and in fact, as we have seen, secured a second extension of its construction deadlines the following year.

LOCAL COMMUNITIES AND THE STATE. Railroad firms could not ignore local importunities indefinitely, however. This was particularly true after the opening of the national legislature in 1890. From that date, if local communities lacked representation on the companies' boards, they did have their spokesmen in the Diet, which, through its legislative power, could vitally affect decision making in the railway enterprises. The capacity of local residents to exert pressure on railway management in this indirect manner appeared most strikingly during the nationalization movement of late 1891. Railway companies, many of which were putting off construction work, confronted the possibility of the Diet's enactment of a railway nationalization bill enthusiastically supported by impatient local interests. Especially vocal in their backing of such legislation were communities along the route of the San'yō Railway, which had repeatedly delayed extension of its line since mid-1890 and, after Nakamigawa's departure, had even begun talking about suspending construction work until the year 1900.[271] The Hiroshima Chamber of Commerce and City Assembly and groups of residents from Okayama and Yamaguchi prefectures were among those petitioning the Diet to pass the nationalization bill in December 1891.[272] The Hiroshima Chamber of Commerce spoke for all these groups when it singled out the San'yō Railway for special criticism. The chamber complained: "Despite the fact that its railroad is a nationally indispensable trunk line, the San'yō Railway Company has applied for postponement of its prescribed completion date, either because it has actually resolved to discontinue permanently construction of said line under the guise of suspension, owing to the difficulty of raising share capital, or because it has decided to embark on a long-term policy of waiting for an opportunity [to begin construction work again]."[273] In view of "the pressing need for completing the San'yō railroad," there seemed no alternative but for the government to buy out and finish the line. Local demands of this kind undoubtedly contributed to the sense of urgency with which the San'yō's new management sought to resume construction work after April 1892.

The localities, of course, were attempting, through the Diet, to prevail on the central bureaucracy and cabinet, and it was ultimately with the latter that the railway companies were more concerned. The parties in the Diet, eager to reduce government expenditures and hence the tax burden on their constituents as well as to increase their power vis-à-vis the oligarchs, were adamantly opposed to the cabinet's nationalization proposal. For their part, cabinet leaders were less committed to nationalization than to the other half of their legislative program, railroad construction. They were thus willing to forgo the purchase bill in exchange for passage in June 1892 of a compromise measure for state railway extension, an item upon which both sides could readily agree. Indeed, top decision makers like Matsukata Masayoshi and Inoue Kaoru continued to be supportive of private railway enterprise, and, for the most part, government policy had a positive, enabling impact on railway-company strategy and planning. The state helped the railroads to weather the financial crisis, for example, by granting subsidies to the principal trunk-line companies and by easing access to bank funds on the part of investors in virtually all the operating railroad firms.

Nevertheless, inasmuch as the government had to balance a number of competing interests, its actions could not always be favorable to the railway companies. In particular, a change in official policy on the acquisition of private land by public utilities that occurred just before the panic broke out resulted in the imposition of a severe constraint on private railroad development during the recession. Until July 1889, the government had aided railway companies in buying rights of way by expropriating whatever private land they had required and then selling the land to them. This administrative practice had received legal confirmation in Article 15 of the 1887 Private Railway Regulations. Then, on July 30, 1889, the government promulgated the Compulsory Land Purchase Law, which included provisions protecting landowner interests. Under this law, the private land expropriation provision of the Private Railway Regulations was repealed, and railroad firms were thenceforth compelled to negotiate for the acquisition of private land directly with the owners.[274]

The railway companies were none too pleased with this development. In a petition to Prime Minister Kuroda Kiyotaka dated August 31, 1889, President Nakamigawa of the San'yō Railway complained that, lacking the coercive powers of the state, a railway enterprise would face endless difficulties in attempting to buy the land it needed from "hundreds and thousands of owners" and asked that the government continue its practice of expropriating right of way on behalf of his company. Otherwise, he warned, "in the future, plans for further construction are liable to collapse in a moment."[275]

In his written opinion on Nakamigawa's petition, Railway Bureau Chief Inoue Masaru was surprisingly sympathetic. Inoue asserted that, "in light of our experience, the request of the San'yō [Railway] Company is entirely unavoidable" and urged that the government grant the request.[276] Yet state leaders had other priorities in mind. In its decision of November 5th, the cabinet denied the San'yō Railway's application on the grounds that making an exception for private railroads would go against the purpose of the new law, namely, "to remove the danger of causing resentment among landowners,"[277] whose land taxes still accounted for the majority of state tax revenues and whose votes would be deciding the first Diet elections the following year. Nevertheless, the cabinet recognized that the law would indeed pose hardships for railway companies; as a way of averting such hardships, one that was "in tune with the objective of protecting and encouraging public utilities," it resolved to have the home minister instruct local officials to assist private railroads in purchasing the land they needed.[278]

The San'yō Railway was by no means the only railroad firm to voice displeasure with the change in procedure for land acquisition. In fact, concern that the new land-purchase law would deal a severe blow to private railroads sparked a concerted movement by railway managers to have it amended. In September 1889, the presidents of nine other railway companies joined Nakamigawa in a second memorial to Prime Minister Kuroda requesting reinstatement of the previous system of land purchase. In their petition, the railway executives protested that, under the new system, "there is hardly any hope of completing construction work within a reasonable period of time" in view of "the delays and obstacles" that were expected to attend the companies' compulsory purchase of land.[279] In November, the government rejected this request as well on the basis that it was "identical to the petition of the San'yō Railway Company president."[280]

With the onset of the tight money situation in late 1889, the timing of the government's enactment of the Compulsory Land Purchase Law could not have been worse for the railroad firms. By early 1890, at the height of the panic, the companies' worst fears concerning the impact of the law, assistance from local officials in the acquisition of land notwithstanding, seemed to be materializing. In May 1890, the *Japan Weekly Mail* offered the following details on the problems private railroads were experiencing as a result of the law:

> Railway companies desirous of acquiring land for carrying on works [have] to deal directly with the landowners, who in some cases number from 120–130 per mile. These people cannot all be assembled together with the view of obtaining their opinions, and yet the process of negotiating with them severally leads to almost interminable delay, while the prices they require are most extravagant. Persons owning land lying on the route of the Kyushu Railway demand figures ranging from ¥8 to ¥130 per *tsubo* [approximately 36 square feet]. The trouble and inconvenience resulting from the present state of matters have at length driven the railway companies to devise concerted action.[281]

The newspaper reported that the railroads were continuing to petition the government for a reinstatement of the previous practice of land expropriation. Their campaign apparently had some effect, for in July 1890, the state issued regulations establishing a formal mechanism for land-purchase negotiations between businessmen and landowners.[282]

The measures implemented by the authorities to facilitate acquisition of land by public utilities, although they undoubtedly eased the burden on railway companies, were nonetheless a far cry from the previous practice. And for several railroads, they were simply not enough to prevent dreaded construction delays. As the following examples suggest, difficulties in purchasing land were perhaps just as responsible for setbacks in private railroad building programs during the recession as were problems in collecting stock payments.

The Kyushu Railway was the first company to put off construction on account of difficulties in buying right of way. In late 1889, the railroad obtained permission from the government to postpone the deadline for completing the last section of the Hakata-Moji line, for which land acquisition had not gone smoothly.[283] In the case of the Chikuhō Industrial Railway, a whole series of disasters, including an outbreak of cholera, a heavy rainfall, and a major flood, impeded construction work from 1890 to 1891.[284] Then, problems in acquiring land and raising capital began to take their toll in 1891. In May of that year, the company petitioned the government for a year's extension of its deadlines for finishing two sections of line, explaining:

> There are various difficulties with respect to the company's negotiating directly with the landowners. Few of them readily comply with the expropriation [of their land], and the majority appeal for a decision by the Compulsory Land Purchase Committee of Inquiry; furthermore, interested parties raise many objections regarding the construction plans, and we are not yet ready to begin work [on the sections in question]. Such being the case, business has slumped badly; in addition, with the current tight money situation, it has been extremely difficult to make headway on the construction work [in progress], and at present, we have only completed half of the entire line. Under these circumstances, there is absolutely no hope of finishing by the deadlines . . . [285]

The government granted the company's request on the grounds that its predicament was, in Railway Bureau Chief Inoue's words, "beyond its control."[286] Even a year's extension proved insufficient, however, as the work continued to stall in the face of exacting landowners and severe flooding. Accordingly, the railroad was forced to apply in May 1892 for yet another one-year postponement of its completion deadlines.[287]

Difficulties in acquiring land often had less to do with the technical problems of negotiating with landowners than with outright opposition to railroad construction from communities along the route of a projected line. At times, such resistance appears to have resulted from the residents' involvement in competing forms of transportation. The Sōbu Railway, for instance, set out to build and operate a line through Chiba prefecture, which boasted an extensive and well-developed river network. Although founded in December 1889, the company was not able to complete its first section of line, a twenty-five-mile stretch, until July 1894 partly because of the opposition of people engaged in inland water transport along the route.[288]

Railway companies were thus forced to make difficult adjustments in purchasing right of way just when they were least able to do so. From the government's standpoint, the railway construction delays occasioned by its change in policy represented a necessary trade-off in its attempt to placate the nation's landowners. Yet, the authorities went to considerable lengths, short of reinstating the old expropriation system, to lighten the increased load on the railroad firms, showing that they were by no means unsolicitous of the railroads' plight. Not only did the state readily grant extensions to the companies, but it sought to facilitate their negotiations with landholders and directed local officials to help them in that task. The latter activity came naturally to prefectural authorities, who had enthusiastically participated in the planning and promotion of such railroads as the Kyushu and San'yō, actively soliciting private investment and state subvention on their behalf.[289] In short, central and local government continued to cooperate with the private railroads in the acquisition of land, though in a fashion that was less generous, if more evenhanded, than before.

WEATHERING THE CRISIS

GOVERNMENT AID. The generally positive character of official attitudes towards private railway companies found its clearest expression in the forms of financial aid that state authorities granted the firms during the panic and recession. The railroads resorted to a variety of emergency measures in order to gain access to funds in the tight money situation and thereby to avoid the more drastic steps of suspending construction work, merging with larger concerns, or selling out to the government. Given the generally supportive nature of state policy and the conservative outlook of the dominant investor groups, it was only natural that the companies should have turned first to the government for relief from the financial crisis. And state officials obliged them with subsidies and indirect loans from the central bank.

During the early 1890s, four railroad firms—the four largest, to be exact—enjoyed government subventions.[290] Actually, all four had applied for their subsidies, and all but the San'yō had won government approval of them, prior to the outbreak of the panic. The San'yō, however, had made its subsidy request on the very eve of the crisis, at a time when business enterprises were already feeling the squeeze of a tightening money market. Moreover, all the subsidized railroads, except for the Hokkaido Colliery, obtained their largest subventions during the period 1890–1891, the only years in which total railway subsidies exceeded ¥1,000,000.

Nevertheless, the Nippon and Hokkaido Colliery railways benefited from government subsidies during the crisis to a much greater degree than did the Kyushu and San'yō. The state subvention supplied the former two with a vital cushion against business fluctuations, inasmuch as the government subsidized these companies before the opening of their lines and guaranteed their profits for substantial periods thereafter. Thus backed by the state, the Nippon Railway had little, if any, difficulty in collecting payments on two new stock issues floated just before and during the panic for construction of the two relatively unprofitable sections north of Sendai. Those issues were both paid up, and the sections completed, by 1891.[291]

Similarly, government subsidies made it possible for the Hokkaido Colliery and Railway to continue construction work during the recession, despite the slump in the coal market. As one of only three railway companies in operation during the crisis years that derived their income primarily from freight traffic,[292] the Hokkaido Colliery naturally experienced a sharp drop in its profit rate at this time, heavily dependent as it was on coal transport. Yet, thanks mainly to the state subvention, the firm was able to offer a dividend of over 7 percent throughout the recession. In consequence, it too had relatively little trouble calling up shares, which, in turn, enabled the company to finish its railway network by 1892.[293]

By comparison, the subvention granted the Kyushu and San'yō railways left their building programs far more vulnerable to disturbances in business activity, for their subsidies were comparatively modest lump-sum payments, contingent on the completion of designated sections of line. The two companies did receive large amounts of this state money at the beginning of the recession. The subsidy played a key role in allowing both firms to offer a dividend of 6 percent during each semester of 1890 and, in the case of the Kyushu Railway, during the first half of 1891 as well.[294] Partly as a result of this, each company was able to make significant additions to its paid-up capital and mileage during 1890 and 1891 (see Table 10). But, with the recession keeping their profits and the collateral value of their stocks at depressed levels, the government subsidy was just not enough to prevent their shareholders from demanding, before long, postponement of both installment payments and construction projects. Forced to heed the shareholders' demands, the two railroads had practically no increase in paid-up capital or mileage during the years 1892–1893. During that period, as neither firm was able to finish a designated section of line, the state subsidy ceased to be awarded to either of them. The dwindling of government support was, in turn, largely responsible for the drop in the companies' dividend rates beginning in 1891. Hence, the San'yō and Kyushu railways, like many of the unsubsidized firms, were caught in a bind between the necessity to complete sections of line in order to raise their income and dividends and the difficulty of procuring construction funds owing to the tight money market and their own poor business results. In the end, therefore, the government subsidy simply did not enable these companies to avoid major setbacks in their building programs.

The other principal form, albeit an indirect one, of state assistance to private railroads during the crisis was the extension of stock-collateral lending by the Bank of Japan. Affecting a much larger number of railroad concerns than did subsidization, this measure proved absolutely crucial to the financing of such hard-hit firms as the San'yō and Kyushu in the first year or so after the panic. Prompting its adoption in May 1890 was a vigorous campaign mounted by private business for government intervention to defuse the crisis. No sooner had the panic broken out than businessmen had begun to inundate the authorities with a variety of general relief proposals. Chambers of commerce in Tokyo and elsewhere had organized special committees to investigate the causes of the tight money situation and to recommend measures for alleviating it. Some of these bodies had urged the government to float a foreign loan; others, to establish an industrial

TABLE 10 Development and Business Results of San'yō and Kyushu Railway Companies, 1889–1894

Year	Length of Line Open (miles)	Paid-up Capital (¥1,000)	Profit (¥1,000)	Profit as Percentage of Capital (%)	State Subsidy (¥1,000)	Dividend (¥1,000)	Dividend Rate (%)
San'yō Railway							
1889	44	2,915	85	2.9	0	77	3.28
							3.0
1890	91 (106.8)	5,720 (96.2)	110	1.9	172	–	6.0
							6.0
1891	140 (53.8)	7,010 (22.6)	200	2.9	36	226	4.1
							2.76
1892	145 (3.6)	7,020 (0.1)	280	4.0	0	257	3.33
							4.0
1893	145 (0)	7,020 (0)	354	5.0	0	312	4.5
							4.5
1894	192 (32.4)	7,794 (11.0)	652	8.4	0	453	5.5
							7.0
Kyushu Railway							
1889	23	2,991	62	2.1	92	154	6.0
							6.0
1890	55 (139.1)	5,036 (68.4)	105	2.1	140	–	6.0
							6.0
1891	137 (149.1)	5,663 (12.5)	243	4.3	41	281	6.0
							4.25
1892	137 (0)	5,700 (0.7)	230	4.0	4	228	4.0
							4.0
1893	137 (0)	5,700 (0)	329	5.8	0	293	4.74
							5.53
1894	146 (6.6)	6,481 (13.7)	506	7.8	0	424	7.0
							7.5

Sources: *Tetsudō-kyoku nenpō, 1907*, appendix, pp. 23–24, 41, 79, 97; *Nihon teikoku tōkei nenkan*, vol. 10 (1891), p. 330, vol. 11 (1892), p. 680, vol. 12 (1893), p. 673, vol. 13 (1894), p. 703, and vol. 14 (1895), p. 711; Table 8 above.

Note: Figures in parentheses represent percentage increase over previous year.

bank. The business-oriented journal *Jiji shinpō* even called for the setting up of a national lottery.[295] The Finance Ministry initially responded to these demands by redeeming ¥8,000,000 in commutation bonds and authorizing the Bank of Japan to exceed its note-issue limit by ¥5,000,000. But, at the continued prodding of private businessmen, the authorities took their most far-reaching step: the broadening of the central-bank policy of discounting bank bills using corporate shares as collateral.

In May 1885, the Bank of Japan had begun accepting the shares of certain "sound" banks and companies, including the Nippon Railway, as security for term loans and discounts on bills. The government had approved this course of action in spite of Article 12 of the Bank of Japan Act, which prohibited lending by the central bank on the security of corporate stock. In the wake of the 1890 Panic, then, as a financial-relief measure, the authorities expanded the list of companies whose shares the Bank of Japan would accept as collateral for discounts on bills. All ten of the firms added to the list were private railroads.[296]

Significantly, it was not the railway companies themselves, but the Tokyo and Osaka bankers' associations that together proposed this measure and pushed for its adoption. The fact that these two groups came forward with a relief plan calling for the acceptance of several additional kinds of railroad stock as security for central-bank loans simply underscores the extent to which the city banks had tied up their capital in stock-collateral loans as well as the degree to which the latter had centered on railway shares.[297] With the liquidity of their capital reduced mainly because of the loans they had made on the security of such shares and with their assets adversely affected by the decline in value of many of the railroad stocks they held as collateral, it is no wonder that members of the Osaka and Tokyo bankers' associations should have focused on railway shares in their relief proposal.

The two associations initially came forward with quite different recommendations. The Osaka bankers, reflecting the greater severity of the financial crisis in their area, put forth the more extreme plan. They decided at first to press the Bank of Japan either to accept a broad range of shares as loan collateral or to extend a special loan of ¥5,000,000 to Osaka prefecture on the joint responsibility of the bankers themselves.[298] In early April, they presented these demands to Finance Minister Matsukata and Bank of Japan Governor Kawada, who had come down to the Kansai area to survey the aftermath of the panic there. Matsukata found the Osaka bankers' proposal to be totally unacceptable apparently for being too radical a departure from central-bank practice. He also realized, however, that to reject it outright would only "heighten the degree of panic among Osaka financial circles."[299] Fortunately for the authorities, the Tokyo bankers favored more moderate remedies. In fact, in late March, Shibusawa Eiichi had argued against relying whatsoever on the government for relief, asserting that "businessmen must be resolved to rescue themselves."[300] After conferring with Kawada, Matsukata decided to summon Shibusawa and other members of the Tokyo Bankers' Association to meet with their Osaka counterparts and to try to come to an agreement with them on a more reasonable relief plan.

Before sending their representatives to Osaka, members of the Tokyo Bankers' Association held a special meeting on April 11th to determine their position on the relief issue. First on the agenda was a request by two representatives of the Kyushu Bankers' Association, both of whom were also directors of the Kyushu Railway Company, that the Tokyo bankers endorse their group's recommendation that Kyushu Railway shares be added to the list of stocks authorized as loan collateral by the central bank.[301] A motion was introduced that the Tokyo Bankers' Association "select, in addition to [Kyushu Railway shares], the stocks of other sound companies"[302] and apply for their acceptance as collateral by the Bank of Japan. In the end, the Tokyo bankers voted to petition the central bank to designate as loan collateral the shares of the Kyushu, San'yō, and Hokkaido Colliery railways and, depending on the course of negotiations in Osaka, to support inclusion of the shares of the Kōbu, Mito, and Ryōmō railways as well.

After a series of consultations in Osaka among the bankers and authorities, a consensus was finally reached in favor of the Tokyo proposal that the Bank of Japan expand its practice of lending on the collateral of sound corporate shares. Representatives of the two bankers' associations then submitted a joint petition to Governor Kawada, requesting that the central bank accept as loan collateral the stocks of ten companies, the six railroads named in the Tokyo bankers' resolution and four of the firms whose shares had already been authorized as collateral items.[303] The financial authorities, in turn, adopted this proposal as the basis of their expanded discount program. Apparently as a concession to the Osaka bankers, they included among the designated collateral items the stocks not only of the subsidized railway companies and the three firms under the Nippon Railway umbrella, but of four relatively unaided railroads—the Kansai, Osaka, Hankai, and Sanuki—that were within the Osaka financial orbit.

The implementation of the enlarged discount system proved a tremendous boon to those commercial banks that had tied up large sums of money in the form of loans secured by railway shares, since the banks could thenceforth, in turn, use those shares to borrow extensively from the Bank of Japan. In its report on the banking industry for 1890, the government's Audit Bureau described the impact of this measure as follows: "Every bank, as if receiving rain after a drought, has raised idle capital and become active, . . . and all are once again enjoying the benefits of the financial community, which had long been dried up."[304]

Banks clearly made heavy use of the system. Of all discounts on domestic bills by the Bank of Japan, discounts on bills with collateral jumped from 28 to 53 percent between 1890 and 1891 and exceeded 50 percent every year thereafter during the first half of the 1890s (see Table 11). At the end of March 1893, railway shares served as collateral for ¥1,840,000 out of ¥2,601,000 in outstanding central-bank discounts on bills with collateral, or approximately 70 percent of the latter (see Table 12). Applying this percentage to discounts on collateralized bills for fiscal-year 1892 as a whole yields an estimate for central-bank discounts on bills using railway shares as collateral that year of ¥16,500,000, an amount equivalent to over one third the total paid-up capital of railway companies in 1892.

During its first year or so in operation, the extended discount program also seems to have greatly benefited the designated private railroads by making it easier for their shareholders to borrow funds from commercial banks in order to meet installment payments. From 1891 to 1893, however, the program generally appears to have been of much less advantage to the companies in view of the sharp drop in the rate of increase in their total paid-up capital and the problems experienced by the San'yō and Kyushu railways, among others, in collecting stock payments during those years. Nonetheless, the fact that the railroad firms enjoyed any increase in paid-up capital at all under the prevailing recession and tight money situation was due in no small measure to the central-bank discounting system.

The financial authorities initially intended the central bank's expanded

TABLE 11 Discounts on Domestic Bills by the Bank of Japan, 1890–1896

Year	Discounts on All Domestic Bills (¥1,000)	Discounts on Bills with Collateral (¥1,000)	Discounts on Bills with Collateral as Percentage of Total (%)
1890	56,983	15,897	27.9
1891	56,769	30,318	53.4
1892	43,454	23,638	54.4
1893	57,856	33,381	57.7
1894	93,295	49,776	53.3
1895	115,009	62,212	54.1
1896	178,546	79,528	44.5

Source: Tsuchiya Takao, "*Nihon ginkō hanki hōkoku* kaidai," in *Nihon kin'yū shi shiryō: Meiji Taishō hen*, vol. 8, Nihon ginkō chōsa-kyoku, ed. (Ōkura-shō insatsu-kyoku, 1956), p. 71.

TABLE 12 Discounts Outstanding on Bills with Collateral by the Bank of Japan, March 31, 1893

Type of Collateral	Total Value of Discounts (¥1,000)
Hokkaido Colliery and Railway Shares	505
Kyushu Railway Shares	473
San'yō Railway Shares	260
Kansai Railway Shares	231
Nippon Railway Shares	189
Ryōmō Railway Shares	92
Kōbu Railway Shares	65
Osaka Railway Shares	25
Total of Railway Shares	1,840
N.Y.K. Shares	440
Osaka Railway Bonds	200
Public Bonds	121
Grand Total	2,601

Source: "Kashidashikin teitōhin shuruibetsu hyō," March 31, 1893, Matsuo ke monjo, 1st ser., vol. 69, no. 28, Finance Ministry Archives, Tokyo.

discount policy to be just a temporary relief measure. In fact, the government approved the policy on the condition that a special bank eventually be established to take over the program.[305] In November 1892, Finance Minister Watanabe Kunitake, in granting the Bank of Japan's request that the program be further extended to cover the corporate bonds of the designated companies, felt constrained to add the following reminder: "Because the collateral system originated as a temporary expedient at the time of the tight money market in 1890, be advised that, once financing has returned to normal, said collateral system will gradually be abolished . . ."[306] The government finally did move to terminate the program in June 1897 as part of the central-bank reform that year. Nevertheless, on the grounds that suddenly to abolish a system that had been in existence for several years would have serious repercussions on the nation's financial markets, the authorities decided essentially to continue the discounting program under a different name.[307] Meanwhile, the plan to set up a special bank to assume discounts on corporate shares never materialized. The Bank of Japan thus remained, in Noda Masaho's words, "an ex-post-facto bearer"[308] of stock-collateral loans from commercial banks to railway shareholders right up until the nationalization of all the railroads in question in 1906–1907.

Pathbreaking Strategies. Besides seeking government assistance, the railroad firms took positive steps on their own to cope with the financial problems they faced during the crisis. In fact, at this time, they pioneered the use by Japanese joint-stock companies of two of those measures, namely, the issuance of preferred stocks and of corporate bonds. In 1892, the Chikuhō Industrial Railway became the first business in Japan to offer preferred stocks. At a special meeting in December 1891, the railroad's stockholders approved a plan to finance new construction by issuing ¥1,500,000 in new shares with a preferred dividend rate of 8 percent. The firm was to allot these shares to the existing stockholders, but, owing to the continued tightness of the money market, it was actually forced to discontinue the offer after the owners had subscribed to less than half the shares involved.[309]

The depressed financial and economic environment plainly limited the effectiveness of both government and corporate measures aimed at enabling private railroads to raise sufficient share capital to meet their fund-

TABLE 13 Aggregate Capital Structure of Private Railway Companies, 1888–1894

Year	Paid up Capital (¥1,000)	Reserves (¥1,000)	Bonds (¥1,000)	Loans (¥1,000)	Construction Costs (¥1,000)	Owned Capital as Percentage of Construction Costs (%)	Total Capital as Percentage of Construction Costs (%)	Loans as Percentage of Construction Costs (%)
	(1)	(2)	(3)	(4)	(5)	(6)	(7)	(8)
1888	14,997	231	0	165	11,834	128.7	130.1	1.4
1889	27,943	367	0	30	20,366	139.0	139.2	0.1
1890	38,493	511	269	1,162	33,816	115.3	119.6	3.4
1891	43,441	649	1,494	843	44,062	100.1	105.4	1.9
1892	46,737	775	1,710	580	47,508	100.0	104.8	1.2
1893	48,870	518	5,680	703	52,050	94.9	107.1	1.4
1894	59,177	1,322	5,778	877	60,794	99.5	110.5	1.4

Source: Tetsudō-kyoku nenpō, 1907, appendix, pp. 44–45.

ing needs during the crisis. Indeed, with the precipitous drop in the rate of increase in paid-up capital for railway companies as a whole in the years following the panic, the sum of the railroads' total paid-up capital and reserves barely matched their overall construction costs in 1891 and 1892 and fell significantly short of the latter in 1893. To cover the difference, several firms resorted to outside capital by negotiating bank loans or issuing corporate bonds (see Table 13, Columns 6 and 7).

For railway companies in general during the recession, borrowing from banks was strictly a stopgap measure. Between 1890 and 1893, six operating railroads had outstanding bank loans; only two of them carried those debts for more than three years running, including the years before and after that period, indicating that the loans were for the most part relatively short-term and probably renewed, if at all, but once or twice.[310] Moreover, the percentage of aggregate construction costs represented by these bank loans in any given year during the early 1890s was never very significant, ranging as it did from 1.2 percent in 1892 to 3.4 percent in 1890 (see Table 13, Column 8). Furthermore, one company, the San'yō Railway, accounted for the vast majority of bank funds advanced to railway enterprises in operation during the period 1890–1892. And, in 1891, the only one of those years in which the San'yō's share of the total fell below 90 percent, the equally distressed Chikuhō Industrial was responsible for most of the remainder; it also had over half the loans outstanding in 1893, by which time the San'yō had liquidated the bank debts it had begun contracting soon after the panic. In the short run, direct bank loans did make a substantial contribution to the financing of these two firms: in 1890, for example, banks lent the San'yō Railway the equivalent of 22 percent of its cumulative construction costs, making it possible for the company to offset overdue stock payments. But this method of capital procurement was clearly a makeshift.

Playing a far more important role in the long-term financing of the San'yō and other railway companies were corporate-bond issues, to which a number of the firms turned heavily in the early 1890s. The issuance of corporate bonds represented the second form of joint-stock-company finance that owed its introduction into Japan to the difficulties experienced by private railroads in the aftermath of the 1890 Panic. The Osaka Railway held the distinction of being the first Japanese business to float securities of this kind. In April 1890, that firm's stockholders voted to issue bonds total-

TABLE 14 Corporate Bonds Outstanding, Selected Railway Companies, 1890–1894
(unit: ¥1,000)

Year	San'yō		Kyushu		Chikuhō Industrial		Osaka	
1890	0		0		0		269	(16.9)
1891	0		0		415	(39.7)	269	(13.9)
1892	0		0		445	(25.4)	0	
1893	2,000	(23.8)	1,500	(23.9)	600	(24.0)	0	
1894	2,000	(21.2)	1,500	(20.1)	600	(19.4)	0	

Source: *Tetsudō-kyoku nenpō, 1907*, appendix, pp. 22–46 passim.
Note: Figures in parentheses represent corporate bonds as percentage of construction costs.

ing ¥268,500 "in order that this company might, for the time being, compensate for the shortage of [construction] capital."[311] The bonds were to pay 10-percent interest and to mature in five years. Other railroads soon followed the Osaka's lead. Besides the Osaka Railway, the four largest rail concerns and the Chikuhō Industrial all issued bonds in the early 1890s. All but the Nippon and Hokkaido Colliery did so to cover shortfalls in construction funds resulting from the companies' inability to collect installment payments or to sell new shares. The percentage of building costs represented by outstanding corporate bonds for each of these four enterprises during the years 1890–1893 ranged from 14 percent in the case of the Osaka Railway in 1891 to 40 percent in the case of the Chikuhō Industrial that same year (see Table 14). In 1893, both the San'yō and Kyushu issued bonds equivalent to nearly a fourth of their respective construction costs.

The Osaka redeemed its bonds in their entirety after only two years, but the other three railroads left most or all of their bonds outstanding for extended periods. In April 1893, the San'yō floated ¥2,000,000 in 6-percent corporate bonds redeemable for a period of ten years after May 1898; in fact, after that date, the company liquidated only a portion of those bonds, redeeming them at the leisurely rate of ¥50,000 a year.[312] In July 1893, the stockholders of the Kyushu Railway decided to issue 5-percent bonds totaling ¥1,500,000 with a ten-year term of redemption. However, in 1906, on the eve of its nationalization, the company still had outstanding bonds in the same amount.[313] In short, there is no question as to the long-term nature of these bonds.

On the other hand, the issuance of corporate bonds was clearly an emergency measure prompted by the financial problems these railway companies faced during the panic and recession. Like the San'yō, for example, the Kyushu "took into consideration the difficulty of raising share capital"[314] when it decided to procure construction funds by floating corporate bonds instead. Accordingly, the railroads stopped issuing bonds altogether at the height of the ensuing boom, when stock subscriptions as well as installment payments were once again proceeding smoothly.

The four largest companies accounted for a growing majority of the bonds issued by railway enterprises prior to 1898 (see Table 15). By 1895, they were responsible for over 90 percent of the outstanding bonds; the San'yō and Kyushu alone, for more than 60 percent. The tide turned dramatically, however, during the Panic of 1897–1898. The strained financial situation at that time triggered a revival of bond issuance among railway companies, but responsible for virtually all of the private railway bonds floated during those years and most of those issued thereafter were small to medium-sized firms, especially those founded during the second railway boom. Consequently, the share of total railway bonds represented by the big four dropped to 50 percent in 1898 and had further declined to 31 percent by 1904. During the panics and recession that followed the second railway boom, the total owned capital of the smaller companies, unlike that of the major railroads, fell substantially short of their aggregate investment needs.[315] As a result, after 1897, firms in the small to medium range accounted not only for most of the bond issues, but also for the majority of the bank loans and all of the preferred stock issues floated by railway companies.

Meanwhile, with the four largest railroads having a total of only three bond issues after 1895, corporate bonds represented on the whole a progressively smaller share of the financing of those firms. Moreover, the Kyushu and San'yō, each of which floated one of those three issues, did so not to raise construction funds during the succession of financial crises around the turn of the century, but rather to finance the purchase of another railway company.[316] Their issuance of bonds for that purpose testified to the stability they had by that time acquired as business enterprises.

TABLE 15 Corporate Bonds Outstanding, Private Railway Companies, 1890–1904
(unit: ¥1,000)

Year	All Railroads	Four Largest Railroads	Bonds Outstanding of Four Largest Railroads as Percentage of Total (%)
1890	269	0	0
1891	1,494	810	54.2
1892	1,710	1,265	74.0
1893	5,680	5,080	89.4
1894	5,778	5,178	89.6
1895	5,552	5,030	90.6
1896	5,350	4,910	91.8
1897	5,410	5,210	96.3
1898	10,174	5,074	49.9
1899	10,640	4,917	46.2
1900	11,018	4,759	43.2
1901	12,839	4,571	35.6
1902	12,853	4,408	34.3
1903	18,364	6,625	36.1
1904	21,022	6,473	30.8

Source: *Honpō shasai ryaku shi,* Takahira Takao, ed. (Nihon kōgyō ginkō chōsa-kakari, 1927), pp. 12–16.

The bond issues these two concerns floated in 1893, however, played a vital role in enabling them to reach a position of soundness in the first place. At a time when stock payments had come to a dead halt for both firms, the Kyushu and San'yō owed their ability to resume construction work in 1893 almost entirely to the successful flotation of those issues (see Table 16, Columns 6, 7, 13, and 14). The two companies actually sold the latter to a comparatively small number of individual and institutional investors. At the end of fiscal-year 1893, for instance, the Kyushu Railway, with an authorized capital stock of ¥7,500,000 and an outstanding bond issue of ¥1,500,000, had 1,858 stockholders, but a mere 218 bondholders.[317] Moreover, because the government requirement that corporate bonds be

TABLE 16 Capital Stuctures of San'yō and Kyushu Railway Companies, 1889–1894
(unit: ¥1,000)

Year	Paid up Capital	Reserves	Bonds	Loans	Construction Costs	Ownd Capital as Percentage of Construction Costs (%)	Total Capital as Percentage of Construction Costs (%)
					San'yō Railway		
	(1)	(2)	(3)	(4)	(5)	(6)	(7)
1889	2,915	5	0	0	2,179	134.0	134.0
1890	5,720	9	0	1,102	4,919	116.5	138.9
1891	7,010	14	0	630	6,647	105.7	115.1
1892	7,020	16	0	525	7,126	98.7	106.1
1893	7,020	31	2,000	0	8,414	83.8	107.6
1894	7,794	61	2,000	280	9,453	83.1	107.2
					Kyushu Railway		
	(8)	(9)	(10)	(11)	(12)	(13)	(14)
1889	2,991	0	0	0	1,254	238.5	238.5
1890	5,036	0	0	0	3,506	143.6	143.6
1891	5,663	0	0	0	5,468	103.6	103.6
1892	5,700	3	0	0	5,854	97.4	97.4
1893	5,700	20	1,500	0	6,289	91.0	114.8
1894	6,481	45	1,500	0	7,476	87.3	107.4

Source: *Tetsudō-kyoku nenpō, 1907*, appendix, pp. 23–24, 41.

registered reduced their negotiability, the bonds tended to remain concentrated in relatively few hands. Prominent among the holders of those bonds were financial institutions. Noda states that, from 1891 to 1892, banks and insurance companies, seeking safe investment opportunities for their deposits, "emerged as large-scale subscribers" to railway and other corporate bonds, and, owing to the bonds' low transferability, "most of the corporate bondholding by institutional investors in effect became nothing but a variety of long-term lending."[318] For railroad concerns hit hard by the financial crisis, the issuance of bonds proved to be a crucial alternative means of finance, an innovative expedient that enabled companies like the San'yō to catapult from the recession into a second round of expansion in the mid-1890s.

On the whole, therefore, railroad firms managed to deal resourcefully with the Panic of 1890 and its aftermath. Their ability to cope depended in large part on the provision of both direct and indirect financing by the government as well as commercial banks. Despite such outside assistance and the basic soundness of the railroads themselves, many of the firms did struggle during the panic and recession; this drove a number of their investors and managers to participate in the nationalization movement that broke out in late 1891. Given the resilience of private railway enterprise, however, the involvement of these individuals proved to be less than wholehearted. Inoue Masaru plainly sought to capitalize on whatever problems the companies did experience during the crisis in order to realize his cherished principle of state ownership and control, for, in July 1891, he baldly asserted in his proposal for a comprehensive railway program that "the present decline in railroad-stock prices is an excellent opportunity for carrying out [the purchase of private railroads]."[319] Nonetheless, in the wake of the 1890 Panic, the call for nationalization of existing private railways was all but drowned out by the cry for construction of new government lines. It was the latter demand that supplied the real impetus behind the railway policy debates and legislative initiatives of the early 1890s.

THREE

The Making of the Railway Construction Law

"Ten last night, bill passed. *Tetsudō banzai!*"
Telegram from Ina-district representatives in Tokyo
to their village headman, June 14, 1892[1]

THE POLICY ARENA

The years 1890–1892 marked a period of great ferment in the ongoing debate over railroad policy. A number of ingredients had combined to produce the lively character of those years. On the one hand, state railway bureaucrats led by Inoue Masaru had seen their monopoly in railroad matters decisively broken during the private railway boom of the late 1880s. They had countered by stepping up their verbal attack on private railway enterprise and by pushing for the enactment of regulations to preserve some measure of official control over private development. Their consistent advocacy of the state-ownership principle had kept that issue alive during a period of active government support of private rail companies. The Railway Bureau thereby helped set the agenda for the policy debate of the early 1890s. Meanwhile, beginning in 1887, the army had added its heightened concern for the planning and construction of railroads to meet military needs.

Most critical to the ruling oligarchs, however, was the fact that the opening in July 1889 of the Tokaido line, the route finally chosen for the Tokyo-Kobe artery, spelled the completion of the government's original plan for railroad building; in the meantime, the licensing and development of private railroads had to a large extent proceeded haphazardly in the absence of an overall blueprint for railroad construction. Furthermore, by this time, the financial constraints that had driven the state to rely substantially on private initiative had been somewhat lifted, thanks to the success of the Matsukata financial reform. These factors alone meant that a thorough rethinking and reformulation of government policy were imminent. Yet the process by which the state charted a new course was accelerated by the Panic of 1890 and its aftermath. Moreover, the establishment of the Diet in 1890 introduced a radically new dimension to railway decision making by opening the process to non-bureaucrats. Not only did the national assembly provide an avenue for businessmen and local leaders to influence government planning, but it increased the importance of political considerations at the center, as the cabinet and opposition parties alike used proposed railway legislation as a weapon in their struggle against each other in the Diet.

Did this ferment represent a major turning point in railroad policy? That the policy debate involved two separate but related issues became strikingly clear when in December 1891 the Matsukata cabinet submitted to the second Diet a bill for the completion of a nationwide railway network and another for the purchase of private railroads by the state. The first addressed the question of long-range planning and finance, the second that of public versus private enterprise. The upshot of this initiative was the Railway Construction Law of 1892. That law resolved one of the two issues by providing a master plan for extending the railway network and a mechanism for putting that plan into effect, but it left the other question open, as was subsequently demonstrated by the continued parallel development of state and private lines. In short, these years constituted a watershed for overall planning and control; they decidedly did not for railway ownership and management.

Analyses of the decision-making process leading to the enactment of the Construction Law typically focus on the state Railway Bureau and, in particular, on Inoue Masaru's "Railroad Policy Proposal" of July 1891. Inoue's proposal, the first comprehensive statement of railroad policy within the government, was adopted almost verbatim by the Matsukata cabinet as its railway legislative program on the eve of the second Diet session. To that extent, therefore, the standard interpretation seems justified. The tendency, however, is to portray the Railway Bureau chief as taking the initiative, dominating the decision-making apparatus to push through his plans for railroad development, which bore fruit, at least partially, in the Railway Construction Law. As one scholar puts it, that law came about "under the strong leadership of the railroad bureaucracy"[2]; it resulted from the Railway Bureau's response to the demands of the bourgeoisie and military bureaucracy and to the financial panic of 1890. In fine, the attitude of the Railway Bureau, as personified by Inoue Masaru, was pivotal in the making of the Construction Law.[3]

I would argue that this portrayal misses the political context of the law. In the early 1890s, the cabinet and the Diet were locked in opposition. The parties controlling the lower house wished to curtail government expenditures and reduce the land tax. The cabinet wanted military and industrial expansion. In the first Diet, the parties had succeeded in cutting administrative expenditure items from the budget, but the upper house had blocked the land-tax reduction bill passed by the lower chamber. The Matsukata cabinet anticipated that in the second Diet, the parties would use the resulting surplus in the 1891 budget as a basis for renewing their demand for an abatement of the land tax.[4] Privy Councilor Inoue Kowashi, the chief architect of the administration's counteroffensive, revealed in a memorandum to Itō Hirobumi in July 1891 the gist of what would become the cabinet's "positive policy," its strategy for dealing with the obstreperous opposition parties. In this document, Inoue urged government leaders to abandon the "siege policy" adopted by the Yamagata cabinet towards the first Diet and instead to take a "positive approach." Specifically, he recommended that the administration submit a bill to the Diet to apply the 1891 budget surplus of six and a half million yen to one of the following four enterprises: riparian works, establishment of industrial banks, nationalization of private railroads, and Hokkaido development.[5] Thus, Inoue sought to have the cabinet undercut the parties' demands by proposing that the budget surplus be earmarked for a project closely connected to local interests, one that could therefore successfully compete with land-tax reduction for lower-house support.

Inoue was seconded on this point by Minister of Agriculture and Commerce Mutsu Munemitsu. In a memorial dated 1891, Mutsu warned that, in the second Diet, the question of land-tax reduction would become a serious political problem unless the cabinet took appropriate measures. He proposed that the authorities decide on a way of spending the surplus that would be "good enough to replace the land-tax issue." Mutsu explicitly singled out the construction of railroads. The administration, he suggested, should recommend that over half the surplus be applied to the extension of railway lines and should in the meantime "order the Railway Bureau to establish a plan of railroad construction that will complete the nation's transportation system . . ."[6]

It was the administration's acceptance of the "positive-policy" idea contained in these opinion papers, and not any presumed leadership on the part of the Railway Bureau, that proved decisive in the initiation of the cabinet's proposed railway legislation. Still, one could argue that Inoue Masaru was largely responsible for drawing attention to the issue of railroad development in the first place by constantly petitioning his superiors throughout the 1880s on the urgency of trunk-line construction and the "evils" of private railroads. Indeed, it seems accurate to say that the Railway Bureau, headed by perhaps the only consistent and outspoken advocate of state ownership of railroads within the Meiji regime, "got nationalization placed on the agenda" after the Panic of 1890.[7]

In making this assertion, however, one should not ignore or discount the role of other subordinate bureaucrats in influencing the views of government leaders on the question of railway nationalization. One such bureaucrat was Ozaki Saburō, chief of the Legal Affairs Bureau, who recorded in his autobiography that, in July 1891, he called on Prime Minister Matsukata to argue for government ownership of railroads, presenting him with an opinion paper to that effect. Ozaki, who in December 1891 went public with his argument in a treatise entitled *On the National Ownership of Railroads* (*Tetsudō kokuyū ron*), noted that, on several occasions after the July meeting, he had the opportunity to express his views to the premier.[8]

Nevertheless, to emphasize the nationalization aspect of the railroad issue is itself a distortion, resulting again from an overestimation of the Railway Bureau's input into the policy-making equation. Inoue Masaru was one of the few government officials with an unshakable commitment to public ownership of railroads, a commitment naturally arising from his desire to protect and expand his bureaucratic empire. This stance is clearly reflected in Inoue's railroad policy proposal, the bulk of which is devoted to the purchase of private lines. Whereas the Railway Bureau chief's position on ownership and control had remained virtually unchanged over the years, that of the government had fluctuated considerably. The most conspicuous case of a shift in state policy on this question had occurred precisely in the years immediately preceding passage of the Railway Construction Law. In the period 1888–1890, the government had come out strongly in support of the private development of trunk lines, granting licenses and subsidies to the Kyushu, San'yō, and Hokkaido Colliery railways and selling its Horonai line to the latter company. Yet, by November 1891, the cabinet had decided to submit a legislative package to the Diet calling for state construction of the principal remaining lines and the nationalization of private railroads. The key, then, is to explain this sudden turnabout in government policy, and, in view of the constancy of Inoue Masaru's stand, no interpretation centering on his influence will suffice.

A satisfactory explanation must take into account the following conjunction of events: the completion of the government's Tokaido line, the opening of the Diet, and the Panic of 1890. Certainly, one factor was political expedience, the attempt to use railroad legislation as a tool to control the Diet. A more basic reason for the change in state policy, however, had to do with the stage of railroad development in Japan. The opening of the Tokaido line in July 1889 marked the fulfillment of the Meiji leaders' original program of railroad construction, but left them without definite plans for the future. Even if the government were to rely henceforth on private enterprise, the proliferation of private rail companies made imperative the establishment of a national plan of development to ensure the orderly extension of the railway system. Nonetheless, many of the lines yet to be built, although they might be economically and militarily important, were not likely to be remunerative, and the financial problems stemming from the panic put in doubt the construction by private concerns even of relatively profitable lines. The probability that private interests would be unable to complete the railway network was a powerful argument for state initiative, a point on which Inoue and top government leaders fully agreed.[9]

The leaders differed sharply from Inoue, however, in their flexible, pragmatic approach to railroad development, and above all, it is this approach that explains the reversal in state policy at this time. The top decision makers in the government were concerned less with the form of railroad ownership and control than with the speed and cost of railway construction. Their real goal was the rapid completion of the main-line network, though at minimal expense to the national treasury. This concern represented the one constant in state railroad policy during the 1880s and 1890s. The government pursued this basic objective by the best available means, which, under one set of conditions, meant subsidization of private lines and, under another, nationalization and railway development by the state. In the aftermath of the panic, it seemed that construction could best be carried out under government auspices; also, provisions for buying up private companies would have to be included in any railway extension plan in view of the financial difficulties and resultant construction delays experienced by such key railroad firms as the San'yō and Kyushu. But nationalization was clearly a secondary issue in the minds of government leaders. Inoue Kowashi indicated as much when he argued in early 1892 that the cabinet had appended the Private Railway Purchase Bill to the Railway Public Bond Bill in order to realize fully the latter's objective of railway extension; therefore, the Diet should properly consider the nationalization measure only after deliberating on the plans for railroad construction contained in the Public Bond Bill.[10] And just as official attitudes towards private enterprise had shifted in the past, so, depending on the circumstances, might they change in the future. In the eyes of the leadership group, the policy of state ownership was definitely not carved in stone.

A preoccupation with the Railway Bureau and its nationalization plans leads to a misreading not only of the policy-making process within the administration, but of the Diet legislative process as well. To assert, as Harada does, that Inoue's proposal gave birth to the Railway Construction Law, albeit in emasculated form, is to relegate the Diet to a largely obstructive role.[11] The story of the making of the law becomes one in which the cabinet's legislative program runs up against, and is partially thwarted by, an unruly lower house. This rendering of the legislative process misrepresents the dynamics of the cabinet-opposition party interaction as well as the nature of the Diet's contribution to the shaping of the law. A positive view of the role played by the political parties and the local elites they represented emerges from a more accurate appraisal of the significance of the law and the legislative proposals on which it was based. That significance, as the very title of the law indicates, is to be found not so much in nationalization or even in state initiative as in railroad construction. The parties did not simply react to the cabinet's bills, but introduced their own construction measures into the Diet. And, in point of fact, a group of lower-house members had moved to establish a special committee to "investigate railroad policy and a construction bill" during the first Diet, well before the cabinet's railway policy-making process had even begun.[12] The Railway Construction Law resulted from the merger of the administration and lower-house bills; it was a compromise act, not a mutilated version of Inoue's proposal.

The Preliminaries: The Railway Bureau and the Army

Still, the Railway Bureau chief's policy proposal did furnish the cabinet with its legislative program, and to that extent at least, it merits close examination.[13] Moreover, in the sparring over bureaucratic turf that preceded the administration's adoption of his scheme, Inoue himself played a prominent role. His main adversary in this jurisdictional conflict was, as usual, the army. Inoue had to go to considerable lengths to placate army officials before the cabinet could reach agreement on a legislative package, one that nevertheless closely mirrored his "Railroad Policy Proposal." In this document, the head of the state railways advocated a two-pronged attack for placing the initiative in railroad development squarely in government hands. His call was for a concerted program of state railroad construction and private railway nationalization.

Inoue opened his proposal by stressing the public character of the railway enterprise. The true value of railroads, he argued, ought to be judged on the basis not of their profit rates, but of the "indirect benefits"—the external economies and national-security contributions—resulting from their operation. In order for the country fully to realize these "indirect benefits," it was necessary to establish a nationwide network with a basic set of connecting and feeder lines. Inoue maintained that to complete this system, excluding Hokkaido, would require the construction of 3,550 miles of railway line, besides the 1,650 miles of line already built or certain to be completed. The cost of constructing the additional mileage, at an estimated rate of ¥60,000 per mile, would amount to ¥213,000,000.

Inoue presented the case for state development of the remaining lines as follows:

> Not only will the carrying out of this railway extension be a difficult undertaking calling for a huge amount of capital, but the majority of the lines will by nature provide mainly indirect benefits; the direct returns on capital will be extremely small. Therefore, to expect these lines to be completed by entrusting them to the management of private companies would be as foolish as to look for fish under a tree. Accordingly, we hold it as a matter of course that the government itself should bear the responsibility of establishing [these lines] as a national enterprise.

As Inoue saw it, the government, by applying the proceeds from money-making railroads to those operating at a loss, would be able to complete the system more readily than would private companies, which sought only profits and controlled but parts of the network.

Yet ¥213,000,000 was an immense sum even for the state. To make the burden more manageable, Inoue recommended that the construction work be divided into several phases and that six lines, with a total length of about eight hundred miles, be built during the first period, which was to last from 1892 to 1898. The lines were chosen on the grounds that they were either urgent from a military standpoint, inexpensive to build, or likely to be profitable. In addition, Inoue urged the construction during the first period of train stations and branch railroads for military use. He estimated the total cost of building the six lines and military facilities to be ¥35,000,000 and proposed that this sum be disbursed at an annual rate of ¥5,000,000. Moreover, to insure the continuous funding of this seven-year program and "to prevent objections . . . from arising midway," he insisted that the construction capital be raised not through budget appropriations, but through public-bond issues based on an independent law approved by the Diet.

Parallel to these plans for state railroad construction, Inoue advocated the government's purchase of selected private lines. The Railway Bureau chief, in what proved to be the culmination of his decade-long assault on private railway enterprise, made the following argument for nationalization:

> By nature, railroads, like the postal service and the telegraph, provide service above all to the general public and represent, so to speak, the pulse of the nation. Hence, hardly anyone disputes the fact that it best conforms to their nature to make them state enterprises rather than

entrusting them to private companies, which aim chiefly at profit-making. Moreover, private lines are unsuitable from the standpoint of national defense . . . [This point] should be obvious from the many recent examples among European countries in which the government nationalizes private railroads and manages them itself.

Inoue scarcely concealed his disdain for private railway companies in assessing the current state of Japanese railroads. In his view, only the government railways and the Nippon Railway Company, which at that time was still virtually a semiofficial concern, had completed their lines as originally planned and were fulfilling their potential as providers of transportation. By contrast, he charged, "the rest of the private railroads have generally failed to achieve their original objectives. Some have not started construction work at all; others have stalled halfway through the work and have not been able to continue whatsoever; while still others, although they have already finished most of the work and have begun operation, have had difficulty supporting themselves because profits have proved unexpectedly small."

Inoue then proceeded to illustrate these claims: the Sōbu and Kōshin railways had yet to begin construction; the Osaka Railway had not started work on its connection with the state railways; the Kansai Railway had indefinitely postponed the building of its Kuwana line; and the Sanuki Railway, which had poor business results, was unlikely to remain in operation for long. In particular, the San'yō and Kyushu railways, "which possess the most important lines among private railroads," had both suspended construction work, the San'yō west of Mihara and the Kyushu south of Kumamoto and west of Saga. In short, Inoue asserted, "one could hardly expect these private railroads to achieve their original objectives and display the true value of railroads." Yet these lines represented important links in the projected national network. "Therefore," Inoue declared, "if it is decided now to have the government carry out the extension of the railroads, these private lines must first be completed . . . and the best way to go about that is for the state to purchase them."

So far, Inoue's argument had focused on the problems that railway companies were experiencing primarily as a result of the 1890 Panic. That he had the financial crisis in mind is clearly evidenced by his oft-cited comment concerning the opportunity presented by the decline in railroad-stock prices at the time. Nevertheless, Inoue built his case for nationalization by referring not only to such transient circumstances, but also to more fundamental considerations. Specifically, he raised three points that he had been making since the early 1880s with regard to the inherent "evils" of private railroads. First, contended Inoue, state construction of the remaining unprofitable sections of the railway network would serve only to increase the earnings of the well-situated private lines: it would profit a small number of railway-company stockholders at the expense of the general population. Second, the division of railway management placed various obstacles in the way of through-traffic. And, third, the relatively high operating costs resulting from that division deterred railway companies from lowering their rates or making capital expenditures. For these reasons, the nationalization of private lines, besides being "the starting point of railway extension," was vital to the realization of the basic public character of railroads.

Inoue then delineated the proper scope and method of nationalization. He urged that, of the seventeen railway companies that up until then had obtained licenses, the following be excluded from government purchase: the Nippon Railway, with its special, protected status; the Mito Railway, which had already concluded a merger agreement with the Nippon; the Kōshin, Sōbu, Hōshū, and Sangū railways, which had yet to begin construction; the Hokkaido Colliery and Railway, whose lines were attached to a mining operation and connected with the policy of Hokkaido colonization; and the Hankai and Iyo railways, each of which provided transportation strictly to a single locality. To buy up the remaining eight companies—the San'yō, Kyushu, Osaka, Kansai, Ryōmō, Kōbu, Sanuki, and Chikuhō Industrial railways—would require an expenditure of about twenty-two million yen, the total value of the firms' equity and loans. Inoue proposed that the government finance this program as well through the issuance of public bonds, part of them to be exchanged for company shares and the rest to be floated on the market.

The Railway Bureau chief presented three alternative ways to purchase the individual companies: (1) to nationalize them at their request; (2) to authorize the state to buy them up at any time; and (3) to purchase them by mutual agreement between the government and the firms, subject to Diet approval. He recommended the third option as avoiding the uncertainty of the first and the arbitrariness of the second and as representing "the usual method of private-railway purchase in the countries of continental Europe." He doubted, however, whether negotiations between the government and companies could actually be concluded in time for the next Diet session, in which case the first option as the one less likely to meet Diet resistance would be the more appropriate of the remaining two.

Inoue appended drafts of proposed legislation to put into effect the first and third purchase options as well as the program of state railroad construction. He concluded his proposal by urging that these drafts be given careful consideration "if indeed it is decided to establish a permanent and far-reaching policy" of railroad development and control.

A prominent feature of Inoue's "Railroad Policy Proposal" was the considerable extent to which he emphasized therein the military necessity of his recommendations and incorporated the railroad demands of the army high command. This concern for the military viewpoint was in sharp contrast to Inoue's position in 1887. At that time, he had flatly rejected the army chief of staff's proposal for building railroads to meet military requirements, bluntly asserting the priority of economic over strategic considerations in railroad construction. In his "Railroad Policy Proposal," however, Inoue stated that three of the six "first-period" lines representing parts of major arteries were "most essential from a military standpoint." Moreover, he recommended that the land required for these railroads be purchased, and the lines built, with the idea eventually of double-tracking them so that they might "fully achieve their [military] purposes." And with regard to another of the six lines, that between Saga and Sasebo, Inoue stressed the urgency of providing rail service to the Sasebo naval base. Also, as noted earlier, he called for the construction or renovation of train stations for military use and the laying of branch lines to local army bases.

In short, the conciliatory attitude towards the military that Inoue expressed in his proposal was a far cry from his earlier intransigence. The concessions he made on strategic matters were so extensive as to amount to more than just lip service. Indeed, Diet members and local leaders typically referred to the government bill embodying Inoue's recommendations on railway extension as a measure for "military-railroad" construction, and local interests found the argument for "military railroads" a convenient justification for pressing the bureaucracy and the Diet to construct lines of local advantage.[14] Likewise, Inoue sought to use the military's demands to bolster his case for state railroad development. In 1887, he had rebuffed the Army General Staff in an effort to preserve the independence and authority of his bureau. In the aftermath of the 1890 Panic, however, the conditions seemed ripe for achieving his objective of placing the initiative in railway extension into government hands. Thus, Inoue shrewdly adopted several items from the army's agenda in a calculated bid for military support, hoping thereby to ensure the swift realization of his program. Yet this dramatic turnabout on his part also demonstrated the extent to which the army, in the context of mounting international tensions particularly on the Korean front, had succeeded in introducing strategic factors into the railway policy-making equation.

Inoue cited military reasons not only for state railroad construction, but also for what he appears to have regarded as the more urgent task, the nationalization of private lines. In view of the army's call for the standardization of railway lines and its interest since the late 1870s in the Prussian model of railroad development, one would expect the Army General Staff to have been a long-standing proponent of railway nationalization. Nevertheless, at least until 1891, army leaders showed little, if any, concern for the issue of railway ownership. Instead, they focused almost exclusively on problems of construction. It seems to have made no difference to the army leadership whether railroads were owned privately or by the government, so long as they were built rapidly and according to military specifications.[15] In fact, in its 1888 pamphlet, the General Staff advocated the construction of strategically important lines by private companies backed financially by the state, a position that made sense during the private railway boom.

Following the 1890 Panic, the army naturally became more receptive to arguments for national ownership of railroads. There are indications, however, that this shift in attitude did not simply represent a pragmatic response to changed circumstances, but reflected a growing realization within army circles that private railroads were intrinsically incapable of providing efficient military transport. In an opinion paper issued in 1891, the Army General Staff, although repeating its traditional demands concerning railroad construction, went beyond those points to advance a comprehensive plan for the building of a nationwide network of "military railroads." Significantly, the General Staff concluded this document by asserting, "In the event of an emergency, in order to have the loading, unloading, and transport of personnel, horses, and materials carried out smoothly, we cannot leave [those tasks], as is presently the case, to be performed by a multitude of small, profit-making companies. The government itself must necessarily intervene in railroads as well as supervise them nationwide."[16] From this position, it was a small step to the advocacy of nationalization. Indeed, Inoue sought to accelerate this shift by explicitly linking the army's program for railroad construction to the government's purchase of private lines. The measure of his success was the extent to which military leaders, notably Army Minister Takajima Tomonosuke and Vice-Chief of Staff Kawakami Sōroku, publicly declared their support for the policy of railway nationalization in late 1891.[17]

That support was not easily won, however. By no means did the army rush to endorse Inoue's proposal when he submitted it to his immediate supervisor, Home Minister Shinagawa Yajirō, in July 1891. In fact, several months passed before the government bureaucracy could reach a consensus on railroad policy, largely because of army objections to the Railway Bureau chief's program. Despite Inoue's emphasis on strategic considerations, the Army General Staff charged that his proposal did not sufficiently take into account its views on railroad development. The points raised by Ozawa Takeo, member of the House of Peers and formerly army chief of staff, in a speech in November 1891 can perhaps be taken as representative of the army's complaints. Having taken part in the compilation of the General Staff's 1888 pamphlet, Ozawa was especially critical of Inoue's plan for "purchasing [private railroads] immediately, without establishing a method of renovating them" along the lines prescribed by the army leadership.[18] Ozawa further argued that, if the attainment of military objectives was to be the basis of nationalization, then the government need only purchase the private trunk lines. Yet Inoue had omitted from his list of railway companies slated for nationalization the Nippon Railway, which, in Ozawa's view, held "the most strategic position among the nation's existing railroads," and had called for the purchase mainly of "militarily useless" branch lines.[19] So long as the regime gave priority to nationalization over renovation, however, even the buying up of trunk lines alone would lead to a situation "differing not in the least from that of today when [these lines] fall under private ownership."[20] In addition, Ozawa attacked Inoue's construction program for envisioning the laying of a line along the Japan Sea coast where it would be "totally unsuitable for military use."[21]

These charges suggest the magnitude of the military opposition that had to be overcome before the cabinet could adopt Inoue's proposal. They also show that the army's construction demands continued to dominate military thinking on railroads and that army leaders were as yet unprepared to accept the principle of national ownership. In fact, it was not until the late 1890s that the army would come forward with its own sophisticated argument for railway nationalization.[22] Still, the military was objecting to Inoue's program largely on technical grounds, and, if some mechanism could be found to give the army a say in the execution of that program, military authorities might be persuaded to support Inoue's plans. Ozawa offered a solution. He urged that the Railway Bureau be reorganized as an office devoted solely to the construction and operation of state railways; meanwhile, the administration of private lines and overall planning would be removed from the bureau's jurisdiction, the responsibility for planning in particular being entrusted to a "railway committee" composed of civil and military bureaucrats selected from the competent ministries.[23] Ozawa's call for reducing the authority of the Railway Bureau suggests that General Staff resentment of Inoue's highhandedness, such as he had exhibited most strikingly in 1887, may have contributed as much to military opposition to his program as did the army's stated concerns. For under the prevailing administrative structure, the implementation of that program would only have enhanced the already considerable powers of the strong-minded Railway Bureau chief. The army no doubt felt that, as long as that structure remained, its interests would be better served through the strict regulation of a predominantly private system than through the unification of railroad management under the control of the state railway bureaucracy.[24] At any rate, Ozawa's proposal for a broadly based railway committee was soon to be realized with the establishment in 1892 of the Railway Council, a deliberative body that was to institutionalize army participation in railroad planning.

The idea of setting up a railroad-planning organ undoubtedly came up during the course of government deliberations on railroad policy beginning in September 1891. The *Tōkyō nichinichi* reported that, on September

19th, Prime Minister Matsukata, Vice-Chief of Staff Kawakami, and Railway Bureau Chief Inoue met to attempt an "adjustment of opinions" on railroad policy.[25] Ozaki Saburō, head of the Legal Affairs Bureau, who also attended that conference, included in his autobiography a summary of the day's discussion. According to Ozaki, Kawakami opened the meeting by voicing the standard military position, urging the improvement of existing railroads and the construction of future ones to suit military needs. Inoue then presented his policy proposal. The discussion ended with a decision to draft two bills largely incorporating Inoue's recommendations, to be submitted to the Diet at its next session. In an apparent move to accommodate the General Staff, however, it was decided to resolve such matters as the routing of lines and the timing of their construction after careful consultation with Kawakami and Inoue.[26]

The army finally gave its imprimatur to the Railway Bureau's program after a series of meetings in mid-November attended by Inoue, Kawakami, and the vice-ministers of finance and home affairs, among others.[27] The General Staff evidently obtained sufficient assurances that, henceforth, its viewpoint would receive full consideration in railroad planning, for, in spite of the objections previously raised by military leaders, the army agreed to a draft of a construction bill that was practically identical to that proposed by Inoue. The only notable change—and a minor one at that—was an extension of the initial period of construction from seven years to ten. In addition, it was decided to recommend a modified version of Inoue's bill for nationalizing railway companies at their request, his preferred option of purchasing them by mutual agreement being considered too difficult and time-consuming to carry out. Home Minister Shinagawa then presented these two bills, to which he appended Inoue's policy proposal, to the cabinet council of November 28th.[28]

The cabinet again revised the first period of construction, shortening it by one year, and increased the amount of funding for the "first-period" lines from ¥35,000,000 to ¥36,000,000, but otherwise, it accepted the construction bill as proposed. On the other hand, the cabinet reversed the decision reached in the lower-level meetings on the method of nationalization, adopting a bill that, following Inoue's recommendation, called for the government to "purchase railway companies immediately through consultation with them rather than waiting for them to request it."[29] The precise motives behind this switch in policy are unclear, but it represented to some degree a vindication of Inoue's relatively strict position on nationalization. In any event, the cabinet submitted the two measures under the titles Railway Public Bond Bill and Private Railway Purchase Bill to the lower house of the Diet on December 14th.[30] The fate of the cabinet's program now lay in the hands of the opposition parties that controlled the lower house.

The Main Event: The Cabinet and the Diet

Parties and Interest Groups Enter the Ring. The introduction of that program into the Diet marked a critical turning point in the formation of Meiji railroad policy. Hitherto, the government bureaucracy had enjoyed a virtual monopoly of decision making in railroad matters, as in other areas of national concern; henceforth, the parties and the local and special interests they represented would have a direct impact on public railroad policy through the legislative process in the Diet. The beginning of lower-house deliberations on the construction and nationalization bills thus signaled the entrance of the Diet into the railway policy-making arena, and from that point on, the competition for influence over state railroad plans was to unfold with an expanded list of contenders, including not only civil and military bureaucrats, but Diet members and local political and business leaders as well.

Chief among the new participants in the process leading to enactment of the Railway Construction Law was a lower-house member and veteran of prefectural politics named Satō Noriharu. The main proponent of state railroad extension in the early Diet, Satō bore a striking resemblance to present-day *zoku*, party legislators who specialize in particular policy fields and capitalize on their expertise and close personal connections to bureaucrats and interest groups to intervene in the decision-making system. This precursor of today's communications *zoku* worked tirelessly to secure passage of railroad-building legislation along the lines of the proposed cabinet bill. In the second Diet session, his efforts were to be thwarted by the opposition parties' policy of total confrontation towards the administration. A subsequent change of tactics on the part of both the cabinet and the parties was to enable Satō in the third Diet to push through a grand compromise measure on railway construction, one that was to reflect as well as shape the new realities of railroad planning in the Meiji regime.

Although party politicians like Satō began to have a direct say in the making of railroad policy during the second Diet, in the months prior to that session, they had already been involved in the process indirectly, influencing the very drafting of the cabinet's pending railway bills. For, as stated earlier, government leaders adopted Inoue's proposal above all because it fit in to the cabinet's emerging strategy for coping with the recalcitrant lower house. The railway program was to form one wing of the administration's "positive policy," aimed at heading off the opposition parties' plans for budget slashing and land-tax reduction. The Matsukata cabinet broadly incorporated into the budget it submitted to the lower house the policy advocated by Privy Councilor Inoue Kowashi. Inoue had urged the cabinet to request that all of the 1891 budget surplus, which the opposition parties hoped to use as a basis for reducing the land tax, be applied to a single industrial or public works project with enough appeal to undermine the tax-relief argument of the parties. Yet, in the 1892 budget, most of the surplus of six and a half million yen was devoted to military expenditures, the remainder—just over one million yen—being earmarked for riparian works and Hokkaido development.[31] In addition, the administration called for the financing of its railroad program through public bond issues based on separate legislation—the above-mentioned railway bills.

As embodied in the budget, therefore, the "positive policy" had, in Banno Junji's words, "become no more than a synonym for armaments expansion,"[32] a far cry from the economic purposes for which Inoue Kowashi had recommended use of the surplus. As such, the policy could hardly have been expected to overwhelm party demands for land-tax reduction. Thus, in its budget, the cabinet had very little to offer the parties' local constituencies—basically ¥945,000 for river works—in return for party acquiescence in its larger policies. The railroad program was an entirely different matter. Not only would that program benefit local interests on a massive scale, but as an independently financed endeavor, it would not compete with the parties' tax-relief program for the same source of revenues, namely, the budget surplus. Inasmuch as the railroad legislation, and in particular the construction bill, was likely to gain widespread support at the local level and offered room for compromise in a way that the budget's "positive-policy" items did not, it had great potential for restraining the anti-cabinet offensive of the opposition parties.

It was some time, however, before that potential was realized. In 1891, opposition party leaders remained committed to the tactics of confrontation and responded to the cabinet's "positive policy" by resolving to reject all new enterprises proposed by the administration. The plan for railway nationalization was no exception. When news leaked in September that the cabinet had decided to buy out private railroads, the two major popular parties announced their unanimous opposition. The Kaishintō, which held 44 of the 300 seats in the lower house and tended to represent urban business interests,[33] declared itself against nationalization as early as mid-September and resolved on October 12th "to prevent passage of the Railway Purchase Bill by attacking it with all our might."[34] On the other hand, the Jiyūtō, the largest party in the lower house with 92 seats, had a primarily rural constituency that was eager for state construction of local lines; as a result, that party was inclined to favor national ownership of railroads. In line with their platform calling for opposition to "unnecessary new enterprises," however, Jiyūtō Diet members agreed on October 12th that, "although of course railroads by their nature should be government-owned, our party will not approve [the Railway Purchase Bill] in this year's Diet."[35]

In spite of the parties' defiant public stance against railway nationalization and all other new government projects, their members were generally in favor of the cabinet's railroad construction bill. They had indicated as much in the first Diet session when Satō Noriharu had introduced a motion, backed by over half the lower-house members representing all factions, to set up a special committee to investigate matters relating to a railway extension bill.[36] And, as Wada Hiroshi notes, the parties' decision to oppose the cabinet's railroad program resulted from considering the issue of nationalization alone.[37] When it was reported in late October that the administration intended to submit a construction bill as well, the opposition parties, particularly the Jiyūtō, began to waver considerably. In the case of the Jiyūtō, not only were party legislators themselves in favor of state railway building, but local leaders started lobbying them persistently to pass construction legislation along the lines of the cabinet proposal.

Hence, the opposition parties fell under intense pressure from their constituencies on the issue of railway extension.

Weaknesses in the parties' program were to make them especially vulnerable to such local importunity. Jiyūtō leader Itagaki Taisuke and his Kaishintō counterpart, Ōkuma Shigenobu, met on November 8th and agreed to join forces in the upcoming Diet in demanding the curtailment of both administrative expenses and the land tax. In order to carry out their plan of using the previous year's budget surplus to cover an abatement of the land tax, however, the parties were compelled to cut not just administrative outlays, but expenditures on new enterprises—the armaments expansion and public works projects proposed under the "positive policy." Yet party men could attack such policies as the strengthening of national defense and the building of economic infrastructure only by questioning the "trustworthiness" of the cabinet, as in the case of railroads, or the urgency of the proposed enterprises. As such, their arguments "could not help but lack persuasiveness."[38]

Another shortcoming of the parties' offensive was that its two aims, the curtailment of administrative expenditures and the abatement of the land tax, differed as to their means of attainment. Even if the parties in the lower house succeeded in trimming the budget through their power of budgetary review, as they had done in the first Diet, such a reduction could not be translated directly into land-tax abatement, for the latter required the house to exercise its power of legislative initiative. Land-tax reduction could only be achieved through the passage of a bill by both chambers of the Diet. In the first Diet session, however, the upper house had dutifully performed its role as bulwark of the throne by defeating the bill for revision of the land-tax law introduced by lower-house members, and it was to do so again in the third and fourth Diets. With this built-in obstruction, the parties had little hope of realizing their goal of tax relief through the legislative authority of the lower chamber.[39]

A further problem with the parties' program was a lack of agreement on objectives. Some party members, notably the leaders, viewed the policy of budget cutting and land-tax reduction primarily as a way to embarrass the government and hasten the establishment of party cabinets. Accordingly, they placed a higher priority on upsetting the administration's budgetary plans than on securing land-tax relief for the largely rural electorate. By contrast, the average party legislator was concerned above all with serving the interests of his constituents. To him, land-tax abatement was the goal, and curtailment of administrative expenditures was simply a means to that end.[40] Insofar as the upper house could prevent the parties from achieving that goal at will, he was prepared at least to some extent to compromise with the cabinet and was receptive to those aspects of the "positive policy" that would benefit his electoral district. And chief among those aspects was the railroad program.

These weaknesses in the platform of the opposition parties became fully apparent only in the course of the second Diet, as local groups intensified their lobbying efforts in behalf of railroad legislation. At the outset of the Diet session, the parties were firmly united in their determination to challenge the Matsukata cabinet. Moreover, Ōkuma's dismissal from government office following the announcement of the opposition-party alliance raised the spirit of defiance among the party rank and file to new heights.[41]

Yet, when the Diet opened on November 21st, the administration had reason to be cautiously optimistic concerning the passage of its railway bills, the adamant stand of the opposition parties notwithstanding. For, as an article in the *Tōkyō nichinichi* indicated, the parties were by no means agreed in their opinions on the cabinet's railroad program. The newspaper divided lower-house members into four groups according to their attitudes towards the cabinet bills:

> First, part of the Jiyūtō maintains that, although we should naturally adopt the principle of national ownership, it would be unwise to do so at present since [land-tax reduction] is a more urgent task. Second, all of the Kaishintō (with the exception of two or three businessmen involved in railroads) and part of the Jiyūtō hold that, regardless of the pros and cons of the principle of national ownership, it would be wrong to entrust this matter to the present government. Third, the Taiseikai and part of the Jiyū Club approve of [railway] extension but disapprove of nationalization. Fourth, the Industrial Association (Jitsugyō kyōkai) and others who aim at relieving the distress of railway companies ... approve of both extension and nationalization, but disapprove of basing them on the principle of national ownership.[42]

The Industrial Association was an ad-hoc grouping of seventy-five legislators representing all factions in the Diet organized by Satō Noriharu and others to push for state railroad construction. As the *Tōkyō nichinichi* pointed out in another article, the group's members were concerned less with nationalization than with the extension and continued operation of railway lines. They held that the purchase of private railroads, if it was to be carried out, should be based not on the principle of public ownership, but "on local or personal interest."[43] Satō, who was to play a major role in the process leading to passage of the Railway Construction Law in the third Diet, personified the primary impetus behind the adoption of that law, namely, the demand for railway extension, especially in the hinterlands of central and northeastern Japan. Born in 1850 into a wealthy farmer's family in present-day Yamagata prefecture, Satō entered politics in 1879 as a member of the prefectural assembly, eventually becoming speaker of that body. In 1881, he formed the first political party in Yamagata and the following year founded the *Yamagata mainichi* newspaper. During the mid-1880s, he was a central figure in the vigorous, though unsuccessful, prefectural campaign to persuade the Railway Bureau to build the main line of the Nippon Railway Company so as to pass through Yamagata. Elected to the lower house in 1890 as a Kaishintō candidate, he plunged into Diet railroad politics with a passion, determined to have railroads constructed in his home prefecture.[44]

Satō seized the opportunity to realize local railroad building presented by the cabinet's decision to introduce railroad legislation into the second Diet. On December 10th, he and thirteen other members of the Industrial Association submitted a Railway Extension Bill to the lower house.[45] Satō and his associates offered this bill as an alternative to the administration's program in the hopes that, should the Diet reject the cabinet's nationalization proposal, it would not throw out the policy of railroad construction as well. The Railway Extension Bill consisted of six articles, the first five of which dealt with railroad construction by the government and the last with the nationalization of private lines. In tune with the group's basic platform, the authors of the bill, unlike the drafters of the cabinet's proposed legislation, devoted little space to the purchase of private railroads—in fact, just two lines. On the other hand, there was hardly any difference between the construction-related articles in the Industrial Association bill and the administration's railway public bond measure. The Railway Extension Bill thus reflected the viewpoint of businessmen who were less than enthusiastic about railway nationalization, as well as local residents calling for the construction of railroads in their localities. Consequently, it was a measure that party legislators who favored railroad extension could readily approve,[46] and Dietmen came under increasing local pressure to do so.

On December 7th, local leaders from ten prefectures met in Tokyo and formed the League for the Promotion of Railroads (Tetsudō kisei dōmeikai) with the aim of lobbying Dietmen to back legislation for state railroad construction. This national organization brought together various local movements whose members were petitioning Diet and cabinet leaders for swift enactment of a railway extension bill.[47] League members came from prefectures such as Yamanashi, Nagano, Ishikawa, and Yamagata in which little, if any, railroad construction had taken place.[48] Alarmed by the growing gap in the level of industrial and transport development between their prefectures and more advanced ones, they were determined to see to it that their localities would not be neglected in the next round of railway extension. In short, they embodied precisely the same drive for regional railroad development as did Dietman Satō Noriharu.

The railway league announced its intention to pursue the following agenda: "to clarify the pros and cons of the [railway] issue; to present opinion papers to the presidents of both the Jiyūtō and the Kaishintō; to appeal to the Diet members' council to investigate new railroads; and, if the parties decide to approve railroad construction, to urge them to change their previous party decisions and adopt the position of the league. . . ."[49] With this program in mind, the members of the group began pressuring Jiyūtō Dietmen to support the extension bill submitted by Satō and other members of the Industrial Association. Furthermore, on December 12th, a league delegation called on Jiyūtō President Itagaki in the hopes of persuading him and other Jiyūtō leaders to soften the party line of total opposition to new government enterprises.[50]

In the meeting with Itagaki, Odagiri Yoshiaki, a railway league member and Jiyūtō affiliate from Yamanashi prefecture, criticized the national Jiyūtō resolution "to reject all new enterprises, regardless of their urgency or appropriateness." In the case of railroad development, he insisted, "public opinion has already approved of [the extension of] military railroads." Moreover, he argued: "The construction of the projected railroads will be independently financed and therefore unrelated to taxes. . . . [The building of] these military railroads is not a project that can be done quickly in the event of an emergency. It is absolutely essential that we start constructing them now."[51] In addition, Odagiri pointed out the economic benefits of state railroad development, in particular the much-needed stimulus it would give to the economy, still in the doldrums following the panic. Finally, he suggested that the parties might reconcile their lack of confidence in the cabinet with approval of the railroad legislation by setting up a standing committee to oversee the execution of the railway program.[52]

Itagaki replied that the party decision on new enterprises was not inflexible, that, "if upon investigation we find that there is nothing improper or unreasonable" with regard to the government office in charge of a particular project, "we will not hesitate in the least" to approve it. "My own opinion," he asserted, "is that all railroads should be state enterprises."[53] Recently, however, he had directed Kōno Hironaka to investigate railway matters, whereupon Kōno had discovered a number of "unspeakable improprieties." Itagaki was presumably referring to the concentration of power in the government's Railway Bureau, which not only built and operated the state lines, but licensed and supervised private ones as well. As a result, Itagaki claimed, in the area of railroads, the party "is concerned entirely with discussing the reform of the Railway Bureau and has not even begun to consider the issue of construction work." He assured his visitors that, "if only a method were established to reform that bureau," he would gladly support the construction program.[54] Itagaki was here expressing the same concern over the state of railway policy making and administration as that of the Army General Staff. Party demands on this front were to merge with those of the military to result in the creation of the Railway Council.

Not surprisingly, Itagaki's argument failed to impress the representatives of the railway league. Odagiri responded by pressing the party leader for his opinion on the cabinet's proposed legislation, particularly its plans for building the Chūō line, a "military railroad" that would run through Odagiri's home prefecture.[55] Itagaki avoided giving a definite answer, stating that, although he naturally favored the construction of military railroads, the Diet faced a surfeit of important bills requiring careful consideration in the present session. Odagiri then emphasized the urgency of railroad construction from the standpoint of his own prefecture:

> This is a matter concerning which all four hundred thousand people of my prefecture cannot help but petition [the Diet]. Although all other localities have railroads and constantly hear the sound of the steam whistle, only in Yamanashi prefecture has there been no railroad construction whatsoever [sic]. . . . It is one of the most isolated areas in the whole country. Consequently, it has fallen behind the currents of society, and the transportation of freight is extremely inconvenient. Comparing this to the human body, it is as if one's entire health were to deteriorate because of the blockage of one part of the blood vessels. Should military railroads now be built, it would bring happiness to one prefecture and wealth and strength to the entire nation.[56]

As Ariizumi Sadao points out, this line of argument suggests the way in which local leaders appropriated the vocabulary and rationale of government authorities in order to legitimate their own demands for local railway development. Odagiri clearly exemplified this tendency in labeling the Chūō line a "military railroad" and in stressing the importance of railroad building for enhancing national power.

Nevertheless, Odagiri was careful to link this national perspective to the particular concerns of his prefecture, as he proceeded to trace the rise of the railway construction movement in Yamanashi. His description, together with Ariizumi's more detailed examination of that movement, offers insight into the development of local lobbying efforts in behalf of railroad legislation. When Yamanashi residents learned in the fall of 1891 that the cabinet's proposed construction bill included plans for a railway line that would pass through their prefecture, they immediately began organizing to push for enactment of the bill. On November 8th, the prefectural assembly invited "all interested people in the prefecture" to a meeting in Kōfu. The 340 residents who attended decided to form an association, which, anticipating the national organization of the same name, they called the League for the Promotion of Railroads, and, in Odagiri's words, "voted unanimously to entreat every Diet member to support the [railway construction] bill."[57] Further, they elected a committee consisting of five to ten people from each of the prefectural districts to spearhead a petition drive as well as a group of seven representatives to go to Tokyo to lobby members of the Diet in person. In the December 12th meeting with Itagaki, Odagiri stated that the representatives of the Yamanashi league would be arriving in Tokyo shortly and would begin their lobbying activities by petitioning Jiyūtō legislators. In the meantime, the movement in Yamanashi had expanded rapidly, as native businessmen, including Nezu Kaichirō, Amenomiya Keijirō, and Ono Kinroku, and prefectural representatives in the Diet had joined the campaign.[58]

Ariizumi notes that members of the Yamanashi branch of the Jiyūtō were especially active in the prefectural railroad movement. They sought to use the railway issue to increase local support for the party, and hence their own chances for election to the Diet, by declaring that they would realize prefectural demands for railroad construction through the power of the Jiyūtō. Accordingly, they put pressure on the national party leadership to back railroad legislation.[59] A prime example of these local Jiyūtō members was Odagiri himself. His membership in the party indicates that he was motivated to participate in the national railway league and to press for local railroad construction not simply to serve local interests, but to satisfy personal political ambitions as well. In order to win election to the Diet as a Jiyūtō candidate, which Odagiri hoped to do in the next general election, he had to convince Yamanashi voters that the Jiyūtō would secure legislation beneficial to the prefecture and that he himself carried weight with the party's central leadership. Odagiri saw the railway issue as a perfect opportunity to achieve these goals.[60]

The party leaders, however, failed him miserably. On December 16th, Jiyūtō Diet members met to determine the party's response to the cabinet's railroad legislation. As in October, it was decided by an overwhelming majority to reject the nationalization bill. Thereupon, Hoshi Tōru, whose faction was engaged in a struggle for party control with the pro-railroad construction group under Ōi Kentarō, strongly insisted that, if the party was going to reject the nationalization proposal, it ought to turn down the construction bill as well. The upshot was that the Jiyūtō Dietmen resolved to oppose both measures. The reason given for this decision was necessarily a forced one: "Even though our party is in favor of the principle of state ownership of railroads, we cannot entrust such a major enterprise to a government that, like the present one, cannot be trusted and especially to one whose railroad policy changes from year to year and has not been settled in the least. Furthermore, the time is not yet right."[61]

Jiyūtō legislators, heavily pressed by their local constituents, undoubtedly wished to approve some form of legislation for railroad building, even if they were against nationalization. The party ended up opposing railroad construction, however, because, in order to preserve internal unity, it had to lump the extension and purchase bills together and to make an all-or-nothing decision regarding them. Another complicating factor was the climate of confrontation in which the opposition parties joined forces to resist all new government enterprises. As Itagaki observed after the second Diet, "truly unfortunate circumstances" led to the party resolution to reject the railroad construction bill, for that decision did not reflect the real desires of the Jiyūtō.[62]

With the opposition parties publicly committed to rejecting the cabinet's railway bills, the prospects for passage of railroad legislation were extremely bleak when the lower house began its first reading of the bills on December 17th. Following Home Minister Shinagawa's explanation of the cabinet's reasons for submitting the legislative proposals and interpellation of administration spokesmen, the house briefly debated the size and number of special committees to which the bills would be referred. Satō Noriharu and his supporters made a last-ditch effort to prevent total rejection of the railroad legislation by proposing that both bills be submitted to a single committee.[63] In view of the strong sentiment for railroad construction within the Diet, they evidently believed that one committee investigating the various railway proposals together might be persuaded to adopt their own extension bill. The factions of the opposition parties that sought to have both cabinet measures defeated insisted on referring each bill to a separate committee. Since Dietmen were certain to turn down the nationalization bill, members of the majority party Jiyūtō at least would be bound by the party resolution to reject the construction bill as well. Moreover, the opposition diehards charged that Satō's proposal was simply a "separate government bill."[64] In the end, the hard-liners prevailed, as the house decided by a vote of 115 to 103 to set up two committees composed of eighteen members each and chose as committee members the candidates put forward by the opposition.[65] Even Satō, the resident house railroad expert, failed to win a seat on either of the committees.

These developments sealed the fate of the cabinet's railway bills. The special committee investigating the Railway Purchase Bill began deliberations on December 21st, subjecting the administration spokesmen to relentless interrogation. Shimada Saburō, a Kaishintō member from Kanagawa prefecture, for example, questioned the sincerity of the administration's claim to be establishing "a permanent and far-reaching policy" when "the government frequently changes its policy, calling for state ownership, then for private ownership, and then for state ownership again."[66] With Shimada's viewpoint typifying the committee's hostile attitude, the outcome was a foregone conclusion. By the end of the day, the members had decided unanimously to recommend rejection of the bill.[67]

In reporting the committee's recommendation to the lower house at the general session on December 23rd, Acting Chairman Nakano Buei, a Kaishintō representative from Kagawa prefecture, cited as the major reason for rejecting the nationalization bill the capriciousness and therefore unreliability of the cabinet's policy on railway ownership. Up until the opening of the Diet, Nakano explained, the administration had been actively promoting private railroads:

> Yet, now, it suddenly reverses that policy and seeks to purchase private lines . . . During this short period, has there really been a change in the times necessitating such a switch in policy? Moreover, might not [the administration] make an about-face regarding the state railways and support the policy of private ownership [again]? Today, when the vestiges of the old custom of issuing an edict in the morning and repealing it in the evening still remain, we cannot easily put our trust in [administration] policy on a matter like railroads that involves long-range planning.[68]

Nakano then proceeded to refute point by point the cabinet's case for nationalization. First, he repudiated the administration's charge that railway companies were an obstacle to efficient military transport by asserting that existing regulations adequately provided for the military use of private railroads in time of emergency. Second, he dismissed the argument that the state should purchase struggling private firms in order to complete the network and realize the basic public character of railroads, contending that nationalization would simply result in unnecessary patronage of the companies involved. Finally, concerning the cabinet's claim that a mixed system would interfere with the orderly development of the railway network, he insisted that nationalization was not the answer, since profitable railroad firms would most likely refuse to sell out.

These statements clearly reflected the arguments of private railway advocates like the journalist Taguchi Ukichi and the railway engineer Saburi Kazushige. Both of these men had published works in which they strongly supported the private ownership of railroads from a laissez-faire perspective and repudiated the charges of nationalization proponents concerning the purported "evils" of private enterprise. And both tried to put their views into practice by engaging in private railway management, Taguchi as president of the Ryōmō Railway and Saburi as director and then president of the Narita Railway.[69] Nakano, himself a businessman who later became president of the Kansai Railway Company, was representing the interests of the Kaishintō's business constituency in borrowing the anti-nationalization arguments of Taguchi and other free-enterprise advocates. Added to Nakano's laissez-faire proclivities, of course, was the adamant political stand of the opposition parties.[70]

Nakano's attack on the nationalization bill was carried further by a Jiyūtō member of the special committee, Ishida Kannosuke, when the issue was brought up for discussion at the general session on December 24th. Ishida declared his opposition to the measure on the following grounds: (1) even after it had initiated the Purchase Bill, the administration was granting licenses to private railroads and therefore had no set policy on railway ownership; (2) private enterprise was preferable since the construction and operating costs of private railroads were lower and their business methods more efficient than those of state lines; and (3) the cabinet's plan to issue railway-purchase bonds bearing 5-percent interest was unreasonable in view of the fact that railway companies were averaging an annual profit rate of only 3.2 percent.[71] Ishida's critique epitomized the overwhelming sentiment of the house, which moved swiftly to vote on the matter that day. At this point, Satō Noriharu made one last attempt to save the construction program. Stating that "to reject the nationalization measure today will make difficult [the subsequent passage] of the extension bill that we desire," Satō introduced a motion to change the agenda so that the construction measure would be considered before the nationalization bill.[72] The motion failed, however, and the house proceeded to reject the Railway Purchase Bill by a wide margin, with only 67 out of the 300 Diet members supporting the measure.[73]

The following day, the special committee investigating the Railway Public Bond Bill concluded its deliberations and voted by a majority of sixteen to two to reject the cabinet's bill. Among the reasons the committee cited for turning down the measure were the following: (1) since the nationalization bill had been rejected, the administration could not realize its plans; (2) the projected lines included several for which licenses had already been granted to private companies, and the Diet had to respect the rights of those firms; and (3) investigation of matters relating to the issue of public bonds was incomplete.[74] The committee was unable to report its decision to the lower house, though, as the cabinet dissolved the Diet that day on the grounds that important government bills were being rejected en masse. As a result, the Railway Public Bond Bill was discarded without having been brought up for discussion, other than at its first reading, on the floor of the lower house.

Party leaders could not have been more relieved by this turn of events. On the one hand, the opposition parties had hewed to their common platform of rejecting new government enterprises by turning down the unpopular nationalization measure. On the other hand, the Diet had been dissolved before the construction bill could be laid before the lower house. In light of the widespread support that measure enjoyed among party members, its submission to the house for further debate would no doubt have caused an uproar and brought to the surface the considerable dissatisfaction among Dietmen over the parties' decision to reject the bill. This discontent was clearly expressed by Inoue Kakugorō, a Jiyūtō Dietman during the second session and backer of the Satō proposal who subsequently left the Jiyūtō. In a speech on January 5, 1892, Inoue assailed the "sinister scheme" of the "subversive" opposition parties, which had conspired to place the extension bill on the agenda after the nationalization measure. The rejection of the latter, he complained, meant that the construction bill, which "was supported by a majority" of the Diet members, could not possibly be adopted, since the construction program required the purchase of private lines, and, once rejected, the same item could not be reintroduced into the Diet.[75]

In the long run, party leaders could ill afford to ignore such displeasure, just as their followers in the Diet could not avoid responding to the demands of local pressure groups. As Itō Miyoji tellingly observed to Itō Hirobumi on December 20, 1891, "[The opposition parties] are again determined to oppose new enterprises for 1892; however, among these, there is the issue of railroads, and the public on the whole tends to favor the government's position. Moreover, when one opposes this, there is *the disadvantage of making enemies of businessmen and [local] leaders* [underlined in the original]. Consequently, one sees evidence of vacillation and indecision [among the parties]."[76] In short, the cabinet's "positive policy," as embodied above all in the railroad program, was beginning to exert a definite impact on the opposition parties' offensive. That policy had whetted the appetite of the parties' local constituents for pork barrel, particularly for state railroad construction. As a result, party leaders found it increasingly difficult to limit their party platforms to curtailment of government expenditures and land-tax reduction. Pressure from disgruntled Diet members and local elites, combined with the basic shortcomings of the parties' retrenchment and tax-relief program, drove leaders of the Jiyūtō in particular to compromise on the issue of railway extension following the second Diet.

CHANGING TACTICS. By the time the third Diet session opened in May 1892, a significant shift had taken place in the attitudes and tactics of both the opposition parties and the cabinet. Each side had reconsidered its position on railroad legislation and become flexible and conciliatory in its approach to the matter. Certainly, interest groups led by the League for the Promotion of Railroads played a big role in pressing party and bureaucratic leaders to modify their strategies and get on with the business of legislating railroad construction; yet equally, if not more, important was the pivotal mediation supplied by two individuals in the government, Dietman Satō Noriharu and Privy Councilor Inoue Kowashi. Not only did these men help build a consensus among their respective colleagues in the Diet and the bureaucracy, but together, they forged a party-bureaucratic link that was to prove critical to successful passage of a railway extension bill in the third Diet.

Facilitating the efforts of Satō and Inoue at the center were timely interventions by the local interests embodied in the national League for the Promotion of Railroads. During the interim between the second and third Diet sessions, the railway league stepped up its lobbying activities in the hopes of persuading the opposition parties to change their policy on state railway construction. League representatives called on Kaishintō President

Ōkuma on January 11, 1892, and on Jiyūtō President Itagaki the following day to impress on them the urgency of railroad building. In their opening statement, the league spokesmen asserted that "it has become increasingly necessary for every locality to seek the extension of railroads" and urged that "a decision for railway extension be reached without fail in the next Diet."[77] They then asked the party chiefs for their opinions on the matter. Ōkuma spoke for his party's business constituency by replying that he was for private ownership of railroads with government assistance and against nationalization and construction by the state. By contrast, Itagaki made clear that he upheld the principle of the national ownership of railroads, but opposed the government's purchase of private lines, which carried "the danger of ruining the national treasury." On the other hand, he expressed support for state railroad construction. Itagaki assured his visitors that he "deeply regretted" the Jiyūtō's resolution of October 1891 to reject the extension measure along with the purchase bill as well as the failure of the lower house to consider the construction bill before the Diet's dissolution in December. He believed that, if the bill had been laid before the house, it would have passed.[78] In light of the impending general election, one might dismiss Itagaki's comments as campaign rhetoric; yet they undoubtedly exemplified the views of Jiyūtō Dietmen and suggest the extent to which the party's leadership felt constrained to alter Jiyūtō policy so as to please the party's supporters at the local level.

The railway league did not limit its activity to interviewing party leaders. In early 1892, the group appealed to the general public by issuing a pamphlet detailing the conversations with Ōkuma and Itagaki as well as a subsequent interview with Prime Minister Matsukata. Despite the considerable divergence among the opinions voiced by the three men, with Matsukata toeing the official administration line, the league concluded, "Leading politicians in the government and in the popular parties uniformly approve of railway extension; hence, there is no difference between the government and the people and no distinction between factions [on this issue]. Such being the case, we believe there are no particular objections to extending railroads throughout the country and putting the means of transportation in order."[79] While publicizing their cause, the group's members constantly visited Dietmen running for reelection from their home prefectures and urged them to back legislation for railroad construction. Moreover, several league members, including Odagiri Yoshiaki, stood as candidates for the Diet themselves in the second general election held in February 1892.[80]

The campaign issues stressed by the men running for election to the Diet from Yamanashi prefecture suggest that the message being broadcast by the national railway league and similar local groups was clearly getting across to members of the opposition parties. During the campaign, all the party candidates in Yamanashi, not just Odagiri and other Jiyūtō members, pledged to support legislation for the construction of "military railroads."[81] Odagiri himself failed to be nominated by the Jiyūtō as its official candidate in his district, the party choosing to endorse instead a man of greater means and therefore with a better chance of winning election.[82] Nevertheless, Odagiri sought to capitalize on his Jiyūtō membership and to impress on the voters the fact that President Itagaki had promised to realize a railroad construction bill in the upcoming Diet. Lacking formal party recognition and the personal wealth of his major opponents, however, he finished a disappointing third in the one-man electoral district.[83] Odagiri's case notwithstanding, a number of candidates in the second Diet election seem to have ridden to victory on the wave of local demands for political patronage, above all for railroad construction. By the same token, the opposition parties' failure to meet those demands in the second Diet may very well have cost the reelection of many a party incumbent. For example, newcomers accounted for over 40 percent of the Jiyūtō's ninety-four members in the third Diet.[84] Certainly, other factors, including the massive election interference carried out by the administration, were involved in this turnover in the party's Diet membership. Nevertheless, local dissatisfaction with the Jiyūtō's uncompromising stand against railroad legislation during the previous session appears to have played a significant part in the membership change. As the March 29, 1892 issue of the *Kokkai* reported, "within the Jiyūtō . . . there is a considerable tendency in favor of [the cabinet's railway bills], there being not a few newly elected Jiyūtō Dietmen."[85] Whatever the precise degree to which the call for railroad building on the part of local leaders was translated into election results, that call was unmistakably heard by Jiyūtō Dietmen-elect, newcomers and returnees alike, as the party's attitude towards railroad legislation following the general election was markedly different from what it had been during the second Diet.

The Jiyūtō was not the only one to undergo a change of heart in early

1892. The administration also began to reconsider its "positive policy" and to show a more conciliatory attitude on the railway question. To be sure, many government officials were still determined to use railroad legislation to confront the opposition parties; as one bureaucrat observed of party Dietmen, "The railroad construction issue is the best measure for splitting the parties. One and all, having come [to the Diet] charged [with enacting a construction bill] by businessmen and ordinary landowners along the prospective routes of railroads in all localities, must want to extricate themselves from party policy and realize the commission with which they came. This is a fact that we should take advantage of . . ."[86] The hostile sentiment expressed here was precisely what the League for the Promotion of Railroads feared most. In its report of early 1892, that group voiced particular concern that the railway issue would be "used as a glorious instrument of war by the various factions" and exhorted the cabinet and parties to set aside their differences and work together in order to achieve the common goal of railway extension.[87] In the aftermath of the second Diet, bureaucratic leaders, despite the continued strength of antiparty feeling, came increasingly to share the league's viewpoint.

The key figure behind the cabinet's reassessment of its railroad legislative strategy was Inoue Kowashi, the originator of the "positive policy." Inoue, who has been described as "a powerful partisan of the Prussian school" of constitutionalism,[88] was also a keen student and admirer of Prussian railroad policy. That he viewed the railway system of Prussia as a model is evidenced by his translation of the Prussian railway nationalization law of December 1879, the contract of June 1879 for the state purchase of the Magdeburg-Halberstadt Railway, and the law of June 1882 establishing railway councils to advise on rates and timetables for the Prussian state lines.[89] In view of the Prussian orientation of Inoue's thinking on railroads, one might expect him to have been as adamant a proponent of railway nationalization as Inoue Masaru, whose "Railroad Policy Proposal" was branded by laissez-faire advocates as "a German-style railway program."[90] Indeed, Inoue Kowashi seems to have had a hand in writing a pamphlet arguing forcefully for national ownership of railroads that was published in April 1892 under the name of Nakane Shigeichi, a secretary in the Legal Affairs Bureau.[91] On the other hand, Inoue was enough of a pragmatist to be willing to compromise on the nationalization issue in order to realize the construction program so eagerly desired by both cabinet leaders and party Dietmen. In addition, his private papers indicate that he was far from a narrow-minded devotee of the nationalized railway regime of Prussia, but showed interest in a wide range of continental European patterns of railroad development. Not only did Inoue translate a French law of 1845 granting concessions to several private companies, but he also solicited the advice of an Italian legal expert employed by the Justice Ministry, Alessandro Paternostro, who, in January 1892, presented Inoue with a series of opinion papers explaining both sides of the debate over railway ownership in Europe as well as the prevailing Italian system wherein the government owned the railroads and private companies operated them.[92]

The reconsideration of the state's railroad legislative program by Inoue Kowashi and other government bureaucrats centered on two problems with the legislation that were believed to have resulted in its rejection. The first was a shortcoming in the presentation of the bills. As a hectograph distributed prior to the third Diet session diagnosed the problem, the cabinet had divided the legislation into two measures and "had not made clear whether it attached greater importance to the policy of railway extension or to that of private railway nationalization."[93] As a consequence, "government policy was dismembered, its ability to be realized weakened, and a bill that ought to have been passed [namely, the construction bill] was also discarded." The second defect in the railroad program was a substantive as opposed to a procedural one. According to the hectograph, the nationalization bill would give the government bureaucracy "such enormous powers of disposition with such a huge amount of capital" that the Diet "could not help but hesitate to approve" the measure; "indeed, this point was one of the main reasons cited in the report of the lower-house committee investigating the Private Railway Purchase Bill for rejecting that measure." The administration's plan for dealing with these shortcomings in its previous strategy consisted, on the one hand, of "combining the railway bills into one measure and making clear that government policy is concerned primarily with planning the extension of the state railways"[94] and, on the other, of establishing a railroad council that would allow the Diet to participate in railway decision making.

Nevertheless, there was considerable opposition within the government bureaucracy to submitting an amended railway bill combining the original proposals. By doing so, it was charged, the cabinet would appear to be yielding to the opposition and admitting that it had erred in its previous approach.[95] Yet, in the February elections, the opposition parties had again captured a majority of the seats in the lower house; hence, if the administration were brazenly to resubmit its railroad legislation without amendment, the lower chamber would almost surely reject it. Thus, the cabinet and the parties, although agreed on the necessity of railroad construction, seemed to be heading perilously towards a deadlock over the means of achieving that goal.

It was Satō Noriharu and his supporters in the Diet who pointed the way out of this impasse. Satō and his associates urged that, in the coming session, the lower house "should first of all deliberate on the Public Bond Bill, which is the extension measure, and define its policy on the railway question . . ."[96] Furthermore, through Inoue Kowashi, they sought to impress on bureaucratic leaders the need to amend the cabinet's railway bills. On March 18, 1892, Inoue wrote to Vice-Minister of Finance Watanabe Kunitake that Satō had visited him the previous evening to discuss the issue of railroad legislation. In the course of their conversation, Inoue reported, Satō had made the following points: "(1) It is certain that the bills will not pass if they are presented just as they were last year; (2) if the two bills are combined and if each [private railroad] purchase is made contingent on [Diet] approval, then [the legislation] will probably pass; (3) either the administration should amend the proposals or (4) [that task] should be entrusted to the Diet."[97] Satō had then asserted that, if the revision were carried out by "a group of important, like-minded Dietmen," the legislation would "have a solid chance of passing." Inoue noted that, at the end of their talk, he had expressed a desire to meet with Satō from time to time to confer on railroad-related matters and that Satō had been "delighted" by this proposal.[98] Inoue's visitor, who left the Jiyūtō to join the Chūō kōshōbu, a union of regional groups of Dietmen formed in April 1892, had established close ties with advocates of railroad construction within the opposition parties, especially through his activity in the suprafactional Industrial Association during the second Diet session. Satō thus had connections with both bureaucratic leaders and opposition-party members. As a result, he was able to perform a key mediating role as well as to win broad support for an expanded version of his original Railway Extension Bill, which he was to present to the lower house on May 6th as an alternative to the cabinet's legislation.

In the meantime, the administration itself continued to give serious thought to amending its railway proposals. On March 26th, the *Yūbin hōchi* reported that "recently, the position in favor of revising the railway bills has been gaining greatly in strength" within the regime and that the government bureaucracy was "roughly divided into two factions" on the issue. On one side of the question was the hard-line group led by Home Minister Fukushima Taneomi; on the other, the pro-revision faction headed by Inoue Kowashi. "In effect," the newspaper maintained, "there are many who argue that last year's railway bills are incomplete and that it would be a mistake to submit them as is." In the midst of this debate, the cabinet on April 15th asked the Legal Affairs Bureau for its opinion on the matter. The bureau replied on April 22nd that, in its view, there was "no particular need to make amendments . . ."[99] Accordingly, on April 28th, the cabinet obtained imperial approval for reintroducing the railway bills in their original form. Right up until it reported the issue to the throne, the administration seems to have considered revising the legislation. In fact, the *Tōkyō nichinichi* claimed on April 27th that the cabinet had decided on a "new railway bill" emphasizing "first of all the necessity of railway extension and second the gradual purchase of lines needed for railway extension." In the end, however, the administration submitted to the lower house on May 7th a railway package that was identical to the one it had laid before the second Diet. Inoue Kowashi and other advocates of revision finally went along with the diehards, it seems, because, even if the lower house rejected the cabinet's legislation, it was almost certain that the policy of railway extension would be realized through an amendment along the lines of the Satō bill.

At the same time that it was debating the question of revising its railroad legislation, the cabinet was steadily developing the idea of establishing a railway council. An internal state document made clear why this idea took hold among government leaders. According to the document, the second Diet had rejected the nationalization measure primarily on the grounds that, "even though we approve the gist of the railway extension and private railway purchase policies, such a major enterprise should not be left to the discretion of one part of the government." Therefore, the cabinet "should, if possible, devise a plan" that would ease these concerns of the Diet and thereby "secure the passage" of the railroad legislation. Not only would the setting up of a railway council serve that purpose, but it would bring additional dividends to the regime. As the document explained, "Rather than taking the dangerous path of acting arbitrarily by assuming sole responsibility for such a major undertaking and attracting public criticism in the future, the government should from the start make its object to be open and impartial and adopt the policy of sharing responsibility with the people."[100]

On April 1st, a formal proposal for creating a railway council was submitted to the cabinet. The first article of the proposal stated that the council would be established by imperial ordinance and that its function would be to "express its opinions, in response to the inquiries of the home minister, on important railroad-related matters such as plans for new railroads and the method and order of purchasing private railroads."[101] The membership would consist of representatives from the Diet as well as military and civil bureaucrats. To a large extent, therefore, the proposal for a railway council was designed to conciliate the lower house. In addition to adjusting the long-standing differences between the Railway Bureau and the army, the council, it was hoped, would serve to placate the opposition parties in the Diet by giving them a say in railway decision making. The proposal submitted to the cabinet can also be seen as the culmination of the demands for a railway council that had been emanating from various quarters, not the least of which were the parties themselves.[102]

On May 2nd, the cabinet approved an imperial ordinance to implement the railway-council proposal. The Legal Affairs Bureau in its written opinion pointed out that the ordinance would also have to be sanctioned by the Diet, since the purchase of private railroads and other expenditure-related matters impinged on the fiscal powers of that body.[103] Nonetheless, the administration made absolutely no mention of the railway council in the bills it presented to the lower house. As Wada puts it, this omission plainly indicates that, "from the time it introduced the bills, the government not only anticipated their revision in the Diet, but was acting on that premise . . ."[104]

Meanwhile, the Jiyūtō, reflecting the shift in attitude towards railroad legislation among its members, was working to come up with its own proposal for railroad construction. The party platform adopted on April 25th stated that the cabinet's nationalization bill "should of course be rejected as in the previous Diet." But it left room for maneuver by providing that the party "should decide, after investigating their pros and cons, whether or not to approve bills on which the second Diet had not yet expressed its opinion [at the time of its dissolution] or measures that the government will submit in the coming session."[105] The party clearly had railroad-building legislation in mind. Yet plans were under way to go beyond this indirection and send a clear signal to the Jiyūtō's local supporters by having the party submit an extension bill of its own. On May 7th and 8th, Jiyūtō Diet members met to discuss whether or not to introduce a measure drafted by party planners. Opponents charged that the party proposal differed "not in the least from the government's bill"; as such, it "should be opposed without fail." Proponents of the measure countered by arguing that, "if this bill is not passed . . . , we should support the [Satō] and government bills."[106] In the end, the Jiyūtō legislators voted by a majority to present to the Diet the party's proposed Railway Construction Bill. The fact that this proposal was very similar to the Satō measure as well as to the cabinet's Public Bond Bill and that party members had indicated their willingness to support the latter two bills shows that the Jiyūtō was far from bent on seeing its proposal adopted as submitted to the Diet; to the contrary, it was prepared from the start to accept amendment of its bill. From the party's standpoint, to introduce an extension bill of its own making had significance in itself as a way of reassuring party constituents that the Jiyūtō was indeed committed to realizing a program of railroad construction.

The third Diet, convoked on May 2nd, opened inauspiciously for supporters of railroad-building legislation, however, as the opposition parties launched a spirited attack on the Matsukata administration for having interfered in the general election. The party-cabinet confrontation reached a climax in mid-May when the lower house passed a resolution censuring the administration for its election interference, prompting the cabinet to retaliate by proroguing the Diet for a week.

Nevertheless, advocates of railroad construction were heartened by the fact that, in the meantime, a variety of groups had introduced railway extension bills into the Diet. Following the presentation of the Satō and cabinet construction measures, the Jiyūtō had submitted its bill on May 10th, and two independent Dietmen, Kawashima Atsushi and Tanaka Gentarō, had introduced a fourth extension proposal on May 12th. The Satō bill bore the signatures of 95 Diet members; the Jiyūtō bill, 79; and the Kawashima bill, 31, for a grand total of 205 endorsements.[107] It appears, though, that several Dietmen backed more than one measure, as was the case with Kagami Kahei, an independent from Yamanashi, who stated in a letter of May 15th to his electoral district that he had signed both the Satō and Kawashima bills.[108] The incidence of such multiple signing further attests to the lack of rigid attachment to any one proposal on the part of Diet members. This pragmatic flexibility was particularly encouraging to proponents of construction legislation.

The various bills, although similar in many ways, were by no means identical. For example, the cabinet's Public Bond Bill specified only the six lines slated for construction during the first period, whereas the Satō bill provided for the laying of twenty-two lines, six of which were to be built during the first phase, and the Jiyūtō, of thirty-two lines, seven of which were scheduled for first-period construction. The Kawashima measure, on the other hand, called merely for the building of seven lines. Not only did the Jiyūtō proposal contain the most scheduled lines, but, for each of those lines, it listed alternate routes (*hikaku sen*), the better to please the party's many constituents. Furthermore, the Jiyūtō measure stipulated that the choice among the alternate routes for each first-period line be made later, subject to the approval of the Diet. It also called for deferring a determination of the timing and cost of first-stage construction. The Satō and cabinet bills, by contrast, insisted on the immediate selection of routes for the railroads to be built during the first phase. In addition, they both provided for the financing of first-stage construction through the issue of ¥36,000,000 in public bonds over a nine-year period beginning in 1892. Meanwhile, the Kawashima bill prescribed a construction period of twenty-five years for lines that were to be determined forthwith; the work was to be funded through the flotation of public bonds, but the amount to be issued was, as in the Jiyūtō measure, to be decided separately with Diet approval.[109]

The proposals also differed somewhat as to the scope and method of nationalization. Not surprisingly, the administration's Private Railway Purchase Bill would have given the government the greatest latitude in buying up private companies. The measure stipulated that the government should gradually purchase "all railroads that provide public service . . . through consultation with the companies."[110] There was no mention whatsoever of the Diet. The Satō bill, however, specified the targets of nationalization as being those railroads "of which [the state purchase] is considered necessary for building" the twenty-two scheduled lines,[111] a definition that was narrowed even further in the Jiyūtō proposal to apply only to the first-period lines. Both these measures and the Kawashima bill made each purchase contingent on Diet approval.[112] Moreover, the Kawashima measure contained an important offsetting provision allowing for the private construction of lines not yet begun by the state.[113]

The Kawashima bill was also the only one to call for the setting up of a railway council. The bill stipulated that this organ was to be established separately by imperial ordinance and that its function was to deliberate on the routing of lines, the order and period of their construction, and the like.[114] These provisions were strikingly similar to those included in the internal administration proposal for a railway council. Kawashima and Co-Sponsor Tanaka, a former member of the pro-administration party Taiseikai, may very well have been in touch with state leaders and have been asked to introduce the idea through their bill.

In short, there were some fairly substantial differences among the railway measures, but the gap between them was not unbridgeable. In particular, the construction-related provisions of the cabinet and Satō proposals were virtually identical. The Jiyūtō bill represented basically a variation on the same theme. On the other hand, the Kawashima measure, with its rather idiosyncratic proposals, appeared to be the odd man out; yet several of those proposals, including that for a railway council, were to be incorporated in the Railway Construction Law. Above all, the Kawashima bill shared with the others a strong emphasis on railroad construction financed by the issuance of public bonds. As Dietmen Kagami declared in his May 15th letter, "since all four bills have [railway] extension as their aim, one must say that passage of an extension bill at any rate is almost certain."[115]

That the lower house finally did agree on a single construction measure, however, was largely owing to the efforts of one man, Satō Noriharu. Satō's proposal appeared on the lower-house agenda on May 10th, the same day the Jiyūtō submitted its bill. Fearing lest head-to-head discussion of the two proposals should trigger a factional struggle on the order of that in the second Diet, Satō had the speaker postpone deliberation on his bill until the next day. In the meantime, he worked to build a consensus among the Jiyūtō, his own Chūō kōshōbu, and the Independent Club that all the railway bills should be referred to one committee.[116] Accordingly, on May 11th, when the lower house began its first reading of the cabinet bills, it decided to set up a special committee of eighteen members to consider the various construction measures together. The house then voted 130 to 121 to refer the administration's nationalization bill to the same committee.[117] The committee's membership, announced at the general session the following day, consisted of seven representatives of the Chūō kōshōbu, six of the Jiyūtō, three of the Kaishintō, and two of the Independent Club.[118] The members included Satō and two of the three sponsors of the Jiyūtō bill and in general held views that were the exact opposite of those of their counterparts in the second Diet. Meeting for the first time on May 13th, the committee elected Satō as chairman and one of the co-sponsors of the Jiyūtō measure as a director.[119]

Satō thus found himself in the driver's seat, backed by a core of like-minded members of the Diet. He now moved to carry out his plan of combining the various railway measures into one bill. As a first step, however, he sought to mobilize support for the idea outside of the committee. Kagami Kahei, for example, noted in his letter of May 15th that he had met with Satō that day and "discussed forming an alliance of Dietmen" with the following platform: "(1) to approve the Jiyūtō bill's inclusion of Hokkaido railroads among the projected lines; (2) to approve the six [first-stage] lines of the Public Bond Bill . . . ; (3) to approve determining the amount of public bonds to be issued and [starting construction] without fail in 1892; (4) to limit the nationalization of railroads to cases in which it is considered necessary and to carry out each purchase after securing the approval of the Diet."[120] As Kagami made clear, Satō's goal was to rally advocates of railroad construction from all factions in the Diet and, by accommodating their respective positions, to secure "the swift passage of an extension bill."[121]

Satō was assisted in this task by the League for the Promotion of Railroads. The group's members, now representing twice as many prefectures as in the second Diet, had resumed their lobbying activities in Tokyo by the end of April.[122] After the four construction bills were introduced into the Diet, the league distributed a pamphlet strongly urging all parties to merge the various proposals. In particular, the group called for adoption of the first-stage lines specified in the Jiyūtō bill, the period of construction prescribed in the Satō and cabinet bills, and the method of nationalization stipulated in the Satō measure.[123]

With the wide-ranging support generated by Satō's campaign as well as that of the railway league, the special committee was able to proceed confidently with the work of amalgamating the railway bills. On May 24th, following the seven-day prorogation of the Diet, Satō appointed a five-member subcommittee headed by himself to draw up a proposal "taking into consideration the government-submitted bills and the other measures."[124] On May 26th, the subcommittee presented its draft proposal, entitled the Railway Construction Bill, to the full committee, which adopted the measure after partial amendment.[125]

The resulting bill represented a skillful compromise among the original proposals, but there was still considerable dissatisfaction among Jiyūtō members over the nationalization provisions of the measure. At a meeting on May 29th, Jiyūtō Dietmen charged that the provisions ran counter to their party's decision to reject the purchase of private lines and declared that they would introduce an amendment to delete the offending articles.[126] This position, however, encountered strong opposition within the party, so on June 2nd, the Jiyūtō legislators held another meeting to discuss the matter. The ensuing debate revealed a sharp conflict of opinion. On the one hand were those who argued that, "since nationalization was a factor in the dissolution of the [second] Diet and is therefore a matter that the party definitely cannot allow, we should flatly oppose it"; and on the other, those who maintained that, "since last year's nationalization bill was based on the principle of national ownership, whereas the measure revised by the committee in the present Diet calls for purchasing sections necessary for extension, the latter is naturally different in purpose and does not contradict the party decision; accordingly, necessary sections ought to be purchased."[127] In the end, through Itagaki's mediation, the party Dietmen managed to avoid a split by deciding that they could vote on the bill as they pleased.[128]

At the general session of the lower house that afternoon, Satō presented the committee's report as well as the Railway Construction Bill. Orita

Kanetaka, a Jiyūtō Dietman from Kagoshima, charged that the special committee had exceeded its authority in combining the two cabinet bills.[129] His criticism notwithstanding, the bill passed its first reading by a majority. The Private Railway Purchase Bill was next on the agenda, but the cabinet, determined this time to prevent opposition to the nationalization measure from derailing the construction bill as well, had asked that consideration of the former be postponed until after a decision had been reached on the construction proposal. In any case, adoption of the Railway Construction Bill with its nationalization provisions would obviate passage of the purchase measure. Amidst a howl of protest from the floor of the chamber, punctuated by shouts of "No precedent!" and "You fool (*bakayarōme*)!" Speaker of the House Hoshi Tōru pronounced the administration's request accepted.[130]

During the second reading of the Construction Bill held on June 4th and 6th, the house adopted several amendments to the projected lines, including a motion to omit the Hokkaido lines as "colonial railroads" requiring separate treatment.[131] On the 6th, Ishida Kannosuke, a Jiyūtō Dietman from Hyōgo prefecture, spoke for the party's anti-nationalization faction by urging removal of the articles providing for the purchase of private railroads.[132] In response, Ushiba Takezō, a member of the Chūō kōshōbu representing Mie prefecture, asserted that the articles were necessary for achieving the bill's objective of railway extension.[133] Ushiba's viewpoint prevailed, as the house quickly dismissed Ishida's motion.

After the Construction Bill had passed its second reading on the 6th, the lower chamber immediately began the third and final reading of the measure. Takasu Hōzō, a Kaishintō member from Ehime, together with the Jiyūtō's Orita Kanetaka, mounted a final attack on the bill. The two Dietmen assailed the measure for prescribing the construction of inadequately surveyed lines as well as the issue of huge amounts of public bonds, which, in Orita's words, would "necessarily cause problems for the future of Japanese finances."[134] Calling these the "dying words" of the opposition, however, a supporter of the bill moved that the debate be closed forthwith. Speaker Hoshi promptly declared this motion accepted, and to a burst of applause, the lower house adopted the railway construction measure as an amendment to the government's Public Bond Bill.[135]

An independent Dietman from Mie prefecture, Kaku Risuke, attested to the magnitude of lower-house support for the policy of railway extension. Kaku stated that it was impossible to know precisely how many Diet members had stood up for the Construction Bill; instead, he offered as a proxy the following factional breakdown of the number of Dietmen who had signed the various railway bills and amendments: 82 out of the 86 Jiyūtō members, 5 out of the 38 Kaishintō members, 10 out of the 11 Dietmen affiliated with the opposition parties, 91 out of the 104 members of the pro-administration party, 13 out of the 15 Dietmen associated with the latter party, and 29 out of the 45 independent Dietmen, for a total of 230 out of the 299 lower-house members. Kaku observed that, "regardless of the issue, the popular and government parties are almost always in the position of dog and monkey. Especially with respect to the issues of dissolution and lack of confidence in administration policy, their battles are furious." By contrast, the railway issue, he complained, "obtained the support of a coalition of popular and government parties and left no room for us independent members to make use of our special skills."[136]

With such extensive backing, the Construction Bill easily passed the lower chamber. Its adoption by the House of Peers, however, was by no means assured. This was especially true in view of the confrontation between the two houses at the time over the lower chamber's right to prior deliberation on the budget. The various interested parties, therefore, made special efforts to avert a possible breakdown in the legislative process. The *Chōya* newspaper reported on June 10th that thirty-six lower-house members representing the Jiyūtō and Chūō kōshōbu had called on leading Dietmen of the upper chamber and urged them to vote for the Construction Bill. The League for the Promotion of Railroads was also active in lobbying members of the upper house. No sooner had the construction measure passed the lower chamber than the league distributed a pamphlet exhorting members of the House of Peers to "approve the bill and enact it swiftly."[137] The cabinet was likewise concerned lest the Construction Bill should run afoul of the inter-house conflict over budgetary powers. On June 6th, the administration notified the upper house that the issue was an "urgent matter" that should be given immediate consideration.[138] The bill itself was submitted to the upper house and referred to a nine-member special committee on the 7th. The committee met on the 8th and approved the bill as amended by the lower house.[139] At the general session on the

11th, when the committee reported back to the full house, Prime Minister Matsukata made explicit the administration's acceptance of the construction measure: "Based on the amended bill of the lower house, the government will in fact be able to achieve its objectives by and large; therefore, the government approves this amended bill and hopes that you will support and quickly pass it."[140]

Several members of the upper house remained unimpressed by the cabinet's assurances. Konoe Atsumaro and others argued on the 11th that the lower-house bill was so different from the administration's proposal that it could not be regarded as an amendment to the cabinet's bill.[141] When the first reading of the measure resumed on the 13th, Viscount Tani Kanjō declared his opposition to the bill on the grounds that the lower house had exceeded its authority in amending the administration's proposal and that the government should establish a comprehensive policy not only for railroads, but for other means of transport as well.[142] Despite Tani's objections, the house voted by a majority to move on to the second reading. During that reading, Murata Tamotsu contended that the bill's title was a misnomer since the measure was concerned more with the issue of public bonds and the nationalization of private lines than with railroad construction per se. He proposed a series of revisions, such as renaming the measure the Railway Public Bond-Purchase Bill and striking from the list of projected railroads all but first-period lines.[143] The house rejected the proposed amendments, however, and adopted the bill as submitted by the lower chamber.

The enactment of the Railway Construction Bill naturally elated those who had been working tirelessly for realization of a program of railway extension. Upon learning that the bill had safely passed the upper house, representatives of the Yamanashi railway league, for example, "could not help but leap for joy, hands waving and feet stomping."[144] Meanwhile, the Private Railway Purchase Bill had died a quiet death, as the lower house had unanimously rejected the measure on June 7th. In trying to explain why "not one person stood up for the bill," one observer speculated that, "prior to [the vote], the government had already realized that the Diet could not possibly accept the principle of national ownership and had privately expressed its approval of the committee's amended bill . . ."[145]

THE CONSTRUCTION LAW AND ITS IMPACT

That bill, with only the minor revisions made during the second reading in the lower house, was promulgated as the Railway Construction Law on June 21st. As a compromise measure, the law contained something for practically everyone concerned.[146] Article 1 affirmed the Railway Bureau's cherished principle of railroad construction by the state. Article 2, on the other hand, reflected the desire of the Jiyūtō and its local supporters for regional railroad development by scheduling thirty-three lines for future construction. Thus, the lower house, while deleting the projected lines for Hokkaido originally proposed in the Jiyūtō bill, substantially increased the number of those for the rest of Japan.[147] Moreover, as in the Jiyūtō proposal, the law listed alternate routes for many of the scheduled lines. The act further called for a program of "first-stage" construction that was basically in accord with the Satō and cabinet measures, though again on a scale more extensive than that of the latter bills. Under the Construction Law, the state was to build nine "first-stage" lines over a period of twelve years, financing the work by floating 5-percent public bonds totaling no more than ¥60,000,000. In addition, the legislation included several articles that met the opposition parties' demand for the institution of checks on bureaucratic power. The cabinet was required to obtain Diet approval of the construction budget for each "first-period" line, decisions on alternate routes, and any changes in the scheduled lines. And, following the Satō bill, the law provided for the negotiated purchase of private railroads in cases where it was deemed necessary for completing the projected lines, subject again to the approval of the Diet.[148] Finally, the act incorporated two crucial provisions from the Kawashima bill that further circumscribed the authority of the government bureaucracy. Article 14 allowed for private building, contingent on Diet approval, of any projected line on which the state "has yet to begin construction." Article 15 provided for the establishment of a Railway Council to advise on the order of construction and the amount of public bonds to be floated for each line, thereby realizing military and party demands for a say in railroad planning.

Inasmuch as the Railway Construction Law represented a merger of proposals differing significantly on the question of nationalization, it was an ambiguous document that brought into an unstable relationship conflicting tendencies on the issue. This ambivalence is plainly mirrored in scholarly appraisal of the law's significance. To some observers, the act was the fulfillment of Inoue Masaru's dreams: it enabled the state once and for all to seize the initiative in railroad development, paving the way for eventual nationalization.[149] Not only did the law establish the principle of state construction based on long-range planning, but it strengthened the government's position of leadership with regard to private railroads by providing for the buying out of railway companies and the setting up of the Railway Council as a central planning organ. In short, the legislation gave "clear direction" to state railroad policy; thereafter, railroads were "to attain rapid development under government guidance."[150]

Other scholars paint a very different picture of the law in terms of its effectiveness as a nationalization act. According to Aoki Eiichi, the law "utterly failed as a measure for the purchase of private railroads."[151] Not only was the government's proposal for nationalization, in Nakanishi's words, "completely emasculated" in the Construction Law,[152] but that act provided for continued private building even of trunk lines. The result was to give legal confirmation to the policy the government had theretofore carried out in practice of promoting parallel state and private development of the main-line network.[153] The law thus represented a major setback for Inoue Masaru's plans for railway nationalization and construction by the state.

Both of these perspectives have some validity, but neither is entirely accurate on its own. Again, this fact stems from the essential ambiguity of the law. Insofar as the act incorporated the often dissonant views of various groups, it was, and still is, subject to a variety of interpretations. Indeed, the manner in which the law was actually interpreted and carried out is the key to understanding its significance. The law certainly laid down the principle of state construction and management and set up a mechanism for nationalization. Yet, the government never put into effect the nationalization provision of the law; to the contrary, it permitted private companies to build many of the scheduled lines, including those that formed parts of major arteries, thereby encouraging the private railway boom of the mid-1890s. On the one hand, the law recognized the preferential right of established firms such as the San'yō and Kyushu to build lines nominally slated for construction by the government under the act for which the companies had already obtained licenses prior to the promulgation of the law.[154] On the other hand, the cabinet exercised the private-construction option for many of the remaining scheduled lines, repeatedly securing Diet approval for the licensing of such new main-line firms as the Hokkaido, Hokuetsu, and Hankaku.[155] The way in which the measure was implemented, therefore, amounted to a reversal of policy. As one popular account aptly puts it, "a construction law for state lines had in no time become a construction law for private railroads."[156] The point, however, is not that the act failed as a nationalization measure, but that, under the enterprise-boom conditions, state leaders simply found it unnecessary to utilize the law's buyout provision in order to achieve their objective of rapid completion of the basic rail network. Hence, in the area of nationalization, the Construction Law was by no means a decisive measure, setting Japan on the road to railway nationalization. Perhaps one can only say, as Ochiai Sadaaki does, that the law was "a turning point that left latitude in railroad policy."[157]

If the law was ambivalent on the question of nationalization, it was far from being so on the issue of construction, reflecting the fundamental agreement on this point among the several extension bills submitted to the Diet. On the construction front, the legislation marked a pivotal change in Meiji railroad policy. The act determined the shape of the evolving trunk-line network by fitting the previously haphazard construction of railroads "into a framework of long-term planning under the control of the Diet."[158] Future main-line railroads would all be bound by the routes specified in the law. The addition or alteration of a scheduled line or the elevation to "first-stage" status of a projected line initially deemed non-urgent would require an amendment to the act. The cabinet would refer such a matter to the Railway Council and, based on the council's recommendations, would submit it to the Diet as a bill requiring the latter's approval. The law thus established a systematic procedure for railroad-construction planning, one in which the Diet would play a major role.

Equally, if not more, important in shaping construction plans was the Railway Council. The Railway Council Regulations, issued as an imperial ordinance on the same day the Construction Law was promulgated, detailed the structure and functions of that deliberative body.[159] Set up to advise the cabinet, the council was to fall under the jurisdiction of the ministry in charge of railroads, initially the Home Ministry and, after July 1892, the Ministry of Communications. Its membership was to consist of a chairman and twenty regular and several ad-hoc members to be drawn from the upper ranks of the service ministries and the General Staff, the Railway Bureau and other related government offices, and the Diet. The ordinance invested the council with a much broader authority than that specified in the Construction Law. Besides determining the order and cost of construction of the projected lines, the council was empowered to investigate the routing of new lines, the purchase of private railroads, the regulation of traffic and fares, and any other matter the supervising ministry might refer to it. The council thus had wide-ranging powers over the planning, construction, and operation of the nation's rail system.

The Railway Council was roughly patterned after the Prussian central railway board established under a law enacted in June 1882. In many respects, the genesis of the Prussian council paralleled that of its Japanese counterpart. In 1879, the Prussian Diet had demanded "certain restrictions on future state railway administration" in return for approving the government's nationalization proposal.[160] This requirement then was partly met by the 1882 law. The purpose of this legislation, according to Inoue Kowashi's translation of a German commentary on it, was to "satisfy . . . those whose interests are affected by railway transportation"; to that end, the law called for the formation of a national railway council, "a mixed official-private organization," to act as an advisory board of the central railway bureaucracy.[161] Insofar as the Japanese Railway Council represented a concession to the Diet's demand for participation in railroad planning, it was very similar in conception to the Prussian board. Further, several provisions of the imperial ordinance, including those specifying the term of office of council members and some of the areas of council jurisdiction, were taken directly from the Prussian law.

The resemblance, however, ends there. The Prussian act provided for the establishment not only of a national railway board, but also of local councils to advise the district branches of the state railway administration. The composition of these advisory boards differed markedly from that of Japan's Railway Council. The local councils were to consist of the representatives of chambers of commerce and industrial and agricultural associations, while the central board was to be composed of thirty members elected by the local councils and ten appointed by the civilian government ministries concerned.[162] The disparity in membership between the Prussian and Japanese councils mirrored the fact that the initiative in Prussia came entirely from the business interests represented in the Diet, and not partly from the military bureaucracy as in Japan. For, unlike the railroad policy of mid-Meiji Japan, that of Prussia in 1879 had long been closely attuned to military strategy.[163] On the other hand, the ordinance governing the Japanese council lacked express provisions for direct business representation, a point on which the Tokyo Chamber of Commerce voiced its displeasure in August 1892.[164] Apparently in an effort to conciliate businessmen, the government appointed Shibusawa Eiichi an ad-hoc member of the first council, convened in December 1892. That Dietmen themselves served on the Railway Council suggests that, in Japan, the motives underlying the Diet's call for a say in railroad planning were more political in nature than they were in Prussia. Legislative leaders in Japan were concerned more with increasing party power than with giving representation to business interests per se.

The Japanese and Prussian councils also diverged in the extent of their respective powers, reflecting the countries' differing stages of railroad development. The Prussian boards, befitting the relative maturity of that state's railway system, were authorized specifically to deliberate on "important matters pertaining to the railway traffic, especially timetables and rate schedules."[165] By contrast, the Japanese Railway Council enjoyed much greater authority, with jurisdiction not only over the operation of railroads, but also over railway construction and the nationalization of private lines. This wider competence corresponded to the comparatively early phase of railroad development in which Japan found itself in 1892.

Despite their differences in organization and jurisdiction, however, the Japanese and Prussian railway councils shared the same basic objective, namely, to broaden the arena of railway decision making. That this was the primary goal of the Japanese council contradicts the view that this organ tended to bolster the bureaucracy's leadership in railway matters.[166] It also puts in doubt the common assertion that the Railway Council served as a mouthpiece for the military.[167] Granted, the council was consistently chaired by a ranking member of the Army General Staff, and military men held six of the twenty-seven positions on the first council.[168] Nevertheless, Dietmen and private citizens comprised fully half of the body's membership. With its broad representation and authority, therefore, the Railway Council ensured that planning under the Construction Law would reflect not the arbitrary decisions of any one section of the civil or military bureaucracy, but a wider, though still firmly elitist, "public opinion."[169]

With the enactment of the Railway Construction Law, Japan entered a new phase of railway-policy formation, as the center of railroad planning gravitated to the Railway Council and the Diet. Following Inoue Masaru's retirement in 1893, the Railway Bureau receded from the political limelight, becoming a more purely technical organ. Meanwhile, local lobbying efforts also underwent a transformation. At the end of 1892, the Railway Council initiated the process of determining the exact routes and order of construction of "first-period" lines, while the Diet began deliberations on the council's initial recommendations. At this point, the common interests that had led prefectural railroad movements to join together in the national League for the Promotion of Railroads dissipated, with the central association breaking up into its constituent local elements. Various localities then organized or reactivated their own railway leagues, each one demanding the selection of a route favorable to its area.[170] Japan thus embarked on a lively period of railroad construction in which local communities contended with one another for the routing of lines through their localities, inundating the Diet and Railway Council with petitions to that effect. The story of this competition, however, is basically a chapter in the development of the state network, specifically its extension into the nation's economic backwater, central and northeastern Japan, whose residents had spearheaded the movement for passage of railway-building legislation in the first place.[171]

With regard to the private sector, the Construction Law as implemented did not mark a dramatic shift in official views and treatment of private railroads. In practice, it imposed few, if any, new restrictions on the establishment and growth of railway enterprises. Granted, the carrot and stick embodied in the private-construction and state-purchase provisions of the act may well have spurred the companies to get on with their construction work, and in that sense, the law may have exerted a strong positive influence on private railroad management. In the area of line selection at least, the law did place the companies under greater state control. Still, the cabinet had exercised strict supervision in this regard, if in a less structured manner, even before passage of the act.

What was different was that the Construction Law introduced into the licensing process two checks on the government bureaucracy in the form of the Railway Council and the Diet. This expansion of the railroad decision-making field had the potential for making it more difficult for railway companies to obtain licenses, given the heightened possibility of political disagreements and attendant delays. Nonetheless, by giving the localities a voice in the process via their representatives in the Diet and by establishing a clear procedure for the licensing of railroad firms, the construction act in the long run facilitated the founding and extension of private railroads. To be sure, state-railway building accelerated under the law, but, while the total length of the state system increased from 551 miles in 1892 to 1,532 miles in 1905, the private network kept pace, growing from 1,320 to 3,251 miles during the same period. Furthermore, of the fifty-seven railway companies that had put track into operation by 1905, thirty-eight—fully two thirds of the total—were licensed after the promulgation of the Railway Construction Law.[172]

Thus, relatively little came of Inoue Masaru's bid for state initiative, let alone nationalization, as embodied in the Construction Law. In fact, at the height of the second private railway boom in the mid-1890s, the government would come under mounting pressure to transfer *its* railways to private firms.[173] Yet, during the panics of 1897–1898 and 1900–1901, business interests would once more urge the state to buy out struggling private lines. As Ōkuma Shigenobu wryly observed in 1902, "The question of railways had become a kind of economical barometer; when times were bad the public wanted the Treasury to buy up the private lines, and when times were good the clamour was for the Treasury to sell the lines owned by the State."[174] In the wake of the financial crises at the turn of the century, Inoue's successors in the communications bureaucracy would once again raise the flag of nationalization within the government. This time they would succeed, not through the 1892 construction act, but through a new piece of legislation—the Railway Nationalization Law of 1906.

Part Three
Towards Nationalization

FOUR

Forging a Consensus

"The unification of railroads under national ownership is the pressing need of the postwar administration, for its implementation will truly cut the Gordian knot for a host of financial, economic, and military problems."

"General Objectives of Railway Nationalization,"
December 1905[1]

In the evening of March 27, 1906, under tumultuous conditions in the House of Representatives, the Diet passed a law that dramatically altered the course of Japanese railroad history. The Railway Nationalization Bill, the centerpiece of the Saionji cabinet's postwar program, had just returned to a restless lower house following its revision in the upper chamber, the very last item of legislation to be considered in the current Diet session. No sooner had the amended bill been placed before the house and endorsed by the prime minister than a Seiyūkai representative leaped up to make an urgent motion that debate be closed and a vote be taken forthwith. The chamber was immediately thrown into an uproar, with shouting and wrestling matches between supporters and opponents of the bill, producing, in the laconic words of contemporary observers, "a very disorderly scene," one "not witnessed of late."[2] In the midst of this confusion, the speaker pronounced the motion accepted. This only compounded the unruliness, prompting one decorum-minded member to exclaim: "Those who are resorting to violence in the chamber will not be forgiven! Who are the scoundrels that are disobeying the speaker's orders?"[3] The outnumbered opponents boycotted the ensuing vote, most of them stalking out of the chamber. In the end, the Nationalization Bill was passed by a tally of 214 to 0. With this explosive beginning, then, Japan was thrust into the age of nationalized railroads.

What were the forces behind the initiation and passage of the Railway Nationalization Law? Why did the government buy out the principal private lines, and why did the railway companies agree to their purchase, following the Russo-Japanese War? These are the major questions to be addressed in this and the ensuing chapter. Viewing these problems in comparative perspective is both useful and suggestive. Beginning in the late nineteenth century, "there was a decisive swing everywhere" on the European continent towards public regulation and ownership of railroads,[4] and even in those so-called paragons of private railway enterprise, Britain and the United States, a heated debate over the issue of state versus private control of railroad networks came to be waged around the same time as in Japan. In fact, British and American publicists produced a flood of literature on the subject from the 1880s through the 1910s.[5] There was a key difference, however, between the Japanese and Western cases. In Western countries, the nationalization debate generally coincided with the maturation of national railway systems, whereas in Japan the debate occurred when the rail network was only partially completed. True, by 1906, many of the arteries and several connecting lines were in place (see Map 5), but the system had yet to be filled out and actually comprised less than one third of its eventual total mileage.[6] In short, Japan had barely begun to experience the "problems of relative maturity," above all the need to build unremunerative branch lines, that had called forth a more extensive government role in the railroad networks of Europe and America.[7] Moreover, with the industrial revolution just getting underway in Japan, rail profits, at least outwardly, were showing no signs of slowing down, and, indeed, railroads were closing in on shipping companies in terms of volume of domestic freight carried.[8]

The fact that private railroads were apparently in sound financial shape and had excellent business prospects around 1906 was a point on which the nationalization movement of the mid-1900s differed markedly from those of the 1890s and early 1900s. The earlier movements had come during financial crises and involved a clear element of providing relief to hard-hit railway companies. In fact, railway investors themselves had participated in

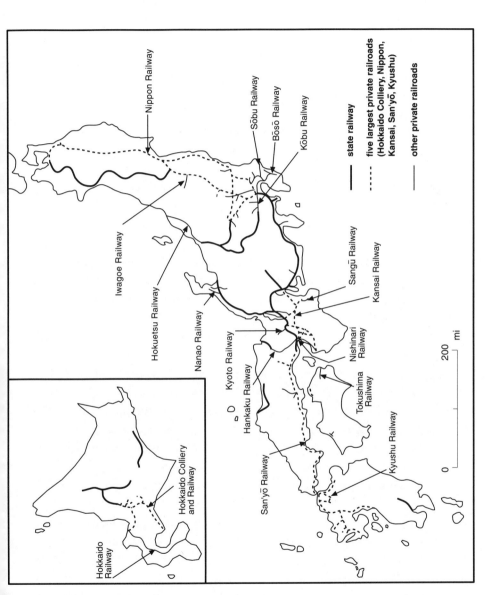

Map 5 Japan's Railway Network in 1906 (nationalized railroads identified by name)

those campaigns in the hopes of restoring the value of their shares. Consequently, their position had been ridiculed by critics like Taguchi Ukichi as a "stockbrokers' nationalization argument."[9] By contrast, the Nationalization Law was enacted during an upswing—the immediate postwar boom—when private railroads were recording sustained high rates of return. This time railway shareholders were by no means clamoring for a government buyout. To the contrary, the riotous Diet scene depicted above suggests that, insofar as opponents in the lower house represented railway business interests, many investors were dead set against nationalization.

In the case of the movement leading up to the 1906 Nationalization Law, the initiative clearly came from the government bureaucracy. The majority-party Seiyūkai, whose antecedent had taken the lead in the nationalization bid of 1899–1900, played more of a supporting role this time. Actually, that party and its predecessors, reflecting the conservative investment attitudes of their landholding and business constituencies, had been fairly consistent advocates of state ownership since the late 1890s. Such had not been the case with the cabinet, however. Indeed, its lack of enthusiasm had spelled failure for the nationalization campaign at the turn of the century. The key then is to explain how a consensus for government purchase was finally reached within the state bureaucracy, a consensus strong enough to enable the Katsura and Saionji cabinets to initiate and successfully carry through the railway nationalization.

Prime Minister Saionji Kinmochi, upon introducing the Nationalization Bill to the lower house on March 6, 1906, asserted that agreement on "the principle of state ownership" had existed from the start, that entrusting railroad construction to private enterprise had been merely "a temporary expedient." Thus, proclaimed Saionji: "To this day, our nation's railway policy has remained consistent from beginning to end."[10] As critics in the Diet were quick to point out, the premier's characterization of the history of Meiji railway policy was plainly distorted. Nonetheless, a similar interpretation has found its way into scholarly writing, which often portrays the nationalization as the inevitable outcome of government planning since at least the early 1890s. This study, however, has demonstrated the definite lack of consensus among state authorities on the question of ownership and control, the result being frequent shifts and even reversals in government railway policy. The one consistent thread was provided by communications officials, backed from the late 1890s by the army. By and large, their advocacy of state ownership had been constant. Resistance to nationalization had come mainly from Finance Ministry bureaucrats, who had continually tried to shift the burden of railroad development on to the private sector, as well as from the oligarchs and their lieutenants, who had tended to share the concerns of finance officials. Explaining the government's decision for nationalization in 1905–1906, therefore, hinges on determining why these authorities ultimately came around to support the railway purchase bill.

Although the state bureaucracy initiated the nationalization bill, its passage still depended on the Diet. Accordingly, another question to be examined is why the Diet, and specifically the Seiyūkai, largely endorsed the administration's proposal, subjecting it to only minor revision compared to what the cabinet's railway program had undergone in 1892. A related issue concerns the response of the railway companies and their principal investors. True, many of the latter, along with their representatives in the Diet, opposed the nationalization. Yet, in view of the profitability of the railway enterprise, why was there not more opposition? Why did the railroads' objections quickly center on the terms of the purchase rather than on the purchase itself? The answers to these questions will go a long way towards explaining this most pivotal of events in Japanese railroad history.

The Communications Ministry

Taking the lead in forging a government consensus on nationalization, not surprisingly, was the Communications Ministry. In doing so, that ministry was simply following in the tracks of former Railway Bureau Chief Inoue Masaru. Communications bureaucrats were undoubtedly in an expansive mood in the early 1900s. Whereas the growth of the private railway network slowed after the panics of 1897–1898 and 1900–1901, the state system actually increased its rate of expansion. Consequently, the state railways' share of the total length of line open rose from 22 percent in 1897 to 32 percent in 1905.[11] Both state and private railroads had initially thrived under the Railway Construction Law, private lines much more so owing to the second enterprise boom. Between 1892 and 1898, the private system had expanded at an annual rate of 12.3 percent, the state system at a comparable rate of 5.7 percent. Yet the government railways had the advantage of guaranteed funding under the Construction Law—some twelve million yen a year in public-bond revenues, to be exact[12]—which enabled them to tide over the crises around the turn of the century. In fact, from 1898 to 1905, the state network grew at an annual rate of 10.4 percent compared to only 2.9 percent for the private network—a complete reversal of their earlier positions.[13] This was surely an exuberant time for communications officials, a factor that may well have quickened their desire to enlarge even further their bureaucratic sphere of influence by realizing the Railway Bureau's cherished principle of national ownership.

This tendency was given clearest expression by Vice-Minister of Communications Den Kenjirō. A former head of the Railway Bureau, Den was in many respects Inoue Masaru's heir as the political spokesman of the railway bureaucracy and the most active bureaucratic proponent of nationalization, a role that led him to become the prime mover in the initial stages of consensus building within the administration. Yet Den did far more than that. He lobbied for nationalization not only among state officials, but also among railway executives and party politicians. In fact, he offers a fascinating case of a top Meiji bureaucrat who descended into the rough-and-tumble of private business and party politics, only to reascend into the state bureaucracy, creating in the process a broad network of contacts that could then be pressed into the service of government policy. Den thereby played no small part in laying the foundation for agreement on railway nationalization among these several groups.

Den was born in 1855 in present-day Hyōgo prefecture. After serving as a police chief in several localities, he entered the Communications Ministry in 1890 and by 1898 had risen to the concurrent positions of vice-minister of communications and railway bureau chief in the third Itō cabinet. He resigned from the government with the collapse of that cabinet in June 1898. The next month, he joined the Kansai Railway Company as a director and general manager and, in December, was elected president. Den's main accomplishment during his roughly two-year term as chief officer of that railroad was to oversee its successful takeover of the Osaka Railway Company.[14] Also during this time, he tried to obtain the cooperation of his counterparts at other leading railroad firms in lobbying for the passage of a railway nationalization bill by the Diet. Den had been a keen advocate of the state ownership of railroads ever since touring Europe in 1896. He had written in his travel diary of having been particularly impressed by the stark contrast between the "divided" and "disorderly" private railway network of Italy and the "systematic and well-regulated" state system of Austria with its "military-style" discipline.[15] The evident superiority of the Austrian system had convinced him that Japan's railroads should also be unified under government control. Once he became president of the Kansai Railway, therefore, Den began exhorting his colleagues in the recession-plagued industry to support the state purchase of their concerns. In February 1900, he met with the presidents of five other railroad firms and urged them to endorse the nationalization proposal that had been submitted to the Diet that month. Den further called on a series of government officials to secure their backing as well. However, "the time was not right," and the proposed legislation ended up being shelved in the lower house.[16]

This bill proved abortive largely on account of financial considerations. To government leaders, armaments expansion had top priority at the time, some 40 percent of the national budget being allocated for that purpose in 1899–1900, and it was felt that the estimated two hundred million yen in public bonds needed to buy up the major private railroads would impose too heavy a burden on the national treasury as well as upset the financial markets.[17] Hence, the nationalization movement that had begun in the private sector in 1898 and that Den had done everything to promote had little chance of succeeding at the time, owing to the financial misgivings of party men and bureaucrats alike. Den, however, simply redirected his efforts, taking an increasing interest in party politics and the financial aspects of nationalization.

No sooner had Itō formed his Seiyūkai cabinet in October 1900 than Den left the Kansai Railway to resume his old position as vice-minister of communications. He wholeheartedly supported Itō's organization of the Seiyūkai as a government party, no doubt viewing it as an excellent opportunity to secure passage of a nationalization law. To his disappointment, the fourth Itō cabinet turned out to be short-lived, wracked as it was by internal conflicts. In the final, climactic dispute, Finance Minister Watanabe Kunitake drew fire from the other cabinet members over his insistence on suspending government enterprises so as to balance the next year's budget. When the resulting deadlock brought down the cabinet in May 1901, Den once again resigned his government post.[18] Before leaving office, however, he penned a sharp rebuttal of Watanabe's retrenchment policy.[19] In this document, which he distributed among other government leaders, Den presented a sophisticated argument on the necessity and feasibility of completing state enterprises in the fields of transportation and communications. His advocacy therein of railway unification, in particular, amounted to an early version of the Communications Ministry's eventual nationalization proposal. Besides advancing the traditional Railway Bureau line that the requirements of transport efficiency and convenience dictated a single state system, Den also addressed the immediate concerns of finance bureaucrats. The government, he asserted, could readily buy up the private railroads by raising foreign loans, which it could then pay off relatively quickly using railway profits. After that, the state railway system would become "an important source of revenue for the national treasury."[20] To support this claim, Den noted that, in Prussia, profits from the state railways had accounted for nearly one fourth of government revenues in 1900 and that, given the many similarities between the Prussian and Japanese systems, comparable results could be fully expected in Japan. He further argued that the current recession offered a "one-in-a-thousand opportunity" to carry out the purchase of private lines, since businessmen were clamoring for nationalization as a relief measure.[21] Much as Inoue Masaru had done a decade earlier, therefore, Den urged that the government take advantage of the economic crisis to realize at one stroke a unified railway network under state control.

Government authorities, however, did not share Den's zeal for capitalizing on the plight of private business. In January 1902, Prime Minister Katsura Tarō responded to a nationalization petition from the Tokyo Chamber of Commerce by stating that, "although I earnestly desire the achievement of railway nationalization, I am against carrying it out as a stopgap measure for economic relief." Instead, he maintained, it should be planned and implemented in conjunction with "the consolidation of finances."[22] Here was the basis of the rationale that would eventually win the day for nationalization within the regime, namely, that a single nationalized railway system would form an integral part of state financial policy—a rationale largely anticipated by Den in his 1901 opinion paper.

Den's proposal may not have met with immediate acceptance by government leaders, but it did serve to impress many with his financial acumen, not the least of whom were officials in the Seiyūkai. In June 1901, shortly after departing the Communications Ministry, Den accepted an invitation from the party to serve in its bureaus for financial and administrative affairs. Thus, in no time, he became a leading member of the Seiyūkai, embarking in earnest on the brief political-party phase of his varied career.[23]

That summer, at the urging of party directors, Den ran as a Seiyūkai candidate in a special lower-house election and won by a landslide.[24] In October, he accompanied party war-horse Itagaki Taisuke on a speaking tour of the Kansai area, reputedly upstaging the veteran politician with his oratorical skills. As a key party official, Den took part in framing the Seiyūkai platform for the upcoming Diet session. He worked hard to get railway nationalization put on the party's legislative agenda, joining hands with other proponents of nationalization among Seiyūkai Diet members in a campaign to that effect. Chief among these was Inoue Kakugorō, managing director of the Hokkaido Colliery and Railway, who had cooperated with Den in pushing for nationalization since the latter's tenure as president of the Kansai Railway Company.[25] Soon after the Diet session opened in December, Den and Inoue called a meeting of these like-minded legislators to discuss strategy. After Den delivered a speech in favor of the state purchase of private lines, the assembled group elected him chairman of their executive committee and voted to introduce a nationalization bill during the current Diet session as well as to begin lobbying for its passage.[26]

In the lower house, Den and Inoue were both elected to the crucial budget committee and appointed to its policy sub-committee. As a result, they found themselves in an excellent position to influence the legislative process. Den himself played a vital role in negotiating the compromise settlement between the Katsura cabinet and the Seiyūkai whereby the latter agreed to support Katsura's budget in return for certain concessions. Needless to say, one of the concessions Den had sought was administration approval of a railway nationalization bill.[27] The cabinet, however, was too pressed at the time to consider such a measure, struggling as it was just to secure funding for its military-expansion program, and as we have seen, Katsura, although sympathetic to the idea, was opposed to what seemed a temporary expedient aimed at relieving private business. Den, therefore, reluctantly withdrew this item, lest it prevent any agreement from being reached with the administration, and decided in consultation with his Seiyūkai supporters to wait for a more opportune time to bring about railway nationalization.[28]

That time arrived when Den left the Seiyūkai with his patron Itō and reentered the government bureaucracy in September 1903. Ōura Kanetake, newly appointed minister of communications, persuaded Den to return to the Communications Ministry to serve for a third time as vice-minister. He did so by promising Den a free hand in running the department. In fact, once Den accepted the offer, Ōura declared that "the Ministry of Communications has two ministers: I am the minister of political affairs and Vice-Minister Den is the minister of administrative affairs. The minister of political affairs must not interfere with the steps taken by the minister of administrative affairs."[29] Now, therefore, Den was in a position to work for nationalization from within the Katsura cabinet. Having laid the groundwork for its acceptance by the business world and the majority party, he now had the opportunity to bring a railroad purchase law one step closer to realization by softening resistance to the idea within the bureaucracy and getting the administration once and for all to take the initiative on the matter.

Den seemed to have chosen an auspicious time to push for a government consensus on nationalization. By the end of 1903, with Russo-Japanese relations rapidly deteriorating, the cabinet had come to recognize the necessity of unifying the nation's railroad network. The ministers, however, were split over whether this should be accomplished by the state or by private enterprise. In November, the two sides worked out a compromise whereby it was agreed to establish a semigovernmental "Imperial Railway Company," and Finance Minister Sone Arasuke was commissioned to draft a bill to that effect. Den reacted vigorously to what he doubtless saw as Finance Ministry meddling in his sphere of jurisdiction, prevailing upon Ōura and Vice-Chief of Staff Kodama to demand the withdrawal of Sone's halfway measure. The upshot was that the cabinet decided anew to have the Communications Ministry draw up a railway nationalization bill.[30]

Den realized that the cabinet's adoption of such a proposal would, in the end, require the approval or at least the acquiescence of finance officials. He therefore wasted no time in seeking their support. In December 1903, he called on Inoue Kaoru, the doyen of the finance bureaucracy, to urge that preparations be made for eventual state purchase of private railroads. Inoue, who had earlier held that nationalization was premature, had "gradually become interested in the issue" in view of the growing crisis on the Russian front.[31] He immediately gave his consent to Den's plan, but insisted that as a first step the government should enact a railroad-collateral law to facilitate foreign borrowing by private railway companies. Den went ahead and drafted a nationalization bill anyway and, in November 1904, met with Vice-Minister of Finance Sakatani Yoshirō and once again with Inoue Kaoru to explain his proposal. He was working out the details of his plan, according to his biographer, "even as the whole country was celebrating the fall of Port Arthur in January 1905."[32] He then made a final round of calls on key cabinet members, after which Communications Minister Ōura presented Den's proposal to the cabinet. Yet, with state finances seriously strained by the war effort, neither the administration nor the Diet was prepared at the time to undertake a major endeavor such as nationalization. So the cabinet decided to postpone submission of a railway purchase bill until the next Diet session and, in the meantime, to conduct further investigations into the financial aspects of such legislation. In lieu of a nationalization measure, the cabinet resolved to introduce in the current Diet session a railroad-collateral bill along the lines that Inoue Kaoru had recommended. This bill, which was also drafted by Den, was readily accepted by all parties concerned, involving as it did no additional imposition on the national treasury.[33] Promulgated in March 1905, the collateral act suggested the powerful influence that finance officials continued to exert on state railroad policy.

Nevertheless, the committee that the cabinet appointed meanwhile to investigate a railway nationalization bill was composed entirely of communications bureaucrats, with the chief of the Railway Bureau serving as chairman. Still, in the two reports it drafted before the war's end in September, the committee was careful to include points calculated to win the support of Finance Ministry officials or, at minimum, to defuse their opposition. Den's hand was clearly evident in these reports, for they followed many of the themes he had raised in his earlier proposals, especially his 1901 opinion paper.[34] The first of these documents, entitled "General Objectives of Railway Nationalization," outlined the rationale for setting about the purchase of private railroads. It began by harking back to the principles espoused by Inoue Masaru, asserting that, "since railways provide public transportation and are therefore no different in character from roads, their management should not be left to private enterprise, but the state itself should administer them." The report then listed several advantages of a unified national system, including lower rates on through-traffic and various economies in operating and equipment expenditures. The latter, it projected, would result in an immediate savings of one and a quarter million yen.

Having presented the traditional Railway Bureau viewpoint, the document then broadened the perspective to portray railway nationalization as the cornerstone of Japan's postwar policy. With the government scrambling to find means of financing its programs, not to mention its huge war debt, railway income could become "a high and mighty source of revenue for the national treasury." And just as Den had done in 1901, the committee members pointed to Prussia as "an excellent example:" "Thirty-three years ago in Germany, that blood-and-iron prime minister [Bismarck] firmly advocated a policy of railway nationalization in order to secure the foundations of Prussian state finances, and as a result of this having been carried out . . . , [railroads] have become the greatest source of government revenue [there]." Continuing along these financial lines, the report also asserted that railroads could serve as collateral to refund the expensive war bonds, which at that time amounted to almost one and a third billion yen, by "facilitating the raising of low-interest foreign loans."

The document further argued that nationalization was necessary for economic and strategic reasons. As a "newly risen power," Japan had to be ready to compete economically with the advanced Western nations after the restoration of peace. To that end, it was absolutely vital to unify and expand the railway network, "the supreme ruler of land transportation means"; moreover, the government itself had to accomplish these tasks, for "it can hardly be expected that [profit-seeking] private companies will build or extend lines with low rates of return or reduce their income to promote the development of industry in general." Finally, the report underscored the urgency of nationalization by raising the specter of a foreign-capital invasion following the war. Again citing Western precedent, the committee noted that European governments had faced "the most obstacles in carrying out the purchase of railroads built with foreign capital . . ."[35] Although foreigners had rarely invested in Japanese railroad firms in the past, they were now showing great interest in Japanese government bonds, and "once it becomes clear that the shares of our major railway companies are sound and profitable, [Westerners] who are quick to discover a profit will be eager to acquire these, and before long, we will see many foreigners among company stockholders." The real danger was that these foreigners might purchase enough shares in the main-line firms to gain control over their management. If that were to happen, the government would find it far more difficult not only to nationalize the railroads in the future, but also to implement rate reductions and other policies aimed at industrial and export promotion in the meantime. Furthermore, in the event of a national crisis, "companies subject to the interference of foreigners" could not be counted on to maintain the secrecy of military transport or to cooperate in conveying troops. Accordingly, the report concluded, the government should seize the occasion to buy out the private railroads in order to nip in the bud the possibility that they might fall into foreign hands.

The second document drawn up by the committee was entitled "Essential Points of the Investigation into the Purchase of Private Railroads." This thirteen-point proposal went into the actual details of the railway buyout, ranging from the method and scope of the nationalization to the calculation of the purchase price, the disposition of nationalized railway employees, and so on. The committee recommended a compulsory purchase over a negotiated one and suggested three alternatives for the number of concerns to be nationalized: either thirty-two or eighteen firms "exclusive of railroads providing local transport" or thirteen main-line companies. Not surprisingly, the communications bureaucrats advised that, "in order to facilitate the future development and completion of the national rail network, the best policy at this time would be to select [the option] with the greatest scope." The report then proposed the following formula for determining the purchase price: the average return on construction costs for the previous three years multiplied by the cumulative construction costs at the end of the past year, the resulting figure multiplied by twenty. Using this method of calculation, the total purchase price would range from ¥343,000,000 for the thirteen trunk-line companies to ¥380,000,000 for the thirty-two "nonlocal" firms. The purchase was to be financed by the issue of public bonds bearing 5-percent interest. The document's framers fully anticipated objections by finance authorities that the sudden increase in government bonds resulting from such an issue would trigger a sharp drop in the price of those bonds and "cause a major financial crisis" by asserting rather optimistically that the issue was "nothing but an exchange of public bonds for stocks."

These reports thus represented the Ministry of Communications' case for nationalization; they clearly revealed its perception that disarming skeptics in the finance bureaucracy was critical to winning over the administration. Before submitting final versions of these documents to the cabinet, Den and his colleagues redoubled their lobbying efforts to ensure the acceptance of their proposals by government leaders. In August 1905, Den accompanied Communications Minister Ōura and Railway Bureau Chief Yamanouchi Kazuji to call yet again on Inoue Kaoru and confirm his endorsement of their plans. Inoue had come to the conclusion that a single nationalized railway system was essential to postwar economic growth. Accordingly, he encouraged his callers, stating that, "to tell you the truth, until now I was not very much in favor of railway nationalization, but I think the time is now ripe. I will give it my support, so do your best."[36] Then, at the end of November, Ōura met with Prime Minister Katsura, Finance Minister Sone, and Army Minister Terauchi Masatake to secure their approval of his ministry's program, and by a memorandum of December 5th, the cabinet unofficially agreed upon the general principles of railway nationalization. Members of the investigative committee thereupon reworked their proposals in light of the discussions they and their superiors had held with officials in the other ministries concerned. They eventually came up with five documents: a nationalization bill, a revised version of the "General Objectives of Railway Nationalization," and protocols concerning calculation of the purchase price, determination of the lines to be bought up, and redemption of the purchase bonds. These the Communications Ministry formally submitted to the cabinet for final approval on December 22nd, by which time Den could confidently state in his cover letter that "we have omitted the signatures of the finance and army ministers, having already completed informal consultations with their ministries."[37]

The investigative committee made two principal changes in its proposals. First, it reduced the number of railroad firms recommended for nationalization from thirty-two to sixteen.[38] The committee did so, one might surmise, as a concession to the Finance Ministry. Second, it recast the latter half of the "General Objectives," that part dealing with the broader reasons for nationalization, to fit the new circumstances in which the country found itself following the conclusion of the Russo-Japanese War in September 1905. The rewrite offered a more detailed, much more effective presentation of the points raised in the original, clearly organizing them under general headings on "industrial promotion," "stockholding by foreigners," and "consolidation of postwar finances." Above all, it related those points far more closely and explicitly to the so-called "postwar management" (*sengo keiei*), the wide-ranging program centering on armaments expansion, heavy industrialization, and colonial development adopted by the Katsura and Saionji cabinets after the victory over Russia. As the new document put it, "the unification of railroads under national ownership is the pressing need of the postwar management, for its implementation will truly cut the Gordian knot for a host of financial, economic, and military problems . . ."[39]

The way in which the revised version of the "General Objectives" realigned the arguments of the original so as to square them with the cabinet's postwar policy is most evident in the section on postwar finances. This section opened by repeating the claims of the initial document that the nationalized railroads would become "a favorable source of revenue" and that the purchase bonds would simply replace corporate securities, adding that the railroad bonds differed from those issued for "unproductive enterprises," meaning military ventures. It then noted with concern that the government had already floated war bonds totaling one and a half billion yen. "However, in order to secure the imperial position in the East, further expansion of armaments will be required. And in order to exercise suzerainty in Korea and carry out the administration of the Liaotung Peninsula and the new possession of southern Sakhalin, expenditures in the hundreds of thousands of yen will be required as well over the next several years . . ." To raise the enormous amounts of capital needed for these tasks, the government had no choice but to rely on bond issues, most of which it would have to float in overseas markets in view of the tight money situation at home. On the other hand, all the domestic bonds outstanding and some of the foreign ones had "exorbitant" rates of interest and short terms of repayment. Therefore, the document asserted, "it is incumbent upon the authorities to devise a way to lighten the burden insofar as they can redeem these [bonds]."

The solution to meeting these multifarious demands for capital was to import low-interest foreign loans. To do so, it was necessary to provide sound collateral, and, as the committee concluded, "the nationalized railways will be the most suitable collateral for these foreign loans. Because of this, there is probably nothing that can compare with them in facilitating the adjustment of postwar finances and the promotion of various enterprises. This, then, is the reason why the policy of purchasing private railroads will serve the postwar consolidation of finances." The new emphasis the document placed on the "postwar management" reflected the broader concerns of the oligarchs and their lieutenants, and, as we shall see, this emphasis was to prove decisive in the cabinet's ultimate acceptance of the nationalization program.

The Katsura cabinet made some minor modifications in the proposals of the investigative committee and tentatively approved them on December 25th. Unfortunately for Den and his associates, however, Katsura had earlier worked out an agreement with the Seiyūkai to transfer the premiership to its president, Saionji, prior to the next Diet session, in return for that party's support of what was expected to be an unpopular peace treaty with Russia.[40] Accordingly, the Katsura cabinet resigned in early January before it had a chance to submit a nationalization bill to the Diet. Nevertheless, one of the conditions set by government leaders in naming Saionji to form a new administration was that he continue Katsura's policies,[41] not the least of which was the buying up of private railroads. It thus fell to the Saionji cabinet to complete the work of nationalization begun by its predecessor. Den left office with Ōura, and in February 1906, their successors in the Communications Ministry submitted a railway purchase proposal to the cabinet that scarcely differed from their own. Following his resignation from the government, Den received an appointment to the House of Peers. As a result, he was to push for nationalization in yet another capacity, this time as a member of the strategic upper house, where the administration's purchase measure was to encounter stiff opposition and undergo considerable revision.[42] It was while serving in this chamber of the Diet that Den would finally see the culmination of his years of effort with the passage of an amended railway nationalization bill on March 27, 1906.

THE ARMY

Among the principal groups of actors in the nationalization drama, one of the few with which Den was not affiliated at one point or another was the army. Although the Communications Ministry took the lead in that drama, the army played an important supporting role. It is not surprising that army authorities should have heartily endorsed the plans of communications bureaucrats, enamored as they both were of the Prussian model, and the strategic reasons for nationalization required little explanation in a country that had just fought two major wars in the space of a decade. Indeed, some would argue that military motives were decisive in the making of the Nationalization Law inasmuch as planning for it began in earnest at a time when the outbreak of hostilities with Russia seemed imminent and passage of the act itself came on the heels of the Russian conflict.[43]

The strategic motive, however, tends to be exaggerated at the expense of other reasons involved, including the aforementioned impulse on the part of communications officials towards bureaucratic aggrandizement. The army had been consistently advocating state ownership of railroads since the late 1890s. Consequently, the military rationale for nationalization had become something of a given by the mid-1900s and cannot in itself account for the cabinet's decision to purchase the private railroads. The Communications Ministry was solicitous of army backing insofar as it made a point of consulting army leaders in drafting its proposals and of incorporating therein military reasons for nationalization. Yet communications bureaucrats were simply taking advantage of strategic concerns to further their own cause, just as in the past they had either accepted or rejected army demands depending on whether or not those demands had served their purposes. And, on the issue of railway ownership, the army's position since the late 1890s had coincided most conveniently with their own.

True, the army's preference for a single state railway system was reinforced by the difficulties it experienced in moving troops by rail during the Russo-Japanese War. The major problem was a lack of equipment standardization, which was only compounded by the network's division among the state railways and nearly forty private companies. The principal concerns all used the same narrow gauge, but they differed greatly in the weight of their rails, the model and tonnage of their rolling stock, and so on. For example, the railroads, as we have seen, imported all manner of locomotives from a variety of manufacturers in Britain, the United States, and Germany; according to Harada and Aoki, "it was as if the makers of various countries were holding a locomotive competition using the whole of the Japanese railroads as their stage."[44] Under these conditions, Den, who took charge of planning and executing the wartime conveyance of troops by rail, found it "difficult even to estimate how many trains would be needed to transport one division."[45] The resulting delays and inefficiencies in military transportation convinced many in the army and elsewhere of the need to nationalize the private railroads so that the government could readily standardize their equipment. And, of course, under unified state management, the rail network could be operated at the beck and call of the government and placed much more rapidly on a war footing. As Army Minister Terauchi testified to members of the lower-house committee investigating the Nationalization Bill in March 1906, "to be able to operate our railroads from the center, just as a person uses his fingers, will make it possible for us not only to employ our military force to advantage, but also to take the initiative against the enemy."[46]

Nevertheless, most observers have overstated the extent to which the fragmented management of the railway system created problems for military transport during the war. In March 1906, critics of the Nationalization Bill were quick to point out that existing regulations contained ample provisions for through-traffic as well as for state takeover of the entire network in time of emergency. As one Diet member asserted, "If the authorities are resourceful, under the Military Requisition Act [promulgated in January 1904], they can at any time use all the country's railroads as they please. At present there is no reason why they cannot attain this objective without nationalizing [the private railroads]."[47] Moreover, many noted that, in practice, the system had actually run quite smoothly during both the Sino-Japanese and Russo-Japanese wars. The railroads had managed to convey vast numbers of troops and supplies with "no particular difficulties," wrote one commentator, adding that, "if state railways are already inferior to private railways in peacetime management, how will they be superior to the latter in wartime?"[48] Even Den found that, in the end, despite the inconveniences caused by the lack of standardization, the system worked "without any hitches to speak of."[49] In short, the situation the army faced during the war was far from the logistical nightmare often suggested. Indeed, in making the strategic case for nationalization, Army Minister Terauchi had to resort to the rather forced argument that the rapid deployment of troops needed to repulse an enemy landing, say, on the Kishū Peninsula could be achieved only if the main lines were all under government control.[50]

A more persuasive reason for nationalization related to military concerns was to prevent direct investment and intervention in Japanese railroads by foreign nationals. This, in fact, was the only strategic motive spelled out in the proposals of Den and other communications bureaucrats. The issue had been first raised in the late 1890s by army officials, fearful lest treaty revision and the other signs of Japan's growing international status should open the floodgates to foreign investment. The army had been particularly concerned that foreign ownership of Japanese corporate shares, which the authorities had interpreted to have been disallowed under the unequal treaties, would be deemed permissible once the revised treaties went into effect in 1899.[51] Army Minister Katsura Tarō had even tried to get the question addressed in the Private Railway Law, passed by the Diet in 1900 to replace the outdated Private Railway Regulations of 1887. Topping the wish list Katsura had sent to the communications minister in 1899 was a request that the pending railway bill prohibit unregistered stockholding in railway companies owning strategically important lines and, furthermore, restrict their shareholders to Japanese nationals. Typically, the Communications Ministry had at first turned a cold shoulder to the army, only to incorporate the latter's viewpoint into its subsequent legislative proposals. In 1899, the communications minister had rebuffed Katsura by stating that his ministry was merely following existing laws and regulations in omitting from the proposed act any limitations on railroad stockholding.[52] Yet, before long, communications bureaucrats had come to see the foreign threat as a useful pretext for railway nationalization and had appropriated the army's position for their own.

On the face of it, the danger of foreign domination of Japanese railroads appeared to be something of a bogeyman with little connection to reality. This view was expressed most forcefully by one member of the Diet who, in March 1906, characterized the nationalization argument centering on that danger as "no more than a dream." This Dietman had investigated all the major railway companies and found not one foreigner among holders of fifty or more shares in those concerns. He went on to lecture his colleagues:

> If foreigners are going to buy anything, they will buy Japanese government bonds. Buying government bonds is much simpler. And if they are going to sell them, they will do so on the London market, so they prefer to deal in public bonds. There may be some among you who imagine that foreigners would willingly buy up railway shares and thereby become directors in this faraway land where the government, which is undecided on ownership rights, meddles excessively.... However, I wish to declare that there is not one among the foreigners [who would do so]. Therefore, I believe [this argument] to be a mere fancy....[53]

Indeed, a look at the lists of principal stockholders for all the private railroads in 1905–1906 generally corroborates the Diet member's finding concerning the extent of direct foreign investment in Japanese railroad firms. Only two foreigners appear on any of the lists—a certain R. W. Irving, who held a 0.5-percent interest in the medium-sized Hokuetsu Railway Company, and another foreigner identified simply as Baelz (perhaps the German physician Erwin Baelz?), who owned a 0.1-percent share in the Kyushu Railway.[54] And a Westerner writing in the *Japan Weekly Mail* in September 1905 seemed to confirm the Dietman's perception of the attitudes of foreign investors by admonishing, "Japan is very different from Europe in point of accessibility to foreign understanding. This country, though much is known about it and though its achievements have attracted world-wide attention, remains a *terra incognita* in the matter of laws and industrial conditions. Foreign capitalists feel like taking a leap in the dark when they invest money here, and they have to be tempted by good terms."[55] In short, Japan's railroads were in no immediate danger of being overrun by foreign capital.

Nonetheless, the concerns of military and civilian authorities in this regard were not totally groundless. The writer of the *Weekly Mail* piece was in fact referring to the successful raising of an overseas loan by the Hokkaido Colliery and Railway, "the first genuine borrowing of foreign money through non-official channels," and reacting to complaints by some Japanese that the firm "might have tried to obtain slightly better terms." The Hokkaido Colliery was soon joined by the Kansai Railway Company in borrowing abroad,[56] and with several other firms, including the San'yō and

Kyushu, planning to follow suit, it may well have seemed to many observers to be only a matter of time before Japan's leading railroads became perilously dependent on external funds. In securing their foreign loans, the Hokkaido Colliery and Kansai railways both made use of the new Railroad Collateral Law, which enabled a railroad concern to mortgage its assets as a whole rather than individually.[57] The latter turned out to be the breakthrough that finally made it possible for private railroads to float corporate bonds overseas.

In truth, Japanese railway companies had been actively soliciting foreign capital for years, although their efforts had borne little fruit prior to the passage of the collateral act. In 1901, for example, the Kyushu and Hokuetsu railways commissioned a British employee of Mitsubishi, Richard Kirby, to help obtain loans for them in England. In June 1901, Kirby wrote to the British minister to Japan requesting his good offices in bringing the matter before the British investing public.[58] He noted that the Kyushu Railway wanted to borrow ¥10,000,000 from abroad. "The line and plant," he assured, "would be mortgaged to the foreign lenders, and I have no doubt but that the Railway people would arrange to nominate as one of the Directors any foreigner or Japanese the lenders should require on the board." Kirby continued, "As you are well aware, the foreigner can have property mortgaged to him, but not being able to own immoveables, could not buy in in case of trouble, and it is proposed to get over this difficulty by establishing a Japanese Company, comprised only of foreign partners or shareholders, which would have all the rights and privileges of any Japanese individual or Company except that it cannot practise law." The thought of a foreign-owned dummy corporation seizing the very lifeblood of Japan's land transportation system would have been enough to terrify any government authority. Kirby suggested that British investors could make even greater inroads into the Japanese economy by means of this strategem: "There is no reason why a foreign-owned Japanese Company should not only lend money to industries such as railways and trams, etc., but undertake the construction and running of them and factories with British capital and products." Stressing that Japan urgently needed funds to develop its resources, he painted a rosy picture for British capitalists: "I think the present an excellent opportunity for the British investor. I am sure after the first start is made there will be a great rush of capital for investment in Japan, and it is the people who first make the start who will reap the most benefit by getting hold of the really good thing." Kirby concluded that, "if the loans for these two railways can be arranged there are other sound railways which would come forward to borrow"; he cited in particular the San'yō Railway Company, which, "should the Kiushiu matter be arranged, I am sure... will be in the market for a loan." Kirby undoubtedly had inside information, for his employer, Mitsubishi, was the principal owner of both the San'yō and Kyushu railways.

Railroad concerns had sought to enlist not only foreign lenders, but also foreign shareholders. In the early 1900s, for instance, the Hokkaido Colliery and Railway had published slick promotional pamphlets in English in an effort to attract Western business and investment. The 1903 edition opened by touting the glories of the firm, "incomparably the largest and most powerful business establishment in Hokkaido," and then noted pointedly: "An important feature is that foreigners are legally entitled to hold shares of the Company in their own names and to subscribe for its debentures. Hence the fact that such a profitable and safe investment is available has much concern for all foreign capitalists."[59] Even though attempts of this kind to recruit foreign investors had fallen short before 1905, the fact that they were being made at all must have alarmed many a government official. And in the wake of the enthusiastic response to Japanese war bonds overseas,[60] the successful flotation of foreign loans by the Hokkaido Colliery and Kansai railways seemed only the beginning of a foreign-capital invasion of the private railroad sector. Even if foreigners did not come forward to purchase railway shares in droves, the steady rise in the ratio of debt capital to equity in the case of many railroads meant that even foreign lenders might gain enough financial leverage to influence management.[61]

The Japanese had a prime example of the foreign domination of a private railroad in their own backyard. This was the largely Japanese-owned Seoul-Pusan Railway Company.[62] The Saionji cabinet submitted legislation for the state purchase of this firm at the same time that it presented the bill for the nationalization of domestic railroad concerns. And in this case, against the backdrop of big-power rivalry for concessions and influence in Korea, the strategic need to keep important railroads out of "foreign" hands took on a particularly urgent, if ironic, note. Moreover, in this instance of "nationalization," the connection with the Russo-Japanese conflict, indeed the role of military considerations in general, was even more pronounced. Insofar as government authorities linked the purchase of the Korean and domestic railroads, therefore, they appeared to underscore the strategic impulse behind the nationalization at home.

The Japanese government had secured the concession for the Seoul-Pusan line from the Korean court in 1898 but, reluctant for financial and diplomatic reasons to build the railroad itself, had encouraged Japanese private business to undertake the task. Armed with promises of a state subsidy, a group of businessmen led by the ubiquitous Shibusawa Eiichi had formally established the Seoul-Pusan Railway Company in 1901. Two years later, the railroad had bought out the Japanese firm founded in 1899 to construct the Seoul-Inchon line. At the end of 1903, with Russo-Japanese relations rapidly deteriorating and the main line only partly completed, the Meiji government had become directly involved in the venture, effectively transforming it into a semiofficial enterprise. On the eve of its purchase by the Japanese state in 1906, the Seoul-Pusan Railway Company, with total equity and loan capital of thirty-one million yen, was operating nearly 300 miles of track, or just under half of the total Korean network, the rest of which was in the hands of the Japanese army.[63]

Strategic motives clearly played a significant, if not an overriding, part in the Meiji government's takeover of the Seoul-Pusan Railway. After all, it was the imminence of war with Russia and the resulting military demand for rapid completion of the company's main line that had prompted direct state intervention in the railroad in the first place. Under the terms of that intervention, approved by the Privy Council in December 1903, the government had provided the firm with extensive financial and technical assistance in return for almost total control over its management.[64] Furthermore, wartime imperatives had led the army itself to extend the central artery northwestward from Seoul to the Manchurian border as well as to build a branch of the Seoul-Pusan line, and after the war, the government moved to buy out the Seoul-Pusan Railway and combine it with these military lines, one of its primary objectives being, in the words of Army Minister Terauchi, "to make secure Japanese communications on Manchurian and Korean soil . . . in case of future emergency."[65]

Military authorities apparently did not experience on the Korean network the same wartime transportation problems that they did on the much more fragmented domestic one. For all practical purposes, they had only one private enterprise to contend with in Korea—the army had in fact usurped from Korean firms the lines it had completed during the war,[66] so that the government buyout there had a certain preventive quality to it. Den's successor as vice-minister of communications suggested as much when, in March 1906, he explained to an interpellator in the lower house that the bill for the purchase of the Seoul-Pusan Railway Company signified that, henceforth, "the important railroads" in Korea would all be built, owned, and managed by the Japanese state.[67]

Preemptive in another sense related to strategic concerns, of course, was the urge to forestall a non-Japanese takeover of such a vital railroad. In truth, the concession for the Seoul-Pusan line restricted the company's shareholders to the Japanese and Korean governments and their subjects, and in 1902, Japanese officials had planned to shield the enterprise from the intervention of overseas lenders by having the semigovernmental Industrial Bank issue foreign bonds on its behalf—in the end, this plan was abandoned, and the firm turned instead to the sale of bonds in Japan.[68] Nonetheless, there had earlier been talk of amending the terms of the concession to permit foreign investment in the company,[69] and as long as that possibility remained, the desire to preclude "foreign" control of the Seoul-Pusan Railway was undoubtedly a compelling motive for its purchase by the Japanese state.

Strategic necessity was the most conspicuous reason for the government's acquisition of the Seoul-Pusan Railway, but it was by no means the only one. Indeed, the initiative for the state intervention beginning in late 1903 appears to have come not from the army but from the Communications Ministry. And the prime mover was once again Vice-Minister of Communications Den Kenjirō. Den, in consultation with army officials, drew up the plan for direct state involvement in the Seoul-Pusan Railway and then called on leading members of the cabinet as well as oligarchs Inoue Kaoru and Yamagata Aritomo to obtain their approval. It was in his meeting with Inoue that Den also recommended making preparations for eventual government purchase of private railroads.[70] In this way, Den established a clear link between rapid completion of the Seoul-Pusan line and railway nationalization. It seems certain that he and others in the Communications Ministry regarded the program of official intervention in the Seoul-Pusan Railway Company as the first step towards the line's ultimate purchase by the Japanese government and integration into the state railway system at home.

Under that program of intervention, the government was to choose the Seoul-Pusan Railway's president and directors, and three of the latter were to be named managing directors specifically by the minister of communications. The government was also to appoint an inspector with considerable powers of oversight.[71] Such interference was by no means unprecedented. The state had regularly reserved for itself similar powers when granting subsidies to domestic railroad firms. What was unusual in the case of the Seoul-Pusan Railway, however, was that this interference was not limited to the duration of the subsidy. In short, official involvement in the Korean concern was apparently meant by communications bureaucrats to be more than just a stopgap. This inference receives some confirmation from the fact that the government immediately appointed as president of the company Chief of the Railway Construction Bureau Furuichi Kōi, a long-standing advocate of railway nationalization.[72] Another Communications Ministry official was chosen to be one of the three managing directors, and a whole army of state railway administrators, engineers, and workmen was sent over to undertake the remaining construction work.[73] All this suggests that a key motive behind the government's purchase of the Seoul-Pusan Railway was, once again, the desire of the Communications Ministry to enlarge its bureaucratic empire by realizing the principle of railway ownership by the state.

Neither the army nor the Ministry of Communications got exactly what it wanted in Korea, however. Army leaders had urged that the "nationalized" Seoul-Pusan line be put under the jurisdiction of the army minister, at least for the time being, whereas officials in the Communications Ministry had called for placing in their hands both the military and nationalized railroads in Korea.[74] But, after Japan established its protectorate over Korea in late 1905, it was decided instead to entrust the administration of the lines to the Korean residency general, and except for a brief period in 1909–1910, when management of the Korean network was transferred to the Japanese railway bureaucracy, domestic and Korean railroads were in fact never "brought into a single united system."[75] Although its hopes for direct control of the Korean lines were dashed, the Communications Ministry undoubtedly could take some solace in the fact that one of its own,

President Furuichi of the Seoul-Pusan Railway, became head of the Railway Administrative Bureau in the residency general.[76]

The prominent role of communications bureaucrats plainly indicates that there were important considerations other than purely military ones involved in the acquisition of the Seoul-Pusan Railway. Yet, even if strategic concerns were in this case ultimately predominant, the parallels drawn by the government between the Korean- and domestic-railway purchases met with far from universal acceptance. In introducing the two purchase bills together in the Diet, the Saionji cabinet intended that they be viewed as integrally related. Finance Minister Sakatani Yoshirō made this explicit at a Diet hearing on the bills by declaring: "it has become most urgent that we endeavor to exploit the opportunity to expand [the] sphere of influence that Japan henceforth deserves to possess [on the continent] by resolving the long-standing question of railway unification and that we make fully serviceable our domestic railroads as well as those in Korea and Manchuria."[77] In addition, Vice-Minister of Communications Nakashōji Ren revealed that the cabinet regarded the two sets of purchases not only as being connected from the standpoint of state policy, but also as being identical in legal terms. Nakashōji did so when he told a lower-house committee member who wondered how the Japanese state could buy out a railroad that operated under a charter granted by the Korean government that "this Seoul-Pusan Railway Company was established in accordance with Japanese law and is therefore not in the least different from domestic [private railroads]."[78]

These arguments proved to be less than persuasive in the Diet. Indeed, most Dietmen drew a sharp distinction between the Seoul-Pusan Railway and railroad companies at home. This differentiation is readily apparent from the way in which they treated the two purchase bills. Whereas the proposal for domestic-railway nationalization aroused lengthy and heated debate in both houses, that for purchase of the Seoul-Pusan Railway received only cursory attention, the chairman of the lower-house committee considering both bills even having to remind his colleagues to deliberate on the latter.[79] There was clearly a broad consensus among opponents and supporters of the domestic nationalization that state purchase of the Seoul-Pusan Railway was both desirable and imperative in view of its close connection with Japan's continental policy. Many, however, refused to buy the government's argument that the railway system at home was equally tied to that policy. As one opponent of the domestic nationalization bill put it, "The Seoul-Pusan Railway is completely different from those at home, being necessary for the management henceforth of Manchuria and the like . . ."[80] In marked contrast to the uproar that attended passage of the domestic-railway purchase bill, that for acquisition of the Seoul-Pusan Railway was approved quickly and unanimously by the lower house and encountered only minor resistance in the upper chamber.

Even within the administration, there was by no means total agreement on the coincidence in character and purpose between the two purchase bills. Foreign Minister Katō Kōmei, the only cabinet member to oppose the domestic nationalization program to the bitter end, ultimately resigning over his objections to it, consented nonetheless to the government's takeover of the Seoul-Pusan Railway. At the time, he explained these apparently contradictory positions by asserting that "the two cases [are] entirely different. The whole history of the building and the strategic uses of the Seoul-Fusan line [makes] the State purchase of that railway desirable. Though built by a private company, it was practically owned by the Government during the war. This purchase does not in any way affect Japanese legal ownership of property in this country."[81] On the other hand, Katō argued, the proposed nationalization of domestic railway companies "will, if carried out arbitrarily, rob private individuals of the rights granted to them" under the Private Railway Law. He went on to state, "Though it is true that what the Law gives the Law can take away, such a radical alteration in the Law as that contemplated by the framers of the Bill now before the Diet ought to be based on State exigencies that do not at present exist in this country. The nationalization of railways is not to-day an indispensable measure. The proposed step is not taken to save the country from great peril or to avoid a threatened calamity. It is merely a commercial undertaking whose ultimate success is by no means assured."[82]

Although Katō was definitely in the minority within the cabinet, appeals to "state exigencies" of a strategic nature simply did not carry the same weight in the case of domestic railroad firms as they did in the case of the Seoul-Pusan Railway. Yet, even though one should guard against overemphasizing the military impetus for nationalization, there is still no gainsaying that the army performed a key auxiliary role in bringing the nationalization about and that a striking harmony of opinions existed on this issue between army authorities, on the one hand, and communications bureaucrats, on the other.

In his efforts to create a consensus for nationalization, Den Kenjirō played a large part in fostering that harmony. We have mentioned that Den was never directly associated with the army. It is true that he remained a civilian bureaucrat, except for brief interludes during which he ventured into the worlds of private business and party politics. As a bureaucrat-turned-politician, he was something of an Itō protege, having served as vice-minister of communications in two of Itō's cabinets and numbered among the many bureaucrats who joined his new political party, the Seiyūkai. But Den also maintained strong ties with the army and civilian officials who made up the Yamagata faction.[83] Like many followers of that soldier-statesman in the civil bureaucracy, he had begun his career in the Home Ministry during Yamagata's long tenure as head of that department. There, Den had become acquainted with Ōura Kanetake, a fellow police chief and Yamagata satellite, and eventually, at Ōura's invitation, he had entered the administration of the Yamagata protege Katsura Tarō. Furthermore, Den had rendered great service to the Army General Staff first as head of the Telegraph Bureau during the Sino-Japanese War and then as coordinator of railroad transport for the military during the Russian conflict.[84] As a consequence, he could expect a ready hearing among army authorities like Vice-Chief of Staff Kodama Gentarō, and in fact, he regularly capitalized on their good will in promoting his views.[85]

Then, too, Yamagata's followers had largely monopolized the post of communications minister, his own nephew and adopted son, Yamagata Isaburō, serving in that capacity in the Saionji cabinet. It is perhaps not surprising, therefore, that a congruence of opinion should have obtained between army and communications officials with both of them being presided over by members of the Yamagata clique. And one might be tempted to ascribe even greater influence in the nationalization movement to the army leaders, such as Katsura and Terauchi, who tended to dominate that clique. Yet, in fairness, it should be pointed out that, factional allegiance notwithstanding, the communications minister was in no way a puppet of the Yamagata group: Yoshikawa Kensei, for example, issued the sharp rebuttal of Army Minister Katsura's demands concerning the Private Railway Bill in 1899. Moreover, Katsura's opposition to immediate nationalization in 1902 indicates that, once in power, even the soldier-statesmen in the faction had to heed more than just their army constituency, constrained as they were by fiscal requirements and the like.[86] In short, there was a real need for someone like Den who could mediate among the various interests concerned, and the fact that Den enjoyed a whole network of contacts cutting across both factional and institutional lines made his efforts on behalf of nationalization all the more effective.

Den's task was naturally facilitated by the consensus for government ownership that already existed within the army. Such agreement had not always prevailed among army authorities, however. In fact, until the late 1890s, army leaders had generally adhered to no principle of railway ownership, being concerned only that the major lines be built rapidly and according to military specifications. As we have seen, during the private railway boom of the late 1880s, the Army General Staff had actually favored the subsidized construction of strategically important railroads by private companies. At the time, that course had appeared much more likely to satisfy the army's requirements than had state construction, given the surge in private investment and the continued tightness of government finances. And Katsura Tarō, in a proposal for the administration of Taiwan he submitted to state leaders before taking up his new post as governor general of that colony in 1896, suggested that army attitudes had changed little by the time of the second railway boom. In this document, Katsura urged that priority be given to the building of a railroad line running the length of Taiwan, his hope being, as he put it, that "this railroad will be completed as quickly as possible regardless of whether it is built by the government or by private interests." State construction would be preferable, he admitted, but since the government was already burdened with mushrooming responsibilities following the Sino-Japanese War and since private businessmen had expressed interest in undertaking the project, he would have "positively no objection to entrusting [the railroad] to private construction . . . if there is a good chance of success." Katsura then recommended that the government indeed "entrust [the work] to a sound private enterprise and grant it sufficient assistance to ensure the rapid completion of construction

... ." He added that there should be "no obstacle to selling off the existing railroad between Taipei and Shinchiku to a private company for a suitable price."[87]

The authorities in fact did commission a private concern, the Taiwan Railway Company, to build the trans-island railroad. Founded by Shibusawa and other Japanese businessmen in 1896, this firm began with high hopes, its initial stock offer being well oversubscribed. The panic that broke out in Japan in 1897, however, put a damper on such optimism. Despite the government's offer of a subsidy of 6 percent, the railroad actually managed to sell only about half its shares. Following hard on this was the failure of foreign and domestic bond issues in 1898. Unable to raise the necessary funds, the company finally dissolved the following year, state authorities having decided in the meantime to have the Taiwan government general build the line instead.[88]

Perhaps partly reflecting this debacle as well as the difficulties that private railroads at home were experiencing during the 1897–1898 recession, the army's railroad policy changed dramatically around 1898. Until then, army demands had centered almost exclusively on matters of construction, with the General Staff calling in particular for the inland routing and double-tracking of trunk lines and the reconstruction of all railroads using the standard gauge. Despite having pressed these demands for the better part of a decade, though, army officials had gotten virtually nowhere with them in the face of spirited opposition from railway bureaucrats. The latter had effectively resisted the army's program on technical and financial grounds, asserting the priority of economic over military considerations in railroad development. The struggle for control of railroad policy seemed to turn in the army's favor, however, when, in 1896, army authorities finally succeeded in having the gauge issue put on the policy-making agenda. In that year, the Diet passed three motions urging the cabinet to further plans for conversion to the standard gauge, and the Communications Ministry obliged by organizing a committee to investigate the matter.[89]

In part, this turn of events resulted from a shift in the balance of power between the General Staff and the Railway Bureau as regards the railroad policy-making process. The army had had its voice in that process institutionalized and therefore strengthened through the Railway Council, which in its very first year had deliberated on a proposal submitted by Tani Kanjō that, since the "chief aim" of the trans-Honshū artery was to serve "military rather than economic" purposes, the broad gauge ought to be employed in building it.[90] On the other hand, the Railway Bureau had seen its influence in the policy-making arena much reduced after the retirement in 1893 of Inoue Masaru, none of whose successors had enjoyed his political clout. Consequently, the bureau had largely retreated into the background, for the most part shedding its political character and becoming a purely technical organ. The developments of 1896, then, can be seen as a temporary triumph for the army, flush from its victory in the China war. And, in the opinion paper it submitted to the gauge investigative committee, the Army General Staff made clear its intention to take advantage of the war and its aftermath in order to realize the army's railway program. In this document, the General Staff insisted that, in view of the restrictions employment of the narrow gauge had imposed on wartime transport, the government should posthaste use the war indemnity to convert all lines to the standard gauge so as to make them more serviceable militarily.[91]

In 1898, however, the investigative committee suddenly broke off its deliberations. The main reason for this was the aforementioned shift in army railroad policy. In that year, the General Staff abruptly replaced gauge conversion with railway nationalization as its top priority.[92] The key figure behind this change was an officer named Ōsawa Kaiyū. After graduating from the Army College, Ōsawa had been despatched overseas to study the strategic role of railroads in Europe, presumably to gather evidence in support of the army's traditional construction demands. Instead, what he brought back with him, as a newspaper noted, was "a firm conviction that private ownership is altogether a mistake."[93] The report that he presented to the General Staff upon his return undoubtedly came as a bombshell to army strategists. Based on his observations particularly of Germany's efficient state system, Ōsawa concluded that the unification of railroad management through state purchase of private lines was the first requisite for effective military transport, while "train speed is rather a secondary issue, and track width is not an important point."[94] Ōsawa's stand prevailed within the General Staff, and accordingly, the gauge issue receded from the political limelight as nationalization took center stage on the army's railway platform.

Ōsawa returned from Europe to become head of the military transport section in the General Staff, establishing himself as the army's resident expert and chief spokesman on railroad matters. He went public with his views in a series of publications in 1898 and 1899.[95] Ōsawa argued therein not only for nationalization of private railroads, but also for improvement of existing facilities and operating procedures so as better to meet the needs of military transport. His viewpoint represented a sharp departure from the army's conventional wisdom, which had pitted the strategic role of railroads against their economic function. By contrast, Ōsawa advocated structuring the system to serve economic purposes in peacetime while allowing for a smooth transition to military use in time of emergency: in other words, a system in which economic and strategic functions would coexist. This stance became the essence of army railroad policy thereafter, and the careful planning of contingency timetables that resulted from this new perspective accounted in good measure for the smooth running of the railway system during the Russo-Japanese War.[96]

Significantly, Ōsawa's views also provided a basis for accommodation with the railway bureaucracy. Besides revising the standard "military-first" position of army planners, Ōsawa echoed the contention of railway bureaucrats, starting with Inoue Masaru, that competition among private railroads inevitably led to mergers and thence to monopolies, causing irreparable harm to the public interest.[97] More than that, he anticipated several of the points subsequently raised by Den Kenjirō and other communications officials in support of nationalization. Admittedly, he differed from them in adamantly opposing the use of railroad profits as a source of revenue for the national treasury. "We must employ every last *sen* of [those] profits for railroad extension, improvement, and development," Ōsawa declared in 1898, "if necessary, separating railway from general finance."[98] On the other hand, Inoue Masaru had long fought for an independent railway account whereby the net earnings of the state railways would be applied to their own capital expenditures rather than simply added to the general revenue, and in fact, his dream was eventually to be realized at least in principle with the passage and subsequent amendment of a special railway account law following the nationalization. In that sense, the argument raised by Den and his associates that the nationalized railways would serve as a moneymaker for the government may have been merely an expedient designed to win the approval of finance authorities.

More important were the points of agreement between Ōsawa and the communications bureaucrats. Like the latter, Ōsawa urged that the government purchase private railroads in order to use them as collateral for low-interest foreign loans. In addition, he was one of the earliest to point up the dangers, both strategic and economic, of letting railway companies slip into foreign hands.[99] In 1898, he warned that, under the revised treaties to take effect the following year, foreign investors could buy into, and ultimately seize control of, Japanese railroad firms, and "once foreigners (*ketōjin*) buy up something, they never let go." Hence, it was absolutely vital for the government to preempt foreign capitalists by immediately nationalizing the private railroads, thereby avoiding what would end up, in the event of a foreign takeover of those lines, "a most disadvantageous way of importing foreign capital . . ."[100]

Needless to say, this argument was very similar to that made later by communications officials. Ōsawa not only may have supplied Den and his colleagues with intellectual ammunition, but he also gave them assistance of a more direct kind. Along with Kodama Gentarō, Ōsawa was Den's principal contact within the army. He worked closely with the vice-minister of communications both in planning the government's 1903 intervention in the Seoul-Pusan Railway and in supervising the movement of troops by rail during the Russo-Japanese War.[101] And one can readily surmise that the communications bureaucrats actively consulted him in devising their nationalization proposal as well. Thus, with the shift in army policy on railroads, the Communications Ministry obtained a powerful ally in its quest for nationalization; and one might say that this change in policy enabled the railway bureaucrats and their immediate superiors to regain the initiative in railroad planning, as the leaders of the Communications Ministry, foremost among them Den Kenjirō, emerged to fill the political vacuum left by Inoue Masaru's departure.

THE FINANCE MINISTRY AND THE OLIGARCHS

The forging of a coalition between the army and the Communications Ministry, however, by no means ensured the success of the nationalization movement after 1898. After all, a similar alliance had failed to achieve state purchase of private railroads in 1892. Just as in that previous bid, the nationalization proposal of 1905–1906 faced stiff opposition both within the administration and without. And the chief source of internal resistance in this case, as it had been in the earlier one, was the Ministry of Finance. From the beginning of the Meiji period, Finance Ministry officials had sought to relieve government finances by actively promoting private railway enterprise, waging a running battle over the issue with the state railway bureaucracy. It was only natural, then, that they should have harbored grave misgivings about the nationalization. Their apprehension was simply compounded by the huge debt of over one and a half billion yen that the Japanese government had contracted during the war. Indeed, it took the best efforts of communications bureaucrats, and more, to persuade the finance authorities ultimately to approve the purchase bill. The latter did so, with great reluctance, only after raising the most serious objections, which, in the meantime, set off a chain reaction of protest within the administration and the Diet. In short, there was nothing inevitable about the railway nationalization. Finance Ministry resistance left in doubt its acceptance by the Saionji cabinet until the very end. And, insofar as such opposition had frustrated attempts to bring about state purchase of private railroads in the past, the attitude of finance bureaucrats—and specifically their eventual acquiescence—proved to be the key to railway nationalization.

We have mentioned the lengths to which Den and his subordinates went in trying to conciliate their counterparts in the Finance Ministry. They evidently succeeded in that endeavor, for, by the end of 1905, finance officials had tentatively agreed to support their nationalization proposal. Railway Bureau Chief Yamanouchi Kazuji later recalled that the committee of communications bureaucrats appointed that year to investigate the railway purchase bill immediately entered into negotiations with the Finance Ministry. Den and members of that committee met repeatedly with Vice-Minister Sakatani Yoshirō and other finance officials. The two sides collided straight away over the method of buying out the private railroads. As Yamanouchi put it:

> Whereas we called for compulsory purchase, the Finance Ministry argued for purchase by mutual consent. We asserted that railways should be regarded as identical in character to roads and different from ordinary private property. European countries all uphold the principle of government privilege and reserve the right to buy back railroads. Therefore, one can treat [railway nationalization] as a form of public expropriation, and

the question is [rather] the purchase price . . . For a long while, we debated the issue, but, in the end, the Finance Ministry agreed to our position.[102]

Finance Ministry approval, though, was not unqualified. Finance authorities were still deeply concerned about the impact that nationalization might have on government finances and particularly on Japanese credit abroad. Once Japan had failed to obtain an indemnity from Russia under the peace treaty of September 1905, it was plain that the administration would have to rely substantially on foreign loans to finance its postwar program, given the tight domestic money market and the relatively limited national tax base. Yet, mainly on account of the wartime loans, over half of which were floated overseas, the total national debt already exceeded two billion yen in 1905. It was now proposed to add to this some four hundred million yen in railway-purchase bonds. This prospect was clearly unsettling to finance officials, none more so, as it would turn out, than Takahashi Korekiyo, then vice-president of the Bank of Japan. Takahashi had gone overseas as Japan's special finance commissioner to negotiate the wartime foreign loans. In September 1905, he telegraphed his home government to urge that it compensate for the lack of reparations by taking various remedial measures, including the postponement of unproductive enterprises.[103] Finance authorities were also anxious to secure alternative means of financing, which meant above all foreign borrowing. As Vice-Minister Sakatani declared in a speech in mid-December:

> The cardinal object kept in view by the compilers of the [national budget] . . . was to adjust the national debt so as to maintain credit abroad. The confidence of foreign lenders depends largely on the market price commanded by bonds. . . . The Japanese Government feels that in view of the many undertakings which will offer themselves in the sequel of the war, it is of prime importance that stores of foreign capital should be accessible, and since that can be achieved only by keeping up the credit of the country's securities, special importance was attached to the latter point by the framers of the Budget.[104]

Against this background of unease among finance officials, Takahashi returned from Europe to deal a near-fatal blow to the recently achieved consensus on nationalization. Giving voice to the worst fears of the finance bureaucracy, he vigorously opposed the nationalization on the grounds that the issue of railway-purchase bonds might trigger a sharp decline in the price of the foreign war bonds and therefore a disastrous loss of Japanese credit overseas.[105] He reportedly went so far as to describe the railway-purchase proposal as a "plan for ruining the country."[106] As we shall see, Takahashi's objections served to harden opposition to nationalization within the Diet. More immediately, however, they produced a dangerous rift among government leaders, which threatened to bring down the nascent Saionji cabinet. First of all, Inoue Kaoru, who as head of wartime budget-making had worked closely with Takahashi, was moved by the latter's argument to withdraw his support of nationalization.[107] Open dissension by these two authorities, in turn, brought to the surface latent resistance within the Finance Ministry, whose bureau heads at one point refused to sign a memorandum circulated by the Communications Ministry concerning the proposed nationalization bill.[108]

The objections of finance officials also played a part in Foreign Minister Katō's vehement opposition to the nationalization proposal. One of the reasons Katō gave for his opposition clearly showed the influence of Takahashi's argument. The foreign minister repeatedly underscored the folly of increasing the already inflated national debt by upwards of four hundred million yen in order to finance the purchase of private railroads, at a time when the government was striving to maintain the value of its outstanding bonds and hence confidence in its credit, particularly among foreign investors.[109] Indeed, one source suggests that this was Katō's principal concern in opposing the nationalization, that, in doing so, he was actually protesting "the government's reckless borrowing policy."[110] This view seems not unreasonable in light of the fact that Katō had begun his official career in the Finance Ministry and that, as an Anglophile who had subsequently served as minister to England and helped negotiate the Anglo-Japanese Alliance of 1902, he was eager to preserve Japan's credit with British investors, who had bought nearly half the war bonds.

In explaining his opposition to the railway purchase bill, however, Katō laid greater stress on reasons that were firmly rooted in liberal laissez-faire doctrines. Above all, he publicly objected to the nationalization on the grounds that the forced sale of private railroads, in the absence of a national emergency that might otherwise justify it, would be "an invasion of private rights"; it would therefore be "most unlawful."[111] Still, Katō was careful to relate this point to the problem of maintaining Japan's international credit. "In particular," he asserted, "since from now on, we will have to rely heavily on foreign capital, if we cause foreigners, who believe strongly in legal guarantees of property rights, to harbor apprehension, it will disturb the basis of trust in our nation and be a very grave matter."[112] Continuing the laissez-faire theme, Katō also argued that public management of the railroads was likely to be less efficient than private management. He specifically pointed out the contradiction between the administration's aim of "making [the railroads] suit the public interest" by upgrading them and lowering rates, and its objective of having them "serve as a source of revenue for the national treasury by earning great profits."[113] In addition, he warned that, under party cabinets, the nationalized railways would be used by the government party to expand its local power, implying that political considerations would overwhelm economic ones in their administration.[114]

In stating the reasons for his opposition to the nationalization program, Katō seems to have emphasized matters of principle largely to demonstrate the purity of his motives, for it was hotly rumored at the time that he was actually opposing the program on behalf of his in-laws, the Iwasaki. In fact, Katō's protest and resignation over the issue of railway nationalization has come to be taken as prima facie evidence that Mitsubishi, the second largest investor in private railroads, also opposed the government's plan. Deferring a more detailed analysis of Mitsubishi's attitude towards nationalization for the time being, we can note in passing that Katō, the former Mitsubishi employee, owed his swift rise in public life in no small measure to the funds and connections provided by his in-laws.[115] And, perhaps not coincidentally, his laissez-faire argument was virtually identical to that of Shōda Heigorō, Mitsubishi's chief executive in Tokyo, who since the late 1890s had been speaking out against nationalization on the grounds that, "if we expect enterprises to progress, they must be left alone—left to natural selection and the survival of the fittest—without artificial intervention."[116] As Shōda summed up his position in 1908, in words closely paralleling those of Katō: "I opposed the nationalization of railways from the beginning. My reasons were that it confiscated the property produced by private individuals, thus disregarding the guarantees under the law, and that the result of unification would be a reduction of competition."[117]

Katō may have had another motive for resigning other than those he made public, a motive more closely linked to his responsibilities as foreign minister. He apparently chafed at having his authority restricted by the army and the oligarchs, who, contrary to his wishes, sought to retain occupation rights in Manchuria even after the withdrawal of Japanese troops following the Russo-Japanese War.[118] As Home Minister Hara Kei recorded in his diary after failing to persuade Katō to agree to the nationalization proposal on February 19th, "it seems that Katō wants to make short the life of this cabinet. He bears ill feeling towards the oligarchic government and wants to restrain the military men."[119] In short, the real reason for Katō's resignation may have had more to do with his opposition to the oligarchs and their army lieutenants than to the railway nationalization.[120]

Whatever his exact motivation, Katō's announcement of his opposition to the nationalization plan and of his determination to resign should the cabinet approve it created quite a sensation. According to one observer, "it was unprecedented for a foreign minister to oppose the financial policy of the government he was serving and to fight it even to the point of resigning his post."[121] Equally unprecedented was the way in which Katō stepped down when he finally did so on March 3rd. Whereas, in the past, ministers of state had customarily resigned on the grounds of health, Katō explicitly cited his objections to the government's nationalization policy.[122]

Saionji, however, managed to prevent Katō's actions from precipitating a full-fledged cabinet crisis by convincing the finance authorities to drop their opposition to the proposed bill, in effect isolating the foreign minister. Just before the cabinet began formal deliberations on the bill in mid-February, Saionji invited Inoue and Takahashi to a meeting with "the ministers concerned," namely, Communications Minister Yamagata, Finance Minister Sakatani, and Army Minister Terauchi. Also present was Vice-Minister of Communications Nakashōji, who sought to allay Takahashi's fears of a sudden collapse of the public-bond market by repeating the Communications Ministry position that the railway-purchase bonds would simply take the place of corporate securities and therefore have little impact on the market and that "there is no comparison between them and public bonds newly issued for unproductive enterprises."[123] However persuasive such arguments were, Finance Minister Sakatani clearly showed their influence when he later testified at an upper-house hearing that bonds floated for "the development of concessions" such as the Seoul-Pusan railway differed from "unproductive" military bonds.[124] Also reassuring was the fact that the administration proposed to grant the purchase bonds not immediately but within a certain period of time, enabling it to spread out the effect of the issue as well as to wait for optimal market conditions.

Nakashōji apparently made no mention of the other pet argument of the communications bureaucracy, namely, that the nationalized railways would become a major source of state revenue. One might expect this point to have had particular appeal to finance officials. Den and his colleagues, of course, had cited Prussian precedent in claiming that nationalization would result in increased revenue for the government, but there is no evidence that finance bureaucrats did likewise. On the contrary, the latter predicted—correctly as it would turn out—that, in spite of their current profitability, the nationalized railways would in the long run prove to be a burden rather than a boon to state finances, owing to the cost of financing the purchase itself as well as subsequent improvements and extensions.[125] At any rate, the points Nakashōji did raise, together with Saionji's resolve to stake the fate of his cabinet on the issue, apparently sufficed to induce Takahashi and Inoue to withdraw their objections.[126] Their compliance then helped to bring the Ministry of Finance around as well, paving the way for a consensus among the three ministers concerned and thereby ensuring the cabinet's final adoption of the nationalization program.

Finance Minister Sakatani himself played an important role in convincing his subordinates to consent to the nationalization, urging them to "just think of it as though the war had lasted another year."[127] What moved the minister of finance to support the railway purchase bill was not so much his colleagues' assurances concerning the nature and timing of bond issues as the administration's larger agenda for postwar Japan. Sakatani gave vivid expression to a major part of that agenda when, at a lower-house hearing in March, he declared:

> At this critical juncture, we must devise a method of economic development so that we do not lag further behind world progress. Needless to say, the best way would be to extend the sphere of influence we have acquired through war. In relation to this, we must devise a method whereby Japanese products can be exported most quickly and cheaply to Korea and China.... Henceforth, how can we wage the economic war [on the continent]? Although we have actually finished the war fought

with arms, we do not know how to wage the war of the abacus. With regard to this, it has become most urgent that we endeavor to exploit the opportunity to expand our sphere of influence ... by resolving the long-pending question of railway unification and that we make fully serviceable both our domestic railroads and those in Korea and Manchuria.[128]

The finance minister's call to arms for the "war of the abacus" echoed the long-standing concern of the oligarchs and their lieutenants for expanding the East Asian markets for Japanese goods, a goal that Sakatani had shared since at least the late 1890s.[129] Unified state ownership of the domestic and Korean railroads would serve that purpose admirably by allowing for cheaper and more efficient transport of Japanese exports.

Indeed, government leaders proclaimed railway nationalization to be the springboard of their postwar program, with Saionji, for example, introducing the purchase bills to the lower house as "the most pressing need of the postwar management."[130] As communications officials had forcefully argued in their nationalization proposals, a united state railway system would not only advance the economic aims of the "postwar management" directly; it would also provide the financial underpinning for the endeavor as a whole. This, it seems to me, is the key to understanding the decision for nationalization particularly on the part of the oligarchs and their lieutenants. Paradoxically, just as in the past, financial considerations had impelled the top decision makers to approve, even promote, the establishment of private railroads and to rule out any serious thought of buying them up, so now did financial considerations prompt them to embrace the nationalization of private lines.

A crucial problem for both the Katsura and Saionji cabinets was how to pay for the postwar program of armaments expansion and industrial and colonial development. Whereas the smaller counterpart to this effort following the Sino-Japanese War had been financed largely by the China indemnity,[131] the post-1905 version, in the absence of a similar windfall from the Russians, would have to rely on other types of funding. Prussian experience suggested that the nationalized railways themselves would prove to be an important source of revenue for the government. Katsura, for one, seems to have accepted this view. In mid-December 1905, for instance, he opined that a compromise could be reached between army and finance authorities over the latter's demand for a reduction in unproductive military expenditures by "applying to industry the profits to be gained from [the nationalized railways]."[132] And, on paper at least, the private railroads *were* highly profitable, returning on average nearly 11 percent on paid-up capital in 1904.[133] State leaders tended, however, to place greater emphasis on the use of the railroads not as moneymakers in themselves, but as security for public loans, particularly of the overseas variety, which were likely to be the principal source of funding for the postwar endeavor. The purchased railroads were expected to serve as excellent collateral for refinancing the enormous war debt as well as for borrowing anew. In short, the oligarchs and their proteges set great store by the nationalization as a way of lending "financial stability" to the postwar management.[134]

There is some indication that, at the outset, government leaders predicated their railway-purchase plans on the acquisition of war reparations from Russia. As one scholar puts it, "the Katsura cabinet, anticipating a war indemnity, planned the railway nationalization as the first step of the postwar management."[135] Some business leaders held similar expectations. In June 1905, Masuda Takashi of Mitsui Bussan, for instance, told Hara Kei and Matsuda Masahisa of the Seiyūkai that, "if we are fortunate enough to obtain an indemnity after the war, I hope that railway nationalization and the conversion of railroads to the broad gauge will be carried out," to which Hara perceptively replied, "on the contrary, it may be that, if we do not obtain an indemnity, we will have to implement railway nationalization."[136] In any event, the prospect of Russian reparations may well have given necessary momentum to nationalization planning during the critical preparatory stages in 1904–1905.

This possibility raises the question of why the procurement of the China indemnity in 1895–1898 did not have the same effect on the nationalization drives of the previous "postwar-management" era. Part of the answer lies in the fact that, in the decade or so following passage of the Railway Construction Law, state rail policy was focused overwhelmingly on railroad building, so that, insofar as the authorities considered applying the indemnity to railroads, they thought almost entirely in terms of promoting the extension of government lines. Between 1895 and 1899, the state railways spent ¥44,450,451 on construction work, more than they had expended for that purpose over the previous twenty-five years, to bring their cumulative construction outlay in 1899 to ¥88,153,497, a sum they would nearly double again over the next five years.[137] The authorities actually applied less than 1 percent of the China indemnity, or some ¥3,000,000, directly to domestic communications enterprises including railroads, although part of the ¥12,000,000 appropriated for the administration of Taiwan went into railroad development there, and the government also drew on the reparations account in lending ¥1,800,000 to the Seoul-Inchon Railway Company.[138] Nevertheless, the indemnity performed a vital role in financing indirectly the construction of state railways at home by providing money for underwriting public-bond issues, which covered about three quarters of the cost of such construction, the rest being met through general-revenue funds.[139] This function became especially important as the government encountered considerable difficulty in floating bonds domestically, particularly after the first postwar recession set in. The authorities partially overcame this problem in 1899 by successfully issuing a foreign loan, the first since 1873, in the amount of ¥98,000,000, roughly a third of which they allotted to the state railways.[140] The indemnity played no small part in making possible this importation of foreign capital, for it had enabled Japan to go on the gold standard in 1897 and thereby to become a full-fledged member of the capitalist club.

Facilitating the introduction of foreign capital was one way in which the China indemnity might indirectly have paved the way for railway nationalization around the turn of the century. Den, for one, stressed in his 1901 proposal the government's ability to finance the purchase of private railroads by floating loans overseas, and to many around that time, the resumption of foreign borrowing must have appeared to be the breakthrough that would finally result in nationalization.[141] There was a key difference, however, between the situations before and after the outbreak of hostilities with Russia, namely, the relatively limited scale of capital importation prior to 1904. The 1899 loan, in fact, was the last one issued overseas until the Russo-Japanese War. True, the government did manage to sell abroad an additional ¥93,000,000 in domestic bonds from 1897 to 1903,[142] but the four war loans and postwar redemption loan floated overseas in 1904–1905 yielded five times the less than ¥200,000,000 imported during the previous seven years.

The dramatic increase in foreign borrowing after 1904 changed the entire context of railroad policy making and helps to explain the suddenness of the decision for nationalization. On the one hand, it made the purchase of private railroads feasible by demonstrating that Japan could raise the necessary capital abroad. Hara Kei exemplified the heightened awareness of the possibilities of overseas borrowing when, in the aforementioned reply to Masuda Takashi, he added: "if we do get an indemnity, it would be best to deposit it in the West as is, and to use the credit to try to improve various enterprises."[143] On the other hand, the steep wartime rise in the country's foreign debt made railway nationalization desirable, some would have said indispensable, in order to provide the government with sound collateral for further loans to refund the national debt as well as to finance the postwar endeavor.

Admittedly, the state tried to deal with its mounting fiscal problems from the late 1890s on, not only by floating bonds at home and abroad, but also by enlarging the government-run postal savings system. In 1875, Japan had followed the lead of Britain to become the fourth nation in the world to establish a system whereby its people could deposit their savings at post offices.[144] The postal service within the Ministry of Communications administered the system, but the Finance Ministry controlled the actual investment of the deposits. Following World War II, the postal savings system was to prove "fabulously successful . . . [as] the institutional linchpin of Japan's high savings rate, which has allowed the country to fund its industrialization more cheaply than virtually any of its competitors."[145] The foundations for this success were laid during the late Meiji period when state leaders recognized the potential contribution of the system to solving Japan's current financial difficulties and began actively promoting postal savings as an integral part of their successive postwar-management programs. The official drive to develop the system into a mass institution for small savers, one that would mobilize funds for the postwar endeavors, originated in 1898 with a hike in the interest rate on postal savings and a general increase and improvement in customer services. Similar changes followed in rapid succession, including the introduction in 1900 of a system for accepting deposits in postage stamps. Aimed at schoolchildren, this program marked the beginning of a systematic effort to instill the habit of institutional saving in the next generation of wage-earners.[146]

The incorporation of postal savings into state financial and industrial policy reached new heights at the end of the Russo-Japanese War when the authorities devised their most ingenious plan. Under the revised Postal Savings Law of July 1905, payments made by the national treasury to service or redeem the public bonds held by postal savers were automatically deposited into their postal-savings accounts. Consequently, the government managed to capture in the form of internal transfer payments a substantial proportion of the vastly increased public expenditures resulting from the war; at the same time, the authorities continued to foster the expansion of postal savings, now as a part of the so-called local improvement movement, through which, during the decade after the war, they sought to mobilize the populace in the service of state goals.[147] The postwar cabinets promoted postal savings not just as a way of preventing the above transfer payments from simply going out as savings withdrawals but also, more positively, as a way of financing state projects, including railway construction and renovation, without excessively floating public bonds.[148] The campaign to encourage postal savings was a resounding success, as total savings rose from less than ¥26,000,000 in 1897 to ¥161,027,000 in 1910, surpassing bank-savings deposits once and for all that year, and the total number of postal savers increased during the same period from under 1,300,000 to over 10,000,000.[149]

The second postwar endeavor, of which railway nationalization and postal savings were to be such vital components, reflected a basic shift in attitude among public officials since the late 1890s on the proper role of government in economic affairs. Reinforcing this change was the growing influence on Japanese bureaucrats of the ideas of the German social policy school, which advocated government takeover of railroads and other forms of state intervention in the economy "in order to ease class conflicts through social welfare legislation."[150] According to Kenneth Pyle, the tenets of this so-called New Historical School exerted a pervasive impact on the bureaucracy from the late 1890s and "became embodied in government policy in a number of highly influential ways."[151] The ideological concerns addressed by this school of thought combined with strategic and financial imperatives to prompt a redefinition of the government's economic role after the Sino-Japanese War. The result, in sharp contrast to the retrenchment policy of the 1880s, was a significant expansion of direct state involvement in industry, beginning with the establishment of government monopolies and the Yawata Iron and Steelworks in the late 1890s and culminating in the nationalization of private railroads. Critics of the railway purchase bill in the Diet were quick to point out this trend, one member of the upper house noting ironically: "The present government is rigorously suppressing socialism; yet, in spite of this, it is carrying out a policy of steadily creating monopolies by usurping private businesses and turning them into state enterprises that is scarcely removed from socialism."[152] The extent to which the planners of the nationalization were actually trying to promote a kind of national socialism is debatable. There is no question, however, that their railway-purchase proposal epitomized the heightened sense of government responsibility for economic welfare and national security embodied in the "postwar-management" program. This expanded definition of the state's role, together with the importance attached to the railway network as both object and facilitator of the postwar endeavor, may best explain why, in the final analysis, agreement was reached among all the authorities concerned to support the government buyout of private railroads in Japan.

The Nationalization Bill, as submitted to the cabinet on February 17th by Communications Minister Yamagata, initially called for the purchase of seventeen railway companies, communications officials having added the Tokushima Railway to the sixteen, mostly main-line firms chosen for nationalization by the previous Katsura administration. At that meeting, however, Hara Kei introduced an amendment to increase the number of railroads to be nationalized from seventeen to thirty-two, raising the total purchase price from ¥410,000,000 to between ¥459,000,000 and ¥471,000,000.[153] Although the first clause of the proposed legislation stipulated that the government purchase "all railroads that provide public transportation" exclusive of firms serving only "one locality," the fifteen companies recommended for inclusion by Hara were almost all railroads of a decidedly local character. Their average length of line was a mere twenty-four miles, and not one of them operated more than fifty miles of track. Their addition would have left in private hands only five of the railroads in operation at the time.[154] Practically every one of these fifteen concerns had been established during the second railway boom following the enactment of the Railway Construction Law. It is commonly maintained that the 1892 law had the effect of limiting private railroad building to local lines that were not scheduled for construction by the government under the act.[155] This assertion clearly ignores the repeated application of the private-construction loophole in the law. Indeed, several rail companies founded after 1892 qualify as main-line firms, such as the Hokkaido and Hokuetsu, both of which were included among the seventeen railroads designated for nationalization in the original proposal. Nevertheless, the trend in private railroad development after 1892 was definitely towards the establishment of small-scale local lines—and necessarily so, construction of the more profitable trunk railroads having already been undertaken during the first railway boom. As we shall see in the next chapter, such local railroads were in general far less remunerative than the older, main-line companies. They were also much harder hit by the recessions of 1897–1898 and 1900–1901 and forced to rely heavily on borrowed capital.

In view of their disappointing business results, it is no wonder to learn from one account that investors in the "shabby railroads (*boro tetsudō*)" excluded from the initial proposal mounted a vigorous campaign to have their companies added to the bill.[156] Such investors were for the most part landlords, merchants, and other men of wealth living along the routes of the lines concerned. The Chūetsu Railway, one of the fifteen firms cited in Hara's amendment, nicely illustrates the predominance of local investment in these railroads. Licensed in 1895, the Chūetsu Railway built a line of twenty-three miles, running inland from the Japan Sea in Toyama prefecture. All thirty-two of its promoters were local men, most of them large landlords involved in a variety of other pursuits as well, ranging from sake brewing and textile manufacturing to trading and banking. The majority of them were also active in politics either as prefectural assemblymen or as National Diet members. These thirty-two individuals accepted over two fifths of the company's 4,400 shares, the rest of which were offered publicly.[157]

The Chūetsu's promoters, who continued to control the railroad on the eve of the nationalization,[158] were precisely the kind of local leaders whose support the Seiyūkai was anxious to gain in order to strengthen its electoral base. As home minister under Saionji, Hara was beginning to push a positive spending policy aimed at extending his party's influence in the provinces by satisfying local economic demands.[159] The nationalization of struggling local railroads fit perfectly into his plans, and it is therefore not surprising that Hara, ever "the party man,"[160] should have responded to pressure from investors in the fifteen companies concerned by insisting on the latter's addition to the purchase bill. Although the political motivation behind the home minister's proposal is clear, it should be recalled that, under Katsura, communications bureaucrats had originally recommended the nationalization of thirty-two, purportedly "nonlocal" railroads, so there could have been no argument from that quarter. By contrast, the Finance Ministry undoubtedly was none too pleased with this proposed expansion in the scope of the nationalization, and perhaps as a concession, it was also proposed that the deadline for issuing the purchase bonds be moved, however slightly, from one and a half years to two years from the date of purchase.[161] The cabinet finally accepted these amendments at the conclusion of a marathon meeting on February 28th, in the middle of which Foreign Minister Katō turned in his letter of resignation and walked out.[162] The administration then submitted the revised bill to the legislature on March 3rd. The fate of the nationalization proposal now lay in the hands of the Diet.

The Diet

Passage of the railway purchase bill at least by the lower house seemed a foregone conclusion with the Seiyūkai and the Daidō Club, the pro-administration party, together commanding a clear majority in that body.[163] Moreover, the Seiyūkai's endorsement of the nationalization program was not simply a matter of political expedience, of concession-making aimed at grasping a share of power. Indeed, the leaders of that party and its predecessors had actively supported railway nationalization since the late 1890s and, during the recent recessions, had actually run ahead of state authorities on the issue. By the time of its short-lived merger with the Shimpōtō in 1898, the old Jiyūtō had largely appropriated the cabinet's "positive policy" for its own. The program of party expansion by pork barrel that Hara would perfect after 1905 was already well in the making under Itagaki Taisuke and Hoshi Tōru in the latter half of the 1890s. Central to that evolving program was the satisfaction of local demands for railroad development under the Railway Construction Law. In the late 1890s, then, the Jiyūtō added to its agenda the state purchase of private railroads. This was in sharp contrast to the ambivalence and outright opposition to nationalization shown by party members in 1891–1892. Once the panic broke out in 1897 and businessmen began calling for railway nationalization as a relief measure, the Jiyūtō lost no time in jumping on the bandwagon.

The party may have done so in part out of a desire to protect the growing railway interests of its traditional landholding constituency; a more important factor in this case, however, was the determination of party leaders to develop closer ties with the rising business class. Forced to share the burden of financing state programs with the enactment of a corporate tax law following the Sino-Japanese War, businessmen vented their dissatisfaction by becoming increasingly active in politics. The antitax movement they launched initially centered on demands for a reduction in military expenditures. With the cabinet refusing to budge on that matter, however, the onset of the recession in 1897 and the resulting critical need for financial relief constrained the business community to change its tactics. Instead of attacking the state's armaments expansion drive, businessmen began pressing the administration to raise the land tax as a way of stabilizing its finances and to float foreign loans as a means of easing the tight money market.[164] The latter demand clearly reflected the new ferment over the possibility of foreign borrowing, and interestingly, in light of the arguments of Den, Ōsawa, and other state bureaucrats, business leaders, too, linked the importation of foreign capital to railway nationalization, calling on the government to buy out private railroads in order to obtain sound collateral for low-interest foreign loans.[165]

Significantly, the leaders of this businessmen's campaign were none other than prominent railway investors and executives such as Amenomiya Keijirō and Inoue Kakugorō. Itagaki and Hoshi were eager to rally such capitalists behind their party, anxious as they were to assure the flow of campaign funds to their followers. This concern, then, accounts for the alacrity with which the Jiyūtō came out in support of the businessmen's position.[166] No sooner had Amenomiya and his colleagues formed an Alliance for the Importation of Foreign Capital in April 1898 than Itagaki appeared before them to declare: "The relief measure [needed] today is to introduce foreign capital and thereby to nationalize the railroads."[167] The party president affirmed in a subsequent newspaper interview "that only by using the Government's credit can foreign capital be procured cheaply, and that the best and simplest form of security Japan can offer to foreign capitalists is her railways."[168] Moreover, in order to raise money to pay back the foreign loans, the Jiyūtō leadership also came around to accept the business demand for an increase in the land tax. This in large part explains the willingness of the party, which now called itself the Kenseitō, to enter into an alliance with the second Yamagata cabinet in November 1898 whereby the Kenseitō agreed to back the administration's legislative program, including a proposal for hiking the land tax, in return for the cabinet's adoption of the party platform.[169] Needless to say, a major item in that platform was railway nationalization. As Banno points out, while the cabinet and the Kenseitō were negotiating the terms of the coalition, railway capitalists and other businessmen put pressure on both sides to reach an agreement, urging the party men in particular to endorse the administration's tax-increase proposal.[170] The Kenseitō was quick to respond. The following January, Itagaki expressed well his party's keen interest in broadening the basis of its support to encompass the rising star of the business community when he asserted, "In the open and enterprising new Japan, agriculture, industry, and commerce all necessarily increase the national wealth, and in terms of [government] protection, no relative importance should be attached to any one; however, since some [areas of the economy] have already developed and others have yet to develop, attention must be paid to their proximate circumstances. To say that agriculture is the foundation of the state is the economic argument of the preceding isolationism."[171]

The new party stance did not mean that the Kenseitō had turned its back on its traditional landlord constituents. It is true that, at this particular juncture, the party's "positive policy" signified a program of economic relief for businessmen at the expense of landowners. In June 1899, Hoshi echoed the business community's own conversion from a policy of military-budget cutting to one of increased spending through capital importation when he proclaimed: "Our objective is to take a positive policy and to hope for the expansion of both armaments and the economy under the postwar management."[172] However, the Kenseitō had never really abandoned its "positive policy" of the local-interest variety, as was made evident by the barrage of pork-barrel legislation it introduced into the Diet in 1899, and in fact, the party was compelled to stress that policy all the more in order to contain the political damage wrought by its endorsement of the land-tax hike.[173] By the time of the Saionji cabinet, the "positive policy" and the nationalization program in particular were very much directed at the localities rather than at the business community, the emphasis having changed decisively from minimizing the loss of landlord support to aggressively expanding party power in the provinces.

In 1898, though, the party was clearly catering to business interests in committing itself to nationalization as a financial-relief measure. And the following year, it moved to make good on its promise. In February 1899, Hoshi and his colleagues submitted to the lower house a proposal for railway nationalization that in wording followed closely the petitions of the business community.[174] There was a subtle but important difference, however, between the lower-house motion and the proposal that the party council had approved the previous month. In the latter, the Kenseitō had urged that the cabinet "decide on an appropriate bill and introduce it during the current session of the Diet";[175] but, in the proposal it actually submitted to the house, the party called on the administration merely to "seek an opportunity" to present a nationalization bill to the Diet, the word "current" having been struck from the original motion.[176] This softening of the party position reflected the fact that the recession in the railroad industry, and with it, the business demand for nationalization, had begun to let up by February 1899. The industry's recovery exposed the basic weakness of the nationalization movement at the turn of the century and accounted in large measure for its ultimate failure.

At the time, however, events seemed to be moving inexorably towards the achievement of nationalization. The lower house adopted the Kenseitō motion by a vote of 145 to 127. On the basis of that motion and in fulfillment of its pledge to the Kenseitō, the Yamagata cabinet established a committee to investigate the purchase of private railroads. Chaired by the minister of communications, the committee consisted of top government bureaucrats, Dietmen, and academic experts. After studying the matter for nearly a year, the committee finally drafted two nationalization bills, which it presented to the cabinet in February 1900. The proposed legislation called for the purchase of nine, primarily main-line firms, including the big five and the Kōbu Railway, precisely the companies in which Amenomiya and his associates had invested most heavily.[177]

The organization of the cabinet investigative committee appeared to mark a crucial turning point in the nationalization movement. Shima Yasuhiko sees the committee as representing "an alliance of railway, military, and finance bureaucrats as well as businessmen" and assigns it considerable historical significance: "It was here that, for the first time, railway nationalization was taken up concretely as a matter that could actually be put into effect."[178] Nevertheless, serious questions can be raised as to whether such unanimity of purpose in fact obtained among the committee members and whether their legislative program stood any real chance of enactment. In the first place, the committee was clearly a vehicle for the Kenseitō's "positive policy," since the cabinet agreed to its formation in line with the party platform and Hoshi Tōru served as head of the committee's executive council. The railway bureaucrats on the committee most certainly had no quarrel with the party program, but the presence thereon of Takahashi Korekiyo and Sakatani Yoshirō, who were charged with investigating sources of financing and the economic impact of bond issues, suggests that there was less than total agreement among government representatives. Indeed, the cabinet itself was far from enthusiastic about the proposed nationalization, burdened as it already was with a huge military budget. Concerned lest the administration should fail to come through with a railway-purchase proposal, Kenseitō members had in fact submitted a compromise bill to the Diet in January 1900. In it, they proposed a single joint enterprise of the kind subsequently considered by the Katsura cabinet. "If, at the present time, it is deemed difficult to obtain adequate sources of funding in order to purchase private railroads," the bill's authors suggested, "an expedient method would be to form a mixed system by merging the state and private trunk lines, to anticipate the unification of management and administration, and to nationalize [the private lines] gradually so as to avoid financial and economic fluctuations."[179] This was a proposal clearly aimed at relieving the financial anxieties of state authorities.

In any case, soon after receiving the nationalization bills from the investigative committee, the cabinet went ahead and introduced them into the Diet. Once they appeared on the agenda, the joint-venture proposal was discarded. It soon became evident, however, that government leaders were simply going through the motions in submitting the nationalization bills. As one source puts it, the administration, "in light of the financial situation, . . . allowed those proposals to lapse."[180] The Kenseitō, for its part, had cooled considerably towards the proposed legislation as well. The businessmen being courted by the party were enjoying the respite from the first postwar recession, the second being some two months in the offing, so there was little pressure from that direction, the efforts of President Den of the Kansai Railway to mobilize the private railway community notwithstanding. Moreover, given the cabinet's lack of enthusiasm, party leaders saw little chance of securing the necessary funding. The extent to which the Kenseitō had lost hope or interest regarding passage of a nationalization bill was made strikingly clear by the fact that the special committee appointed by the lower house to deliberate on the purchase proposals never once convened. As one newspaper reported, "Chairman Hoshi and the Kenseitō committee members decided to table [the bills] because there was hardly any prospect of reaching agreement within the party."[181]

The cabinet investigative committee and its abortive bills may have prefigured the eventual consensus on nationalization, but there was little direct connection between the committee's proposal and that of the Katsura and Saionji administrations, except with regard to language. Both called for the nationalization of all railroads providing "general transportation," meaning primarily trunk lines, a principle to which the investigative committee, unlike the Saionji cabinet with its addition of conspicuously local lines, by and large adhered. Yet therein lay the key difference as far as the backing of the majority party was concerned. Hoshi and his colleagues had shown that support for a nationalization bill aimed at relieving the financial world was too unstable to ensure Diet approval, subject as it was to fluctuating business cycles. By contrast, Hara would demonstrate that, when linked to local interests, railway nationalization would prove far more compelling to the majority of Diet members.

True, as suggested earlier, the Saionji cabinet's proposal contained an element of providing financial relief to struggling local railroads, but equally, if not more, important was the desire of party men to use the profits from the nationalized railway companies to build new lines in their home districts. Local demand for the state construction of such lines had, if anything, intensified since the 1890s, especially since many of the local lines yet to be built had little prospect of making money and therefore could be constructed only with difficulty by private concerns. For example, in late 1902, on the eve of the seventeenth Diet session, local branches of the Seiyūkai bombarded party headquarters with petitions for railroad construction. Typical was the memorial of the Yamagata prefectural chapter, which, besides seconding the national-party platform, urged Seiyūkai leaders to "be resolved to complete the railroads."[182] Similarly, the Toyama prefectural branch added to its endorsement of central policy three local demands, including one calling on party headquarters to "work for the rapid construction of the Toyama-Naoetsu railroad."[183] That local importunities were becoming increasingly focused on state railway building is evidenced by President Itō's admonition to party regulars at the time that, "as regards the railroad question, when it comes to sinking money into their own localities, Diet members until now have all been engaged in a tug of war, proposing anything and everything regardless of the expense to the state."[184] It was precisely Hara's wish to bind such local demands for railroad development to the bureaucracy's plan for nationalization that led him to recommend the purchase of additional local lines, perhaps as much to assure the improvement as the extension of those lines. The connection between "railway unification and diffusion" was expressed most clearly by a spokesman for the Daidō Club who, during the first reading of the purchase bill in the lower house on March 6, 1906, affirmed that, "when the state adopts a policy of extending [railroads] even to remote mountain villages, this will of course stimulate the growth of productivity and the development of manufacturing and commerce in those areas . . ."[185] This was a statement guaranteed to play well among rural representatives in the Diet as well as their constituents back home.[186]

In short, it appeared that the Railway Nationalization Bill would have an easy time of it in the lower house, but such a scenario would by no means prove to be the case. For one thing, the Kenseihontō, with its close ties to Mitsubishi and its desire to obstruct the Seiyūkai-backed cabinet, was determined to put up a fight. It was joined by the Seikō Club, a grouping of former independents, and together, the two parties controlled over a third of the lower-house membership.[187] Their pugnacious stance ensured that government representatives would have to endure intense grilling during committee hearings and that the bill itself would come under fierce attack on the house floor. Of far greater concern, however, was the attitude of the Daidō Club, which held the all-important swing vote. Although ostensibly a pro-cabinet party, that group would remain dangerously divided on the issue until relatively late in the session. It would take considerable concessions on other matters as well as a fair dose of bribery by the administration to bring the Daidō Club in line, thereby securing passage of the railway purchase bill by the lower house.

The opposition parties made certain, though, that the bill's passage would be anything but smooth. In denouncing the proposed legislation, members of the Kenseihontō and Seikō Club found particularly useful ammunition in the arguments of Katō and Takahashi. Several of them echoed Katō's laissez-faire stand, Taketomi Tokitoshi of the Kenseihontō declaring, for instance, that "progress is the result of competition.... For that reason, it is beyond question that, if [railroads] became a state monopoly, progress will at that point cease."[188] Shimada Saburō of the Seikō Club was more concrete, backing his assertion that "all competition is the friend of progress" by citing the example of the San'yō Railway. As Shimada pointed out, the latter had been "pressed by its competition" in the shipping industry to improve passenger service and lower freight rates, which had, in turn, induced the state railways to do likewise.[189] Like Katō, opponents of the nationalization argued that the management of the state railways was less efficient than that of their private counterparts, Taketomi in particular parading statistics showing the average operating expenditure per mile for the state system to be ¥6,800 compared to only ¥5,300 for the private network.[190] Opposition members wondered, therefore, how the administration could expect the purchase to result in a reduction of operating costs.

Taketomi also repeated almost verbatim Katō's charge concerning the unlawfulness of the nationalization act. "Because this railway nationalization takes away rights that have been legally granted to people for a fixed period of time," the Dietman maintained, "it will break the guarantees of the constitution and undermine trust in the law and, by extension, confidence in the state both at home and abroad..."[191] In addition, Taketomi offered the following variation on Katō's warning that the nationalized railroads would fall prey to politics: "since the government attends to all kinds of business, once the railroads come under state management, they will be influenced at all times by the [general] circumstances of the government." In particular, the Dietman asserted, if a "nominal official" were to become head of the Communications Ministry, the ministry's leverage would diminish in government counsels and railroad construction would suffer accordingly, experience having shown that, "even if the extension of railroads is necessary, the cabinet will not accept the requests of a nominal minister." Taketomi then rebuked the bill's supporters in the house by exclaiming: "Do you mean to put all the nation's railroads into this kind of state?"[192]

Opponents of the Nationalization Bill were also quick to voice Takahashi's concern as to the potential impact that the tremendous issue of purchase bonds would have on the public-bond market as well as on Japanese credit abroad.[193] Shimada specified as his authority on the matter not only the opinion of Takahashi, but also that of his superior, President Matsuo Shinzen of the Bank of Japan, who as a bureau head in the Finance Ministry in 1899 had "used the same reasoning" to caution against government borrowing to finance nationalization.[194] Yet spokesmen for the opposition added twists of their own to the arguments of finance officials. Asano Yōkichi of the Seikō Club, for instance, predicted that the government would be hard pressed to maintain the value of the nearly three billion yen in public bonds expected to be outstanding by 1911. To do so, the authorities, he feared, would be forced "to follow at all times a financial policy of trading furiously" in public bonds. Asano warned that such a course would "move Japan's finances practically into a Russian mode," presumably the ultimate pejorative at the time, with the government "barely supporting [its finances] through a Witteesque policy," the latter referring to the Russian finance minister's program of industrialization through massive foreign borrowing. "I believe it to be extremely frightful," Asano concluded, "that the finances of this magnificent victorious nation should be turned into Russian-style [finances] and wind up in a stockjobber's mode as well."[195]

The opposition further criticized specific reasons for nationalization raised by various cabinet representatives. As for Premier Saionji's contention that nationalization was the natural outcome of a policy that state authorities had been pursuing since the Meiji Restoration, opponents retorted: "up to the present, the government has never had a fixed policy towards railroads."[196] As proof, Taketomi noted that, "while on the one hand purporting to uphold the principle of national ownership, the government in 1889 sold the railroads it had built in Hokkaido dirt cheap to private interests for a price that hardly amounted to a year's construction costs."[197] Shimada added that, in the beginning, it was not the case that state leaders consciously adopted a policy of national ownership; "in fact, it was only that, at the time our first railroads were built, the government itself undertook [the task] because there was nobody in the private sector who would do so, the level of our nation being such that the distinction between state and private ownership did not cross our people's minds ...."[198] Moreover, Taketomi cleverly turned against the bill's proponents Saionji's argument that state approval of private railroads had been merely a stopgap aimed at promoting the rapid completion of rail lines. The Dietman maintained that, under the postwar management, the advancement of railroad construction was even more urgent than it had been in the past. Therefore, "the need is all the more pressing [for the government] to continue this policy of approving private construction as a temporary expedient in order to promote the rapid completion and improvement of railroads."[199] For that policy, Taketomi gloated, "has truly hit the mark, its effect being strikingly apparent today." Whereas the state had been able to build only 1,300 miles of line over a period of three and a half decades, he pointed out, private companies, starting ten to fifteen years later, had managed to complete almost two and a half times that amount.[200]

Saionji was not the only administration spokesman to come under fire. Opponents of the bill assailed with equal relish the positions of both communications bureaucrats and army officials. Communications Minister Yamagata had announced that railway unification was necessary for economic development. Taketomi responded by asking what connection there was between railway unification and nationalization. The former, he contended, could just as easily be achieved under private ownership. All that was needed was adequate supervision. The government had plenty of means at its disposal, including the Private Railway Law, to ensure proper connections among the railroad concerns. The fact that the system was still not totally integrated simply meant that the government had neglected those means and thus shown itself to be "incompetent as a supervisor."[201] Asano pointed out that a de facto unification was already in the making on a regional level because of the trend towards the absorption of smaller railroad firms by such major ones as the Kyushu, Kansai, and San'yō. Before long, there would be relatively few companies left, and if the government made sure that the railroads were fully connected, "the benefits of unification [would] by no means obtain only on the basis of national ownership."[202]

Meanwhile, Army Minister Terauchi had asserted that nationalization was essential so that the railroads could be operated at the beck and call of the government in time of emergency as well as be outfitted to meet military needs. Asano, however, countered that the Order for the Military Requisition of Railroads already empowered the authorities to take over all the private railroads and "use them as they please" in the event of a national crisis.[203] In addition, Taketomi disputed Terauchi's argument that only the state could afford the improvements army authorities desired, specifically, the upgrading of rolling stock to enable a single train to carry upwards of a thousand men and the construction of stations to handle the same. These were "impossible requests" not only for private companies, but also for the government, for the latter "does not have limitless funds to invest in railroads," and "whether managed publicly or privately, railroads are commercial enterprises [that] are kept going by making ends meet . . ."[204] Shimada chimed in by asking rhetorically how such local railroads as the Takano, Toyokawa, and Narita had anything to do with military affairs. All three of those railroads, he observed, had been built to transport visitors to local temples or shrines. To applause from his colleagues, Shimada repeated: "What do these railroads have to do with the nationalization?"[205] "If any of them is said to have a bearing on military affairs," he continued,

> perhaps harking back to the Ashikaga period and beyond, it is for the purpose of offering prayers at Mount Takano when there is a national crisis, or going back even further to the age of the Minamoto and Taira, of praying for victory to the god of fire (*fudō*) at Narita. I believe there is no way to evaluate the assertion that in the Meiji era, the Narita, Takano, and Toyokawa railroads have any connection to military matters other than simply to laugh at it. (Someone calls out [from the floor], 'You should argue with sincerity!') What I have said is the absolute truth without any mistake . . . [Therefore] you ought to listen to what I have to say.[206]

By this time, advocates of nationalization were becoming incensed over Shimada's derisive comments, not the least of which was his charge, perhaps not unwarranted, that these local railroads were actually added to the bill as a form of "patronage" aimed at buying the votes of Diet members with interests in those lines and thereby "securing a majority."[207] His remarks finally prompted one Dietman to shout: "How can one depart from principle on account of one or two minor companies?"[208] Shimada was not finished, however. Hecklers notwithstanding, he forged on with his speech, which lasted a total of about two hours. At the end of it, he threw the chamber into an uproar by introducing a newspaper article suggesting that the purchase bill had in fact originated with the demands of railway businessmen, who, using insider information, had positioned themselves to profit handsomely by the nationalization.[209]

Besides such provocative and largely unsubstantiated points, Shimada made several substantive comments of great interest concerning Western precedents. All parties to the debate took pains to cite examples from the West in support of their arguments, and the comparisons they drew with their own country tell a great deal about contemporary Japanese perceptions of Western railroads as well as notions about what constituted the ideal pattern for Japan. Most Dietmen in favor of nationalization followed the lead of government bureaucrats in upholding the German state system as the proper model for Japan. Sasa Tomofusa of the Daidō Club, for instance, reiterated the rosy view of communications officials that, judging from the experience of Germany, the nationalized railways should prove to be "an unparalleled source of state revenue."[210] Sasa further maintained that railway nationalization was a "worldwide trend." Nationalization fever, he noted, was sweeping the European continent, infecting one nation after another, from Germany, Austria, and Hungary to Belgium, Denmark, and Switzerland. Moreover, it was not at all improbable, he asserted, that "this kind of argument will win out . . . in England, France, and America as well."[211]

Meanwhile, opponents of the purchase bill were highly critical of what they saw as the reckless embrace of the German model by nationalization advocates. At a committee hearing, Asano, for example, worried that the cabinet had adopted wholesale "the Bismarckian policy imported directly from Germany by Minister Yamagata" and was "retailing it without understanding [its implications]." Government leaders, he charged, had failed to see that "the conditions of Germany at the time Bismarck carried out his policy and those of our nation [today] are very different." Bismarck's main objective in implementing nationalization had been to further German unification, whereas "the national polity and situation of Japan" rendered such a policy "politically unnecessary."[212] Shimada elaborated on this theme in his Diet speech by underscoring the fact that Bismarck had started out by nationalizing only the Prussian railroads and "had not done anything so reckless as to buy up at once all the railroads of the German federation." Furthermore, he argued, Germany had financed the purchase of private railroads "not by increasing the public debt, as in the case of Japan, but by using the indemnity it had gained from France as a result of its victory [in the Franco-Prussian War]; consequently, from an economic standpoint as well, the circumstances were completely different."[213]

Shimada also questioned his opponents' claim that railway nationalization was the trend of the times by citing cases in which the state ownership of railroads had failed. In particular, he disputed a Seiyūkai spokesman's characterization of the Belgian system as a "remarkably successful" example of government ownership by asserting that the Belgian national railways had in fact turned out to be "highly unprofitable." In addition, he observed, "Italy went through a similar experience, which finally gave rise to the opinion that the railroads must be turned over to private management."[214] It was clear which model Shimada preferred when he noted approvingly, if somewhat wishfully, that "from the beginning, our railroads have followed the British pattern . . ." This was only natural, he maintained, seeing that Railway Commissioner Inoue Masaru had been trained in England and the government had imported from that country the technicians and materials needed to build the first railroads. Moreover, Japan had adopted not only British technology, but also "British-style regulations." Turning Saionji's argument on its head, Shimada then affirmed that "the British way" meant private railway enterprise, and, "although [Japan] has gone through many vicissitudes since [Inoue's time], it can be regarded by and large as a nation of private railroads." This pattern was set from the start, he contended, and "in no way was the principle of national ownership established in our nation's past."[215] Shimada was clearly following in the tradition of Taguchi Ukichi and other proponents of laissez-faire in advocating the British model of railroad development.

Interestingly, Takekoshi Yōsaburō of the Seiyūkai sought to undercut the free-enterprise argument of the opposition by claiming that the principle of state ownership had in fact originated in England. As Takekoshi explained in his speech before the lower house, "Opponents call this bill a Bismarckian or a German imitation, but that is not the case at all. This is an issue that was first settled by Gladstone, whom you profess to be your guiding light. In 1844, as secretary of agriculture and commerce, Gladstone decided on a nationalization bill and submitted it to Parliament. It gained unanimous approval and became law. The reason it could not be carried out at the time was simply that the influence of railway shareholders in the houses was strong enough to prevent it from being put into practice."[216] Takekoshi then proceeded to rebut the opposition argument that railway nationalization would constitute "an invasion of private rights." In the first place, he asserted, railway companies were established on the basis not of private rights but of special rights, inasmuch as the government granted them tax exemptions and a variety of other privileges. Accordingly, "the Railway Nationalization Law will cause companies that are the embodiment of special rights to be broken up, [their holdings] distributed equally among the people, thereby turning all the people into shareholders."[217]

The two others who spoke for the purchase bill in the house, Sasa of the Daidō Club and Mochizuki Kotarō, nominally a member of the Seikō Club, also attacked the opposition's stand on this issue, albeit from different angles. Mochizuki appealed to the constitution itself. He admitted that he himself had "once wandered about in delusion," having been led astray by the opponents' "seductive" battle cry that railway nationalization was "a violation of the constitution and an infringement upon private rights." But he had no such delusions now. The constitutional guarantee of private rights, Mochizuki pointed out, was "not absolute and unlimited." The constitution specified that, in cases where it was deemed "necessary for the public interest," the state could legally restrict, nay, even take away, the property rights of Japanese subjects. And such a case, clearly, was railway nationalization. Sasa, on the other hand, cited the authority of Western precedent in dismissing the opposition's argument on this point. In 1898, he noted, the Swiss government had carried out the compulsory purchase of private railroads. Nationalization had thus taken place "in the European country that most values private rights, and in a republic, to boot." In view of that fact, Sasa concluded, "we believe that this [talk of] private rights invasion is not worth listening to in the least."[218]

Just as the bill's opponents largely repeated the objections of dissenting government authorities, so did its advocates, for the most part, echo the official cabinet position. For example, Takekoshi and his colleagues reiterated the administration's claim that the railway-purchase bonds would be "productive bonds" and would simply take the place of stocks.[219] In a variation on Finance Minister Sakatani's argument, Mochizuki added that the nationalization would free up capital for the development of Japanese business interests on the Asian continent.[220] As a result of its alliance with England and its victory over Russia, Mochizuki exulted, Japan had truly become "a world nation (*sekai no Nihon*)," but in considering ways to exploit the economic opportunities that attended its new status, the nation could do without arguments of a "village-schoolmaster" variety such as propounded by opponents of nationalization.[221] The supporters of the purchase bill also iterated the views of communications officials. Takekoshi, for instance, stressed the need for unification of the railway network so as to make long-distance transportation faster and more predictable, stating that present conditions were such that, "to use a metaphor, if one were to send eggs from Nagasaki to Tokyo, by the time they reach Tokyo, the eggs will have become chickens . . ."[222] The advocates of nationalization likewise reflected the social-policy thinking of government bureaucrats, none more so than Takekoshi. If left to themselves, Takekoshi warned, the private railroads will continue to consolidate, eventually forming a giant monopoly. Should that happen, instead of the state owning the railroads, "the railway companies will end up owning the state." Moreover, the result will be none other than "class warfare," with "the poor laying siege to the wealthy by the tens of thousands." Thus, one purpose of the nationalization, Takekoshi suggested, was to interpose the government between the capitalists and the lower classes in order to prevent social upheaval.[223]

These, then, were the arguments raised by members of the lower house for and against the Railway Nationalization Bill. In the end, however, the bill's passage by the lower chamber depended not so much on the rhetorical skills of Dietmen as on timely inducements by the administration. The house referred the nationalization measure, together with the bill for the purchase of the Seoul-Pusan Railway, to a forty-five-member special committee. The Seiyūkai and Daidō Club held a solid majority on the committee with twenty-six members combined, so it appeared that the Nationalization Bill would pass through that body without too much difficulty. To the alarm of government leaders, though, a group within the Daidō Club strongly opposed the nationalization, and as late as March 12th, just days before the committee vote, the party had yet to reach a decision on the bill. At this point, Home Minister Hara went into action. Working through a minor club member, he sought to induce other members of the faction to endorse the cabinet's proposal. He then summoned club leaders and exhorted them to support the original bill and to allow no amendments whatsoever.[224] The upshot was that, on March 14th, Diet members affiliated with the Daidō Club held a conference and voted unanimously to back the administration's proposal.[225] Members of the Seiyūkai in the Diet did likewise that day, and, as Hara noted with relief in his diary, "the issue has been completely decided."[226]

Hara claimed that affiliates of the Daidō Club had agreed to support the nationalization program "without requiring any particular recompense."[227] The press, however, suggested otherwise. As one newspaper reported, the authorities had promised to approve the establishment of various enterprises in the Kansai area including an electric railway and a hydroelectric plant in which club members held interests. Cash had also changed hands, although the administration had gotten "a big bargain" inasmuch as it had had to pay out only a few tens of thousands of yen. The paper speculated that Daidō Club members "had been forced to put up" with that amount because their allies in the Seiyūkai had served as intermediaries.[228] So perhaps Hara was not so far off after all!

In any case, there was no longer any doubt as to the bill's adoption by the lower house. On March 15th, the committee approved the cabinet's proposal, without amendment, by a vote of 30 to 14, the members for the most part balloting along straight party lines. The committee chairman reported back to the chamber the next day, and following the speeches cited above, the lower house passed the Railway Nationalization Bill by a wide margin, 243 to 109, the pro-cabinet parties having even managed to pry a few votes from the opposition.[229] The bill then moved on to the House of Peers, where it awaited a considerably different fate.

In view of the Yamagata faction's strength in the upper house, one would expect the peers to have looked favorably on what was essentially the proposal of Yamagata's protege. Nevertheless, the conservative peers were evidently unhappy with the party coloration of the present cabinet, its avowal to continue Katsura's policies and the preponderance in it of nonparty men notwithstanding, and perhaps nothing reflected the Seiyūkai's influence on the administration more clearly than the inflated Nationalization Bill. The result was that the cabinet's proposal was in for serious resistance in the upper chamber. As the *Japan Weekly Mail* reported after the proposal's submission to that body, "The Railway Bill created much more excitement in the House of Peers than it did in the House of Representatives. No sooner was Marquis Saionji's address finished than he and other Ministers present were accosted with a whole shower of questions. . . . It looks at present as though the Bill might be somewhat roughly handled by the Peers, who have shown a good deal of spirit this session in dealing with important Government Bills."[230]

The nationalization proposal indeed met with harsh treatment by members of the upper house. The staunchest opponents relentlessly cross-examined cabinet spokesmen in committee meetings and railed against the bill in the general session, in the process echoing many of the points raised by their counterparts in the lower chamber. The dissenting peers, however, were even more vociferous than the latter in repeating the objections of finance authorities. As one peer put it, the purchase bill was "inopportune" since the government was already burdened with a huge and growing debt "owing to the Russo-Japanese War, nay, to the diplomatic failure at Portsmouth."[231] Under these conditions there was no telling what impact the issue of nearly half a billion yen in railway-purchase bonds might have on the public-bond market. To say that it would have no effect at all was simply "a fallacious view."[232] Another peer called the assertion that railway profits would increase markedly following the nationalization "a big lie," given the diminishing returns on subsequent expansion of the system and the ample inclusion of "good-for-nothing railroads (*yakuza tetsudō*)" in the bill.[233]

To the consternation of the cabinet, such arguments only caused opposition to spread among the peers. On March 24th, Hara noted anxiously that, "regarding the Railway Nationalization Bill, the situation in the upper house is not good. Even some of the original supporters have suddenly come to profess opposition or become genuine opponents."[234] Considering the extent of resistance in the house, it became increasingly apparent that the administration's proposal stood little chance of passage in its original form. In fact, the special committee appointed to investigate the proposal ultimately responded to the financial concerns of house members by substantially revising the Nationalization Bill. First of all, the committee extended the period for buying up the railroads from six to ten years and the period for issuing the purchase bonds from two to five years. The objective in both cases, the chairman reported to the chamber, was to avoid "disturbing the market by handing over the public bonds as slowly as possible."[235] Second, the committee slashed the number of companies to be nationalized by eliminating the fifteen local railroads that the cabinet had added at Hara's insistence. The committee undoubtedly took this action not only to lighten the financial burden on the government, but also to excise the party imprint from the Nationalization Bill.

These amendments apparently succeeded in overcoming the opposition of all but the diehards among upper-house members. One peer seemed to voice the opinion of many when he declared, "I am one who cannot support this bill. However, because I believe these amendments have lessened the possibility that it will disturb the economy . . . , I will support the revised bill. . . . If, unfortunately, the final bill increases the number of companies even by one firm or greatly shortens the [purchase] period or the like, I will come back to express my disapproval of it. ('Hear! Hear!')"[236] With this sentiment prevailing, the bill as amended passed the first reading on March 27th by a vote of 205 to 62 and immediately went through the final two readings.[237] The revised proposal was then hurriedly sent to the lower house with only hours remaining in the current Diet session.

There was a distinct possibility that the peers' amendments were of such a magnitude that the lower chamber would simply refuse to accept them. And, with hardly any time to work out a compromise, the bill would wind up being shelved, which, according to one source, was the peers' intention all along.[238] Even if there had been time to refer the proposal to a joint committee, it was "doubtful," Hara noted, "whether the upper house would ever have approved the committee's bill . . ."[239] In particular, he observed, "members of the previous cabinet at bottom desired the amended bill," suggesting that Katsura and his colleagues may actually have been behind the peers' revision. In any event, the situation was "extremely hazardous." However unpalatable the revised proposal may have been to him personally, Hara concluded that "we must firmly agree to the upper-house bill" and pressed the Seiyūkai and Daidō Club to take that position.[240] Saionji expressed well the cabinet's attitude when he asserted: "The amendments of the House of Peers are regrettable; however, we recognize that, in this case, we must consent to them."[241] The pro-administration parties fell in line, and at 7:30 p.m. on the last day of the Diet session, the lower house approved the amended purchase proposal in the raucous scene portrayed at the beginning of this chapter. The Railway Nationalization Bill thus became law.

FIVE

The Business Response

How it pulls at our hearts,
Even though we are only giving up a metal road.
                    Hara Rokurō, on the nationalization
                    of the San'yō Railway Company,
                            December 1, 1906[1]

How did the railway companies and business in general respond to the initiation and passage of the Nationalization Law? Certainly, there was no public movement for railway nationalization such as businessmen had mounted during the panics and recessions of the previous decade and a half. Indeed, the railroads themselves were not in the kind of desperate financial situation that, during those earlier crises, had driven many of their owners to press for a government buyout as a relief measure. Far from it. On the eve of the nationalization, private rail concerns as a whole were showing excellent business results, in several cases recording their highest returns ever. In 1905–1906, for instance, the industry giant, the Nippon Railway, was able to offer dividends in the 12–14 percent range, 12 percent having been its previous high, set in 1888.[2] In 1905, the thirty-eight private railroads in operation had an average profit rate of 9.5 percent against total construction expenditures; the seventeen firms soon to be nationalized had an average return of 10.1 percent.[3] With the boom immediately following the Russo-Japanese War in full swing, the future looked extremely promising for private railway enterprise. As one newspaper noted in early 1906, "the revival of trade consequent upon the restoration of peace has set in, and . . . one of its results has been such a large movement of goods and passengers as to open very bright prospects for the railways and greatly enhance the market value of their shares."[4] From this, it would seem only natural that the private railroads and their stockholders would have resisted the government's plan—in the words of a Nippon Railway executive—"to take away railway companies" and thereby cause "already profitable enterprises [to] be wiped out of existence . . ."[5] And, as we have suggested, such was indeed the case with major railway capitalists like the Iwasaki who were represented in the Diet by the Kenseihontō.

The Smaller Railway Companies

Although railroad concerns in general appeared to be highly profitable, underlying their strong business performance were serious problems of finance and construction. To begin with, there was a sizable difference in profit and dividend rates between large main-line firms such as the Nippon and smaller companies like the Chūetsu Railway, which returned only 5.7 percent on total construction costs in 1905.[6] We have indicated that owners of small to medium-sized local railroads like the Chūetsu, which were largely eschewed by the big investors, welcomed the nationalization and in fact scrambled to have their lines included in the purchase bill. It was not as if their companies were on the verge of collapse. Yet, financially they were on much less secure ground than were the large trunk-line concerns.

The financial instability of the smaller railroads had much to do with the problems they had experienced during the panics of 1897–1898 and 1900–1901. Much as in the case of the 1890 Panic and ensuing recession, those crises were in good part a reaction to the feverish speculation and investment that accompanied the second enterprise boom of the mid-1890s. That boom, which once again centered on railway companies, reached its peak in 1896. In that year, private rail promotion rose to unprecedented levels with applicants inundating the government with 450 requests for provisional railway licenses.[7] In fact, the authorities approved only 29 of these applications, the rest failing as competitive bids for the same line or being rejected on the grounds of inadequate planning. And, between 1893 and 1906, only about half the recipients of temporary licenses, most of them granted during the boom years, actually managed to obtain full licenses;

yet half of the latter, in turn, ended up being invalidated.⁸ In short, the railroad mania produced countless speculative and unsound schemes. As one source describes the period:

> The situation was such that retired government officials and unsavory businessmen (*jitsugyōkai no goro*) would meet on the second floor of a tea house or in the corner of a shop and use a ruler to draw a line on one of the maps put out by the General Staff. Enlisting men of reputation, they would then float stocks, and in no time at all, a railway company of hundreds of thousands or millions of yen would be established, its potential shares yielding a margin of ¥3 to ¥5 a share. Indeed, in meeting the needs of such railroad planning, the maps of the General Staff were completely sold out.⁹

The second railway boom certainly had its share of excesses, but like the first boom, it also gave rise to a number of successful ventures. As noted earlier, the majority of these were local railroads that operated relatively short interurban or suburban lines. In most cases connecting with the trunk railroads, these lines played an important role in helping to fill out the system. Nevertheless, when the panics broke out, the railway companies founded during the boom were in an extremely precarious position, since most of them had yet to finish their lines. Even in the best of times, the smaller railroads often had trouble covering construction costs. For example, in 1895, the medium-sized Ryōmō Railway, which was actually launched during the first boom, was reprimanded by the Railway Bureau for misappropriating part of its reserves to make up for a shortage of building funds.¹⁰ No wonder, then, that such firms should have experienced all the more difficulty raising capital during the postwar panics. The result, as one member of the Railway Council observed in 1899, was that, "owing to economic fluctuations, more and more private railroads are returning the [construction] licenses they have already obtained or requesting that their licenses be granted at a later date."¹¹

To avoid postponement of construction work, many of the smaller concerns were forced to rely extensively on borrowed money. Even then, their total capital fell well short of their combined construction costs in 1902 (see Table 17). By contrast, the dependence on loan capital of the five largest railroads had declined steadily since the early 1890s to the point where, in 1902, their total equity alone more than covered their cumulative building expenses. Whereas the major railroad firms had turned heavily to bond issues in the aftermath of the 1890 Panic, after 1897, it was primarily small to medium-sized railroad firms who took that route. The smaller enterprises, however, were by no means able to secure terms as favorable as those obtained earlier by the trunk-line companies. All nine of the issues floated in 1898 bore interest in the 10–12 percent range, that of the Chūetsu Railway, for example, having a 12-percent interest rate and a two-year term of redemption.[12] Many of these firms were then compelled to borrow from banks at the prevailing high interest rates in order to service their bonded debt. For railroads with lines in operation, the combined weight of interest payments on bank loans and bond issues meant a steep decline in profit rates. As Table 18 indicates, the operating revenue of the smaller railroads actually increased during the second panic, so the drop in net earnings was clearly due to the sudden rise in expenditures, especially in the subcategory of "general expenses," which included interest payments. While the five "majors" were maintaining high rates of return, the small to medium-sized firms saw their profits continue to decline. Those companies that had fallen most heavily into debt were hard pressed to pay interest to lenders, let alone dividends to investors. Indeed, the number of railroads that were unable to offer any dividends at all increased from five in 1899 to nine the following year and to thirteen in 1901.[13] Moreover, some firms even had to default on their loans; in 1901, for instance, both the Toyokawa and Nishinari railroads were attached by banks for nonpayment of promissory notes.[14]

After the turn of the century, a number of the smaller rail concerns took extraordinary steps in order to extricate themselves from spiraling indebtedness. From 1900 to 1903, eleven firms moved to readjust their finances by reducing their capital stock. Five of these companies then joined four other railroads in issuing preferred stocks between 1900 and 1902. Under the recessionary conditions that lasted until 1903, however, the effort to raise construction funds through preferred-stock issues for the most part failed miserably, as the companies faced immense difficulty in placing the stocks or in collecting payments from subscribers. In the end, several firms resorted to the ultimate relief measure, namely, corporate dissolution. Between 1900 and 1904, eleven railroads, including three of those that had reduced capital or issued preferred stock, were broken up through acquisition or conveyance.[15]

TABLE 17 Aggregate Capital Structure of the Five Largest and the Remaining Railway Companies, 1902

Railway Companies	Paid-up Capital (¥1,000)	Reserves (¥1,000)	Bonds (¥1,000)	Loans (¥1,000)	Construction Costs (¥1,000)	Owned Capital as Percentage of Construction Costs (%)	Total Capital as Percentage of Construction Costs (%)
Five Largest Companies	149,898	4,371	5,075	0	149,753	103.0	106.4
Remaining Companies	52,706	785	7,778	1,583	66,996	79.8	93.8

Source: Sugiyama Kazuo, "Kabushiki kaisha seido no hatten: bōseki, tetsudō gyō o chūshin ni," in Kobayashi Masaaki et al., eds., Nihon keiei shi o manabu, vol. 1, Meiji keiei shi (Yūhikaku, 1976), pp. 122-123.

The Karatsu Railway Company, which operated eighteen miles of line in Kyushu, illustrates all the tendencies exhibited by the recession-plagued local railroads. Admittedly, this firm differed from most such enterprises in that it derived the bulk of its income from the transportation of freight, particularly coal. It was therefore much harder hit by the economic slump that attended the panics than the majority of local railroads, which generally based their operations on passenger transport. The difference, however, was only a matter of degree, for, even in the case of firms that experienced no decline in revenues, the panics usually caused earnings to fall well below expectations, certainly below the level necessary to meet interest payments. And the Karatsu reacted to the crises in ways that were typical of smaller railway companies as a whole.

No sooner had the Karatsu Railway opened its first line in 1898 than it was already in deep trouble. With profits kept down by the recession in the coal market, the firm went increasingly into debt and "was not even able to pay its first dividend."[16] This situation produced a classic split among the directors over the issue of whether or not to continue with planned construction work. One faction representing management insisted on "completion of the unfinished lines in anticipation of [future] profits,"[17] while the other spoke for many of the stockholders in demanding suspension of the remaining construction work. The controversy finally led to the resignation of the president, and in February 1900, the stockholders elected Minami Kiyoshi to replace him. Minami immediately launched a multifaceted program designed to rescue the company from its financial plight. "On the one hand, he carried out a major reduction in the staff . . . and, on the other hand, floated bonds in an effort to raise capital." Then, in March 1901, "seeing the decline in the current stock price as a golden opportunity,"[18] Minami reduced the company's capital by redeeming some 40 percent of its shares. He did this by exchanging preferred stocks for the redeemed securities, waiving the first payment on the preferred stocks in lieu of a refund. By this means, the company netted ¥178,940 in depreciated earnings.[19] As a result, the firm's business results improved markedly, enabling it to offer a dividend that year of over 10 percent.

These halcyon days were short lived, however. Even as it moved to restructure its capital stock, the Karatsu had outstanding bonds in an amount equivalent to that of its paid-up capital. Added to these was ¥48,000 in

TABLE 18 Business Results of Private Railway Companies, 1899–1901 (unit: ¥1,000)

	Major Trunk-Line Railroads			Smaller Railroads		
Year	1899	1900	1901	1899	1900	1901
No. of Companies	5	5	5	35	34	35
Paid-up Capital	112,646	128,203	144,598	46,892	49,784	52,562
Income	19,135	23,490	26,737	5,631	6,509	7,047
Expenditure						
General Expenses	1,545	2,325	2,576	792	1,436	1,957
Total	9,642	10,832	12,408	2,773	4,043	4,798
Net Profit	9,493	12,658	14,329	2,858	2,466	2,249
Profit as Percentage of Capital	8.4	9.9	9.9	6.1	5.0	4.3

Source: *Nihon teikoku tōkei nenkan,* vol. 19 (Naikaku tōkei-kyoku, 1900), pp. 699–701, 704–706, vol. 20 (1901), pp. 763–765, 768–770, and vol. 21 (1902), pp. 704–706, 709–711.

Note: The table excludes the three railway companies that were bought out by major trunk-line firms in 1900–1901.

short-term bank loans bearing high interest.[20] Before long, therefore, the railroad "had to put all its earnings into [servicing these debts] . . ."[21] The second panic then began to take its toll, and the company once again fell into desperate straits. In the end, despite Minami's best efforts to save the firm, he was forced to accept the stockholders' demand that the company sell out to the Kyushu Railway. In December 1901, Minami concluded a merger agreement with his counterpart in that firm, thereby putting an end to the Karatsu Railway and its financial woes.

The Kyushu Railway's acquisition of the Karatsu was part of a general trend towards amalgamation among business enterprises at the time. In both of the leading sectors of Meiji industrialization, cotton spinning and railroads, the successive panics triggered a rash of mergers after the turn of the century, as is suggested by the decline in the number of enterprises in each of these fields after 1900 (see Table 19). We mentioned that eleven railroad firms were absorbed by others during the period 1900–1904. Of these, two were tiny railroads in Shikoku that combined with another, slightly larger, local concern, the Iyo Railway. A third was a small, heavily indebted company in the Kantō area that sought to avoid bankruptcy by setting up a new firm with a reduced capital stock, to which it conveyed all its assets. The remaining cases, however, all involved the acquisition of struggling local railroads by trunk-line concerns. The Kansai Railway Company was the most active amalgamator, taking over four of the eleven railroads in question, with the Kyushu and San'yō each accounting for two mergers. The consolidation movement had actually begun with the Nippon Railway's purchase of the Ryōmō in 1896, and both the Kansai and Kyushu had had their first taste of amalgamation during the latter half of the 1890s.

The government appears to have welcomed and even encouraged this tendency toward railroad consolidation. Railway Bureau Chief Inoue, of course, had long decried the fragmentation of the railway network, and under the Construction Law, state authorities evidently sought to regulate private development in such a way as to create coherent subsystems under the control of as few companies as possible. They did so in part by refusing to "sanction the construction of competing lines," a policy that had the added benefit of avoiding the "disastrous waste of none-too-plentiful capital . . ."[22] The Construction Law had in several instances listed alternative routes for the lines scheduled for construction by the state, but in every case approved for private development, the Railway Council had decided upon only one of those routes, choosing from among the several bids made by private promoters. This process typically induced erstwhile competitors to join forces in a single project.[23] Another way in which government officials tried to further the orderly development of the private system, then, was to promote mergers among established companies. This policy was made explicit in a memorandum submitted by the Railway Council to the Communications Ministry in 1893. The Railway Bureau had asked the council to consider "ways to prevent the harmful effects caused by the division [of the network] into small railway companies." In its memorandum, the council responded by stating that "the appropriate method would be to establish the termini of railway lines as well as regional districts and to place the lines within each district under the management of one company." However, since it would take years to put such a program into effect, the council concluded that a more "timely" approach would be to make the railroads "merge or else connect with each other to the extent that their operations allow it . . ."[24]

TABLE 19 Total Number of Railway and Spinning Companies, 1897–1905

Year	Railway Companies	Spinning Companies
1897	66	65
1898	58	74
1899	58	78
1900	55	79
1901	50	66
1902	50	56
1903	46	51
1904	39	49
1905	39	49

Source: Noda Masaho, *Nihon shōken shijō seiritsu shi: Meiji ki no tetsudō to kabushiki kaisha kin'yū* (Yūhikaku, 1980), p. 157.

With the authorities taking this kind of attitude, therefore, the major railway companies had little difficulty in swallowing up local concerns that were reeling under the impact of successive panics. Indeed, after 1897, the Kyushu and San'yō railroads annexed most of the smaller firms in their respective regions. Likewise, the Kansai Railway took over a good number of the many local companies in the Kansai area. And even the Nippon, which had earlier absorbed the Mito and Ryōmō railroads, attempted in 1904 to buy out two other local lines in the Kantō region.[25] Thus, the trend towards amalgamation enabled the five major railroads to reverse the steady decline in their share of the private rail system that had accompanied the proliferation of railway companies during the second boom. Whereas the "big five" had accounted for 88 percent of the paid-up capital as well as the operating mileage of all private railroads in 1891, their share in both categories had fallen to around 65 percent in 1899. But by 1905, thanks mainly to the amalgamation movement, they had raised their proportion of the total paid-up capital to 75 percent and of the total length of line open to 68 percent.[26] In retrospect, the consolidation trend fashioned the railway giants all the more into the building blocks of nationalization, making it that much easier for the government to purchase the bulk of the private network.

The smaller railroads that managed to survive the panics without being taken over by the "majors" often did so by persuading banks to invest in their shares or debentures. Indeed, one of the important effects of the crises was to trigger the rise of institutional investors in the smaller railway enterprises. For example, the Kyoto Railway, founded in 1895 mainly on the basis of noble and local-business capital, saw its profit rate plunge during the first postwar panic, at which time it began to receive some investment from local banks. After the turn of the century, however, the company turned with a vengeance to wealthy Yokohama bankers, who, by 1905, had come to own 47 percent of the railroad's stock and to occupy six of the top ten spots on its shareholders' list.[27] In the case of the Nishinari Railway Company, an overzealous director of the Kitahama Bank of Osaka bought up about a fifth of the railroad's shares in the aftermath of the 1897–1898 Panic. Under the tight-money conditions, though, he had great difficulty raising funds to meet his stock payments. The bank finally came to his rescue, lending him the necessary capital on the security of his personal property. Then, in 1902, the director settled with the bank by transferring to it his entire interest in the railroad, which, by that time, had grown to over a quarter of the company's total stock.[28]

Besides investing in railway shares, beginning in 1898, the Kitahama and other banks moved aggressively into the business of underwriting railway bonds. And almost all the bonds they accepted were issued by small to medium-sized firms that were struggling to make ends meet during the postwar financial crises. Banks affiliated with the Yasuda group were especially active in this field. Altogether, they accounted for over 40 percent of all the railway bonds underwritten by banks between 1898 and 1906, including those floated by the Chūgoku in 1898 and the Tokushima in 1899.[29] Banks welcomed the bonds even of the less-sound local railroads in part because the bonds invariably yielded high interest, in part because the railroads themselves constituted excellent security. On top of this, the banks could readily borrow money from the semiofficial Industrial Bank using the railway bonds as collateral.[30] The emergence of banks as major investors in the smaller railroads had important implications for railway nationalization: the generally conservative outlook of such financial institutions made them especially amenable to a government buyout that would enable them to exchange the risks of corporate investment for the security of public bondholding.

One other significant byproduct of the panics was the outbreak of a nationalization movement among private businessmen. As we noted earlier, this movement centered on Amenomiya Keijirō and other railway owners, and not surprisingly, most of them were investors in small to medium-sized railroads whose profits and stock prices plummeted during the postwar crises. Insofar as these businessmen were merely seeking relief from the panics, their demand for state purchase was basically no different from that raised by businessmen in 1891; as such, it was castigated by laissez-faire advocates as a "stockbrokers' argument."[31] And, just like the 1891 campaign, the postwar nationalization movement took the form of a petition drive by chambers of commerce. Specifically, in 1898, both the Tokyo and Kyoto chambers of commerce petitioned the cabinet and the Diet to purchase private railroads. In their memorials, the two chambers stressed the need for unification of the railway network on economic as well as strategic grounds and observed that, under the existing fragmented system, small railroads were having difficulty carrying out scheduled construction work for lack of capital, to say nothing of creating a unified network; hence, they exhorted the authorities to resolve this situation by nationalizing the railway companies.[32]

The petition presented by the Tokyo Chamber of Commerce was largely the work of Amenomiya, Inoue Kakugorō, and their associates. Admittedly, Inoue was affiliated not with any of the smaller railroads but with one of the five majors, the Hokkaido Colliery and Railway. Nonetheless, as an enterprise heavily dependent on the transport of coal, his company was harder hit by the panics and resulting market slumps than most of the other trunkline firms. In addition, Amenomiya was a principal owner and director of the highly profitable Kōbu Railway, but he was also the largest shareholder in a less-successful local firm, the Kawagoe Railway Company.[33] In the case of the petition made by the Kyoto Chamber of Commerce, however, there is no doubt that the blow dealt by the panic to smaller railroads was far and away the chief stimulus. For the sponsors of that chamber's memorial, businessmen like Tanaka Gentarō and Hamaoka Kōtetsu, were all involved in the hard-pressed Kyoto Railway Company.[34]

As noted earlier, the Kenseitō took up these groups' demand and managed to get railway nationalization put on the legislative agenda. No sooner had the lower house tabled the resulting purchase bills, however, than the second postwar panic broke out. With stock prices tumbling once again, Amenomiya and his friends redoubled their efforts and, in September 1901, succeeded in getting the National Federation of Chambers of Commerce to pass a resolution supporting the state buyout of private railroads through the flotation of foreign bonds. It was also decided to have the Tokyo Chamber of Commerce submit a petition to that effect to the cabinet and the Diet.[35] This, then, was the petition that Katsura rebuffed in January 1902 on the grounds that it called for nationalization merely as "a stopgap relief measure."

The nationalization movement of the panic years may have helped to make businessmen in general more receptive to the state purchase of private rail companies, but inasmuch as that movement was a reaction to the panics themselves, it had little direct bearing on the final passage of the Railway Nationalization Law, occurring as the latter did during an economic upswing.[36] Nevertheless, the panics left an important legacy for the smaller railroad concerns by highlighting their financial instability and forcing them to resort increasingly to bank investment. Even if they were in much better shape financially by the time of the nationalization, the large debts that many of them had carried over from the crisis years continued to weigh down their operations. Small wonder that local railroads, for the most part, should have welcomed their purchase by the government.

The Major Railroads

In contrast to most of the smaller rail companies, the principal trunk-line firms had weathered the panics with relative ease and had enjoyed increasingly high rates of return since the turn of the century. Inasmuch as the five largest railroads accounted for about four fifths of both the paid-up capital and operating mileage of the seventeen nationalized concerns, the attitude of their owners was decisive to the companies' overall reception of the nationalization proposal. In view of their lofty profit and dividend rates, the big five apparently had good reason to oppose the nationalization, and several of them did indeed object to it.

The large railroad concerns of western Japan put up the strongest fight. In particular, the Kansai Railway resisted the government purchase to the bitter end. As late as December 1906, the company petitioned the cabinet and both houses of the Diet to be exempted from the nationalization, arguing somewhat lamely that, under the stated restriction of the purchase to nonlocal railroads, its lines "should naturally be excluded since [they all] fall within a particular region and lack the characteristics of a trunk line . . ."[37] The Kansai Railway Company had had a history of antagonism towards the state, so its resistance to the nationalization came as no surprise. Backed by local Kansai capitalists and outside investors like Mitsubishi, the firm had been almost the embodiment of free enterprise. The only one of the five biggest railroads never to receive government subsidies, the Kansai Railway had developed a fiercely independent spirit and aggressively expanded its network by buying up smaller railway companies in the Kansai area. By the turn of the century, it had extended its main line from Nagoya to Osaka, setting the stage for the furious rate war it waged against the parallel state line beginning in 1902.[38]

By the time the rate war came to a close in 1904, government authorities were clearly shaken by the severe competition the Kansai Railway had given their biggest moneymaker, the Tokaido line. This became especially apparent when, later that year, the authorities rushed to lease the Nishinari Railway Company's short line between the city and bay of Osaka. Since the late 1890s, the Kansai Railway had been planning to purchase the Nishinari and thereby secure an outlet on Osaka Bay. Had this plan been realized, the state railways would have been placed all the more at a competitive disadvantage. An even greater threat arose in 1904 as businessmen began to consider the formation of a grand union of private railroads in the Kansai region. Such a union would have controlled all the freight traffic involving sea connections in the Osaka area as well as passenger traffic to the sightseeing mecca of Nara and thus have dealt a serious blow to the Tokaido line. As the largest railroad concern in the area, the Kansai Railway would naturally have dominated the union, which undoubtedly would also have included the tiny but strategic Nishinari Railway.[39]

Alarmed by these plans, government officials moved quickly to gain control of the Nishinari's line. In August 1904, a section head in the state railways submitted a report to the communications minister urging that the government buy up the company, taking advantage of the recent deterioration in its business performance and the resulting decline in the price of its stock. After further investigating the matter, this official then presented a follow-up report in November in which he declared:

> If the present situation continues, the [Nishinari Railway] will go bankrupt and will have to merge with another railroad. And the railroad it will merge with is probably none other than the Kansai Railway. If that were to happen, the Kansai Railway would become all the more powerful an enemy of the state railways. . . . What if [this company], which has already subjected the state railways to various disadvantages, were also to gain possession of a railroad to the head of Osaka Bay? The Kansai Railway would end up gripping the throat of Osaka city, and our state railways would sustain serious losses indeed. Therefore, to preserve our interests, we should either lease the Nishinari Railway for an appropriate fee and have the Railway Bureau operate it or go ahead and purchase it.[40]

The government heeded this bureaucrat's advice and decided to lease the Nishinari Railway for the time being, eventually buying it out under the Railway Nationalization Law.

As this episode plainly indicates, the competition that erupted between the Kansai and state railways left a deep impression on government authorities. This was one of the few cases of overt antagonism between railway companies and the state, a far cry from the harmony of interests that generally prevailed. Yet, for that very reason, it struck a sharply discordant note, with the result that, for communications officials at least, preventing a reprise of the Kansai rivalry became yet another motive for nationalization.

The Kansai Railway's opposition to state purchase apparently stemmed from its natural antagonism towards the government bureaucracy as well as the independence of its local owners, but it may also have had to do with the presence of Mitsubishi among its top shareholders.[41] The most vocal opponent of nationalization, Mitsubishi had motives for private rail investment that differed from those of the majority of principal railway shareholders. Dominating the stockholders' lists of private railroads on the eve of the nationalization were institutional investors led by banks, insurance companies, and the Imperial Household Ministry and private investors such as nobles, landlords, and big-city capitalists ranging from stockbrokers to textile merchants.[42] Whereas such owners tended to be concerned mainly with the direct return on their investment, Mitsubishi was interested more in the wider benefits of railroad development. In particular, the control and extension of private railroads had become a key part of Mitsubishi's overall business strategy in western Japan, as the emergent combine sought to integrate the roads with its other activities, above all mining and shipbuilding. Mitsubishi, therefore, had a strong vested interest in keeping the railroads under private ownership and management.

This concern for the external economies of railroad development led Mitsubishi to sink even more money into the San'yō and Kyushu railroads. In fact, these two companies became the prime targets of railway investment for this nascent zaibatsu. In 1905, Iwasaki Hisaya was the biggest shareholder in both firms, and together, he and Iwasaki Yanosuke held 8 percent of the San'yō's total stock and 12 percent of that of the Kyushu Railway. At the same time, Hisaya was the fourth largest stockholder in the Kansai, but his holdings in that company amounted to less than 1 percent of its shares.[43] The fact that Mitsubishi remained the leading investor in both the San'yō and Kyushu railways largely explains why these two trunk-line concerns of western Japan also resisted the nationalization.

Mitsubishi had invested heavily in Kyushu railroads in connection with its extensive coal-mining operations there. Such investment had given Mitsubishi a potent weapon in its rivalry with Mitsui over control of the Kyushu coal industry. Around the time of the nationalization, Kyushu's share of total domestic coal production amounted to nearly 80 percent, of which mines owned by Mitsui and Mitsubishi accounted for some two fifths. By accepting sales commissions from smaller coal-mine operators, however, Mitsui had gained command over half the distribution of coal in Kyushu.[44] Mitsubishi, therefore, sought to counter Mitsui's overwhelming advantage in sales by building its own strength in transportation. Besides taking the largest share of stock in the Kyushu Railway, Mitsubishi also became the top shareholder in the Chikuhō Industrial. Mitsubishi's support enabled the latter company to overcome its financial problems and to continue extending its lines within the rich coal fields of the Chikuhō region.

Before long, however, Mitsubishi demanded control over the Chikuhō Industrial's management and, in 1896, succeeded in having its candidate, Sengoku Mitsugu, appointed chief officer of the firm (see Figure 11).[45]

Born into the family of a Tosa samurai in 1857, Sengoku had graduated from the Engineering College in Tokyo and had eventually become a state-railway engineer. On loan from the Railway Bureau, he had supervised line construction work for both the Nippon and Kōbu rail companies.[46] In 1896, then, Sengoku resigned from the state railways to launch a career in private-railroad management. Bursting onto the Kyushu railway scene, he developed in no time into a professional manager par excellence. Backed by Mitsubishi, he relentlessly pursued a program of business expansion, ignoring the protestations of more conservative stockholders and prompting his peers to describe him as being "cold and stubborn as a rock."[47] When the Chikuhō Industrial merged with the Kyushu in 1897, Sengoku became vice-president and managing director of the latter and, the following year, rose to the presidency. As the top executive of the Kyushu Railway, Sengoku "changed the previous conservative policy and firmly adopted a positive strategy."[48] On the one hand, he vigorously expanded the company's network by buying up the construction licenses of other railroads and, on the other hand, invested extensively in upgrading its existing lines.[49]

Sengoku's aggressive pursuit of his program elicited a sharp reaction from the more conservative owners who had their sights set on higher dividends. Compounding the problem was the fact that the Kyushu Railway, like other Meiji railroad firms, had no system of depreciation accounting and therefore financed improvements out of operating revenues. As a result, Sengoku's heavy investment in renovations, together with his expansion of the maintenance and other staff, put pressure on the company's profits. These steps only exacerbated the impact of the 1897 Panic, causing the dividend rate to plunge from 10 percent that year to 6.5 percent in 1899.[50] Dismayed by this outcome, a group of stockholders began vehemently criticizing management's expansionary policy and, in July 1899, launched a campaign to oust Sengoku from the presidency.[51] The upshot was yet another classic confrontation between ownership and management with "the stockholders desiring an increase in dividends even to the point of reducing the business, and the directors insisting on expanding the business even if it means cutting dividends."[52] The critics, led by bankers, stockbrokers, and other railroad capitalists, were opposed by Mitsubishi and local mine owners, who since the Chikuhō merger had gained control of the Kyushu board.[53] Through the mediation of oligarch Inoue Kaoru,

Figure 11 Sengoku Mitsugu (1857–1931), second president of the Kyushu Railway Company, 1898–1907. Photograph: courtesy of the Transportation Museum, Tokyo.

the conflict was eventually settled in management's favor, it being determined that Sengoku's program had simply been making up for the serious neglect of essential capital expenditures by the previous administration.[54] As the *Japan Weekly Mail* reported in August 1899:

> The truth, as now established, is that, instead of being content to follow the example of other Japanese lines, and, eschewing every improvement of a costly character, make the payment of fat dividends the unique consideration, a spirit of progress was infused into the management of the Kiushiu road by its superintendent, Mr. Sengoku, and instead of banking all the traffic receipts for the purposes of the half-yearly accounts, reasonable sums were devoted to improving the rolling stock, repairing the line, and putting things generally in creditable condition.[55]

With continued support from Mitsubishi, Sengoku went on pursuing his positive policies, thrusting aside a second attempt by disgruntled stockholders to interfere with his program in 1902.[56] By the mid-1900s, thanks to his success in extending and renovating the company's network, the Kyushu Railway had become vital to Mitsubishi's strategy of expansion in the coal-mining industry: between 1897 and 1906, the railroad nearly quintupled its freight income and raised the latter's share of total revenues from 41 to 58 percent.[57] Evidently, Mitsubishi had much to lose from the railway nationalization and every reason to oppose it.

It should therefore come as no surprise that, once the cabinet submitted its nationalization bill to the Diet in March 1906, Sengoku set out to derail the proposed legislation. On March 14th, Home Minister Hara received police reports that Sengoku had joined forces with other railroad executives to lobby against the bill among lower-house members. Hara thereupon instructed the police "to be on the lookout for bribery" and eventually, through Inoue Kaoru, warned Sengoku to desist from further intervention.[58] In the end, the Kyushu Railway president was forced to acquiesce in the state purchase, but defeat was most grudgingly acknowledged, as the firm suggested in the short history it published in 1907. "This company regrets having to transfer all its assets to the government at this time," company officials lamented therein, for "henceforth, [the railroad's] profits will see no end . . ."[59] Apparently, Mitsubishi simply had too much at stake to give in lightly.

The Iwasaki put even more money into the San'yō Railway than they did into the Kyushu.[60] Like the Kyushu Railway, the San'yō also had strategic importance for Mitsubishi's other operations. Besides it role in transshipping coal from Kyushu, the railroad offered Mitsubishi and its shipping affiliate, the N.Y.K. (Nippon yūsen kaisha), a means of competing with the O.S.K. (Osaka shōsen kaisha), which controlled much of the freight business in the Inland Sea. As we have seen, in the early years, competition from the O.S.K. and other steamship companies had exerted constant pressure on the San'yō to lower rates and improve service. Beginning in the late 1890s, however, it was the railroad that took the offensive. In 1898, the O.S.K. inaugurated a direct line between Osaka and Moji "to connect with the Tokaido state railway and the Kyushu Railway,"[61] in effect totally bypassing the San'yō and thus posing an even greater threat to the railroad. The latter responded with a vengeance. It set up its own steamship company to provide service between the western terminus of its railroad line and Moji, made arrangements for through-traffic with the Tokaido and Kyushu railways, and launched a fierce rate war between its new steamship firm and the O.S.K.[62] The rate war involved passenger fares, but, in mid-1898, the San'yō also displayed an aggressive attitude towards freightage, adopting the policy that, "when it is judged to be in our interest to reduce our rates, we should try to attract freight by cutting the rates 10–15 percent and [thereby] plan to compete with the O.S.K. and other steamship companies."[63] These tactics dealt a sharp blow to the O.S.K., which saw its business stagnate after 1898. Meanwhile, the San'yō enjoyed a steady rise in its operating income, in large part owing to the sudden increase in through-traffic revenues.[64]

Investment in the San'yō Railway had other indirect benefits for Mitsubishi. In particular, the rivalry between the railroad and the O.S.K. resulted in increased business for Mitsubishi's Nagasaki shipyard, for the railroad's steamship subsidiary placed all its orders for new vessels with the Nagasaki yard.[65] That Shōda Heigorō, who was both manager of the shipyard and a director of the San'yō Railway, sought to promote such complementary development is clearly evidenced by his recommendation in 1906 that the railroad install in its new ferryboats the latest British turbines then under trial production at the Nagasaki shipyard.[66] In addition, Mitsubishi had a variety of interests along the route of the railroad, including the mining division's big moneymakers, the Yoshioka and Ikuno mines, and a number of investments in the port of Kobe.[67]

Mitsubishi's concern for the wider benefits of railroad investment led it to support the emergence in the San'yō, as in the Kyushu, of full-time salaried managers devoted to expansion of the enterprise. Sengoku's counterpart in the San'yō was Ushiba Takuzō. A Keiō graduate, Ushiba had served in the Finance Ministry and on the boards of several business concerns before coming to the San'yō Railway in 1894 as general superintendent. In that position, he had assisted President Matsumoto Jūtarō, an Osaka entrepreneur who personified traditional railroad management. In drawing up plans for the Hankai Railway Company in the mid-1880s, for example, Matsumoto had stood by the old Sakai highway and estimated the traffic volume by counting beans in the sleeve pocket of his kimono.[68] As president of the 130th National Bank and a major stockholder in several of the private railroads, he exemplified railway owner-executives who served part-time on the boards of rail companies while simultaneously engaging in other business enterprises. Matsumoto was unusual, however, in the number of railroad firms over which he concurrently presided—five, to be exact, in the early 1900s![69] Needless to say, he was unable to supervise the day-to-day operation of these roads; that task he left to full-time lieutenants like Ushiba. Under the aegis of Mitsubishi, then, the San'yō Railway Company joined the Kyushu in the late 1890s in moving steadily towards the appointment of full-time career managers to the highest decision-making posts. Paralleling the rise of Sengoku in the Kyushu Railway, Ushiba was promoted to managing director of the San'yō in 1898 and finally succeeded Matsumoto as chairman of the board in 1904.[70] As administrative experts with little share in their companies' ownership, Ushiba and Sengoku lent a high degree of professionalism to the top managements of the San'yō and Kyushu railways.

Like Sengoku, Ushiba also called for expanded investment in the railroad, but he was more tactful in dealing with shareholders. Beginning in the late 1890s, he sought to rally the owners of the San'yō behind his program of plant renovation by urging them to extend their time horizons and appealing to their sense of civic duty. Stockholders ought not to begrudge the huge outlay of capital needed to upgrade the railroad, he argued in 1899, since such investment would "open a permanent source of profits and, at the same time, fulfill [the company's] grave responsibility towards society."[71] By January 1906, Ushiba had refined his position considerably. In a series of articles he published that month, he insisted that private railroads must restrict their dividends and use the resulting surplus to carry out needed improvements. Ushiba went on to criticize the general tendency whereby railway companies "compete for the highest dividend rate," and "the more their profits increase, the more they have to pay them out to shareholders." If the firms fail to restrain their dividend rates, he warned, they "will block the source of progress and improvement and thus lose their permanent interests."[72]

Although forthright and sensible, Ushiba's stand nevertheless went against the profit-seeking proclivities of many stockholders. Yet he managed to avoid the problems Sengoku faced not only because of his appeals to investors, but also because of the transformation that had taken place among the principal owners themselves. By 1905, the Osaka investors who had given Nakamigawa such a hard time had largely disappeared from the San'yō's list of major stockholders, with Mitsubishi and Mitsui being joined at the top of the list by Sumitomo and various banks and insurance companies (see Table 20). With this more stable ownership, Ushiba had less trouble selling his message.

Also, unlike Sengoku, Ushiba did not take up the fight against nationalization himself. That task was left to Shōda Heigorō. As a founder and director of the San'yō and leading executive of Mitsubishi, Shōda nicely personified the coincidence of interests between the railroad and the zaibatsu. We have noted in connection with Katō Kōmei that Shōda vigorously opposed the nationalization on the grounds that it would reduce competition, and without competition, there would be no progress. By "progress," Shōda specifically meant "improvement of facilities," and it should be pointed out that, by 1905, his laissez-faire position had departed significantly from "the classic Anglo-American argument."[73] Shōda was against price competition, for, in his view, the latter inevitably produced damaging rate wars and ended in price-fixing agreements anyway. Instead, what he advocated was "a competition in facilities" whereby companies would vie to upgrade their plant and equipment through rationalization of management while maintaining a "fixed level of profits."[74] Moreover,

Shōda's brand of "free enterprise" thinking led him to favor not an all-private network, but rather the existing mixed system. As he put it, "It is harmful to leave the management of railroads entirely to private enterprise, just as it is to nationalize them completely. Only by having both [private interests and the state] manage them can we expect to make progress in improvements."[75] In short, the more diversified the competition, the better.

Behind all this talk of railroad improvement lay a serious problem confronting the San'yō and other railway companies at the time, namely, the need for massive capital investments to upgrade the inadequately built or rapidly depreciating railway lines. Opponents of the nationalization liked to make comparisons between the state and private railways, pointing out the much lower construction costs and higher profitability of the latter.[76] Indeed, in 1905, the cumulative building expense per mile of line for the state railways was ¥104,385, while the comparable figure for the seventeen companies that were eventually nationalized was only ¥80,407. Partly because of their cheaper construction, the nationalized private lines as a whole proved to be considerably more profitable than their government counterparts, returning 10.1 percent on construction costs in 1905 compared to 7.4 percent for the state lines.[77] The disparity is explained in part by the lower efficiency of state management and the greater difficulty of construction of many government lines, particularly the trans-Honshū railroads, which were built as much for political and strategic as for economic reasons. Yet equally, if not more, important was the fact that private railroads had managed to reduce their construction expenses and thereby achieve relatively high profit rates by neglecting or postponing necessary repairs and improvements.

In the San'yō Railway, for example, the "Osaka economizers" who ousted Nakamigawa succeeded in slashing the construction cost per mile from around fifty-nine thousand yen in 1889 to less than fifty thousand in 1892 (see Table 21). Under Matsumoto and Ushiba, however, the company reversed this trend, sharply raising the rate of expenditure on plant and rolling stock so as to meet the demands of the growing economy for increased carrying capacity. The upshot was that, by the early 1900s, the San'yō was rapidly approaching the level of fixed investment on the state lines.

By that time, the San'yō Railway had clearly achieved high standards of construction and service compared to other Japanese railroads. Neverthe-

TABLE 20 Top Ten Shareholders in the San'yō Railway Company, 1905

Name	Number of Shares
Iwasaki Hisaya	44,103
Mitsui Bank	39,065
Iwasaki Yanosuke	13,507
Meiji Life Insurance Co.	12,316
Nihon Savings Bank	9,490
Sumitomo Bank	9,059
Sumitomo Kichizaemon	7,077
Meiji Fire Insurance Co.	5,635
Tatsuuma Kichizaemon	5,126
Terada Jin'yomo	5,114

Source: *Teikoku tetsudō yōkan,* 3rd ed. (Tetsudō jihō-kyoku, 1906), p. 182.

less, management was painfully aware that, at least in the area of double-tracking, the company still had a long way to go in order to satisfy the growing demand for rail transportation. Ushiba gave voice to this concern when he declared at the general stockholders' meeting in 1904, "[H]aving only double-tracked the section between Kobe and Himeji, before long, we will be pressed by the need to double-track the line west of Himeji to Shimonoseki."[78] Accordingly, after the Russo-Japanese War, the company drew up plans for a major expansion program, including not only the double-tracking of existing lines, but also the building of new feeder lines.[79]

With the sudden increase in funding needs attending this postwar program, it was only natural that the San'yō's management should have changed its thinking on profit distribution and begun advocating the restriction of dividends so as to build up the company's internal supply of expansion capital. The railroad had actually started to limit dividend payouts as early as 1903, when the percentage of profits allocated for dividends began a steady decline while that assigned to retained earnings rose proportionately (see Table 22). These trends, however, accelerated dramatically in the first semester of 1904. At that time, despite a sharp increase in profits, the company held the dividend rate at 8 percent, the same level as in the previous term. As Ushiba explained at the aforementioned stockholders' meeting that year, the reason the firm was retaining the surplus profits rather than applying them to dividends was that, "presently, there is a great need to take precautions and prepare for [the expected growth in capital expenditures]."[80] Thus, it was against this background that, in January 1906, Ushiba made one final appeal to the investing public to support his dividend-limitation policy.

The institutional investors who dominated the San'yō's ownership may have been more willing to accept reduced but stable dividends than more profit-minded individual investors. But banks and insurance companies were also cautious investors, and those who held interests in the San'yō were undoubtedly concerned over the prospect of having to tie up huge additional sums of capital in the railroad, should dividend restriction fail to produce sufficient funds for Ushiba's program.

The biggest railway investor among financial institutions was the Mitsui Bank, which, in the San'yō Railway, was the second largest stockholder after Mitsubishi. In sharp contrast to the latter, Mitsui openly supported the state purchase of private railroads. Many have explained Mitsui's endorsement of nationalization in terms of its rivalry with Mitsubishi for supremacy over the Kyushu coal industry.[81] By getting the government to buy out the Kyushu and San'yō railways in particular, it is reasoned, Mitsui would be able to thwart its rival's attempt to use railroad investment as a means of countering Mitsui's control over the distribution of Kyushu coal. This viewpoint receives some confirmation from the fact that the most vocal proponent of nationalization among Mitsui executives was Masuda Takashi of the combine's trading company, which handled Mitsui's sales operations in Kyushu as elsewhere.

Mitsui, however, had additional reasons for supporting the government's purchase of private railroads. Taking a position that was virtually identical to that of Finance Minister Sakatani and other state authorities, Mitsui also advocated nationalization as a way of enabling the government to improve the rail network and thereby to promote Japanese exports. Representative of the views of Mitsui executives in this regard were those of Hatano Shōgorō, a director of the Mitsui Bank. Hatano noted in late 1905 that the state would have to rely heavily on foreign loans to finance its postwar program, but in order to obtain the foreign exchange to redeem those loans, it also needed to adopt an aggressive export-promotion policy. A key part of

TABLE 21 Construction Expenses, San'yō Railway Company, 1889–1905

Year	Construction Expenses						Total (¥1,000)	Average Length of Line Open (miles)	Construction Expenses per Mile of Line Open (¥1,000 per mile)
	Track (%)	Land (%)	Tunnel (%)	Station (%)	Machine Shop (%)	Rolling Stock (%)	Merger (%)		
1889	–	–	–	–	–	–	–	2,179	37	58.9
1892	–	–	–	–	–	–	–	7,125	144	49.5
1897	16.6	12.7	6.0	3.4	1.0	15.0	0	16,342	231	70.7
1902	15.2	12.0	5.1	4.8	2.3	17.5	0	26,795	332	80.7
1905	13.9	10.8	4.6	5.1	2.5	17.5	6.6	35,835	416	86.1

Source: Sakurai Tōru, "San'yō tetsudō kabushiki kaisha no shihon chikuseki jōken to kokuyūka mondai," *Shōgaku shūshi*, vol. 49, no. 3, p. 67 (February 1980).

that policy, then, was to upgrade service on the nation's railway system. As Hatano asserted, the government could help make China in particular into a "great market for our manufactured goods" by "lowering freightage" and "correcting defects" in the railway network.[82] Furthermore, in his talk with Hara earlier that year, Masuda, as we have noted, linked railway nationalization to standard-gauge reconstruction, offering additional evidence that Mitsui set great store by the government's renovation of the nationalized railroads. And Masuda had good reason to welcome the stimulus such improvement would give to the export trade since, in the mid-1900s, his company handled 10–15 percent of Japan's total exports.[83] Moreover, the fact that the San'yō Railway accounted for fully one fifth of the total volume of raw cotton and cotton goods transported on the nation's railroads in 1905 would make its renovation at government hands a vital part of Mitsui Bussan's strategy for invading the Chinese cotton-textile market.[84]

Another reason Mitsui backed railway nationalization had to do with a change in investment policy on the part of the bank itself. After Nakamigawa left the San'yō Railway to become head of the Mitsui Bank in 1891, the combine, in line with the policy he instituted of expanding its industrial assets, had embarked on an aggressive program of railway investment through stock acquisition by the bank. Thus, from virtually no interest in the San'yō in 1891, Mitsui, through its bank, had purchased nearly 7 percent of the railroad's stock by 1893. This program climaxed in 1899 when the bank bought a huge block of shares in the Hokkaido Colliery to become the largest stockholder in that railroad.[85]

After Nakamigawa died in 1901, however, the bank's management adopted a more conservative policy towards industrial investments and launched a full-scale program of conversion to ordinary commercial-bank status. In accordance with this new strategy, therefore, the bank let its interest in the San'yō decline to some 5 percent by 1905, even as the Iwasaki were increasing their share.[86] In September 1902, the bank's auditors had recommended the following policy on stock ownership: "From the standpoint of [building] the reserve fund for deposits, it is all right to hold stocks that are accepted as collateral by the Bank of Japan. . . . [However,] it would appear that we have a bit too many shares of the San'yō and Nippon railways, and as for our other stockholdings, we should of course dispose of them quickly."[87] Thus, by the mid-1900s, railway stockholding had

TABLE 22 Profit Distribution, San'yō Railway Company, 1901–1905

Year	Semester	Dividend (%)	Directors' Bonus (%)	Reserve (%)	Retained Earnings (%)	Total Profit (¥)	Dividend Rate (%)
1901	2nd	93.9	0.7	5.0	0.4	919,752	7.6
1902	1st	94.1	0.7	5.0	0.2	969,021	7.6
	2nd	94.1	0.6	5.0	0.3	1,004,959	7.9
1903	1st	88.6	0.5	5.0	5.9	1,354,655	10.0
	2nd	83.7	0.5	4.7	11.0	1,184,525	8.0
1904	1st	66.2	0.4	4.6	28.8	1,571,751	8.0
1905	1st	58.9	0.5	3.7	37.0	2,601,301	10.0

Source: Sakurai, "San'yō tetsudō," p. 70.

become something of a nuisance to the Mitsui Bank, at best a way of increasing its reserves for the deposit and discount operations it was seeking to enlarge. Moreover, the fact that the bank was also attempting to "switch from investment in stocks with their high potential for the long-term fixation [of capital] to investment in public bonds with their short-term convertibility"[88] rendered it doubly receptive to a nationalization that would bring about the replacement of its railway shares by government bonds.

This attitude on the part of its principal owner explains to a great extent why the Hokkaido Colliery and Railway put up no resistance to the nationalization and, in fact, embraced it with enthusiasm in the person of its managing director, Inoue Kakugorō. Morikawa Hidemasa notes that Mitsui had been "at a loss as to how to dispose of the Hokkaido Colliery shares procured during the Nakamigawa period,"[89] and perhaps it was no coincidence that it was in the year of Nakamigawa's death that Inoue joined forces with Den Kenjirō to push for a nationalization bill in the Diet.

At any rate, Mitsui's attitude towards railway nationalization contrasted strikingly with that of Mitsubishi. The difference can be accounted for in large part by reference to disparities in their business operations. Besides their common emphasis on mining, Mitsubishi had centered its activities on transportation, investing first in shipping and then in railroads, whereas Mitsui had focused on trade and finance.[90] For Mitsubishi, therefore, railway investment was an integral component of its business strategy; for Mitsui, it was simply a means to other ends, specifically, bank-reserve accumulation and export promotion, which could be better served through the government's purchase and improvement of private railroads.

As far as its bank was concerned, Mitsui's views on railway-stock ownership were probably no different from those of most financial institutions that held railway interests. By 1905, banks and insurance companies had emerged as railway investors to such an extent that those appearing on major stockholders' lists alone that year possessed fully a sixth of all the shares of the five largest railroads combined.[91] As a result, in the San'yō and Kyushu in particular,[92] the rise of professional managers backed by Mitsubishi and committed to the expansion and continued existence of their enterprise was to a considerable degree offset by the ascendance of conservative institutional investors.

The openness of such investors to nationalization was also evidenced by the 15th National Bank, Japan's leading railway shareholder, whose stand on the issue largely determined that of the Nippon Railway. By the mid-1900s, the latter company was facing the same need for renovation as the Kyushu and San'yō railways, but, in its case, the need was even greater, for lacking career managers with the progressiveness and enterprise displayed by Sengoku and Ushiba, the Nippon had barely begun to make the necessary improvements.

Japan's biggest railway company had initially drawn most of its income from passenger transport. The situation began to change, however, with the completion of the Jōban line in 1897. From that year on, freight earnings increased rapidly, thanks mainly to the growing conveyance of coal from the Jōban region. They eventually overtook passenger revenues and, on the eve of the nationalization, made up some three fifths of the company's total income.[93] The Nippon thus developed into what Japanese scholars like to call "an industrial railroad." The firm's managers were clearly aware at the time that such a change had taken place. As one of them put it in 1902, "Now railroads can be roughly divided into two kinds, namely, passenger railroads and freight railroads. . . . The Nippon Railway, which falls into the second category, carries, for the most part, Jōban coal, Ōshū rice, forest products, firewood and charcoal, and so on. Therefore, our business policy is aimed at satisfying [the shippers of these goods]."[94]

The railroad, however, seemed to fall short of this goal. In May 1905, for example, the coal-mine owners in the Jōban area complained to the government about the inadequacy of the Nippon's carrying capacity.[95] They were also unhappy about the rates charged by the firm. In February 1903, the Jōban mine operators requested that the company lower its rates so that they might cope with the influx of Kyushu coal into the Tokyo market. The Nippon responded by reducing its coal freightage for the rest of the month from ¥0.018 to ¥0.015 per ton-mile. The collier operators were incensed at this paltry reduction and demanded that the rate be further reduced. "However," reported the *Tōkyō keizai zasshi*, "the Nippon Railway holds that it would be difficult to comply with this request . . . and has not taken any action. Consequently, the coal-mine owners have all resolved to cut production by a third if the Nippon Railway does not agree to lower its rate."[96] This threat evidently prompted the company to agree at least to maintain the reduced rate beyond the end of the month. Despite this concession, freightage came to weigh increasingly on the management of coal-mining enterprises in the Jōban area. The Iwaki Coal-Mining Company, for example, saw its dividend drop from 10 percent in 1902 to around 5 percent in the latter half of 1903. The reason for this decline, according to the *Tōyō keizai shinpō*, was a sharp increase in operating costs, which took up 80–90 percent of the firm's income, "and railroad freightage represents the bulk of these operating expenses; plainly speaking, it is as if most of the income were simply absorbed as freightage by the Nippon Railway Company."[97] Yet, not until after the Nationalization Law was passed did the Nippon consent to lower its coal freightage again.[98]

The railroad refused to do so prior to that time mainly because it experienced a constant shortage of funds in the early 1900s. For, besides the demands from users, the company was also faced with the need to make huge capital expenditures during that time. Following the enactment of the Nationalization Law, the firm reported to the government that, from 1902 to 1905, there had often been a shortfall in its capital account; each time that had occurred, it had applied to the shortfall surplus funds appropriated from its profit account. The amount thus appropriated had risen steeply during those years, reaching some ¥4,000,000 at its height.[99] The basic cause of this growing shortage of capital was a rapid increase in expenditures on rolling stock and a gradual rise in station and machine-shop outlays. As Sakurai points out, the company had completed its "extensive" development with the purchase of the Ryōmō Railway in 1896 and the opening of the Jōban line the following year; thereafter, it turned to "intensive" development of its network. The "age of renovation" had arrived.[100] The result was a rise in average fixed investment per mile of operating line from ¥47,167 in 1897 to ¥62,051 in 1905. Yet even this substantial increase represented far less than what was accomplished in terms of "intensive" development at the San'yō and Kyushu railroads, which saw their average fixed investment per mile of open line soar during that same period from ¥58,366 to ¥88,266 and from ¥61,034 to a staggering ¥114,232, respectively.[101] Mitsubishi virtually guaranteed the supply of capital required by the latter two companies, but evidently, its counterpart at the Nippon, the 15th National Bank, was not as forthcoming with financial support, for that railroad's managers complained constantly about the lack of funding for improvements.[102]

By the turn of the century, the top executives of the Nippon Railway Company were keenly aware of the need to upgrade the enterprise, but hamstrung by shortage of capital and lacking the initiative of their colleagues at the San'yō and Kyushu, they did relatively little to meet that need. In 1900, President Soga Sukenori admitted that private lines, including his own, were poorly equipped as compared to those of the state. "In station facilities," he noted, "whereas the government railways build tile-roofed or stone warehouses, the private railroads use shingle roofing.... In addition, because the platform facilities of private lines are somewhat inferior to those of the state railways, [shippers] experience some inconvenience in loading goods, and passengers, in boarding and disembarking from [trains]."[103] The situation, however, was unavoidable: "since the funding needed to [improve facilities] is lacking," Soga explained, "circumstances do not permit it."

The company eventually had to come up with some money for improvements after the enactment of the Private Railway Law in 1900. Under this law, the government issued a series of directives aimed at standardizing the facilities on the various lines. Among the most important of these was the Railway Construction Regulations. The latter required railroad concerns to meet certain standards for plant and equipment, resulting in at least some increase in average construction outlays for all the railroads. The Nippon was no exception. But like most of the other firms, it finished only part of the rebuilding work prescribed under the regulations:[104] in March 1905, the estimated cost of the work it had yet to complete came to almost half a million yen, or over 10 percent of the total for all seventeen railroads eventually slated for nationalization.[105] Moreover, the authorities had to revise the construction regulations immediately after the nationalization, the standards they had set in 1900 having quickly become outmoded in the face of exploding demand for rail transportation.[106] The Nippon Railway thus fell short of meeting construction requirements that were already becoming obsolete, much less of carrying out improvements on a scale demanded by the growing economy.

The Nippon failed to satisfy the need not only to upgrade its stations and lines, but also to renovate its rolling stock. As noted earlier, Meiji railroads had no system of depreciation accounting,[107] so money spent on the renovation of rolling stock generally appeared as an operating expenditure in company accounts. In the case of the Nippon Railway, the rapid increase in this expenditure after 1897 naturally produced a decline in the firm's profit rate. Yet the demand for such outlays was only bound to intensify, as is suggested by the fact that, at the end of 1904, the company determined that nearly a quarter of its 350 locomotives were superannuated.[108] In 1901, the railroad seemed to take the necessary countermeasure by setting up a special reserve fund for renovating its rolling stock; however, this fund also took the form of an operating expenditure, and in any case, it barely scratched the surface of the problem. From 1903 to 1904, for example, the fund grew by ¥250,000; of this, about half was spent on improvements, but the rest was applied to the shortage in the capital account.[109] Hence, not even this modest increase in the special reserve fund was entirely devoted to upgrading the company's rolling stock. Of small scale to begin with, the fund was thus woefully inadequate to the task at hand. Full-scale renovation of the Nippon's rolling stock simply had to wait until after the nationalization.

The Nippon Railway boasted one of the highest profit rates in the industry. Yet its excellent business results masked, and were partly made possible by, its serious neglect of capital expenditures. Sooner or later, therefore, the company would have to put out substantial amounts of money in order to carry out vital improvements to its plant and equipment. But the magnitude of the required investment made it apparent that stockholders would have to tie up all the more capital in the railroad while receiving a lower, if more accurate, return on their investment.

These problems were by no means lost on the railroad's largest shareholder, the 15th National Bank. Like the Mitsui Bank, it too had undergone a change in policy on stock ownership by the time of the nationalization. The 15th National had been founded mainly for the purpose of financing railroads, and even after 1897, when the bank shed its national-bank status and made public its holdings of Nippon Railway stock, railroad investments—the vast majority of them in the Nippon—continued to account for almost half the bank's total assets.[110] Naturally, therefore, the vicissitudes of the Nippon Railway had a direct impact on the business results of the bank. This became painfully clear in 1898, at the height of the panic, when a drop in the price of Nippon stock triggered a corresponding decline in that of 15th Bank shares. Consequently, a growing minority within the 15th began urging that the bank get rid of its Nippon Railway shares. The views of this group were rejected at the time, but in October 1898, the stockholders elected a new president, Sonoda Kōkichi, who established the policy of converting the 15th into an ordinary commercial and deposit bank.[111] Under this new policy, the bank's massive holdings of Nippon stock suddenly became a burden in the eyes of management, which, like its counterpart at the Mitsui Bank, was hard pressed to dispose of the 15th's railway interests. No wonder, then, that the 15th Bank should have supported the nationalization movement of 1899.[112]

Adding to the sense of urgency with which the bank sought to unload its railway investments was alarm at the growing capital requirements of the Nippon Railway. The bank, of course, had enjoyed consistently high dividends on its Nippon shares. Government subsidies had played a big part in maintaining the dividend rate at around 10–11 percent during the first decade and a half. At their height in 1890–1891, the subsidies had accounted for almost half the dividend payout. Thereafter, the importance of the state subsidy had steadily declined, so that in 1905, the last year in which a subvention was made, it represented less than 1 percent of total dividends. Yet, during most of the 1890s, the government's largesse had enabled the company to ignore the emerging need for renovations. By 1898, however, the subsidy's share of dividends had fallen to the point where it was unable to shield the railroad from the blow of the panic, with the result that the dividend rate plunged to 5.5 percent in the first half of 1898 and to 7.0 percent for the year as a whole.[113] The crisis only underscored the alarming fact that state aid was disappearing precisely when the demand for unmet capital expenditures was becoming too great for the railroad to ignore.

As a consequence, the Nippon was forced to put into effect its own, albeit limited, version of Ushiba's dividend-restriction policy. The company's dividend rate recovered to 10.0 percent in 1900, but, despite an increase in the profit rate from 11.6 percent that year to 12.8 in 1904, the firm never raised the annual dividend by more than half a percentage point during that period. The reason, as President Soga publicly revealed in 1900, was that the railroad had adopted a policy of limiting dividends. After explaining the urgent need for capital expenditures in order to expand the railroad's carrying capacity, Soga declared that "our company's policy is first of all to reduce the stockholders' dividend and invest [the resulting surplus] in the improvement of facilities and to make up for any additional shortage [of capital] by raising fares."[114] Soga's threatened "reduction" of dividends was translated in practice into a mild limitation of dividends. In any event, the resulting accumulation of internal reserves was hardly sufficient to meet the enormous capital expenditures required.[115]

For the 15th Bank, determined as it was to expand its ordinary-banking operations and disturbed by the scale of investment that had yet to be made in the Nippon, the nationalization came as a godsend. By then, the bank had long since abandoned its original policy of centering its activities on railroad stockholding, and the issue quickly became the purchase price. When government authorities asked Sonoda for his opinion on the proposed nationalization, he replied that, "as president of the 15th Bank, I see the issue as being the price; if it is the government's intention to purchase [the railroad's stock] for less than ¥120 a share, I will have to protect the interests of the [bank's] majority stockholders . . . ."[116] As Sonoda explained later in a newspaper interview, the granting of purchase bonds at the rate of ¥120 per share would enable Nippon stockholders to maintain their current return of 12 percent. Since the government had indeed decided to issue the railroad's stockholders public bonds at the rate of slightly more than ¥120 per paid-up share, he had "no particular objections to the state's purchase measure." Sonoda made explicit why his bank was more than willing to accept these terms. Pointing out the need for capital expenditures on the Nippon's lines, he doubted that the dividend would rise above 12 percent even if profits were to increase. Moreover, he added, "Even though railroads show considerable revenues, if they covet all their profits and fail to carry out various improvements, they cannot escape vicious slander from the standpoint of the public interest."[117] Sonoda's comments reveal the extent to which the problem of upgrading the Nippon had come to weigh on the minds of bank officials. To their relief, the nationalization "removed this burden" and, by converting Nippon stock into public bonds, "added a large measure of stability to the management of the 15th Bank."[118]

The 15th not only held a majority interest in the Nippon Railway, but it also participated heavily in its management. On the eve of the nationalization, a bank director was serving concurrently as one of the two managing directors of the Nippon, and President Sonoda and a former bank executive were members of its board. As a result, the 15th by and large succeeded in imposing its views on the railroad. Admittedly, President Soga, as a member of the upper house, expressed opposition to the Nationalization Bill, and Hara Kei attributed growing resistance among the peers entirely to "the campaign headed by the Nippon Railway Company."[119] Yet, as Hara pointed out, Soga's objections centered almost exclusively on the purchase price. As a member of the special committee considering the proposed bill, Soga fought unsuccessfully for amendments to "safeguard the rights of the companies" by requiring that the government buy out the railroads through negotiation and exchange purchase bonds for the companies' shares based on their current rather than par value.[120] In a newspaper interview earlier that year, the managing director of the Nippon who was not affiliated with the 15th had left little doubt that the railroad's management was by no means opposed to nationalization in principle. This executive had asserted that he was "objecting to the method of calculating the purchase price, not to the purchase itself." If the government nationalized the railroads without making that method more favorable to investors, it would end up "sacrificing the interests of the shareholders."[121] Such views were very much in tune with those of Sonoda, suggesting a close agreement between the managements of the bank and railroad, the presence of a Mitsubishi executive on the Nippon's board notwithstanding.

Yet, for all we have said about Mitsubishi's vital stake in railway ownership and control, it too may have been willing to sell out for the right price. And, as we will see, investors in the larger railroads got a generous price indeed. Certainly, President Sengoku of the Kyushu Railway lobbied hard against the proposed Nationalization Bill, but Hara in his diary offered no details as to the nature of Sengoku's objections, except to say that he had joined forces with "Soga of the Nippon Railway and the like."[122] In fact, another source claims that "Sengoku's opposition lay with the method of purchase . . ."[123] If so, then perhaps in the final analysis, the attitude of the Kyushu Railway, and, by extension, of Mitsubishi, was not far removed from that of the 15th Bank. At any rate, it seems safe to say that the 15th's qualified endorsement of nationalization epitomized the general stance of financial institutions that had come to dominate the ownerships of the major railroad firms. That position was doubtless also shared by the Imperial Household, the fourth largest shareholder in private railroads—the third biggest in the Nippon and second in the Hokkaido Colliery[124]—which, in many ways, functioned as a conservative investment house. Such railway investors, in particular, would have been only too happy to shift the burden of required capital expenditures on to the state, receiving in the case of the more profitable railroads a most generous settlement in return.

THE BUSINESS COMMUNITY AT LARGE

On the whole, therefore, the owners and financiers of private rail companies welcomed the nationalization. They were joined by most shippers, who were hopeful that a single national railroad system would result in cheaper and more efficient transportation of freight. The Jōban coal-mine operators may have been exceptional in the degree of difficulty they experienced with private railway management, but an article in the *Tōkyō asahi* newspaper on May 9, 1905, suggested that there was widespread dissatisfaction among businessmen over the fragmented state of the country's rail network. Calling for "a major reform" of the Railway Operating Law, the author of this article complained:

> First of all, the companies do not have uniform rates, that is, they lack what in English are called "through-rates." . . . Because there are no "through-rates," passengers have to pay short-distance fares on the state lines and the Nippon Railway [even when traveling long distances over the two]. . . . So not only must they endure the inconvenience of transfers and worry about the calculation of fares, but they have to pay the highest short-distance fare for each line. The loss they sustain is not inconsiderable. . . . Furthermore, with regard to freight, because the aforementioned "through-rates" are lacking, shippers truly suffer immense losses. . . . If one company operated the railroad from Yokohama to Kōfu or if "through-rates" were available, shippers would be able to send their goods [on that line] for only one sixth the present rate.[125]

This commentator added that another source of aggravation was the late arrival of freight. According to one trading company's survey, it took three days for goods to cover one forty-seven-mile stretch—an average of less than sixteen miles a day. "Today's commercial and industrial world can hardly be satisfied with this."

The cabinet clearly sought to capitalize on this kind of discontent, stressing in its presentation of the Nationalization Bill to the Diet the increase in transport convenience and especially the reduction in rates that would ensue. One member of the lower house asked Prime Minister Saionji to clarify his statement that railway nationalization would strengthen the nation's finances: Did he mean that the measure would indirectly strengthen those finances by promoting the development of industry, or did he mean that it would do so directly by helping raise money? Saionji shot back that he meant the former.[126] The emphasis on the benefits to private industry, particularly the improvement in services and lowering of rates implied in Saionji's answer, was necessary to ensure the bill's acceptance by the Diet. The considerable lengths to which cabinet leaders went to underscore those benefits reflected the change in character of business demands for nationalization since the turn of the century. Earlier, it had been railway investors and financiers who had clamored for state purchase of railroads as a relief measure; now it was railway users who were pressing for nationalization as a promising means of industrial promotion.

The business community, though, was by no means unanimous in its support of railway nationalization. A number of businessmen openly questioned whether the administration could in fact realize the ambitious goals it had set for its railroad-acquisition program. State authorities predicted that the return on the nation's rail system as a whole would continue to rise following the nationalization. Consequently, the government would easily be able to finance both the making of improvements and the redemption of purchase bonds out of the proceeds of the railroads, while at the same time reducing rates. Businessmen were quick to challenge these rosy projections. Many agreed with the observation of one newspaper that the proposed standardization of the network and lowering of rates "would, if carried out, render substantial profits very uncertain."[127] Representatives of the railroad industry emphasized the enormous increase in outlays that the nationalized railways were bound to require. Once the government had bought out the private lines, they argued, it would undoubtedly extend them, but, because the extensions would be into remote areas, construction costs would be higher and profits lower. Thus, as a Hankaku Railway manager noted, "on the one hand, expenditures will rise, while, on the other, revenues will decline. Therefore, . . . repayment of [the railway loan] itself is doubtful."[128] The *Jiji shinpō*, an organ of the business community, pointed out the additional burden of paying for badly needed renovations by declaring, "Another point on which the Government's forecast is at fault is in the amount of money that will be required for improvements. Some of the lines to be purchased are in such a poor condition that heavy outlays will be required for alterations and improvements even during the first few years of State ownership. The sums of money spent on this will reduce the fund available for the payment of interest and the other objects specified . . ."[129] Hence, to many critics in the business community and the press, it seemed highly unlikely that the cabinet would be able to achieve its stated goals.

Businessmen also noted the inherent conflict between the administration's twin objectives of cutting rates and strengthening state finances, charging that what the authorities were really after were the profits of the private railroads. And, like opponents of nationalization in the Diet, they decried the rising tide of state intervention in the economy that had resulted from the quest for additional sources of revenue. As the *Japan Weekly Mail* reported in March 1906, "There are Japanese . . . who regard with no little alarm the recent attitude of the Government towards private enterprises. To them it seems that the Government is aiming at getting every paying concern into its own hands. The chief reason for the proposed purchase of the railways is alleged to be the profits that will accrue from them later on . . ."[130] The aforementioned managing director of the Nippon Railway exemplified this perception of growing state interventionism when he asserted, "The government has previously taken away the private tobacco and salt industries and is now likewise planning to take away railway companies. If the government goes on to nationalize the sake and sugar industries as well, already profitable enterprises will be wiped out of existence, and the development of private industry will ultimately grind to a halt."[131] Another businessman, anticipating the sharply critical comments of Diet members, exclaimed that, "for a government to seize and operate a private business and to try to improve its financial situation with the profits from that business is the *Russian way* [underlined in the original]."[132]

State authorities, though, managed to quiet most of this business opposition, much of which came from leading railway investors like Hara Rokurō.[133] Generous compensation helped, of course. So did the efforts of Inoue Kaoru, who appears to have played a particularly important role in placating the dissenters among private businessmen. Once he had finally agreed to support the nationalization program, Inoue threw himself into mediating between the government and the business community. Hara Kei recorded on March 2, 1906, that, for the past few days, Inoue had been "endeavoring to pacify businessmen." He had met with several of them that day and had agreed to deliver their demands to the cabinet. The following day, Hara noted that the cabinet had decided to accept "in general" the requests of the businessmen. Inoue's efforts of the past several days, he concluded, had been "truly immense," for he had persuaded the opposing businessmen by and large to consent to the nationalization while having them "present only a few requests" to the government.[134]

For the majority of business leaders, no such persuasion was necessary. Shibusawa Eiichi spoke for many of them when, on the eve of the Diet deliberations on the Nationalization Bill, he declared:

> To further national development, [the government] must afford facilities for commerce and industry by attending carefully to such matters as freight rates. For example, it must lower rates in order to promote major export items, and it must also give facilities and reduce the cost of transportation for coal, the motive power of industry. No matter how much control the government has, so long as there are moneymaking private companies, they will be slow to comply with the government's orders. Under these conditions, we cannot hope to achieve satisfactory results. Rather, it would probably be better to nationalize [the private railroads]. . . . Japan's present situation indicates that this is by no means a time to take England as a model. If the current administration advocates railway nationalization from the standpoint of paying close attention to exports and imports and of increasing national strength through railroad policy, I may under the present circumstances be obliged to support [nationalization], even though it is a policy I originally opposed.[135]

Earlier that year, Shibusawa had criticized private rail companies for their "lack of mutual connections" and "extremely high rates" and had urged the government to unify them "through nationalization or other means" and to afford facilities and reduce rates "at least for key industries." He had then linked this need for unification of domestic railroads to that of Japanese railway interests on the continent by asserting that "coordinating the railroads of Manchuria and Korea" should be given top priority in the administration of those areas.[136] Shibusawa's insistence that the government use railroad policy as an engine for promoting private business concerns, especially those in export industries, mirrored perfectly the demands of the great majority of Japanese businessmen, from Mitsui Bussan executives down to the Jōban coal-mine operators. It was also a position shared by government leaders, with Shibusawa's views practically coinciding with those subsequently advanced by his son-in-law, Finance Minister Sakatani.

Shibusawa had indeed originally objected to nationalization. In fact, in mid-1894, with the economy entering an upswing, he had joined with Nakamigawa of the Mitsui Bank, Mitsubishi's Suehiro Michinari, and other prominent businessmen to press for the transfer of state railways into private hands. Their plan was for the government to sell off all its lines for a price roughly equivalent to the latter's cumulative construction costs.[137] The plan collapsed, however, with the outbreak of the Sino-Japanese War. Then, when businessmen launched their campaign for the state purchase of private railroads during the Panic of 1897–1898, Shibusawa at first resisted, charging that supporters of nationalization "are taking advantage of military men and politicians and have as their real aim the appreciation of stock prices and nothing else. . . . I am totally opposed to the government ownership argument. Because of that [stance], some years ago, we applied for the sale of state railways, and we hold the same view today."[138]

By November 1898, however, Shibusawa had changed his tune, for, in that month, he petitioned the upper house on behalf of the Tokyo Chamber of Commerce to push for nationalization. Shibusawa also backed the nationalization petition that the chamber presented to the cabinet in late 1901.[139] Nakanishi claims that Shibusawa and other big-business leaders had not in fact abandoned their commitment to the private ownership of railroads. They "tentatively" endorsed the nationalization movement only because "they could not openly oppose [it] as a measure of relief from the panics." Their position at that time "was basically different from their attitude in 1906, when they came to accept nationalization as inevitable and withdrew their own private-ownership argument."[140] Although the nationalization petitions appeared to represent the demands of businessmen as a whole, in actuality, the impetus came from one segment of the business community, namely, "speculative elements and small to medium railway capitalists" like Amenomiya Keijirō.[141] Be that as it may, the fact that the 15th Bank welcomed railway nationalization in 1899 suggests that the movement may have been broader than Nakanishi maintains. Yet, to be sure, the nature of the business demand for state purchase of private railroads had changed dramatically by the mid-1900s, owing to the shift in leadership and policy at the Mitsui Bank, for instance, and the rapid growth in industrial transportation needs. Moreover, Shibusawa's conversion in the end made it all the easier for government leaders to rally the majority of the business community behind their nationalization program.[142]

BUYING OUT THE COMPANIES

A broad consensus for railway nationalization thus prevailed among investors and users alike. State authorities, therefore, had good reason to expect that they would have little trouble in putting the Nationalization Law into effect. Prior to the law's enactment, however, the *Japan Weekly Mail* had not been so sanguine. In February 1906, that paper had cautioned that, in view of the current prosperity of the railway companies, "insuperable difficulties may arise in attempting to carry [the law] into operation."[143] Yet the government managed to avoid such problems by providing favorable, if not munificent, compensation to railway shareholders and by repeatedly acquiescing in their demands to make the terms of the settlement even more advantageous to them.

The nationalization act called for the purchase of the seventeen firms originally recommended for nationalization by Communications Minister Yamagata. These concerns ranged from the five biggest railroads down to such small but strategically important lines as the Nishinari and Kyoto. As noted earlier, the law stipulated that "railroads whose object is to furnish transportation to one locality are to be excluded [from the nationalization]." This rather vague definition of the scope of the measure was clarified by the chairman of the upper-house committee investigating the purchase bill. The committee chairman explained that, in reducing the number of companies to be nationalized, the committee had "mainly taken those [railroads] that come under the category of scheduled lines listed in the Railway Construction Law and added a few others deemed necessary." The 1892 Construction Law, then, was used as "the basis for deleting the remaining fifteen [railroads]" that the cabinet had included at Hara's insistence.[144] The Chūgoku Railway Company, which had built a railroad inland from Okayama city to connect with a planned state line to the Japan Sea, was the only one of the railroads struck from the bill whose line was in fact designated for completion in the Construction Law. Yet, government officials had decided to move the route of their projected cross-island railroad further eastward, so the Chūgoku had in practice ceased to be regarded as a "scheduled line."[145] Other factors were also involved in the exclusion of railway companies from the buyout. For example, the Nankai Railway, one of the largest of the deleted firms, was omitted partly because of the military's objection that it operated a vulnerable coastal line.[146]

The other principal revision made by the upper house was the extension of the purchase period. The authorities quickly realized, however, that, although prolonging the nationalization would cushion the impact on the bond market, it might also result in raising the purchase price to prohibitive levels. Communications Minister Yamagata explained why in a memorandum he presented to the cabinet on July 18, 1906, urging the government to expedite the implementation of the law. The formula for determining the purchase price of the railroads, as spelled out in the law, was to multiply by twenty the product of the average return on construction costs for the years 1903–1905 and the total construction costs on the date of purchase. In other words, the government used as the basis for calculating the price a profit rate of 5 percent,[147] which meant a huge windfall for companies like the Nippon and Kōbu that had recorded profits in excess of 10 percent. Yamagata warned, however, that extending the nationalization over a ten-year period might enable the railroads to secure changes in the law that would make the formula even more favorable to them. As he pointed out, during the recent Diet session, "some major railway companies schemed to introduce amendments concerning the method of calculating the price," and they might continue to do so, attempting, for example, "to revise the figure used to multiply the profits from twenty to twenty-two or twenty-three."[148] Hara suggested that President Soga of the Nippon Railway had in fact introduced an amendment in the upper house to that very effect.[149]

A more immediate concern raised by Yamagata was that various companies were seeking to raise their cumulative construction costs by "suddenly carrying out works they have neglected such as expanding facilities and extending and double-tracking lines."[150] Under the pricing formula, he noted, a railroad firm with a return on construction costs of over 5 percent was legally guaranteed a profit on any fixed investment it made until the date of purchase. Yamagata presented data for eight such railroads, ranging from the Kōbu with nearly a 15-percent profit rate to the Kansai with a return of almost 6 percent. The purchase prices of the three most profitable concerns, the Kōbu, Hokkaido Colliery, and Nippon, would come out to more than double their construction costs.[151] Consequently, Yamagata observed, for every ¥100 increase in building expenses made by the Kōbu Railway, for example, it would reap a profit of over ¥190 at the time of its purchase. As a result, the moneymaking railroads were scrambling to increase their construction costs, and the situation, the minister noted, was "giving rise to a multitude of abuses and almost getting out of hand."[152] Within just a little over a month of the law's enactment, the government had received applications for construction work involving a total expenditure of more than ¥12,000,000. This amount converted into a purchase price of nearly ¥24,000,000. Since most of the work applied for was "essential for the promotion of industry," the authorities felt constrained to give permission, even though doing so meant inflating the cost of nationalization. And there was no doubt that such applications would continue to pour in; accordingly, Yamagata concluded, "every day's delay increases [the government's] loss, and before long the purchase price will have reached an appallingly large amount. . . . The damage inflicted on state finances will not be light by any means."[153] Such arguments were bound to convince finance officials, and, as the communications minister assured them, even if the government were to nationalize the railroads forthwith, it would still have five years to issue the purchase bonds and thereby avoid a precipitous drop in bond prices.[154] The cabinet promptly accepted Yamagata's proposal and decided to buy up all the railroads by October 1907, beginning in the fall of 1906 with the three most profitable companies and the Iwagoe Railway, whose principal owners included the 15th Bank and the Nippon Railway itself.[155]

Needless to say, the relatively profitable railroads frantically carried out construction work right up until the date of their purchase. The law stipulated that railway companies had to obtain state approval for any increase or reduction in construction costs and that the government would refuse to accept changes made without its permission; but the proviso that followed this stipulation effectively nullified whatever control it gave the authorities by stating that, retroactively, "the government may approve [such changes] after assessing the amount and collecting a suitable compensation." Moreover, Satō Yūnō, head of the special government office set up to audit the railroads in preparation for their nationalization, later recalled that the government had little hope of restraining the companies anyway since their presidents "were all first-class people."[156] The upshot was that railroads like the Kōbu embarked on crash expansion programs with or without state approval. As Satō put it, "they were all working day and night, . . . making a commotion as though a fire had started." The Nippon Railway, he noted, had hastened to double-track what is now the Yamanote line, while the Sōbu, Kansai, and Sangū had carried out similar work on their lines. Further, the Kōbu Railway, which had suspended construction at Ochanomizu, suddenly extended its line to Manseibashi. In the end, the government was compelled to accept some sixteen million yen in total construction expenditures after March 1906. The Kyushu Railway topped the list with more than five million yen in additional investment, followed by the San'yō, Kansai, Nippon, and Kōbu, each with over one million yen.[157]

The Nippon Railway in fact made over 500 applications for construction-cost increases totaling more than six million yen. Of these, the government approved 330 requests calling for a combined investment of nearly five million yen. Renovation of rolling stock and double-tracking accounted for about 60 percent of the total, although, by the purchase date, the firm had actually been able to spend only about half that amount.[158] Meanwhile, in December 1906, the stockholders of the Kansai Railway, as a hedge against failure of their request for exemption from the nationalization, endorsed management's proposal to double-track and electrify the company's lines so as to make the terms of purchase more favorable to the investors. In their resolution, the owners lamented the fact that the government was going to buy out the railroad just when its foundations were becoming "extremely secure," but then added that "we cannot thank you directors enough for saving us stockholders from a difficult situation by planning such major improvements as double-tracking and electrification . . ."[159]

The railway companies sought to raise the figure not only for their cumulative construction costs at the date of purchase, but also for their average profit rates for the years 1903–1905. They attempted the latter by pressing the authorities to accept a wide range of accounting devices aimed at increasing the total profits and reducing the total building expenses for that period. Chief among these devices were the inclusion of income taxes in the profit account and the deduction of expenditures on unopened lines from total construction costs. The government finally gave in to the companies and agreed to both these forms of accounting manipulation in November 1907.[160] Thus, the Nippon Railway, for example, was able to raise its average profit rate from the 11.98 percent calculated by the government in 1906 to a final figure of just under 12.5 percent. This meant that, in the end, the company received a nominal profit of ¥150 for every ¥100 in construction costs, an increase of about ¥10 over the figure Yamagata had cited in his memorandum of July 1906.[161] Satō could only conclude his reminiscences by exclaiming that the calculation of purchase prices had been "astonishingly liberal. It is a wonder that we settled so many things that way."[162]

For companies whose lines had been open less than three years at the end of 1905 or for whom the pricing formula yielded a figure below construction cost, the law prescribed a different method for determining the purchase price. In such cases, the government and the company were to negotiate a price within the cost of construction. As it turned out, the authorities had to apply this provision to eight of the seventeen railroads, and, in this instance, they did encounter some difficulty in carrying out the nationalization. The railroad concerns that came under this stipulation were for the most part smaller firms that had been hit hard by the panics; their owners were therefore generally receptive to the state purchase. Nevertheless, most of these railroads had shown improvement in their business results during the postwar upswing, and, in any event, their shareholders must have been dissatisfied no end by the gaping disparity between their compensation and that enjoyed by investors in the more lucrative established firms. For the Saionji administration and the Diet were soon flooded with petitions from these companies demanding more favorable treatment.

The Hokuetsu Railway, for example, memorialized both houses of the Diet in January 1907, objecting that, as the law stood, its owners would recoup only about 80 percent of their entire investment. "To have the railroad purchased at [such] an unexpectedly low price and to incur [such] huge losses," the company bemoaned in its petition, "is something the investors cannot bear." It was simply "unthinkable in this glorious age of respect for the ownership rights of the people."[163] Consequently, the railway requested that the Diet make an exception for the Hokuetsu whereby the government would calculate its purchase price using the average return for the period 1904–1906, since the firm's profit rate had recently surpassed the 5-percent threshold. As an alternative, the company proposed that the Diet postpone the railroad's purchase until the projected completion of its Toyama-Naoetsu line in 1913. The firm argued that, at present, it had the character of being merely a "local transportation facility." It was only with the opening of the Toyama-Naoetsu railroad that it would become part of the main-line system. Therefore, delaying its purchase would not interfere with the government's objective of unifying the nation's principal railroads. And, as the company pointed out, "if the stockholders obtain considerable dividends during the period of postponement, it will serve as some consolation to them"; moreover, since it was likely that the price of public bonds would gradually increase, the investors would be able "to reduce greatly the loss" they would sustain when their stocks were finally converted to bonds.[164]

Similarly, the Kyoto Railway, which had originally planned to build a line from Kyoto to the naval port of Maizuru, appealed to both the Diet and the Communications Ministry in 1907 to improve the terms of its purchase. As the railroad complained in its petition to the communications minister: "from the time of its founding, the company has been privately exhorted by competent authorities in the army and navy and driven by a sense of nationalism" to make enormous construction expenditures. The difficulty of its route notwithstanding, it had constructed its line using gentle gradients and curves; it had planned its major stations "on a grand scale," had bought enough land in the vicinity of Kyoto for double-tracking, and had "striven to build its facilities in accordance with the broad-gauge system."[165] Despite its extraordinary efforts to meet the military's requirements—and the Kyoto was definitely exceptional in the extent to which it came under such demands—the company was now being asked to sell out for a price below construction costs. This was unconscionable.

The government denied almost all these requests for rendering the settlement more advantageous to the younger or less profitable firms. Nevertheless, it made every effort to accommodate their stockholders within the limits of the law. What this meant in practice was that the authorities took the companies' total construction costs as their purchase prices, although shareholders were generally unable to recover their entire investment since the government issued the purchase bonds at par. In the case of the Hankaku Railway, the state had initially announced that it would exchange public bonds valued at ¥42 for each Hankaku share with a paid-up value of ¥50. The company had repeatedly petitioned the government for special treatment,[166] but when that tack failed, it commissioned Shibusawa Eiichi and the hard-nosed Sengoku Mitsugu to negotiate with the authorities on its behalf. In the end, the government agreed to grant the full ¥50 for each share. And, as one source puts it, "the stockholders were all very satisfied."[167]

The employees of the railway companies were also generally pleased with the nationalization, for the government had made it clear that, with the exception of the top management and temporary workers, all the staff would continue to be employed by the state railways. They were also assured that, for the most part, their pay would remain the same, and no doubt, many were heartened by the fact that, as a whole, state-railway employees received a higher average wage than did their counterparts in any of the five major private railroads.[168] As a result, by October 1907, the government had managed to take over all seventeen railroads without any particular difficulty. The transfer of the Kyoto Railway, for example, went smoothly in the end, the stockholders having in the meantime secured a purchase price at least roughly equivalent to the total paid-up capital. On August 1, 1907, President Tanaka Gentarō and state representatives completed the conveyance of the enterprise at the firm's main office in Kyoto. Thereupon, the company dissolved and its employees all came under the jurisdiction of the Kobe branch of the newly established Imperial Railway Department. As one of the staff later recalled of that day, "We thought there should at least be a farewell ceremony, but Mr. Tanaka said, 'It's better not to do anything that ostentatious. For, from now on, you are going to be government officials and render further service to the railroad world.' With that, after just posing for a commemorative picture in front of the cherry tree at the company entrance, we ended up parting. It was truly a depressing conclusion."[169] Hara Rokurō, a principal owner and director of five railroads including the Kyushu and San'yō, was considerably more sentimental when he and other San'yō directors met with state officials to convey that company's assets to the government on December 1, 1906. An opponent of nationalization to the last, Hara marked the occasion with the following plaintive verse:

> How it pulls at our hearts,
> Even though we are only giving up a metal road.[170]

In return for handing over their railroads, however, the owners of nationalized railway stock began receiving 5-percent interest on the purchase price beginning in May 1907. The government continued to compensate them in this way until it finally granted the 5-percent railroad-purchase bonds in 1909.[171] A number of issues such as the aforementioned tax-accounting question still remained, so that, in most cases, the authorities simply had to estimate the purchase price; for instance, the final price of the Nippon Railway was not decided until April 1908. In the meantime, investors were free to speculate in the shares of the nationalized companies. Since the stock exchanges removed those shares from their boards, most of the trading actually took place on the spot market.[172] The announcement in July 1906 of the cabinet's decision to speed up the nationalization had triggered a sharp rise in the prices of the nationalized railway shares, but with the collapse of the postwar boom in 1907, those same prices dropped just as sharply. The government's delay in determining the purchase prices of the railroads, let alone the issue date and redemption period of the purchase bonds, merely aggravated the situation. Because of the resulting uncertainty, banks hesitated to accept the railway stocks as collateral for loans.[173] Consequently, holders of nationalized railway shares who were in need of cash were constrained to sell their stocks even at a loss. This, of course, only accelerated the decline in prices, as the market became inundated with stocks for sale.

As early as April 1907, investors and financiers began calling on the authorities to resolve the crisis by granting the purchase bonds forthwith. Bankers in western Japan, for example, complained in a petition to the communications minister that, "since the stocks of the purchased railroads have yet to be exchanged for public bonds, they are neither pure stocks nor public bonds. As a result, they are unable to afford facilities for finance."[174] The price of public bonds, though, was also falling steadily at the time.

Hence, government leaders naturally feared that issuance of the purchase bonds then would only exacerbate the drop in the public-bond price. As one observer noted, they continued to maintain an attitude of "procrastination . . . , waiting earnestly until the time was ripe."[175] Nevertheless, the authorities responded to the pressure from businessmen and bankers by setting at least provisional purchase prices for the nationalized railroads beginning in May 1907 and by directing the Bank of Japan to treat the railway shares as public bonds for collateral purposes and to raise their collateral value. These measures, however, failed to stem the decline in the prices of nationalized railway stocks, as heavy selling continued on the market. The stock prices finally bottomed out in mid-1908, at which point they began to recover, although only slowly compared to the rebound in the price of public bonds.

By the middle of 1908, the gradual retirement of outstanding public bonds, the curtailment of the national budget, and the importation of foreign capital had all combined to ease the money market and reduce interest rates. The latter, in turn, caused the price of public bonds, which had been falling since early 1906, to begin a strong recovery. Seizing the occasion, the government finally granted the railway-purchase bonds in two installments in 1909.[176] To the relief of all concerned, the authorities managed to issue ¥456,195,000's worth of public bonds within the space of five months without adversely affecting the bond market. The nationalization was thus brought to a successful conclusion.

CAPITAL UNBOUND: INVESTING THE COMPENSATION

The total purchase price of the nationalized railways had ballooned to some ¥471,000,000, or nearly twice their combined construction costs. After adding to that sum the value of inventories and subsidiaries, the government had subtracted the railroads' outstanding debt to arrive at the final figure of ¥456,195,000. Stockholders received 5-percent bonds with a total par value in that amount in exchange for stocks with an overall paid-up value of ¥217,590,000. This settlement meant that on the average the new bondholders drew interest equivalent to a return of about 10.5 percent on their investment in the nationalized companies. All but one eighth of the bonds went to holders of stock in the five largest railroads, and investors in all of these except the Kansai obtained bonds with a value more than double that of their investment. Owners of the Sangū and especially the Kōbu and Sōbu railroads also profited handsomely as a result of the nationalization (see Table 23).

Some writers have argued that, as a whole, the compensation granted the stockholders of the nationalized railways represented an enormous windfall.[177] This was definitely the case with certain firms, most notably the Kōbu. But, as one railway bureaucrat noted, "the objective in calculating the purchase price was to have the interest on public bonds replace the dividend the companies' stockholders had been receiving on their shares. The general principle was that the income enjoyed by bondholders should remain the same so as not to inflict loss on the companies and stockholders."[178] Since the nationalized railways had recorded an average dividend of around 9.3 percent in 1905,[179] the government, by converting the railroads' stocks into public bonds at a rate that gave the former shareholders an equivalent, if somewhat higher, return, had by and large adhered to this basic principle. In that sense, the settlement, although favorable, was not as munificent as often portrayed.

On the other hand, the nationalization *was* a tremendous boon to investors inasmuch as government bonds were generally more marketable and more attractive as loan collateral than were corporate shares. This advantage was only magnified by the drop and slow recovery in railroad-stock prices, which, at their nadir in mid-1908, amounted on average to a mere 62 percent of face value. By contrast, the market price of public bonds hit bottom at around 80 percent of par and, as noted above, rebounded more quickly than did the current prices of railway shares.[180] Moreover, investors in the smaller railway companies founded since the Panic of 1890 were particularly appreciative of the borrowing power of government bonds since the Bank of Japan as a rule had not accepted their shares as collateral for discounts to commercial banks, and the latter therefore had been less than enthusiastic about lending on the security of those shares.

These points were not missed by either Dietmen or government officials, who anticipated that former railway shareholders would swiftly liquidate their bondholdings or else borrow extensively on them and would sink the cash thus realized in a variety of business ventures. In the lower house, for example, Sasa Tomofusa of the Daidō Club asked rhetorically,

TABLE 23 The Nationalized Railway Companies

Company	Date of Purchase	Length of Line Open (miles)	Paid up Capital (¥1,000)	Final Purchase Price (¥1,000)
Nippon	Nov. 1906	860	58,200	142,524
Kyushu	July 1907	446	50,300	118,508
San'yō	Dec. 1906	406	36,100	76,639
Hokkaido Col.	Oct. 1906	208	12,650	30,997
Kansai	Oct. 1907	280	24,180	30,438
Kōbu	Oct. 1906	28	2,670	14,600
Sōbu	Sep. 1907	73	5,760	12,406
Hokkaido	July 1907	159	6,340	6,132
Sangū	Oct. 1907	26	3,100	5,729
Hankaku	Aug. 1907	70	4,000	4,284
Hokuetsu	Aug. 1907	86	3,700	3,722
Kyoto	Aug. 1907	22	3,420	3,296
Iwagoe	Nov. 1906	49	2,640	2,422
Nishinari	Dec. 1906	5	1,650	1,847
Nanao	Sep. 1907	34	1,100	994
Bōsō	Sep. 1907	39	1,040	960
Tokushima	Sep. 1907	21	750	697
Totals		2,812	217,590	456,195

Sources: Hoshino Takao, "Meiji sanjū-ku nen no tetsudō kokuyūka: shitetsu no chihō tetsudōka," in Nakagawa Keiichirō, Morikawa Hidemasa, and Yui Tsunehiko, eds., *Kindai Nihon keiei shi no kiso chishiki* (Yūhikaku, 1974), p. 158; *Tetsudō-kyoku nenpō, 1907*, appendix, pp. 22–46 passim; *Nihon kokuyū tetsudō hyaku nen shi*, vol. 4 (1972), pp. 250–251.

"What will the major stockholders—those first-rate men of wealth—and many other shareholders do with the enormous sums of capital they will obtain as a result of the purchase?" and answered his own question by predicting: "Since they cannot afford to sit idly by, being content with the public bonds, they are certain to look in other directions and establish all kinds of enterprises."[181] Or, as Finance Minister Sakatani put it somewhat more graphically at an upper-house hearing, "If [former railway investors] sell the bonds issued by the government, how will they use the proceeds? By no means will they use the latter for eating and drinking sake. I am sure they are bound to set up spinning and shipping companies in Japan or invest willingly in such enterprises in Manchuria and Korea."[182]

To the Diet and cabinet, therefore, an expected bonus of railway nationalization was that it would promote the expansion and diversification of private industry by releasing venture capital hitherto tied up in railroads. The predictions of Sasa and Sakatani proved to be right on target, as many of the former railway capitalists took advantage of the occasion to reinvest their money. This opportunity was in a very real sense the dividend accruing to the ex-owners of the nationalized railway companies from shifting the burden of railroad development onto the state. Amenomiya Keijirō, a principal stockholder in the Kōbu and Hokkaido Colliery railways, suggested that railroad investors had fully shared the expectations of government spokesmen in this regard. For, in his unpublished memoirs, Amenomiya wrote that he himself had pressed for nationalization as a way of "enabling the private sector, which had theretofore concentrated on the construction of [standard] railroads, to apply its capital to other enterprises,"[183] presumably in newer, more profitable industries with higher growth potential both at home and in Japan's overseas possessions.

One such industry at home consisted of light railways, an area in which Amenomiya himself invested heavily after the nationalization. Between 1906 and 1907, this wide-ranging businessman established steam-powered tramways in various localities across Japan. In 1908, he combined eight of these to form the Greater Japan Tramway Company (Dai Nippon kidō kaisha). Amenomiya was the president and majority owner of the firm, which operated a total of nearly one hundred miles of track and initially paid a dividend of around 6 percent. Just as important to Amenomiya as the direct return on his investment in tramways, though, was the business they provided another of his enterprises, namely, an ironworks he founded in 1907 to produce rolling stock and other equipment for light railways.[184] Through his participation in the financing and management of tramways, therefore, Amenomiya was able to ensure the continued expansion of his new iron-manufacturing plant as well. The steam-driven tramways he thus developed were immediate forerunners of the private light railways that the government began to promote in the 1910s as a way of meeting the growing demand for local rail transportation. Amenomiya's business ventures in this field were, according to Aoki Eiichi, "especially large-scale, and both as a tramway manager and as a rail car manufacturer he left a great mark on the history of Japan's local railways."[185] It was mainly through the sale of his standard-railway interests that Amenomiya obtained the wherewithal to make such an impact in the first place.

The rise of light railways was but part of a third railroad boom, paradoxically triggered in large measure by the nationalization, that centered on the establishment of electric commuter railroads and the South Manchuria Railway Company. In 1907, for example, the directors and shareholders of the nationalized Hankaku Railway founded the Mino-Arima Electric Railway Company, predecessor of the Hankyū Electric Railway and prototype of the private-rail conglomerates of modern Japan. The Mino-Arima was the first Japanese railroad concern to follow an aggressive strategy of purchasing and developing residential land along the route of its line. This management innovation provided the base for the company's diversification into a variety of leisure-related activities. Between 1910 and 1929, it moved successively into the business of operating a zoo, a hot-springs resort, the forerunner of the Takarazuka all-women's revue, a baseball park, and a station department store.[186]

The other force behind the third railroad boom, the South Manchuria Railway Company, also drew capital from the former owners of nationalized railways, although not as much as the enormous scale of this concern might suggest. The South Manchuria Railway was a semiofficial joint-stock venture organized in late 1906 to manage the rail lines and ancillary enterprises that Japan had won in southern Manchuria as a result of its recent victory over Russia. Besides furnishing half the total authorized capital of ¥200,000,000 in the form of these spoils of war, the government guaranteed a return of 6 percent for fifteen years on the shares subscribed by private investors. This guarantee naturally made the railroad firm an attractive target of investment to private capitalists, especially those seeking an alternative to the soon-to-be-nationalized domestic railroads, whose shares had generally been regarded as among the most "secure investment objects."[187] Consequently, the offer of South Manchuria Railway shares in September 1906 gave rise to a frenzied stock mania, with the 99,000 shares offered being oversubscribed by a factor of more than a thousand.[188] At the top of the subscribers' list was Ōkura Kihachirō, a principal stockholder in the Hokkaido Colliery, who put in a bid for all 99,000 shares. Other stockholders of rail companies slated for nationalization among the highest bidders were the Mitsui and Yasuda banks and Mitsubishi, each of which applied for 30,000 shares.[189] Because of the stock boom, however, the shares had to be alloted to over 9,000 subscribers, twice the number of shareholders in the biggest nationalized railroad, the Nippon, so that Ōkura actually ended up receiving only 91 shares in the South Manchuria Railway; Mitsui, Yasuda, and Mitsubishi received only 27 each. These four, together with the head of the emerging Furukawa combine, were in fact the only private stockholders with over 5 shares in the company at the end of 1906. The allocative process, whereby the shares were distributed among all the subscribers in proportion to their bids, was presumably a normal procedure, but the effect of this dispersal of stock ownership was to prevent the zaibatsu from gaining a controlling interest in the firm.[190]

In any event, from its inception until 1912, the South Manchuria Railway raised over 80 percent of its funding through foreign-bond issues, for, with the government guaranteeing payment of principal and interest, the company was able to borrow overseas without mortgaging the railroad and thereby compromising its independence.[191] Private share capital was to the end merely a supplement to foreign loans and the government's original investment. The joint-stock form itself was basically a sop to the Western powers, who were demanding that Manchuria be kept open to private enterprise. In fact, after making an initial payment in 1907 of just ¥2,000,000, one tenth the total par value of their shares, the railroad's stockholders waited until 1912 to pay the second installment totaling ¥10,000,000.[192] In short, the South Manchuria Railway, despite having an authorized capital roughly equivalent to that of the seventeen nationalized railroads combined, had definite limits as an object of investment for the former owners of nationalized railway stock.

Domestic electric railroads possessed slightly more potential for absorbing funds formerly invested in the nationalized railway companies. Such enterprises, which mushroomed after the nationalization, already boasted a total paid-up capital of over thirty-seven million yen in 1906.[193] As Table 24 indicates, however, the biggest opportunities for investment were in such emerging growth sectors as the electric-power and light, iron-and-steel, and chemical industries. The figures in this table suggest that railroads, spinning companies, and banks, which had spearheaded business

TABLE 24 New Projected Capital by Industry,
August 1905–February 1907
(unit: ¥1,000)

Industry	New Projected Capital
Electric Power and Light	709,913
Iron and Steel	121,460
Chemical	82,700
Railway	80,945
Spinning	75,700
Shipping	62,000
Finance	61,730
Food	55,800
Marine Products	32,200
Lumber	13,500
Warehousing	7,600
Other	452,625
Total	1,756,173

Source: *Mitsubishi ginkō shi* (Mitsubishi ginkō shi hensan iinkai, 1954), p. 113.

development in the mid-Meiji years, were beginning to give way to heavy industries centered in electric power as the generator of Japanese economic growth. Railway nationalization contributed to this shift both by depriving investors of the largest, most capital-intensive railroads at home and by making funds available for reinvestment in the new wave of leading economic sectors.

The latter did indeed receive huge transfusions of capital from nationalized railroads. This was particularly true of electric-power companies, which expanded rapidly in both number and scale after the Russo-Japanese War, replacing the nationalized rail concerns as the primary targets of stock investment.[194] Given the conservative behavior of most investors, no doubt many of the former shareholders in the nationalized railroads simply hung on to their purchase bonds. Still, they could readily borrow on the security of those bonds,[195] and the blue-chip stocks of electric and gas companies presented especially attractive investment opportunities. The Tokyo Electric Light Company, for example, offered a return on investment of over 10 percent throughout the years 1905–1909, while the dividend of the Tokyo Gas Company was generally in the 11–14 percent range during the 1900s.[196] The Imperial Household, the epitome of the cautious railway investor, acquired substantial interests in both these firms around the time of the nationalization.[197]

Financial institutions that had invested heavily in the nationalized railroads were particularly active in financing electric and gas companies following the nationalization. Many had increased their ability to do so by snatching up nationalized railway shares at depressed prices during the three-year interval between the promulgation of the Nationalization Law and the granting of the railroad-purchase bonds. In fact, Shibusawa Eiichi later recalled that he had advised the 1st Bank and other institutions to buy up the railway shares while their prices were low, figuring that the latter were bound to rise as the shares came to be exchanged for public bonds.[198] Squeezed by the tight money market, however, many smaller stockholders simply could not afford to wait. The result was that the shares of nationalized railroads became increasingly concentrated in the hands of banks and other investors of means. The number of stockholders declined accordingly, that in the Nippon Railway, for instance, falling from 4,497 in June 1906 to 4,018 in March 1909.[199]

Financial institutions were not the only ones who augmented their railway interests during this period. Wealthy individual investors did so too, as evidenced by the case of the Ōhara family of Kurashiki. The second largest landowner in Okayama prefecture, the Ōhara family had branched out into spinning and banking in mid-Meiji and into railroads soon after, having purchased 700 shares in the San'yō and 100 in the Seoul-Pusan Railway by 1901.[200] After the passage of the Nationalization Law, the Ōhara stepped up their investment in the San'yō Railway. They must have felt strongly about the advantages of owning nationalized railway stock, for they were willing to pay a premium for the additional shares they purchased. In June 1906, the Ōhara bought 500 shares of San'yō stock for 1.7 times the par value; in the panic year of 1907, they acquired another 100 shares for 1.6 times par and in 1909, 267 shares for 1.9 times par. In the end, the Ōhara held 2,301 shares of San'yō stock with a total par value of ¥115,050, for which they received public bonds in the amount of ¥240,600 at par.[201] Since they had actually invested nearly ¥148,000 in San'yō shares, the interest on their purchase bonds was equivalent to about an 8-percent return on their total investment in San'yō stock. This was a fairly substantial drop from the annual dividend of 10 percent that the railway company had paid in 1905 and 1906.[202] Therefore, in aggressively buying up San'yō shares after March 1906, the Ōhara evidently had their sights set on the collateral value of the public bonds they would eventually acquire. Indeed, after obtaining those bonds, the family may well have borrowed against them in order to acquire shares in other enterprises such as the Kurashiki Electric Light Company, in which the Ōhara began to invest in September 1909.[203]

There is no doubt that banks and insurance companies set store by the borrowing power of railroad-purchase bonds, for most of them held on to the bonds granted them in exchange for the nationalized railway shares they had eagerly bought up before and especially after the nationalization. That ordinary commercial banks had invested heavily in the nationalized railroads is made clear by the fact that, during the year 1909, the total value of their holdings of government bonds nearly doubled, from ¥101,668,000 to ¥200,929,000, while that of their stockholdings declined from ¥82,660,000 to ¥36,040,000.[204] Largely accounting for these changes, of course, was the conversion that year of nationalized railway shares to public bonds, the latter having as they did a combined par value roughly twice that of the liquidated shares. The 15th Bank alone received ¥31,578,505's worth of government bonds at par for its holdings of Nippon and Iwagoe stock. The bank actually kept the resulting appreciation of its assets to a minimum by putting a valuation of only ¥21,110,000 on these bonds.[205] By comparison, its railway shares had had an estimated market value of about ¥18,000,000. The bank's earnings from the nationalization, therefore, were not as large as some have maintained; nevertheless, the greater price stability and collateral value of the national bonds proved a tremendous boon to the 15th, enabling it to enlarge steadily its ordinary banking operations. In his interview of April 1906, President Sonoda had revealed that the bank had "no particular plans to sell the [railroad-purchase] bonds . . . We will have the bonds, as we do [now] the railway stocks, form part of the bank's assets."[206] In fact, just as Sonoda had stated, after the 15th finally received its purchase bonds in early 1909, it made no move to unload them, with the result that, between 1908 and 1909, the share of national bonds in the bank's assets rose from 11 to 54 percent while that of corporate stocks fell from 44 to 1 percent.[207] Thus, in Hoshino's words, "the 15th Bank was transformed from a stockholder of the Nippon Railway into an owner of public bonds."[208] The next two biggest recipients of railroad-purchase bonds among banks were the Mitsui and Sumitomo. The Mitsui Bank held some ¥8,000,000 in blue-chip nationalized railway shares in January 1909, and Sumitomo, more than ¥2,000,000 in June 1909.[209] The bonds they received in exchange for those shares, with a total par value well over twice the combined paid-up value of the stocks, added a large measure of stability to the management of these banks as well.

The most aggressive buyers of nationalized railway shares were not banks, however, but insurance firms. The prime example was the Tokio Marine Insurance Company, whose railroad stockholdings in 1905 consisted of 5,000 shares in the Kyushu and 2,800 in the San'yō. By 1907, the firm had increased its stake in those two railroads to 13,224 and 7,296 shares, respectively, and had acquired new interests of 6,233 shares in the Nippon and 784 in the Kōbu. It also held 7,700 shares of Kyushu Railway stock as loan collateral and ¥100,000's worth of bonds in both the Hokuetsu and Sōbu railroads.[210] The other leading railroad stockholders among insurance companies—Meiji Life, Meiji Fire, and Nihon Life—had invested much more heavily in private railroads prior to the nationalization than had Tokio Marine, but they had been steadily enlarging their railway interests during the early 1900s and continued to do so after the passage of the Nationalization Law. Nihon Life began purchasing railroad stocks in 1897, when its articles of incorporation were amended so as to permit investment by the company in corporate shares as well as in bank deposits and bonds. By 1902, it had bought up over 9,000 shares in railroads that would eventually be nationalized and, within three years, had raised that figure to almost 14,000. In 1908, corporate stocks, the vast majority of them nationalized railway shares, represented one fourth of the firm's total assets; however, as a result of the granting of purchase bonds the following year, stocks' share of total assets plummeted to 4 percent, while that of public bonds shot up proportionately.[211] Meiji Life, the largest railway investor among insurance companies, recorded a similar expansion of its railroad stockholdings following the Sino-Japanese War. After 1902, by which time the company had acquired over 18,000 railway shares, corporate stocks generally accounted for two fifths of the firm's assets. By 1905, the company had augmented the number of railway shares it held to nearly 31,000. This situation changed dramatically in 1909, when the issue of railroad-purchase bonds caused a sharp drop in the ratio of stock holdings to total assets from 0.39 to 0.05 and a corresponding rise in the ratio of public bonds.[212]

For the most part, the insurance companies retained their railroad-purchase bonds and, instead of reinvesting in other corporate stocks, used the bonds as the basis for expanded lending to business enterprises. The chief beneficiaries of the liberalized lending policies of insurance firms were electric-railway, gas, and, above all, electric-power companies. Tokio Marine, whose loans climbed from 5 percent of assets in 1908 to 39 percent in 1913, lent primarily to shipping companies,[213] but other insurance firms, including both Nihon and Meiji Life, clearly hit upon electric-power companies as objects of investment that would largely replace the nationalized railroads. In the case of Nihon Life, long-term loans to electric-power and electric-railway concerns increased rapidly following the nationalization, and in 1913, loans accounted for nearly three fifths of the company's total assets.[214] Meiji Life sharply raised its lending rate as well from around 20 percent of assets in 1910 to over 50 percent in 1914; in its case, too, most of the loans went to "corporate enterprises such as electric-power and railway companies."[215] In 1915, the firm also began to invest heavily in corporate bonds, the issue of which increased markedly with the expansion of various industries, "especially the electric-power industry, which required huge fixed assets."[216] Meanwhile, the insurance companies continued to make little, if any, investment in corporate shares, although, when they did, they usually chose the "sound stocks" of electric and gas companies.[217] It was mainly through loans and bond purchases, made possible in large part by the railway nationalization, that insurance firms promoted the rapid postwar growth of the electric-power industry.[218]

Another emerging sector that benefited directly from the nationalization was the iron-and-steel industry. The Nippon Steelworks, founded in 1907 by the former owners of the Hokkaido Colliery and Railway, presents the most striking case in this field. The Hokkaido Colliery was the only former railway company that remained in existence, albeit in substantially altered form, following the nationalization. In line with the government's expanded definition of its role in the economy, state authorities had originally intended to buy out the company's coal mines as well as its rail network. Under the nationalization act, however, the government had no power to expropriate the firm's coal-mining division, since the latter was not, strictly speaking, a subsidiary of the railroad. State officials, therefore, had to resort to persuasion. The head of the Railway Bureau, for example, urged the firm to agree to the sale of its coal-mining business, explaining that for some time the government had wanted to possess its own coal mines so that it could be at least partly self-sufficient in fuel.[219] At the time, the net assets of the company's colliery and railroad divisions were roughly equal. The returns of the colliery division, although less stable, were generally higher than those of its railroad counterpart. Yet, despite the greater profitability of the firm's coal-mining operations, it appeared that the company would get no more for them than it would for its railway lines. Furthermore, Managing Director Inoue Kakugorō had been planning to establish an iron and steelworks since the early 1890s and had purchased iron-ore fields in anticipation of that eventuality.[220] Inoue saw the railway nationalization as a golden opportunity to realize his dream by having the Hokkaido Colliery use its compensation to embark on iron-and-steel manufacturing in conjunction with its coal-mining business. In the end, after determining that profits from the colliery division were likely to increase, the firm decided to sell only its railway interests to the government. Accordingly, the Diet struck the company's coal-mining division from the list of enterprises slated for nationalization by the cabinet.[221]

After giving up its railroads in October 1906, the firm renamed itself the Hokkaido Colliery and Steamship Company. In December, the stockholders unanimously approved Inoue's proposal that the company initiate an iron foundry and a steelworks. In making this proposal, Inoue received strong backing within the company from Amenomiya Keijirō, who was then in the process of setting up his own ironworks, and outside of it from navy officials, who were anxious to foster the domestic production of steel for their naval expansion program. The latter introduced Inoue to the Tokyo representative of Armstrong, the British munitions firm, and in July 1907, Inoue and officials of Armstrong and Vickers, which had joined the negotiations in the meantime, signed a contract to establish a joint steelworks venture in Muroran, Hokkaido.[222] The result was the Nippon Steelworks, founded in November 1907 with a total capital of ¥10,000,000, half of it provided by the Hokkaido Colliery and half by the two British companies. The Hokkaido Colliery applied to its share part of the proceeds from the liquidation of its railroad-purchase bonds. The money thus raised came to ¥10,705,641. Of this sum, the company had by mid-1909 invested ¥5,625,000 in the Nippon Steelworks and another ¥630,000 in a separate ironworks established in 1908.[223] The Nippon Steelworks successfully imported the latest steel-making technology, thanks to its tie-up with the British munitions makers and direct assistance from the Japanese navy. As the prototype of the large-scale private munitions manufacturer, it had a major impact on the development of the steel industry in Japan. The nationalization settlement played no small part in bringing about its establishment by supplying fully half the initial investment in the enterprise. In addition, although navy orders accounted for the vast majority of the company's business in its early years, the new Imperial Railway Department, saddled as it was with the rapidly deteriorating equipment of the nationalized railroads, began increasingly to place orders for rolling-stock parts and the like.[224] In short, the railway nationalization contributed in several significant ways to the beginnings of heavy industrialization in Japan.

In the case of the Hokkaido Colliery and Nippon Steelworks, one can tell with exceptional precision how the former stockholders of a nationalized rail concern invested at least part of their income from the sale of the railroad. In most instances, however, such documentation is simply lacking. Nonetheless, one can probably attribute in large measure to the compensation granted the ex-owners of nationalized railway stock any increase in investment activity on their part following the nationalization. Such an inference can be made, for example, in the case of Mitsubishi. Despite its opposition to the railway nationalization, Mitsubishi profited immensely from the state purchase of private railroads, and, as William Wray notes, the compensation Mitsubishi received for its railway interests "was a major stimulus to its diversification into other industries."[225] Based on its holdings of nationalized railway stock in 1905, Mitsubishi would have gotten railroad-purchase bonds with a total par value on the order of ¥15,000,000. These bonds would have commanded a market price of about ¥12,000,000, compared to the roughly ¥7,000,000 that the combine had actually sunk in the railroads. Thus, Mitsubishi's net gain from the liquidation of its purchase bonds would have come to around ¥5,000,000, a considerable sum indeed.[226] Anticipating the vast resources it would have at its disposal following the purchase settlement, Mitsubishi branched out into a number of new fields after the promulgation of the Nationalization Law. Iwasaki Hisaya, for instance, invested in the Kirin Beer Company in 1907 and in the Nippon Nitrogenous Fertilizer and Nippon Celluloid companies in 1908. Meanwhile, in 1907, Yanosuke founded the Asahi Glass Company, capitalized at ¥1,000,000; the Iwasaki and Mitsubishi executives held five sixths of its shares. Mitsubishi also enlarged its existing operations around this time, increasing the authorized capital stock of the Tokyo Warehousing Company, for example, from ¥300,000 in 1905 to ¥2,000,000 in 1907. Reflecting this heightened investment activity, the Mitsubishi holding company raised its capital as well from ¥5,000,000 to ¥15,000,000 in 1907. Among established Mitsubishi enterprises, the largest recipients of increased investment following the nationalization were shipbuilding and especially mining, the latter representing the fastest-growing asset category in the decade prior to World War I.[227]

The nationalization likewise provided the occasion for a significant expansion of Mitsubishi's colonial interests. In Korea, the zaibatsu began purchasing tenant farm land in 1907 and exploiting the Kyŏmip'o iron-ore district in 1911.[228] It also established a bamboo plantation in Taiwan in 1908. This was done in conjunction with the Mitsubishi Paper Company, which planned to manufacture pulp using bamboo. In 1911, Mitsubishi set up a pulp factory at the site of the plantation, but the factory actually remained in operation for only two years.[229] Although the nature and scale of these initiatives abroad may not have been particularly striking, they nevertheless present a marked contrast to Mitsubishi's overseas activities prior to the nationalization, typified as the latter were by the Iwasaki's relatively limited participation in the Seoul-Pusan Railway.[230]

Mitsubishi was not the only former railway owner to show a more positive attitude towards colonial investment following the nationalization. Ex-railroad capitalists of all stripes began pouring money into sugar-manufacturing companies in Taiwan in particular from around this time. One such firm was the Taiwan Sugar Company. Formed in 1900 with Mitsui Bussan and the Imperial Household as its top shareholders, this concern had seen its dividend rise steadily from 5 percent in 1901–1902 to 10 percent in 1904–1905.[231] The company carried out its first capital-stock increase in

1906, raising the number of its shares from 20,000 to 100,000. In 1907, Hara Rokurō, also a major stockholder in the firm, helped to negotiate its acquisition of another sugar manufacturer, thereby doubling its capital stock.[232] The company bought out yet another rival in 1909 and increased its authorized capital stock a second time in 1910, by which time the number of its shares had climbed to 480,000. With its excellent business record, the firm naturally "became an object of investment by insurance companies, banks, trust companies, and the like."[233] Former railway owners also numbered among the promoters of the Meiji Sugar Company, founded in 1907, which, by 1912, had raised its paid-up capital to ¥7,500,000 and its dividend rate to 12 percent.[234] No doubt, the willingness of private investors to pull out of railroads and sink their funds into such lucrative enterprises both at home and abroad played a key role in facilitating the railway nationalization.

Conclusion

The nationalizations of 1906–1907 brought to a tentative conclusion the long-running debate over state versus private ownership of principal railway lines. If the Construction Law of 1892 had left the door open for private development of nonlocal lines, the nationalization act made it clear that, henceforth, private railroads would be restricted to the field of local transport. On the other hand, the 1906 law was ambiguous as to what constituted "the provision of transportation to one locality," the criterion for exclusion from state purchase. Subsequent administrations were free to interpret this provision as they wished, the result being that, from 1917 to 1945, the government bought out nearly seventy additional railway companies, most of them operating lines of a decidedly local character.[1] The Railway Council in fact paved the way for the state purchase of private railroads licensed after 1906. In approving the construction applications of two companies in the Kantō area in late 1907, the council laid down the following policy:

> Since the Nationalization Law has been promulgated, we are to put trunk lines under government management and allow private operation of local railroads ... We regard the [lines in question] as having the objective strictly of servicing the localities along their routes; accordingly, we will grant them licenses as lines of local transportation. However, because this area has the prospect of becoming quite urbanized in the future, although we do not consider it necessary at present, it may some day be extremely useful from the standpoint of national transportation to have lines of this sort, too, operated as part of the trunk-line network ... Therefore, we will issue them licenses on the condition that, in the future, the government may purchase them under the provisions of the present Nationalization Law.[2]

As the council thus intimated, the year 1907 would by no means see the last of railway nationalization.

Nevertheless, the first set of nationalizations was by far the most momentous. As a result of it, the state's share of the total length of railway line open leaped from about 30 percent in 1905 to over 90 percent in 1907.[3] At one stroke, the state railways ingested what amounted to nearly twice themselves in terms not only of open track but also of rolling stock and operating revenue. "In other words," as one writer graphically puts it, "it was as though a one-meter snake had swallowed a two-meter snake, and it was only natural that this would give rise to indigestion and diarrhea."[4] The government, however, sought to minimize the ill effects of the nationalization by moving quickly to regulate its suddenly bloated system. The first and perhaps simplest task was to bring about a unification of rates. As early as October 1906, the authorities began offering uniform rebates for long-distance freight. Then, in November of the following year, they established a single passenger-fare schedule for the entire state network and, in October 1912, did the same for freight rates.[5] The government also began to tackle the more difficult job of standardizing the equipment on the various lines it had taken over. The magnitude of this assignment is suggested by the fact that, at the end of 1907, the private railroads employed at least twenty-four varieties of rails.[6] State officials worked steadily to create order out of this chaos, allocating substantial sums of money in order to finance the necessary equipment purchases and improvements.

In so doing, government authorities by and large made good on their promises to lower rates and to rationalize the rail-transport system. Rate standardization was accompanied by a substantial reduction in freight charges, which dropped on average by 21 percent per ton-mile between 1905 and 1913. Also, during that period, the state railways steadily increased the speed and frequency of through-trains.[7] At the same time, they recorded a significant decline in overhead, the ratio of administrative to total operating expenses falling from nearly 9 percent in 1905 to below 3 percent in 1908.[8]

In improving its efficiency and service, the government system was aided in no small measure by the infusion of private managerial talent from the nationalized railroads. Out of the 48,409 employees transferred from the latter to the state railways, 340 were in a category just below the top management. A number of these became prominent officials in the new Imperial Railway Department; for example, a manager of the Kyushu Railway took charge of the Kyushu branch office and two San'yō executives headed the department's transportation and engineering divisions, respectively.[9] Engineers carried over from the nationalized companies also made their mark in the government railways, an ex-Kansai Railway engineer earning the sobriquet "the father of rolling stock" for his contributions in that area and a former San'yō man designing the superexpress Tsubame train in 1930.[10] Yet, the highest posts in the railway administration continued to be held by officials of government stock, causing many an ambitious ex-officer of the nationalized railroads to seek opportunity elsewhere, especially in the booming field of colonial railroads.[11] Those who stayed, however, accounted in large part for the vitality of the national railway system in the early decades of this century.

With help from innovative ex-officers of the purchased railroads, the government was able to deliver on much of its program for the nationalized system. That program had looked splendid on paper. The state would borrow primarily overseas to buy out and renovate the private railroads, while the compensation granted the former owners would provide venture capital for a variety of other enterprises. Meanwhile, the upgraded and unified rail network would promote industrial growth and exports, which, in turn, would increase the national tax base, the influx of foreign currency, and the income of the state railways. All these would enable the government to liquidate the railway debt in a relatively short period of time. With the railroad loans repaid, the authorities could then lower rates, upgrade the system, and foster industrial expansion all the more.

Judging from the marked improvement in rail service and the tremendous growth of the Japanese economy after the 1900s, one would have to say that the government succeeded admirably in the industrial-stimulation part of its program. That success came at a heavy price, however, as the authorities failed miserably in the other part of their plan, namely, to clear the railway debt within a few decades. The main reason for this failure was the shortsightedness of government planners, who seriously underestimated the cost of upgrading the purchased railroads. The nationalization imposed on the state railways the huge burden of financing not only the purchase itself, but also the renovation work inherited from the delinquent companies. As it turned out, the profits of the railroads were barely sufficient to pay interest on the purchase bonds. In order to carry out the massive improvements required, therefore, the government was constantly forced to raise additional loans. By 1912, the amount of funds committed to renovation work, much of it representing the legacy of the nationalized railroads, had snowballed to over four hundred fifty million yen.[12]

State officials also failed to anticipate fully the cost of expanding the system. This problem was only compounded by the intrusion of the Seiyūkai, whose zeal for satisfying local demands for state-railway building led to a sharp increase in construction expenditures. By 1912, mainly owing to Hara's positive spending policy, the amount of money set aside for the extension of state railways had risen to more than two hundred fifty million yen.[13] In the long run, the resulting proliferation of nonpaying local lines severely undercut the government's program, proving an enormous drain on the state system. This trend represented a major reason for the financial crisis in which the Japanese National Railways found itself by the late 1970s. At that time, such lines accounted for more than a quarter of the corporation's annual deficit of over eight hundred billion yen. The authorities raised the possibility then of transferring the majority of these local lines to private railway or bus companies.[14] By 1985, privatization of the entire public-rail network had emerged as the official objective, becoming the centerpiece of Prime Minister Nakasone Yasuhiro's administrative-reform program aimed at reducing government spending. With the breakup of the national railways into several private companies on April 1, 1987, state railroad policy had come full circle from the early Meiji efforts to promote private railway enterprise. In light of these recent developments, the following prediction by the *Jiji shinpō* at the time of the nationalization takes on an uncannily prophetic note:

> It seems to us that after all the railways have been put into proper repair and the new gigantic system has been duly organized the Government will only just manage to pay interest on their loans. As for their reducing the rates all over the country and still being able to gradually redeem the loans by means of surplus profit, it is the wildest of chimeras. As a financial scheme the proposed measure will not bear examination. If it is carried out it will land us in untold difficulties. The railways instead of becoming a valuable source of revenue may well become a perfect white

elephant which the Government may be glad to put up to auction in years to come.[15]

In addition to the mixed legacy of the railway nationalization, two other conclusions stand out in this study. The first speaks more to scholarship in Japan. Harada Katsumasa, the doyen of Japanese railroad historians, exemplifies the standard Japanese view of Meiji railroad policy when he writes, "The [Meiji] government, while holding state construction and state management as its fundamental policy, had to approve private railroads . . . But [the growth of private lines] naturally went against the government's policy of national ownership."[16] In contrast to this interpretation, I would argue that the Meiji leadership had a much more favorable attitude towards private railway enterprise. From the beginning, state authorities, far from seeing private initiative in this field as a necessary evil, were generally eager to promote private railroads. The government extended various forms of assistance, ranging from subsidies and profit guarantees to technology and personnel transfers, to ensure the successful launching of private rail companies and later provided crucial indirect support through the expanded central-bank discount program. State involvement in the private railway sector was indeed extensive, but it was largely market-conforming, with the emphasis mainly on encouragement rather than control of private firms. To be sure, all railroad concerns faced strict government supervision in the selection of lines, and subsidized companies were required, for the duration of their subvention, to furnish detailed reports to the authorities and to obtain state approval of management changes. Yet, as the lines were completed and the terms of the subsidies expired, the government came to treat the railroads, for the most part, like other joint-stock ventures, without trying to regulate excessively their internal management. All these points suggest that Meiji leaders regarded private railway companies as more than temporary phenomena destined from the start for eventual nationalization and that state railroad policy and the attitudes that shaped it were more liberal than previously maintained.

Certainly, there was no "road to nationalization," no consistent, underlying impulse towards public ownership and control. Instead, government policy throughout the first three decades of the Meiji era remained fluid and ambiguous. In fact, one can say that the authorities had no policy to speak of until late in the period when a consensus for nationalization was finally achieved. The primary reason for the lack of a coherent policy prior to that time is that a number of groups had an input into state railroad plans. By no means was railway decision making a monopoly of the government bureaucracy. Indeed, this study has highlighted the critical importance of the Diet, which exerted considerable influence on railroad planning through its legislative power. Even within the state bureaucracy, finance and army authorities were often at odds with their communications counterparts over the proper role of the government in the railway field. A coalescence of official views did not occur until after the turn of the century. In the meantime, the policies and programs adopted along the way were largely based on expedience, on pragmatic compromises among rival groups, rather than on any hard-and-fast principle.

The picture of policy formation that emerges for the Meiji railroad industry displays pronounced similarities with that of industrial policy making in Japan since World War II. A comparison of the patterns for Meiji railroads and postwar telecommunications offers a vivid illustration of the parallels. In each case, during the initial decades of the period, bureaucrats had virtually complete control over the policy-making process in the context of a single-minded national pursuit of domestic development. Politicians then began to play an increasingly larger role against a common background of interministerial clashes, economic crises, and mounting foreign pressures and commitments, including capital liberalization. On the latter point, MPT officials in 1982 clearly echoed the arguments of their turn-of-the-century forebears when they fought with MITI bureaucrats for control over telecommunications business by raising the specter of an "invasion of foreign capital," specifically an American takeover of the industry.[17] The actual mechanism by which politicians intervened in the decision-making system was similar in the two cases. As railroad experts in the Meiji Diet with extensive ties to bureaucrats and interest groups, Satō Noriharu and to some extent Den Kenjirō appear as forerunners of today's *zoku*, veteran Diet politicians who take part in the central decision-making process in certain areas where they have developed substantial policy expertise and personal bureaucratic connections.[18] Just as the Communications Ministry had Den as its party ally in the early 1900s, so too did MPT have its postal-*zoku* and ex-bureaucratic supporters in the Diet during the 1980s.

Close party-bureaucratic linkages thus reflected Japanese political practices in the latter half of Meiji as well as in recent decades. Moreover, in both eras, party politicians performed the important function of mediating interministerial conflict on particular issues by enacting "omnibus pork barrel bill[s] that [gave] something to everybody."[19]

The second major conclusion of this work speaks more to American scholarship on Japan. This study suggests the need for substantial revision of current views on the role of the state as well as of banks in Meiji economic development. The recent trend, led by Kozo Yamamura and others, has been to minimize the contribution of both and, by implication, to deny the applicability of the Gerschenkronian late-development model to Japan. The Meiji government, it is asserted, confined itself mainly to providing a favorable institutional environment for private enterprise. After the first decade of the Meiji period, the state directly intervened only in military-related fields. Similarly, banks, it is claimed, played only a small part in the financing, and therefore management, of Meiji industry. Thus, surprisingly, the pattern of industrialization in Meiji Japan appears to have approximated that in Britain much more than those in follower countries like Germany and Russia during the nineteenth century. I would argue that these generalizations stem from an overemphasis on industries such as cotton-spinning, which, given its relatively low capital needs and small scale of operation, did not require the participation of banks or the state. Yet hardly any attention has been paid to the important field of railroads. In the latter, one finds fairly extensive involvement by the government and commercial banks alike. Besides direct action through its own railways, the state gave support both directly and indirectly to private firms and also intervened in their managements for the duration of subsidies. Meanwhile, although, as Yamamura maintains, the contribution of banks to industrial financing in the aggregate may have been relatively small during the Meiji period,[20] much of the funding they did provide went to the strategic sector of private railroads. Banks performed a vital indirect role in the supply of railway share capital through large-scale lending on the security of shares, and by the turn of the century, such institutions had emerged as prominent railroad stockholders in their own right. As a result, banks accounted for a substantial proportion of the total capital of railway companies and, by the same token, played an increasingly significant part in their administration—not unlike the case of investment banking in continental Europe. In short, the experience of Meiji railroads indicates that Gerschenkron's thesis concerning the late-comer's need for "special institutional devices"[21] to substitute for individual private enterprise still has relevance for the Japanese case.

This statement, however, does not mean that either German-style investment banking or Russian-style state intervention dominated the railroad industry in Meiji Japan. In fact, the Meiji experience represented a hybrid of British and continental patterns of railroad development. There was heavy bank involvement in the financing of Meiji railroads, but until late in the period, such involvement was primarily indirect, taking the form of loans to individual railway stockholders on the collateral of their shares. Hence, like their British counterparts, Meiji railway companies depended largely on ordinary share capital supplied by individual investors. Further, the magnitude of government aid to private railroads, although considerable in Meiji Japan, was far less there than in continental European countries or, for that matter, in the United States.[22] On the whole, the Meiji regime followed a quasi-laissez-faire strategy in the railway field as in most other industrial sectors.

Yet, with the nationalization of 1906–1907, Japanese railroads seemed to move decisively in a statist direction very much along Prussian lines. The government buyout resulted in the near-complete displacement of private enterprise from the field of standard railroads. It involved an uncommon degree of state leadership as well as coercion of private economic interests, as demonstrated by the initiation of the program by the communications bureaucracy and the opposition of Mitsubishi and other railroad investors. The nationalization thus appears to lend firm support to the notion of the Meiji regime as a "strong state" flexing its bureaucratic muscle to take control of a particular industry.

On closer inspection, however, it seems that, in this case, the Japanese government actually fell in between the strong, smart state of Chalmers Johnson's "developmental" model and the constrained, not-so-smart one of Richard Samuels' "reciprocal consent" model.[23] On the one hand, state bureaucrats took charge in proposing the railway purchase and showed considerable prescience in their plan for using the national rail network as an instrument of economic development. On the other hand, inasmuch as the nationalization was a legislative rather than administrative action, the

Diet with its control over legislation and its representation of railroad users and investors placed important constraints on the power of the government bureaucracy. In order to secure passage of the Nationalization Bill, communications officials had to modify their proposal, essentially dropping the goal of having the railroads serve as moneymakers for the national treasury, with serious long-term implications for the financial health of the state railway system. In addition, the private railroads themselves had close connections with the government: in particular, the Imperial Household Ministry was a major stockholder in several companies, and a number of Diet members and ex-bureaucrats were owners or managers of railroad concerns. The upshot of this interpenetration of government and business was that the bureaucracy was constrained as well to negotiate with the rail companies over the terms of their acquisition. In the final analysis, bureaucratic prescience on the issue of industrial promotion must be balanced against the decided lack of foresight on the question of railway finance, as the huge debt incurred by the state in purchasing and upgrading the railroads foreshadowed the financial difficulties that would plague the national railway system in years to come.

One needs to qualify the extent to which the railway nationalization represented not only a case of bureaucratic dominance and autonomy, but also an aberration from the generally market-conforming behavior of the Meiji regime. Certainly, the government effectively eliminated private enterprise from this field, but the heavy indebtedness and low profitability of the smaller railway companies and the serious neglect or deferment of renovations by almost all the firms suggest that stockholders as a whole may have been only too willing to shift the burdens of ownership onto the state. As Samuels notes, private investors in Japan have frequently sought to socialize risk or to transfer costs to the government. They did so in this case by supporting or acquiescing in the nationalization of transport infrastructure. But, unlike the example of the energy industries that Samuels examines, in this instance, private interests failed to "separate state aid from state control."[24] Willingly or not, they had little choice, in the face of a broad consensus for nationalization within the government, but to relinquish control over this industry and move on to other fields.

Yet, despite having a number of statist goals reflecting the agendas of the communications, military, and finance bureaucracies, the government basically had the interests of the private sector at heart. State officials showed this concern by their readiness to offer generous compensation to the owners of the more profitable railway companies and to negotiate the terms of the settlement so as to make it even more rewarding to them. The authorities were also aware that, by nationalizing the capital-intensive railroads and using them as collateral to raise low-interest foreign loans, they would not only ease the domestic money market but also free up private capital for investment in other, faster-growing industries.

This redirecting of private investment exemplified a more general process by which the industrial structure of modern Japan has undergone rapid and progressive transformation. During the Meiji period, the experience of the railroad industry closely paralleled that of shipping: In each case, the government initially attracted private capital to an emergent growth industry by offering subsidies and other forms of assistance; once the industry was well-established, however, the state adopted policies that, wittingly or not, prompted or compelled the owners of that capital to reinvest it in new sunrise industries such as shipbuilding, steel, and electric power.[25] Since World War II, this kind of government intervention has become much more intentional, with the state targeting successive waves of industries for special promotion or phaseout depending on whether they represent "the growing ducklings" or "the lame old ducks."[26] One can also find suggestive parallels at the enterprise level in the case of businesses that abandoned or downsized their original activities to pursue a broader strategy of diversification. Prominent examples of this pattern include the mid-Meiji conversion of Mitsubishi from shipping firm into mining-based combine, the interwar transformation of Nitchitsu from fertilizer maker into diversified chemical company,[27] and the postwar expansion of Kanebō from textiles into cosmetics, pharmaceuticals, and a wide range of other consumer goods.[28]

To say that the Meiji government nationalized the railroads partly to engineer the transfer of private capital into new growth industries is not to say that railroads constituted a mature, let alone declining, industry at the time. Indeed, we noted earlier that, by the mid-1900s, the Japanese railway system had barely begun to experience the problems of relative maturity that had already been afflicting the more developed rail networks of the West for decades. In terms of Japan's capital supply, though, perhaps its system *had* reached a certain maturity by that time. For, in an aggregate sense, the nation faced a serious shortage of funding, as evidenced by the increasingly severe financial crises from 1890 onward. It was this overall capital scarcity that provoked growing business demands for the importation of foreign capital, often linked to calls for the state purchase of private railroad lines. At least in part, then, government officials were responding to private initiative in advocating railway nationalization as a means to borrowing capital from abroad and, at the same time, releasing private funds currently tied up in railroads. Following the nationalization, the authorities proceeded to carry through on their promise to aid other industrial sectors by lowering rates and improving service on the newly unified rail network. From a macroeconomic standpoint, therefore, the railway buyout can be seen essentially as a market-conforming measure, with the state supplying an efficient transportation infrastructure to foster the growth of private business and industry as a whole. In that sense, although the government did far more than just provide a favorable climate for private investment in railroads, state intervention in this field ultimately had the effect of promoting the expansion and diversification of private enterprise. The railway purchase of 1906–1907 thus represented not so much a case of government intrusion leading to the displacement of private initiative as it did of public support resulting in the release of private capital for productive employment in other sectors of the economy. This, then, was the real legacy of railway nationalization for Japanese business.

List of Abbreviations Used in the Notes
Notes
List of Works Cited
Index

List of Abbreviations Used in the Notes

NKTH   *Nihon kokuyū tetsudō hyaku nen shi*
NTS   *Nihon tetsudō shi*
SEDS   *Shibusawa Eiichi denki shiryō*
TKN   *Tetsudō-kyoku nenpō*

Notes

INTRODUCTION

1. Jeffrey Richards and John M. MacKenzie, *The Railway Station: A Social History* (Oxford: Oxford University Press, 1986), p. 2.
2. Francis L. Hawks, comp., *Narrative of the Expedition of an American Squadron to the China Seas and Japan*, vol. 1, Sidney Wallach, ed. (London: MacDonald, 1952), p. 171; William Heine, *With Perry to Japan*, Frederic Trautmann, tr. (Honolulu: University of Hawaii Press, 1990), p. 93.
3. Heine, p. 126.
4. Hawks, comp., p. 194.
5. Ibid., p. 171.
6. Cited in *Nihon kokuyū tetsudō hyaku nen shi: tsū shi* (Nihon kokuyū tetsudō, 1974), p. 8.
7. Paul H. Noguchi, *Delayed Departures, Overdue Arrivals: Industrial Familialism and the Japanese National Railways* (Honolulu: University of Hawaii Press, 1990), pp. 30–31; "All aboard the gravy train," *The Economist*, June 16, 1990, p. 38. The latest generation of Tokaido Shinkansen, called "Nozomi," made its debut in 1992 and has a top speed of 167.4 mph: "New 'bullet' out to regain rail speed record," *Japan Access*, May 11, 1992, p. 6.
8. *Tetsudō ichibetsu* (Tetsudō-shō, 1921), pp. 27–30.
9. Noguchi, p. 33.
10. Thomas C. Smith, "Preface to the Second Printing," in his *Political Change and Industrial Development in Japan: Government Enterprise, 1868–1880* (Stanford: Stanford University Press, 1955), p. v.
11. On state promotion of shipping in the Meiji period, see William D. Wray, *Mitsubishi and the N.Y.K., 1870–1914: Business Strategy in the Japanese Shipping Industry* (Cambridge: Council on East Asian Studies, Harvard University, 1984).
12. The one exception is Toshiharu Watarai, *Nationalization of Railways in*

Japan (New York: Columbia University Press, 1915). Among the available works on particular aspects of Meiji railroad development are Eiichi Aoki, *Railway Construction as Viewed from Local Society* (Tokyo: United Nations University, 1980); Katsumasa Harada, "Technological Independence and Progress of Standardization in the Japanese Railways," *Developing Economies*, vol. 18, no. 3, pp. 313–332 (September 1980); Masaho Noda, "Corporate Finance of Railroad Companies in Meiji Japan," in Keiichiro Nakagawa, ed., *Marketing and Finance in the Course of Industrialization* (Tokyo: University of Tokyo Press, 1978), pp. 87–101; Yoshinobu Oikawa, "Market Structure and the Construction of Rural Railways during the Formative Period of Industrial Capitalism in Japan," *The Journal of Transport History*, 3rd ser., vol. 5, no. 2, pp. 34–46 (September 1984); Thomas Richard Schalow, "Transforming Railroads into Steamships: Banking with the Matsukata Family at the 15th Bank," *Hitotsubashi Journal of Commerce and Management*, vol. 22, no. 1, pp. 55–67 (December 1987); and Tokihiko Tanaka, "Meiji Government and the Introduction of Railways," *Contemporary Japan*, vol. 28, no. 3, pp. 567–588 (May 1966) and vol. 28, no. 4, pp. 750–788 (May 1967).

13. On the absorption of railway technology, see Harada Katsumasa, *Tetsudō shi kenkyū shiron: kindaika ni okeru gijutsu to shakai* (Nihon keizai hyōronsha, 1989); and his "Technological Independence."
14. Harada Katsumasa and Aoki Eiichi, *Nihon no tetsudō: hyaku nen no ayumi kara* (Sanseidō, 1973), p. 22.
15. See, in particular, Shima Yasuhiko, *Nihon shihonshugi to kokuyū tetsudō* (Nihon hyōronsha, 1950).
16. Nakanishi, however, has refined the argument to place equal emphasis on the economic impulse behind the "Bismarckian nationalization": Nakanishi Ken'ichi, *Nihon shiyū tetsudō shi kenkyū: toshi kōtsū no hatten to sono kōzō*, 2nd ed. (Minerva shobō, 1979), pp. 126–173.
17. *Nihon kokuyū tetsudō hyaku nen shi*, 14 vols. (Nihon kokuyū tetsudō, 1969–1974), hereafter cited as *NKTH*.
18. Outstanding among the business history studies are Hoshino Takao, "Nippon tetsudō kaisha to dai jūgo kokuritsu ginkō (1)-(3)," *Musashi daigaku ronshū*, vol. 17, pp. 77–109 (June 1970), vol. 19, no. 1, pp. 1–22 (August 1971), and vol. 19, nos. 5–6, pp. 117–183 (March 1972); and Sugiyama Kazuo, "Kigyō no zaimu, tōshi katsudō to bunkateki haikei: Meiji ki no tetsudō gyō, men-bōseki gyō o jirei to shite," *Keiei shi gaku*, vol. 10, pp. 54–86 (August 1975).

A. tremendous boon for students of Meiji railroad history has been the recent publication of the following massive collections of railroad-related materials under the editorial direction of Noda Masaho, Harada Katsumasa, and Aoki Eiichi (with Oikawa Yoshinobu for the 2nd ser. of the

Meiji collection): *Meiji ki tetsudō shi shiryō*, 1st ser., 17 vols., 2nd ser., 43 vols. (Nihon keizai hyōronsha, 1980–1989); and *Taishō ki tetsudō shi shiryō*, 1st ser., 24 vols., 2nd ser., 20 vols. (Nihon keizai hyōronsha, 1983–1985).

19. See Smith's *Political Change and Industrial Development*.
20. Alexander Gerschenkron, *Economic Backwardness in Historical Perspective: A Book of Essays* (Cambridge: Belknap Press of Harvard University Press, 1962), pp. 5–30.
21. Barry Supple, "The State and the Industrial Revolution, 1700–1914," in Carlo M. Cipolla, ed., *The Fontana Economic History of Europe*, vol. 3, *The Industrial Revolution* (London: Fontana Books, 1973), pp. 326–327.
22. Carter Goodrich, *Government Promotion of American Canals and Railroads, 1800–1890* (New York: Columbia University Press, 1960).
23. Supple, pp. 328–329.
24. Ibid., p. 329; W. O. Henderson, *The Rise of German Industrial Power, 1834–1914* (London: Temple Smith, 1975), p. 211.
25. These various types of market intervention by the state are discussed in Richard J. Samuels, *The Business of the Japanese State: Energy Markets in Comparative and Historical Perspective* (Ithaca: Cornell University Press, 1987), p. 13ff.
26. Chalmers Johnson, *MITI and the Japanese Miracle: The Growth of Industrial Policy, 1925–1975* (Stanford: Stanford University Press, 1982), p. 88.
27. Kozo Yamamura, *A Study of Samurai Income and Entrepreneurship: Quantitative Analyses of Economic and Social Aspects of the Samurai in Tokugawa and Meiji Japan* (Cambridge: Harvard University Press, 1974), pp. 137–187; and his "Entrepreneurship, Ownership, and Management in Japan," in Peter Mathias and M. M. Postan, eds., *The Cambridge History of Europe*, vol. 7, pt. 2 (Cambridge: Cambridge University Press, 1978), pp. 217–238.

For a more recent critique of state enterprise in the 1870s, see Stephen W. McCallion, "Trial and Error: The Model Filature at Tomioka," in William D. Wray, ed., *Managing Industrial Enterprise: Cases from Japan's Prewar Experience* (Cambridge: Council on East Asian Studies, Harvard University, 1989).
28. Nakanishi, p. 53.
29. See Johnson, *MITI*, especially pp. 19–23.
30. Samuels develops this interpretation in his *The Business of the Japanese State*.
31. Chalmers Johnson, "MITI, MPT, and the Telecom Wars: How Japan Makes Policy for High Technology," in Chalmers Johnson, Laura D. Tyson, and John Zysman, eds., *Politics and Productivity: The Real Story of Why Japan Works* (Cambridge, Mass.: Ballinger Publishing Company, 1989).

32. See especially Bruce Mazlish, ed., *The Railroad and the Space Program: An Exploration in Historical Analogy* (Cambridge: M.I.T. Press, 1965).
33. Johnson, "MITI, MPT, and the Telecom Wars," p. 225.
34. Ezra F. Vogel, *Comeback Case by Case: Rebuilding the Resurgence of American Business* (New York: Simon and Schuster, 1985), p. 162.
35. Fujii Nobuyuki, "Yūsen kisen Mitsubishi kaisha ni okeru denshin riyō: Meiji zenki kaiun gyō no jōhō system," *Keiei shi gaku*, vol. 25, no. 3, p. 41 (October 1990).
36. Fujii Nobuyuki, "Meiji zenki no denshin seisaku," *Nihon rekishi*, no. 479, p. 74 (April 1988).
37. Ibid., pp. 75–84.
38. D. Eleanor Westney, *Imitation and Innovation: The Transfer of Western Organizational Patterns to Meiji Japan* (Cambridge: Harvard University Press, 1987), p. 126.
39. Hirofumi Yamamoto, ed., *Technological Innovation and the Development of Transportation in Japan* (Tokyo: United Nations University Press, 1993), pp. 9–14, 34–37. Mitsui's monopoly lasted from 1873 to 1875. During that time, the company maintained exclusive agencies at Shinbashi, Yokohama, and Kanagawa stations and handled some 70–80 percent of the freight carried on the Shinbashi line. Then, in 1875, the government terminated this privilege by permitting Inland Transport and other companies to compete with Mitsui in collecting and delivering goods for the expanding state railway system: Tanaka Tokihiko, "Tetsudō yusō," in Matsuyoshi Sadao and Andō Yoshio, eds., *Nihon yusō shi* (Nihon hyōronsha, 1971), pp. 218–219.
40. Johnson, "MITI, MPT, and the Telecom Wars," p. 187; Westney, p. 127; Yūsei-shō, ed., *Yūsei hyaku nen no ayumi* (Shōgakkan, 1971), p. 57.

1. The Transformative Power of Meiji Railroads

1. Masaru Inouye, "Japanese Communications: Railroads," in Shigenobu Okuma, ed., *Fifty Years of New Japan*, vol. 1 (London: Smith, Elder, & Co., 1910), p. 446.
2. Nicholas Faith, *The World the Railways Made* (London: Bodley Head, 1990), p. 1.
3. B. R. Mitchell, *European Historical Statistics, 1750–1970*, abridged ed. (New York: Columbia University Press, 1978), pp. 315–318.
4. Thomas W. Cleaver, "Regional Income Differentials in Japanese Economic Growth" (Ph.D. dissertation, Harvard University, 1970), appendix, p. 629; *Tetsudō-kyoku nenpō, 1907,* Teishin-shō tetsudō-kyoku, ed. (Tetsudō-in, 1909), appendix, pp. 1–4, hereafter cited as *TKN, 1907.*
5. For a description of travel on this line prior to completion of the Usui

"abt" railway, see Percival Lowell, *Noto: An Unexplored Corner of Japan* (Boston: Houghton, Mifflin, 1891), especially pp. 17–51.
6. *TKN, 1907*, appendix, pp. 4–13.
7. Daigohō Toshio, "Tetsudō shōka to Ōwada Takeki," in Watanabe Kōhei et al., eds., *Kiteki issei: tetsudō hyaku nen bungaku to zuihitsu senshū* (Jitsugyō no Nihonsha, 1972), pp. 487–488; Komota Nobuo et al., *Nihon ryūkōka shi* (Shakai shisōsha, 1970), p. 29; Dallas Finn, *Meiji Revisited: The Sites of Victorian Japan* (New York: Weatherhill, forthcoming), p. 280 of manuscript. The text of Ōwada's *Railway Song (Chiri kyōiku tetsudō shōka dai isshū)* is reprinted in Daigohō, pp. 482–498.
8. Ibid., pp. 482–483, 489. For examples of local railroad songs, see *Monogatari Tōhoku honsen shi*, Nihon kokuyū tetsudō Sendai chūzai riji-shitsu, ed. (Sendai: Tetsudō kōsaikai Tōhoku shibu, 1971), pp. 143–146; and *Tsuyama-shi shi*, vol. 6, Tsuyama-shi shi hensan iinkai, ed. (Tsuyama: Tsuyama shiyakusho, 1980), pp. 256–257.
9. *TKN, 1907*, appendix, pp. 13–18; Thomas W. Cleaver, "Railways," in *Kodansha Encyclopedia of Japan*, vol. 6 (Tokyo: Kodansha, 1983), p. 278.
10. Daigohō, pp. 491–497.
11. Cleaver, "Railways," p. 278; and his "Regional Income Differentials," p. 643.
12. For a critique of this revisionist view, see Patrick O'Brien, *The New Economic History of the Railways* (New York: St. Martin's Press, 1977).
13. Tominaga Yūji, *Kōtsū ni okeru shihonshugi no hatten: Nihon kōtsū gyō no kindaika katei* (Iwanami shoten, 1953), p. 54. Examples of recycled German and American rails from mid-Meiji, clearly imprinted with maker and date of manufacture, can still be seen bracing the platform roofs of train stations in Tokyo and elsewhere: Harada Katsumasa, *Tetsudō no kataru Nihon no kindai* (Soshiete, 1977), pp. 167–171.
14. Noda Masaho et al., *Nihon no tetsudō: seiritsu to tenkai* (Nihon keizai hyōronsha, 1986), pp. 82–83.
15. Sawa Kazuya, *Nihon no tetsudō: hyaku nen no hanashi* (Tsukiji shokan, 1972), pp. 102–104.
16. Sawai Minoru, "Senzenki Nihon tetsudō sharyō kōgyō no tenkai katei, 1890 nendai–1920 nendai," *Shakai kagaku kenkyū*, vol. 37, no. 3, p. 22 (1985). By the mid-1890s, Japan had already become largely "self-sufficient" in the production of freight and passenger carriages, but until the country acquired a steel-making capability in the early 1900s, the chassis and other metal parts were all imported. The same arrangement, of course, applied to the steel components of the domestic-made locomotives prior to that time.
17. Natsume Sōseki, *Botchan*, Umeji Sasaki, tr. (Rutland, Vt.: Charles E. Tuttle Company, 1968), p. 29.

18. *Nihon kokuyū tetsudō hyaku nen shi: tsū shi*, p. 60; Finn, p. 277.
19. The British engineer, Edmund Morell, was a veteran of railroad construction in the British empire, where the narrow gauge was widely in use; apparently, he convinced his Japanese employers that this gauge was best suited to the special circumstances of Japan, specifically its mountainous terrain and shortage of capital: Sawa, pp. 22–23.
20. *Nihon tetsudō ukeoi gyō shi: Meiji hen* (Tetsudō kensetsu gyō kyōkai, 1967), p. 63.
21. *Kyūshū tetsudō kensetsu no onjin Hermann Rumschöttel* (Moji tetsudō kanrikyoku Rumschöttel kenshōkai, 1960), pp. 1–3; Sorimachi Shōji, *Tetsudō no Nihon shi* (Bunken shuppan, 1982), pp. 278–279.
22. *Kyū-tetsu nijū nen shi* (Kyūshū tetsudō kabushiki kaisha sōmu-ka, 1907), pp. 81–83. Of the remaining engines, nine were made in Britain and four in Switzerland.
23. The felicitous phrase is Dallas Finn's: Finn, p. 275.
24. *Hokkaidō tetsudō hyaku nen shi*, vol. 1 (Sapporo: Nihon kokuyū tetsudō Hokkaidō sō-kyoku, 1976), p. 39; Sawa, pp. 92–94.
25. Finn, p. 275.
26. Harada, *Tetsudō no kataru Nihon no kindai*, pp. 177–183; Harada and Aoki, pp. 114–115.
27. Sawai, pp. 56–61; Harada and Aoki, pp. 114, 122; Harada, *Tetsudō no kataru Nihon no kindai*, pp. 183, 186.
28. *Kōhon Mitsui bussan kabushiki kaisha 100 nen shi*, vol. 1, Nihon keiei shi kenkyūjo, ed. (Mitsui bussan kabushiki kaisha, 1978), p. 250.
29. Sawai, pp. 27–28.
30. Matsumoto Hiroshi, *Mitsui zaibatsu no kenkyū* (Yoshikawa kōbunkan, 1979), pp. 418–419.
31. Sawai, pp. 28, 56; Takamura Naosuke, "Dokusen soshiki no keisei," in Takamura Naosuke, ed., *Nichi-Ro sengo no Nihon keizai* (Hanawa shobō, 1988), pp. 171–172; Harada and Aoki, p. 120; Harada, *Tetsudō no kataru Nihon no kindai*, p. 186. For more on the rolling-stock manufacturers' cartel, formed in 1909, and the "designated factory" system that replaced it in 1912, see the above articles by Takamura and Sawai.
32. With the achievement of tariff autonomy in July 1911, the tariff rate for locomotives jumped from 5 percent to 20 percent and for carriages from 5 percent to 30 percent: Takamura, "Dokusen soshiki no keisei," p. 173.
33. Patrick O'Brien, "Transport and Economic Development in Europe, 1789–1914," in Patrick O'Brien, ed., *Railways and the Economic Development of Western Europe, 1830–1914* (New York: St. Martin's Press, 1983), p. 17.
34. The following figures suggest that it was not until 1911 or 1912 that trains surpassed coastal vessels in the movement of domestic goods:

Transport of Domestic Freight (unit: million tons)

Year	Sea-borne	By Rail
1908	n.a.	25.9
1909	n.a.	26.2
1910	36.6[a]	28.2
1911	34.5[a]	32.8
1912	32.4[a]	36.7
1913	30.3	41.2
1914	28.4	40.9
1915	26.1	42.3
1916	28.3	50.4
1917	30.8	58.9
1918	30.6	64.8
1919	33.1	73.5
1920	32.5	69.8

Source: Kokaze Hidemasa, "Tetsudō kokuyūka to un'yu mō no saihen," in Takamura, ed., p. 61.

[a] estimates derived by extrapolating backwards from the figures for 1913–1915, prior to the wartime boom.

As Kokaze and Ishii Kanji point out, however, such data are misleading, for in terms of ton-miles, coastal shipping undoubtedly continued to outdistance rail transport well beyond the Meiji era, given the relatively short-haul nature of most of the freight carriage by rail: Kokaze, "Tetsudō kokuyūka," p. 61; Ishii Kanji, "Kokunai shijō no keisei to tenkai," in Yamaguchi Kazuo and Ishii Kanji, eds., *Kindai Nihon no shōhin ryūtsū* (Tōkyō daigaku shuppankai, 1986), p. 8.

35. For Japan as a whole, as late as 1912, marine transport alone still accounted for more rice carried than did rail transport, with coastal vessels delivering a total of 7,015 *koku* as opposed to the 6,857 *koku* arriving by train that year: Ishii Kanji, "Kokunai shijō," p. 27.
36. *Monogatari Tōhoku honsen shi*, pp. 157–160.
37. Nobutaka Ike, "The Pattern of Railway Development in Japan," *Far Eastern Quarterly*, vol. 14, p. 229 (February 1955).
38. *TKN, 1907*, appendix, pp. 46–75 passim.
39. Watarai, p. 23.
40. Takafusa Nakamura, *Economic Growth in Prewar Japan*, Robert A. Feldman, tr. (New Haven: Yale University Press, 1983), p. 74. See *Japan Weekly Mail*, July 31, 1886, p. 105, citing an article in the *Jiji shinpō* complaining of the "exorbitant" freight rates charged by the Shinbashi-Yokohama and other lines, with the result that "slower modes of traffic," especially ship-

ping, continued to dominate goods transport. From the late 1890s, railroads faced competition far less from riverine than from coastal shipping, as the emphasis of national riparian policy shifted from support of boat transportation to flood control, and prefectural administrations began to invest more in road improvement than in river works: Oikawa Yoshinobu, *Meiji ki chihō tetsudō shi kenkyū: chihō tetsudō no tenkai to shijō keisei* (Nihon keizai hyōronsha, 1983), p. 238.
41. William W. Lockwood, *The Economic Development of Japan* (Princeton: Princeton University Press, 1954), pp. 107–108.
42. *TKN, 1907*, p. 151.
43. Tanaka, "Tetsudō yusō," p. 233.
44. Sumiya Mikio, *Nihon sekitan sangyō bunseki* (Iwanami shoten, 1968), pp. 244, 247; Shinya Sugiyama, *Japan's Industrialization in the World Economy, 1859–1899* (London: The Athlone Press, 1988), p. 170; Wray, p. 284.
45. Ishii Kanji, "Kokunai shijō," p. 50.
46. Yamaguchi shows that by the mid-1900s, in advance of the national trend, the Japan Sea-side prefectures of Fukui and Ishikawa had already switched to primary reliance on railroads for the export of rice: Yamaguchi Kazuo, "Kindaiteki yusō kikan no hattatsu to shōhin ryūtsū: Hokuriku, Hokuetsu chihō no baai," in Yamaguchi and Ishii, eds., pp. 99, 102.
47. The same appears to have been true of cement, which increasingly traveled by rail over short distances but remained dependent on marine transport for long-haul movement: Imuta Toshimitsu, "Semento gyō ni okeru kokunai shijō no keisei," in Yamaguchi and Ishii, eds., p. 346.

The railway tunnel connecting Kyushu, the top coal-producing island, with Honshū was not completed until 1942. On the other hand, the national railways began ferrying freight cars between Moji and Shimonoseki in 1911 and between Hakodate and Aomori in 1914. With the inauguration of this service and the provision of special rates and rebates for Kyushu rice, trains did overtake ships in the conveyance of rice from Kyushu to the main island, but evidently the cost reductions were not enough to induce a similar shift in the inter-island movement of coal: Kokaze, "Tetsudō kokuyūka," pp. 57, 66, 74.
48. Takafusa Nakamura, *Economic Growth*, p. 62; Sumiya, p. 295; *Honpō tetsudō no shakai oyobi keizai ni oyoboseru eikyo*, vol. 2 (Tetsudō-in, 1916), pp. 780–781.
49. Sumiya, pp. 220–221, 295.
50. *Honpō tetsudō*, vol. 2, pp. 833–835.
51. Sumiya, p. 295. The Miike and Hokkaido coal mines did not benefit as remarkably from railroad development in the 1890s and early 1900s as did their Chikuhō and Jōban counterparts. The Kyushu Railway's main line

reached the Miike region in 1891, but between that year and 1906, Miike's share of total Japanese coal production declined from 18.1 percent to 11.4 percent: ibid., pp. 220–221, 295. In fact, in the 1900s, Miike's owner, Mitsui, sought to reduce the cost of haulage from the mines by developing harbor facilities at nearby Ōmuta and switching from rail to ship transport: Johannes Hirschmeier and Tsunehiko Yui, *The Development of Japanese Business, 1600–1980*, 2nd ed. (London: George Allen & Unwin Ltd., 1981), p. 181. The Hokkaido coal fields, being located in the interior rather than at tidewater, were almost totally dependent on railroad transportation for their development. By 1892, several important mines had been connected by rail to the ports of Otaru and Muroran. Coal production grew steadily in Hokkaido, as the island increased its proportion of Japan's total output from 3.4 percent in 1887 to 7.2 percent in 1890 and then to 11.2 percent in 1906: Sumiya, pp. 220–221, 295. On the other hand, the Hokkaido Colliery and Railway, which monopolized railroad transport in the central coal fields, hindered the expansion of mines other than its own by restricting their access to its rail network, so that full-scale development of the island's coal-mining industry had to await the nationalization of the Hokkaido Colliery lines in 1906, which made rail service equally available to all mines: Sumiya, p. 294.

52. Takamura Naosuke, "Sangyō, bōeki kōzō," in Ōishi Kaichirō, ed., *Nihon sangyō kakumei no kenkyū*, vol. 1 (Tōkyō daigaku shuppankai, 1975), p. 50. By comparison, estimates of the share of coal output delivered to railroads in the United States range from 2 percent for 1859 to 20 percent for 1880, and in England and Wales, from 2 percent to 14 percent for 1865: O'Brien, *The New Economic History*, p. 59.
53. This rather startling but apt simile was suggested to me by Albert Craig.
54. In 1890, for instance, Nagano was the top producer of raw silk among Japanese prefectures, accounting for 21 percent of total national output, followed by Gunma (15 percent), Fukushima (9 percent), and Yamanashi (5 percent). Close behind Yamanashi were Saitaima (5 percent) and Gifu (4 percent), two other landlocked prefectures: Shinya Sugiyama, p. 117.
55. Harada, "Technological Independence," p. 318.
56. E. Sydney Crawcour, "Industrialization and Technological Change, 1885–1920," in John W. Hall et al., gen. eds., *The Cambridge History of Japan*, vol. 6, *The Twentieth Century*, Peter Duus, ed. (Cambridge: Cambridge University Press, 1988), p. 423.
57. In fact, Lockwood writes that raw silk was "Japan's premier export for over 60 years," probably financing "no less than 40 percent of Japan's entire imports of foreign machinery and raw materials" from 1870 to 1930. As he concludes, in one of his more memorable statements: "That the

lowly silkworm should play such a massive role in Japanese industrialization is truly astonishing": Lockwood, p. 94.
58. "Tōkaidō suji tetsudō junransho," 1870, Tetsudō-ryō jimubō, vol. 1, Japan Railway Archives, Tokyo.
59. *Nihon kokuyū tetsudō hyaku nen shi: tsū shi*, pp. 75–76.
60. *Gunma-ken shi: shiryō hen*, vol. 18 (Maebashi: Gunma-ken shi hensan iinkai, 1978), p. 80, cited in Oikawa, *Meiji ki chihō tetsudō shi kenkyū*, p. 237n5.
61. Harada, *Tetsudō no kataru Nihon no kindai*, p. 97; Shinya Sugiyama, p. 117.
62. Shinya Sugiyama, p. 117.
63. Ibid., pp. 117, 122–123.
64. *Honpō tetsudō*, vol. 1, p. 379.
65. Chūō tetsudō kisei sanshi gyō rengōkai, *Tai Chūō tetsudō sanshi gyōsha iken*, December 1892, p. 18, Transportation Museum Archives, Tokyo.
66. *Nihon tetsudō shi*, vol. 2 (Tetsudō-shō, 1921), pp. 140–141, hereafter cited as *NTS*; Kawada Reiko, "Chūō sen no kensetsu to sono keizaiteki haikei," *Kōtsū bunka*, no. 5, pp. 32–33 (1965). The Suwa men proposed to use the money specifically to purchase public bonds through the Japan Industrial Bank, which was then to forward the funds to the national treasury earmarked for extension of the Chūō line.
67. Harada Katsumasa et al., eds., *Tetsudō to bunka* (Nihon keizai hyōronsha, 1986), p. 15.
68. *Nagano kensei shi*, vol. 1 (Nagano: Nagano-ken, 1971), p. 456.
69. "Railways," *Japan Weekly Mail*, May 6, 1905, p. 479.
70. "Chūō tetsudō no Yamanashi-ken ni oyoboshitaru eikyō (2)," *Tōkyō keizai zasshi*, November 28, 1903, p. 1021.
71. Takafusa Nakamura, *Economic Growth*, p. 62; *Honpō tetsudō*, vol. 2, p. 893.
72. *Ina kōhō*, no. 12 (1893), cited in *Nagano kensei shi*, vol. 1, p. 453.
73. Shimo Ina-gun railroad committee members to Zakōji village headman Imamura Zengo, June 14, 1892, in Nagano-ken, ed., *Nagano-ken shi: kindai shiryō hen*, vol. 7, *Kōtsū, tsūshin* (Nagano: Nagano-ken shi kankōkai, 1981), p. 565.
74. Telegram dated May 23, 1894, in Nagano-ken, ed., p. 571.
75. *Nagano kensei shi*, vol. 1, p. 453.
76. Harada and Aoki, p. 49; "Dai ikkai tetsudō kaigi giji sokkiroku," 15th and 20th sessions, December 1892, Tetsudō kaigi giji sokkiroku, Japan Railway Archives, Tokyo.
77. *Nagano kensei shi*, vol. 1, p. 453.
78. Harada and Aoki, p. 49; *Nagano kensei shi*, vol. 1, p. 454.
79. A private electric railroad was finally built through the valley in the Tai-

shō period and linked to the Tokaido line in 1937: *Nihon kokuyū tetsudō hyaku nen shi: tsū shi,* appended map.
80. *Japan Weekly Mail,* June 27, 1891, p. 728; Saburi Kazutsugu, *Nihon no tetsudō* (1891).
81. *NTS,* vol. 1, p. 878.
82. This impulse became all the more pronounced following the Sino-Japanese War of 1894–1895, with the government pressed by the need to finance its ambitious postwar program of armaments expansion and heavy industrialization: Oikawa, *Meiji ki chihō tetsudō shi kenkyū,* pp. 58, 119; and his "Market Structure and the Construction of Rural Railways," p. 45.
83. Uda Tadashi, "Waga kuni tetsudō jigyō keiei shi ni okeru seifu to kigyō: 'tetsudō seiryaku' no tenkai katei," *Keiei shi gaku,* vol. 6, no. 1, pp. 137–138 (September 1971).
84. In 1908, for instance, the rail network hauled about half of all the raw cotton supplied to spinning mills and over half their combined output of cotton yarn: Harada, "Technological Independence," pp. 318–319.
85. Roy E. H. Mellor, *German Railways: A Study in the Historical Geography of Transport* (Aberdeen: University of Aberdeen, 1979), p. 35.
86. Carol Gluck pairs the locomotive with the emperor as the two most powerful symbols of modernity in the Meiji era: Carol Gluck, *Japan's Modern Myths: Ideology in the Late Meiji Period* (Princeton: Princeton University Press, 1985), p. 101.
87. Leo Marx, *The Machine in the Garden: Technology and the Pastoral Ideal in America* (New York: Oxford University Press, 1964), pp. 191–192.
88. Cited in ibid., p. 191.
89. The words in quotations are from Marx's discussion of the cultural symbolism of the railroad in antebellum America, which seems equally applicable to Meiji Japan: ibid., pp. 193, 197. See also his "The Impact of the Railroad on the American Imagination, as a Possible Comparison for the Space Impact," in Mazlish, ed., especially pp. 207–213.
90. For British and American antecedents of the same phenomenon, see Michael Adas, *Machines as the Measure of Men: Science, Technology, and Ideologies of Western Dominance* (Ithaca: Cornell University Press, 1989), pp. 222–223; and Marx, *The Machine,* p. 191.
91. *Tōkyō nichinichi shinbun,* 1872/9/6.
92. Shioda Ryōhei, ed., *Narushima Ryūhoku, Fukube Bushō, Kurimoto Joun shū,* vol. 4 of *Meiji bungaku zenshū* (Chikuma shobō, 1969), pp. 180, 420–421.
93. Takami Sawashige, *Tōkyō kaika hanjō shi* (1874), in Yoshino Sakuzō, ed., *Meiji bunka zenshū,* vol. 19 (Nihon hyōronsha, 1928), p. 264.
94. Watanabe et al., eds., pp. 528–529. A typical railroad "travel account"

(*kikōbun*)—a description by the poet Masaoka Shiki of a ride he took on the recently opened Sōbu Railway in Chiba prefecture—appeared in the journal *Nihon* on December 30, 1894.

95. "Tōkyō han'ei mari uta," *Yūbin hōchi*, December 8, 1874, in *Shinbun shūsei Meiji hennen shi*, vol. 2 (Shinbun shūsei Meiji hennen shi hensankai, 1936), p. 244. For other examples of ditties and counting songs from early Meiji, see Ishii Mitsuru, *Nihon tetsudō sōsetsu shiwa* (Hōsei daigaku shuppan-kyoku, 1952), pp. 364, 367.
96. Ibid., p. 364.
97. Gluck, p. 101. Gluck has the train chugging its way "to the remote and distant parts" and becoming an unqualified "fact of daily life" by the end of Meiji. Considering the relatively limited reach of the network as late as 1912, one would have to qualify the *direct* impact of railroads on everyday life even at the close of the period.
98. Charles Dickens, "A Flight," in his *Reprinted Pieces* (Chapman and Hall, 1868), p. 238, cited in T. R. Gourvish, *Railways and the British Economy, 1830–1914* (Cambridge: Economic History Society, 1980), p. 9.
99. Charles Dickens, *Dombey and Son*, Alan Horsman, ed. (Oxford: Oxford University Press, 1982), pp. ix, 184; "mad dragon" cited in James A. Ward, *Railroads and the Character of America, 1820–1887* (Knoxville: University of Tennessee Press, 1986), p. 29.
100. Marx, "The Impact of the Railroad," pp. 211–213; Wayne H. Cole, "The Railroad in Canadian Literature," *Canadian Literature*, no. 77, pp. 124–130 (Summer 1978).
101. D. T. Timins, "By Rail in Japan," *The Railway Magazine*, vol. 2, p. 230 (March 1898).
102. Junichiro Tanizaki, *Seven Japanese Tales*, Howard Hibbett, tr. (New York: Alfred A. Knopf, 1963), p. 86.
103. Natsume Sōseki, *The Three-Cornered World*, Alan Turney, tr. (New York: G. P. Putnam's Sons, 1965), pp. 181–182.
104. Ibid., p. 183.
105. Gluck, p. 247.
106. John F. Embree, *Suye Mura: A Japanese Village* (Chicago: University of Chicago Press, 1939), p. 258. For a reference to a story of a late-Meiji badger train, see Harada et al., eds., p. 250.
107. The quote represents one of several arguments made by opponents of railroad construction in Nagano in the mid-Meiji period: cited in *Nagano kensei shi*, vol. 1, p. 457.
108. The quoted phrase is from a petition of 1869/12 from the Board of Censors (Danjōdai, later merged with the Justice Ministry) to the Council of State, in *Hōki bunrui taizen* (Naikaku kiroku-kyoku, 1889), 1st ser., kan-

shoku mon, kansei, Minbu-shō, p. 37, cited in Tanaka Tokihiko, *Meiji ishin no seikyoku to tetsudō kensetsu* (Yoshikawa kōbunkan, 1963), p. 306.
109. Tsumaki Chūta, *Maebara Issei den* (Sekibunkan, 1934), p. 868.
110. *Nihon kokuyū tetsudō hyaku nen shi: tsū shi*, p. 23; Masaru Inouye, p. 431.
111. Petition by Hiji domain retainer Ishii Torao, in Ōkuma monjo, cited in Harada and Aoki, p. 28.
112. Harada Katsumasa, "Maejima Hisoka to tetsudō," *Teishin kyōkai zasshi*, April 1969, p. 28.
113. *Kido Kōin nikki*, vol. 2, Tsumaki Chūta, ed. (Nihon shiseki kyōkai, 1933), p. 84.
114. *Ōkubo Toshimichi nikki*, vol. 2 (Nihon shiseki kyōkai, 1927), p. 190.
115. Edward Seidensticker, *Low City, High City: Tokyo from Edo to the Earthquake* (New York: Alfred A. Knopf, 1983), p. 49. Seidensticker actually makes the point that the railroad aroused less opposition than did the telegraph. This may have been true of the Tokyo area, but in less "enlightened" rural communities, the two innovations often seem to have elicited equally hostile reactions.
116. Ogawa Tameji, *Kaika mondō* (Sanshoten, 1874), pp. 126–127, in Yoshino Sakuzō, ed., *Meiji bunka zenshū*, vol. 20 (Nihon hyōronsha, 1929).
117. *Shinshū hyaku nen* (Nagano: Shinano mainichi shinbunsha, 1967), p. 84.
118. Ishii Mitsuru, p. 276.
119. *Nagano kensei shi*, vol. 1, p. 458.
120. Nagata Hiroshi, ed., *Meiji no kisha: tetsudō sōsetsu 100 nen no kobore banashi kara* (Kōtsū Nihonsha, 1964), pp. 183–188.
121. Hayashi Rikio, ed., *Kyōdo shi jiten: Ōsaka-fu* (Shōheisha, 1980), pp. 170–171.
122. *Kanagawa no hyaku nen*, vol. 2, Asahi shinbunsha Yokohama shi-kyoku, ed. (Yokohama: Yūrindō, 1968), p. 21.
123. *NKTH*, vol. 1 (1969), p. 170; Shibusawa Keizō, comp. and ed., *Japanese Life and Culture in the Meiji Era*, Charles S. Terry, tr. (Tokyo: Ōbunsha, 1958), pp. 220–221. For other examples of popular protest leading to the rerouting of railway lines, see Harada Katsumasa, *Eki no shakai shi: Nihon no kindaika to kōkyō kūkan* (Chūō kōronsha, 1987), pp. 55–56; and Robert Leslie August, "Urbanization and Local Government in Japan: A Study of Shibuya, 1889–1932" (Ph.D. dissertation, University of Pittsburgh, 1975), pp. 46–47.
124. Sawa, p. 97.
125. Aoki in fact argues that the opposition was more limited than is commonly maintained, although the evidence offered here suggests that he perhaps understates the extent of resistance: Aoki Eiichi, "Tetsudō kihi densetsu ni taisuru gimon," *Shin chiri*, vol. 29, no. 4, pp. 1–11 (March 1982); Harada et al., eds., pp. 7–8.

126. Ueda Hiroshi, *Inoue Masaru den* (Kōtsū Nihonsha, 1956), p. 95.
127. "Opening of the Railway," *The Far East*, October 16, 1872, p. 113.
128. Ibid., p. 116.
129. Ibid., p. 118.
130. Ibid.
131. Ishii Mitsuru, pp. 361–362.
132. Kōbun ruiju, 6th ser., vol. 55, un'yu mon, cited in *NKTH*, vol. 1, p. 170.
133. *Shinshū hyaku nen*, p. 84.
134. *Japan Weekly Mail*, July 10, 1886, p. 31, citing an article in the *Jiji shinpō*.
135. "Yo wa tetsudō no yo no naka: Ryōmō tetsudō mōshikomi chōka," *Tōkyō nichinichi shinbun*, December 23, 1886, in *Shinbun shūsei Meiji hennen shi*, vol. 6, p. 375.
136. Tetsudō-kyoku jimu shorui, vol. 1, no. 48, cited in Sawa, p. 56.
137. *Japan Weekly Mail*, June 16, 1888, p. 551, citing an article in the *Tōkyō nichinichi shinbun*.
138. Harada makes a similar point, stressing the importance attached by local boosters to "being connected to the center by rail": Harada, *Eki no shakai shi*, p. 58.
139. *Japanese Railways: Annual Report of the Imperial Railway Department for 21st Fiscal Year of Meiji (April 1888 to March 1889)* (Imperial Railway Department, 1889), p. 25, Transportation Museum Archives, Tokyo.
140. *Nihon kokuyū tetsudō hyaku nen shi: tsū shi*, p. 124.
141. "Railway News," *Japan Weekly Mail*, December 14, 1895, p. 646.
142. Isogai Masayoshi and Iida Bun'ya, *Yamanashi-ken no rekishi* (Yamakawa shuppansha, 1973), p. 241.
143. Shibata Hajime and Asamori Kaname, eds., *Kyōdo shi jiten: Okayama-ken* (Shōheisha, 1980), p. 188; Harada Katsumasa, *Kisha, densha no shakai shi* (Kōdansha, 1983), p. 81.
144. "Kisha no hayasa: kodomo no neta aida ni Yokohama-Shinagawa kan ōfuku," *Shinbun zasshi*, June 1873, in *Shinbun shūsei Meiji hennen shi*, vol. 2, p. 52.
145. *Japan Weekly Mail*, February 27, 1886, p. 199.
146. Harada, *Kisha, densha*, p. 81.
147. *TKN, 1907*, appendix, p. 75.
148. Harada et al., eds., p. 226. The guidebook, founded with the encouragement of Fukuzawa Yukichi and modeled after similar Western publications, was a monthly magazine that included editorials, news, and short stories, together with timetables and other useful travel information.
149. *Nihon kokuyū tetsudō hyaku nen shi: tsū shi*, pp. 81–82; Shibusawa, comp. and ed., p. 229.
150. "Tōkaidō tetsudō zentsū mo ato ikka getsu," *Chōya shinbun*, March 17, 1889, in *Shinbun shūsei Meiji hennen shi*, vol. 7, p. 248.

151. Shibusawa, comp. and ed., p. 229.
152. Marx, *The Machine*, p. 194; Wolfgang Schivelbusch, *The Railway Journey: The Industrialization of Time and Space in the Nineteenth Century* (Berkeley: University of California Press, 1986), p. 33.
153. Cited in Ward, p. 110.
154. Richards and MacKenzie, p. 3.
155. Cited in Schivelbusch, pp. 15, 37.
156. Ibid., p. 53.
157. Nagata, ed., pp. 1, 30.
158. Shibusawa, comp. and ed., p. 223.
159. Ishii Mitsuru, pp. 364–365 (italics added).
160. Saitō Ryokuu, *Hikaechō* (1898), cited in Nagata, ed., p. 31. An American tourist made the same observation in 1891 when he wrote of his travels by rail in Japan: "One of the things which imitation of Western ways is annihilating is distance. Japan, like the rest of the world, is shrinking": Lowell, p. 40.
161. David S. Landes, *Revolution in Time: Clocks and the Making of the Modern World* (Cambridge: Belknap Press of Harvard University Press, 1983), p. 285.
162. *Japan Weekly Mail*, November 20, 1886, p. 498.
163. Thomas C. Smith, "Peasant Time and Factory Time in Japan," in his *Native Sources of Japanese Industrialization, 1750–1920* (Berkeley: University of California Press, 1988), p. 220.
164. Cited in Harada et al., eds., p. 41.
165. Richards and MacKenzie, p. 98.
166. *Honpō tetsudō*, vol. 1, p. 191.
167. Nagata, ed., p. 173.
168. Sawa, p. 39. This notice represented a revision of instructions announced four months earlier, at the time of the provisional opening of the Shinagawa-Yokohama section of the line, that customers should arrive fifteen minutes, and the gates be closed five minutes, before departure. The Railway Bureau was strictly enforcing a similar rule on its Takasaki line as late as 1891 when an American tourist wrote of the frustrating experience of just missing his train, which was still standing at the platform at Ueno station but within the "imported five-minute regulation": "Here I was, the miserable victim of a punctuality my own people [sic] had foisted on a land only too happy without it!" For time, as this traveler saw it, had been "the one thing worthless in old Japan." The American's journey resumed when "sufficiently punctual passengers [were] permitted to board the next train": Lowell, pp. 12–14, 17.
169. Harada et al., eds., pp. 42, 44–46.
170. Saitō, *Hikaechō*, cited in Nagata, ed., p. 31.

171. Harada Katsumasa, *Meiji tetsudō monogatari* (Chikuma shobō, 1983), p. 92.
172. Tetsudō-ryō jimubō, vol. 3, no. 3, cited in Nagata, ed., p. 174; also, Harada, *Meiji tetsudō*, p. 93.
173. Harada, *Meiji tetsudō*, p. 93.
174. Smith, "Peasant Time," p. 221.
175. Nagata, ed., p. 57.
176. "The Japan Railway Company," *Japan Weekly Mail*, February 14, 1903, p. 162.
177. "Behaviour of Travellers by Railway in Japan," *Japan Weekly Mail*, May 4, 1901, p. 468.
178. Timins, pp. 232–233.
179. Shimazaki Tōson, *The Broken Commandment*, Kenneth Strong, tr. (Tokyo: University of Tokyo Press, 1974), p. 119.
180. Smith, "Peasant Time," p. 225.
181. Constantine N. Vaporis, "Caveat Viator: Advice to Travelers in the Edo Period," *Monumenta Nipponica*, vol. 44, no. 4, p. 463 (Winter 1989). On the recreational character of pilgrimage during the Tokugawa era, see also Harada et al., eds., pp. 123, 182.
182. Harada notes that, contrary to received opinion, the very first set of cars imported into Japan, for use on the Shinbashi line, were in fact American-style carriages with central corridors: Harada, *Meiji tetsudō*, pp. 102–103. It appears that, for the next twenty-five years, subsequent cars were almost all compartmentalized.
183. Lowell, p. 36.
184. Timins, p. 234.
185. In the first decade of railroad operation, newspapers reported several cases of riders fined for passing water or gas while on board. See, for example, "Kisha untenchū ni shōben: bakkin jū en nari," *Tōkyō nichinichi shinbun*, April 15, 1873, and "Kisha chū de hōhi shite, bakkin go en," *Tōkyō nichinichi shinbun*, November 19, 1881, in *Shinbun shūsei Meiji hennen shi*, vol. 2, p. 31 and vol. 4, p. 491; also, Sawa, pp. 34–35. As a comic song of early Meiji put it, in a play on homonyms: "Passing water from the window of the train, that makes twice I've put out my train *chin*": Nagata, ed., p. 157.
186. Tetsudō-kyoku jimu shorui, vol. 4 (1889), no. 14, cited in Sawa, p. 36.
187. Richards and MacKenzie, p. 11.
188. "Hida goryō-kyoku chō bossu: kisha ni benjo naki gisei," *Jiji shinpō*, April 29, 1889, in *Shinbun shūsei Meiji hennen shi*, vol. 7, p. 263. The accident was a sad endnote to the illustrious career of Hida, a marine engineer by training, who had helped to introduce modern shipbuilding technology into Japan and, ironically, had chaired the founding commit-

tee of the country's first and largest private railroad, the Nippon. For more on Hida's career and demise, see Tsuchiya Shigeaki, *Kindai Nihon zōsen kotohajime: Hida Hamagorō no shōgai* (Shin jinbutsu ōraisha, 1975).

189. "Kisha ni benjo—botsubotsu toritsukeru," *Jiji shinpō*, May 26, 1889, in *Shinbun shūsei Meiji hennen shi*, vol. 7, p. 275.
190. "Chūō tetsudō no Yamanashi-ken ni oyoboshitaru eikyō (1)," *Tōkyō keizai zasshi*, November 21, 1903, p. 16.
191. Shiga Naoya, "Abashiri made," in Watanabe et al., eds., pp. 11–17.
192. Emi Suiin, *Kisha no taizoku* (Aoki Sūzandō, 1901), cited in Harada, *Kisha, densha*, p. 101.
193. Natsume Sōseki, *Sanshirō: A Novel*, Jay Rubin, tr. (Seattle: University of Washington Press, 1977), pp. 4–5.
194. "State Purchase of Private Railways," *Japan Weekly Mail*, December 14, 1898, p. 632.
195. "Japanese Railways," *Japan Weekly Mail*, August 9, 1902, p. 138, citing an article in the *Tōkyō nichinichi shinbun*.
196. *Tōkyō shin hanjō ki* (1874), cited in Shibusawa, comp. and ed., pp. 223–224.
197. Sawa, p. 39; "role models" in Noguchi, p. 49.
198. Nagata, ed., p. 33, citing a newspaper in Shizuoka; and "Tetsudō no benri oyobi fuhei no ki," *Tōkyō keizai zasshi*, July 20, 1889, pp. 74–76, which lists passenger grievances concerning railroads in general, with specific references to the state and Nippon Railway lines.
199. Petition to the Home Ministry, December 1897, cited in *Nagano kensei shi*, vol. 1, p. 459.
200. *Gunma no Meiji hyaku nen* (Maebashi: Mainichi shinbun Maebashi shikyoku, 1968), pp. 242–243.
201. "The Japan Railway Company," *Japan Weekly Mail*, February 14, 1903, p. 162, citing the *Jiji shinpō*.
202. Alfred D. Chandler, Jr., and Richard S. Tedlow, *The Coming of Managerial Capitalism: A Casebook on the History of American Economic Institutions* (Homewood, Ill.: Richard D. Irwin, Inc., 1985), p. 183.
203. George H. Burgess and Miles C. Kennedy, *Centennial History of the Pennsylvania Railroad Company, 1846–1946* (Philadelphia: The Pennsylvania Railroad Company, 1949), pp. 757–760.
204. Jack Simmons, *The Railways of Britain: An Historical Introduction* (London: Routledge & Kegan Paul, 1961), p. 147.
205. "Tetsudō no benri oyobi fuhei no ki," p. 76.
206. Chandler and Tedlow, p. 183.
207. "Tetsudō no benri oyobi fuhei no ki," p. 76.
208. *Jiji shinpō*, cited in "State Purchase of Private Railways," *Japan Weekly Mail*, December 14, 1898, p. 632.

209. "Sandai tetsudō no sokuryoku chinsen hikaku," *Tōkyō keizai zasshi*, February 28, 1903, p. 31.
210. Alfred W. Arthurton, "The Railways of Japan," *The Railway Magazine*, vol. 15, p. 503 (December 1904).
211. Sawa, p. 125.
212. For more on the "administrative backwardness of most Meiji railroads," see my "Private Railroads in the Meiji Era: Forerunners of Modern Japanese Management?" in Tsunehiko Yui and Keiichiro Nakagawa, eds., *Japanese Management in Historical Perspective* (Tokyo: University of Tokyo Press, 1989).
213. Arthurton, p. 503.
214. Albert Fishlow, *American Railroads and the Transformation of the Antebellum Economy* (Cambridge: Harvard University Press, 1965), p. 308.
215. Chandler and Tedlow, p. 183.
216. "Japanese Railways from a Military Point of View," *Japan Weekly Mail*, October 21, 1893, p. 466.
217. Cited in Sakurai Tōru, "Nippon tetsudō kabushiki kaisha no shihon chikuseki jōken to kokuyūka mondai (1): kokka dokusen seisei ni kansuru junbiteki kōsatsu," *Ōsaka shidai ronshū*, no. 25, p. 73 (1976).
218. "Sir William Bisset," *Japan Weekly Mail*, May 24, 1902, p. 560.
219. "Bisset-shi no honpō tetsudō hyō," *Tōyō keizai shinpō*, June 5, 1902, pp. 29–30.
220. *Nagano kensei shi*, vol. 1, p. 459.
221. Shimazaki, p. 75.
222. *Yomiuri shinbun*, November 1909, cited in Nagata, ed., p. 22.
223. "Railways in Japan," *Japan Weekly Mail*, May 15, 1909, p. 635.
224. In *Shinbun shūsei Meiji hennen shi*, vol. 6, p. 242.
225. *Tōkyō nichinichi shinbun*, May 1, 1890, cited in Shibusawa, comp. and ed., p. 228.
226. *Tōkyō nichinichi shinbun*, September 12, 1891, cited in Shibusawa, comp. and ed., p. 225.
227. Shibusawa, comp. and ed., p. 226.
228. *Nihon kokuyū tetsudō hyaku nen shi: tsū shi*, pp. 127–128; *NKTH*, vol. 4 (1972), pp. 425–427; Aoki Kaizō, *Jinbutsu kokutetsu hyaku nen* (Chūō senkyō kabushiki kaisha shuppan-kyoku, 1969), p. 66; Harada, *Eki no shakai shi*, p. 127.
229. Cited in *NKTH*, vol. 4, p. 425.
230. "Railway and Steamship Competition," *Japan Weekly Mail*, September 3, 1898, p. 239.
231. The handbook, the fourth edition of *The Working and Management of an English Railway* (London, 1891), was authored by George Findlay, general manager of the London & North Western Railway Company, and trans-

lated by a San'yō Railway official as *Eikoku tetsudō ron* (Kobe: San'yō tetsudō kabushiki kaisha, 1894).

The state railways actually seem to have taken the lead in sending officials on overseas inspection tours in the latter half of Meiji; as the *Japan Weekly Mail* reported on March 21, 1896:

> Japanese or foreign experts who are occupying leading positions in this country are unable to keep in close touch with the latest ideas of the West. . . . Most of [the] foreign advisers came to Japan in the early part of the Meiji era and their knowledge is now rather antiquated. . . . The inspection of railway affairs in the West by Japanese experts is regarded by the Government as a matter of urgent importance, and hereafter steps will be taken to despatch abroad an expert or two every year with that end in view: "Railways," p. 24.

A state engineer named Oka Seii, who was sent on the first such tour in 1897, later became freight-office manager in the Nippon Railway: *Tetsudō senjin roku*, Nihon kōtsū kyōkai, ed. (Nihon teishajō kabushiki kaisha, 1972), p. 98.

232. Sawa, p. 100.
233. Harada, *Meiji tetsudō*, pp. 102–103.
234. In *Shinbun shūsei Meiji hennen shi*, vol. 4, p. 336.
235. Emi, *Kisha no taizoku*, cited in Harada, *Kisha, densha*, pp. 97–102.
236. Harada, *Meiji tetsudō*, p. 204; *Nihon kokuyū tetsudō hyaku nen shi: tsū shi*, p. 128.
237. The following description is based on Harada and Aoki, pp. 104–105; Harada, *Tetsudō no kataru Nihon no kindai*, pp. 102–105; and *Nihon kokuyū tetsudō hyaku nen shi: tsū shi*, pp. 129–131.
238. Cited in Harada and Aoki, p. 104.
239. For more on Kinoshita, see Aoki Kaizō and Yamanaka Tadao, *Kokutetsu kōryū jidai: Kinoshita un'yu nijū nen* (Nihon kōtsū kyōkai, 1957), especially pp. 16–39; and *Tetsudō senjin roku*, pp. 126–127.
240. "Japanese Railways," *Japan Weekly Mail*, August 9, 1902, p. 138.
241. Cited in "Railway Fares," *Japan Weekly Mail*, February 28, 1903, p. 218.
242. *Tōkyō nichinichi shinbun*, November 18, 1903, cited in Sawa, p. 100.
243. Cited in Shibusawa, comp. and ed., p. 225.
244. Cited in ibid., pp. 225–226. I have slightly modified the translation, changing "middle-" and "upper-class" to "second-" and "first-class."
245. Inaba Hiroshi, ed., *Kyōdo shi jiten: Kanagawa-ken* (Shōheisha, 1978), p. 221; Harada and Aoki, pp. 70–71.
246. Cited in Shibusawa, comp. and ed., p. 227.
247. *Niroku shinbun*, September 3, 1909, cited in Shibusawa, comp. and ed., p. 228.

248. Shibusawa, comp. and ed., p. 228.
249. "Railway Fares," *Japan Weekly Mail*, February 28, 1903, p. 218.
250. Paul Waley, "Tokyo: Urban Change in the Meiji and Taishō Eras," *The Japan Foundation Newsletter*, vol. 18, no. 3, p. 17 (January 1991).
251. Harada et al., eds., p. 31.
252. Cited in Richards and MacKenzie, p. 123. On early American promoters, see Ward, pp. 12–27.
253. Such prefectures included Yamanashi and those in the Hokuetsu region: Eiichi Aoki, *Railway Construction*, pp. 15–16; Yamaguchi Kazuo, pp. 132–133.
254. *Honpō tetsudō*, vol. 3, p. 1620.
255. Ibid., p. 1615.
256. Ibid., vol. 1, p. 383.
257. "Chūō tetsudō no Yamanashi-ken ni oyoboshitaru eikyō (2)," p. 1021.
258. Ishikawa Tōji, *Kokkai giin senkyo kokoroe* (1889), pp. 6–8, cited in Gluck, p. 64.
259. Isogai and Iida, p. 241.

2. The First Two Decades

1. *NTS*, vol. 1, p. 663.
2. See Tanaka, *Meiji ishin*, especially pp. 116–123, 305–317.
3. Smith, *Political Change and Industrial Development*, p. 36.
4. *NKTH*, vol. 1, p. 112.
5. Ibid., pp. 45–54.
6. *Dai Nihon gaikō bunsho*, vol. 2, pt. 3, Gaimu-shō chōsa-bu, ed. (Nihon kokusai kyōkai, 1938), pp. 269–274. As Hoshino points out in a revisionist article, however, Parkes originally recommended to Foreign Ministry officials that construction of the Shinbashi-Yokohama line be financed by "Japanese merchants"; it was only after government authorities had arranged for a loan to be raised in England on the security of Japan's customs and future railway revenues that the British minister came out in support of public initiative: Hoshino Takao, "Meiji shonen no shitetsu seisaku: 'tetsudō kokuyū shugi setsu,' 'kansen kansetsu shugi setsu' no saikentō," *Musashi daigaku ronshū*, vol. 27, nos. 3–5, pp. 126, 134–135 (December 1979). Parkes had in fact introduced the Japanese to the loan contractor, a former inspector general of the Chinese maritime customs service named Horatio Nelson Lay.
7. Petition from the Board of Censors to the Council of State, 1869/12, cited in Tanaka, *Meiji ishin*, p. 306.

8. *Iwakura Tomomi kankei monjo*, vol. 8, Ōtsuka Takematsu, ed. (Nihon shiseki kyōkai, 1935), p. 115.
9. The state railways carried more than 26,000 military personnel from Tokyo to Yokohama during the rebellion, which lasted from February to September 1877, and nearly 32,000 personnel between Kyoto and Kobe from July 1877 to June 1878: *NKTH*, vol. 1, pp. 538–539.
10. *Maejima Hisoka jijoden* (Hayama-chō: Maejima Hisoka denki kankōkai, 1956), pp. 70–71.
11. From 1871 to 1881, Maejima headed the postal service. After leaving the government with his patron Ōkuma, he became the first president of the Kansai Railway Company in 1887 and of the Hokuetsu Railway in his home prefecture in 1896. He was also active as a promoter and director of the Seoul-Pusan Railway after the turn of the century: Harada, "Maejima," pp. 30–31; "Maejima Hisoka nenpu," *Teishin kyōkai zasshi*, April 1969, pp. 59–61.
12. Harada, "Maejima," p. 29.
13. *Maejima*, p. 71.
14. Maejima forecasted rather optimistically that the Tokyo-Kobe artery would pay for itself within five years, after which it would yield an annual profit on construction costs of fully 36 percent; after it was finally completed in 1889, the Tokaido line would indeed prove to be the big moneymaker for the state railways, but it would show a rate of return less than half that predicted by Maejima: *NTS*, vol. 1, pp. 35–40; Tominaga, p. 184.
15. *NTS*, vol. 1, pp. 40–43.
16. *Shibusawa Eiichi jijoden*, cited in *Tetsudō senjin roku*, p. 181.
17. Tanaka, *Meiji ishin*, p. 339.
18. *NTS*, vol. 1, pp. 35–36.
19. Ochiai Sadaaki, "Meiji shonen no tetsudō seisaku: Nihon tetsudō seisaku shi josetsu (1)," *Un'yu to keizai*, vol. 17, no. 2, p. 25 (1957).
20. On the Kansai Railway, see Yamaguchi Eizō, "Kansai tetsudō kaisha shimatsu," *Kōtsū bunka*, no. 8, pp. 729–740 (October 1939); and Yoshikawa Kanji, "Waga kuni shitetsu no hōga to Kansai tetsudō kaisha," *Dōshisha shōgaku*, vol. 2, no. 1, pp. 32–59 (July 1950). Primary materials are included in Mitsui ke monjo, 2nd ser., vols. 2280–2281, 2284, 2288–2289, 2293, Mitsui bunko, Tokyo. This firm is not to be confused with the Kansai Railway Company that was licensed in 1888 and nationalized in 1907.
21. Tanaka, *Meiji ishin*, p. 341.
22. *NTS*, vol. 1, p. 361.
23. Ibid., pp. 361–362.
24. Ibid., p. 362.
25. *NKTH*, vol. 1, p. 113.
26. *NTS*, vol. 1, p. 128. The line was completed in February 1877, just in time

to transport troops during the Satsuma Rebellion: *TKN, 1907*, appendix, p. 1.
27. Francis H. Trevithick, "The History and Development of the Railway System in Japan," *Transactions of the Asiatic Society of Japan*, vol. 22, p. 121 (September 1894).
28. *Segai Inoue-kō den*, vol. 2, Inoue Kaoru-kō denki hensankai, ed. (Naigai shoseki kabushiki kaisha, 1933), p. 496.
29. Ochiai Sadaaki, "Meiji shonen no tetsudō seisaku: Nihon tetsudō seisaku shi josetsu (2)," *Un'yu to keizai*, vol. 17, no. 3, p. 60 (1957).
30. In 1871, for example, the government disbursed a total of ¥22,657,948 in samurai stipends: Smith, *Political Change and Industrial Development*, p. 32.
31. Ochiai, "Meiji shonen (2)," p. 58; "Donzō Takashima Kaemon-ō kaikyū dan," manuscript photocopy, Transportation Museum Archives, Tokyo.
32. Ochiai, "Meiji shonen (2)," p. 58.
33. *Iwakura-kō jikki*, vol. 2, Tada Kōmon, ed. (Iwakura-kō kyūseki hozonkai, 1927), p. 1017.
34. *NKTH*, vol. 1, pp. 115–116. On the Tokyo Railway Association, see also *Kōbu-shō kiroku: tetsudō no bu*, vol. 5 (Nihon kokuyū tetsudō, 1963); and *Shibusawa Eiichi denki shiryō*, vol. 8, Shibusawa seien kinen zaidan ryūmonsha, ed. (Shibusawa Eiichi denki shiryō kankōkai, 1956), hereafter cited as *SEDS*.
35. Cited in Ochiai, "Meiji shonen (2)," p. 60.
36. *Segai Inoue-kō den*, vol. 2, p. 543; *NKTH*, vol. 1, pp. 116–117.
37. Hoshino Takao, "Shitetsu no seiritsu to hatten: Nippon tetsudō kaisha to tetsudō netsu," in Nakagawa Keiichirō, Morikawa Hidemasa, and Yui Tsunehiko, eds., *Kindai Nihon keiei shi no kiso chishiki* (Yūhikaku, 1974), p. 79.
38. *Segai Inoue-kō den*, vol. 2, p. 543.
39. *NTS*, vol. 1, p. 355.
40. Cited in Nakanishi, p. 15.
41. Watarai, p. 36.
42. Nakanishi, p. 15.
43. Hoshino, "Nippon tetsudō (1)," p. 80.
44. *NKTH*, vol. 1, p. 120; Dajō ruiten, 3rd ser. (1878–1879), vol. 42, no. 31, Kokuritsu kōbunshokan, Tokyo.
45. *NKTH*, vol. 2 (1970), pp. 415–416.
46. Nakanishi, p. 11.
47. *NKTH*, vol. 2, p. 416; Watarai, p. 34. These funds enabled the state railways to begin work on the Kyoto-Tsuruga line in 1879. That line was finally completed in 1884: *TKN, 1907*, appendix, p. 1.
48. On the 15th National Bank, see Hoshino Takao, "Meiji ki no shitetsu to

ginkō: Nippon tetsudō kaisha to dai jūgo ginkō to o chūshin ni," *Kōtsū bunka*, no. 5, pp. 65–72 (1965); and Hoshino, "Nippon tetsudō (1)-(3)."
49. *NKTH*, vol. 2, p. 416; Nakanishi, p. 11.
50. Dajō ruiten, 4th ser. (1880), vol. 30, no. 5.
51. Cited in Smith, *Political Change and Industrial Development*, p. 99.
52. *Meiji zenki zaisei keizai shiryō shūsei*, vol. 1, Ōkura-shō, ed. (Kaizōsha, 1931), p. 519.
53. Supple, pp. 328–329; Edwin A. Pratt, *State Railways: Object Lessons from Other Lands* (London: P. S. King & Co., 1907), pp. 41–44; Kimon A. Doukas, *The French Railroads and the State* (New York: Columbia University Press, 1945), pp. 20–43.
54. Yamada Eitarō, "Nippon tetsudō kabushiki kaisha enkakushi," vol. 1, p. 173, Hitotsubashi University Library, Tokyo.
55. *NKTH*, vol. 2, pp. 416–417. Also on the Nippon Railway, see *SEDS*, vol. 8; *Kōbu-shō kiroku*, vols. 13, 22, 26, 28, 33, 39; and the rich collections of documents in "Nippon tetsudō kaisha sōritsu ki," Iwakura Tomomi monjo, no. 191, Kensei shiryō-shitsu, National Diet Library, Tokyo, and Tetsudō-in monjo, Nippon tetsudō, vols. 1–10 (1881–1903), Transportation Museum Archives, Tokyo.
56. Hoshino, "Nippon tetsudō (2)," pp. 9–11.
57. *Iwakura-kō jikki*, vol. 2, p. 790.
58. *NKTH*, vol. 2, pp. 417–418.
59. Noda Masaho, "Meiji ki ni okeru shiyū tetsudō no hattatsu to kabushiki hakkō shijō no tenkai: waga kuni ni okeru shiyū tetsudō no hattatsu to shōken shijō no keisei (1)," *Keizai shirin*, vol. 32, p. 126 (January 1964).
60. Ochiai Sadaaki, "Meiji jū nendai no tetsudō seisaku (1)," *Un'yu to keizai*, vol. 17, no. 6, p. 24 (1957).
61. Yamada, vol. 1, p. 173.
62. *NKTH*, vol. 2, p. 416; Noda, "Meiji ki shiyū tetsudō," p. 125.
63. *NKTH*, vol. 2, p. 399.
64. Trevithick, p. 123.
65. Ochiai, "Meiji jū nendai (1)," p. 22.
66. *NTS*, vol. 1, p. 747.
67. *SEDS*, vol. 8, p. 560.
68. Watarai, p. 38.
69. *NTS*, vol. 1, p. 700. The railroad was obliged to furnish state officials with a constant stream of documents in order to meet this requirement. At one point, the company, complaining about the burden of having to prepare "tens of thousands of documents throughout the year," petitioned the authorities to shorten the period of subvention and to pay the subsidy as a lump sum: Yamada, vol. 2, p. 185. The government and railroad were

unable to agree on the size of the payment, however, so the company finally withdrew its petition: *NTS*, vol. 2, pp. 303–305.
70. Ibid., vol. 1, p. 701.
71. Smith, *Political Change and Industrial Development*, p. 99. For more on the sale of government enterprises during the Meiji period, see Kobayashi Masaaki, *Nihon no kōgyōka to kangyō haraisage: seifu to kigyō* (Tōyō keizai shinpōsha, 1977).
72. Memorandum from Itō Hirobumi to Chief Councilor Sanjō Sanetomi, December 1881, in Kōbun ruiju, 6th ser. (1882), vol. 55, no. 26, Kokuritsu kōbunshokan, Tokyo.
73. Ibid.
74. *NKTH*, vol. 1, p. 340.
75. Ibid., p. 348.
76. *NKTH*, vol. 2, p. 431.
77. Kōbun ruiju, 13th ser. (1889), vol. 48, no. 24.
78. *NTS*, vol. 1, p. 784.
79. Nakanishi, p. 31.
80. Noda Masaho, *Nihon shōken shijō seiritsu shi: Meiji ki no tetsudō to kabushiki kaisha kin'yū* (Yūhikaku, 1980), p. 64; Hoshino, "Shitetsu no seiritsu," p. 77.
81. Nakanishi, p. 31.
82. *Kin'yū rokujū nen shi* (Tōyō keizai shinpōsha, 1924), p. 358.
83. Watarai, p. 39.
84. Hoshino, "Shitetsu no seiritsu," p. 80.
85. *TKN, 1907*, p. 31.
86. Sugiyama Kazuo, "Kigyō no zaimu, tōshi katsudō," pp. 58–59.
87. The bureau's draft proposal for the regulations is included in Tetsudōkyoku jimu shorui, vol. 2 (1887), no. 3, Japan Railway Archives, Tokyo.
88. *NKTH*, vol. 1, p. 177; Kōbun ruiju, 11th ser. (1887), vol. 38, no. 8.
89. *NKTH*, vol. 2, pp. 566–572, 602–605, 647–651.
90. Ochiai, "Meiji jū nendai (1)," p. 25.
91. Ibid.
92. Shima, p. 79.
93. Trevithick, p. 138.
94. *Shishaku Inoue Masaru-kun shōden*, Murai Masatoshi, ed. (Inoue shishaku dōzō kensetsu dōshikai, 1915), p. 6.
95. Uda, "Waga kuni tetsudō," p. 127.
96. Cited in Tanaka, "Tetsudō yusō," pp. 181–182.
97. Harada Katsumasa, "Tetsudō fusetsu hō seitei no zentei," *Nihon rekishi*, no. 208, p. 37 (September 1965).
98. *NTS*, vol. 1, p. 392.
99. Ibid., p. 394.

100. The government had given the Railway Bureau the go-ahead to complete this line in 1883. Coming in the wake of "the period of extreme dullness," this authorization, Inoue later recalled, had brought him "almost boundless satisfaction": Masaru Inouye, p. 439. See also *Shishaku Inoue Masaru-kun shōden*, pp. 34–35.
101. *NKTH*, vol. 1, p. 178 and vol. 2, p. 395.
102. Cited in Ochiai Sadaaki, "Meiji jū nendai (2)," vol. 17, no. 7, p. 33.
103. Cited in ibid.
104. *NKTH*, vol. 2, p. 402.
105. *NKTH*, vol. 1, p. 172; Harada, "Tetsudō fusetsu hō," pp. 26–27.
106. Sanbō honbu rikugun-bu, *Tetsudō ron* (1888), University of Tokyo Faculty of Economics Library, Tokyo.
107. This section and the following one draw on my article "Railroads in Crisis: The Financing and Management of Japanese Railway Companies during the Panic of 1890," in Wray, ed.
108. The 1893 Commercial Code stipulated that a company's shareholders pay up at least one quarter of the par value of their shares at the time of the company's establishment. In 1895, however, the government reduced the immediate-payment requirement for railroad firms to one tenth or more of the par value of subscribed stock: Nagaoka Shinkichi, *Meiji kyōkō shi josetsu* (Tōkyō daigaku shuppankai, 1971), p. 21; Noda, *Nihon shōken shijō*, p. 212.
109. That banks regularly made loans on partially paid-up shares is evidenced by a warning from the Mitsui Bank to its branches in October 1893 that, because of the difficulties attending company confiscation or bank foreclosure of partially paid-up shares, they should be "extremely cautious about accepting such stock as collateral": "Gōmei kaisha Mitsui ginkō reiki isan," cited in Sugiyama Kazuo, "Kin'yū," in Furushima Toshio and Andō Yoshio, eds., *Ryūtsū shi*, pt. 2 (Yamakawa shuppansha, 1975), p. 395.

    On the installment payment system and stock-collateral lending by banks in connection with private railroads, see Noda, *Nihon shōken shijō*, pp. 189–231; also, his "Corporate Finance of Railroad Companies," pp. 90–96. The "gradual calling up of instalments on shares" appears to have been a common practice in the early British railways and was by no means a unique characteristic of the Japanese version of capitalist industrial development, as some writers have suggested. The above quote is from M. C. Reed, *Investment in Railways in Britain, 1820–1844: A Study in the Development of the Capital Market* (London: Oxford University Press, 1975), p. 236.
110. "Kyūshū tetsudō kabushiki kaisha chōsa hōkokusho," February 1900, in *SEDS*, vol. 9 (1956), p. 277; Noda, *Nihon shōken shijō*, pp. 72–73.
111. In April 1890, the Osaka Chamber of Commerce reported that "[share-

holders] have come to accept shares beyond their means, . . . and when they need financing, they generally borrow from banks using the shares as collateral": "Kin'yū enkatsu o hakaru gi ni tsuki jōshin," April 1890, in *Ōsaka shōhō kaigisho shiryō*, vol. 3, cited in Takamura Naosuke, *Nihon bōseki gyō shi josetsu*, vol. 1 (Hanawa shobō, 1971), p. 169.

112. In the late 1880s, the average authorized capital stock of operating railway companies was roughly a hundred times that of joint-stock ventures as a whole: *TKN, 1907*, appendix, pp. 22–46 passim; *Nihon teikoku tōkei nenkan*, vol. 13 (Naikaku shokikan-shitsu tōkei-ka, 1894), p. 655.

Trunk-line railroads generally required seven to ten years to complete their lines; smaller railroads, two to three years: Sugiyama Kazuo, "Kigyō no zaimu, tōshi katsudō," p. 60. These terms, however, were not equivalent to the gestation periods of fixed investment, since rail concerns foreshortened those periods by raising share capital on installment and by opening short sections of line as they were finished.

113. *TKN, 1907*, appendix, p. 44; *Nihon teikoku tōkei nenkan*, vol. 13, p. 655. The latter yearbook does not provide figures for the total paid-up capital of joint-stock companies prior to 1889.

114. See Ericson, "Railroads in Crisis," p. 167; and Takamura Naosuke, "Meiji 23 nen kyōkō no seikaku: Nagaoka Shinkichi cho *Meiji kyōkō shi josetsu* ni yosete," *Nihon rekishi*, no. 332, pp. 87–91 (January 1976).

115. The market prices of all but a handful of the stocks listed on the Tokyo and Osaka stock exchanges fell below their paid-up values in 1890: *Tōkyō kabushiki torihikijo gojū nen shi* (Tōkyō kabushiki torihikijo, 1928), p. 126; *Ō-kabu gojū nen shi* (Ōsaka kabushiki torihikijo, 1928), p. 589.

116. "Shibusawa Eiichi-kun no kin'yū hippaku dan," *Tōkyō keizai zasshi*, March 22, 1890, in *SEDS*, vol. 5 (1955), pp. 212–213.

117. *NTS*, vol. 1, p. 663; *Japanese Railways*, p. 24.

118. *NKTH*, vol. 2, pp. 390–391.

119. Noda, *Nihon shōken shijō*, p. 75.

120. Reed, p. 96.

121. *TKN, 1907*, appendix, p. 44.

122. Ibid., p. 31, appendix, pp. 22–46 passim.

123. *Tetsudō iken zenshū* (Otani Matsujirō, 1892), pp. 397–398.

124. Nakanishi, p. 40.

125. For more on the difficulties experienced by these main-line railroads of western Japan, see Kokaze Hidemasa, "Kōtsū shihon no keisei," in Takamura Naosuke, ed., *Kigyō bokkō: Nihon shihonshugi no keisei* (Minerva shobō, 1992).

126. *NTS*, vol. 1, p. 899.

127. "Shin jigyō no shihonkin roku oku en ni noboru," *Tōyō keizai shinpō*, April 5, 1896, cited in Noda, *Nihon shōken shijō*, p. 98.

128. *NTS*, vol. 1, p. 878.
129. Takamura, *Nihon bōseki gyō shi*, vol. 1, pp. 169–170, 172n28. Takamura notes that, in both semesters of 1890, over 40 percent of the spinning companies whose dividend rates could be determined offered no dividends whatsoever.
130. The 1890 expansion of central-bank discounting using railway shares as collateral will be discussed later in this chapter.
131. For example, in fiscal-year 1900, when the Railway Bureau began to report complete data on the capital structure of the private railroads in operation, the aggregate paid-up capital of those companies accounted for 79 percent of their total capital: *Tetsudō-kyoku nenpō, 1900* (Teishinshō tetsudō-kyoku, 1901), pp. 55, 203.
132. Ishii Tsuneo, "Ryōmō tetsudō kaisha ni okeru kabunushi to sono keifu," *Meidai shōgaku ronsō*, vol. 41, nos. 9–10, pp. 142–146 (July 1958).
133. "San'yō tetsudō kaisha kabunushi meibo," September 1891, in *Nakamigawa Hikojirō denki shiryō*, Nihon keiei shi kenkyūjo, ed. (Tōyō keizai shinpōsha, 1969), p. 170. Other bank officers holding 1,000 or more shares in the San'yō Railway at that time included Tamaki Jirōsaburō (3,070 shares), Itō Chōjirō (1,973), Inoue Yasujirō (1,100), Imai Shōgorō (1,012), and Satsuma Jihei (1,000). These stockholders have been identified as bank executives on the basis of Takechi Kyōzō, "Nisshin sensōgo tetsudō kaisha no kabunushi to sono keifu," *Seitō joshi tanki daigaku kiyō*, no. 6, pp. 22–23 (September 1976); and Ishii Tsuneo, "Ryōmō kabunushi," p. 146. Several of these bankers had rather diversified interests in railway companies. Inoue Yasujirō, president of the 136th National Bank and director of the 130th, held 1,520 shares of the Kyushu Railway's first stock issue in March 1896, 3,000 of that of the Kansai in June 1894, and 200 shares in the Ryōmō in October 1890: "Kaku shisetsu tetsudō dai kabunushi ichiranhyō," *Tetsudō zasshi*, no. 5, p. 22 (June 1896); Kansai tetsudō kabushiki kaisha, *Dai jūnikai hōkoku*, 1894, p. 36; Ishii Tsuneo, "Ryōmō kabunushi," p. 144. Besides the 4,615 shares he had in the San'yō Railway in 1891, Imamura Seinosuke, president of his own private bank, held 1,100 shares of the Kyushu Railway's first issue in March 1896 and 4,437 of that of the Kansai Railway in June 1894: "Kaku shisetsu tetsudō dai kabunushi ichiranhyō," no. 5, p. 23; Kansai tetsudō, *Dai jūnikai hōkoku*, p. 36. Imamura, 130th National Bank president Matsumoto, and Yokohama Specie bank director Hara were still among the leading railway investors in 1902–1903, with total holdings of over 10,000 shares apiece: Sugiyama Kazuo, "Meiji 30 nendai ni okeru tetsudō kaisha no dai kabunushi to keieisha," *Seikei daigaku keizai gakubu ronshū*, vol. 7, no. 2, p. 155 (1977).

Noda has shown that the aggregate turnover in railway shares on the nation's stock exchanges declined dramatically during the panic and recession, and remained at a moderate level through 1895: Noda, *Nihon shōken shijō*, p. 238. In most cases, therefore, one can probably regard the number of first-issue shares held by an investor, say, at the end of fiscal-year 1895 (that is, March 1896) as a fairly accurate approximation of the number he possessed during the financial crisis (most railroads did not issue new shares until after 1892).

134. Ishii Tsuneo, "Ryōmō kabunushi," pp. 142–143, 147.
135. See Hoshino, "Nippon tetsudō (2)," p. 22, on the 15th National Bank's conversion to ordinary bank status in 1897 and its appearance from that year on Nippon Railway stockholders lists; and Sugiyama Kazuo, "Kabushiki kaisha seido no hatten: bōseki, tetsudō gyō o chūshin ni," in Kobayashi Masaaki et al., eds., *Nihon keiei shi o manabu*, vol. 1, *Meiji keiei shi* (Yūhikaku, 1976), pp. 117–118, on the rise of institutional investors in railway companies after the turn of the century.
136. "San'yō kabunushi meibo," pp. 170–171.
137. Hoshino, "Nippon tetsudō (1)-(3)."
138. Hugh Patrick, "Japan, 1868–1914," in Rondo Cameron et al., *Banking in the Early Stages of Industrialization: A Study in Comparative Economic History* (New York: Oxford University Press, 1967), pp. 258–259; Kozo Yamamura, *A Study of Samurai Income,* and his "Japan, 1868–1930: A Revised View," in Rondo Cameron, ed., *Banking and Economic Development: Some Lessons of History* (New York: Oxford University Press, 1972), p. 175.
139. Hoshino, "Nippon tetsudō (3)," pp. 155–156, 182.
140. The 9 percent figure was arrived at by dividing the bank's total minimum investment ("*shoyū daka* [sic]," in ibid., p. 165, Table 36) in the Nippon Railway for the years 1890–1893 by the total paid-up capital of private railroads for those years (*TKN, 1907*, appendix, pp. 44–45). Hoshino suggests that the actual percentage may have been nearly twice that figure: Hoshino, "Nippon tetsudō (3)," p. 164.
141. Ibid., p. 155.
142. Ibid., pp. 164–165.
143. Ibid., p. 155. I have calculated the total paid-up value by multiplying the ratio of the railroad's paid-up capital to the combined par value of its stock issues in March 1897 (Hoshino, "Nippon tetsudō (2)," pp. 4, 19) by the total par value of the bank's estimated holding of 260,000 shares in May 1897 (0.78 x ¥13 million).
144. The firm in question was the medium-sized Iwagoe Railway, founded in 1897. At the time of the Iwagoe's purchase by the government in 1906, the 15th National held 5,000 shares in the railroad: Hoshino, "Nippon tetsudō (3)," pp. 180–181.
145. Of these shares, 25,490 were held in Iwasaki Hisaya's name, and 2,881 in

the names of Mitsubishi executives Shōda Heigorō and Teranishi Seiki: "San'yō kabunushi meibo," p. 170.

146. In 1881, Mitsubishi accepted, under the names of Iwasaki family members and Mitsubishi executives, about 9,000 shares of Nippon Railway stock: Hoshino, "Nippon tetsudō (2)," p. 11. If Mitsubishi had retained its initial shares and taken all of its subsequent capital-stock-increase allocations, its total holdings in 1891 would have been about 28,000 shares. This clearly did not happen, for Mitsubishi's interest in the railroad fell from about 8 percent in 1881 to 4.1 percent in 1886 and to 3.2-percent in 1896: Nippon tetsudō kaisha, "Hyakkabu ijō kabunushi jinmeibo," September 21, 1886, in *SEDS*, vol. 8, p. 572; Hoshino, "Nippon tetsudō (3)," p. 166, and "Nippon tetsudō (2)," p. 19. Using the 3.2-percent figure, one would arrive at a conservative estimate of 11,000–12,000 shares for the amount of Nippon Railway stock held by Mitsubishi in 1891.

147. Kokaze, "Kōtsū shihon," p. 100; Tōjō Tadashi, "Meiji ki tetsudō kaisha no keiei funsō to kabunushi no dōkō: 'Kyūshū tetsudō kaikaku undō' o megutte," *Keiei shi gaku*, vol. 19, no. 4, pp. 8, 11 (January 1985).

148. In 1905–1906, the 15th National held 308,773 shares of railway stock; Mitsubishi (Iwasaki Hisaya and Iwasaki Yanosuke), 157,122 shares; Mitsui (Mitsui Bank and its president, Mitsui Takayasu), 126,752 shares; and the Imperial Household, 63,326 shares: Sugiyama Kazuo, "Meiji 30 nendai," pp. 156–157, 160–161, 170.

149. The available lists indicate that Mitsui maintained its approximately 1-percent stake in the Nippon from 1881 to 1896: Hoshino, "Nippon tetsudō (2)," pp. 10, 19–20, and "Nippon tetsudō (3)," p. 166. Mitsui apparently held 1,000 shares in the Ryōmō under the names of two Mitsui Bussan employees: Ishii Tsuneo, "Ryōmō kabunushi," p. 143.

150. Takechi, "Nisshin sensōgo," p. 10. Mitsui's interest in the San'yō Railway at this time appears to have been limited to the 1,012 shares held under the name of the aforementioned Kobe branch manager of the Mitsui Bank: "San'yō kabunushi meibo," p. 170.

151. "Kaku shisetsu tetsudō dai kabunushi ichiranhyō," no. 5, p. 22; Takechi, "Nisshin sensōgo," p. 22.

152. Takechi, "Nisshin sensōgo," pp. 10, 15, 30; Hoshino, "Nippon tetsudō (2)," pp. 19–20, and "Nippon tetsudō (3)," p. 166.

153. Hoshino, "Nippon tetsudō (2)," p. 16n4; Takechi, "Nisshin sensōgo," pp. 14–17. For more on noble investment in railway companies in the late 1890s, see Imuta Toshimitsu, "Kazoku shisan to tōshi kōdō: kyū daimyō no kabushiki tōshi o chūshin ni," *Chihō kin'yū shi kenkyū*, no. 18, pp. 1–49 (March 1987); on the formation and investment of peers' capital in general, see the following by Senda Minoru: "Kazoku shihon no seiritsu, tenkai: ippanteki kōsatsu," *Shakai keizai shi gaku*, vol. 52, no. 1, pp. 1–37

(April 1986); and "Kazoku shihon no seiritsu, tenkai: Meiji, Taishō ki no kyū Tsuchiura hanshu Tsuchiya ke ni tsuite," *Shakai keizai shi gaku*, vol. 55, no. 1, pp. 1-36 (April 1989).

Kokaze makes the interesting observation that the designation of Kyushu and San'yō railway shares as hereditary peerage assets in March and April 1890 helped keep their prices from falling as much as spinning-company shares: Kokaze, "Kōtsū shihon," pp. 95, 105n38.

154. Sugiyama Kazuo, "Kigyō no zaimu, tōshi katsudō," p. 57. In September 1891, Fujita held 300 shares in the San'yō Railway, for which his group undertook most of the construction work (see Nakamigawa Hikojirō to Motoyama Hikoichi, February 2, 1887, in *Nakamigawa*, p. 188), and one of his managers, Motoyama Hikoichi, had another 300: "San'yō kabunushi meibo," p. 172. In addition, in March 1895, Fujita and Motoyama together possessed 2,420 shares of the Chikuhō Industrial's first stock issue, a total second only to that of the Iwasaki: *Chikuhō tetsudō kabushiki kaisha kabunushi jinmeihyō*, 1895, Teishin-shō kōbunsho, vol. 9 (1895), no. 8, Japan Railway Archives, Tokyo.
155. In September 1894, Amenomiya had a 9-percent interest in the Hokkaido Colliery and Railway, second only to that of the Imperial Household, and in March 1894, he was the largest holder of the Kōbu Railway's first stock issue with 2,224 shares, or 12 percent of the total: Takechi, "Nisshin sensōgo," p. 10; *Kōbu tetsudō kabushiki kaisha, Dai jūnikai hōkoku*, 1894, Teishin-shō kōbunsho, vol. 7 (1893-1894), no. 6.
156. In March 1896, Moroto was the largest holder (2,750 shares) of the Hōshū Railway's first stock issue: "Shisetsu tetsudō kaisha dai kabunushi ichiranhyō," *Tetsudō zasshi*, no. 7, p. 23 (July 1896).
157. Tanaka held 3,320 shares in the Hokkaido Colliery and Railway in September 1894, 1,236 shares in the San'yō Railway in September 1891, and 850 shares of the Kansai Railway's first issue in June 1894: Takechi, "Nisshin sensōgo," p. 10; "San'yō kabunushi meibo," p. 170; Kansai tetsudō, *Dai jūnikai hōkoku*, p. 36. In 1902-1903, Tanaka, with a total of 27,217 shares, appears to have been the fifth largest railway stockholder after the 15th National Bank, Mitsubishi, Mitsui, and the Imperial Household: Sugiyama Kazuo, "Meiji 30 nendai," pp. 155-156.
158. Sugiyama Kazuo, "Kabushiki kaisha seido," p. 116.
159. "San'yō kabunushi meibo," p. 170.
160. Ishii Tsuneo, "Ryōmō kabunushi," pp. 142-147. As far as can be determined, there were only three local textile producers among the major stockholders.
161. Ono Kazushige, "Kōbu tetsudō to Tachikawa," *Tachikawa-shi shi kenkyū*, no. 2, p. 116 (December 1965).
162. Ishii Tsuneo, "Ryōmō kabunushi," pp. 141-142. The prefectures holding

second and third place in terms of percentage of total stock accounted for were Niigata (22.7 percent) and Wakayama (13.1 percent).
163. Takechi, "Nisshin sensōgo," pp. 53–55; Ishii Tsuneo, "Ryōmō kabunushi," pp. 143–145.
164. Sugiyama Kazuo, "Meiji 30 nendai," p. 159n1.
165. Noda gives the somewhat misleading impression that the Railway Construction Law of 1892 marked a sharp dividing line between eras of trunk- and local-railroad incorporation, respectively: Noda, "Corporate Finance of Railroad Companies," p. 88. Sugiyama makes clear that the majority of railroads founded during the 1880s and early 1890s were relatively small in terms of projected operating mileage; of the eighteen companies that applied for licenses before 1890 and eventually received them, twelve planned to build less than fifty miles of line each: Sugiyama Kazuo, "Kigyō no zaimu, tōshi katsudō," p. 60.
166. Murakami Teiichi, *Minami Kiyoshi den* (Hayami Tarō, 1909), pp. 69–70.
167. Tagawa-shi, ed., *Tagawa-shi shi*, vol. 2 (Tagawa: Tagawa shiyakusho, 1976), pp. 912–913.
168. "San'yō kabunushi meibo," pp. 173–174.
169. Noda, *Nihon shōken shijō*, p. 263.
170. Sugiyama Kazuo, "Kigyō no zaimu, tōshi katsudō," p. 57.
171. Fishlow, p. 308.
172. "Kyūshū tetsudō hōkokusho," p. 278.
173. Kikuchi Takenori, *Nakamigawa Hikojirō-kun* (Jinmin shinbunsha shuppan-bu, 1903), pp. 57–59. In late 1890, for example, the railroad sought to keep construction costs down by laying track over a mountain pass on the Hakata-Moji section using a maximum gradient of 1/44, more than twice the usual limit, instead of building a tunnel: *NKTH*, vol. 2, pp. 608–609.
174. "Kyūshū tetsudō hōkokusho," p. 278.
175. *NKTH*, vol. 2, pp. 582–584.
176. Kikuchi, p. 60.
177. Murakami Sadamu, "Keiroku," in *Nakamigawa*, p. 185. On June 23, 1892, for example, the *Tōkyō nichinichi* reported that the Nippon Railway had arranged to buy 122 cars from the San'yō for ¥110,000; the San'yō planned to use this money to pay off debts or to raise the dividend by depositing it and "distributing the interest as much as possible among the stockholders," the latter being a clear indication of the extent to which investors had gained control over decision making in the company.
178. Murakami Sadamu, p. 185.
179. "Kyūshū tetsudō hōkokusho," p. 277.
180. Memorandum from Matsukata Masayoshi to Prime Minister Yamagata Aritomo, April 25, 1891, *Kōbun ruiju*, 15th ser. (1891), vol. 37, no. 8.

181. "Kyūshū tetsudō hōkokusho," p. 277. The firm did not resume collection of stock payments until 1894: *NKTH*, vol. 4, p. 537.
182. Cited in memorandum from Home Minister Soejima Taneomi to Prime Minister Matsukata Masayoshi, April 9, 1892, Kōbun ruiju, 16th ser. (1892), vol. 38, no. 4.
183. *NKTH*, vol. 4, pp. 537–539.
184. *Nihon teikoku tōkei nenkan*, vol. 10 (Naikaku tōkei-kyoku, 1891), p. 330, vol. 11 (1892), p. 680, and vol. 12 (1893), p. 673. A profit account is not available for 1890, but the dividend rate suggests that stock dividends took up the entire profits and subsidies for that year.
185. *TKN, 1907*, appendix, p. 41.
186. President Nakamigawa of the San'yō Railway, in a petition dated October 9, 1889, to Prime Minister Kuroda Kiyotaka requesting that the government grant his firm a special construction subsidy, vividly described the predicament of a recently established railway company caught between stockholder expectations of immediate dividends and the long gestation period of railway capital:

> The raising of capital is not proceeding as we had hoped. This has resulted from the fact that we cannot really distribute suitable returns on the capital we use to defray building expenses during [the period of] railroad construction work. Even if the outlook for profit making following the opening of the entire line is good, the situation during the coming nine years [the projected total construction time] is such that one is forced to leave huge sums of capital in a state no different from that of being interest-free. Accordingly, it is truly unavoidable that, with the common stockholder unable to bear this hardship and stock payments likely to be long delayed, the company's affairs are not going as we had hoped: Nakamigawa, p. 165.

187. Patrick, p. 283.
188. Ibid.
189. *TKN, 1907*, appendix, pp. 44–45.
190. *NTS*, vol. 1, p. 729.
191. Ibid., pp. 779, 781.
192. *Teikoku tetsudō yōkan*, 3rd ed. (Tetsudō jihō-kyoku, 1906), p. 364; *NKTH*, vol. 2, pp. 492, 502.
193. *NKTH*, vol. 2, pp. 512, 517.
194. I was able to identify the residences of six of the railroad's seven directors; of these, four were nonlocal: ibid., pp. 494, 502.
195. *NTS*, vol. 1, p. 782. Documents concerning the merger can be found in Kōbun ruiju, 15th ser., vol. 31, nos. 13–15.

196. "Ryōmō tetsudō kaisha dokuritsu ni kessu," *Tōkyō keizai zasshi*, May 28, 1892, p. 759.
197. "Ryōmō tetsudō kaisha no rinji sōkai," *Tōkyō keizai zasshi*, July 30, 1892, pp. 170–171.
198. *NKTH*, vol. 2, p. 491.
199. Nakanishi, p. 59.
200. Adachi Ritsuen, *Imamura Seinosuke-kun jireki* (Otani Matsujirō, 1906), p. 165.
201. Ishii Tsuneo, "Ryōmō kabunushi," pp. 130–131, 134.
202. Ibid., pp. 142–146.
203. Adachi, pp. 166–167.
204. Ibid., pp. 167–168.
205. Ibid., p. 169.
206. A budget was prepared for the railroad in 1886 with the expectation that freight transport would account for well over half the company's revenue: Ishii Tsuneo, "Ryōmō tetsudō kaisha no keiei shiteki kenkyū," *Meiji daigaku shōgaku kenkyūjo nenpō*, no. 4, pp. 168–171 (1958).
207. *NKTH*, vol. 2, p. 492.
208. Sugiyama Kazuo, "Kigyō no zaimu, tōshi katsudō," pp. 58–60.
209. *Tōkyō kabushiki torihikijo*, p. 127; *Ō-kabu*, p. 589.
210. *Tōkyō nichinichi shinbun*, September 17–18 and November 12, 1891, cited in Wada, pp. 33–34; *Tōkyō kabushiki torihikijo*, p. 127.
211. In the early 1890s, railway shares probably accounted for over half of all shares held as loan collateral by the large city banks and for about three quarters of the volume of exchange on the Tokyo stock market: Ericson, "Railroads in Crisis," pp. 167, 178; Noda, *Nihon shōken shijō*, p. 234.
212. The petitions are contained in *Tetsudō iken zenshū*, pp. 95–99, 389–393, 396–400. Three to six members of each group appear on the major stockholders list for the Ryōmō in October 1890 or the San'yō in September 1891, or both.
213. Ibid., pp. 378–381, 387–389, 394–396, 534–538.
214. Harada, "Tetsudō fusetsu hō," pp. 25–26. A quick check of the membership lists for the Tokyo and Osaka chambers of commerce at the time of the nationalization movement revealed that three of the fifty members of the Tokyo chamber, besides Mitsui Bussan under the names of different representatives, appear on the 1890 list of major stockholders in the Ryōmō Railway, and six of the fifty members of the Osaka chamber appear on the 1891 list of principal investors in the San'yō: Ishii Kanji, "Kaidai: Shōgyō kaigisho hōkoku," in *Kindai Nihon shōhin ryūtsū shi shiryō*, vol. 6, pt. 2, Shōhin ryūtsū shi kenkyūkai, ed. (Nihon keizai hyōronsha, 1979), pp. 5–6.

215. *Tetsudō iken zenshū*, pp. 389–538 passim; "San'yō kabunushi meibo," pp. 170–173.
216. "San'yō kabunushi meibo," pp. 170–174.
217. "Tetsudō dai kabunushi no kesshin ikaga," in *Tetsudō iken zenshū*, pp. 198–200.
218. "Tetsudō kaiage ni kanshi Kawada Nihon ginkō sōsai kaku ginkōka to kyōgisu," *Tōkyō keizai zasshi*, November 28, 1891, in *Tetsudō iken zenshū*, pp. 105–107.
219. *SEDS*, vol. 9, pp. 532, 546. The texts of both documents and a record of the discussion of the bankers' petition by the chamber of commerce are included in *Tetsudō iken zenshū*, pp. 95–104, 357–361.
220. Tōkyō ginkō shūkaijo, "Seifu min'yū no tetsudō o baishū shi, sono enchō kantsū o reito subeki no gi," November 30, 1891, in *Tetsudō iken zenshū*, pp. 97–98.
221. "Tetsudō dai kabunushi," p. 198.
222. "San'yō kabunushi meibo," p. 171; Ishii Tsuneo, "Ryōmō kabunushi," pp. 143–144.
223. Nakanishi, p. 90.
224. Ibid., p. 95.
225. "Tetsudō kaiage Kawada Nihon ginkō sōsai," p. 106.
226. Ibid., p. 107.
227. "Tetsudō kaiage ni kansuru chōsa-iin hōkokusho," in *Tetsudō iken zenshū*, pp. 39, 41. The petition of the Osaka Chamber of Commerce to the Diet is also included in ibid., pp. 361–370.
228. Ibid., pp. 51–52.
229. *Tōkyō kabushiki torihikijo*, p. 127.
230. In twelve of the twenty-one railroads licensed before 1893, forty-two of the seventy-five directors in June 1896 appear on their companies' major stockholders lists for either March or September 1896: "Kaku shisetsu tetsudō dai kabunushi ichiranhyō," *Tetsudō zasshi* (retitled *Tetsudō* from no. 19), no. 5, pp. 21–23 (June 1896), no. 8, pp. 22–24 (July 1896), and no. 26, pp. 30–32 (November 1896); "Shisetsu tetsudō kaisha"; "Kaku shisetsu tetsudō jūyaku oyobi kachō shimei ichiranhyō," *Tetsudō zasshi*, no. 9, pp. 29–31 (July 1896) and no. 10, pp. 23–26 (July 1896). The definition of "major stockholders" ranges from owners of 100 or more shares in the case of the smaller companies to owners of 1,000 or more in that of the largest firm.
231. "San'yō tetsudō kaisha teikanchū kōsei no ken," Kōbun ruiju, 13th ser., vol. 46, no. 36.
232. "San'yō kabunushi meibo," pp. 170–174.
233. *Nakamigawa*, p. 135.
234. Sugiyama Kazuo, "Kigyō no zaimu, tōshi katsudō," p. 71.

235. Ishii Tsuneo, "Ryōmō kabunushi," pp. 137, 145.
236. The average number of names on the major stockholders lists for the twelve companies in the 1896 sample is twenty-seven. At least half of the twelve presidents or managing directors of these railroads appear among the thirty largest shareholders in their companies; one fourth, among the ten largest.
237. "San'yō kabunushi meibo," pp. 170–174.
238. Tsunehiko Yui, "The Personality and Career of Hikojirō Nakamigawa, 1887–1901," *Business History Review*, vol. 44, no. 1, p. 45 (Spring 1970).
239. Nakamigawa Hikojirō, letter to Motoyama Hikoichi, February 2, 1887, in *Nakamigawa*, pp. 187–189.
240. Yui, p. 45. For a detailed description of Nakamigawa's policies as San'yō Railway president, see Kikuchi, pp. 53–69, also reprinted in *Nakamigawa*, pp. 137–142.
241. Murakami Sadamu, in *Nakamigawa*, p. 183; Kikuchi, p. 57.
242. Ida Seiza, "San'yō tetsudō jidai," in *Nakamigawa*, p. 178.
243. Kikuchi, p. 63.
244. *Imanishi Rinzaburō ibunroku*, vol. 1, suppl., Komatsu Mitsuo, ed. (Osaka: Imanishi Yosaburō, 1925), p. 4.
245. Yui, p. 47.
246. *NKTH*, vol. 2, p. 585; "San'yō kabunushi meibo," pp. 170–174.
247. *Imanishi*, vol. 1, suppl., p. 4b.
248. *Tōkyō nichinichi shinbun*, June 17, 1892, cited in *NKTH*, vol. 2, p. 587.
249. Adachi, p. 177.
250. Ibid., p. 179.
251. Ibid., pp. 180–181.
252. Ibid., pp. 178, 181. For a contrary view of Imamura as representing "a class of stable shareholders"—"the so-called railroad bourgeoisie"—that rose to prominence in the wake of the 1890 Panic, see Kokaze, "Kōtsū shihon," p. 101.
253. *Tetsudō senjin roku*, pp. 217–218, 247.
254. *NKTH*, vol. 2, p. 596.
255. See Article 2 of the government orders (*meireisho*) specifying the terms of the subsidy granted the Hokkaido Colliery and Railway in November 1889: ibid., p. 651. The San'yō and Kyushu subsidy orders also stipulated that, for the duration of the subvention, the appointment and dismissal of the president and vice-president would require the approval of the finance minister: ibid., pp. 572, 602, 605.

A parallel case of state intervention in private railway management in the United States was that of the Union Pacific Railroad. Under the Pacific Railroad Act of 1864, the government, as a condition for providing the Union Pacific with a generous land grant and loan, was to appoint

five of the railroad's twenty directors, with each of the firm's standing and special committees to include one of those five: Goodrich, pp. 184–185.
256. *NKTH*, vol. 2, pp. 645, 653.
257. On the careers of Minami and Sengoku, see *Tetsudō senjin roku*, pp. 201–202, 344–346; and Murakami Teiichi.
258. *Tetsudō senjin roku*, pp. 305–306; *NKTH*, vol. 2, p. 662.
259. *Tetsudō senjin roku*, p. 356.
260. See *Kōgaku hakushi Shiraishi Naoji den* (Kōgaku hakushi Shiraishi Naoji den hensankai, 1943), pp. 77–108.
261. The two smaller companies were the Ryōmō and Mito, of which President Narahara of the Nippon Railway was serving concurrently as chief officer.
262. *Sōken Matsumoto Jūtarō-ō den* (Matsumoto-ō dōzō kensetsukai, 1922), p. 29; *Shōin Motoyama Hikoichi-ō*, Ko Motoyama shachō denki hensan iinkai, ed. (Osaka: Ōsaka mainichi shinbunsha, 1937; Tōkyō nichinichi shinbunsha, 1937), p. 141; *Hayami Tarō den* (Osaka: Ko Hayami Tarō-shi hensan-kakari, 1939), p. 74.
263. Shiraishi Naoji et al., "Tetsudō kakuchō narabini baishū ni tsuki seigan," undated, in *Tetsudō iken zenshū*, pp. 400–404. The other two companies represented were the Mito and Sangū railways. Even after the defeat of the nationalization bill, President Takahashi of the Kyushu Railway continued to recommend that his company sell out to the government, actually securing informal agreement on that course of action from both the directors and shareholders in October 1892: Kokaze, "Kōtsū shihon," p. 97.
264. *Tetsudō senjin roku*, pp. 300–301.
265. Ban Naonosuke, "Zenkoku tetsudō kaiage ni kansuru seifu no hōryaku o ronzu," *Tōkyō keizai zasshi*, September 26, 1891, in *SEDS*, vol. 9, pp. 541–543.
266. For a look at Ban's counterparts in the early American railroads, see Alfred D. Chandler, Jr., *The Visible Hand: The Managerial Revolution in American Business* (Cambridge: Belknap Press of Harvard University Press, 1977), pp. 97–101.
267. This provision, included in Article 20, read as follows: "At the time of establishment, the promoters... must appoint [to the board of directors] one person from each prefecture along the railway line": Hoshino, "Nippon tetsudō (1)," p. 100.
268. Tagawa-shi, ed., vol. 2, pp. 912–913.
269. Ishii Tsuneo, "Ryōmō kabunushi," pp. 136–138, 147.
270. Adachi, p. 180.
271. *Hara Rokurō-ō den*, vol. 2 (Hara Kunizō, 1937), p. 257.
272. *Tetsudō iken zenshū*, pp. 374–378, 387–389, 419–427, 458–476, 489–519.

The petition of the Hiroshima Chamber of Commerce is also included in *Hiroshima-ken shi: kindai gendai shiryō hen*, vol. 2 (Hiroshima-ken, 1975), pp. 563–565.
273. *Tetsudō iken zenshū*, pp. 377–378.
274. *NKTH*, vol. 2, p. 414; *NTS*, vol. 1, p. 829.
275. Kōbun ruiju, 13th ser., vol. 50, cited in *NKTH*, vol. 2, pp. 564–565. As the *Japan Weekly Mail* explained to its Western readers on October 12, 1889, "land is here owned by so many small proprietors that the difficulty of transacting business is very greatly enhanced": "The Grievances of Private Railway Companies," p. 325.
276. Kōbun ruiju, 13th ser., vol. 50.
277. Ibid.
278. Ibid.
279. *NTS*, vol. 1, p. 735.
280. *NKTH*, vol. 2, p. 566. The fact that Nakamigawa spearheaded the movement to revise the Compulsory Land Purchase Law casts doubt on the assertion that he took an enlightened view of that act, thinking it "natural to protect proprietorship in a modern civilized society, and did not agree with the other managers": Yui, p. 58, citing Kikuchi, pp. 59–60.
281. "The Protection of Railway Operations," *Japan Weekly Mail*, May 17, 1890, p. 495.
282. *NKTH*, vol. 2, p. 414.
283. Ibid., p. 608.
284. *Kyū-tetsu*, pp. 27–28.
285. Memorial from President Hotta Masayasu of the Chikuhō Industrial Railway to Home Minister Saigō Tsugumichi, May 14, 1891, Tetsudō-in monjo, Chikuhō kōgyō tetsudō, vol. 1 (1888–1893), no. 7.
286. Memorandum from Inoue Masaru to the cabinet, May 27, 1891, ibid.
287. The company managed to finish the sections concerned by the end of this second extension: *NKTH*, vol. 2, p. 639.
288. Ibid., p. 362.
289. Noda, *Nihon shōken shijō*, p. 71.
290. The Hokkaido Railway, licensed in 1900, became the fifth recipient of government railroad subsidies in 1902: *Hokkaidō tetsudō hyaku nen shi*, vol. 1, pp. 218–219.
291. Hoshino, "Nippon tetsudō (2)," pp. 17–18.
292. The other two firms, the Chikuhō Industrial and Kushiro, were also industrial railroads closely tied to mining enterprises.
293. On the Hokkaido Colliery, see Hirose Takiji, "Hokkaidō ni okeru shiyū tetsudō no seikaku: tankō tetsudō to Hokkaidō tetsudō," *Atarashii dō shi*, no. 29, pp. 11–23 (September 1968) and no. 30, pp. 15–25 (November 1968).

294. Actual figures on dividend payouts are unavailable for 1890, but multiplying the average paid-up capital by the dividend rate for each company that year yields estimated payouts of ¥259,000 for the San'yō Railway and ¥241,000 for the Kyushu. The subsidies these firms received in 1890 amounted to 66 percent and 58 percent, respectively, of these estimates.
295. Takizawa Naoshichi, *Kōhon Nihon kin'yū shi ron* (Yūhikaku, 1912), p. 270.
296. *Nihon ginkō enkakushi*, 1st ser., vol. 2, pt. 1 (Nihon ginkō enkakushi hensan-iin, 1913), pp. 170–174; memorial from Bank of Japan governor Kawada Koichirō to Finance Minister Matsukata Masayoshi, May 8, 1890, Matsuo ke monjo, 1st ser., vol. 82, no. 21, Finance Ministry Archives, Tokyo.

In its announcement of the measure, the bank actually designated fifteen kinds of shares as authorized collateral, but it had actually begun accepting five of them—N.Y.K., Tokio Marine Insurance, and three issues of Nippon Railway stock—before the announcement. Noda and Hoshino point out, however, that the expanded discount program included qualitative as well as quantitative changes. Whereas, prior to 1890, the central bank had accepted as loan collateral the stocks of selected business institutions on the grounds that they were under "the special supervision and protection of the government and Imperial Household" and were therefore "different from ordinary banks and companies" (*Meiji zaisei shi*, vol. 14 [Meiji zaisei shi hakkōsho, 1927], p. 406), in 1890, it broadened the scope of authorized collateral to include such "ordinary companies" as the Osaka and Sanuki railroads: Noda, *Nihon shōken shijō*, p. 222. Furthermore, under the extended system, the Bank of Japan abolished the restriction of a given share's collateral value to its paid-up value as well as the limitation on the amount of funds that the central bank could lend to a single commercial bank by means of bill discounting. Together, these changes made it easy for commercial banks to borrow large sums of money from the Bank of Japan: Hoshino, "Nippon tetsudō (2)," p. 18n1.
297. For estimates on the proportion of the railway companies' total paid-up capital for which bank loans secured by railroad stocks accounted in the early 1890s, see Ericson, "Railroads in Crisis," pp. 167, 178.
298. "Kin'yū kyūsai ni kansuru Ōsaka kaigi," *Tōkyō keizai zasshi*, April 26, 1890, and "Ōsaka hyōtei no kekka ikaga," *Tōkyō nichinichi shinbun*, May 9, 1890, both in *SEDS*, vol. 5, pp. 216–218.
299. "Seien sensei den shokō" (1919–1923), in *SEDS*, vol. 5, p. 211.
300. "Shibusawa Eiichi-kun no kin'yū hippaku dan," p. 212.
301. "Dōmei ginkō rinji shūkai rokuji," April 11, 1890, *Kaigi rokuji*, January 1889–December 1890, and "Migi no rinjikai o unagashitaru in'yu," *Chūgai shōgyō shinpō*, April 11, 1890, both in *SEDS*, vol. 6 (1955), pp. 187, 209–210. According to one newspaper report, the Kyushu Railway had in

fact originally proposed this measure to the Kyushu Bankers' Association: "Ōsaka ni okeru kin'yū hippaku no kyūsai saku," *Tōkyō nichinichi shinbun*, April 15, 1890, in *SEDS*, vol. 5, p. 213.
302. *SEDS*, vol. 6, p. 187.
303. Tōkyō dōmei ginkō, "Dai hyaku-nikai teishiki shūkai rokuji," May 15, 1890, in *SEDS*, vol. 6, pp. 187–189.
304. Ōkura-shō kansa-kyoku, "Dai jūsanji ginkō eigyō hōkoku," 1890, in *Nihon kin'yū shi shiryō: Meiji Taishō hen*, vol. 7, pt. 1, Nihon ginkō chōsa-kyoku, ed. (Ōkura-shō insatsu-kyoku, 1960), p. 482.
305. *Meiji zaisei shi*, vol. 14, p. 942.
306. Directive from Watanabe Kunitake to the Bank of Japan, November 21, 1892, Matsuo ke monjo, 1st ser., vol. 82, no. 39.
307. "Nihon ginkō enkaku teiyō (shuyō nisshi)," 1882–1905, in *Nihon kin'yū shi shiryō: Meiji Taishō hen*, vol. 10, suppl. (1957), p. 181.
308. Noda, *Nihon shōken shijō*, p. 224.
309. *Kyū-tetsu*, pp. 22–23; Shibusawa Eiichi, letter to Itō Hirobumi, March 18, 1893, in *SEDS*, vol. 9, pp. 6–7.
310. *TKN, 1907*, appendix, pp. 22–46 passim.
311. *Honpō shasai ryaku shi*, Takahira Takao, ed. (Nihon kōgyō ginkō chōsa-kakari, 1927), p. 3. The firm planned to apply the proceeds from its bond issue to construction of the Nara and Sakurai stations: "Ōsaka tetsudō kaisha," *Dai Nihon tetsudō zasshi*, no. 9, p. 21 (June 21, 1890).
312. *Sōken Matsumoto*, p. 30; "San'yō tetsudō kaisha no shasai boshū," *Tōkyō keizai zasshi*, March 18, 1893, pp. 394–395; *TKN, 1907*, appendix, p. 24.
313. Kyūshū tetsudō kabushiki kaisha, *Dai jukkai hōkoku*, 1893, p. 8, cited in Noda, *Nihon shōken shijō*, p. 90; *TKN, 1907*, appendix, p. 41.
314. "Kyūshū tetsudō hōkokusho," p. 278.
315. Sugiyama Kazuo, "Kabushiki kaisha seido," pp. 122–123.
316. *Honpō shasai ryaku shi*, pp. 13–16; Noda, *Nihon shōken shijō*, p. 130.
317. Kyūshū tetsudō kabushiki kaisha, *Dai jūikkai hōkoku*, 1894, p. 14, cited in Noda, *Nihon shōken shijō*, p. 95.
318. Noda, *Nihon shōken shijō*, pp. 93, 96.
319. *NTS*, vol. 1, pp. 929–930.

3. The Making of the Railway Construction Law

1. Cited in Nagano-ken, ed., vol. 7, p. 565.
2. Harada, "Tetsudō fusetsu hō," p. 40.
3. Ibid., p. 30.
4. For a fuller treatment of party and administration strategies in the early sessions of the Diet, see Banno Junji, *Meiji kenpō taisei no kakuritsu* (Tōkyō daigaku shuppankai, 1971). Also important in the preparation of

this chapter were Ariizumi Sadao, *Meiji seiji shi no kiso katei: chihō seiji jōkyō shi ron* (Yoshikawa kōbunkan, 1980); Toriumi Yasushi, "Tetsudō fusetsu hō seitei katei ni okeru tetsudō kisei dōmeikai no atsuryoku katsudō," *Tōkyō daigaku kyōyō gakubu jinbunkagaku-ka kiyō*, no. 43, pp. 139–157 (August 1967); and especially Wada Hiroshi, "Shoki gikai to tetsudō mondai," *Shi gaku zasshi*, vol. 84, pp. 31–52 (October 1975).

5. *Inoue Kowashi den: shiryō hen*, vol. 1, Inoue Kowashi denki hensan iinkai, ed. (Kokugakuin daigaku toshokan, 1966), pp. 383–390.
6. "Chiso kaisei ni tsuite," 1891, Mutsu Munemitsu kankei monjo, Kensei shiryō-shitsu, National Diet Library, Tokyo.
7. Harada, "Tetsudō fusetsu hō," p. 24.
8. *Ozaki Saburō jijo ryaku den*, vol. 2 (Chūō kōronsha, 1977), p. 272.
9. This agreement is evidenced by the fact that Home Minister Shinagawa Yajirō, Prime Minister Matsukata, and Inoue Kowashi, in their Diet speeches and memorials, repeated practically word for word the argument made by Inoue Masaru in his policy proposal.
10. *Inoue Kowashi den*, vol. 2 (1968), p. 455.
11. *Nihon kagaku gijutsu shi taikei*, vol. 16, *Doboku gijutsu*, Nihon kagaku shi gakkai, ed. (Daiichi hōki kabushiki kaisha, 1970), p. 103.
12. Wada, p. 32.
13. The text of Inoue's proposal can be found in *NTS*, vol. 1, pp. 916–943, from which the following quotations are drawn.
14. See, for example, Ariizumi, p. 218, on the use of the "military-railway" argument by opinion makers in Yamanashi prefecture.
15. Harada, "Tetsudō fusetsu hō," p. 41n20.
16. *Tetsudō iken zenshū*, p. 10.
17. For Takajima's statement in favor of nationalization, made at the time of the first reading of the cabinet's Public Bond Bill in the lower house, see *Dai Nihon teikoku gikai shi*, vol. 1 (Shizuoka: Dai Nihon teikoku gikai shi kankōkai, 1926), p. 1429; for Kawakami's, see *Tetsudō iken zenshū*, pp. 10–25.
18. Ozawa Takeo, "Tetsudō ni kansuru iken," p. 10, Transportation Museum Archives, Tokyo. Reprinted in revised form under the title "Tetsudō ron" in *Tetsudō iken zenshū*, pp. 272–281, to which the following notes refer.
19. Ibid., pp. 274, 276.
20. Ibid., p. 276.
21. Ibid., p. 278.
22. Aoki Eiichi, Harada Katsumasa, and Miyazawa Motokazu, "Meiji hyaku nen kinen tokushū gō," *Han kōtsū*, vol. 68, p. 31 (October 1968).
23. Ozawa, "Tetsudō ron," pp. 279–280.
24. Shima, pp. 107–108.
25. "Tetsudō tōgi," *Tōkyō nichinichi shinbun*, September 22, 1891.

26. *Ozaki*, vol. 2, pp. 286–289. Ozaki gives the date of the meeting as September 17th.
27. Ibid., p. 295.
28. *NTS*, vol. 1, pp. 946–948.
29. Ibid., p. 949.
30. For the documents detailing the decision-making process culminating in the cabinet's acceptance of these two railway bills, see Kōbun ruiju, 15th ser., vol. 37, no. 21.
31. Banno, p. 54. The military outlays included ¥2,300,000 for the establishment of a steelworks under the jurisdiction of the Navy Ministry.
32. Ibid., p. 56.
33. *Gikai seido shichijū nen shi: seitō, kai, ha hen* (Shūgi-in, Sangi-in, 1961), p. 260. For a listing of lower-house members in the second Diet by party affiliation, see ibid., pp. 254–258; for rough data on their occupations, though often referring to positions they held after serving in the Diet, a useful source is *Shūgi-in meikan*, Nihon kokusei chōsakai, ed. (Kokusei shuppan-shitsu, 1977).
34. *Kokkai*, October 15, 1891.
35. *Tōhō*, no. 1, p. 30 (October 25, 1891).
36. Wada, pp. 32, 48n18.
37. Ibid., p. 33.
38. Banno, p. 64.
39. Ibid., pp. 62–63.
40. Ibid., p. 65; Ariizumi, pp. 201–202.
41. Wada, p. 34.
42. *Tōkyō nichinichi shinbun*, December 22, 1891.
43. Ibid., December 19, 1891.
44. Uda Tadashi, "Meiji zenki Tōhoku kansen tetsudō kensetsu keikaku to chihō jijō: shiryō shōkai o chūshin ni," *Ōtemon keizai ronshū*, vol. 4, no. 1, pp. 98–99 (September 1969).
45. The bill is included in *Tetsudō iken zenshū*, pp. 252–256.
46. Wada, p. 35.
47. Petitions calling for government railway construction submitted to the Diet by residents of three of the prefectures represented in the Railroad Promotion League—Niigata, Ishikawa, and Fukui—are contained in *Tetsudō iken zenshū*, pp. 381–387, 538–546, 546–572.
48. Four of the prefectures represented in the railway league—Fukui, Nagano, Niigata, and Fukushima—had some railroad line in 1891; the rest, including Toyama and Akita, had none.
49. *Kokkai*, December 10, 1891.
50. A summary of part of the discussion between Itagaki and the delegation leader, Odagiri Yoshiaki, is included in *Tetsudō iken zenshū*, pp. 109–112.

A more complete account is to be found in the December 18, 1891 issue of *Kyōchū nippō*, cited in Ariizumi, pp. 213–214.
51. *Tetsudō iken zenshū*, p. 110.
52. Ibid., p. 111.
53. Ibid.
54. Ibid., p. 112.
55. Ariizumi, p. 213.
56. Ibid.
57. Ibid.
58. Ibid., pp. 211–212.
59. Ibid., p. 212.
60. Ibid., pp. 214–215.
61. *Tōhō*, no. 5, p. 23 (December 25, 1891).
62. *Tetsudō kisei dōmeikai hōkoku* (Tetsudō kisei dōmeikai, 1892), p. 31.
63. *Dai Nihon teikoku gikai shi*, vol. 1, p. 1436.
64. Wada, p. 37.
65. *Dai Nihon teikoku gikai shi*, vol. 1, p. 1436. See ibid., p. 1442, for a list of the committee members.
66. "Shūgi-in tetsudō baishū hōan shinsa tokubetsu iinkai sokkiroku," 1st session, December 21, 1891, p. 1, *Shūgi-in iinkai kaigiroku*, National Diet Library, Tokyo.
67. Ibid., 2nd session, p. 6.
68. *Dai Nihon teikoku gikai shi*, vol. 1, p. 1496.
69. Aoki, Harada, and Miyazawa, pp. 32, 48; *NKTH*, vol. 1, p. 186.
70. While serving as a member of the second Diet, Nakano was concurrently vice-president of the Tokyo stock exchange. He came under intense pressure there from the stockbrokers, who were clamoring for nationalization as a relief measure following the 1890 Panic, and was eventually forced to resign from the exchange in January 1892: Yamamura Akira, "Meiji 25 nen no tetsudō fusetsu hō ni tsuite: hō o meguru rongi o chūshin to shite," *Un'yu to keizai*, vol. 24, no. 6, pp. 69–70 (June 1964).
71. *Dai Nihon teikoku gikai shi*, vol. 1, pp. 1515–1516.
72. Ibid., p. 1513.
73. *Tōhō*, no. 10, p. 14 (April 10, 1892).
74. Wada, p. 38.
75. *Inoue Kakugorō-kun enzetsu hikki: gikai kaisan iken* (1892), pp. 65–66.
76. *Itō Hirobumi kankei monjo*, vol. 2 (Hanawa shobō, 1974), p. 167.
77. *Tetsudō kisei dōmeikai hōkoku*, pp. 3–4.
78. Ibid., p. 30.
79. Ibid., p. 48.
80. Toriumi, pp. 147–148.
81. Ariizumi, p. 219.

82. Ibid., p. 225.
83. Ibid., pp. 224, 228.
84. *Gikai seido*, pp. 254–270.
85. Cited in Wada, p. 42.
86. Shimizu Ichitarō, "Tai gikai saku," in Itō Hirobumi, ed., *Hisho ruisan: teikoku gikai shiryō*, vol. 1 (1934), p. 507.
87. *Tetsudō kisei dōmeikai hōkoku*, pp. 50–51.
88. George Akita, *Foundations of Constitutional Government in Modern Japan, 1868–1900* (Cambridge: Harvard University Press, 1967), p. 10. Akita discusses Inoue's role in the making of the Meiji Constitution.
89. Inoue Kowashi monjo, B-3762, B-3783, B-3794, Kokugakuin daigaku, Tokyo.
90. Ban, pp. 541–543.
91. Inoue's private papers contain several manuscript drafts of the first part of the pamphlet, which was entitled *Tetsudō ron* (Treatise on Railroads), as well as a newspaper clipping of a lengthy review of the work: Inoue Kowashi monjo, B-3768, B-3769, B-3785.
92. Ibid., B-3788, B-3790, B-3791, B-3792. On Paternostro and other foreign employees of the Meiji government, see H. J. Jones, *Live Machines: Hired Foreigners and Meiji Japan* (Vancouver: University of British Columbia Press, 1980).
93. "Shisetsu tetsudō baishū hōan ni kansuru ken," Mutsu Munemitsu kankei monjo.
94. Ibid.
95. See, for example, the editorial in the April 28, 1892 issue of *Nihon*.
96. *Yūbin hōchi shinbun*, April 7, 1892.
97. *Inoue Kowashi den*, vol. 4 (1971), p. 693.
98. Ibid.
99. Kōbun ruiju, 16th ser., vol. 8, no. 41.
100. "Tetsudō kaigi o mōkuru no gi," Matsukata ke monjo, vol. 61, no. 1, Finance Ministry Archives, Tokyo.
101. Kōbun ruiju, 16th ser., vol. 8, no. 41.
102. Private business was also in on the act, as the Tokyo Chamber of Commerce, in its nationalization petition of December 1891, called for the establishment of an organ that would enable businessmen to participate in railway policy making: *Tetsudō iken zenshū*, p. 361.
103. Kōbun ruiju, 16th ser., vol. 8, no. 41.
104. Wada, p. 42.
105. *Jiyū*, April 26, 1892.
106. Detection letter of May 8, 1892, Matsukata ke monjo, vol. 61.
107. Yamamura Akira, p. 70.
108. *Yamanashi-ken gikai shi*, vol. 2 (Kōfu: Yamanashi-ken gikai, 1970), p. 109.

109. Toriumi, pp. 149–152.
110. *NTS*, vol. 1, p. 950.
111. Inoue Kowashi monjo, B-3786.
112. Toriumi, p. 151.
113. Yamamura Akira, p. 70.
114. Toriumi, p. 151.
115. *Yamanashi-ken gikai shi*, vol. 2, p. 109.
116. *Chōya shinbun*, May 12, 1892. At the start of the third session, the Jiyūtō and Chūō kōshōbu each controlled ninety-five seats in the lower house; the Independent Club had thirty-one seats. The Kaishintō, with thirty-seven lower-house members, had declared its opposition to both government bills in line with its policy of private-railway ownership: *Gikai seido*, p. 265.
117. *Dai Nihon teikoku gikai shi*, vol. 1, p. 1829.
118. Ibid., p. 1830; *Gikai seido*, pp. 266–270.
119. "Shūgi-in tetsudō kōsai hōan shisetsu tetsudō baishū hōan shinsa tokubetsu iinkai," May 13, 1892, p. 111, *Shūgi-in iinkai kaigiroku*.
120. *Yamanashi-ken gikai shi*, vol. 2, p. 109.
121. Ibid.
122. Toriumi, p. 151.
123. "Dai san teikoku gikai teishutsu no tetsudō hōan ni taisuru tetsudō kisei dōmeikai no kibō," Transportation Museum Archives, Tokyo.
124. "Shūgi-in tetsudō kōsai hōan tokubetsu iinkai," May 24, 1892, pp. 124–125.
125. Ibid., May 26, 1892, pp. 126–138.
126. *Kokkai*, May 31, 1892.
127. Ibid., June 3, 1892.
128. *Tōhō*, no. 14, p. 16 (June 10, 1892).
129. *Dai Nihon teikoku gikai shi*, vol. 1, pp. 2047–2048.
130. Ibid., p. 2051.
131. Ibid., p. 2084.
132. Ibid., pp. 2090–2091.
133. Ibid., pp. 2093–2095.
134. Ibid., p. 2097.
135. Ibid., pp. 2097–2098.
136. Kaku Risuke, *Dai sanki gikai* (1892), pp. 44–45.
137. Tetsudō kisei dōmeikai, *Tetsudō an ni taisuru kibō*, 1892, p. 1, University of Tokyo Faculty of Economics Library, Tokyo.
138. Kōbun ruiju, 16th ser., vol. 8, no. 41.
139. "Tetsudō fusetsu hōan tokubetsu iinkai kaigiroku," June 8, 1892, p. 421, *Kizoku-in tokubetsu iinkai giji sokkiroku*, National Diet Library, Tokyo.
140. *Dai Nihon teikoku gikai shi*, vol. 1, p. 1742.

141. Ibid., p. 1744.
142. Ibid., pp. 1765–1769.
143. Ibid., pp. 1773–1775.
144. *Yamanashi-ken gikai shi*, vol. 2, p. 87.
145. Shimizu Ichitarō, p. 507.
146. See *NTS*, vol. 1, pp. 955–961, for the text of the law.
147. As Toriumi notes, Hokkaido residents had yet to be given voting rights to the lower house; hence, the parties had no incentive to retain the projected Hokkaido lines from the standpoint of increasing electoral support: Toriumi, p. 154. The Diet eventually passed a separate Hokkaido Railway Construction Law in May 1896: Harada and Aoki, p. 46.
148. The administration, though finally accepting these conditions as the price for securing passage of the law, was none too pleased with them. A memorandum in Inoue Kowashi's personal papers exemplifies this dissatisfaction. According to this document, the provisions for Diet control over line selection and the licensing of private railroads represented "an encroachment on the executive sphere"; in the case of Prussia and the German Empire, the memorandum stated, the government had to obtain Diet approval only to make appropriations for the purchase of private railroads or the building of new lines: Inoue Kowashi monjo, B-3761.
149. See, for example, *NKTH*, vol. 2, p. 399; and *Nihon kagaku gijutsu shi taikei*, vol. 16, p. 193.
150. *NKTH*, vol. 1, p. 189.
151. Aoki, Harada, and Miyazawa, p. 30.
152. Nakanishi, p. 98.
153. Aoki, Harada, and Miyazawa, p. 30; Harada and Aoki, p. 46.
154. Article 13 of the Railway Construction Law: *NTS*, vol. 1, p. 961. The government interpreted this provision even to include companies that had acquired only temporary licenses to build what were subsequently incorporated into the law as "scheduled lines": *NTS*, vol. 2, pp. 257–258.
155. *NKTH*, vol. 4, pp. 222, 225.
156. Shimizu Keijirō, *Shitetsu monogatari* (Shunjūsha, 1930), p. 45.
157. Ochiai Sadaaki, "Tetsudō fusetsu hō no seiritsu: Meiji jū nendai no tetsudō seisaku, zokuhen," *Un'yu to keizai*, vol. 17, no. 9, p. 37 (1957).
158. Aoki, Harada, and Miyazawa, p. 30.
159. Kōbun ruiju, 16th ser., vol. 8, no. 41.
160. Gustav Cohn, "The Railway Policy of Prussia," *Journal of Political Economy*, vol. 1, p. 187 (March 1893).
161. Inoue Kowashi monjo, B-3783.
162. Balthasar H. Meyer, "Railroad Ownership in Germany," in William Z. Ripley, ed., *Railway Problems* (Boston: Ginn & Company, 1907), pp. 664–666.

163. On the beginnings of military involvement in Prussian railroads, see Dennis E. Showalter, "Soldiers and Steam: Railways and the Military in Prussia, 1832 to 1848," *The Historian*, vol. 34, pp. 242–259 (February 1972).
164. Nakanishi, p. 100.
165. Meyer, p. 663.
166. See, for example, *Nihon kagaku gijutsu shi taikei*, vol. 16, pp. 193, 195.
167. Aoki, Harada, and Miyazawa, p. 128, is representative of this view.
168. *Nihon kokuyū tetsudō hyaku nen shi: tsū shi*, pp. 89–90.
169. Harada and Aoki, p. 44.
170. For an example of such local railway leagues, see *Tanaka Gentarō-ō den* (Kyoto: Miura Toyoji, 1934), p. 118.
171. For more on state railroad building under the construction act, see Eiichi Aoki, *Railway Construction*, pp. 10–16; and Harada and Aoki, pp. 46–49.
172. *TKN, 1907*, pp. 30–31, appendix, pp. 22–46 passim.
173. See, for example, the articles on "Railways" in the *Japan Weekly Mail* for May 19, 1894, p. 585; February 1, 1896, p. 120; and February 15, 1896, p. 187.
174. "The Imperial Railway Society," *Japan Weekly Mail*, May 31, 1902, p. 583.

4. Forging a Consensus

1. *Tetsudō kokuyū shimatsu ippan* (Teishin-shō, 1909), p. 66.
2. "The Railway Nationalization Bill," *Japan Weekly Mail*, March 31, 1906, p. 328; *Hara Kei nikki*, vol. 2, Hara Keiichirō, ed. (Fukumura shuppan kabushiki kaisha, 1965), p. 174.
3. *Dai Nihon teikoku gikai shi*, vol. 6 (1928), p. 1120.
4. Alan S. Milward and S. B. Saul, *The Development of the Economies of Continental Europe, 1850–1914* (Cambridge: Harvard University Press, 1980), p. 42.
5. See, for example, Simon Sterne, *Report to the Honorable Thomas F. Bayard, Secretary of State, on the Relations of the Governments of the Nations of Western Europe to the Railways* (Washington, D. C., 1887); Charles Waring, *State-Purchase of Railways* (London, 1887); Clement Edwards, *Railway Nationalization* (London, 1898); William Cunningham, *Should Our Railways Be Nationalised? A Comparison of British, German, and American Systems* (Dunfermline, 1903); Edwin A. Pratt, *State Railways and his The Case against Railway Nationalisation* (London, 1913); and W. M. Acworth, *Historical Sketch of Government Ownership of Railroads in Foreign Countries* (Washington, D.C., 1917).
6. Andō Yoshio, ed., *Kindai Nihon keizai shi yōran* (Tōkyō daigaku shuppankai, 1975), p. 12.
7. Supple, p. 330.

8. Kokaze estimates that it was in 1911 or 1912 that trains finally surpassed coastal vessels in the transport of domestic freight: Kokaze, "Tetsudō kokuyūka," pp. 60–61.
9. See, for example, "Shisetsu tetsudō kaiage no gi," *Tōkyō keizai zasshi*, May 7, 1898, pp. 953–955.
10. *Dai Nihon teikoku gikai shi*, vol. 6, p. 892.
11. *TKN, 1907*, p. 30.
12. Ochiai Sadaaki, "Kokuyū made no tetsudō seisaku (zoku): tetsudō kokuyū hō no seiritsu," *Un'yu to keizai*, vol. 18, no. 10, p. 46 (1958).
13. Calculated from *TKN, 1907*, p. 30; Shima, pp. 86–87.
14. *Den Kenjirō den* (Den Kenjirō denki hensankai, 1932), pp. 122–124.
15. Ibid., pp. 97–98.
16. Ibid., p. 126.
17. *NKTH*, vol. 3 (1971), p. 145.
18. *Den*, p. 131.
19. Excerpts from Den's opinion paper were published in *Tetsudō jihō*, nos. 90–94 (March 1901), and included in *Jū nen kinen Nihon no tetsudō ron*, Kinoshita Ritsuan, ed. (Tetsudō jihō-kyoku, 1909), pp. 138–164.
20. *Jū nen kinen Nihon no tetsudō ron*, p. 142.
21. Ibid., p. 160.
22. "Tōkyō shōgyō kaigisho chinjō iin no shushō hōmon," *Tōkyō keizai zasshi*, January 11, 1902, p. 30.
23. *Den*, p. 132.
24. Ibid., pp. 133–136.
25. On Inoue's advocacy of railway nationalization, see *Inoue Kakugorō-kun ryaku den*, Furushō Yutaka, ed. (Inoue Kakugorō-kun kōrō hyōshōkai, 1919), p. 90.
26. *Den*, p. 140.
27. Ibid., p. 143.
28. Ibid., p. 146.
29. Cited in ibid., pp. 166–167.
30. Ibid., pp. 167–168.
31. *Segai Inoue-kō den*, vol. 5 (1934), p. 159.
32. *Den*, p. 201.
33. Ibid., pp. 201–202; *Segai Inoue-kō den*, vol. 5, pp. 159–160.
34. The reports are included in Kōbun ruiju, 30th ser. (1906), vol. 16, no. 6; and in *Tetsudō kokuyū shimatsu ippan*, pp. 20–45.
35. The later version of this document made it clear that the committee members specifically had in mind the experience of Switzerland. On the Swiss case, see Horace Micheli, *State Purchase of Railways in Switzerland*, John Cummings, tr. (New York: Macmillan Company, 1898); and Hans

Dietler, *The Regulation and Nationalization of the Swiss Railways* (Philadelphia: American Academy of Political and Social Science, 1899).
36. *Segai Inoue-kō den*, vol. 5, p. 161.
37. Memorandum from Den Kenjirō to the cabinet chief secretary, December 22, 1905, Kōbun ruiju, 29th ser. (1905), vol. 18, no. 14–2.
38. These comprised all but one of the companies eventually bought out by the government. The exception was the Tokushima Railway, which was added in the revised bill that Ōura's successor presented to the Saionji cabinet in February 1906.
39. *Tetsudō kokuyū shimatsu ippan*, p. 66.
40. Shumpei Okamoto, *The Japanese Oligarchy and the Russo-Japanese War* (New York: Columbia University Press, 1970), pp. 187–191, citing *Hara Kei nikki*, vol. 2, pp. 129–145 passim.
41. Roger F. Hackett, *Yamagata Aritomo in the Rise of Modern Japan, 1838–1922* (Cambridge: Harvard University Press, 1971), pp. 233–234; Tetsuo Najita, *Hara Kei in the Politics of Compromise, 1905–1915* (Cambridge: Harvard University Press, 1967), p. 29.
42. *Den*, pp. 210–211.
43. See, for instance, Ōshima Fujitarō, *Kokka dokusen shihon to shite no kokuyū tetsudō no shiteki hatten* (Itō shoten, 1949), pp. 34–38; and Noda, *Nihon shōken shijō*, p. 291.
44. Harada and Aoki, p. 113.
45. *Den*, p. 184. As it turned out, it took fourteen trains per day for a period of ten days to move just one combat division from Tokyo to Hiroshima.
46. "Shūgi-in tetsudō kokuyū hōan hoka ikken iinkai kaigiroku," 2nd session, March 9, 1906, p. 5, *Shūgi-in iinkai kaigiroku*, 5th ser., no. 36.
47. *Dai Nihon teikoku gikai shi*, vol. 6, p. 976.
48. Noritake Kōtarō, "Tetsudō baishū wa danjite hi nari," *Tōkyō keizai zasshi*, March 10, 1906, in *SEDS*, vol. 9, pp. 595–599. See also the interpellation by Ōishi Masaoto in "Shūgi-in iinkai kaigiroku," 2nd session, March 9, 1906, p. 3, *Shūgi-in iinkai kaigiroku*, 5th ser., no. 36.
49. *Den*, p. 184.
50. "Shūgi-in iinkai kaigiroku," 5th session, March 13, 1906, pp. 32–33, *Shūgi-in iinkai kaigiroku*, 5th ser, no. 36.
51. "Foreign Ownership of Shares in Japanese Companies," *Japan Weekly Mail*, July 16, 1898, p. 53.
52. *NKTH*, vol. 3, p. 34.
53. *Dai Nihon teikoku gikai shi*, vol. 6, p. 986. For a similar critique by a railway-company president, see Ogawa Isao, "Kansai tetsudō no kokuyūka hantai undō no saihyōka: Kataoka Naoharu no shoron shōkai," *Un'yu to keizai*, vol. 42, no. 10, p. 58 (October 1982).
54. *Teikoku tetsudō yōkan*, pp. 149, 274.

55. "The Tanko Railway Company," *Japan Weekly Mail*, September 23, 1905, p. 330.
56. For more on these companies' foreign loans, see Noda, *Nihon shōken shijō* pp. 184–185.
57. *NTS*, vol. 2, pp. 755–756.
58. Richard J. Kirby, letter to Sir Claude Macdonald, June 3, 1901, Foreign Office Records, FO 800/134, Public Record Office, London. I wish to thank William D. Wray for showing me a copy of this letter.

    For earlier efforts by the Kyushu, San'yō, and nine other railway companies to borrow capital from abroad, see the following articles in the *Japan Weekly Mail*: "Capital for Railways," May 21, 1898, p. 529; and "Foreign Capital for Japanese Railways," November 19, 1898, p. 502.
59. *Hokkaido Tanko Tetsudo Kaisha* (1903), p. 1, Hakodate City Library.
60. See Gary Dean Best, "Financing a Foreign War: Jacob H. Schiff and Japan, 1904–05," *American Jewish Historical Quarterly*, vol. 61, no. 4, pp. 313–324 (June 1972).
61. The ratio of borrowed money to paid-up capital for private railroads as a whole had increased from 7.5 percent in 1900 to 14.9 percent in 1905: *TKN, 1907*, appendix, p. 45.
62. On the Seoul-Pusan Railway, see Janet Hunter, "Japanese Government Policy, Business Opinion and the Seoul-Pusan Railway, 1894–1906," *Modern Asian Studies*, vol. 11, no. 4, pp. 573–599 (October 1977); and Peter Duus, "Economic Dimensions of Meiji Imperialism: The Case of Korea, 1895–1910," in Ramon H. Myers and Mark R. Peattie, eds., *The Japanese Colonial Empire, 1895–1945* (Princeton: Princeton University Press, 1984), pp. 128–171.
63. Murakami Katsuhiko, "Shokuminchi," in Ōishi Kaichirō, ed., vol. 2, pp. 295, 298; *NKTH*, vol. 3, pp. 86–88.
64. *Chōsen tetsudō shi*, vol. 1 (Seoul: Chōsen sōtokufu tetsudō-kyoku, 1937), pp. 232–234.
65. "Kizoku-in tetsudō kokuyū hōan hoka ikken tokubetsu iinkai giji sokkiroku," 6th session, March 26, 1906, p. 70, *Kizoku-in tokubetsu iinkai giji sokkiroku*.
66. Ko Pyon'un, *Kindai Chōsen keizai shi no kenkyū* (Yūsankaku, 1978), pp. 178–179, 181, 184.
67. "Shūgi-in iinkai kaigiroku," 7th session, March 15, 1906, p. 65, *Shūgi-in iinkai kaigiroku*, 5th ser., no. 36.
68. Murakami Katsuhiko, pp. 304–305, 311n42.
69. *Chōsen tetsudō shijū nen ryaku shi* (Seoul: Chōsen sōtokufu tetsudō-kyoku, 1940), p. 32.
70. *Den*, p. 170; *Segai Inoue-kō den*, vol. 5, p. 159.
71. *Chōsen tetsudō shi*, vol. 1, pp. 232–234.

72. *Tetsudō senjin roku*, p. 319.
73. *Chōsen tetsudō shi*, vol. 1, p. 234; *Den*, p. 173; *SEDS*, vol. 16 (1957), p. 482.
74. *Chōsen tetsudō shijū nen ryaku shi*, p. 69.
75. Hunter, p. 598.
76. *Chōsen tetsudō shijū nen ryaku shi*, p. 75.
77. "Shūgi-in iinkai kaigiroku," 2nd session, March 9, 1906, p. 6, *Shūgi-in iinkai kaigiroku*, 5th ser., no. 36.
78. Ibid., 6th session, March 14, 1906, p. 47.
79. Ibid., p. 46.
80. "Kizoku-in tokubetsu iinkai giji sokkiroku," 6th session, March 26, 1906, p. 71, *Kizoku-in tokubetsu iinkai giji sokkiroku*.
81. "Nationalization of the Railways," *Japan Weekly Mail*, March 17, 1906, p. 278, citing an article in *Tōkyō nichinichi shinbun*, March 10, 1906. See also *Katō Kōmei*, vol. 1, Itō Masanori, ed. (Katō-haku denki hensan iinkai, 1929), p. 575.
82. "Nationalization of the Railways," p. 278.
83. For more on the Yamagata clique, see Hackett, pp. 144–147.
84. *Den*, pp. 79–85, 183–184.
85. See, for example, ibid., pp. 166–168.
86. Nakanishi generally overstates the importance of the Yamagata clique in the trend towards nationalization; in particular, he largely ignores Katsura's opposition to it in 1902: Nakanishi, pp. 110n1, 111–112, 113n4.
87. "Katsura Tarō jiden," vol. 2, pp. 66b-67, Katsura Tarō kankei monjo, no. 77–1, Kensei shiryō-shitsu, National Diet Library, Tokyo.
88. On the Taiwan Railway Company, see *Taiwan tetsudō shi*, vol. 1 (Taiwan sōtokufu tetsudō-bu, 1910), pp. 407–482; and *SEDS*, vol. 9, pp. 199–225.
89. Mitani Taiichirō, *Nihon seitō seiji no keisei: Hara Kei no seiji shidō no tenkai* (Tōkyō daigaku shuppankai, 1967), p. 138.
90. *NTS*, vol. 2, p. 761; "Dai ikkai tetsudō kaigi giji sokkiroku," 2nd session, January 28, 1893, pp. 3–18.
91. *NTS*, vol. 2, pp. 779–782.
92. *Segai Inoue-kō den*, vol. 5, p. 166.
93. "Railways," *Japan Weekly Mail*, September 3, 1898, p. 236.
94. *NTS*, vol. 2, p. 795; Aoki, Harada, and Miyazawa, pp. 31, 139.
95. Ōsawa Kaiyū, *Tetsudō no kairyō ni kansuru iken* (1898), in Aoki, Harada, and Miyazawa, pp. 138–152; Ōsawa Kaiyū, "Tetsudō kokuyū ron," *Tetsudō kyōkai shi*, vol. 1, no. 2, pp. 234–280 (1898); Ōsawa Kaiyu, "Minami-kun cho 'Tetsudō keiei no hōshin' o yomu," *Tetsudō jihō*, no. 35 (December 1899), in *Jū nen kinen Nihon no tetsudō ron*, pp. 108–121.
96. Aoki, Harada, and Miyazawa, pp. 129–132.
97. Ōsawa, "Minami-kun cho," p. 117.
98. Ōsawa, "Tetsudō kokuyū ron," p. 272.

99. Ibid., pp. 267–274.
100. Ibid., p. 274.
101. *Den*, p. 170.
102. Shirayanagi Shūko, *Zoku zaikai taihei ki* (Nihon hyōronsha, 1930), p. 82, citing an article in the *Tōkyō asahi*.
103. *Takahashi Korekiyo jiden* (Chikura shobō, 1936), pp. 766–767; Masazo Ohkawa, "The Armaments Expansion Budgets and the Japanese Economy after the Russo-Japanese War," *Hitotsubashi Journal of Economics*, vol. 5, pp. 72–73 (January 1965).
104. "Mr. Sakatani on Japanese Finance," *Japan Weekly Mail*, December 23, 1905, p. 675.
105. *Segai Inoue-kō den*, vol. 5, p. 162.
106. Shirayanagi, p. 83.
107. *Segai Inoue-kō den*, vol. 5, p. 163.
108. *Ōkura-shō hyaku nen shi*, vol. 1 (Ōkura zaimu kyōkai, 1969), p. 203.
109. *Katō Kōmei*, vol. 1, pp. 567, 569; *Katō Kōmei den* (Katō Kōmei den kankōkai, 1928), pp. 60–61.
110. *Katō Kōmei den*, p. 60.
111. *Katō Kōmei*, vol. 1, pp. 568–569.
112. Ibid.
113. Ibid., pp. 569–570.
114. Ibid., pp. 566–567.
115. Peter Duus, *Party Rivalry and Political Change in Taishō Japan* (Cambridge: Harvard University Press, 1968), pp. 54–55. According to a source cited by Duus, Katō's wife, the eldest daughter of Iwasaki Yatarō, brought a dowry later estimated at ¥3,000,000, bearing an annual interest of ¥150,000.
116. From a speech before the Railway Council in December 1898, in Tsubotani Zenshirō, ed., *Tōdai meiryū gojūka hōko roku* (Hakubunkan, 1899), pp. 42–56, cited in Byron K. Marshall, *Capitalism and Nationalism in Prewar Japan: The Ideology of the Business Elite, 1868–1941* (Stanford: Stanford University Press, 1967), p. 23.
117. *Tōyō keizai shinpō*, February 15, 1908, p. 206, cited in Marshall, p. 23.
118. Duus, *Party Rivalry*, p. 58.
119. *Hara Kei nikki*, vol. 2, p. 169.
120. For more on this interpretation, see Nakayama Naoichi, "Dai ichiji Saionji naikaku Katō gaisō no jishoku riyū ni tsuite," *Ōsaka shidai jinbun kenkyū*, vol. 12, no. 8, cited in Sakurai Tōru, "San'yō tetsudō kabushiki kaisha no shihon chikuseki jōken to kokuyūka mondai: kokka dokusen seisei ni kansuru kisoteki kōan," *Shōgaku shūshi*, vol. 49, no. 3, p. 74n79 (February 1980).
121. Shirayanagi, p. 55.

122. Ibid.; Duus, *Party Rivalry*, p. 58.
123. *Segai Inoue-kō den*, vol. 5, p. 164.
124. "Kizoku-in iinkai giji sokkiroku," 3rd session, March 23, 1906, p. 28, *Kizoku-in iinkai giji sokkiroku*.
125. *Ōkura-shō*, vol. 1, p. 203.
126. *Segai Inoue-kō den*, vol. 5, pp. 164–165.
127. *Ōkura-shō*, vol. 1, p. 203.
128. "Shūgi-in iinkai kaigiroku," 2nd session, March 9, 1906, p. 6, *Shūgi-in iinkai kaigiroku*, 5th ser., no. 36.
129. Duus, "Economic Dimensions of Meiji Imperialism," pp. 136–137.
130. *Dai Nihon teikoku gikai shi*, vol. 6, p. 892.
131. The war reparations Japan obtained from China, totaling over ¥360,000,000, represented some 80 percent of all government expenditures on "postwar-management" enterprises between 1896 and 1903: Giichi Ono, *Expenditures of the Sino-Japanese War* (New York: Oxford University Press, 1922), pp. 117–119.
132. *Hara Kei nikki*, vol. 2, p. 159.
133. *TKN, 1907*, appendix, pp. 45, 103.
134. Saionji's address to the lower house, March 6, 1906, in *Dai Nihon teikoku gikai shi*, vol. 6, p. 892.
135. Takizawa, p. 815.
136. *Hara Kei nikki*, vol. 2, p. 140.
137. *TKN, 1907*, appendix, pp. 20–21.
138. For more on the China indemnity, see Takahashi Makoto, *Meiji zaisei shi kenkyū* (Aoki shoten, 1964); and Nagaoka Shinkichi, "Nisshin sengo no zaisei seisaku to baishōkin: 'sengo keiei' no seisaku kettei o megutte," in Andō Yoshio, ed., *Nihon keizai seisaku shi ron*, vol. 1 (Tōkyō daigaku shuppankai, 1973), pp. 111–158. On the postwar management in general, refer to Ishii Kanji, "Nisshin sengo keiei," in *Iwanami kōza: Nihon rekishi*, vol. 16, *Kindai*, pt. 3 (Iwanami shoten, 1976), pp. 47–94.
139. Giichi Ono, p. 106.
140. Junnosuke Inouye, *Problems of the Japanese Exchange, 1914–1926* (London: Macmillan and Company, 1931), pp. 230–231; Watarai, p. 34.
141. For more on the upsurge in demands for railway nationalization through foreign borrowing around the turn of the century, see Noda, *Nihon shōken shijō*, p. 180. Proposals along those lines began to emerge as early as the 1897–1898 Panic. See, for example, "State Purchase of Railways," *Japan Weekly Mail*, February 5, 1898, p. 133.
142. Lockwood, p. 254.
143. *Hara Kei nikki*, vol. 2, p. 140.
144. Westney, p. 117.
145. Johnson, "MITI, MPT and the Telecom Wars," p. 208.

146. Sugiura Seishi, "Taishūteki reisai chochiku kikan toshite no yūbin chokin no seiritsu: Nisshin sengo no yūbin chokin no tenkai to sono seikaku," *Shakai keizai shi gaku*, vol. 52, no. 4, pp. 70, 86 (October 1986); Kenjiro Den, "Japanese Communications: The Post, Telegraph, and Telephone," in Okuma, ed., vol. 1, p. 416.
147. Sugiura Seishi, "Nichi-Ro sengo no yūbin chokin no tenkai to chochiku shōrei seisaku," *Shakai keizai shi gaku*, vol. 56, no. 1, pp. 37, 44 (April 1990); for more on the local improvement movement, see Kenneth B. Pyle, "The Technology of Japanese Nationalism: The Local Improvement Movement, 1900–1918," *Journal of Asian Studies*, vol. 33, no. 1, pp. 51–65 (November 1973).
148. Sugiura, "Nichi-Ro sengo," pp. 49, 53–54.
149. Ibid., p. 33; Yūsei-shō, ed., pp. 68, 97.
150. Kenneth B. Pyle, "Advantages of Followership: German Economics and Japanese Bureaucrats, 1890–1925," *Journal of Japanese Studies*, vol. 1, no. 1, p. 133 (Autumn 1974).
151. Ibid., p. 141. Also, on the growing interest in "social policy" among Meiji bureaucrats, see Sheldon Garon, *The State and Labor in Modern Japan* (Berkeley: University of California Press, 1987), pp. 25–26.
152. *Dai Nihon teikoku gikai shi*, vol. 6, p. 698. On March 4, 1899, after the Diet had approved a massive subsidization program to encourage shipping and shipbuilding interests, the *Japan Weekly Mail* had noted the "very marked tendency among the Japanese" under "the *post-bellum* programme" to move away from the system whereby "the Government [had] carefully abstained from meddling in industrial or commercial affairs.... The present session of the Diet is distinctly remarkable for a disposition on the part of the members to draw officialdom once more into the [industrial] sphere of affairs": "Sōul-Fusan Railway," p. 214.
153. *Katō Kōmei*, vol. 1, p. 572; *Hara Kei nikki*, vol. 2, p. 168; *NKTH*, vol. 3, p. 180.
154. *NKTH*, vol. 3, pp. 182, 185–186; *TKN, 1907*, appendix, pp. 22–46 passim.
155. See, in particular, Noda, *Nihon shōken shijō*, p. 98; and his "Corporate Finance of Railroad Companies," p. 88.
156. *Katō Kōmei*, vol. 1, p. 572.
157. Awaji Kenji, "Chūetsu tetsudō fusetsu to jinushi zō to no kanren," *Fudai keizai ronshū*, vol. 12, no. 2, pp. 248–249, 266–267 (July 1966).
158. The president and one of the four directors in 1905 had been promoters of the railroad, and another director, also a local man, had been one of the company's original directors: Sugiyama Kazuo, "Meiji 30 nendai," p. 177; Awaji, pp. 249, 268.
159. For more on Hara's "cultivation of a local power base" in late Meiji, see Najita, pp. 58–79.

160. *Katō Kōmei*, vol. 1, p. 572.
161. *NKTH*, vol. 3, p. 181.
162. *Hara Kei nikki*, vol. 2, p. 170.
163. At the end of the Diet session in question, the Seiyūkai had 149 members and the Daidō Club 76, out of a total Diet membership of 379: *Gikai seido*, p. 368.
164. Banno, pp. 207–209.
165. Noda, *Nihon shōken shijō*, p. 180. The *Japan Weekly Mail* reported on May 7, 1898, that "so-called 'businessmen' in the Diet and manufacturers in general" were advocating railway nationalization and that "the introduction of foreign capital [was their] final goal": "Railways and the Indemnity," p. 473. As the same journal pointed out later that month, foreign loans could be obtained at 5 percent interest compared to 10 percent interest for money borrowed at home: "Capital for Railways," May 21, 1898, p. 529.
166. As the *Japan Weekly Mail* observed on August 27, 1898, "the Liberals . . . are anxious to secure the allegiance of the 'Business Men' by openly associating themselves with the State purchase problem": "State Purchase of Private Railways," p. 210. For more on Hoshi's efforts to cultivate business support, see Arthur E. Tiedemann, "Big Business and Politics in Prewar Japan," in James W. Morley, ed., *Dilemmas of Growth in Prewar Japan* (Princeton: Princeton University Press, 1971), pp. 274–275.
167. *Tōyō keizai shinpō*, May 5, 1898, p. 35.
168. "State Purchase of Private Railways," *Japan Weekly Mail*, August 27, 1898, p. 210, citing an interview published in the *Jiji shinpō*.
169. Hackett, p. 193; Akita, p. 142.
170. Banno, pp. 211–212.
171. Itagaki Taisuke, "Shin nen shokan," *Kenseitō tōhō*, vol. 1, no. 4, p. 177 (January 20, 1899), cited in Banno, p. 212.
172. Cited in Maejima Shōzō, *Meiji chū-makki no kanryō seiji* (Kyoto: Sekibunsha, 1964), p. 171.
173. Banno, pp. 211, 224–225.
174. *NTS*, vol. 2, p. 802; Ochiai Sadaaki, "Kokuyū made no tetsudō seisaku," *Un'yu to keizai*, vol. 18, no. 4, p. 47 (1958).
175. "Tetsudō kokuyū ron no yurai," *Ginkō tsūshin roku*, no. 159 (February 15, 1899), in *SEDS*, vol. 9, p. 560.
176. Ibid.
177. *Nihon kokuyū tetsudō hyaku nen shi: tsū shi*, p. 148; *NTS*, vol. 2, pp. 805–808.
178. Shima, p. 100.
179. *NTS*, vol. 2, p. 810.

180. *Kōtsū hattatsu shi*, special edition of *Taiyō*, November 1906, p. 151, cited in Ikeda Hiroyuki, *Kōtsū shihon no ronri* (Minerva shobō, 1972), p. 309.
181. *Kokumin shinbun*, February 22, 1900, in *Shinbun shūsei Meiji hennen shi*, vol. 11, p. 27.
182. *Seiyū*, no. 27, p. 32 (December 10, 1902), cited in Mitani, p. 134.
183. *Seiyū*, no. 27, p. 34, cited in Mitani, p. 135.
184. *Seiyū*, no. 27, p. 8, cited in Mitani, p. 135.
185. *Dai Nihon teikoku gikai shi*, vol. 6, p. 975.
186. Incidentally, this Dietman's own prefecture, Kumamoto, was serviced at the time only by the Kyushu Railway's trunk line, which ran about halfway down the length of the prefecture.
187. The Kenseihontō had ninety-eight Diet members and the Seikō Club, thirty-six: *Gikai seido*, p. 368.
188. *Dai Nihon teikoku gikai shi*, vol. 6, p. 971.
189. Ibid., p. 983.
190. Ibid., p. 971.
191. Ibid., p. 973.
192. Ibid., p. 972.
193. See, for example, Taketomi's remarks in ibid., p. 973.
194. Ibid., pp. 986–987.
195. Ibid., p. 978.
196. Ibid., p. 969.
197. Ibid., pp. 969–970.
198. Ibid., p. 981.
199. Ibid., p. 970.
200. Taketomi was a bit loose with his figures, for, in March 1906, the government actually had over 1,500 miles of open track, an amount equal to nearly half the private total: *TKN, 1907*, p. 30.
201. *Dai Nihon teikoku gikai shi*, vol. 6, p. 971.
202. Ibid., p. 977.
203. Ibid., p. 976.
204. Ibid., p. 970.
205. Ibid., p. 985.
206. Ibid., p. 986.
207. Ibid., pp. 985–986.
208. Ibid., p. 986.
209. Ibid., p. 988.
210. Ibid., p. 974.
211. Ibid.
212. "Shūgi-in iinkai kaigiroku," 7th session, March 15, 1906, p. 50, *Shūgi-in iinkai kaigiroku*, 5th ser., no. 36.
213. *Dai Nihon teikoku gikai shi*, vol. 6, p. 982.

214. Ibid., p. 987.
215. Ibid., p. 981.
216. Ibid., p. 979.
217. Ibid.
218. Ibid., p. 975.
219. Ibid., pp. 975, 980, 990.
220. Ibid., p. 990.
221. Ibid., p. 991.
222. Ibid., p. 980.
223. Ibid., p. 981.
224. *Hara Kei nikki*, vol. 2, p. 171.
225. "Tekkoku an to giin betsu," *Tōkyō keizai zasshi*, March 17, 1906, in *SEDS*, vol. 9, p. 600.
226. *Hara Kei nikki*, vol. 2, p. 171.
227. Ibid.
228. *Tōkyō asahi*, March 15, 1906, in *Shinbun shūsei Meiji hennen shi*, vol. 13, p. 60.
229. The ballot broke down as follows: 141 Seiyūkai, 72 Daidō Club, 14 independent, 8 Kenseihontō, and 8 Seikō Club members supporting the bill; 84 Kenseihontō, 21 Seikō Club, and 4 independent members opposing it: "The Railway Nationalization Bill Passes," *Japan Weekly Mail*, March 24, 1906, p. 302.
230. Ibid.
231. *Dai Nihon teikoku gikai shi*, vol. 6, p. 697.
232. Ibid., p. 698.
233. Ibid., pp. 709–711.
234. *Hara Kei nikki*, vol. 2, p. 173.
235. *Dai Nihon teikoku gikai shi*, vol. 6, p. 696.
236. Ibid., p. 704.
237. Ibid., p. 711.
238. *Katō Kōmei*, vol. 1, p. 577.
239. *Hara Kei nikki*, vol. 2, p. 173.
240. Ibid., p. 174.
241. *Kōtsū hattatsu shi*, p. 161, cited in Ikeda, p. 313.

5. The Business Response

1. *Hara Rokurō*, vol. 2, p. 264.
2. Hoshino, "Nippon tetsudō (3)," p. 122.
3. *TKN, 1907*, appendix, pp. 22–46, 78–104.
4. "The Nationalization of the Railways," *Japan Weekly Mail*, February 17, 1906, p. 169, citing an article in the *Asahi shinbun*.

5. "Tetsudō no baishū kakaku ni tsuite," *Tōkyō keizai zasshi*, February 24, 1906, p. 281.
6. *TKN, 1907*, appendix, pp. 31, 87.
7. Takechi Kyōzō, *Meiji zenki yusō shi no kisoteki kenkyū* (Yūsankaku, 1978), pp. 78–79.
8. *NTS*, vol. 2, pp. 258–261.
9. *Kin'yū rokujū nen shi*, p. 404.
10. Memorandum from Railway Bureau Chief Matsumoto Sōichirō to the Ryōmō Railway Company, September 12, 1895, Teishin-shō kōbunsho, vol. 9, no. 15.
11. Cited in Oikawa, *Meiji ki chihō tetsudō shi kenkyū*, p. 48.
12. Noda, *Nihon shōken shijō*, p. 129; Awaji, p. 270.
13. Takamura Naosuke, "Kyōkō," in Ōishi, ed., vol. 2, p. 202.
14. Noda, *Nihon shōken shijō*, pp. 142–143.
15. Ibid., pp. 144, 146, 152–155, 162.
16. *NTS*, vol. 2, p. 550.
17. Murakami Teiichi, p. 75.
18. Ibid., p. 76.
19. Noda, *Nihon shōken shijō*, p. 145.
20. *TKN, 1907*, appendix, p. 42; Murakami Teiichi, p. 77.
21. Murakami Teiichi, p. 77.
22. "Nihon no tetsudō," *Tetsudō kyōkai shi*, vol. 1, no. 3, p. 361 (1898).
23. See *Wakayama-ken shi: kin-gendai shiryō*, vol. 4 (Wakayama: Wakayama-ken, 1978), pp. 912–913, for an example of a merger between two promoters' groups.
24. Memorandum from Railway Council Chairman Kawakami Sōroku to Communications Minister Kuroda Kiyotaka, 1893, Teishin-shō kōbunsho, vol. 7, no. 2.
25. The attempt failed, however, as the companies were unable to reach agreement on the terms of the merger: *Hara Rokurō*, vol. 2, pp. 294–295.
26. *TKN, 1907*, appendix, pp. 22–46 passim.
27. Oikawa, *Meiji ki chihō tetsudō shi kenkyū*, pp. 40–47.
28. *Iwashita Seishū den*, Ko Iwashita Seishū-kun denki hensankai, ed. (Kondō Otokichi, 1931), p. 27.
29. Sugiyama Kazuo, "Kabushiki kaisha seido," pp. 123–124.
30. Noda, *Nihon shōken shijō*, p. 136.
31. "Shisetsu tetsudō kaiage no gi," p. 953; *Kin'yū rokujū nen shi*, p. 415.
32. *NTS*, vol. 2, pp. 797–802.
33. Takechi, "Nisshin sensōgo," pp. 15–16.
34. Nakanishi, p. 105.
35. Ibid., p. 109.
36. Marshall treats business support of nationalization as a sustained phe-

nomenon, overlooking the close connection between the incidence of nationalization demands and financial crises: Marshall, pp. 22–24.
37. *NTS*, vol. 2, p. 367.
38. Ironically, Den Kenjirō had helped pave the way for this rivalry by negotiating the company's purchase of the Osaka Railway in 1900; this acquisition had given the firm a direct route between Nagoya and Osaka. The rate war actually broke out nearly two years after Den resigned as president of the company: *Den*, pp. 122–124; Harada and Aoki, pp. 53–54.
39. Shima, pp. 89–90.
40. *NTS*, vol. 2, p. 215.
41. Ogawa explains the Kansai's resistance to nationalization in terms of the strong opposition of its president, Kataoka Naoharu, and, by extension, of one of its principal investors, the Nippon Life Insurance Company, over which Kataoka was concurrently presiding, but his evidence appears inconclusive: Ogawa Isao, pp. 56–57.
42. Sugiyama Kazuo, "Meiji 30 nendai," pp. 153–181.
43. Ibid., pp. 160–161.
44. Shima, p. 114.
45. *Asō Takichi den* (Asō Takichi den kankōkai, 1934), p. 349.
46. In his later years, Sengoku was to serve as head of the Railway Ministry and president of the South Manchuria Railway Company: *Tetsudō senjin roku*, pp. 201–202.
47. Murakami Teiichi, p. 77.
48. Adachi, p. 198.
49. *NKTH*, vol. 4, pp. 546–549, 551–554.
50. *Kyū-tetsu*, p. 113.
51. Ibid., pp. 17–18. See also *SEDS*, vol. 9, pp. 237–302.
52. "Kyū-tetsu jiken no saitei," *Tōkyō keizai zasshi*, February 17, 1900, p. 276.
53. Tōjō, pp. 21–25.
54. "Kyūshū tetsudō hōkokusho," p. 278.
55. "The Kiushiu Railway," *Japan Weekly Mail*, August 26, 1899, p. 209.
56. *Kyū-tetsu*, p. 18.
57. *TKN, 1907*, appendix, p. 69.
58. *Hara Kei nikki*, vol. 2, pp. 171–172.
59. *Kyū-tetsu*, p. 118.
60. The following discussion of the San'yō and Nippon railway companies draws heavily on Sakurai Tōru, "San'yō tetsudō," and his "Nippon tetsudō (1)-(2)," *Ōsaka shidai ronshū*, no. 25, pp. 59–84 (1976) and no. 26, pp. 45–65 (1977).
61. Ōsaka shōsen kabushiki kaisha, *Eigyō hōkokusho*, 1899.
62. Sakurai, "San'yō tetsudō," p. 59.

63. "San'yō tetsudō nimotsu unchin hikisage no keikaku," *Tōyō keizai shinpō*, July 5, 1898, p. 35.
64. Sakurai notes that, between 1898 and 1901, proceeds from through-traffic rose from 15 percent to 24 percent of the San'yō's total passenger income and from 13 percent to 21 percent of its total freight income: Sakurai, "San'yō tetsudō," p. 61.
65. *Iwasaki Yanosuke den*, vol. 2 (Iwasaki Yatarō, Iwasaki Yanosuke denki hensankai, 1971), p. 325.
66. *NKTH*, vol. 4, p. 429; *Kan-Pu renrakusen shi* (Hiroshima: Hiroshima tetsudō kanri-kyoku, 1979), p. 18.
67. *Iwasaki Yanosuke den*, vol. 2, pp. 99–121, 326–345.
68. Kamemura Masanao and Makimura Shiyō, eds., *Ōsaka ben*, vol. 3 (Osaka: Seibundō shoten, 1951), p. 116.
69. Sugiyama Kazuo, "Kigyō no zaimu, tōshi katsudō," p. 77n42.
70. *Tetsudō senjin roku*, p. 57.
71. Ushiba Takuzō, "Tetsudō eigyō no hōshin," *Tetsudō jihō*, no. 14 (May 1899), in *Jū nen kinen Nihon no tetsudō ron*, pp. 274–286.
72. Ushiba Takuzō, "Shisetsu tetsudō rieki haitō seigen ron," *Tetsudō jihō*, nos. 329–334 (January 1906), in *Jū nen kinen Nihon no tetsudō ron*, pp. 185–219.
73. Marshall, p. 23.
74. "Shōrai no tetsudō seisaku," *Tōyō keizai shinpō*, July 15, 1905, p. 12.
75. Ibid.
76. See, for example, "The Railway Nationalization Bill," *Japan Weekly Mail*, March 31, 1906, p. 328, citing figures published in the *Tōkyō nichinichi*.
77. *TKN, 1907*, appendix, pp. 21–46, 77–104 passim.
78. "San'yō tetsudō Ushiba senmu no enzetsu," *Tetsudō jihō*, November 5, 1904, p. 10.
79. Sakurai, "San'yō tetsudō," p. 69.
80. "San'yō tetsudō Ushiba senmu," p. 10.
81. See, for example, Shima, p. 115.
82. Hatano Shōgorō, "Sengo keiei ron," *Tōkyō keizai zasshi*, November 4, 1905, p. 883.
83. Matsumoto, p. 420.
84. Sakurai, "San'yō tetsudō," pp. 63, 76.
85. *Nakamigawa Hikojirō-kun denki shiryō* (1927), pp. 157–158, cited in Sakurai, "San'yō tetsudō," p. 76.
86. Sakurai, "San'yō tetsudō," p. 72.
87. *Mitsui jigyō shi: shiryō hen*, vol. 3 (Mitsui bunko, 1977), p. 423.
88. Matsumoto, pp. 527–528.
89. Morikawa Hidemasa, "Mitsui zaibatsu no takakuteki jū kōgyōka katei (2)," *Keiei shirin*, vol. 5, no. 1, p. 6 (April 1968).

90. Hatate Isao, *Nihon no zaibatsu to Mitsubishi: zaibatsu kigyō no Nihonteki fūdo* (Rakuyū shobō, 1978), p. III; Matsumoto, p. 380.
91. *Teikoku tetsudō yōkan*, passim. Excluding the 15th National Bank, the proportion would fall to about one tenth.
92. In 1905, banks and insurance companies among the leading shareholders together owned 12 percent of the San'yō's total stock and 10 percent of that of the Kyushu Railway; such institutions also held over a quarter of the Kyushu's outstanding bonds that year: ibid.
93. Sakurai, "Nippon tetsudō (1)," pp. 63, 66; Ikeda, p. 305.
94. Kume Ryōsaku, "Tetsudō no kafū," *Tōkyō keizai zasshi*, October 25, 1902, p. 785.
95. *NKTH*, vol. 4, p. 312ff.
96. "Kyūshū tan to Jōban tan," *Tōkyō keizai zasshi*, February 28, 1903, p. 363.
97. "Banjō tankō kabushiki kaisha no saikin seiseki," *Tōyō keizai shinpō*, November 15, 1904, p. 28.
98. *Honpō tetsudō*, vol. 2, p. 791.
99. *Tetsudō kokuyū shimatsu ippan*, pp. 881–882.
100. Sakurai, "Nippon tetsudō (1)," pp. 72–73.
101. *TKN, 1907*, appendix, pp. 22, 24, 41.
102. In March 1906, for instance, the head of the Nippon's General Affairs Department emphasized the inadequacy of the firm's annual expenditure of about three million yen on renovations: "Tekkoku an to chōsa no gobyū," *Tōyō keizai shinpō*, March 25, 1906, p. 398.
103. *Tōyō keizai shinpō*, 1900, p. 463, cited in Sakurai, "Nippon tetsudō (1)," p. 73.
104. In March 1906, at an upper-house hearing on the Nationalization Bill, Railway Bureau Chief Yamanouchi indicated that the majority of private railroads had yet to complete the required reconstruction work: "Kizoku-in tokubetsu iinkai giji sokkiroku," 4th session, March 24, 1906, p. 39, *Kizoku-in iinkai giji sokkiroku*.
105. *Tetsudō kokuyū shimatsu ippan*, p. 43.
106. *NKTH*, vol. 6, p. 27.
107. There was one minor exception, however; in the case of workshop machinery, the Nippon did carry out depreciation accounting: Sakurai, "Nippon tetsudō (2)," p. 64n2.
108. Sakurai, "Nippon tetsudō (1)," pp. 78–79.
109. *Tetsudō kokuyū shimatsu ippan*, p. 882.
110. Hoshino, "Nippon tetsudō (3)," p. 180.
111. *Mitsui ginkō hachijū nen shi* (Mitsui ginkō, 1957), p. 563.
112. "Kaku tetsudō kaisha no naii," *Tōkyō keizai zasshi*, February 18, 1899, pp. 313–314.
113. Hoshino, "Nippon tetsudō (3)," p. 122.

114. Soga Sukenori, "Tetsudō dan," *Tōyō keizai shinpō*, no. 156, p. 463 (1900), cited in Sakurai, "Nippon tetsudō (2)," p. 49.
115. In spite of their massive investment programs, the San'yō and Kyushu railroads managed, respectively, to almost triple and quadruple their reserves between 1900 and 1905, whereas the Nippon, its much smaller program of renovation notwithstanding, only doubled its reserves during that period: *TKN, 1907*, appendix, pp. 22, 24, 41.
116. Cited in Hoshino, "Nippon tetsudō (3)," p. 180.
117. "Tetsudō kabuken ni kawarubeki kōsai," *Tōkyō keizai zasshi*, April 14, 1906, pp. 589–590.
118. *Mitsui ginkō hachijū nen shi*, p. 567.
119. *Hara Kei nikki*, vol. 2, p. 173.
120. *Dai Nihon teikoku gikai shi*, vol. 6, p. 696.
121. "Tetsudō no baishū kakaku ni tsuite," pp. 280–281.
122. *Hara Kei nikki*, vol. 2, p. 171.
123. *Katō Kōmei*, vol. 1, p. 580.
124. Sugiyama Kazuo, "Meiji 30 nendai," pp. 156–157, 160–161.
125. "Tetsudō eigyō hō kaikaku," *Tōkyō asahi shinbun*, May 9, 1905, cited in *NKTH*, vol. 3, pp. 500–502.
126. *Dai Nihon teikoku gikai shi*, vol. 6, p. 893. Earlier, Railway Bureau Chief Hirai Seijirō had assured businessmen that, with regard to railway nationalization, "the official view is chiefly inspired by solicitude for the development of trade and industry": "Nationalization of Railways," *Japan Weekly Mail*, February 3, 1906, p. 110.
127. "Nationalization of the Railways," *Japan Weekly Mail*, March 17, 1906, p. 278, citing an article in the *Asahi shinbun*.
128. *Hayami*, p. 100.
129. Cited in "Nationalization of the Railways," *Japan Weekly Mail*, March 17, 1906, p. 279.
130. Ibid., p. 278.
131. "Tetsudō no baishū kakaku ni tsuite," p. 281.
132. Adachi Tarō, "Tetsudō tōitsu ni tsuite," *Tetsudō jihō*, no. 335 (February 1906), in *Jū nen kinen Nihon no tetsudō ron*, p. 228.
133. For Hara's objections to the nationalization, see his "Tetsudō kokuyū zengo saku," *Tōkyō keizai zasshi*, April 7, 1906, in *SEDS*, vol. 9, pp. 605–607.
134. *Hara Kei nikki*, vol. 2, p. 170.
135. "Seien sensei no tetsudō kokuyū dan," *Ryūmon zasshi*, February 25, 1906, pp. 6–8.
136. "Kongo no zaisei keizai saku," *Jitsūgyō no Nihon*, January 1906, cited in Nakanishi, pp. 116–117.
137. Nakanishi, pp. 102–103; *TKN, 1907*, appendix, p. 21.

138. "Shibusawa Eiichi-shi no hi-tetsudō kan'yū ron," *Jiji shinpō*, August 30, 1898, in *SEDS*, vol. 21 (1958), p. 364.
139. *NTS*, vol. 2, p. 800; Ikeda, p. 310.
140. Nakanishi, p. 113n3.
141. Ibid., p. 106.
142. Marshall, citing Shibusawa's article in the August 30, 1898 issue of the *Jiji shinpō*, states that Shibusawa opposed railway nationalization on the grounds that it would lead to excessive military influence over railroad planning, but he fails to point out that Shibusawa eventually came around to support nationalization: Marshall, p. 22.
143. "The Nationalization of the Railways," *Japan Weekly Mail*, February 17, 1906, p. 169.
144. *Dai Nihon teikoku gikai shi*, vol. 6, p. 695.
145. Fujisawa Susumu and Arima Nobehisa, "Chūgoku tetsudō no setsuritsu to sono shihon, eigyō no tenkai katei: shitetsu no setsuritsu, keiei to sono kokuyūka o meguru mondai to shite," *Okayama daigaku kyōiku gakubu kenkyū shūroku*, no. 28, p. 59 (September 1969).
146. *Kaitsū gojū nen* (Osaka: Nankai tetsudō kabushiki kaisha, 1936), p. 30.
147. Nakagawa Seiza, *Teikoku tetsudō seisaku ron* (Tetsudō kenkyūsha, 1928), p. 71.
148. *Tetsudō kokuyū shimatsu ippan*, p. 156.
149. *Hara Kei nikki*, vol. 2, p. 173.
150. *Tetsudō kokuyū shimatsu ippan*, p. 154.
151. Not surprisingly, these three companies, and particularly the Kōbu and Hokkaido Colliery, were the railroads that welcomed the nationalization the most, whereas the Kansai, with the lowest profit rate and hence the lowest purchase price among the major railroads, was the one that most resisted it.
152. *Tetsudō kokuyū shimatsu ippan*, p. 152.
153. Ibid., pp. 154–155.
154. Ibid., p. 157.
155. Kōbun ruiju, 30th ser., vol. 16, no. 9; *Teikoku tetsudō yōkan*, p. 306.
156. Shimizu Keijirō, ed., *Kōtsū konjaku monogatari* (Kōyūsha, 1933), pp. 23–24.
157. *Tetsudō kokuyū shimatsu ippan*, appendix, Table 10.
158. Sakurai, "Nippon tetsudō (2)," pp. 55–56.
159. Tetsudō-in monjo, Kansai tetsudō, vol. 1 (1887–1906), no. 19.
160. "Tetsudō baishū kakaku to kōsai," *Tōyō keizai shinpō*, November 25, 1907.
161. Teishin-shō, *Nippon tetsudō baishū kagaku keisansho*, 1908, Table 1–3.
162. Shimizu, ed., p. 26.
163. *Hokuetsu tetsudō kokuyū no ken ni tsuki seigansho*, 1907, pp. 2a-b, University of Tokyo Faculty of Economics Library, Tokyo.

164. Ibid., pp. 3a-b.
165. *NTS*, vol. 2, p. 510.
166. Ibid., p. 460.
167. *Hayami*, p. 95.
168. In fiscal-year 1905, the average monthly wage for all employees on the state railways was ¥15.57; on the San'yō, ¥15.47; on the Hokkaido Colliery, ¥15.13; on the Kyushu, ¥14.37; on the Nippon, ¥13.09; and on the Kansai, ¥11.28: Hoshino, "Nippon tetsudō (3)," p. 138.
169. Ōe Soten, "Watashi no onjin Tanaka-san," *Tanaka Gentarō-ō den*, cited in *NKTH*, vol. 4, p. 450.
170. *Hara Rokurō*, vol. 2, p. 264.
171. The bonds for the Seoul-Pusan Railway were granted the year before: *Ōkura-shō*, vol. 1, p. 204.
172. Noda, *Nihon shōken shijō*, p. 301.
173. "Kabushiki shijō no kinkyō," *Tōyō keizai shinpō*, December 5, 1907.
174. *Tetsudō kokuyū shimatsu ippan*, appendix, p. 12.
175. Yamagata Toshikazu, *Zaisei jū nen* (Momiyama shoten, 1914), p. 172.
176. Noda, *Nihon shōken shijō*, pp. 299, 302, 304–305.
177. See, for example, Shima, p. 119.
178. Nakagawa Seiza, p. 70.
179. *Nihon teikoku tōkei nenkan*, vol. 25 (Naikaku tōkei-kyoku, 1906), pp. 514, 518–519.
180. Noda, *Nihon shōken shijō*, pp. 299–300.
181. *Dai Nihon teikoku gikai shi*, vol. 6, p. 975.
182. "Kizoku-in tokubetsu iinkai giji sokkiroku," 5th session, March 25, 1906, p. 53, *Kizoku-in tokubetsu iinkai giji sokkiroku*.
183. "Amenomiya Keijirō-shi kokka jigyō keireki dan," Chapter 11 (unpaginated manuscript), University of Tokyo Faculty of Economics Library, Tokyo.
184. Ibid., Chapter 10; "Amenomiya Keijirō-shi kiroku" (unpaginated manuscript), University of Tokyo Faculty of Economics Library, Tokyo.
185. Eiichi Aoki, *Railway Construction*, p. 31.
186. Sakudo Yōtarō, "Shitetsu keiei no seiritsu to sono tenkai: Mino-Arima dentetsu no baai o chūshin to shite," *Ōsaka keidai ronshū*, nos. 117–118, pp. 105, 108–110, 114 (July 1977); Takechi Kyōzō, *Toshi kinkō tetsudō no shiteki tenkai* (Nihon keizai hyōronsha, 1986), pp. 103–108, 116–118.
187. Noda, *Nihon shōken shijō*, p. 310.
188. Minami Manshū tetsudō kabushiki kaisha, ed., *Jū nen shi* (Dairen: Minami Manshū tetsudō kabushiki kaisha, 1919), pp. 911–912.
189. Takizawa, p. 844. Mitsubishi made its bid under the names of Iwasaki Hisaya and the Mitsubishi Bank.
190. Miyazaki Hiroshi and Andō Minoru, "Mantetsu no sōritsu," in Andō

Hikotarō, ed., *Mantetsu: Nihon teikokushugi to Chūgoku* (Ochanomizu shobō, 1965), p. 53.
191. Minami Manshū tetsudō, ed., p. 925; Kaneko Fumio, "Sōgyō ki no Minami Manshū tetsudō, 1907–1916 nen," *Shakai kagaku kenkyū*, vol. 31, no. 4, pp. 178–179 (January 1980).
192. Minami Manshū tetsudō, ed., p. 925.
193. "Honpō sangyō no taisō wa nanzo," *Tōyō keizai shinpō*, June 15, 1909.
194. Noda, *Nihon shōken shijō*, pp. 315–316.
195. As the *Japan Weekly Mail* noted on May 5, 1906, "it is not probable that the ex-holders of railway shares will unload any large blocks of bonds after the railways have passed into the State's hands. The main object of such unloading would be to obtain capital for other enterprises, and the banks are always willing to advance money on the security of bonds . . .": "The Railway Question," p. 461.
196. *Tōkyō dentō kabushiki kaisha kaigyō gojū nen shi* (Tōkyō dentō kabushiki kaisha, 1936), appendix, Table 1; *Tōkyō gasu gojū nen shi* (Tōkyō gasu kabushiki kaisha, 1935), pp. 125–126.
197. *Tōkyō dentō*, pp. 86–87; *Tōkyō gasu*, p. 103.
198. *Seien kaikoroku*, vol. 1, Konuki Shūichirō, ed. (Seien kaikoroku kankōkai, 1927), p. 479.
199. Nippon tetsudō kabushiki kaisha, *Hōkoku* and *Seisan hōkoku*, cited in Noda, *Nihon shōken shijō*, p. 345.
200. Nakamura Masanori, *Kindai Nihon jinushi sei shi kenkyū: shihonshugi to jinushi sei* (Tōkyō daigaku shuppankai, 1979), pp. 92, 106.
201. Ibid., p. 111.
202. Ibid., p. 109. In calculating the return on the Ōhara's investment in the San'yō, Nakamura ignores the premium they had paid for their additional shares, which leads him to conclude that, even in terms of the dividend-interest differential, the Ōhara case demonstrates that "the railway nationalization did indeed profit the local landlord class": ibid., p. 111.
203. Ibid., p. 105. The family also bought twenty-one shares in the South Manchuria Railway in 1907: ibid., p. 106.
204. Noda, *Nihon shōken shijō*, pp. 346–347.
205. Hoshino, "Nippon tetsudō (3)," p. 181.
206. "Tetsudō kabuken," in *SEDS*, vol. 9, p. 611.
207. Hoshino, "Nippon tetsudō (3)," p. 176.
208. Ibid., p. 181.
209. "Eigyō hōkoku," *Tōyō keizai shinpō*, January 15, 1909 and July 15, 1909.
210. *Teikoku tetsudō yōkan*, pp. 149, 182; *Tōkyō kaijō kasai hoken kabushiki kaisha hyaku nen shi*, vol. 1, Nihon keiei shi kenkyūjo, ed. (Tōkyō kaijō kasai hoken kabushiki kaisha, 1979), pp. 244–245.

211. *Nippon seimei kyūjū nen shi* (Osaka: Nihon seimei hoken sōgo kaisha, 1980), p. 307; Sugiyama Kazuo, "Meiji 30 nendai," pp. 155, 157.
212. *Meiji seimei hoken kabushiki kaisha rokujū nen shi* (Meiji seimei hoken kabushiki kaisha, 1942), pp. 251–252; Sugiyama Kazuo, "Meiji 30 nendai," pp. 156–157.
213. *Tōkyō kaijō*, pp. 320, 325.
214. *Nippon seimei*, p. 307.
215. *Meiji seimei*, p. 252.
216. Ibid., p. 253.
217. Noda, *Nihon shōken shijō*, p. 319.
218. According to Allen, "capital invested in electric supply companies rose from ¥2 million in 1893 to ¥12 million in 1907 and to nearly ¥200 million in 1913": G. C. Allen, *A Short Economic History of Modern Japan*, 4th ed. (New York: St. Martin's Press, 1981), p. 86.
219. Inoue Kakugorō, *Hokkaidō tankō kisen kabushiki kaisha no jūshichi nenkan* (Inoue Gorō, 1940), p. 24.
220. Ibid., pp. 23, 25; *Inoue Kakugorō-kun ryaku den*, p. 117; *Muroran seitetsujo gojū nen shi* (Muroran: Fuji seitetsu kabushiki kaisha Muroran seitetsujo, 1958), pp. 37–38.
221. *NKTH*, vol. 4, p. 272.
222. Hokkaidō tankō kisen kabushiki kaisha, ed., *Gojū nen shi* (Hokkaidō tankō kisen kabushiki kaisha, 1939), pp. 63–64; *Muroran seitetsujo*, p. 48; *Inoue Kakugorō-kun ryaku den*, pp. 117–119; J. D. Scott, *Vickers: A History* (London: Weidenfeld and Nicolson, 1962), p. 85.
223. *Hokkaidō tankō kisen kabushiki kaisha shichijū nen shi*, Shichijū nen shi hensan iinkai, ed. (Hokkaidō tankō kisen kabushiki kaisha, 1958), pp. 84, 103.
224. *Hokkaidō tankō shichijū nen shi*, p. 102; Kozo Yamamura, "Success Illgotten? The Role of Meiji Militarism in Japan's Technological Progress," *Journal of Economic History*, vol. 37, no. 1, pp. 128–129 (March 1977).
225. Wray, p. 285.
226. *Teikoku tetsudō yōkan*, passim; *Tetsudō kokuyū shimatsu ippan*, appendix, Table 18; *TKN, 1907*, appendix, pp. 22–46 passim.
227. Hatate, p. 85; *Asahi garasu kabushiki kaisha sha shi*, Asahi garasu kabushiki kaisha rinji sha shi hensan-shitsu, ed. (Asahi garasu kabushiki kaisha, 1967), p. 36; *Mitsubishi ginkō shi* (Mitsubishi ginkō shi hensan iinkai, 1954), p. 114; Wray, pp. 458–459.
228. Hatate, pp. 143–145.
229. Ibid., p. 84; *Iwasaki Hisaya den* (Iwasaki Hisaya den hensan iinkai, 1961), pp. 531–532.
230. At the end of 1905, Mitsubishi held 1,000 shares out of a total of 500,000 in that railroad: *Teikoku tetsudō yōkan*, p. 224.

231. *Taiwan seitō kabushiki kaisha shi* (Taiwan seitō kabushiki kaisha, 1939), pp. 83, 294.
232. *Hara Rokurō*, p. 407; *Taiwan seitō*, p. 270.
233. *Taiwan seitō*, p. 271.
234. *Meiji seitō kabushiki kaisha sanjū nen shi* (Meiji seitō kabushiki kaisha Tōkyō jimusho, 1936), pp. 4–5, 68.

Conclusion

1. For details, see the appended map "Baishū shisetsu tetsudō zu" in *Nihon kokuyū tetsudō hyaku nen shi: tsū shi*.
2. "Dai jūhachi kai tetsudō kaigi giji sokkiroku," 2nd session, December 27, 1907, pp. 19–20, Tetsudō kaigi giji sokkiroku.
3. *TKN, 1907*, p. 30.
4. Miyano Takeo, "Tetsudō kokuyū hō ni yoru shisetsu tetsudō no baishū to sonogo (Taishō zenhan ki goro made) no sochi," *Kōeki jigyō kenkyū*, vol. 24, p. 107 (February 1973).
5. Ikeda, pp. 315–316; *Honpō tetsudō*, vol. 1, pp. 121–122; Kokaze, "Tetsudō kokuyūka," pp. 59–60.
6. Miyano, p. 120.
7. Kokaze, "Tetsudō kokuyūka," pp. 58–59.
8. *Kokuyū jū nen shi: honpō tetsudō kokuyūgo no shisetsu narabi ni seiseki* (Tetsudō-shō, 1920), p. 58. For more on the post-1906 program of rationalization and standardization with particular reference to locomotive works, see Eisuke Daito, "Railways and Scientific Management in Japan, 1907–30," *Business History*, vol. 31, no. 1, pp. 1–28 (January 1989).
9. Miyano, pp. 107, 109.
10. Aoki and Yamanaka, p. 50.
11. Miyano, p. 109. As Morikawa points out, there was also a fair amount of managerial spinoff from the nationalized railroads to other private businesses: Morikawa Hidemasa, *Nihon keiei shi* (Nihon keizai shinbunsha, 1981), pp. 98–99.

    Daito notes that, both before and after the nationalization, the state railways themselves were a source of technical and managerial talent for private industry, as a number of engineers transferred from the national railways to private locomotive manufacturers: Daito, p. 22.
12. Nagaoka Shinkichi, "Nichi-Ro 'sengo keiei,'" in Ōishi Kaichirō and Miyamoto Ken'ichi, eds., *Nihon shihonshugi hattatsu shi no kiso chishiki* (Yūhikaku, 1975), p. 226.
13. Ibid.; Najita, p. 70.
14. "Kokutetsu *rōkaru* sen no shujutsu," *Asahi shinbun*, January 31, 1979, p. 5.

15. Cited in "Nationalization of the Railways," *Japan Weekly Mail*, March 17, 1906, p. 279.
16. Harada, "Tetsudō fusetsu hō," pp. 22–23.
17. Johnson, "MITI, MPT, and the Telecom Wars," pp. 211–212.
18. Gerald L. Curtis, *The Japanese Way of Politics* (New York: Columbia University Press, 1988), pp. 112–116; Johnson, "MITI, MPT, and the Telecom Wars," p. 203.
19. Johnson, "MITI, MPT, and the Telecom Wars," p. 227.
20. See Kozo Yamamura, "Japan, 1868–1930"; and his "Entrepreneurship."
21. Gerschenkron, p. 14.
22. For example, by the early 1860s, the government had provided about one fourth of the total financing for private-railroad construction in France and at least that amount in the United States: C. B. Derosne, *Ten Years of Imperialism in France: Impressions of a Flaneur* (1862), in S. Pollard and C. Holmes, eds., *Documents of European Economic History*, vol. 1, *The Process of Industrialization, 1750–1870* (London: Edward Arnold, 1968), p. 426; Goodrich, p. 271. By contrast, even at its height in the 1880s and early 1890s, the ratio of cumulative state subsidies to cumulative construction costs for private railroads in Japan never exceeded one eighth: *TKN, 1907*, appendix, pp. 44–45, 102–103.
23. See Johnson, *MITI*; and Samuels, *The Business of the Japanese State*.
24. Samuels, p. 261.
25. Wray, pp. 250–255.
26. Ronald Dore, *Flexible Rigidities: Industrial Policy and Structural Adjustment in the Japanese Economy, 1970–80* (Stanford: Stanford University Press, 1986), p. 148. For an excellent case study on government involvement and structural change in the postwar energy industries, see Laura Hein, *Fueling Growth: The Energy Revolution and Economic Policy in Postwar Japan* (Cambridge: Council on East Asian Studies, Harvard University, 1990).
27. Barbara Molony, *Technology and Investment: The Prewar Japanese Chemical Industry* (Cambridge: Council on East Asian Studies, Harvard University, 1990), p. 139.
28. Dore, p. 215.

List of Works Cited

Adachi Ritsuen. *Imamura Seinosuke-kun jireki* (Career of Imamura Seinosuke). Otani Matsujirō, 1906.
Adachi Tarō. "Tetsudō tōitsu ni tsuite" (On Railway Unification), *Tetsudō jihō* (Railway Review), no. 335 (February 1906), in *Jū nen kinen Nihon no tetsudō ron* (q.v.).
Adas, Michael. *Machines as the Measure of Men: Science, Technology, and Ideologies of Western Dominance.* Ithaca: Cornell University Press, 1989.
Akita, George. *Foundations of Constitutional Government in Modern Japan, 1868–1900.* Cambridge: Harvard University Press, 1967.
"All aboard the gravy train," *The Economist*, June 16, 1990, p. 38.
Allen, G. C. *A Short Economic History of Modern Japan.* 4th ed. New York: St. Martin's Press, 1981.
"Amenomiya Keijirō-shi kiroku" (Records on Amenomiya Keijirō). University of Tokyo Faculty of Economics Library, Tokyo.
"Amenomiya Keijirō-shi kokka jigyō keireki dan" (Narrative of the Patriotic Enterprises of Amenomiya Keijirō). University of Tokyo Faculty of Economics Library, Tokyo.
Andō Yoshio, ed. *Kindai Nihon keizai shi yōran* (Handbook of Modern Japanese Economic History). Tōkyō daigaku shuppankai, 1975.
Aoki, Eiichi. *Railway Construction as Viewed from Local Society.* Tokyo: United Nations University, 1980.
———. "Tetsudō kihi densetsu ni taisuru gimon" (Doubts about the Tradition of Challenges to Railroads), *Shin chiri* (New Geography), vol. 29, no. 4, pp. 1–11 (March 1982).
———, Harada Katsumasa, and Miyazawa Motokazu. "Meiji hyaku nen kinen tokushū gō" (Special Edition on the Meiji Centennial), *Han kōtsū* (Universal Transportation), vol. 68 (October 1968).
Aoki Kaizō. *Jinbutsu kokutetsu hyaku nen* (Hundred Years of People in the National Railways). Chūō senkyō kabushiki kaisha shuppan-kyoku, 1969.
——— and Yamanaka Tadao. *Kokutetsu kōryū jidai: Kinoshita un'yu nijū*

nen (The Golden Age of the National Railways: Twenty Years of Transportation under Kinoshita). Nihon kōtsū kyōkai, 1957.

Ariizumi Sadao. *Meiji seiji shi no kiso katei: chihō seiji jōkyō shi ron* (Foundations of Meiji Political History: Historical Essay on Local Political Conditions). Yoshikawa kōbunkan, 1980.

Arthurton, Alfred W. "The Railways of Japan," *The Railway Magazine*, vol. 15, pp. 496–504 (December 1904).

Asahi garasu kabushiki kaisha sha shi (History of Asahi Glass Company, Inc.). Asahi garasu kabushiki kaisha rinji sha shi hensan-shitsu, ed. Asahi garasu kabushiki kaisha, 1967.

Asō Takichi den (Biography of Asō Takichi). Asō Takichi den kankōkai, 1934.

August, Robert Leslie. "Urbanization and Local Government in Japan: A Study of Shibuya, 1889–1932." Ph.D. dissertation. University of Pittsburgh, 1975.

Awaji Kenji. "Chūetsu tetsudō fusetsu to jinushi zō to no kanren" (The Relationship between the Construction of the Chūetsu Railroad and the Landlord Class), *Fudai keizai ronshū* (Toyama University Economic Studies), vol. 12, no. 2, pp. 240–271 (July 1966).

Ban Naonosuke. "Zenkoku tetsudō kaiage ni kansuru seifu no hōryaku o ronzu" (On the Government's Plan Regarding the Purchase of Railroads Nationwide), *Tōkyō keizai zasshi,* September 26, 1891, in *Shibusawa Eiichi denki shiryō,* vol. 9 (q.v.).

"Banjō tankō kabushiki kaisha no saikin seiseki" (The Recent Results of the Banjō Coal-Mining Company, Inc.), *Tōyō keizai shinpō,* November 15, 1904, p. 28.

Banno Junji. *Meiji kenpō taisei no kakuritsu* (Establishment of the Meiji Constitutional System). Tōkyō daigaku shuppankai, 1971.

"Behaviour of Travellers by Railway in Japan," *Japan Weekly Mail,* May 4, 1901, p. 468.

Best, Gary Dean. "Financing a Foreign War: Jacob H. Schiff and Japan, 1904–05," *American Jewish Historical Quarterly*, vol. 61, no. 4, pp. 313–324 (June 1972).

"Bisset-shi no honpō tetsudō hyō" (Mr. Bisset's Evaluation of Our Country's Railroads), *Tōyō keizai shinpō,* June 5, 1902, pp. 29–30.

Burgess, George H., and Miles C. Kennedy. *Centennial History of the Pennsylvania Railroad Company, 1846–1946.* Philadelphia: The Pennsylvania Railroad Company, 1949.

"Capital for Railways," *Japan Weekly Mail,* May 21, 1898, p. 529.

Chandler, Alfred D., Jr. *The Visible Hand: The Managerial Revolution in American Business.* Cambridge: Belknap Press of Harvard University Press, 1977.

———, and Richard S. Tedlow. *The Coming of Managerial Capitalism: A Casebook on the History of American Economic Institutions*. Homewood, Ill.: Richard D. Irwin, Inc., 1985.
Chikuhō tetsudō kabushiki kaisha kabunushi jinmeihyō (Stockholders List of the Chikuhō Railway Company, Inc.), 1895. Teishin-shō kōbunsho (q.v.), vol. 9, no. 8.
"Chiso kaisei ni tsuite" (On Land Tax Reform), 1891. Mutsu Munemitsu kankei monjo (q.v.).
Chōsen tetsudō shijū nen ryaku shi (Short History of the Forty Years of Korean Railroads). Seoul: Chōsen sōtokufu tetsudō-kyoku, 1940.
Chōsen tetsudō shi (History of Korean Railroads), vol. 1. Seoul: Chōsen sōtokufu tetsudō-kyoku, 1937.
Chōya shinbun (Whole Nation Newspaper), 1889–1892.
Chūō tetsudō kisei sanshi gyō rengōkai (Silk-Industry League for Promotion of the Chūō Railroad). *Tai Chūō tetsudō sanshi gyōsha iken* (Opinion of Silk-Industry Members Concerning the Chūō Railroad), December 1892. Transportation Museum Archives, Tokyo.
"Chūō tetsudō no Yamanashi-ken ni oyoboshitaru eikyō (1)-(2)" (Effects of the Chūō Railway on Yamanashi Prefecture), *Tōkyō keizai zasshi,* November 21 and 28, 1903.
Cleaver, Thomas W. "Railways," in *Kodansha Encyclopedia of Japan*, vol. 6. Tokyo: Kodansha, 1983.
———. "Regional Income Differentials in Japanese Economic Growth." Ph.D. dissertation. Harvard University, 1970.
Cohn, Gustav. "The Railway Policy of Prussia," *Journal of Political Economy*, vol. 1, pp. 179–192 (March 1893).
Cole, Wayne H. "The Railroad in Canadian Literature," *Canadian Literature*, no. 77, pp. 124–130 (Summer 1978).
Crawcour, E. Sydney. "Industrialization and Technological Change, 1885–1920," in John W. Hall et al., gen. eds., *The Cambridge History of Japan*. Vol. 6, *The Twentieth Century*, Peter Duus, ed. Cambridge: Cambridge University Press, 1988.
Curtis, Gerald L. *The Japanese Way of Politics*. New York: Columbia University Press, 1988.

"Dai ikkai tetsudō kaigi giji sokkiroku" (Minutes of the First Railway Council), December 1892–March 1893. Tetsudō kaigi giji sokkiroku (q.v.).
"Dai jūhachi kai tetsudō kaigi giji sokkiroku" (Minutes of the Eighteenth Railway Council), January 1907–January 1908. Tetsudō kaigi giji sokkiroku (q.v.).
Dai Nihon gaikō bunsho (Japanese Diplomatic Documents), vol. 2, pt. 3. Gaimu-shō chōsa-bu, ed. Nihon kokusai kyōkai, 1938.

Dai Nihon teikoku gikai shi (Japanese Imperial Diet Records), vols. 1, 6. Shizuoka: Dai Nihon teikoku gikai shi kankōkai, 1926, 1928.

"Dai san teikoku gikai teishutsu no tetsudō hōan ni taisuru tetsudō kisei dōmeikai no kibō" (Hopes of the Railroad Promotion League concerning the Railway Bills Introduced into the Third Imperial Diet). Transportation Museum Archives, Tokyo.

Daigohō Toshio. "Tetsudō shōka to Ōwada Takeki" (The Railway Song and Ōwada Takeki), in Watanabe et al., eds., *Kiteki issei* (q.v.).

Daito, Eisuke. "Railways and Scientific Management in Japan, 1907–30," *Business History*, vol. 31, no. 1, pp. 1–28 (January 1989).

Dajō ruiten (Council of State Documents), 3rd–4th ser. (1878–1880). Kokuritsu kōbunshokan, Tokyo.

Den, Kenjiro. "Japanese Communications: The Post, Telegraph, and Telephone," in Okuma, ed., *Fifty Years of New Japan* (q.v.).

Den Kenjirō. Memorandum to the Cabinet Chief Secretary, December 22, 1905. Kōbun ruiju, 29th ser., vol. 18, no. 14–2 (q.v.).

Den Kenjirō den (Biography of Den Kenjirō). Den Kenjirō denki hensankai, 1932.

Derosne, C. B. *Ten Years of Imperialism in France: Impressions of a Flaneur, 1862*. In S. Pollard and C. Holmes, eds. *Documents of European Economic History*, vol. 1, *The Process of Industrialization, 1750–1870*. London: Edward Arnold, 1968.

Detection Letter, May 8, 1892. Matsukata ke monjo, vol. 61 (q.v.).

Dickens, Charles. *Dombey and Son*. Alan Horsman, ed. Oxford: Oxford University Press, 1982.

Dietler, Hans. *The Regulation and Nationalization of the Swiss Railways*. Philadelphia: American Academy of Political and Social Science, 1899.

"Dōmei ginkō rinji shūkai rokuji" (Bankers' Association Special Meeting Minutes), April 11, 1890, *Kaigi rokuji* (Minutes of Meetings), January 1889–December 1890, in *Shibusawa Eiichi denki shiryō*, vol. 6 (q.v.).

"Donzō Takashima Kaemon-ō kaikyū dan" (Reminiscences of the Venerable Takashima Kaemon). Manuscript photocopy. Transportation Museum Archives, Tokyo.

Dore, Ronald. *Flexible Rigidities: Industrial Policy and Structural Adjustment in the Japanese Economy, 1970–80*. Stanford: Stanford University Press, 1986.

Doukas, Kimon A. *The French Railroads and the State*. New York: Columbia University Press, 1945.

Duus, Peter. "Economic Dimensions of Meiji Imperialism: The Case of Korea, 1895–1910," in Ramon H. Myers and Mark R. Peattie, eds., *The Japanese Colonial Empire, 1895–1945*. Princeton: Princeton University Press, 1984.

———. *Party Rivalry and Political Change in Taishō Japan*. Cambridge: Harvard University Press, 1968.

"Eigyō hōkoku" (Business Reports), *Tōyō keizai shinpō,* January 15, 1909 and July 15, 1909.

Embree, John F. *Suye Mura: A Japanese Village.* Chicago: University of Chicago Press, 1939.

Ericson, Steven J. "Private Railroads in the Meiji Era: Forerunners of Modern Japanese Management?" in Tsunehiko Yui and Keiichiro Nakagawa, eds., *Japanese Management in Historical Perspective.* Tokyo: University of Tokyo Press, 1989.

———. "Railroads in Crisis: The Financing and Management of Japanese Railway Companies during the Panic of 1890," in Wray, ed., *Managing Industrial Enterprise* (q.v.).

Faith, Nicholas. *The World the Railways Made.* London: Bodley Head, 1990.

Findlay, George. *The Working and Management of an English Railway.* 4th ed. London, 1891. Translated by Hayami Tarō as *Eikoku tetsudō ron* (Treatise on English Railroads). Kobe: San'yō tetsudō kabushiki kaisha, 1894.

Finn, Dallas. *Meiji Revisited: The Sites of Victorian Japan.* New York: Weatherhill, forthcoming.

Fishlow, Albert. *American Railroads and the Transformation of the Ante-bellum Economy.* Cambridge: Harvard University Press, 1965.

"Foreign Capital for Japanese Railways," *Japan Weekly Mail,* November 19, 1898, p. 502.

"Foreign Ownership of Shares in Japanese Companies," *Japan Weekly Mail,* July 16, 1898, p. 53.

Fujii Nobuyuki. "Meiji zenki no denshin seisaku" (Telegraph Policy in the Early Meiji Period), *Nihon rekishi,* no. 479, pp. 71–88 (April 1988).

———. "Yūsen kisen Mitsubishi kaisha ni okeru denshin riyō: Meiji zenki kaiun gyō no jōhō system" (Telegraph Use by the Mitsubishi Mail Steamship Company: The Information System of the Shipping Industry in the Early Meiji Period), *Keiei shi gaku* (Japan Business History Review), vol. 25, no. 3, pp. 40–57 (October 1990).

Fujisawa Susumu and Arima Nobehisa. "Chūgoku tetsudō no setsuritsu to sono shihon, eigyō no tenkai katei: shitetsu no setsuritsu, keiei to sono kokuyūka o meguru mondai to shite" (The Establishment of the Chūgoku Railway and the Development of Its Capital and Business: Problems in the Founding, Management, and Nationalization of Private Railroads), *Okayama daigaku kyōiku gakubu kenkyū shūroku* (Studies of the Okayama University Education Department), no. 28, pp. 43–60 (September 1969).

Garon, Sheldon. *The State and Labor in Modern Japan.* Berkeley: University of California Press, 1987.

Gerschenkron, Alexander. *Economic Backwardness in Historical Perspective: A Book of Essays*. Cambridge: Belknap Press of Harvard University Press, 1962.

Gikai seido shichijū nen shi: seitō, kai, ha hen (Seventy-Year History of the Diet System: Political Party, Association, Faction Volume). Shūgi-in, Sangi-in, 1961.

Gluck, Carol. *Japan's Modern Myths: Ideology in the Late Meiji Period*. Princeton: Princeton University Press, 1985.

Goodrich, Carter. *Government Promotion of American Canals and Railroads, 1800–1890*. New York: Columbia University Press, 1960.

Gourvish, T. R. *Railways and the British Economy, 1830–1914*. Cambridge: Economic History Society, 1980.

"The Grievances of Private Railway Companies," *Japan Weekly Mail*, October 12, 1889, p. 325.

Gunma no Meiji hyaku nen (Gunma's Meiji Centennial). Maebashi: Mainichi shinbun Maebashi shi-kyoku, 1968.

Hackett, Roger F. *Yamagata Aritomo in the Rise of Modern Japan, 1838–1922*. Cambridge: Harvard University Press, 1971.

Hankai tetsudō keireki shi (History of the Hankai Railway). Matsumoto Jūtarō, 1899.

Hara Kei nikki (Diary of Hara Kei), vol. 2. Hara Keiichirō, ed. Fukumura shuppan kabushiki kaisha, 1965.

Hara Rokurō. "Tetsudō kokuyū zengo saku" (Railway Nationalization Countermeasure), *Tōkyō keizai zasshi*, April 7, 1906, in *Shibusawa Eiichi denki shiryō*, vol. 9 (q.v.).

Hara Rokurō-ō den (Biography of the Venerable Hara Rokurō), vol. 2. Hara Kunizō, 1937.

Harada Katsumasa. *Eki no shakai shi: Nihon no kindaika to kōkyō kūkan* (Social History of the Station: Japan's Modernization and Public Space). Chūō kōronsha, 1987.

―――. *Kisha, densha no shakai shi* (Social History of Trains and Streetcars). Kōdansha, 1983.

―――. "Maejima Hisoka to tetsudō" (Maejima Hisoka and Railroads), *Teishin kyōkai zasshi* (Communications Society Journal), April 1969, pp. 28–31.

―――. *Meiji tetsudō monogatari* (Tales of Meiji Railroads). Chikuma shobō, 1983.

―――. "Technological Independence and Progress of Standardization in the Japanese Railways," *Developing Economies*, vol. 18, no. 3, pp. 313–332 (September 1980).

―――. "Tetsudō fusetsu hō seitei no zentei" (Prerequisites to the Enactment of the Railway Construction Law), *Nihon rekishi*, no. 208, pp. 22–41 (September 1965).

———. *Tetsudō no kataru Nihon no kindai* (Japan's Modern History as Told through Railroads). Soshiete, 1977.

———. *Tetsudō shi kenkyū shiron: kindaika ni okeru gijutsu to shakai* (Studies in Railway History: Technology and Society in the Process of Modernization). Nihon keizai hyōronsha, 1989.

——— and Aoki Eiichi. *Nihon no tetsudō: hyaku nen no ayumi kara* (Japanese Railroads: A Century of Progress). Sanseidō, 1973.

——— et al., eds. *Tetsudō to bunka* (Railroads and Culture). Nihon keizai hyōronsha, 1986.

Hatano Shōgorō. "Sengo keiei ron" (On the Postwar Management), *Tōkyō keizai zasshi,* November 4, 1905, p. 883.

Hatate Isao. *Nihon no zaibatsu to Mitsubishi: zaibatsu kigyō no Nihonteki fūdo* (Japan's Zaibatsu and Mitsubishi: The Japanese Features of Zaibatsu Enterprise). Rakuyū shobō, 1978.

Hawks, Francis L., comp. *Narrative of the Expedition of an American Squadron to the China Seas and Japan,* vol. 1. Sidney Wallach, ed. London: MacDonald, 1952.

Hayami Tarō den (Biography of Hayami Tarō). Osaka: Ko Hayami Tarō-shi hensan-kakari, 1939.

Hayashi Rikio, ed. *Kyōdo shi jiten: Ōsaka fu* (Dictionary of Local History: Osaka Prefecture). Shōheisha, 1980.

Hein, Laura. *Fueling Growth: The Energy Revolution and Economic Policy in Postwar Japan.* Cambridge: Council on East Asian Studies, Harvard University, 1990.

Heine, William. *With Perry to Japan.* Frederic Trautmann, tr. Honolulu: University of Hawaii Press, 1990.

Henderson, W. O. *The Rise of German Industrial Power, 1834–1914.* London: Temple Smith, 1975.

"Hida goryō-kyoku chō bossu: kisha ni benjo naki gisei" (Imperial Property Bureau Chief Hida Dies: Victim of the Lack of Toilets on Trains), *Jiji shinpō,* April 29, 1889, in *Shinbun shūsei Meiji hennen shi,* vol. 7, p. 263 (q.v.).

Hirose Takiji. "Hokkaidō ni okeru shiyū tetsudō no seikaku: tankō tetsudō to Hokkaidō tetsudō" (The Nature of Private Railroads in Hokkaido: The Colliery and Railway and the Hokkaido Railway), *Atarashii dō shi* (New History of Hokkaido), no. 29, pp. 11–23 (September 1968), and no. 30, pp. 15–25 (November 1968).

Hiroshima-ken shi: kindai gendai shiryō hen (History of Hiroshima Prefecture: Modern Historical Materials), vol. 2. Hiroshima-ken, 1975.

Hirschmeier, Johannes, and Tsunehiko Yui. *The Development of Japanese Business, 1600–1980*. 2nd ed. London: George Allen & Unwin Ltd., 1981.
Hokkaidō tankō kisen kabushiki kaisha (Hokkaido Colliery and Steamship Company, Inc.), ed. *Gojū nen shi* (Fifty-Year History). Hokkaidō tankō kisen kabushiki kaisha, 1939.
Hokkaidō tankō kisen kabushiki kaisha shichijū nen shi (Seventy-Year History of Hokkaido Colliery and Steamship Company, Inc.). Shichijū nen shi hensan iinkai, ed. Hokkaidō tankō kisen kabushiki kaisha, 1958.
Hokkaido Tanko Tetsudo Kaisha (Hokkaido Colliery and Railway Company), 1903. Hakodate City Library.
Hokkaidō tetsudō hyaku nen shi (Centennial History of Hokkaido Railways), vol. 1. Sapporo: Nihon kokuyū tetsudō Hokkaidō sō-kyoku, 1976.
Hokuetsu tetsudō kokuyū no ken ni tsuki seigansho (Petition of the Hokuetsu Railway on the Matter of Nationalization), 1907. University of Tokyo Faculty of Economics Library, Tokyo.
Honpō shasai ryaku shi (Short History of Japanese Corporate Bonds). Takahira Takao, ed. Nihon kōgyō ginkō chōsa-kakari, 1927.
"Honpō sangyō no taisō wa nanzo" (What Is the State of Our Country's Industry?), *Tōyō keizai shinpō,* June 15, 1909.
Honpō tetsudō no shakai oyobi keizai ni oyoboseru eikyō (The Influence of Japanese Railroads on Society and the Economy). 3 vols. Tetsudō-in, 1916.
Hoshino Takao. "Meiji ki no shitetsu to ginkō: Nippon tetsudō kaisha to dai jūgo ginkō to o chūshin ni" (Private Railroads and Banks in the Meiji Period: The Case of the Nippon Railway Company and the 15th Bank), *Kōtsū bunka* (Transportation Culture), no. 5, pp. 65–72 (1965).

———. "Meiji sanjū-ku nen no tetsudō kokuyūka: shitetsu no chihō tetsudōka" (The 1906 Railway Nationalization: The Localization of Private Railroads), in Nakagawa, Morikawa, and Yui, eds., *Kindai Nihon keiei shi no kiso chishiki* (q.v.).

———. "Meiji shonen no shitetsu seisaku: 'tetsudō kokuyū shugi setsu,' 'kansen kansetsu shugi setsu' no saikentō" (Policy on Private Railroads in Early Meiji: A Reexamination of Views Concerning the "Principle of Railway National Ownership" and the "Principle of Trunk-Line Government Construction"), *Musashi daigaku ronshū* (Musashi University Studies), vol. 27, nos. 3–5, pp. 117–143 (December 1979).

———. "Nippon tetsudō kaisha to dai jūgo kokuritsu ginkō (1)-(3)" (The Nippon Railway Company and the 15th National Bank), *Musashi daigaku ronshū,* vol. 17, pp. 77–109 (June 1970), vol. 19, no. 1, pp. 1–22 (August 1971) and vol. 19, nos. 5–6, pp. 117–183 (March 1972).

———. "Shitetsu no seiritsu to hatten: Nippon tetsudō kaisha to tetsudō netsu" (The Formation and Development of Private Railroads: The Nippon Railway Company and the Railway Mania), in Nakagawa, Morikawa, and Yui, eds., *Kindai Nihon keiei shi no kiso chishiki* (q.v.).

Hotta Masayasu. Memorial to Saigō Tsugumichi, May 14, 1891. Tetsudō-in monjo, Chikuhō kōgyō tetsudō, vol. 1, no. 7 (q.v.).

Hunter, Janet. "Japanese Government Policy, Business Opinion and the Seoul-Pusan Railway, 1894–1906," *Modern Asian Studies*, vol. 11, no. 4, pp. 573–599 (October 1977).

Ida Seiza. "San'yō tetsudō jidai" (The San'yō Railway Period), in *Nakamigawa Hikojirō denki shiryō* (q.v.).

Ike, Nobutaka. "The Pattern of Railway Development in Japan," *Far Eastern Quarterly*, vol. 14, pp. 217–229 (February 1955).

Ikeda Hiroyuki. *Kōtsū shihon no ronri* (The Logic of Transportation Capital). Minerva shobō, 1972.

Imanishi Rinzaburō ibunroku (Posthumous Writings of Imanishi Rinzaburō), vol. 1, suppl. Komatsu Mitsuo, ed. Osaka: Imanishi Yosaburō, 1925.

"The Imperial Railway Society," *Japan Weekly Mail*, May 31, 1902, p. 583.

Imuta Toshimitsu. "Kazoku shisan to tōshi kōdō: kyū daimyō no kabushiki tōshi o chūshin ni" (Peerage Assets and Investment Behavior: With Emphasis on the Stock Investments of Former Daimyo), *Chihō kin'yū shi kenkyū* (Studies in the History of Local Finance), no. 18, pp. 1–49 (March 1987).

———. "Semento gyō ni okeru kokunai shijō no keisei" (Formation of the Domestic Market in the Cement Industry), in Yamaguchi and Ishii, eds., *Kindai Nihon no shōhin ryūtsū* (q.v.).

Inaba Hiroshi, ed. *Kyōdo shi jiten: Kanagawa-ken* (Dictionary of Local History: Kanagawa Prefecture). Shōheisha, 1978.

Inoue Kakugorō. *Hokkaidō tankō kisen kabushiki kaisha no jūshichi nenkan* (Seventeen Years with Hokkaido Colliery and Steamship Company, Inc.). Inoue Gorō, 1940.

Inoue Kakugorō-kun enzetsu hikki: gikai kaisan iken (Speech Notes of Inoue Kakugorō: Opinion on the Diet Dissolution), 1892.

Inoue Kakugorō-kun ryaku den (Short Biography of Inoue Kakugorō). Furushō Yutaka, ed. Inoue Kakugorō-kun kōrō hyōshōkai, 1919.

Inoue Kowashi den: shiryō hen (Biography of Inoue Kowashi: Historical Materials), vols. 1–2, 4. Inoue Kowashi denki hensan iinkai, ed. Kokugakuin daigaku toshokan, 1966, 1968, 1971.

Inoue Kowashi monjo (Inoue Kowashi Papers), B-3761–B-3794. Kokugakuin daigaku, Tokyo.

Inoue Masaru. Memorandum to the Cabinet, May 27, 1891. Tetsudō-in monjo, Chikuhō kōgyō tetsudō, vol. 1, no. 7 (q.v.).

Inouye, Junnosuke. *Problems of the Japanese Exchange, 1914–1926*. London: Macmillan and Company, 1931.

Inouye Masaru. "Japanese Communications: Railroads," in Okuma, ed., *Fifty Years of New Japan* (q.v.).

Ishii Kanji. "Kaidai: Shōgyō kaigisho hōkoku" (Explanatory Notes: Chambers of Commerce Reports), in *Kindai Nihon shōhin ryūtsū shi shiryō* (Historical Materials on Commodity Distribution in Modern Japan), vol. 6, pt. 2, Shōhin ryūtsū shi kenkyūkai, ed. Nihon keizai hyōronsha, 1979.

―――――. "Kokunai shijō no keisei to tenkai" (Formation and Development of the Domestic Market), in Yamaguchi and Ishii, eds., *Kindai Nihon no shōhin ryūtsū* (q.v.).

―――――. "Nisshin sengo keiei" (The Post-Sino-Japanese War Management), in *Iwanami kōza: Nihon rekishi* (Iwanami Lectures: Japanese History). Vol. 16, *Kindai* (Modern Period), pt. 3. Iwanami shoten, 1976.

Ishii Mitsuru. *Nihon tetsudō sōsetsu shiwa* (Historical Tales of the Founding of Japanese Railroads). Hōsei daigaku shuppan-kyoku, 1952.

Ishii Tsuneo. "Ryōmō tetsudō kaisha ni okeru kabunushi to sono keifu" (Stockholders in the Ryōmō Railway Company and Their Lineages), *Meidai shōgaku ronsō* (Meiji University Commercial Science Studies), vol. 41, nos. 9–10, pp. 129–152 (July 1958).

―――――. "Ryōmō tetsudō kaisha no keiei shiteki kenkyū" (Business-History Study of the Ryōmō Railway Company), *Meiji daigaku shōgaku kenkyūjo nenpō* (Annual Report of the Meiji University Commercial Science Research Institute), no. 4, pp. 161–207 (1958).

Isogai Masayoshi and Iida Bun'ya. *Yamanashi-ken no rekishi* (History of Yamanashi Prefecture). Yamakawa shuppansha, 1973.

Itō Hirobumi kankei monjo (Papers Relating to Itō Hirobumi), vol. 2. Hanawa shobō, 1974.

Iwakura Tomomi kankei monjo (Papers Relating to Iwakura Tomomi), vol. 8. Ōtsuka Takematsu, ed. Nihon shiseki kyōkai, 1935.

Iwakura-kō jikki (Records on Prince Iwakura), vol. 2. Tada Kōmon, ed. Iwakura-kō kyūseki hozonkai, 1927.

Iwasaki Hisaya den (Biography of Iwasaki Hisaya). Iwasaki Hisaya den hensan iinkai, 1961.

Iwasaki Yanosuke den (Biography of Iwasaki Yanosuke), vol. 2. Iwasaki Yatarō, Iwasaki Yanosuke denki hensankai, 1971.

Iwashita Seishū den (Biography of Iwashita Seishū). Ko Iwashita Seishū-kun denki hensankai, ed. Kondō Otokichi, 1931.

"The Japan Railway Company," *Japan Weekly Mail*, February 14, 1903, p. 162.
Japan Weekly Mail, 1886–1909.
"Japanese Railways," *Japan Weekly Mail*, August 9, 1902, p. 138.
Japanese Railways: Annual Report of the Imperial Railway Department for 21st

Fiscal Year of Meiji (April 1888 to March 1889). Imperial Railway Department, 1889. Transportation Museum Archives, Tokyo.
"Japanese Railways from a Military Point of View," *Japan Weekly Mail*, October 21, 1893, p. 466.
Jiyū (Liberty), April 26, 1892.
Johnson, Chalmers. *MITI and the Japanese Miracle: The Growth of Industrial Policy, 1925–1975*. Stanford: Stanford University Press, 1982.
———. "MITI, MPT, and the Telecom Wars: How Japan Makes Policy for High Technology," in Chalmers Johnson, Laura D. Tyson, and John Zysman, eds., *Politics and Productivity: The Real Story of Why Japan Works*. Cambridge, Mass.: Ballinger Publishing Company, 1989.
Jones, H. J. *Live Machines: Hired Foreigners and Meiji Japan*. Vancouver: University of British Columbia Press, 1980.
Jū nen kinen Nihon no tetsudō ron (Tenth-Anniversary Views on Japanese Railroads). Kinoshita Ritsuan, ed. Tetsudō jihō-kyoku, 1909.

"Kabushiki shijō no kinkyō" (The Recent Condition of the Stock Market), *Tōyō keizai shinpō*, December 5, 1907.
Kaitsū gojū nen (Fifty Years since the Opening [of the Nankai Railway]). Osaka: Nankai tetsudō kabushiki kaisha, 1936.
Kaku Risuke. *Dai sanki gikai* (The Third Diet), 1892.
"Kaku shisetsu tetsudō dai kabunushi ichiranhyō" (Major Stockholders List for Each of the Private Railroads), *Tetsudō zasshi* (Railroad Journal; retitled *Tetsudō* [Railroads] from no. 19), no. 5, pp. 21–23 (June 1896), no. 8, pp. 22–24 (July 1896), and no. 26, pp. 30–32 (November 1896).
"Kaku shisetsu tetsudō jūyaku oyobi kachō shimei ichiranhyō" (List of Names of Directors and Section Heads for Each of the Private Railroads), *Tetsudō zasshi* (Railroad Journal), no. 9, pp. 29–31 (July 1896) and no. 10, pp. 23–26 (July 1896).
"Kaku tetsudō kaisha no naii" (The Intentions of Each Railway Company), *Tōkyō keizai zasshi*, February 18, 1899, pp. 313–314.
Kamemura Masanao and Makimura Shiyō, eds. *Ōsaka ben* (Osaka Dialect), vol. 3. Osaka: Seibundō shoten, 1951.
Kanagawa no hyaku nen (Hundred Years of Kanagawa [since the Restoration]), vol. 2. Asahi shinbunsha Yokohama shi-kyoku, ed. Yokohama: Yūrindō, 1968.
Kaneko Fumio. "Sōgyō ki no Minami Manshū tetsudō, 1907–1916 nen" (The South Manchuria Railway during Its Founding Period, 1907–1916), *Shakai kagaku kenkyū* (Social Science Studies), vol. 31, no. 4, pp. 171–201 (January 1980).
Kan-Pu renrakusen shi (History of the Shimonoseki-Pusan Ferry). Hiroshima: Hiroshima tetsudō kanri-kyoku, 1979.

Kansai tetsudō kabushiki kaisha (Kansai Railway Company, Inc.). *Dai jūnikai hōkoku* (Twelfth Report), 1894.
"Kashidashikin teitōhin shuruibetsu hyō" (List of Loan Collateral by Type), March 31, 1893. Matsuo ke monjo, 1st ser., vol. 69, no. 28 (q.v.).
Katō Kōmei (Biography), vol. 1. Itō Masanori, ed. Katō-haku denki hensan iinkai, 1929.
Katō Kōmei den (Biography of Katō Kōmei). Katō Kōmei den kankōkai, 1928.
"Katsura Tarō jiden" (Autobiography of Katsura Tarō), vol. 2. Katsura Tarō kankei monjo (Papers Relating to Katsura Tarō), no. 77.1. Kensei shiryō-shitsu, National Diet Library, Tokyo.
Kawada Koichirō. Memorial to Matsukata Masayoshi, May 8, 1890. Matsuo ke monjo, 1st ser., vol. 82, no. 21 (q.v.).
Kawada Reiko. "Chūō sen no kensetsu to sono keizaiteki haikei" (Construction of the Chūō Line and Its Economic Setting), *Kōtsū bunka* (Transportation Culture), no. 5, pp. 19–35 (1965).
Kawakami Sōroku. Memorandum to Kuroda Kiyotaka, 1893. Teishin-shō kōbunsho, vol. 7, no. 2 (q.v.).
Kido Kōin nikki (Diary of Kido Kōin), vol. 2. Tsumaki Chūta, ed. Nihon shiseki kyōkai, 1933.
Kikuchi Takenori. *Nakamigawa Hikojirō-kun* ([Biography of] Mr. Nakamigawa Hikojirō). Jinmin shinbunsha shuppan-bu, 1903.
"Kin'yū kyūsai ni kansuru Ōsaka kaigi" (The Osaka Conference Regarding Financial Relief), *Tōkyō keizai zasshi*, April 26, 1890, in *Shibusawa Eiichi denki shiryō*, vol. 5 (q.v.).
Kin'yū rokujū nen shi (Sixty-Year History of Finance). Tōyō keizai shinpōsha, 1924.
Kirby, Richard J. Letter to Sir Claude Macdonald, June 3, 1901. Foreign Office Records, FO 800/134. Public Record Office, London.
"Kisha chū de hōhi shite, bakkin go en" (Five-Yen Fine for Breaking Wind on the Train), *Tōkyō nichinichi shinbun*, November 19, 1881, in *Shinbun shūsei Meiji hennen shi*, vol. 4, p. 491 (q.v.).
"Kisha ni benjo—botsubotsu toritsukeru" (Toilets Gradually Being Installed on Trains), *Jiji shinpō*, May 26, 1889, in *Shinbun shūsei Meiji hennen shi*, vol. 7, p. 275 (q.v.).
"Kisha no hayasa: kodomo no neta aida ni Yokohama-Shinagawa kan ōfuku" (The Speed of the Train: A Round Trip between Yokohama and Shinagawa while a Child Slept), *Shinbun zasshi* (News Journal), June 1873, in *Shinbun shūsei Meiji hennen shi*, vol. 2, p. 52 (q.v.).
"Kisha untenchū ni shōben: bakkin jū en nari" (Urinating while the Train Is Moving: The Fine Is Ten Yen), *Tōkyō nichinichi shinbun*, April 15, 1873, in *Shinbun shūsei Meiji hennen shi*, vol. 2, p. 31 (q.v.).
"The Kiushiu Railway," *Japan Weekly Mail*, August 26, 1899, p. 209.

"Kizoku-in tetsudō kokuyō hōan hoka ikken tokubetsu iinkai giji sokkiroku" (Minutes of the House of Peers Special Committee on the Railway Nationalization Bill and One Other Item), 3rd–6th sessions, March 23–26, 1906. *Kizoku-in tokubetsu iinkai giji sokkiroku* (q.v.).
Kizoku-in tokubetsu iinkai giji sokkiroku (Minutes of House of Peers Special Committees), 1892, 1906. National Diet Library, Tokyo.
Ko Pyon'un. *Kindai Chōsen keizai shi no kenkyū* (A Study of Modern Korean Economic History). Yūsankaku, 1978.
Kobayashi Masaaki. *Nihon no kōgyōka to kangyō haraisage: seifu to kigyō* (Japan's Industrialization and the Sale of State Enterprises: The Government and Business). Tōyō keizai shinpōsha, 1977.
Kōbu-shō kiroku: tetsudō no bu (Records of the Public Works Ministry: The Railway Section), vols. 5, 13, 22, 26, 28, 33, 39. Nihon kokuyū tetsudō, 1963–1964, 1969, 1977–1978, 1980.
Kōbu tetsudō kabushiki kaisha (Kōbu Railway Company, Inc.). *Dai jūnikai hōkoku* (Twelfth Report), *1894*. Teishin-shō kōbunsho, vol. 7, no. 6 (q.v.).
Kōbun ruiju (Collected Official Documents [of the Cabinet]), 6th–30th ser. (1882–1906). Kokuritsu kōbunshokan, Tokyo.
Kōgaku hakushi Shiraishi Naoji den (Biography of Shiraishi Naoji, Doctor of Engineering). Kōgaku hakushi Shiraishi Naoji den hensankai, 1943.
Kōhon Mitsui bussan kabushiki kaisha 100 nen shi (Manuscript Centennial History of Mitsui & Co.), vol. 1. Nihon keiei shi kenkyūjo, ed. Mitsui bussan kabushiki kaisha, 1978.
Kokaze Hidemasa. "Kōtsū shihon no keisei" (Formation of Transportation Capital), in Takamura Naosuke, ed., *Kigyō bokkō: Nihon shihonshugi no keisei* (Enterprise Boom: Formation of Japanese Capitalism). Minerva shobō, 1992.
———. "Tetsudō kokuyūka to un'yu mō no saihen" (The Railway Nationalization and the Reorganization of the Transport Network), in Takamura, ed., *Nichi-Ro sengo no Nihon keizai* (q.v.).
Kokkai (The National Diet), 1891–1892.
Kokumin shinbun, February 22, 1900, in *Shinbun shūsei Meiji hennen shi*, vol. 11 (q.v.).
"Kokutetsu *rōkaru* sen no shujutsu" (Surgical Operation on the Local Lines of the National Railways), *Asahi shinbun*, January 31, 1979, p. 5.
Kokuyū jū nen shi: honpō tetsudō kokuyūgo no shisetsu narabi ni seiseki (History of the First Decade after the Nationalization: Post-Nationalization Facilities and Performance of Japanese Railroads). Tetsudō-shō, 1920.
Komota Nobuo et al. *Nihon ryūkōka shi* (History of Japanese Popular Songs). Shakai shisōsha, 1970.
Kume Ryōsaku. "Tetsudō no kafū" (The Family Traditions of Railways), *Tokyo keizai zasshi*, October 25, 1902, p. 785.

"Kyūshū tan to Jōban tan" (Kyushu Coal and Jōban Coal), *Tōkyō keizai zasshi,* February 28, 1903, p. 363.

"Kyūshū tetsudō kabushiki kaisha chōsa hōkokusho" (Report on Investigation into the Kyushu Railway Company, Inc.), February 1900, in *Shibusawa Eiichi denki shiryō,* vol. 9 (q.v.).

Kyūshū tetsudō kensetsu no onjin Hermann Rumschöttel (Hermann Rumschöttel, Benefactor of Kyushu Railroad Construction). Moji tetsudō kanrikyoku Rumschöttel kenshōkai, 1960.

"Kyū-tetsu jiken no saitei" (The Decision in the Kyushu Railway Case), *Tōkyō keizai zasshi,* February 17, 1900, p. 276.

Kyū-tetsu nijū nen shi (Twenty-Year History of the Kyushu Railway Company). Kyūshū tetsudō kabushiki kaisha sōmu-ka, 1907.

Landes, David S. *Revolution in Time: Clocks and the Making of the Modern World.* Cambridge: Belknap Press of Harvard University Press, 1983.

Lockwood, William W. *The Economic Development of Japan.* Princeton: Princeton University Press, 1954.

Lowell, Percival. *Noto: An Unexplored Corner of Japan.* Boston: Houghton, Mifflin, 1891.

McCallion, Stephen W. "Trial and Error: The Model Filature at Tomioka," in Wray, ed., *Managing Industrial Enterprise* (q.v.).

Maejima Hisoka jijoden (Autobiography of Maejima Hisoka). Hayama-chō: Maejima Hisoka denki kankōkai, 1956.

"Maejima Hisoka nenpu" (Chronological Record of Maejima Hisoka). *Teishin kyōkai zasshi* (Communications Society Journal), April 1969, pp. 59–61.

Maejima Shōzō. *Meiji chū-makki no kanryō seiji* (Bureaucratic Politics from the Mid- to Late-Meiji Period). Kyoto: Sekibunsha, 1964.

Marshall, Byron K. *Capitalism and Nationalism in Prewar Japan: The Ideology of the Business Elite, 1868–1941.* Stanford: Stanford University Press, 1967.

Marx, Leo. "The Impact of the Railroad on the American Imagination, as a Possible Comparison for the Space Impact," in Mazlish, ed., *The Railroad and the Space Program* (q.v.).

———. *The Machine in the Garden: Technology and the Pastoral Ideal in America.* New York: Oxford University Press, 1964.

Matsukata ke monjo (Matsukata [Masayoshi] Papers), vol. 61. Finance Ministry Archives, Tokyo.

Matsukata Masayoshi. Memorandum to Yamagata Aritomo, April 25, 1891. Kōbun ruiju, 15th ser., vol. 37, no. 8 (q.v.).

Matsumoto Hiroshi. *Mitsui zaibatsu no kenkyū* (A Study of Mitsui Zaibatsu). Yoshikawa kōbunkan, 1979.

Matsumoto Sōichirō. Memorandum to the Ryōmō Railway Company, September 12, 1895. Teishin-shō kōbunsho, vol. 9, no. 15 (q.v.).
Matsuo ke monjo (Matsuo [Shigeyoshi] Papers), 1st ser., vols. 69, 82. Finance Ministry Archives, Tokyo.
Mazlish, Bruce, ed. *The Railroad and the Space Program: An Exploration in Historical Analogy*. Cambridge: M.I.T. Press, 1965.
Meiji ki tetsudō shi shiryō (Historical Materials on Meiji-Period Railroads). Noda Masaho, Harada Katsumasa, and Aoki Eiichi (with Oikawa Yoshinobu for 2nd ser.), eds. 1st ser., 17 vols.; 2nd ser., 43 vols. Nihon keizai hyōronsha, 1980–1989.
Meiji seimei hoken kabushiki kaisha rokujū nen shi (Sixty-Year History of Meiji Life Insurance Company, Inc.). Meiji seimei hoken kabushiki kaisha, 1942.
Meiji seitō kabushiki kaisha sanjū nen shi (Thirty-Year History of Meiji Sugar Company, Inc.). Meiji seitō kabushiki kaisha Tōkyō jimusho, 1936.
Meiji zaisei shi (Meiji Financial History), vol. 14. Meiji zaisei shi hakkōsho, 1927.
Meiji zenki zaisei keizai shiryō shūsei (Collection of Historical Materials on Finance and the Economy in the Early Meiji Period), vol. 1. Ōkura-shō, ed. Kaizōsha, 1931.
Mellor, Roy E. H. *German Railways: A Study in the Historical Geography of Transport*. Aberdeen: University of Aberdeen, 1979.
Meyer, Balthasar H. "Railroad Ownership in Germany," in William Z. Ripley, ed., *Railway Problems*. Boston: Ginn & Company, 1907.
Micheli, Horace. *State Purchase of Railways in Switzerland*. John Cummings, tr. New York: Macmillan Company, 1898.
"Migi no rinjikai o unagashitaru in'yu" (Factors Prompting the Above Special Meeting), *Chūgai shōgyō shinpō* (Domestic and Foreign Commercial News), April 11, 1890, in *Shibusawa Eiichi denki shiryō*, vol. 6 (q.v.).
Milward, Alan S., and S. B. Saul. *The Development of the Economies of Continental Europe, 1850–1914*. Cambridge: Harvard University Press, 1980.
Minami Manshū tetsudō kabushiki kaisha (South Manchuria Railway Company, Inc.), ed. *Jū nen shi* (Ten-Year History). Dairen: Minami Manshū tetsudō kabushiki kaisha, 1919.
"Mr. Sakatani on Japanese Finance," *Japan Weekly Mail*, December 23, 1905, p. 675.
Mitani Taiichirō. *Nihon seitō seiji no keisei: Hara Kei no seiji shidō no tenkai* (Formation of Japanese Party Politics: Development of Hara Kei's Political Leadership). Tōkyō daigaku shuppankai, 1967.
Mitchell, B. R. *European Historical Statistics, 1750–1970*. Abridged ed. New York: Columbia University Press, 1978.
Mitsubishi ginkō shi (History of Mitsubishi Bank). Mitsubishi ginkō shi hensan iinkai, 1954.

Mitsui ginkō hachijū nen shi (Eighty-Year History of Mitsui Bank). Mitsui ginkō, 1957.
Mitsui jigyō shi: shiryō hen (History of Mitsui Enterprises: Historical Materials), vol. 3. Mitsui bunko, 1977.
Mitsui ke monjo (Mitsui Family Papers), 2nd ser., vols. 2280–2281, 2284, 2288–2289, 2293. Mitsui bunko, Tokyo.
Miyano Takeo. "Tetsudō kokuyū hō ni yoru shisetsu tetsudō no baishū to sonogo (Taishō zenhan ki goro made) no sochi" (Purchase of Private Railroads under the Railway Nationalization Law and Steps Taken Thereafter [until about the First Half of the Taishō Period]), *Kōeki jigyō kenkyū* (Studies on Public Utilities), vol. 24, pp. 93–123 (February 1973).
Miyazaki Hiroshi and Andō Minoru. "Mantetsu no sōritsu" (Establishment of the South Manchuria Railway), in Andō Hikotarō, ed., *Mantetsu: Nihon teikokushugi to Chūgoku* (The South Manchuria Railway: Japanese Imperialism and China). Ochanomizu shobō, 1965.
Molony, Barbara. *Technology and Investment: The Prewar Japanese Chemical Industry*. Cambridge: Council on East Asian Studies, Harvard University, 1990.
Monogatari Tōhoku honsen shi (Narrative History of the Tōhoku Main Line). Nihon kokuyū tetsudō Sendai chūzai riji-shitsu, ed. Sendai: Tetsudo kosai-kai Tōhoku shibu, 1971.
Morikawa Hidemasa. "Mitsui zaibatsu no takakuteki jū kōgyōka katei (2)" (Process of Diversified Heavy Industrialization of the Mitsui Zaibatsu), *Keiei shirin* (Business Studies), vol. 5, no. 1, pp. 1–26 (April 1968).
———. *Nihon keiei shi* (Japanese Business History). Nihon keizai shinbunsha, 1981.
Murakami Katsuhiko. "Shokuminchi" (Colonies), in Ōishi, ed., *Nihon sangyō kakumei no kenkyū*, vol. 2. (q.v.).
Murakami Sadamu. "Keiroku" (Odds and Ends), in *Nakamigawa Hikojirō denki shiryō* (q.v.).
Murakami Teiichi. *Minami Kiyoshi den* (Biography of Minami Kiyoshi). Hayami Tarō, 1909.
Muroran seitetsujo gojū nenshi (Fifty-Year History of Muroran Ironworks). Muroran: Fuji seitetsu kabushiki kaisha Muroran seitetsujo, 1958.
Mutsu Munemitsu kankei monjo (Documents Relating to Mutsu Munemitsu). Kensei shiryō-shitsu, National Diet Library, Tokyo.

Nagano-ken (Nagano Prefecture), ed. *Nagano-ken shi: kindai shiryō hen* (History of Nagano Prefecture: Modern Historical Materials). Vol. 7, *Kōtsū, tsūshin* (Transportation, Communications). Nagano: Nagano-ken shi kankōkai, 1981.

Nagano kensei shi (History of Constitutional Government in Nagano), vol. 1. Nagano: Nagano-ken, 1971.

Nagaoka Shinkichi. *Meiji kyōkō shi josetsu* (Introduction to the History of Meiji Financial Panics). Tōkyō daigaku shuppankai, 1971.

————. "Nichi-Ro 'sengo keiei'" ("Postwar Management" Following the Russo-Japanese War), in Ōishi Kaichirō and Miyamoto Ken'ichi, eds., *Nihon shihonshugi hattatsu shi no kiso chishiki* (Basic Information on the Historical Development of Japanese Capitalism). Yūhikaku, 1975.

————. "Nisshin sengo no zaisei seisaku to baishōkin: 'sengo keiei' no seisaku kettei o megutte" (Financial Policy and the Indemnity Following the Sino-Japanese War: On Policy Making for the "Postwar Management"), in Andō Yoshio, ed., *Nihon keizai seisaku shi ron* (Studies in the History of Japanese Economic Policy), vol. 1. Tōkyō daigaku shuppankai, 1973.

Nagata Hiroshi, ed. *Meiji no kisha: tetsudō sōsetsu 100 nen no kobore banashi kara* (Meiji Trains: Gleanings on the Centennial of the Inauguration of Railroads). Kōtsū Nihonsha, 1964.

Najita, Tetsuo. *Hara Kei in the Politics of Compromise, 1905–1915*. Cambridge: Harvard University Press, 1967.

Nakagawa Keiichirō, Morikawa Hidemasa, and Yui Tsunehiko, eds. *Kindai Nihon keiei shi no kiso chishiki* (Basic Information on Modern Japanese Business History). Yūhikaku, 1974.

Nakagawa Seiza. *Teikoku tetsudō seisaku ron* (Treatise on Imperial Railway Policy). Tetsudō kenkyūsha, 1928.

Nakamigawa Hikojirō. Letter to Motoyama Hikoichi, February 2, 1887, in *Nakamigawa Hikojirō denki shiryō* (q.v.).

Nakamigawa Hikojirō denki shiryō (Biographical Materials on Nakamigawa Hikojirō). Nihon keiei shi kenkyūjo, ed. Tōyō keizai shinpōsha, 1969.

Nakamura Masanori. *Kindai Nihon jinushi sei shi kenkyū: shihonshugi to jinushi sei* (A Study on the History of the Modern Japanese Landlord System: Capitalism and the Landlord System). Tōkyō daigaku shuppankai, 1979.

Nakamura, Takafusa. *Economic Growth in Prewar Japan*. Robert A. Feldman, tr. New Haven: Yale University Press, 1983.

Nakanishi Ken'ichi. *Nihon shiyū tetsudō shi kenkyū: toshi kōtsū no hatten to sono kōzō* (A Study on the History of Private Railroads in Japan: The Development and Structure of Urban Transportation). 2nd ed. Minerva shobō, 1979.

"Nationalization of Railways," *Japan Weekly Mail,* February 3, 1906, p. 110.

"Nationalization of the Railways," *Japan Weekly Mail,* February 17, 1906, p. 169, and March 17, 1906, pp. 278–279.

Natsume Sōseki. *Botchan* (Little Master). Umeji Sasaki, tr. Rutland, Vt.: Charles E. Tuttle Company, 1968.

———. *Sanshirō: A Novel*. Jay Rubin, tr. Seattle: University of Washington Press, 1977.

———. *The Three-Cornered World*. Alan Turney, tr. New York: G. P. Putnam's Sons, 1965.

"New 'bullet' out to regain speed record," *Japan Access*, May 11, 1992, p. 6.

Nihon, 1892–1894.

"Nihon ginkō enkaku teiyō (shuyō nisshi)" (Summary of the Bank of Japan's History [Record of Principal Developments]), 1882–1905, in *Nihon kin'yū shi shiryō: Meiji Taishō hen,* vol. 10, suppl. (q.v.).

Nihon ginkō enkakushi (History of the Bank of Japan), 1st ser., vol. 2, pt. 1. Nihon ginkō enkakushi hensan-iin, 1913.

Nihon kagaku gijutsu shi taikei (Collection on the History of Japanese Science and Technology). Vol. 16, *Doboku gijutsu* (Civil-Engineering Technology). Nihon kagaku shi gakkai, ed. Daiichi hōki kabushiki kaisha, 1970.

Nihon kin'yū shi shiryō: Meiji Taishō hen (Historical Materials on Japanese Finance: Meiji, Taishō), vol. 7, pt. 1, vol. 8, vol. 10, suppl. Nihon ginkō chōsa-kyoku, ed. Ōkura-shō insatsu-kyoku, 1956–1957, 1960.

Nihon kokuyū tetsudō hyaku nen shi (Centennial History of the Japanese National Railways). 14 vols. Nihon kokuyū tetsudō, 1969–1974.

Nihon kokuyū tetsudō hyaku nen shi: tsū shi (Centennial History of the Japanese National Railways: General Survey). Nihon kokuyū tetsudō, 1974.

"Nihon no tetsudō" (Japanese Railways), *Tetsudō kyōkai shi* (Journal of the Railway Society), vol. 1, no. 3, pp. 360–366 (1898).

Nihon teikoku tōkei nenkan (Annual Statistics of the Japanese Empire), vols. 10–25. Naikaku tōkei-kyoku or Naikaku shokikan-shitsu tōkei-ka, 1891–1906.

Nihon tetsudō shi (History of Japanese Railroads). 3 vols. Tetsudō-shō, 1921.

Nihon tetsudō ukeoi gyō shi: Meiji hen (History of the Japanese Railroad Contracting Business: Meiji Volume). Tetsudō kensetsu gyō kyōkai, 1967.

Nippon seimei kyūjū nen shi (Ninety-Year History of Nippon Life Insurance). Osaka: Nippon seimei hoken sōgo kaisha, 1980.

Nippon tetsudō kaisha (Nippon Railway Company). "Hyakkabu ijō kabunushi jinmeibo" (List of Stockholders with 100 Shares or More), September 21, 1886, in *Shibusawa Eiichi denki shiryō,* vol. 8 (q.v.).

"Nippon tetsudō kaisha sōritsu ki" (Records on the Founding of the Nippon Railway Company). Iwakura Tomomi monjo (Iwakura Tomomi Papers), no. 191. Kensei shiryō-shitsu, National Diet Library, Tokyo.

Noda, Masaho. "Corporate Finance of Railroad Companies in Meiji Japan," in Keiichiro Nakagawa, ed., *Marketing and Finance in the Course of Industrialization*. Tokyo: University of Tokyo Press, 1978.

———. "Meiji ki ni okeru shiyū tetsudō no hattatsu to kabushiki hakkō shijō no tenkai: waga kuni ni okeru shiyū tetsudō no hattatsu to shōken shijō no keisei (1)" (Development of Private Railroads and the Stock Market in the Meiji Period: Development of Japanese Private Railroads and the Formation of the Securities Market), *Keizai shirin* (Economic Studies), vol. 32, pp. 114–165 (January 1964).

———. *Nihon shōken shijō seiritsu shi: Meiji ki no tetsudō to kabushiki kaisha kin'yū* (History of the Formation of the Japanese Securities Market: Meiji-Period Railroads and Joint-Stock-Company Finance). Yūhikaku, 1980.

——— et al. *Nihon no tetsudō: seiritsu to tenkai* (Japanese Railroads: Formation and Development). Nihon keizai hyōronsha, 1986.

Noguchi, Paul H. *Delayed Departures, Overdue Arrivals: Industrial Familialism and the Japanese National Railways*. Honolulu: University of Hawaii Press, 1990.

Noritake Kōtarō. "Tetsudō baishū wa danjite hi nari" (The Railway Purchase Is Decidedly a Mistake), *Tōkyō keizai zasshi*, March 10, 1906, in *Shibusawa Eiichi denki shiryō*, vol. 9 (q.v.).

O'Brien, Patrick. *The New Economic History of the Railways*. New York: St. Martin's Press, 1977.

———. "Transport and Economic Development in Europe, 1789–1914," in Patrick O'Brien, ed., *Railways and the Economic Development of Western Europe, 1830–1914*. New York: St. Martin's Press, 1983.

Ochiai Sadaaki. "Kokuyū made no tetsudō seisaku" (Railroad Policy until the Nationalization), *Un'yu to keizai* (Transport and the Economy), vol. 18, no. 4, pp. 38–54 (1958).

———. "Kokuyū made no tetsudō seisaku (zoku): tetsudō kokuyū hō no seiritsu" (Railroad Policy until the Nationalization [sequel]: Formation of the Railway Nationalization Law), *Un'yu to keizai*, vol. 18, no. 10, pp. 43–50 (1958).

———. "Meiji jū nendai no tetsudō seisaku (1)-(2)" (Railroad Policy during the Second Decade of Meiji), *Un'yu to keizai*, vol. 17, no. 6, pp. 18–26 (1957) and vol. 17, no. 7, pp. 30–35 (1957).

———. "Meiji shonen no tetsudō seisaku: Nihon tetsudō seisaku shi josetsu (1)-(2)" (Railroad Policy in the Early Years of Meiji: Introduction to the History of Japanese Railroad Policy), *Un'yu to keizai*, vol. 17, no. 2, pp. 20–25 (1957) and vol. 17, no. 3, pp. 54–62 (1957).

———. "Tetsudō fusetsu hō no seiritsu: Meiji jū nendai no tetsudō seisaku, zokuhen" (Formation of the Railway Construction Law: Sequel to Railroad Policy during the Second Decade of Meiji), *Un'yu to keizai*, vol. 17, no. 9, pp. 31–37 (1957).

Ogawa Isao. "Kansai tetsudō no kokuyūka hantai undō no saihyōka: Kataoka Naoharu no shoron shōkai" (Reevaluation of the Kansai Railway's Move-

ment Opposing Nationalization: Introducing the Views of Kataoka Naoharu), *Un'yu to keizai*, vol. 42, no. 10, pp. 48–62 (October 1982).
Ogawa Tameji. *Kaika mondō* (Dialogue on Enlightenment). Sanshoten, 1874. In Yoshino Sakuzō, ed., *Meiji bunka zenshū* (Complete Collection on Meiji Culture), vol. 20. Nihon hyōronsha, 1929.
Ohkawa, Masazo. "The Armaments Expansion Budgets and the Japanese Economy after the Russo-Japanese War," *Hitotsubashi Journal of Economics*, vol. 5, pp. 68–83 (January 1965).
Oikawa, Yoshinobu. "Market Structure and the Construction of Rural Railways during the Formative Period of Industrial Capitalism in Japan," *The Journal of Transport History*, 3rd ser., vol. 5, no. 2, pp. 34–46 (September 1984).
————. *Meiji ki chihō tetsudō shi kenkyū: chihō tetsudō no tenkai to shijō keisei* (Studies in the Local Railroad History of the Meiji Period: Development of Local Railroads and Market Formation). Nihon keizai hyōronsha, 1983.
Ōishi Kaichirō, ed. *Nihon sangyō kakumei no kenkyū* (Studies on the Japanese Industrial Revolution). 2 vols. Tōkyō daigaku shuppankai, 1975.
Ō-kabu gojū nen shi (Fifty-Year History of the Osaka Stock Exchange). Ōsaka kabushiki torihikijo, 1928.
Okamoto, Shumpei. *The Japanese Oligarchy and the Russo-Japanese War*. New York: Columbia University Press, 1970.
Ōkubo Toshimichi nikki (Diary of Ōkubo Toshimichi), vol. 2. Nihon shiseki kyōkai, 1927.
Okuma, Shigenobu, ed. *Fifty Years of New Japan*, vol. 1. London: Smith, Elder, & Co., 1910.
Ōkura-shō hyaku nen shi (Centennial History of the Finance Ministry), vol. 1. Ōkura zaimu kyōkai, 1969.
Ōkura-shō kansa-kyoku (Finance Ministry Audit Bureau). "Dai jūsanji ginkō eigyō hōkoku" (Thirteenth Report on Bank Operations), 1890, in *Nihon kin'yū shi shiryō: Meiji Taishō hen,* vol. 7, pt. 1 (q. v.).
Ono, Giichi. *Expenditures of the Sino-Japanese War*. New York: Oxford University Press, 1922.
Ono Kazushige. "Kōbu tetsudō to Tachikawa" (The Kōbu Railway and Tachikawa), *Tachikawa-shi shi kenkyū* (Studies in the History of Tachikawa City), no. 2, pp. 99–123 (December 1965).
"Opening of the Railway," *The Far East*, October 16, 1872.
"Ōsaka hyōtei no kekka ikaga" (Results of the Osaka Conference), *Tōkyō nichinichi shinbun,* May 9, 1890, in *Shibusawa Eiichi denki shiryō,* vol. 5 (q.v.).
"Ōsaka ni okeru kin'yū hippaku no kyūsai saku" (Plan for Relieving the Financial Stringency in Osaka), *Tōkyō nichinichi shinbun,* April 15, 1890, in *Shibusawa* Eiichi denki shiryō, vol. 5 (q.v.).

Ōsaka shōsen kabushiki kaisha (O.S.K.). *Eigyō hōkokusho* (Business Report), 1899.

"Ōsaka tetsudō kaisha" (Osaka Railway Company), *Dai Nihon tetsudō zasshi* (Japanese Railway Journal), no. 9, p. 21 (June 21, 1890).

Ōsaka tetsudō ryaku reki (Brief History of the Osaka Railway). Osaka: Kakehi Teizō, 1901.

Ōsawa Kaiyū. "Minami-kun cho 'Tetsudō keiei no hōshin' o yomu" (On Reading "Railway Management Policy" by Mr. Minami), *Tetsudō jihō* (Railway Review), no. 35 (December 1899), in *Jū nen kinen Nihon no tetsudō ron* (q.v.).

———. "Tetsudō kokuyū ron" (Treatise on Railway National Ownership), *Tetsudō kyōkai shi* (Journal of the Railway Society), vol. 1, no. 2, pp. 234–280 (1898).

———. *Tetsudō no kairyō ni kansuru iken* (Opinion Concerning the Improvement of Railroads), 1898, in Aoki, Harada, and Miyazawa, "Meiji hyaku nen kinen" (q.v.).

Ōshima Fujitarō. *Kokka dokusen shihon to shite no kokuyū tetsudō no shiteki hatten* (Historical Development of the National Railways as a Form of State Monopoly Capital). Itō shoten, 1949.

Ozaki Saburō jijo ryaku den (Short Autobiography of Ozaki Saburō), vol. 2. Chūō kōronsha, 1977.

Ozawa Takeo. "Tetsudō ni kansuru iken" (Opinion Concerning Railroads). Transportation Museum Archives, Tokyo.

———. "Tetsudō ron" (Treatise on Railroads), in *Tetsudō iken zenshū* (q.v.).

Patrick, Hugh. "Japan, 1868–1914," in Rondo Cameron et al., *Banking in the Early Stages of Industrialization: A Study in Comparative Economic History*. New York: Oxford University Press, 1967.

Pratt, Edwin A. *State Railways: Object Lessons from Other Lands*. London: P. S. King & Co., 1907.

"The Protection of Railway Operations," *Japan Weekly Mail*, May 17, 1890, p. 495.

Pyle, Kenneth B. "Advantages of Followership: German Economics and Japanese Bureaucrats, 1890–1925," *Journal of Japanese Studies*, vol. 1, no. 1, pp. 127–164 (Autumn 1974).

———. "The Technology of Japanese Nationalism: The Local Improvement Movement, 1900–1918," *Journal of Asian Studies*, vol. 33, no. 1, pp. 51–65 (November 1973).

"Railway and Steamship Competition," *Japan Weekly Mail*, September 3, 1898, p. 239.

"Railway Fares," *Japan Weekly Mail*, February 28, 1903, p. 218.

"The Railway Nationalization Bill," *Japan Weekly Mail,* March 31, 1906, p. 328.
"The Railway Nationalization Bill Passes," *Japan Weekly Mail,* March 24, 1906, p. 302.
"Railway News," *Japan Weekly Mail,* December 14, 1895, p. 646.
"The Railway Question," *Japan Weekly Mail,* May 5, 1906, p. 461.
"Railways," *Japan Weekly Mail,* May 19, 1894, p. 585, February 1, 1896, p. 120, February 25, 1896, p. 187, March 21, 1896, p. 24, September 3, 1898, p. 236, and May 6, 1905, p. 479.
"Railways and the Indemnity," *Japan Weekly Mail,* May 7, 1898, p. 473.
"Railways in Japan," *Japan Weekly Mail,* May 15, 1909, p. 635.
Reed, M. C. *Investment in Railways in Britain, 1820–1844: A Study in the Development of the Capital Market.* London: Oxford University Press, 1975.
Richards, Jeffrey, and John M. MacKenzie. *The Railway Station: A Social History.* Oxford: Oxford University Press, 1986.
"Ryōmō tetsudō kaisha dokuritsu ni kessu" (The Ryōmō Railway Company Decides for Independence), *Tōkyō keizai zasshi,* May 28, 1892, p. 759.
"Ryōmō tetsudō kaisha no rinji sōkai" (Special General Meeting of the Ryōmō Railway Company), *Tōkyō keizai zasshi,* July 30, 1892, pp. 170–171.

Saburi Kazutsugu. *Nihon no tetsudō* (Japanese Railroads), 1891.
Sakudo Yōtarō. "Shitetsu keiei no seiritsu to sono tenkai: Mino-Arima dentetsu no baai o chūshin to shite" (The Formation and Development of Private Railway Management: The Case of the Mino-Arima Electric Railway), *Ōsaka keidai ronshū* (Studies of the Osaka University of Economics), nos. 117–118, pp. 105–123 (July 1977).
Sakurai Tōru. "Nippon tetsudō kabushiki kaisha no shihon chikuseki jōken to kokuyūka mondai (1)-(2): kokka dokusen seisei ni kansuru junbiteki kōsatsu" (Conditions of Capital Accumulation in the Nippon Railway Company and the Nationalization Issue: Preliminary Study Concerning the Formation of a State Monopoly), *Ōsaka shidai ronshū* (Studies of Osaka City University), no. 25, pp. 59–84 (1976) and no. 26, pp. 45–65 (1977).
———. "San'yō tetsudō kabushiki kaisha no shihon chikuseki jōken to kokuyūka mondai: kokka dokusen seisei ni kansuru kisoteki kōan" (Conditions of Capital Accumulation in the Sanyō Railway Company and the Nationalization Issue: Basic Ideas Concerning the Formation of a State Monopoly), *Shōgaku shūshi* (Studies in Commercial Science), vol. 49, no. 3, pp. 55–77 (February 1980).
Samuels, Richard J. *The Business of the Japanese State: Energy Markets in Comparative and Historical Perspective.* Ithaca: Cornell University Press, 1987.
Sanbō honbu rikugun-bu (Army General Staff). *Tetsudō ron* (Treatise on Railroads), 1888. University of Tokyo Faculty of Economics Library, Tokyo.
"Sandai tetsudō no sokuryoku chinsen hikaku" (Comparison of the Speeds

and Rates of the Three Major Railways), *Tōkyō keizai zasshi,* February 28, 1903, p. 31.
"San'yō tetsudō kaisha kabunushi meibo" (San'yō Railway Company Stockholders List), September 1891, in *Nakamigawa Hikojirō denki shiryō* (q.v.).
"San'yō tetsudō kaisha no shasai boshū" (Flotation of Corporate Bonds by the San'yō Railway Company), *Tōkyō keizai zasshi,* March 18, 1893, pp. 394–395.
"San'yō tetsudō kaisha teikanchū kōsei no ken" (Matter Concerning Revision of the Articles of Incorporation of the San'yō Railway Comapny). Kōbun ruiju, 13th ser. (1889), vol. 46, no. 3 (q.v.).
"San'yō tetsudō nimotsu unchin hikisage no keikaku" (Plans by the San'yō Railway to Reduce Freight Charges), *Tōyō keizai shinpō,* July 5, 1898, p. 35.
"San'yō testsudō Ushiba senmu no enzetsu" (Speech by Managing Director Ushiba of the San'yō Railway), *Tetsudō jihō* (Railway Review), November 5, 1904, p. 10.
Sawa Kazuya. *Nihon no tetsudō: hyaku nen no hanashi* (Japanese Railroads: A Century of Stories). Tsukiji shokan, 1972.
Sawai Minoru. "Senzenki Nihon tetsudō sharyō kōgyō no tenkai katei, 1890 nendai-1920 nendai" (Development of the Prewar Japanese Railway Rolling-Stock Industry, 1890s-1920s), *Shakai kagaku kenkyū* (Social Science Studies), vol. 37, no. 3, pp. 1–200 (1985).
Schalow, Thomas Richard. "Transforming Railroads into Steamships: Banking with the Matsukata Family at the 15th Bank," *Hitotsubashi Journal of Commerce and Management,* vol. 22, no. 1, pp. 55–67 (December 1987).
Schivelbusch, Wolfgang. *The Railway Journey: The Industrialization of Time and Space in the Nineteenth Century.* Berkeley: University of California Press, 1986.
Scott, J. D. *Vickers: A History.* London: Weidenfeld and Nicolson, 1962.
Segai Inoue-kō den (Biography of Marquis Inoue), vols. 2, 5. Inoue Kaoru-kō denki hensankai, ed. Naigai shoseki kabushiki kaisha, 1933–1934.
Seidensticker, Edward. *Low City, High City: Tokyo from Edo to the Earthquake.* New York: Alfred A. Knopf, 1983.
Seien kaikoroku (Reminiscences of Shibusawa Eiichi), vol. 1. Konuki Shūichirō, ed. Seien kaikoroku kankōkai, 1927.
"Seien sensei den shokō" (Biography of Shibusawa Eiichi, First Proof), 1919–1923, in *Shibusawa Eiichi denki shiryō,* vol. 5 (q.v.).
"Seien sensei no tetsudō kokuyū dan" (Shibusawa Eiichi on Railway Nationalization), *Ryūmon zasshi* (Ryūmon Journal), February 25, 1906, pp. 6–8.
Senda Minoru. "Kazoku shihon no seiritsu, tenkai: ippanteki kōsatsu" (Formation and Development of Peerage Capital: A General Study), *Shakai keizai shi gaku* (Studies in Socioeconomic History), vol. 52, no. 1, pp. 1–37 (April 1986).
———. "Kazoku shihon no seiritsu, tenkai: Meiji, Taishō ki no kyū Tsu-

chiura hanshu Tsuchiya ke ni tsuite" (Formation and Development of Peerage Capital: On the Tsuchiya Family, Former Daimyo of Tsuchiura, during the Meiji and Taishō Periods), *Shakai keizai shi gaku*, vol. 55, no. 1, pp. 1–36 (April 1989).

Shibata Hajime and Asamori Kaname, eds. *Kyōdo shi jiten: Okayama-ken* (Dictionary of Local History: Okayama Prefecture). Shōheisha, 1980.

Shibusawa Eiichi. Letter to Itō Hirobumi, March 18, 1893, in *Shibusawa Eiichi denki shiryō*, vol. 9 (q.v.).

Shibusawa Eiichi denki shiryō (Biographical Materials on Shibusawa Eiichi), vols. 5–6, 8–9, 16, 21. Shibusawa seien kinen zaidan ryūmonsha, ed. Shibusawa Eiichi denki shiryō kankōkai, 1955–1958.

"Shibusawa Eiichi-kun no kin'yū hippaku dan" (Mr. Shibusawa Eiichi on the Tight Money Market), *Tōkyō keizai zasshi*, March 22, 1890, in *Shibusawa Eiichi denki shiryō*, vol. 5 (q.v.).

"Shibusawa Eiichi-shi no hi-tetsudō kan'yū ron" (Mr. Shibusawa Eiichi's Opinion against Government Ownership of Railroads), *Jiji shinpō*, August 30, 1898, in *Shibusawa Eiichi denki shiryō*, vol. 21 (q.v.).

Shibusawa Keizō, comp. and ed. *Japanese Life and Culture in the Meiji Era*. Charles S. Terry, tr. Tokyo: Ōbunsha, 1958.

Shiga Naoya. "Abashiri made" (To Abashiri), in Watanabe et al., eds., *Kiteki issei* (q.v.).

Shima Yasuhiko. *Nihon shihonshugi to kokuyū tetsudō* (Japanese Capitalism and the National Railways). Nihon hyōronsha, 1950.

Shimazaki Tōson. *The Broken Commandment*. Kenneth Strong, tr. Tokyo: University of Tokyo Press, 1974.

Shimizu Ichitarō. "Tai gikai saku" (Plans for the Diet), in Itō Hirobumi, ed., *Hisho ruisan: teikoku gikai shiryō* (Classified Secretarial Collection: Materials on the Imperial Diet), vol. 1, 1934.

Shimizu Keijirō. *Shitetsu monogatari* (Tales of Private Railroads). Shunjūsha, 1930.

―――, ed. *Kōtsū konjaku monogatari* (Tales of Transportation, Past and Present). Kōyūsha, 1933.

Shinbun shūsei Meiji hennen shi (Newspaper-Collection Chronicle of Meiji), vols. 2, 4, 6–7, 11, 13. Shinbun shūsei Meiji hennen shi hensankai, 1936.

Shinshū hyaku nen (Hundred Years of Shinshū [since the Restoration]). Nagano: Shinano mainichi shinbunsha, 1967.

Shioda Ryōhei, ed. *Narushima Ryūhoku, Fukube Bushō, Kurimoto Joun shū* (Collected Works of Narushima Ryūhoku, Fukube Bushō, and Kurimoto Joun), vol. 4 of *Meiji bungaku zenshū* (Complete Collection of Meiji Literature). Chikuma shobō, 1969.

Shiraishi Naoji et al. "Tetsudō kakuchō narabini baishū ni tsuki seigan" (Petition Concerning the Extension and Purchase of Railroads), undated, in *Tetsudō iken zenshū* (q.v.).

Shirayanagi Shūko. *Zoku zaikai taihei ki* (Sequel to Chronicle of Great Peace in the Business World). Nihon hyōronsha, 1930.

"Shisetsu tetsudō baishū hōan ni kansuru ken" (The Matter of the Private Railway Purchase Bill). Mutsu Munemitsu kankei monjo (q.v.).

"Shisetsu tetsudō kaiage no gi" (The Matter of the Private Railway Purchase), *Tōkyō keizai zasshi,* May 7, 1898, pp. 953–955.

"Shisetsu tetsudō kaisha dai kabunushi ichiranhyō" (Major Stockholders Lists for Private Railway Companies), *Tetsudō zasshi* (Railroad Journal), no. 7, pp. 23–24 (July 1896).

Shishaku Inoue Masaru-kun shōden (Biographical Sketch of Viscount Inoue Masaru). Murai Masatoshi, ed. Inoue shishaku dōzō kensetsu dōshikai, 1915.

Shōin Motoyama Hikoichi-ō (The Venerable Motoyama Hikoichi). Ko Motoyama shachō denki hensan iinkai, ed. Osaka: Ōsaka mainichi shinbunsha, 1937; Tōkyō nichinichi shinbunsha, 1937.

"Shōrai no tetsudō seisaku" (Railroad Policy in the Future), *Tōyō keizai shinpō,* July 15, 1905, p. 12.

Showalter, Dennis E. "Soldiers and Steam: Railways and the Military in Prussia, 1832 to 1848," *The Historian,* vol. 34, pp. 242–259 (February 1972).

Shūgi-in iinkai kaigiroku (Minutes of House of Representatives Committees), 1891–1892, 1906. National Diet Library, Tokyo.

Shūgi-in meikan (House of Representatives Directory). Nihon kokusei chōsakai, ed. Kokusei shuppan-shitsu, 1977.

"Shūgi-in tetsudō baishū hōan shinsa tokubetsu iinkai sokkiroku" (Stenographic Record of the House of Representatives Special Committee Investigating the Railway Purchase Bill), 1st session, December 21, 1891. *Shūgi-in iinkai kaigiroku* (q.v.).

"Shūgi-in tetsudō kokuyū hōan hoka ikken iinkai kaigiroku" (Minutes of the House of Representatives Committee on the Railway Nationalization Bill and One Other Item), 2nd and 5th–7th sessions, March 9 and 13–15, 1906. *Shūgi-in iinkai kaigiroku,* 5th ser., no. 36 (q.v.).

"Shūgi-in tetsudō kōsai hōan shisetsu tetsudō baishū hōan shinsa tokubetsu iinkai" (House of Representatives Special Committee Investigating the Railway Public Bond Bill and the Private Railway Purchase Bill), May 13, 24, and 26, 1892. *Shūgi-in iinkai kaigiroku* (q.v.).

Simmons, Jack. *The Railways of Britain: An Historical Introduction.* London: Routledge & Kegan Paul, 1961.

"Sir William Bisset," *Japan Weekly Mail,* May 24, 1902, p. 560.

Smith, Thomas C. "Peasant Time and Factory Time in Japan," in his *Native*

Sources of Japanese Industrialization, 1750–1920. Berkeley: University of California Press, 1988.

———. *Political Change and Industrial Development in Japan: Government Enterprise, 1868–1880*. Stanford: Stanford University Press, 1955.

Soejima Taneomi. Memorandum to Matsukata Masayoshi, April 9, 1892. Kōbun ruiju, 16th ser., vol. 38, no. 4 (q.v.).

Sōken Matsumoto Jūtarō-ō den (Biography of the Venerable Matsumoto Jūtarō). Matsumoto-ō dōzō kensetsukai, 1922.

Sorimachi Shōji. *Tetsudō no Nihon shi* (Japanese History through Railroads). Bunken shuppan, 1982.

"Sōul-Fusan Railway," *Japan Weekly Mail,* March 4, 1899, p. 214.

"State Purchase of Private Railways," *Japan Weekly Mail,* August 27, 1898, p. 210, and December 14, 1898, p. 632.

"State Purchase of Railways," *Japan Weekly Mail,* February 5, 1898, p. 133.

Sugiura Seishi. "Nichi-Ro sengo no yūbin chokin no tenkai to chochiku shōrei seisaku" (Development of Postal Savings after the Russo-Japanese War and Savings-Promotion Policy), *Shakai keizai shi gaku* (Studies in Socioeconomic History), vol. 56, no. 1, pp. 31–61 (April 1990).

———. "Taishūteki reisai chochiku kikan toshite no yūbin chokin no seiritsu: Nisshin sengo no yūbin chokin no tenkai to sono seikaku" (Establishment of Postal Savings as a Mass Small-Savings Institution: The Development and Character of Postal Savings after the Sino-Japanese War), *Shakai keizai shi gaku,* vol. 52, no. 4, pp. 64–92 (October 1986).

Sugiyama Kazuo. "Kabushiki kaisha seido no hatten: bōseki, tetsudō gyō o chūshin ni" (Development of the Joint-Stock-Company System: The Cases of the Spinning and Railway Industries), in Kobayashi Masaaki et al., eds., *Nihon keiei shi o manabu* (Learning about Japanese Business History). Vol. 1, *Meiji keiei shi* (Meiji Business History). Yūhikaku, 1976.

———. "Kigyō no zaimu, tōshi katsudō to bunkateki haikei: Meiji ki no tetsudō gyō, men-bōseki gyō o jirei to shite" (Financial and Investment Activities of Enterprises and Their Cultural Setting: The Cases of the Railway and Cotton-Spinning Industries during the Meiji Period), *Keiei shi gaku* (Japan Business History Review), vol. 10, pp. 54–86 (August 1975).

———. "Kin'yū" (Finance), in Furushima Toshio and Andō Yoshio, eds., *Ryūtsū shi* (History of Distribution), pt. 2. Yamakawa shuppansha, 1975.

———. "Meiji 30 nendai ni okeru tetsudō kaisha no dai kabunushi to keieisha" (Major Stockholders and Managers of Railway Companies during the Fourth Decade of Meiji), *Seikei daigaku keizai gakubu ronshū* (Studies of the Seikei University Faculty of Economics), vol. 7, no. 2, pp. 153–181 (1977).

Sugiyama, Shinya. *Japan's Industrialization in the World Economy, 1859–1899*. London: The Athlone Press, 1988.

Sumiya Mikio. *Nihon sekitan sangyō bunseki* (Analysis of the Japanese Coal-Mining Industry). Iwanami shoten, 1968.
Supple, Barry. "The State and the Industrial Revolution, 1700–1914," in Carlo M. Cipolla, ed., *The Fontana Economic History of Europe*. Vol. 3, *The Industrial Revolution*. London: Fontana Books, 1973.

Tagawa-shi (Tagawa City), ed. *Tagawa-shi shi* (History of Tagawa City), vol. 2. Tagawa: Tagawa shiyakusho, 1976.
Taishō ki tetsudō shi shiryō (Historical Materials on Taishō-Period Railroads). Noda Masaho, Harada Katsumasa, and Aoki Eiichi, eds. 1st ser., 24 vols., 2nd ser., 20 vols. Nihon keizai hyōronsha, 1983–1985.
Taiwan seitō kabushiki kaisha shi (History of Taiwan Sugar Company, Inc.). Taiwan seitō kabushiki kaisha, 1939.
Taiwan tetsudō shi (History of Taiwanese Railroads), vol. 1. Taiwan sōtokufu tetsudō-bu, 1910.
Takahashi Korekiyo jiden (Autobiography of Takahashi Korekiyo). Chikura shobō, 1936.
Takahashi Makoto. *Meiji zaisei shi kenkyū* (A Study of Meiji Financial History). Aoki shoten, 1964.
Takami Sawashige. *Tōkyō kaika hanjō shi* (Record of Tokyo's Enlightenment and Prosperity), 1874, in Yoshino Sakuzō, ed., *Meiji bunka zenshū* (Complete Collection of Meiji Culture), vol. 19. Nihon hyōronsha, 1928.
Takamura Naosuke. "Dokusen soshiki no keisei" (Formation of Monopolies), in Takamura Naosuke, ed., *Nichi-Ro sengo no Nihon keizai* (q.v.).
———. "Kyōkō" (Financial Panics), in Ōishi, ed., *Nihon sangyō kakumei no kenkyū*, vol. 2 (q.v.).
———. "Meiji 23 nen kyōkō no seikaku: Nagaoka Shinkichi cho *Meiji kyōkō shi josetsu* ni yosete" (The Nature of the Panic of 1890: In Connection with *Introduction to the History of Meiji Financial Panics* by Nagaoka Shinkichi), *Nihon rekishi*, no. 332, pp. 80–98 (January 1976).
———. *Nihon bōseki gyō shi josetsu* (Introduction to the History of the Japanese Spinning Industry), vol. 1. Hanawa shobō, 1971.
———. "Sangyō, bōeki kōzō" (Structure of Industry and Trade), in Ōishi, ed., *Nihon sangyō kakumei no kenkyū*, vol. 1. (q.v.).
———, ed. *Nichi-Ro sengo no Nihon keizai* (The Japanese Economy after the Russo-Japanese War). Hanawa shobō, 1988.
Takechi Kyōzō. *Meiji zenki yusō shi no kisoteki kenkyū* (Basic Study on the History of Early Meiji Transport). Yūsankaku, 1978.
———. "Nisshin sensōgo tetsudō kaisha no kabunushi to sono keifu" (Railway Company Stockholders and Their Lineages Following the Sino-Japanese War), *Seitō joshi tanki daigaku kiyō* (Bulletin of the Seitō Women's Junior College), no. 6, pp. 1–61 (September 1976).

──────. *Toshi kinkō tetsudō no shiteki tenkai* (Historical Development of Suburban Railroads). Nihon keizai hyōronsha, 1986.
Takizawa Naoshichi. *Kōhon Nihon kin'yū shi ron* (Manuscript Historical Treatise on Japanese Finance). Yūhikaku, 1912.
Tanaka Gentarō-ō den (Biography of the Venerable Tanaka Gentarō). Kyoto: Miura Toyoji, 1934.
Tanaka, Tokihiko. "Meiji Government and the Introduction of Railways," *Contemporary Japan*, vol. 28, no. 3, pp. 567–588 (May 1966) and vol. 28, no. 4, pp. 750–788 (May 1967).
──────. *Meiji ishin no seikyoku to tetsudō kensetsu* (The Political Situation at the Time of the Meiji Restoration and Railroad Construction). Yoshikawa kōbunkan, 1963.
──────. "Tetsudō yusō" (Railway Transport), in Matsuyoshi Sadao and Andō Yoshio, eds., *Nihon yusō shi* (History of Japanese Transport). Nihon hyōronsha, 1971.
Tanizaki, Junichiro. *Seven Japanese Tales*. Howard Hibbett, tr. New York: Alfred A. Knopf, 1963.
"The Tanko Railway Company," *Japan Weekly Mail*, September 23, 1905, p. 330.
Teikoku tetsudō yōkan (Imperial Railway Handbook). 3rd ed. Tetsudō jihōkyoku, 1906.
Teishin-shō (Communications Ministry). *Nippon tetsudō baishū kagaku keisansho* (Account Statement for the Purchase Price of the Nippon Railway), 1908.
Teishin-shō kōbunsho (Official Documents of the Communications Ministry), vols. 7, 9 (1893–1894, 1895). Japan Railway Archives, Tokyo.
"Tekkoku an to chōsa no gobyū" (The Railway Nationalization Bill and Errors in the Inquiry), *Tōyō keizai shinpō*, March 25, 1906, p. 398.
"Tekkoku an to giin betsu" (The Railway Nationalization Bill and the Division among Diet Members), *Tōkyō keizai zasshi*, March 17, 1906, in *Shibusawa Eiichi denki shiryō*, vol. 9 (q.v.).
"Tetsudō baishū kakaku to kōsai" (Railroad Purchase Prices and Public Bonds), *Tōyō keizai shinpō*, November 25, 1907.
"Tetsudō dai kabunushi no kesshin ikaga" (What Are the Intentions of Major Railway Stockholders?), in *Tetsudō iken zenshū* (q.v.).
"Tetsudō fusetsu hōan tokubetsu iinkai kaigiroku" (Proceedings of the Special Committee [Investigating] the Railway Construction Bill), June 8, 1892. *Kizoku-in tokubetsu iinkai giji sokkiroku* (q.v.).
Tetsudō ichibetsu (Glimpses of Railways). Tetsudō-shō, 1921.
Tetsudō iken zenshū (Complete Collection of Opinions on Railroads). Otani Matsujirō, 1892.
Tetsudō jihō (Railway Review), 1899–1906.

"Tetsudō kabuken" (Railroad Stocks), in *Shibusawa Eiichi denki shiryō,* vol. 9 (q.v.).

"Tetsudō kabuken ni kawarubeki kōsai" (Public Bonds That Are to Replace Railroad Stocks), *Tōkyō keizai zasshi,* April 14, 1906, pp. 589–590.

"Tetsudō kaiage ni kanshi Kawada Nihon ginkō sōsai kaku ginkōka to kyōgisu" (Bank of Japan President Kawada Confers with Bankers about the Purchase of Railroads), *Tōkyō keizai zasshi,* November 28, 1891, in *Tetsudō iken zenshū* (q.v.).

"Tetsudō kaiage ni kansuru chōsa-iin hōkokusho" (Report of the Investigative Committee on the Purchase of Railroads), in *Tetsudō iken zenshū* (q.v.).

Tetsudō kaigi giji sokkiroku (Railway Council Minutes), 1891–1893, 1907–1908. Japan Railway Archives, Tokyo.

"Tetsudō kaigi o mōkuru no gi" (Matter Concerning the Establishment of a Railway Council). Matsukata ke monjo, vol. 61, no. 1 (q.v.).

Tetsudō kisei dōmeikai (Railroad Promotion League). *Tetsudō an ni taisuru kibō* (Hopes Concerning the Railway Bill), 1892. University of Tokyo Faculty of Economics Library, Tokyo.

Tetsudō kisei dōmeikai hōkoku (Report of the Railroad Promotion League). Tetsudō kisei dōmeikai, 1892.

"Tetsudō kokuyū ron no yurai" (History of the Railway Nationalization Debate), *Ginkō tsūshin roku* (Banking News), no. 159 (February 15, 1899), in *Shibusawa Eiichi denki shiryō,* vol. 9 (q.v.).

Tetsudō kokuyū shimatsu ippan (Outline of the Railway Nationalization Settlement). Teishin-shō, 1909.

"Tetsudō no baishū kakaku ni tsuite" (On the Purchase Prices of the Railroads), *Tōkyō keizai zasshi,* February 24, 1906, pp. 280–281.

"Tetsudō no benri oyobi fuhei no ki" (A Description of the Conveniences and Shortcomings of the Railroads), *Tōkyō keizai zasshi,* July 20, 1889, pp. 74–76.

Tetsudō senjin roku (Records on Railway Predecessors). Nihon kōtsū kyōkai, ed. Nihon teishajō kabushiki kaisha, 1972.

"Tetsudō tōgi" (Railroad Deliberations), *Tōkyō nichinichi shinbun,* September 22, 1891.

Tetsudō-in monjo (Documents of the Railway Department), Chikuhō kōgyō tetsudō (Chikuhō Industrial Railway), vol. 1 (1888–1893), Kansai tetsudō (Kansai Railway), vol. 1 (1887–1906), and Nippon tetsudō (Nippon Railway), vols. 1–10 (1881–1903). Transportation Museum Archives, Tokyo.

Tetsudō-kyoku jimu shorui (Business Papers of the Railway Bureau), vol. 2 (1887). Japan Railway Archives, Tokyo.

Tetsudō-kyoku nenpō (Annual Report of the Railway Bureau), *1900.* Teishin-shō tetsudō-kyoku, 1901.

——, *1907.* Teishin-shō tetsudō-kyoku, ed. Tetsudō-in, 1909.

Tiedemann, Arthur E. "Big Business and Politics in Prewar Japan," in James W. Morley, ed., *Dilemmas of Growth in Prewar Japan*. Princeton: Princeton University Press, 1971.

Timins, D. T. "By Rail in Japan," *The Railway Magazine*, vol. 2, pp. 230–236 (March 1898).

Tōhō (Party Report), 1891–1892.

Tōjō Tadashi. "Meiji ki tetsudō kaisha no keiei funsō to kabunushi no dōkō: 'Kyūshū tetsudō kaikaku undō' o megutte" (Management Disputes and Stockholder Tendencies in Meiji-Period Railway Companies: The Case of the "Kyushu Railway Reform Movement"), *Keiei shi gaku*, vol. 19, no. 4, pp. 1–35 (January 1985).

"Tōkaidō suji tetsudō junransho" (Report on Survey of a Railroad along the Tokaido), 1870. Tetsudō-ryō jimubō (Business Records of the Railway Office), vol. 1. Japan Railway Archives, Tokyo.

"Tōkaidō tetsudō zentsū mo ato ikka getsu" (One Month until the Opening of the Tokaido Railway), *Chōya shinbun* (Whole Nation Newspaper), March 17, 1889, in *Shinbun shūsei Meiji hennen shi*, vol. 7, p. 248 (q.v.).

Tokyo asahi, March 15, 1906, in *Shinbun shūsei Meiji hennen shi*, vol. 13 (q.v.).

Tōkyō dōmei ginkō (Tokyo Bankers' Association). "Dai hyaku-nikai teishiki shūkai rokuji" (Minutes of the 102nd Regular Meeting), May 15, 1890, in *Shibusawa Eiichi denki shiryō*, vol. 6 (q.v.).

Tōkyō dentō kabushiki kaisha kaigyō gojū nen shi (Fifty-Year History of Tokyo Electric Light Company, Inc.). Tōkyō dentō kabushiki kaisha, 1936.

Tōkyō gasu gojū nen shi (Fifty-Year History of Tokyo Gas). Tōkyō gasu kabushiki kaisha, 1935.

Tōkyō ginkō shūkaijo (Tokyo Bankers' Association). "Seifu min'yū no tetsudō o baishū shi, sono enchō kantsū o reito subeki no gi" (The Government Should Buy up Private Railroads and Strive for Their Extension and Completion), November 30, 1891, in *Tetsudō iken zenshū* (q.v.).

"Tōkyō han'ei mari uta" (Tokyo Prosperity Ball Song), *Yūbin hōchi shinbun* (Postal Information Newspaper), December 8, 1874, in *Shinbun shūsei Meiji hennen shi*, vol. 2, p. 244 (q.v.).

Tōkyō kabushiki torihikijo gojū nen shi (Fifty-Year History of the Tokyo Stock Exchange). Tōkyō kabushiki torihikijo, 1928.

Tōkyō kaijō kasai hoken kabushiki kaisha hyaku nen shi (Centennial History of Tokio Marine & Fire Insurance Co., Inc.), vol. 1. Nihon keiei shi kenkyūjo, ed. Tōkyō kaijō kasai hoken kabushiki kaisha, 1979.

Tōkyō keizai zasshi, 1889–1906.

Tōkyō nichinichi shinbun, 1872–1892.

"Tōkyō shōgyō kaigisho chinjō iin no shushō hōmon" (Interview with the Prime Minister by the Petition Committee Members of the Tokyo Chamber of Commerce), *Tōkyō keizai zasshi*, January 11, 1902, p. 30.

Tominaga Yūji. *Kōtsū ni okeru shihonshugi no hatten: Nihon kōtsū gyō no kindaika katei* (Development of Capitalism in the Transport Field: The Modernization Process in the Japanese Transportation Industry). Iwanami shoten, 1953.

Toriumi Yasushi. "Tetsudō fusetsu hō seitei katei ni okeru tetsudō kisei dōmeikai no atsuryoku katsudō" (Lobbying Activities of the Railroad Promotion League in the Process Leading to Enactment of the Railway Construction Law), *Tōkyō daigaku kyōyō gakubu jinbunkagaku-ka kiyō* (Bulletin of the University of Tokyo Faculty of General Education Humanities Division), no. 43, pp. 139–157 (August 1967).

Tōyō keizai shinpō, 1898–1909.

Trevithick, Francis H. "The History and Development of the Railway System in Japan," *Transactions of the Asiatic Society of Japan*, vol. 22, pp. 115–252 (September 1894).

Tsuchiya Shigeaki. *Kindai Nihon zōsen kotohajime: Hida Hamagorō no shōgai* (Beginnings of Modern Japanese Shipbuilding: The Life of Hida Hamagorō). Shin jinbutsu ōraisha, 1975.

Tsuchiya Takao. *"Nihon ginkō hanki hōkoku* kaidai" (Explanatory Notes for *Semiannual Report of the Bank of Japan*), in *Nihon kin'yū shi shiryō: Meiji Taishō hen*, vol. 8 (q.v.).

Tsumaki Chūta. *Maebara Issei den* (Biography of Maebara Issei). Sekibunkan, 1934.

Tsuyama-shi shi (History of Tsuyama City), vol. 6. Tsuyama-shi shi hensan iinkai, ed. Tsuyama: Tsuyama shiyakusho, 1980.

Uda Tadashi. "Meiji zenki Tōhoku kansen tetsudō kensetsu keikaku to chihō jijō: shiryō shōkai o chūshin ni" (Construction Plans for the Tōhoku Trunk-Line Railroad and Local Conditions in Early Meiji: With Emphasis on the Introduction of Historical Materials), *Ōtemon keizai ronshū* (Economic Studies of Ōtemon University), vol. 4, no. 1, pp. 75–111 (September 1969).

———. "Waga kuni tetsudō jigyō keiei shi ni okeru seifu to kigyō: 'tetsudō seiryaku' no tenkai katei" (Government and Private Enterprise in the Business History of the Japanese Railroad Industry: The Development of "Railway Policy"), *Keiei shi gaku*, vol. 6, pp. 124–139 (September 1971).

Ueda Hiroshi. *Inoue Masaru den* (Biography of Inoue Masaru). Kōtsū Nihonsha, 1956.

Ushiba Takuzō. "Shisetsu tetsudō rieki haitō seigen ron" (Treatise on the Limitation of Dividends in Private Railroads), *Tetsudō jihō*, nos. 329–334 (January 1906), in *Jū nen kinen Nihon no tetsudō ron* (q.v.).

———. "Tetsudō eigyō no hōshin" (Railroad Business Policy), *Tetsudō jihō*, no. 14 (May 1899), in *Jū nen kinen Nihon no tetsudō ron* (q.v.).

Vaporis, Constantine N. "Caveat Viator: Advice to Travelers in the Edo Period," *Monumenta Nipponica*, vol. 44, no. 4, pp. 461–483 (Winter 1989).
Vogel, Ezra F. *Comeback Case by Case: Rebuilding the Resurgence of American Business*. New York: Simon and Schuster, 1985.

Wada Hiroshi. "Shoki gikai to tetsudō mondai" (The Early Diet and the Railway Question), *Shi gaku zasshi*, vol. 84, pp. 31–52 (October 1975).
Wakayama-ken shi: kin-gendai shiryō (History of Wakayama Prefecture: Modern Historical Materials), vol. 4. Wakayama: Wakayama-ken, 1978.
Waley, Paul. "Tokyo: Urban Change in the Meiji and Taishō Eras," *The Japan Foundation Newsletter*, vol. 18, no. 3, pp. 16–20 (January 1991).
Ward, James A. *Railroads and the Character of America, 1820–1887*. Knoxville: University of Tennessee Press, 1986.
Watanabe Kōhei et al., eds. *Kiteki issei: tetsudō hyaku nen bungaku to zuihitsu senshū* (With One Sound of the Whistle: An Anthology of Literature and Miscellaneous Writings Depicting a Century of Railroads). Jitsugyō no Nihonsha, 1972.
Watanabe Kunitake. Directive to the Bank of Japan, November 21, 1892. Matsuo ke monjo, 1st ser., vol. 82, no. 39 (q.v.).
Watarai, Toshiharu. *Nationalization of Railways in Japan*. New York: Columbia University Press, 1915.
Westney, D. Eleanor. *Imitation and Innovation: The Transfer of Western Organizational Patterns to Meiji Japan*. Cambridge: Harvard University Press, 1987.
Wray, William D. *Mitsubishi and the N.Y.K., 1870–1914: Business Strategy in the Japanese Shipping Industry*. Cambridge: Council on East Asian Studies, Harvard University, 1984.
——————, ed. *Managing Industrial Enterprise: Cases from Japan's Prewar Experience*. Cambridge: Council on East Asian Studies, Harvard University, 1989.

Yamada Eitarō. "Nippon tetsudō kabushiki kaisha enkakushi" (History of the Nippon Railway Company). 2 vols. Hitotsubashi University Library, Tokyo.
Yamagata Toshikazu. *Zaisei jū nen* (Ten Years of Finance). Momiyama shoten, 1914.
Yamaguchi Eizō. "Kansai tetsudō kaisha shimatsu" (Circumstances of the Kansai Railway Company), *Kōtsū bunka* (Transportation Culture), no. 8, pp. 729–740 (October 1939).
Yamaguchi Kazuo. "Kindaiteki yusō kikan no hattatsu to shōhin ryūtsū: Hokuriku, Hokuetsu chihō no baai" (Development of Modern Transportation Facilities and Commodity Distribution: The Case of the Hoku-

riku and Hokuetsu Districts), in Yamaguchi and Ishii, eds., *Kindai Nihon no shōhin ryūtsū* (q.v.).

Yamaguchi Kazuo and Ishii Kanji, eds. *Kindai Nihon no shōhin ryūtsū* (Commodity Distribution in Modern Japan). Tōkyō daigaku shuppankai, 1986.

Yamamoto, Hirofumi, ed. *Technological Innovation and the Development of Transportation in Japan*. Tokyo: United Nations University Press, 1993.

Yamamura Akira. "Meiji 25 nen no tetsudō fusetsu hō ni tsuite: hō o meguru rongi o chūshin to shite" (On the 1892 Railway Construction Law: With Emphasis on the Debate Surrounding the Law), *Un'yu to keizai* (Transport and the Economy), vol. 24, no. 6, pp. 66–71 (June 1964).

Yamamura, Kozo. "Entrepreneurship, Ownership, and Management in Japan," in Peter Mathias and M. M. Postan, eds., *The Cambridge Economic History of Europe*, vol. 7, pt. 2. Cambridge: Cambridge University Press, 1978.

———. "Japan, 1868–1930: A Revised View," in Rondo Cameron, ed., *Banking and Economic Development: Some Lessons of History*. New York: Oxford University Press, 1972.

———. *A Study of Samurai Income and Entrepreneurship: Quantitative Analyses of Economic and Social Aspects of the Samurai in Tokugawa and Meiji Japan*. Cambridge: Harvard University Press, 1974.

———. "Success Illgotten? The Role of Meiji Militarism in Japan's Technological Progress," *Journal of Economic History*, vol. 37, no. 1, pp. 113–135 (March 1977).

Yamanashi-ken gikai shi (History of the Yamanashi Prefectural Assembly), vol. 2. Kōfu: Yamanashi-ken gikai, 1970.

"Yo wa tetsudō no yo no naka: Ryōmō tetsudō mōshikomi chōka" (We Live in a Railway Age: Ryōmō Railway [Shares] Oversubscribed), *Tōkyō nichinichi shinbun,* December 23, 1886, in *Shinbun shūsei Meiji hennen shi,* vol. 6, p. 375 (q.v.).

Yoshikawa Kanji. "Waga kuni shitetsu no hōga to Kansai tetsudō kaisha" (The Germination of Private Railroads in Japan and the Kansai Railway Company), *Dōshisha shōgaku* (Dōshisha University Commerical Studies), vol. 2, no. 1, pp. 32–59 (July 1950).

Yūbin hōchi shinbun (Postal Information Newspaper), 1892.

Yui, Tsunehiko. "The Personality and Career of Hikojirō Nakamigawa, 1887–1901," *Business History Review*, vol. 44, no. 1, pp. 39–61 (Spring 1970).

Yūsei-shō (Ministry of Posts and Telecommunications), ed. *Yūsei hyaku nen no ayumi* (A Century of Posts and Telecommunications). Shōgakkan, 1971.

Index

Akita, George, 433n88
Allen, G. C., 455n218
Alliance for the Importation of Foreign Capital, 292
Amenomiya Keijirō, 141, 292, 294, 321–322, 350, 362–363, 370, 420n155
American Locomotive Company, 34
Anglo-Japanese Alliance, 280
Aoki Eiichi, 237, 262, 362, 403n125
Ariizumi Sadao, 214
Armstrong, 370
Army: construction demands of, 121, 202, 203–204, 274–275, 356; and railroad policy-making process, 121–122, 191, 202, 204–205, 274–277; and conflict with Railway Bureau, 122, 197, 203–204, 274; on railway ownership and nationalization, 202–203, 204, 249, 261–263, 271–274, 275–277; and Railway Council, 204, 213, 227, 240, 274; and communications bureaucracy, 261, 263, 272–273, 274, 276–277, 380; and Korean railroads, 267–268, 269; and Katō Kōmei, 282. *See also* Bureaucracy; Military
Army General Staff. *See* Army
Asahi Glass Company, 372
Asano Yōkichi, 299, 300–301, 302
Austria, 251

Ban Naonosuke, 167–168
Bank of Japan, 115, 176–182, 279, 299, 359, 360, 428n296
Banks: in Europe, 14; stock- and bond-collateral lending by, 123, 124, 126, 134–138, 178–182, 320, 358, 359, 360, 381, 382, 415n109, 415–416n111, 423n211, 454n195; as railroad stockholders, 133–138, 144–145, 320, 324, 331, 334, 336–339, 342–343, 381, 417n133, 450n92; and 1891 nationalization movement, 156–158, 343; direct loans to private railroads by, 184, 186, 314; as bondholders, 188–189, 320, 367–368; and railway nationalization of 1906–1907, 320, 322, 336–339, 344, 345, 366, 367–368; role of, in Meiji industrial development, 364–365, 381–382. *See also* Financing; Investment in railroads
Banno Junji, 207, 293
Belgium, 32, 303
Benkei, 34
Bismarck, Otto von, 256, 302–303
Bisset, Sir William, 81
Bonds: public, 108, 250, 256, 258, 259, 266, 278, 279, 280, 286, 288, 299, 356, 358–359, 360; corporate, 182, 184–189, 265, 268, 274, 314, 369; railway-purchase, 257–258, 259, 279–280, 282–283, 291, 299, 304–305, 307, 308, 344, 345, 347, 353, 357, 358–361, 365, 366–368, 369, 371, 378, 453n171, 454n195. *See also* Financing; Loans.
Botchan, 33
Britain: railroads in, 14, 76, 78–79, 128, 246, 303–304, 415n109; telegraphs in, 20; and rail and rolling-stock exports to Japan, 32, 33, 34, 146–147; and influence on Japanese railroads, 84, 85, 303; postal savings in, 287; and Meiji patterns of industrialization and railroad development, 381, 382
Broken Commandment, The, 73, 81
Bureaucracy: and railway policy making,

Bureaucracy *(continued)*
16–17, 206, 223–227, 380, 382–383; and interministerial conflict, 103–104, 117–118, 121–122, 197, 203–204, 254, 274, 278, 280, 380, 381; party and business linkages of, 220, 225, 250, 380–381, 383; and railway nationalization, 248–249, 250, 254–260, 382–383; influence of social policy school on, 288–289. *See also* Army; Communications, Ministry of; Finance, Ministry of; Railway Bureau

Carnegie Steel, 32
Carriages. *See* Passenger carriages
Chambers of commerce, 156, 159, 169–170, 240, 252, 321–322, 350
Chemical industry, 364
Chikuhō coal fields, 28, 41, 52, 325. *See also* Coal-mining industry
Chikuhō Industrial Railway Company: stockholders in, 138, 141, 143, 325; management of, 168–169, 325–326; and construction delays, 173; financing of, 182, 184, 185; as an "industrial railroad," 427n292
China, 336
China indemnity, 38, 275, 284, 285–286, 442n131
Chūetsu Railway Company, 290, 312, 314, 443n158
Chūgoku Railway Company, 320, 351–352
Chūō line, 30, 44, 46–50, 65–66, 77, 93, 213, 400n66
Chūō kōshōbu, 225, 231, 234, 434n116
Coal-mining industry: and railroad connections, 28, 48; economic impact of railroads on, 40–42, 52, 398–399n51; and railroad investment, 143, 325, 328; and Mitsubishi-Mitsui rivalry, 325, 334; and Nippon Railway, 339–340; and Hokkaido Colliery and Railway, 370, 399n51
Colonial investments by former railway owners, 372–373
Commercial Code of 1893, 123, 415n108
Communications, Ministry of: as predecessor of Ministry of Posts and Telecommunications, 18; establishment and growth of, 20–21; and railway nationalization of 1906–1907, 249–250, 251–252, 254–260, 291, 302, 356, 382, 383; and army, 261, 263, 272–273, 274, 277, 380; and Seoul-Pusan Railway, 268–270, 277; and Finance Ministry, 278–279, 280, 282–283, 380; and postal savings, 287; and party-bureaucratic linkage, 380. *See also* Bureaucracy; Railway Bureau

Communications network, Meiji, 18–21
Commutation of stipends, 106, 107
Compulsory Land Purchase Law (1889), 171–172, 427n280
Construction, railway: 26–31, 246. *See also* Private railroads; Railway Construction Law; State railways
Cotton-spinning industry, 7, 132, 317, 364–365, 381, 417n129
Council of State, 72, 97–108 passim, 112, 114
Craig, Albert, 399n53

Dai Nippon kidō kaisha (Greater Japan Tramway Company), 362
Daidō Club, 291, 297–298, 305–306, 308, 444n163
Daito, Eisuke, 456n11
Den Kenjirō: as consensus builder, 250, 254–255, 258, 273, 278; as bureaucrat, 250, 251–252, 254–255, 258; as Kansai Railway president, 250–251, 296, 448n38; and 1901 opinion paper, 252, 255, 286; as Seiyūkai Diet member, 253–254, 338, 380; as peer, 260; and army, 261, 268, 272, 276, 277; and military transport, 262, 272, 277; and Seoul-Pusan Railway, 268–269, 277
Depreciation accounting, 326, 341, 450n107
Dialogue on Civilization, A (Kaika mondō), 59
Diet: and pork-barrel politics, 7; and railway policy making, 17, 192, 206, 241–242, 380, 382–383; and 1891 nationalization movement, 153–159 passim, 169–170; and Railway Construction Law, 196–197, 236, 238; second- and third-session deliberations of, 216–219, 230–235; elections for, 222, 228; and Railway Nationalization Law, 245–246, 249, 280, 296, 355–356, 370; and Seoul-Pusan Railway Purchase Law, 270–271; on conversion to standard gauge, 274. *See also* House of Peers; Legislation, railroad; Lobbying; Parties, political
Discount system, central-bank, 178–182, 360, 379, 428n296

Dividends. *See* Private railroads: profit distribution by
Duus, Peter, 441n115

Electric railroads, 92, 363, 364, 369, 400–401n79
Electric-power industry, 364, 365–366, 369, 455n218
Embree, John, 57
Employees, railway, 72–73, 74, 77–78, 357, 376, 453n168
Engels, Friedrich, 12
Engineers, state railway, 117, 166–167, 377, 456n11
Engines. *See* Locomotives
"Essential Points of the Investigation into the Purchase of Private Railroads," 257–258

Fares. *See* Rates, railway
15th National Bank (peers' bank; 15th Bank): and founding of Nippon Railway, 108, 109, 110; as railroad investor, 134–138, 340, 342–343, 353, 418n144; and railway nationalization, 338–339, 343, 344, 345, 350, 367–368
Finance, Ministry of: and conflict with public works and communications bureaucrats, 104, 118, 254, 278, 380; on Tokyo Railway Association, 105–106; and Panic of 1890, 178; and railway nationalization, 249, 254–255, 258, 259, 278–280, 282–284, 291; and postal savings, 287. *See also* Bureaucracy
Financing: themes concerning, 8, 9–12; and foreign loans, 9–10, 98, 252, 255, 256; of state railways, 10, 98–99, 100–101, 102, 103, 108, 207, 236, 250, 285–286, 288, 377–378, 412n47; of private railroads, 10–12, 110, 123–126, 133–145, 174–189, 264–266, 313–317, 319–320, 322, 381–382, 417n131; of joint-stock companies, 123–126; of railway nationalization, 257, 383. *See also* Banks; Bonds; Investment in railroads; Loans; Stockholders, railway
Findlay, George, 408n231
1st Bank, 366
Fishlow, Albert, 145–146
5,000-Mile Celebration, 26
France, 14, 20, 26, 38–39, 109, 457n22
Freight transport. *See* Transport
Fujita Denzaburō, 141, 160, 164, 420n154

Fukushima Taneomi, 226
Fukuzawa Yukichi, 404n148
Furuichi Kōi, 269, 270
Furukawa, 364

Gas industry, 365–366, 369
Gauge, rail: 2'6", 32; narrow, 33, 80, 261, 396n19; standard (broad), 121, 274–275, 285, 336, 356
"General Objectives of Railway Nationalization," 255–257, 258, 259–260
German social policy school, 288, 305
Germany (and Prussia): railroads in, 14–15, 26, 80, 302–303, 435n148; and rail and locomotive exports to Japan, 32–33, 34–36; economic impact of railroads in, 38–39, 53; taken as model in Japan, 122, 223–224, 239–240, 252, 256, 261, 275, 283, 284, 302; and Meiji patterns of industrialization and railroad development, 381, 382
Gerschenkron, Alexander, 14, 15, 381, 382
Gladstone, William, 303–304
Gluck, Carol, 401n86, 402n97
Gold standard, adoption of, 286
Government, Meiji: economic role of, 14, 15, 38, 288–289, 369–370, 381, 382, 384, 385, 443n152; intervention in railroads by, 15–16, 51–52, 97–98, 110–113, 166, 318, 323–324, 379, 381, 382–385, 425n255; and telegraphs, 18–20; initiation of steel industry by, 38, 288; enlistment of private capital by, 98–99, 102, 103, 104, 112; and Seoul-Pusan Railway, 266–271; intervention in the economy by, 288–289, 348, 384. *See also* State railway policy
Great Western Railway, 78–79
Greater Japan Tramway Company (Dai Nippon kidō kaisha), 362
Gunma prefecture, 42–44, 45

Hachisuka Mochiaki, 105
Handa Ryōhei, 70
Hankai Railway Company, 330
Hankaku Railway Company, 347, 357, 363
Hankyū Electric Railway Company, 363
Hara Kei: on Katō Kōmei, 282; on war reparations from Russia, 285, 287; and Railway Nationalization Bill, 289, 290–291, 296, 297, 306, 307, 308, 328, 345, 349, 351, 352; and positive spending policy, 290, 291, 378

Hara Rokurō, 348, 357–358, 373
Harada Katsumasa, 154, 196, 262, 379, 404n138, 406n182
Hatano Shōgorō, 334–336
Hida Hamagorō, 76, 78, 406–407n188
Hirai Seijirō, 167, 451n126
Hiroshima Chamber of Commerce, 169–170
Historiography: on railroad policy, 12–13, 379; on economic role of Meiji government and banks, 14, 15, 381; on economic impact of railroads, 31–32; on Railway Construction Law, 192–193, 196, 237; on railway nationalization of 1906–1907, 248
Hokkaido, 33, 233, 398–399n51
Hokkaido Colliery and Railway Company: and Meiji government, 114, 117, 166, 175; stockholders in, 140, 141, 336, 345; enlistment of foreign capital by, 264–265, 266; and Mitsui Bank, 336, 338; and railway nationalization of 1906–1907, 338, 353, 369–371, 399n51, 452n151
Hokkaido Colliery and Steamship Company, 370–371
Hokkaido Railway Company, 427n290
Hokkaido Railway Construction Law (1896), 435n147
Hokuetsu Railway Company, 265, 355–356
Honshū, 28, 34, 40
Hori Motoi, 166
Hoshi Tōru, 215, 233, 291–296 passim
Hoshino Takao, 136, 368, 410n6, 428n296
House of Peers (upper house): 193, 209, 234–235, 306–308, 351, 352. *See also* Diet; Legislation, railroad
House of Representatives (lower house), 245. *See also* Diet; Legislation, railroad; Parties, political

Ikuno mines, 28, 330
Imamura Seinosuke, 151–152, 165, 425n252
Imperial Household Ministry, 49, 140, 324, 345, 366, 372, 383
Imperial Railway Company, 254
Imperial Railway Department, 357, 371, 377
Ina basin, 49–50, 63, 400–401n79
Indemnity. *See* China indemnity
Independent Club, 231, 434n116
India, 81
Industrial Association (Jitsugyō kyōkai), 210–211, 212, 225

Industrial Bank of Japan, 268, 320, 400n66
Industrial policy (targeting), 7, 17–18, 380, 384
Inland Transport Company (Naikoku tsuun kaisha), 20, 394n39
Inoue Kakugorō, 219, 253, 292, 321, 338, 370
Inoue Kaoru: during the 1870s, 104, 105–106; and railway nationalization, 254–255, 258, 280, 282, 283; and Kyushu Railway mediation, 326–328; as government-business intermediary, 328, 348–349
Inoue Kowashi, 193, 196, 207, 220, 223–224, 225, 226, 430n9
Inoue Masaru: as advocate of state railways, 117–118, 194–195; background of, 118, 303; on private railroads, 118–121, 171, 173, 189, 191, 198–200, 276; and army, 121–122, 197, 201–205; on railway promoters, 127; "Railroad Policy Proposal" of, 153, 192–193, 197–201, 205, 207, 223, 430n9; and Railway Construction Law, 237, 242; retirement of, 275, 277; for separate railway account, 276. *See also* Railway Bureau
Insurance companies: as railway stockholders, 134, 324, 331, 334, 338, 368–369, 450n92; as bondholders, 188–189, 368, 369
International Trade and Industry, Ministry of (MITI), 17, 380
Investment in railroads: motives for, 51, 144–145, 157, 324–325; by zaibatsu, 51, 138–140, 144, 157, 324–325, 329–330, 331, 334, 336–338, 340; economizing on, 80–82, 145–147; enlistment of private capital for, 98–99, 100–101, 102, 103, 104, 110; by merchants and landlords, 102, 104, 141; by nobles, 104–108, 110, 140, 144–145; speculative, 115, 127–128, 141, 144, 160, 312–313; by banks, 133–138, 144–145, 320, 322, 334, 336–338, 340; by industrial capitalists, 140–141; by stockbrokers, 141, 144; by local residents, 142–144, 290; direct foreign, 256–257, 263–264, 266, 268, 277; fixed, 332, 340, 352–354; and reinvestment after 1906–1907, 360–373. *See also* Banks; Bonds; Financing; Loans; Stockholders, railway
Iron-and-steel industry, 32, 38, 288, 362, 364, 369–371, 431n31
Ishida Kannosuke, 218, 233
Ishii Kanji, 397n34

Itagaki Taisuke, 209, 212–213, 216, 221, 232, 253, 291, 292–293
Italy, 26, 92, 251, 303
Itō Hirobumi, 94, 98, 99, 113–114, 251, 254, 272, 297
Itō Miyoji, 219–220
Iwagoe Railway Company, 353, 367, 418n144
Iwaki Coal-Mining Company, 41, 340
Iwakura Mission, 58–59
Iwakura Tomomi, 105, 106, 108, 109–110, 111, 134
Iwasaki family, 281, 312, 329, 372. *See also* Mitsubishi
Iwasaki Hisaya, 138, 140, 325, 372, 418n145
Iwasaki Yanosuke, 325, 372
Iyo Railway Company, 32–33, 317

Japanese National Railways, 6, 13, 378
Jitsugyō kyōkai (Industrial Association), 210–211, 212, 225
Jiyū Club, 210
Jiyūtō: stance on 1891 railway bills, 208, 210, 215–216; and local lobbying, 212, 215; and railroad-building legislation, 220, 221, 222; Railway Construction Bill of, 227–228, 229, 230, 231, 232, 236; on railway nationalization, 232, 291–293, 444n166; seats in third Diet, 434n116. *See also* Diet; Legislation, railroad; Lobbying; Parties, political
Jōban coal fields, 28, 41–42, 48. *See also* Coal-mining industry
Jōban line, 41–42, 339
Johnson, Chalmers, 15, 16, 17–18, 382

Kagami Kahei, 229, 230, 231
Kaika mondō (*A Dialogue on Civilization*), 59
Kaishintō, 208, 210, 434n116
Kaku Risuke, 233–234
Kanebō, 384
Kansai Railway Company (1871–1874), 102–103, 104
Kansai Railway Company (1888–1907): and competition with state railways, 77, 86–88, 323–324, 448n38; customer service of, 83, 85–88; under Den Kenjirō, 250–251, 448n38; foreign borrowing by, 264–265; and mergers, 318, 319, 323, 324; on railway nationalization, 322–323, 324, 448n41; 452n151; investors in, 323, 324, 325; capital expenditures by, 354
Kansai region, 92, 103
Kantō region, 48
Karatsu Railway Company, 316–317
Kataoka Naoharu, 448n41
Katō Kōmei, 271, 280–282, 291, 298, 441n115
Katsura Tarō: on railway nationalization, 252, 253, 258, 273, 284–285, 322; and agreement with Seiyūkai, 260, 306; as army minister, 263, 273; as Yamagata protégé, 272; on railroads in Taiwan, 273–274; and revised Railway Nationalization Bill, 308
Kawada Koichirō, 156, 157, 158, 178–179
Kawagoe Railway Company, 321
Kawakami Sōroku, 203, 205
Kawasaki Shipbuilding Company, 36
Kawashima Atsushi, 229, 230
Kawashima bill, 229, 230, 236
Kenseihontō, 297, 298, 312, 445n187
Kenseitō, 293–296, 321
Kido Takayoshi, 58
Kinoshita Yoshio, 89
Kirby, Richard, 265–266
Kirin Beer Company, 372
Kisha seizō kaisha (Train Manufacturing Company), 36
Kiso River valley, 49–50
Kitahama Bank, 320
Kiyohara Tama, 61
Kobe port, 330
Kōbu Railway Company: local opposition to, 61; stockholders in, 140, 142; and Amenomiya Keijirō, 141, 321; and Nippon Railway, 150; and railway nationalization of 1906–1907, 352, 353, 354, 360, 452n151
Kodama Gentarō, 254, 272, 277
Kōfu city, 46, 48, 65–66, 93
Kokaze Hidemasa, 397n34, 420n153, 437n8
Kōno Hironaka, 213
Konoe Atsumaro, 235
Korea, 266–270 passim, 349, 362, 372
Korean residency general, 269, 270
Kōshin Railway Company, 50–51, 132
Kōshū highway, 45, 46, 61
Krauss engines, 32–33
Kurashiki Electric Light Company, 367
Kuroda Kiyotaka, 171, 172
Kushiro Railway Company, 427n292
Kyŏmipʻo iron-ore district, 372

Kyoto Chamber of Commerce, 321
Kyoto Railway Company, 320, 321, 351, 356, 357
Kyushu, 32, 33, 41, 325
Kyushu Bankers' Association, 179, 428–429n301
Kyushu Railway Company: capital expenditures by, 33, 326–328, 340, 354; and Panic of 1890, 81, 129, 132, 146, 147–148, 165, 169, 176, 421n173, 428–429n301; and Mitsubishi, 81, 138, 325, 326–328, 330, 338, 340, 345; state subsidies to, 116–117, 175–176; and stock payments and construction, 123–124, 173, 176; and Mitsui, 140, 334; profit distribution by, 148, 326, 428n294; financing of, 185–187, 265–266, 450n92; and mergers, 317, 318, 319, 326; and railway nationalization of 1906–1907, 325, 328, 345

Lay, Horatio Nelson, 410n6
League for the Promotion of Railroads (Tetsudō kisei dōmeikai), 212, 220–222, 223, 231–232, 234, 241, 431n47, 431n48
Legislation, railroad: and pork-barrel politics, 7, 290–291, 293–294, 296–297; decision-making process for, 12, 17, 192–197, 204–207, 220–228, 253–260, 278–279, 282–283, 293, 294–296, 382–383; proposals for, in 1891–1892, 153–154, 158, 159, 170, 192, 196–201, 205–206, 211–212, 216–219, 226, 227–228, 228–232; and cabinet-Diet conflict, 193–194, 195, 207–208, 215–216, 223; Diet deliberations on, 216–219, 230–235, 297–305, 306–309; nationalization proposal of 1900, 250–251, 294–296, 321; nationalization proposal of 1902, 253–254; Railroad Collateral Law, 255, 265; Private Railway Law, 263, 271, 273, 300, 341; Seoul-Pusan Railway Purchase Law, 266, 268, 270–271; railway account law, 276; Hokkaido Railway Construction Law, 435n147. *See also* Diet; Lobbying; Railway Construction Law; Railway Nationalization Law
Liberal Democratic Party, 17
Life insurance companies. *See* Insurance companies
Light railways, 32, 362–363
Line selection, 44, 49–50, 63, 236, 238–239, 241, 318, 379

Liverpool and Manchester Railway, 76, 152
Loans: foreign, 9–10, 98, 252, 255, 264–265, 266, 279, 286–287, 292–293, 322, 364, 384, 385, 410n6, 444n165; stock-collateral, 123, 124, 126, 134–138, 176, 178–182, 358, 360, 381, 382, 415n109, 415–416n111, 423n211, 428n296; bond-collateral, 182, 320, 360, 367, 454n195; direct corporate, 184, 186, 314, 369; railroads as collateral for foreign, 255, 256, 260, 265, 277, 285, 287, 292, 384. *See also* Bonds; Financing
Lobbying: for state railway construction, 46–47, 49–50, 201, 208–209, 241, 296–297, 431n47; and Panic of 1890, 122, 169, 176–179; and nationalization movements, 153–160, 167, 169–170, 250–251, 290, 292–293, 321–322, 350; by League for the Promotion of Railroads, 212–215, 220–222, 231–232, 234; on Railway Nationalization Bill, 328, 345, 355–356
Local improvement movement, 288
Lockwood, William, 399–400n57
Locomotives: models of, 4; imports of, 32–36, 80, 83, 262; domestic production of, 32, 34, 36, 38, 395n16; as symbol, 53, 55, 93, 401n86; early reactions to, 59, 60, 61, 62, 70; of Nippon Railway, 342
Lower house (House of Representatives), 245. *See also* Diet; Legislation, railroad; Parties, political

Maebashi city, 45
Maejima Hisoka, 99, 100–102, 103, 411n11, 411n14
"Maglev" supertrain, 4–6
Management, private railway: shortcomings of, 80, 408n212; stockholder influence on, 81, 133, 145–160, 162–164, 165, 325–328, 330, 338–339, 344, 345; and full-time career managers, 83, 168, 330, 338, 339; and overlap with ownership, 160–161, 165, 168, 330, 331, 344, 424n230, 425n236; and conflict with ownership, 162–164, 316, 326–328; ex-journalists in, 165, 167–168; former state officials in, 166–167, 326; state intervention in, 166, 267, 269, 379, 425n255; local participation in, 168–169, 426n267; after railway nationalization of 1906–1907, 357, 376–377, 456n11. *See also* Private railroads

Manchuria, 270, 271, 282, 349, 362, 363, 364
Man-powered railroad, 90
Marshall, Byron, 447–448n36, 452n142
Marx, Leo, 53, 401n89
Masaoka Shiki, 401–402n94
Masuda Takashi, 285, 287, 334, 336
Matsuda Masahisa, 285
Matsukata financial reform, 10, 108, 113, 115, 124, 192
Matsukata Masayoshi, 108–109, 111, 116, 118, 178–179, 221, 235, 430n9
Matsumoto city, 50, 63
Matsumoto Jūtarō, 161, 330, 332
Matsuo Shinzen, 299
Meiji emperor, 6, 34, 61, 401n86
Meiji Fire Insurance Company, 368. *See also* Insurance companies
Meiji Life Insurance Company, 368–369. *See also* Insurance companies
Meiji Sugar Company, 373
Mergers, railway, 132, 149–153, 300, 314, 317–319, 340
Miike coal mine, 398–399n51. *See also* Coal-mining industry
Military, 49, 58, 99, 240, 352, 356. *See also* Army
Military Requisition of Railroads Act (1904), 262, 301
Military transport by rail: and Satsuma Rebellion, 99, 121, 411n9; influence of German experience in, 122, 275; and private railroads, 217, 257, 261–262, 301; during Sino- and Russo-Japanese wars, 261, 262–263, 267–268, 275, 276, 277, 438n45; Ōsawa Kaiyū on, 275–276
Minami Kiyoshi, 166, 316, 317
Mino-Arima Electric Railway Company, 363
MITI (Ministry of International Trade and Industry), 17, 380
Mito Railway Company, 132, 149–150, 319
Mitsubishi: shipping monopoly of, 20; and Kyushu Railway, 81, 138, 325, 326–328, 330, 338; and San'yō Railway, 83, 138, 161, 325, 329–330, 331, 338; as railway stockholder, 138–140, 157, 324–325, 364; and Nippon Railway, 138, 345, 419n146; and Chikuhō Industrial Railway, 138, 325–326; and foreign borrowing by private railroads, 265, 266; and railway nationalization, 281, 297, 324–325, 338, 345, 371–372, 382; and Kansai Railway, 323, 324, 325; and South Manchuria Railway, 364, 453n189; diversification of, 371, 384
Mitsubishi Paper Company, 372
Mitsui: as handler of railroad freight, 20, 394n39; and abortive Kansai Railway, 102; as railroad stockholder, 138, 140, 157, 336, 419n149, 419n150; and Hokkaido Colliery and Railway, 140, 336; and San'yō Railway, 140, 331, 334, 336; and rivalry with Mitsubishi, 325, 334; on railway nationalization of 1906–1907, 334–338; and Miike coal mine, 399n51
Mitsui Bank, 334, 336–338, 351, 364, 368, 415n109
Mitsui Bussan (Mitsui & Co.), 36, 38, 285, 334, 336, 350, 372
Mochizuki Kotarō, 304, 305
Morell, Edmund, 396n19
Mōri Jūsuke, 167
Morikawa Hidemasa, 338, 456n11
Moroto Seiroku, 141, 420n156
Motoyama Hikoichi, 420n154
MPT (Ministry of Posts and Telecommunications), 17–18, 380
Murano Sanjin, 161, 162, 164, 167
Murata Tamotsu, 235
Muroran city, 370
Mutsu Munemitsu, 193–194

N.Y.K. (Nippon yūsen kaisha), 329
Nagano prefecture, 42–51 passim, 59, 60, 78, 81
Nagasaki shipyard, 329
Naikoku tsuun kaisha (Inland Transport Company), 20, 394n39
Nakamigawa Hikojirō: positive investment strategy of, 146–147, 162, 164–165; and 1891 nationalization movement, 156–157; as San'yō Railway stockholder, 160–161; and Osaka investors, 162–164, 331, 332; government petitions by, 171, 172, 422n186, 427n280; as head of Mitsui Bank, 336, 338, 350
Nakamura Masanori, 454n202
Nakane Shigeichi, 223
Nakanishi Ken'ichi, 107, 129, 158, 237, 350, 392n16, 440n86
Nakano Buei, 217–218, 432n70
Nakasendō (interior route), 44, 45, 63

Nakashōji Ren, 270, 282, 283
Nakasone Yasuhiro, 378
Nankai Railway Company, 352
Narahara Shigeru, 150, 161, 166, 426n261
National Bank Act of 1883, 136
National banks, 134–138. *See also* Banks
National Federation of Chambers of Commerce, 322
National railways. *See* State railways
Natsume Sōseki, 32–33, 54, 56–57, 77
Navy, 356, 370, 371, 431n31
New Historical School, 288
Nihon Life Insurance Company, 368, 369, 448n41. *See also* Insurance companies
Nikkō line, 83, 91
Nippon Celluloid Company, 372
Nippon Nitrogenous Fertilizer Company, 372
Nippon Railway Company: founding and early development of, 20, 45, 62, 63, 108, 109–113, 114, 115, 117, 118, 140; facilities and rolling stock of, 39, 77, 79, 81, 341–342, 421n177; management of, 72–73, 168, 339, 341, 344–345; customer service of, 78, 82–83, 339; capital expenditures by, 80, 81, 339, 340–342, 343–344, 354, 450n102; and 15th National Bank, 134–138, 140, 339, 340, 342–343, 344, 345, 367–368; stockholders in, 136–138, 140, 364, 366; profit distribution by, 148–149, 311, 340, 343–344; and mergers, 149–153, 318, 319, 340; state subsidies to, 175, 343, 413–414n69; and coal-mining industry, 339–340; and railway nationalization of 1906–1907, 344–345, 352, 353, 355, 358
Nippon Steelworks, 369, 370–371
Nippon yūsen kaisha (N.Y.K.), 329
Nishinari Railway Company, 314, 320, 323–324, 351
Nitchitsu, 384
Nobles, 104–108, 110, 140, 144–145
Noda Masaho, 182, 188, 417–418n133, 421n165, 428n296
North British Company, 34
Notorious Train Robber, The (*Kisha no taizoku*), 85
Nozomi, 391n7

O.S.K. (Ōsaka shōsen kaisha), 329
Ochiai Sadaaki, 238
Odagiri Yoshiaki, 212–215, 222

Ogawa Isao, 448n41
Ōhara family, 366–367, 454n202, 454n203
Ōi Kentarō, 215
Oka Seii, 409n231
Ōkubo Toshimichi, 58
Ōkuma Shigenobu, 98, 99, 100, 106, 209, 210, 221, 242
Ōkura Kihachirō, 363, 364
Oligarchs, 170, 195–196, 238, 249, 260, 282, 284. *See also* Government, Meiji
1,000–Mile Celebration, 26
Onga River (Ongagawa), 41
Onishi Shin'yuemon, 142
Ono merchant house, 102
Ono Yoshimasa, 152
Orita Kanetaka, 232–233
Osaka Bankers' Association, 154, 158, 178–179
Osaka Chamber of Commerce, 159, 415–416n111, 423n214
Osaka city, 60, 124–126, 141, 142, 323–324
Osaka Railway Company, 142, 184–185, 250, 429n311, 448n38
Ōsaka shōsen kaisha (O.S.K.), 329
Ōsawa Kaiyū, 275–277, 292
Ōtsuka Osamu, 160, 162
Ōura Kanetake, 254, 255, 258, 260, 272
Ōwada Takeki, 28–30, 31
Ownership, private railway. *See* Stockholders, railway
Ozaki Saburō, 194, 205
Ozawa Takeo, 203–204

Panic of 1890: as catalyst for change, 12, 122, 195–196; impact of, on private railroads, 50, 51, 80–81, 128–132, 143, 146–148, 149–159, 162, 165, 169–170, 176, 182–185, 186, 189, 314, 425n252; causes of, 123–126
Panics of 1897–1898 and 1900–1901: as catalysts for change, 12, 320, 322; impact of, on private railroads, 186, 249–250, 274, 290, 312–318, 319–322, 326, 342, 343; and nationalization movements, 242, 246–248, 252, 291–296, 350
Parkes, Sir Harry, 98, 410n6
Parties, political: and railway policy making, 17, 196–197, 206–207, 294–296, 380–381; and private business, 17, 292–294; opposition of, to railway nationalization, 170, 208, 297–303, 306–307; struggle of, with cabinet, 192, 193, 207–208, 209–210, 215–

216, 228; and Railway Council, 213, 227, 236, 240; and railroad-building legislation, 219–220; bureaucratic linkages of, 220, 225, 250, 380–381. *See also* Diet; Legislation, railroad; Lobbying

Passenger carriages: imported from Germany, 33; early occupancy rate of, 68; facilities in, 74–77, 83, 86, 406n185; compartmentalized, 74–76, 84–85; open, 83, 84–85, 406n182; sleeping cars, 83, 84; for light railways, 362–363; domestic production of, 395n16

Passenger transport. *See* Transport; Travel, railway

Paternostro, Alessandro, 224

Patrick, Hugh, 134, 149

Pennsylvania Railroad Company, 78

Perry, Commodore Matthew, 3–4

Pope, Alexander, 69

Popular Rights Movement, 84

Pork-barrel politics, 7, 290–291, 293–294, 296–297, 378. *See also* Lobbying; Parties, political

Postal Savings Law (1905), 288

Postal savings system, 287–288

Posts and Telecommunications, Ministry of (MPT), 17–18, 380

Post-station towns, 60–61, 65

Postwar management (*sengo keiei*), 259–260, 279, 284–289, 300, 401n82, 442n131, 443n152

Preferred stocks, 182, 186, 314, 316

Private business: and railway policy making, 16–17, 433n102; and Panic of 1890, 176–178; and railway nationalization, 292–294, 295–296, 321–322, 346–351, 444n165, 447–448n36; diversification strategy of, 384

Private railroads: since 1987, 6; share of total network, 7, 116, 128, 242; financing of, 10–12, 123–126, 133–145, 174–189, 255, 264–266, 313–317, 319–320, 322, 381–382, 439n61, 457n22; construction of, 45, 50, 116, 128, 146, 147–148, 162, 169–170, 173–174, 249–250, 289–290, 332, 352–354; investors in, 51, 144, 290, 338, 345; proposals for, 64–65, 100–103, 104–110, 115, 127, 312–313; management of, 80, 160–169, 330, 338, 339; capital expenditures by, 80–81, 146, 283, 326, 332, 339, 340–342, 343–344, 347–348, 352–354, 383, 450n104, 451n115; and Panic of 1890, 80–81, 122–123, 128–132, 143, 146–148, 149–159, 162, 165, 169–170, 174–189; trunk-line firms, 130, 142, 144, 145, 186, 290, 313–314, 318, 319, 322–346; smaller firms, 130, 140, 142–143, 168–169, 186, 289–290, 312–322, 355–357, 360, 383; mergers between, 132, 149–153, 300, 314, 317–319, 340; profit distribution by, 148–149, 314, 451n115; land acquisition by, 170–174, 427n275; under Railway Construction Law, 237–238, 241–242, 249–250; and railway nationalization, 246–248, 249, 250–251, 290, 312, 322–323, 324, 325, 328, 338, 344–345, 351–358, 359–360, 375; in Korea and Taiwan, 266–269, 274; profitability of, 285, 311, 314, 332; lack of depreciation accounting in, 326, 341; average capital stock and construction time of, 416n112. *See also* Management, private railway; Stockholders, railway; *individual railway companies*

Private railway boom: first, 20, 50, 63–65, 114–116, 123, 124, 127–128, 273; second, 65, 143, 237, 242, 273, 289, 312–313, 319; third, 363

Private Railway Law (1900), 263, 271, 273, 300, 341

Private Railway Purchase Bill (1891–1892), 196, 206, 208, 216–218, 224, 229–230, 233, 235

Private Railway Regulations (1887), 116, 121, 159, 171, 263

Privatization, railroad, 6, 106–107, 113–114, 242, 350, 378

Privy Council, 267

Prussia. *See* Germany

Public Works, Ministry of, 44, 103–104, 105, 117, 118. *See also* Bureaucracy

Purchase price of nationalized railroads, 257, 289, 344, 345, 352–357, 358, 359, 360. *See also* Bonds: railway-purchase; Railway Nationalization Law

Putiatin, E. V., 4

Pyle, Kenneth, 288

Ragusa, Vincenzo, 61

Railroad Collateral Law (1905), 255, 265

Railroads: images of, 3, 53–57, 70, 401n89; enthusiasm for, 4, 58, 62–66, 404n138; and debate over state versus private enterprise, 6–7, 246; as leading economic sector, 7,

Railroads *(continued)*
  317, 364–365; social impact of, 25, 66, 402n97; economic impact of, in the West, 31–32, 38–39, 399n52; and backward linkages, 32–39, 42, 53; and export promotion, 38, 51–52, 284; and forward linkages, 39–49, 52–53, 398–399n51; written accounts of, 54, 401–402n94; in song and art, 54–55; opposition to, 58, 59–61, 99–100, 174, 403n115, 403n125; impact of, on conceptions of time and space, 69–72, 405n160, 405n168; lax management of, 72–73; treatment of passengers by, 74–76, 77–78, 82–83, 84, 86–90; economizing on fixed investments by, 80–82; impact of, on travel and recreation, 82–83, 90–91, impact of, on work and residence patterns, 91–92; and nation-building, 92–94; and standardization of styles and tastes, 93. *See also* Private railroads; State railways
Rails, 32, 33, 38, 376, 395n13
Railway Bureau: line selection and construction by, 44, 49–50, 415n100; on railway promoters, 64–65; time discipline promoted by, 71, 72; and customer service, 89; for railroads as public enterprise, 103, 256; and private railroads, 111, 112, 116, 150, 151, 153, 370; and railway policy-making process, 117–118, 122, 191, 192–193, 194, 241, 274–275, 277; criticized by Jiyūtō, 213; and army, 227, 274, 276. *See also* Inoue Masaru
Railway companies. *See* Private railroads; *individual railway companies*
Railway Construction Law (1892): as turning point, 12, 192, 238, 241–242, 421n165; and Chūō line, 44, 46, 49–50; historical interpretations of, 192–193, 196, 237; party and Diet input into, 196–197, 236, 435n147, 435n148; army input into, 204–205, 236; as compromise measure, 232, 236; Diet deliberations on, 232–235; as nationalization act, 236–238; railroad development under, 236, 237–238, 241–242, 249–250, 285–286, 289–290, 291, 318, 375, 435n154; and Railway Nationalization Bill, 351–352. *See also* Legislation, railroad; Railway Council
Railway Construction Regulations (1900), 341, 450n104
Railway Council: and army, 204, 227, 236, 240, 274; and opposition parties, 213, 227, 236; proposed, 224, 226–227, 230; regulations for, 238–239; compared to Prussian central railway board, 239–240; and private business, 240, 433n102; and railway decision making, 240–241, 242, 318; and railway nationalization, 375–376. *See also* Railway Construction Law
"Railway Estimates" (Tetsudō okusoku), 99, 100–102, 103
Railway nationalization, pre-1903: movement of 1891, 153–160, 167, 169–170, 246–248, 423n214; proposed by Inoue Masaru in 1891, 198–201; under Railway Construction Law, 236–238; movements of 1898–1902, 242, 246–248, 250–251, 252, 253–254, 285, 291–296, 321–322, 343, 350; proposed by army in 1898, 275–277. *See also* Private Railway Purchase Bill
Railway nationalization of 1906–1907: as turning point, 7–8, 12, 375, 382; and historical interpretations, 12–13, 14, 15–16, 248; as "Bismarckian nationalization," 12, 392n16; motives behind, 12–13, 250, 261, 267, 284–285, 293–294, 296–297, 324, 383–384; and economic and business development, 38, 284, 334–336, 347, 349, 362, 365, 377, 382, 385, 451n126; movement leading up to, 246–249, 254–260, 277–285, 286–287, 288–289, 290–291; and railway nationalization in the West, 246, 256, 302–303; attitudes of private railroads and business towards, 248, 249, 312, 322–323, 324, 325, 328, 338, 344–345, 347–348, 358; and postwar management, 259–260, 284–285, 286–287, 288–289; and Seoul-Pusan Railway, 266–267, 268–269, 270–271; bureaucratic and Diet opposition to, 271, 279–282, 297–303, 306–307; freeing up of private capital by, 305, 360–373, 384, 385; and merger trend, 319; and financial investors, 320, 336–339, 344, 345–346. *See also* State railway policy
Railway Nationalization Law (1906): passage of, 245–246, 260, 308–309, 322, 446n229; amendments to, 289–291, 307–308, 351–352, 370; Diet deliberations on, 297, 298–305, 306–309, 346–347; party positions on, 297–298, 305–306; implementation of,

324, 351, 352–360, 375–379; and lobbying by private railroads, 328, 345, 355–356
Railway policy. *See* State railway policy
Railway Public Bond Bill (1891–1892), 196, 206, 218–219, 229, 231, 233
Railway Song, The, 28–31, 55
Rates, railway: freight, 40, 329, 339–340, 346, 376, 397–398n40; passenger, 66, 82–83, 89, 91–92, 329, 346, 376; and Kansai-state rate war, 77, 86–88, 323, 448n38; and railway nationalization of 1906–1907, 346–347, 348, 349, 376, 385
Rebates, railway, 38, 376, 398n47
Record of Tokyo's New Prosperity, A (Tōkyō shin hanjō ki), 54
Reed, M. C., 128
Regulation, railroad: and Nippon Railway, 112–113, 413n69; under Private Railway Regulations, 116, 121; of stock payment and ownership, 123, 263; and line selection and subsidies, 241, 379, 425n255; for military transport, 262; of connections and competition, 300, 318; under Railway Construction Regulations, 341. *See also* Government, Meiji: intervention in railroads
Rice transport, 39, 40, 398n46, 398n47
Rickshaws, 40, 61, 66, 68
River transport, 41, 45, 398n40
Rolling stock. *See* Locomotives; Passenger carriages
Rumschöttel, Hermann, 33, 146
Russia, 14, 260, 284, 299, 348, 363, 381, 382
Russo-Japanese War, 46, 259, 261–263, 266–267, 276, 277, 286, 311. *See also* Postwar management
Ryōmō Railway Company: at time of incorporation, 64, 423n206; stockholders in, 134, 140, 142–143; and merger with Nippon Railway, 149–153, 318, 319; local participation in management of, 169; financial difficulties of, 313

Saburi Kazutsugu, 50–51, 218
Saigō Takamori, 99
Saionji Kinmochi: and Railway Nationalization Bill, 248, 282, 284, 299, 300, 303, 307, 308–309, 347; named prime minister, 260
Sakatani Yoshirō: in decision-making process on railway nationalization, 255, 278, 282, 295; on railway nationalization and business expansion overseas, 270, 283–284, 305, 334, 350, 361–362; on foreign borrowing, 279; on reinvestment of nationalized-railway capital, 361–362
Sakurai Tōru, 340, 449n64
Samuels, Richard, 17, 382, 383
Sangū Railway Company, 131, 354, 360
Sanjō Sanetomi, 114
Santama region, 142
Sanuki Railway Company, 61
San'yō Railway Company: acquisition of rolling stock by, 34, 83–84, 85, 146–147; customer service of, 77, 79, 83–84, 164, 298; management of, 80, 160–165, 330, 338; and competition with steamship companies, 83, 164, 298, 329, 449n64; and Mitsubishi, 83, 138, 161, 325, 329–330, 331, 338, 340; state subsidies to, 116–117, 175–176; and Panic of 1890, 129, 132, 146–147, 162, 169–170, 176, 421n177; stockholders in, 134, 138, 140, 142, 144, 154–155, 160–161, 162–164, 331, 334, 336, 366–367, 450n92, 454n202; and Mitsui, 140, 331, 334, 336; capital expenditures by, 146–147, 162, 330–334, 340, 354; government petitions by, 171, 422n186; financing of, 184, 185–187, 189, 266; and mergers, 318, 319; and railway nationalization of 1906–1907, 325, 331–332, 357–358, 377; profit distribution by, 331, 333–334, 428n294
Sasa Tomofusa, 302, 304, 360–361, 362
Sasago tunnel, 30–31, 46, 70–71, 94
Satō Noriharu: as precursor of *zoku*, 206–207, 225–226, 380; in first Diet, 208; in second Diet, 210–212, 216, 218; background of, 211; and Railway Extension Bill (Satō bill), 211–212, 226, 228, 229, 230, 232, 236; in third Diet, 230–231, 232
Satō Yūnō, 354, 355
Satsuma Rebellion, 99, 121, 411n9, 412n26
Seidensticker, Edward, 403n115
Seikō Club, 297, 298, 445n187
Seiyūkai: and railway nationalization, 248, 249, 253–254, 291, 305, 306, 308; founding of, 251; and Den Kenjirō, 253–254, 272; agreement of, with Katsura, 260; and pork-barrel politics, 290–291, 296–297, 378; Diet seats held by, 444n163. *See also* Diet; Parties, political

Sengo keiei. See Postwar management
Sengoku Mitsugu, 166, 325–328, 330, 331, 339, 345, 357, 448n46
Seoul-Inchon Railway Company, 267, 286
Seoul-Pusan Railway Company, 266–271, 277, 305, 366, 372, 411n11, 453n171, 455n230
Shibusawa Eiichi: as Finance Ministry official, 101; on Panic of 1890, 126–127; as member of Tokyo Bankers' Association, 156, 158, 179; on first Railway Council, 240; and railway companies, 267, 274, 357; and railway nationalization, 349–351, 366, 452n142
Shiga Naoya, 77
Shikoku, 28, 32–33
Shima Yasuhiko, 294–295
Shimada merchant house, 102
Shimada Saburō, 216–217, 298, 299–300, 301–303
Shimazaki Tōson, 73, 81
Shimpōtō, 291
Shinagawa Yajirō, 203, 205, 216, 430n9
Shinbashi-Yokohama line: opening of, 6, 61–62; construction and financing of, 10, 26, 410n6; in print and song, 54, 55; opposition to, 58, 60; early travel on, 66–68, 69–70, 71, 72, 84; plans for privatization of, 106–107
Shin'etsu line, 60, 73, 78, 81–82
Shinkansen ("bullet train"), 4, 74, 391n7
Shiojiri, 48, 50
Shipbuilding, 329, 372
Shipping, coastal: state intervention in, 20, 384; and railroad competition and displacement, 39, 40, 246, 396–397n34, 397n35, 397–398n40; and complementarity with rail transport, 40; in Tokugawa period, 42; and competition with San'yō Railway, 83, 164, 298, 329. *See also* Transport
Shiraishi Naoji, 167
Shōda Heigorō, 281, 329, 331–332, 418–419n145
Silk industry, 42–44, 45–49, 50, 52
Silk, raw, 38, 40, 44, 45–46, 48–49, 399n54, 399–400n57
Sino-Japanese War of 1894–1895, 38, 262, 272, 273, 284, 288, 350, 401n82. *See also* China indemnity; Postwar management
Smith, Thomas, 6, 14, 70, 72

Sōbu Railway Company, 91, 131–132, 140, 174, 354, 360
Soga Sukenori, 341, 343–344, 344–345, 352
Sone Arasuke, 254, 258
Sonoda Kōkichi, 343, 344, 345, 367
South Manchuria Railway Company, 363–364, 448n46, 454n203
State railway policy: and economic and business development, 7, 36, 38, 284, 349–350, 377, 382, 451n126; towards private enterprise, 8, 10–14, 108, 114–115, 116–117, 170, 241, 378, 379; on ownership and control, 8, 10, 98, 101–104, 105–107, 111–112, 113, 114, 118, 120–121, 195–196, 238, 248–249, 375, 379–380; on finance, 10–12, 98–99, 100–101, 102–103, 112, 174–182, 255; formation of, 12, 16–17, 21, 104, 191–197, 204–207, 220, 242, 254–255, 258, 274–277, 278–279, 282–287, 289, 290–291, 293, 294–296, 380–381, 382–383; on construction, 195–196, 238, 285. *See also* Government, Meiji; Regulation, railway; Subsidies
State railways: inauguration of, 6; financing of, 10, 98–99, 100–101, 102, 103, 108, 207, 250, 285–286, 288; facilities and rolling stock of, 32, 34–36, 74–77, 81–82, 84–85, 341; capital expenditures by, 34–36, 376, 377–378; construction of, 44, 46–48, 49–50, 103, 107–108, 249–250, 285–286, 332, 378; management efficiency of, 73, 298, 332, 376; customer service of, 77–78, 89–90, 91, 92; and competition with Kansai Railway, 77, 86–88, 323–324, 448n38; share of total network, 116, 128, 242, 376; as source of state revenue, 252, 256, 259, 276, 281, 283, 284–285, 302, 383; and railway nationalization of 1906–1907, 376–379; managerial and technical spinoffs from, 456n11
State support for private railroads, 170, 171, 174, 379. *See also* Discount system, central bank; Subsidies
Steel industry. *See* Iron-and-steel industry
Stock-collateral lending. *See* Loans: stock-collateral
Stockholders, railway: influence of, on management, 81, 133, 145–160, 162–164, 165, 325–328, 330, 338–339, 344, 345; installment payments and stock-collateral borrowing by, 123–126; and Panic of 1890,

128–129, 143, 146–148, 149–159, 162; leading investors among, 133–141, 324, 419n148; local versus metropolitan, 141–144; attitudes of, towards investment, 144–145, 149, 157, 324–325; in pre-1903 nationalization movements, 153–160, 246–248, 321–322, 343; and overlap with management, 160–161, 165, 168, 330, 331, 344, 424n230, 425n236; and conflict with management, 162–164, 316, 326–328; and foreigners, 263–264, 266; and railway nationalization of 1906–1907, 281, 290, 312, 320, 324–325, 334–339, 344–346, 354, 355–357, 359–360, 383; reinvestment of nationalized-railway capital by, 360–373. *See also* Investment in railroads; Private railroads

Stocks, railway: payments on, 123–126, 364; as loan collateral, 126, 134–138, 178–182, 358, 359, 360, 368, 381, 382, 415n109, 415–416n111, 423n211; market prices of, 129, 153–154, 158–159, 358, 359, 360, 366, 368, 416n111, 420n153; preferred, 182, 186, 314, 316; foreign ownership of, 263–264, 266; of nationalized firms, 358–359, 360, 366–367, 368; turnover of, 417–418n133

Subsidies: to trunk-line firms, 51, 323; to Nippon Railway, 111, 175, 343, 413–414n69; and state intervention in management, 113, 166, 269, 425n255; to Kyushu and San'yō railways, 116–117, 175–176; to Hokkaido Colliery and Railway, 117, 175; and Panic of 1890, 130, 175–176; to Taiwan Railway, 274; to Hokkaido Railway, 427n290; cumulative, 457n2

Suehiro Michinari, 350
Sugar-manufacturing industry, 372–373
Sugiyama Kazuo, 142, 143, 145, 153, 161, 421n165
Sumitomo, 331
Sumitomo Bank, 368
Superheater locomotives, 34–36, 80
Suwa, 45–49, 50, 52
Switzerland, 304, 437n35

Taguchi Ukichi, 152, 165, 218, 248, 303
Taiseikai, 210, 230
Taishō period, 39, 92
Taiwan, 36, 273–274, 286, 372
Taiwan government general, 274
Taiwan Railway Company, 274

Taiwan Sugar Company, 372–373
Takahashi Korekiyo, 279–280, 282, 283, 295, 298, 299
Takahashi Shinkichi, 147–148, 165, 166, 167, 426n263
Takajima Tomonosuke, 203
Takarazuka all-women's revue, 363
Takasaki line (to Ueno, Tokyo), 45, 107, 108
Takashima Kaemon, 104–105
Takasu Hōzō, 233
Takechi Kyōzō, 143
Takekoshi Yosaburō, 303–305
Taketomi Tokitoshi, 298–299, 300, 301, 445n200
Tanaka Gentarō, 229, 230, 357
Tanaka Shinshichi, 141, 420n157
Tani Kanjō, 235, 274–275
Tanizaki Jun'ichirō, 56
Tariff protection, 34, 36, 38, 396n32
Technology, railroad, 4–6, 8–9, 117, 166, 409n231
"Telecom" wars of 1983–1985, 17–18
Telecommunications, 17–18, 380
Telegraphs, 18–20, 21, 59, 98, 102, 103, 403n115
Temiya-Horonai line, 114
Terajima Munenori, 111
Teranishi Seiki, 418–419n145
Terauchi Masatake, 258, 262, 263, 267, 272, 282, 300–301
Tetsudō kisei dōmeikai. *See* League for the Promotion of Railroads
"Tetsudō okusoku" (Railway Estimates), 99, 100–102, 103
Through-traffic, 39, 329, 346, 376, 449n64
Time and space, 69–73
Tōhoku line, 93
Tokaido line: completion of, 10, 26, 191, 195; in *Railway Song*, 30; facilities and rolling stock on, 34, 76, 77, 79–80, 81, 82; versus Nakasendō route, 44, 63; and post-station towns, 60–61, 65; and travel and recreation, 68–69, 89, 90; leisurely operation of, 73; and Kansai Railway, 89, 323; as moneymaker, 323, 411n14
Tokio Marine Insurance Company, 368, 369. *See also* Insurance companies
Tokugawa period, 8, 42, 58, 71, 74
Tokushima Railway Company, 289, 320, 438n38
Tokutomi Roka, 54

Tokyo, 93, 141, 142
Tokyo Bankers' Association, 154, 156–158, 178–179
Tokyo Chamber of Commerce, 156, 240, 252, 321, 322, 350, 423n214, 433n102
Tokyo Electric Light Company, 365–366
Tokyo Gas Company, 366
Tokyo Railway Association, 105–107, 108, 109
Tōkyō shin hanjō ki (*A Record of Tokyo's New Prosperity*), 54
Tokyo Warehousing Company, 372
Tone River, 45
Toriumi Yasushi, 435n147
Toyokawa Railway Company, 314
Tōzan Company, 107–108, 109, 110, 111
Trading companies, 36–38, 334, 336
Train Manufacturing Company (Kisha seizō kaisha), 36
Trains: speed of, 4, 54, 66, 68, 69–70, 79–80; in woodblock prints, 8, 55; frequency of, on Shinbashi-Yokohama line, 66; passenger amenities on, 74–77, 83, 86. *See also* Railroads
Tramways, 362–363
Transport: by road, 20, 40, 45–46, 66, 68, 70; waterborne, 20, 39, 40–41, 45, 66, 396–397n34, 397n35, 397–398n40, 398n47, 399n51; competition between railroads and other modes of, 39–41, 45, 61, 66, 68, 83, 164, 174, 298, 329, 396–397n34, 397n35, 397–398n40, 398n47, 437n8; passenger, by rail, 39, 68, 130, 145, 153; freight, by rail, 39–42, 45–46, 48, 130, 175, 246, 316, 336, 339, 346, 396–397n34, 398n46, 398n47, 399n51, 401n84, 437n8; in Tokugawa period, 42, 68, 69, 71, 74. *See also* Military transport by rail
Travel, railway, 8–9, 66–80, 81–92, 404n148
Treaty revision, 33, 34, 263, 277
Trevithick, Richard Francis, 32
Tsubame superexpress train, 377

Union Pacific Railroad, 425–426n255
United States: state intervention in railroads of, 14, 246, 382, 425–426n255, 457n22; and rail and locomotive exports to Japan, 32, 33–34, 36; passenger amenities on railroads in, 78, 79; economizing by railroads in, 80, 145–146
Upper house. *See* House of Peers
Ushiba Takezō, 233
Ushiba Takuzō, 330–331, 332, 333–334, 339
Usui Pass, 28, 45, 46

Vickers, 370

Wada Hiroshi, 208, 227
Wada Pass, 46
War, Ministry of, 58
Watanabe Kunitake, 182, 251, 252
Witte, Sergei, 299
Wray, William, 371

Yamagata Aritomo, 94, 114, 268, 272, 293, 294, 306, 440n86
Yamagata Isaburō, 272, 282, 289, 300, 302, 351, 352–353, 355
Yamaguchi Kazuo, 398n46
Yamamura, Kozo, 15, 134–135, 381
Yamanashi prefecture, 42–44, 46, 48, 50, 94, 214–215, 235
Yamanote line, 45, 83, 354
Yamanouchi Kazuji, 258, 278, 450n104
Yamao policy (memorial), 102–103, 104, 105, 106, 111–112, 121
Yamao Yōzō, 102–103, 118
Yasuda, 320, 364
Yasuda Zenjirō, 156–157
Yawata Iron and Steelworks, 32, 38, 288
Yoshikawa Kensei, 272–273
Yoshioka mines, 330
Yoshitsune, 34
Yui, Tsunehiko, 162

Zaibatsu, 51, 138, 144, 157, 364. *See also* Mitsubishi; Mitsui
Zōjō-ji, 72
zoku ("tribesmen"), 17, 206, 380

Harvard East Asian Monographs

1. Liang Fang-chung, *The Single-Whip Method of Taxation in China*
2. Harold C. Hinton, *The Grain Tribute System of China, 1845–1911*
3. Ellsworth C. Carlson, *The Kaiping Mines, 1877–1912*
4. Chao Kuo-chün, *Agrarian Policies of Mainland China: A Documentary Study, 1949–1956*
5. Edgar Snow, *Random Notes on Red China, 1936–1945*
6. Edwin George Beal, Jr., *The Origin of Likin, 1835–1864*
7. Chao Kuo-chün, *Economic Planning and Organization in Mainland China: A Documentary Study, 1949–1957*
8. John K. Fairbank, *Ch'ing Documents: An Introductory Syllabus*
9. Helen Yin and Yi-chang Yin, *Economic Statistics of Mainland China, 1949–1957*
10. Wolfgang Franke, *The Reform and Abolition of the Traditional Chinese Examination System*
11. Albert Feuerwerker and S. Cheng, *Chinese Communist Studies of Modern Chinese History*
12. C. John Stanley, *Late Ch'ing Finance: Hu Kuang-yung as an Innovator*
13. S. M. Meng, *The Tsungli Yamen: Its Organization and Functions*
14. Ssu-yü Teng, *Historiography of the Taiping Rebellion*
15. Chun-Jo Liu, *Controversies in Modern Chinese Intellectual History: An Analytic Bibliography of Periodical Articles, Mainly of the May Fourth and Post-May Fourth Era*
16. Edward J. M. Rhoads, *The Chinese Red Army, 1927–1963: An Annotated Bibliography*
17. Andrew J. Nathan, *A History of the China International Famine Relief Commission*
18. Frank H. H. King (ed.) and Prescott Clarke, *A Research Guide to China-Coast Newspapers, 1822–1911*
19. Ellis Joffe, *Party and Army: Professionalism and Political Control in the Chinese Officer Corps, 1949–1964*

20. Toshio G. Tsukahira, *Feudal Control in Tokugawa Japan: The Sankin Kōtai System*
21. Kwang-Ching Liu, ed., *American Missionaries in China: Papers from Harvard Seminars*
22. George Moseley, *A Sino-Soviet Cultural Frontier: The Ili Kazakh Autonomous Chou*
23. Carl F. Nathan, *Plague Prevention and Politics in Manchuria, 1910–1931*
24. Adrian Arthur Bennett, *John Fryer: The Introduction of Western Science and Technology into Nineteenth-Century China*
25. Donald J. Friedman, *The Road from Isolation: The Campaign of the American Committee for Non-Participation in Japanese Aggression, 1938–1941*
26. Edward LeFevour, *Western Enterprise in Late Ch'ing China: A Selective Survey of Jardine, Matheson and Company's Operations, 1842–1895*
27. Charles Neuhauser, *Third World Politics: China and the Afro-Asian People's Solidarity Organization, 1957–1967*
28. Kungtu C. Sun, assisted by Ralph W. Huenemann, *The Economic Development of Manchuria in the First Half of the Twentieth Century*
29. Shahid Javed Burki, *A Study of Chinese Communes, 1965*
30. John Carter Vincent, *The Extraterritorial System in China: Final Phase*
31. Madeleine Chi, *China Diplomacy, 1914–1918*
32. Clifton Jackson Phillips, *Protestant America and the Pagan World: The First Half Century of the American Board of Commissioners for Foreign Missions, 1810–1860*
33. James Pusey, *Wu Han: Attacking the Present through the Past*
34. Ying-wan Cheng, *Postal Communication in China and Its Modernization, 1860–1896*
35. Tuvia Blumenthal, *Saving in Postwar Japan*
36. Peter Frost, *The Bakumatsu Currency Crisis*
37. Stephen C. Lockwood, *Augustine Heard and Company, 1858–1862*
38. Robert R. Campbell, *James Duncan Campbell: A Memoir by His Son*
39. Jerome Alan Cohen, ed., *The Dynamics of China's Foreign Relations*
40. V. V. Vishnyakova-Akimova, *Two Years in Revolutionary China, 1925–1927*, tr. Steven I. Levine
41. Meron Medzini, *French Policy in Japan during the Closing Years of the Tokugawa Regime*
42. *The Cultural Revolution in the Provinces*
43. Sidney A. Forsythe, *An American Missionary Community in China, 1895–1905*
44. Benjamin I. Schwartz, ed., *Reflections on the May Fourth Movement: A Symposium*
45. Ching Young Choe, *The Rule of the Taewŏn'gun, 1864–1873: Restoration in Yi Korea*

46. W. P. J. Hall, *A Bibliographical Guide to Japanese Research on the Chinese Economy, 1958–1970*
47. Jack J. Gerson, *Horatio Nelson Lay and Sino-British Relations, 1854–1864*
48. Paul Richard Bohr, *Famine and the Missionary: Timothy Richard as Relief Administrator and Advocate of National Reform*
49. Endymion Wilkinson, *The History of Imperial China: A Research Guide*
50. Britten Dean, *China and Great Britain: The Diplomacy of Commercial Relations, 1860–1864*
51. Ellsworth C. Carlson, *The Foochow Missionaries, 1847–1880*
52. Yeh-chien Wang, *An Estimate of the Land-Tax Collection in China, 1753 and 1908*
53. Richard M. Pfeffer, *Understanding Business Contracts in China, 1949–1963*
54. Han-sheng Chuan and Richard Kraus, *Mid-Ch'ing Rice Markets and Trade: An Essay in Price History*
55. Ranbir Vohra, *Lao She and the Chinese Revolution*
56. Liang-lin Hsiao, *China's Foreign Trade Statistics, 1864–1949*
57. Lee-hsia Hsu Ting, *Government Control of the Press in Modern China, 1900–1949*
58. Edward W. Wagner, *The Literati Purges: Political Conflict in Early Yi Korea*
59. Joungwon A. Kim, *Divided Korea: The Politics of Development, 1945–1972*
60. Noriko Kamachi, John K. Fairbank, and Chūzō Ichiko, *Japanese Studies of Modern China Since 1953: A Bibliographical Guide to Historical and Social-Science Research on the Nineteenth and Twentieth Centuries, Supplementary Volume for 1953–1969*
61. Donald A. Gibbs and Yun-chen Li, *A Bibliography of Studies and Translations of Modern Chinese Literature, 1918–1942*
62. Robert H. Silin, *Leadership and Values: The Organization of Large-Scale Taiwanese Enterprises*
63. David Pong, *A Critical Guide to the Kwangtung Provincial Archives Deposited at the Public Record Office of London*
64. Fred W. Drake, *China Charts the World: Hsu Chi-yü and His Geography of 1848*
65. William A. Brown and Urgunge Onon, translators and annotators, *History of the Mongolian People's Republic*
66. Edward L. Farmer, *Early Ming Government: The Evolution of Dual Capitals*
67. Ralph C. Croizier, *Koxinga and Chinese Nationalism: History, Myth, and the Hero*
68. William J. Tyler, tr., *The Psychological World of Natsume Sōseki,* by Doi Takeo

69. Eric Widmer, *The Russian Ecclesiastical Mission in Peking during the Eighteenth Century*
70. Charlton M. Lewis, *Prologue to the Chinese Revolution: The Transformation of Ideas and Institutions in Hunan Province, 1891–1907*
71. Preston Torbert, *The Ch'ing Imperial Household Department: A Study of its Organization and Principal Functions, 1662–1796*
72. Paul A. Cohen and John E. Schrecker, eds., *Reform in Nineteenth-Century China*
73. Jon Sigurdson, *Rural Industrialism in China*
74. Kang Chao, *The Development of Cotton Textile Production in China*
75. Valentin Rabe, *The Home Base of American China Missions, 1880–1920*
76. Sarasin Viraphol, *Tribute and Profit: Sino-Siamese Trade, 1652–1853*
77. Ch'i-ch'ing Hsiao, *The Military Establishment of the Yuan Dynasty*
78. Meishi Tsai, *Contemporary Chinese Novels and Short Stories, 1949–1974: An Annotated Bibliography*
79. Wellington K. K. Chan, *Merchants, Mandarins and Modern Enterprise in Late Ch'ing China*
80. Endymion Wilkinson, *Landlord and Labor in Late Imperial China: Case Studies from Shandong by Jing Su and Luo Lun*
81. Barry Keenan, *The Dewey Experiment in China: Educational Reform and Political Power in the Early Republic*
82. George A. Hayden, *Crime and Punishment in Medieval Chinese Drama: Three Judge Pao Plays*
83. Sang-Chul Suh, *Growth and Structural Changes in the Korean Economy, 1910–1940*
84. J. W. Dower, *Empire and Aftermath: Yoshida Shigeru and the Japanese Experience, 1878–1954*
85. Martin Collcutt, *Five Mountains: The Rinzai Zen Monastic Institution in Medieval Japan*
86. Kwang Suk Kim and Michael Roemer, *Growth and Structural Transformation*
87. Anne O. Krueger, *The Developmental Role of the Foreign Sector and Aid*
88. Edwin S. Mills and Byung-Nak Song, *Urbanization and Urban Problems*
89. Sung Hwan Ban, Pal Yong Moon, and Dwight H. Perkins, *Rural Development*
90. Noel F. McGinn, Donald R. Snodgrass, Yung Bong Kim, Shin-Bok Kim, and Quee-Young Kim, *Education and Development in Korea*
91. Leroy P. Jones and Il SaKong, *Government, Business, and Entrepreneurship in Economic Development: The Korean Case*
92. Edward S. Mason, Dwight H. Perkins, Kwang Suk Kim, David C. Cole, Mahn Je Kim, et al., *The Economic and Social Modernization of the Republic of Korea*

93. Robert Repetto, Tai Hwan Kwon, Son-Ung Kim, Dae Young Kim, John E. Sloboda, and Peter J. Donaldson, *Economic Development, Population Policy, and Demographic Transition in the Republic of Korea*
94. Parks M. Coble, Jr., *The Shanghai Capitalists and the Nationalist Government, 1927–1937*
95. Noriko Kamachi, *Reform in China: Huang Tsun-hsien and the Japanese Model*
96. Richard Wich, *Sino-Soviet Crisis Politics: A Study of Political Change and Communication*
97. Lillian M. Li, *China's Silk Trade: Traditional Industry in the Modern World, 1842–1937*
98. R. David Arkush, *Fei Xiaotong and Sociology in Revolutionary China*
99. Kenneth Alan Grossberg, *Japan's Renaissance: The Politics of the Muromachi Bakufu*
100. James Reeve Pusey, *China and Charles Darwin*
101. Hoyt Cleveland Tillman, *Utilitarian Confucianism: Ch'en Liang's Challenge to Chu Hsi*
102. Thomas A. Stanley, *Ōsugi Sakae, Anarchist in Taishō Japan: The Creativity of the Ego*
103. Jonathan K. Ocko, *Bureaucratic Reform in Provincial China: Ting Jih-ch'ang in Restoration Kiangsu, 1867–1870*
104. James Reed, *The Missionary Mind and American East Asia Policy, 1911–1915*
105. Neil L. Waters, *Japan's Local Pragmatists: The Transition from Bakumatsu to Meiji in the Kawasaki Region*
106. David C. Cole and Yung Chul Park, *Financial Development in Korea, 1945–1978*
107. Roy Bahl, Chuk Kyo Kim, and Chong Kee Park, *Public Finances during the Korean Modernization Process*
108. William D. Wray, *Mitsubishi and the N.Y.K., 1870–1914: Business Strategy in the Japanese Shipping Industry*
109. Ralph William Huenemann, *The Dragon and the Iron Horse: The Economics of Railroads in China, 1876–1937*
110. Benjamin A. Elman, *From Philosophy to Philology: Intellectual and Social Aspects of Change in Late Imperial China*
111. Jane Kate Leonard, *Wei Yuan and China's Rediscovery of the Maritime World*
112. Luke S. K. Kwong, *A Mosaic of the Hundred Days: Personalities, Politics, and Ideas of 1898*
113. John E. Wills, Jr., *Embassies and Illusions: Dutch and Portuguese Envoys to K'ang-hsi, 1666–1687*
114. Joshua A. Fogel, *Politics and Sinology: The Case of Naitō Konan (1866–1934)*

115. Jeffrey C. Kinkley, ed., *After Mao: Chinese Literature and Society, 1978–1981*
116. C. Andrew Gerstle, *Circles of Fantasy: Convention in the Plays of Chikamatsu*
117. Andrew Gordon, *The Evolution of Labor Relations in Japan: Heavy Industry, 1853–1955*
118. Daniel K. Gardner, *Chu Hsi and the Ta Hsueh: Neo-Confucian Reflection on the Confucian Canon*
119. Christine Guth Kanda, *Shinzō: Hachiman Imagery and its Development*
120. Robert Borgen, *Sugawara no Michizane and the Early Heian Court*
121. Chang-tai Hung, *Going to the People: Chinese Intellectual and Folk Literature, 1918–1937*
122. Michael A. Cusumano, *The Japanese Automobile Industry: Technology and Management at Nissan and Toyota*
123. Richard von Glahn, *The Country of Streams and Grottoes: Expansion, Settlement, and the Civilizing of the Sichuan Frontier in Song Times*
124. Steven D. Carter, *The Road to Komatsubara: A Classical Reading of the Renga Hyakuin*
125. Katherine F. Bruner, John K. Fairbank, and Richard T. Smith, *Entering China's Service: Robert Hart's Journals, 1854–1863*
126. Bob Tadashi Wakabayashi, *Anti-Foreignism and Western Learning in Early-Modern Japan: The New Theses of 1825*
127. Atsuko Hirai, *Individualism and Socialism: The Life and Thought of Kawai Eijirō (1891–1944)*
128. Ellen Widmer, *The Margins of Utopia: Shui-hu hou-chuan and the Literature of Ming Loyalism*
129. R. Kent Guy, *The Emperor's Four Treasuries: Scholars and the State in the Late Ch'ien-lung Era*
130. Peter C. Perdue, *Exhausting the Earth: State and Peasant in Hunan, 1500–1850*
131. Susan Chan Egan, *A Latterday Confucian: Reminiscences of William Hung (1893–1980)*
132. James T. C. Liu, *China Turning Inward: Intellectual-Political Changes in the Early Twelfth Century*
133. Paul A. Cohen, *Between Tradition and Modernity: Wang T'ao and Reform in Late Ch'ing China*
134. Kate Wildman Nakai, *Shogunal Politics: Arai Hakuseki and the Premises of Tokugawa Rule*
135. Parks M. Coble, *Facing Japan: Chinese Politics and Japanese Imperialism, 1931–1937*
136. Jon L. Saari, *Legacies of Childhood: Growing Up Chinese in a Time of Crisis, 1890–1920*
137. Susan Downing Videen, *Tales of Heichū*

138. Heinz Morioka and Miyoko Sasaki, *Rakugo: The Popular Narrative Art of Japan*
139. Joshua A. Fogel, *Nakae Ushikichi in China: The Mourning of Spirit*
140. Alexander Barton Woodside, *Vietnam and the Chinese Model: A Comparative Study of Vietnamese and Chinese Government in the First Half of the Nineteenth Century*
141. George Elison, *Deus Destroyed: The Image of Christianity in Early Modern Japan*
142. William D. Wray, ed., *Managing Industrial Enterprise: Cases from Japan's Prewar Experience*
143. T'ung-tsu Ch'ü, *Local Government in China under the Ch'ing*
144. Marie Anchordoguy, *Computers, Inc.: Japan's Challenge to IBM*
145. Barbara Molony, *Technology and Investment: The Prewar Japanese Chemical Industry*
146. Mary Elizabeth Berry, *Hideyoshi*
147. Laura E. Hein, *Fueling Growth: The Energy Revolution and Economic Policy in Postwar Japan*
148. Wen-hsin Yeh, *The Alienated Academy: Culture and Politics in Republican China, 1919–1937*
149. Dru C. Gladney, *Muslim Chinese: Ethnic Nationalism in the People's Republic*
150. Merle Goldman and Paul A. Cohen, eds., *Ideas Across Cultures: Essays on Chinese Thought in Honor of Benjamin I. Schwartz*
151. James Polachek, *The Inner Opium War*
152. Gail Lee Bernstein, *Japanese Marxist: A Portrait of Kawakami Hajime, 1879–1946*
153. Lloyd E. Eastman, *The Abortive Revolution: China under Nationalist Rule, 1927–1937*
154. Mark Mason, *American Multinationals and Japan: The Political Economy of Japanese Capital Controls, 1899–1980*
155. Richard J. Smith, John K. Fairbank, and Katherine F. Bruner, *Robert Hart and China's Early Modernization: His Journals, 1863–1866*
156. George J. Tanabe, Jr., *Myōe the Dreamkeeper: Fantasy and Knowledge in Kamakura Buddhism*
157. William Wayne Farris, *Heavenly Warriors: The Evolution of Japan's Military, 500–1300*
158. Yu-ming Shaw, *An American Missionary in China: John Leighton Stuart and Chinese-American Relations*
159. James B. Palais, *Politics and Policy in Traditional Korea*
160. Douglas Reynolds, *China, 1898–1912: The Xinzheng Revolution and Japan*
161. Roger Thompson, *China's Local Councils in the Age of Constitutional Reform*

162. William Johnston, *The Modern Epidemic: History of Tuberculosis in Japan*
163. Constantine Nomikos Vaporis, *Breaking Barriers: Travel and the State in Early Modern Japan*
164. Irmela Hijiya-Kirschnereit, *Rituals of Self-Revelation: Shishōsetsu as Literary Genre and Socio-Cultural Phenomenon*
165. James C. Baxter, *The Meiji Unification through the Lens of Ishikawa Prefecture*
166. Thomas R. H. Havens, *Architects of Affluence: The Tsutsumi Family and the Seibu-Saison Enterprises in Twentieth-Century Japan*
167. Anthony Hood Chambers, *The Secret Window: Ideal Worlds in Tanizaki's Fiction*
168. Steven J. Ericson, *The Sound of the Whistle: Railroads and the State in Meiji Japan*